NEWNES
DICTIONARY OF DATES

NEWNES
DICTIONARY OF DATES

Compiled by

Lewis wright

ROBERT COLLISON, *compiler*

NEWNES: LONDON

First published 1961

Second Impression 1962

SET IN EIGHT POINT PLANTIN
MADE AND PRINTED IN GREAT BRITAIN BY
MORRISON AND GIBB LIMITED, LONDON AND EDINBURGH
FOR GEORGE NEWNES LIMITED, TOWER HOUSE
SOUTHAMPTON STREET, LONDON, W.C.2

When all its work is done, the lie shall rot ;
The truth is great, and shall prevail,
When none cares whether it prevail or not.

Coventry Patmore.

PREFACE

A BOOK of this size must necessarily be selective : its success will depend on how closely it reflects current tastes and interests. I have tried to follow the present vogue for facts and allusions many of which relate to scientific and technological achievements rather than wars and battles, and for cultural and sociological leaders in preference to field-marshals and admirals. The result will be seen to be an amalgam of people and subjects : some people appear under their names (and perhaps under the fields of their work or hobbies as well) because they have an additional importance to the public as personalities, while others are to be found only under their inventions or discoveries since they themselves have otherwise remained unnoticed or obscure beyond their immediate circles. In addition, there are entries for events which, as far as I can judge, are liable to arise in conversation or dispute or in the newspapers or on the air. A certain number of entries are devoted to the first appearance of things that have contributed very considerably to the advancement of the material or moral status of mankind.

Any research worker knows that there is nothing so difficult to discover as the unchallengeable date. Even a man's birth or death date is not always known beyond doubt : for example, there are still controversies over the birth dates of such famous persons in recent times as Puccini and Conrad ; how much more difficult is it therefore to be certain of the correct dates of those who lived in the fourteenth or fifteenth century. Indeed, as the search goes on, it becomes increasingly obvious that our own preoccupation with birthdays and anniversaries is as recent in its origin as is the present zest for first editions or manuscripts of important books. Again, in the case of inventions, what is the important date—the date of ' Eureka ! I have found it ! ', the date of the public announcement when the discoverers hares his knowledge with the world, or the date of the first patent or publication when the find can at last be shared ? In every case where the dates have proved doubtful, I have tried to define the circumstances, and have based the dates I give on the best current available evidence, and have—in the more problematical instances—indicated the alternatives.

Some of the entries may, in comparison with their neighbours, seem trivial, but it does seem that life being not wholly serious there is scope for items which, in spite of their poor claim to immortality, have an immediate interest for the curious. That they should have driven out more weighty items which have long graced the magnificent pages of the noble Haydn will, I hope, encourage the reader to recourse once again to that matchless work.

This may in fact be the moment to draw attention to those other works that may help the reader in other ways : Steinberg's *Historical Tables* and its French parallel *Clio* both tabulate dates chronologically and break them up into categories. The old Haydn and the smaller dictionary issued by Nelson are both still of great use in spite of their last editions having appeared early in this century ; while Langer's revision of the famous Ploetz supplements its detailed chronological summary with a full index. And, of course, the Everyman Dictionary is an invaluable desk companion.

In the lists of anniversaries similar emphasis has been laid on scientific and technological discoveries and personalities, and on sociological and political reforms and achievements. Among the names so baldly listed there may be some that at first sight appear obscure or unexciting. The reader who, however, cares to follow these names to their description in the larger dictionaries of national biography and in the national and international encyclopædias will, I believe, invariably find an interesting or unusual story to justify their inclusion. At the moment there is no good list of anniversaries, and it is hoped that the present book will do something to remedy that deficiency.

To acknowledge satisfactorily all the help I have had in the compiling and preparation of this volume would fill many pages. Hardly a conversation I have had during the past two years has failed to start some line of enquiry that has resulted in a useful new entry or modified an existing one. To all my friends and acquaintances who have—wittingly or unwittingly—thus contributed to the usefulness of this work I offer my sincere thanks while, at the same time, exonerating them from any blame which must indeed remain my sole charge.

R. C.

DICTIONARY
OF
DATES

A

A 1, first British car registration, issued to the 2nd Earl Russell 1903.

'AE' (George William Russell), Irish poet, b. 1867, d. 1935.

A.R.P. Act, enacted in Britain to ensure air-raid precautions 1938.

À Becket, Thomas, Archbishop of Canterbury, b. 1118, assassinated 1170.

À Beckett, Gilbert, English humorous writer, b. 1811, d. 1856.

Aachen (Aix-la-Chapelle), founded 125 ; Charlemagne's capital, free city of the Holy Roman Empire, burnt 1656 ; captured by American troops 1944.

Aalto, Hugo Alvar, Finnish architect, b. 1898.

Abadan, Persian port and refinery, founded 1909, evacuated by British 1951.

Abbas I, Egyptian pasha, b. 1813, assassinated 1854.

Abbas the Great, Shah of Persia, b. about 1557, d. 1628.

Abbasid Dynasty, founded by Abdul Abbas 750, ended 1258.

Abbeville, Treaty of (Treaty of Paris), relinquishing English claims to several French territories, signed 20 May 1259.

Abbey, Edwin Austin, American-born painter, b. 1852, d. 1911.

Abbot, George, Archbishop of Canterbury (1611–1633), b. 1562, d. 1633.

Abd Al Kader, Algerian revolutionary leader, b. 1808, d. 1883.

Abd Al Krim, Rif revolutionary leader, b. 1882.

Abdication of King Edward VIII, 10 Dec. 1936.

Abdominal Operation, first successfully performed by the American surgeon Ephraim McDowell, b. 1771, d. 1830.

Abdul Latif, Arabian writer, b. 1162, d. 1231.

Abdur Rahman Khan, Emir of Afghanistan, b. about 1844, d. 1901.

Abel, Sir Frederick Augustus, scientist, inventor (1879) of apparatus for determining flashpoint of petroleum, b. 1827, d. 1902.

Abelard, Peter, French philosopher, lover of Héloïse, b. 1079, d. 1142.

Abercrombie, Lascelles, English poet, b. 1881, d. 1938.

Abercromby, Sir Robert, commander of the Indian forces, b. 1740, d. 1827.

Aberdeen, incorporated by David I, granted charter by William the Lion 1179, burnt by Edward III 1336.

Aberdeen, George Gordon, Earl of, British statesman (Prime Minister, 1852–1855), b. 1784, d. 1860.

Aberration of Light, discovered 1729 by the English astronomer James Bradley, b. 1693, d. 1762.

Abershaw, Jerry, English highwayman, b. about 1773, hanged 1795.

Aberystwyth, founded 1109, granted first charter 1277, College erected there 1872.

Abhorrers, political group (connected with Tories), first came into prominence 1680.

Abingdon School, Berkshire, British public school, founded in pre-Norman days, re-endowed by John Roysse 1563

Abington, Mrs Frances, English actress, b. 1737, d. 1815.

Abjuration Oath, rejecting the Stuarts, first required 1701.

Abolition of Slavery, in British possessions 1834 ; in French possessions 1848 ; throughout U.S.A. 1862.

Abortion, made statutory offence in Britain 1803.

Aboukir Bay, Battle of (the Battle of the Nile), fought by Lord Nelson 1 Aug. 1798.

About, Edmond, French writer (*Le roi des montagnes,* 1856), b. 1828, d. 1885.

Abraham (Abram), Hebrew patriarch, travelled from Ur to Palestine about 2000–1500 B.C.

Abraham, Battle of the Heights of, fought near Quebec between British and French 13 Sept. 1759.

Abraham, Robert, English architect, b. 1773, d. 1850.

Abruzzi Earthquake, Italy, destroying 15,000, 3 Nov. 1706.

Absolute Zero (−273° F.), idea introduced by Lord Kelvin, b. 1824, d. 1907.

Abu Nuwas, Arabian poet, b. about 756, d. 810.

Abyssinia, introduced to Christianity by Frumentius about 329.

Abyssinian Expedition, carried out by British troops from India 1867–1868.

Académie des Jeux Floreux, Paris, constituted an academy by Louis XIV 1694.

Académie Française, Paris, founded 10 Feb. 1635.

Accademia Della Crusca, Italy, leading Italian academy, founded 1582.

Accoramboni, Vittoria (Webster's ' White Devil '), b. 1557, assassinated 1585.

Accordion, invented by the German Friedrich Buschmann 1822.

Accountants, Institute of Chartered, in England and Wales, founded (as the Institute of Accountants) 1870 ; chartered 1880.

Accra, Ghana, founded by the Swedes 1657.

Acetylene, discovered 1836 by the British scientist Edmund Davy, b. 1785, d. 1857.

Achæan League, Greece, formed about 280, dissolved 146 B.C.

Achæmenid Dynasty, ruled Persia from about 550 to 300 B.C.

Achromatic Telescope, invented about 1757 by the English optician John Dollond, b. 1706, d. 1761 ; and, independently, in 1733 by the English amateur Chester Moor Hall, b. 1703, d. 1771.

Ackermann, Rudolph, German-born publisher of illustrated books, b. 1764, d. 1834.

Aconcagua, highest mountain in the Andes, first climbed by the Fitzgerald Expedition 1897.

Acre, taken by the Crusaders 1110, captured by Saladin 1187, recaptured by Richard Cœur de Lion 1191, finally lost to Christendom 1291. Battle of Acre 1189.

Acridine, chemical compound, isolated by the German scientists Carl Graebe and H. Caro 1890.

Act of Settlement, securing Hanoverian succession to the English throne, passed 1701.

Actinium, radio-active element, discovered 1900 by the French scientist André Debierne, b. 1874.

Actinometer, invented 1825 by Sir John Herschel, b. 1792, d. 1871.

Actium, Battle of, between Octavian and Marc Antony, 2 Sept. 31 B.C.

Acton, John Dalberg, Lord, English historian, b. 1834, d. 1902.

Actress, First English (name uncertain), played Desdemona 8 Dec. 1660.

Adalbert, St, b. about 957, martyred 997.

Adalbert, German archbishop, b. about 1000, d. 1072.

Adam, James, Scottish architect, b. 1730, d. 1794.

Adam, Robert, Scottish architect and brother of James, b. 1728, d. 1792.

Adam de la Halle, French troubadour, b. about 1240, d. 1287.

Adams, Francis William Lauderdale, Australian writer, b. 1862, committed suicide 1893.

Adams, Henry, American historian, b. 1838, d. 1918.

Adams, John, 2nd U.S. President (1797–1801), b. 1735, d. 1826.

Adams, John Couch, English astronomer (predicted position of the planet Neptune 1845), b. 1819, d. 1892.

Adams, John Quincey, 6th U.S. President (1825–1829), b. 1767, d. 1848.

Adams, Samuel, American statesman, b. 1722, d. 1803.

Adams, Sarah Flower, English hymnwriter (*Nearer to Thee*), b. 1805, d. 1848.

Adams, William Bridges, English inventor, b. 1797, d. 1872.

Adding Machines, first model built 1642 by the French scientist Blaise Pascal, b. 1623, d. 1662.

Addington, Henry, 1st Viscount Sidmouth, President of the Council, b. 1757, d. 1844.

Addinsell, Richard, English composer of incidental music (*Warsaw Concerto*), b. 1904.

Addis Ababa, founded by Menelek II as Abyssinian capital 1892.

Addison, Joseph, English author—with Steele—of *The Spectator,* b. 1672, d. 1719.

Addison, Thomas, English discoverer 1855 of Addison's disease, b. 1793, d. 1860.

Addled Parliament, of James I's reign, sat 5 Apr. to 7 June 1614.

Adelaide, Queen, wife of William IV, b. 1792, d. 1849.

Adelaide, South Australia, founded 1836 and named after Queen Adelaide.

Aden, annexed to British India, 16 Jan. 1839; became Crown Colony 1 Apr. 1937; Legislative Council established Jan. 1947.

Adenauer, Konrad, German Chancellor since 1949, b. 1876.

Adler, Alfred, Austrian psychologist, b. 1870, d. 1937.

Adler, Larry, American harmonica-player, b. 1914.

Adler, Nathan Marcus, Chief Rabbi and founder 1855 of Jews' College, London, b. 1803, d. 1890.

Adler, Viktor, Austrian politician, b. 1852, d. 1918.

Admiralty, London, founded 1512.

Admiralty Islands, Bismarck Archipelago, discovered by the Dutch 1616.

Adoption, made legal in England in 1926.

Adrenaline, a hormone, isolated 1901 by the Japanese scientist Jokichi Takamine, b. 1854, d. 1922.

Adrian, St, martyred 4 Mar. 303.

Adrian I, Pope, 772–795.

Adrian II, Pope, 867–872.

Adrian III, St, Pope, 884–885.

Adrian IV (Nicolas Breakspear), Pope, first and only English Pope, 1154–1159.

Adrian V, Pope, 1276.

Adrian VI (Adrian Florensz), Pope, 1522–1523, b. 1459, d. 1523.

Adrian, Edgar Douglas, Baron, English physiologist, b. 1889.

Adrianople, Battle of, 378; taken by the Ottomans, 1360, and their capital 1366–1453.

Advent, Christian festival comprising the period encompassed by the four Sundays before Christmas.

Advertisement Duty, Newspaper, introduced in England under Cromwell, abolished 1853.

Ady, Endre, Hungarian poet, b. 1877, d. 1919.

Ælfric, scholar and writer, b. about 955, d. about 1020.

Æmilian Way, Roman road, constructed 187 B.C.

Aerodynamics, study founded by Sir George Cayley 1809.

Aeroplane, steam model patented 1842 by W. S. Henson; successful model flown 1903 by Wright brothers; flights of Blériot, Brabazon and Cody 1909.

Æschines, Greek orator, b. 389, d. 314 B.C.

Æschylus, Greek dramatist (*Seven against Thebes,* 467 B.C.), b. 525, d. 456 B.C.

Æsop, Greek writer of fables, b. about 620, d. about 560 B.C.

Ætius, Flavius, Roman leader (defeated Attila 451), b. about 390, murdered 454.

Afghanistan, independent kingdom since 1747; treaty with Britain 1855; independence recognised by Anglo-Russian Convention signed 31 Aug. 1907.

Afghan Wars, between British and Afghans, 1839–1842, 1879–1180, 1919.

Agadir, Incident of, 1911; earthquake, 1960.

Agapemonites, religious sect founded 1846 by the Rev. Henry James Prince, b. 1811, d. 1899.

Agapitus, St, Pope, 535–536.

Agapitus II, Pope, 946–955.

Aga Khan I, spiritual leader of Ismaili sect of Islam, b. 1800, d. 1881.

Aga Khan II, spiritual leader of the Ismaili sect of Islam, d. 1885.

Aga Khan III, spiritual leader of the Ismaili sect of Islam, b. 1877, d. 1957.

Aga Khan IV, spiritual leader of the Ismaili sect of Islam, b. 1936.

Agassiz, Jean Louis Rodolphe, Swiss naturalist, b. 1807, d. 1873.

Agatha, St, martyred 5 Feb. 251.

Agatho, St, Pope 678–681.

Aghrim, Battle of, fought in Ireland against James II 12 July 1691.

Agincourt, Battle of, fought between Henry V and the French 25 Oct. 1415.

Agnes' Eve, St, 20–21 Jan.

Agnostic, term first introduced 1869 by the English scientist Thomas Henry Huxley, b. 1825, d. 1895.

Agricola (Georg Bauer), German 'father of mineralogy', b. 1490, d. 1555.

Agricola, Gnaeus Julius, Roman general, b. 37, d. 93.

Agriculture, Board—now Ministry—of, formed 1889.

Agriculture, Department of, U.S.A., created 15 May 1862.

Agrigentum, Sicily, founded about 582 B.C.

Agrippa, Marcus Vipsanius, Roman general, b. 63, d. 12 B.C.

Aguilar, Grace, English writer (*The Vale of Cedars*, 1850), b. 1816, d. 1847.

Ahmed I, Turkish sultan (from 1603), b. 1589, d. 1617.

Ahmed II, Turkish sultan (from 1691), b. 1643, d. 1695.

Ahmed III, Turkish sultan (1703–1730), b. 1637, d. 1736.

Ahmedabad, Indian city, founded by Ahmed Shah 1411.

Ahmediya Movement, Muslim sect founded 1889 by Mirza Ghulam Ahmed, b. 1839, d. 1908.

Ahmed Khan, Sir Syed, Indian educationist, b. 1817, d. 1898.

Ahmednagar, Indian city, founded by Ahmed Nizam Shah 1494.

Aidan, St, first bishop of Lindisfarne, d. 31 Aug. 651.

Ainsworth, William Harrison, English historical novelist (*The Tower of London*, 1840), b. 1805, d. 1882.

Air, composition first analysed 1771 by the French chemist Antoine Laurent Lavoisier, b. 1743, d. 1794.

Airdrie, Lanarkshire, founded 1695.

Air Gun, invented 1656 by Guter of Nuremberg.

Airmail Post, first organised in Britain by the *Empire Illustrated* 10 Aug. 1910.

Airmail Service, first regular, inaugurated by the U.S. Government 1918.

Air Ministry, London, constituted separate Ministry 1917.

Air-pump, invented by the German scientist Otto von Guericke, b. 1602, d. 1686.

Air-ship, models constructed by Giffard in 1852 and by Renard and Krebos in 1884 ; rigid model constructed by Zeppelin in 1900.

Air Training Corps, formed in Britain 1 Feb. 1941.

Airy, Sir George Biddell, Astronomer Royal (1835–1881), b. 1801, d. 1892.

Aisne, Battle of the, World War I, 13–28 Sept. 1914.

Aix-la-Chapelle (Aachen), founded 125. Congresses 1668, 1748 and 30 Sept–21 Nov. 1818.

Ajaccio, Corsica, founded 1492 by Genoese.

Ajanta Cave Paintings, India, dated approximately 600.

Akbar, Jalaluddin Mohammed, Mogul Emperor of India (1556–1605), b. 1542, d. 1605.

Akerman, John Yonge, English founder of the *Numismatic Journal*, b. 1806, d. 1873.

Akhnaton, heretic pharaoh of Egypt (Amenhotep IV), lived during 14th century B.C.

Akron, Ohio, founded 1825, chartered 1865.

Aksakov, Sergei Timofeievich, Russian writer (*Family Chronicle*, 1846–1856), b. 1791, d. 1859.

Alabama, U.S.A., created Territory 1817, admitted as State to the Union 1819.

Alabama, The, Confederate warship, built at Birkenhead 1862, attacked U.S. shipping 1862–1864, sunk by *Kearsage* 1864. Britain paid compensation for her depradations in 1873.

Alamein, Battle of, World War II, 23 Oct.–4 Nov. 1942.

Alanbrooke, Alan Brooke, Viscount, British soldier, b. 1887.

Alaric, Visigoth king, d. 410.

Alaska, discovered by Vitus Bering 1741 ; purchased from the Russians by U.S.A. 1867 ; incorporated as Territory 1912 ; became 49th State 1959.

Alba, Ferdinand Alvarez de Toledo, Duke of, Spanish soldier, b. 1507, d. 1582.

Albania, under Turkish suzerainty 1467–1912 ; Principality 1912–1924 ; Republic 1925–1928 ; Monarchy 1928–1946 ; Republic from 1946.

Albany, Louisa, Countess of, wife of Prince Charles Edward, b. 1753, d. 1824.

Albeniz, Isaac, Spanish composer (*Iberia*, 1906), b. 1860, d. 1909.

Alberoni, Giulio, Italian statesman, b. 1664, d. 1752.

Albert, Anti-Pope, 1102.

Albert, Prince Consort of England (from 1840), b. 1819, d. 1861.

Albert I, King of the Belgians (from 1909), b. 1875, d. 1934.

Albert Hall, Kensington, built in memory of Prince Albert 1867–71.

Albert Memorial, Hyde Park, begun 1864, completed 1876.

Albert Nyanza, lake, discovered 1864 by Sir Samuel White Baker, b. 1821, d. 1893.

Alberta, Canada, organised as district 1875 ; created Province 1905.

Alberti, Domenico, Italian composer (*Endimione*), b. about 1710, d. 1740.

Albertini, Leone Battista, Italian painter and sculptor, b. 1404, d. 1472.

Albertus, Magnus, German philosopher, b. about 1200, d. 1280.

Albigenses, French heretics, active about 1200, destroyed 1209–1229.

Albuera, Battle of, Peninsular War, fought between British and French 16 May 1811.

Albuquerque, Alphonso, Portuguese statesman, b. 1453, d. 1515.

Albuquerque, New Mexico, founded 1706.

Alcibiades, Greek general, b. about 451, d. 404 B.C.

Alcock, Sir John William, pioneer aviator, b. 1892, d. 1919.

Alcott, Louisa May, American writer (*Little Women*, 1868–1869), b. 1832, d. 1888.

Alcuin, English scholar, b. about 735, d. 804.

Aldenham School, English public school, founded by Richard Platt 1597.

Aldershot Camp, English military camp, founded 1854.

Aldhelm, bishop of Sherborne, b. about 640, d. 709.

Aldington, Richard, English writer (*Death of a Hero*, 1929), b. 1892.

Aldol, chemical compound discovered by the French chemist Charles Adolphe Wurtz, b. 1817, d. 1884.

Aldwych, opened 18 Oct. 1905.

' Aleichem, Sholem ' (Shalom Rabinovich), Yiddish writer, b. 1859, d. 1916.

Aleman, Mateo, Spanish writer (*Guzmár de Alfarache*, 1599–1604), b. 1547 d. about 1616.

d'Alembert, Jean le Rond, French scientist and philosopher, b. 1717, d. 1783.

Aleutian Islands, discovered by Vitus Bering 1725 ; bought from Russia by U.S.A. 1867.

Alexander, St, Pope 105–119.

Alexander II (Anselmo Baggio), Pope 1061–1073.

Alexander III (Rolando Bandinelli), Pope 1159–1181.

Alexander IV (Rinaldo di Segni), Pope 1254–1261.

Alexander V (Peter Philargès), Anti-Pope 1409–1410.

Alexander VI (Rodrigo Borgia), Pope 1492–1503, b. 1431, d. 1503.

Alexander VII (Fabio Chigi), Pope 1655–1667, b. 1599, d. 1667.

Alexander VIII (Pietro Ottoboni), Pope 1689–1691, b. 1610, d. 1691.

Alexander the Great, of Macedon, ruler of Greece (336–323 B.C.) and conqueror of Persia (334–330 B.C.), b. 356, d. 323 B.C.

Alexander I, Russian emperor (from 1801), b. 1777, d. 1825.

Alexander II, Russian emperor (from 1855), b. 1818, assassinated 1881.

Alexander III, Russian emperor (from 1881), b. 1845, d. 1894.

Alexander I, King of Scotland (from 1107), b. about 1078, d. 1124.

Alexander II, King of Scotland (from 1214), b. 1198, d. 1249.

Alexander III, King of Scotland (from 1249), b. 1241, d. 1285.

Alexander, King of Yugoslavia (from 1921), b. 1888, assassinated at Marseilles 9 Oct. 1934.

Alexander, Mrs Cecil Frances, hymn-writer ('There is a green hill far away'), b. 1818, d. 1895.

Alexander, Sir George, English actor-manager, b. 1858, d. 1918.

Alexander, Harold, Viscount, British soldier, b. 1891.

Alexander, Michael Solomon, first Anglican bishop of Jerusalem, b. 1799, d. 1845.

Alexandra, Queen, wife of Edward VII, b. 1844, d. 1925.

Alexandria, founded 331 B.C. ; library founded during 3rd century B.C., damaged 47 B.C., destroyed A.D. 272.

Alexandria, Battle of, fought between British and French 21 March 1801.

Alexandrian Era, began 5503 B.C.

Alexios Comnenos, Byzantine Emperor (1081-1118), b. 1048, d. 1118.

Alfarabi, Arabian musician, b. about 900, d. 950.

Alfieri, Vittorio, Italian poet (*Saul*, 1782), b. 1749, d. 1803.

Alfonso, see **Alphonso.**

Alford, Henry, first editor of the *Contemporary Review*, b. 1810, d. 1871.

Alfred the Great, King of England (from 871), b. 849, d. 899.

'Alfred Jewel, The ', Ashmolean Museum, Oxford, found at Athelney, 1693.

Algeciras, Conference of, concerning Morocco, held 1906.

Algeria, annexed to France 1842 ;

conquered by Allies from Axis 1942 ; nationalist revolt began 1954.

Alhambra, The, Moorish palace near Granada, built between 1248 and 1354.

Ali, Muslim leader, b. about 600, killed 660.

Ali, Mehemet, Pasha, Turkish Grand Vizier and ruler of Egypt, b. 1815, d. 1871.

Aliens Act, Great Britain, passed 1793.

Aliwal, Battle of, first Sikh War, fought between the British and the Sikhs 28 Jan. 1846.

Alizarin, red dye, synthesised 1868 by the German scientist Karl Liebermann, b. 1842, d. 1914.

Aiken, Henry, English etcher, d. 1831.

All-Blacks, New Zealand Rugby team, made unbeaten tour of British Isles 1924-1925.

All Hallows' Eve, 31 Oct.

All Saints, festival instituted 625 ; celebrated at Rome 13 May.

All Souls' Day, celebrated 2 Nov. (except when Sunday of festival is of the first class when it is celebrated 3 Nov.).

All Souls' College, Oxford University, founded 1437 by Henry Chichele, b. 1362, d. 1443.

Allan, David, Scottish painter, b. 1744, d. 1796.

Allen, Grant, Canadian-born writer (*The Woman Who Did*, 1895), b. 1848, d. 1899.

Allenby, Edmund, Viscount, British soldier, b. 1861, d. 1936.

Alleyn, Edward, English actor-manager, founder of Dulwich College 1619, b. 1566, d. 1626.

Alleyn's School, English public school, founded by Edward Alleyn 1619.

'All the Talents', Administration of, Cabinet formed under Grenville 1806, resigned 1807.

Allhallows School, Dorset, British public school founded in Devon in early 16th century. Removed to Dorset 1938.

Alma, Battle of the, Crimean War, in which the Allies fought the Russians, 20 Sept. 1854.

Almack's, London club founded 1763 by William Almack (d. 1781) ; established as Brooks's 1778.

Almanac Duty, abolished in Britain 1834.

Almanza, Battle of, War of the Spanish Succession, French fought British and Portuguese, 25 April 1707.

Alma-Tadema, Sir Lawrence, Dutchborn painter, b. 1836, d. 1912.

Almeida, Portugal, captured by the Spaniards 25 Aug. 1762 ; by the French 1810 ; and recaptured by the Allies under Wellington 1811.

Almeida, Francisco de, Portuguese statesman, killed 1509.

Almohades (*Muwahhidim*), Berber Muslim sect, ruled N. Africa and Spain during 12th and 13th centuries.

Almond, Dr Hely Hutchinson, Scottish educational reformer, b. 1832, d. 1903.

Almoravides (*Murabitim*), Berber Muslim sect, ruled N. Africa and Spain during 11th and 12th centuries.

Almqvist, Karl, Swedish writer, b. 1793, d. 1866.

Alpaca Fabrics, first manufactured (1852) in England by Sir Titus Salt, b. 1803, d. 1876.

Alpha Rays, discovered 1896 by Lord Rutherford, b. 1871, d. 1937.

Alphage, St, Archbishop of Canterbury, b. 954, d. 1012.

Alphonso I, King of Portugal (from 1112), b. 1094, d. 1185.

Alphonso the Fat, King of Portugal (from 1211), b. 1185, d. 1223.

Alphonso III, King of Portugal (from 1248), b. 1210, d. 1279.

Alphonso IV, King of Portugal (from 1325), b. 1290, d. 1357.

Alphonso Africano, King of Portugal (from 1438), b. 1432, d. 1481.

Alphonso VI, King of Portugal (from 1656 to 1668), b. 1643, d. 1675.

Alphonso I, King of Spain, 739–757.

Alphonso the Chaste, King of Spain, 789–842.

Alphonso the Great, King of Spain, 866–914.

Alphonso IV, King of Spain, 924–931.

Alphonso V, King of Spain, 999–1028.

Alphonso VI, King of Spain, 1065–1109.

Alphonso the Emperor, King of Spain, 1126–1157.

Alphonso the Noble, King of Castile, 1158–1214.

Alphonso IX, King of Leon, 1188–1230.

Alphonso the Wise, King of Spain, 1252–1284.

Alphonso XI, King of Spain, 1312–1350.

Alphonso XII, King of Spain (from 1870), b. 1857, d. 1885.

Alphonso XIII, King of Spain, b. 1886, acceded to the throne 1902, abdicated 14 Apr. 1931.

Alsace-Lorraine, ruled by Germany 1871–1918, by France 1918–1940, by Germany 1940–1944, by France since 1944.

Altamira Cave Paintings, Santander, Spain, discovered by the daughter of Marcelino de Sautuola 1879.

Altdorfer, Albrecht, German artist, b. about 1480, d. 1538.

Altmark, Battle of the, 16 Feb. 1940.

Aluminium, isolated 1854 by the French colonial scientist Henri Ste.-Claire Deville, b. 1818, d. 1881.

Amateur Athletic Association, United Kingdom, founded 1880.

Amateur Athletic Union, U.S.A., founded under the name of National Association of Amateur Athletes of America 1880. Assumed present name 1888.

Amati, Niccolo, Italian violin-maker, b. 1596, d. 1684.

Amazon River, discovered 1500 by the Spanish navigator Vicente Yañez Pinzón, b. about 1460, d. about 1524.

Ambassadors, first legally protected in England 1708.

Amboyna, Molucca island and town, discovered by the Portuguese 1511 ; seized by the Dutch 1605 ; Massacre of, 1623.

Ambrose, St, bishop of Milan, b. about 340, d. 397.

Ambulances, introduced 1792 by Baron Dominique Jean Larrey, b. 1766, d. 1842.

Amelia, Princess, daughter of George III, b. 1783, d. 1810.

America, discovered by Christopher Columbus 1492. Vikings believed to have reached America about 1000.

American Academy in Rome, founded 1905.

American Academy of Arts and Sciences, chartered at Boston 1780.

American Antiquarian Society, founded 1812.

American Bar Association, organised 1878.

American Bible Society, founded 1816.

American Civil War, fought 1861 to 1865.

American Civil War Veteran, last surviving, Walter Williams, b. 1843, d. 1959.

American Constitution, came into force 21 June 1788.

American Declaration of Independence, made 4 July 1776.

American Dialect, of English, first mentioned 1740.

American Duties Act, passed 1764 ; on tea 1767.

American Ephemerus and Nautical Almanac, founded 1849 by Charles Henry Davis, b. 1807, d. 1877.

American Federation of Labor, founded 1886.

American Football, adopted present form 1880.

American Legion, founded 1919.

American Philosophical Society, founded by Benjamin Franklin at Philadelphia 1734.

American Society for the Prevention of Cruelty to Animals, founded 1866.

American States, Organisation of, formed 1948.

American War of Independence, fought 1775 to 1783.

Ames, Joseph, English bibliographer (*Typographical Antiquities*, 1749), b. 1689, d. 1759.

Amfiteatrov, Daniele, Russian-born composer, b. 1901.

Amherst College, Hampshire Co., Mass., U.S.A., opened 1821, chartered 1825.

Amiel, Henri Frédéric, Swiss philosopher, b. 1821, d. 1881.

Amiens, Treaty of, between Great Britain, France, Spain and the Netherlands, signed 25 March 1802.

Amiens Cathedral, constructed 1220–1288.

Amines, derivatives of ammonia, discovered 1849 by the French chemist Charles Adolphe Wurtz, b. 1817, d. 1843.

Amis, Kingsley, British writer (*Lucky Jim*, 1954), b. 1922.

Amman, Jost, Swiss artist, b. 1539, d. 1591.

Amœba, described 1775 by Rösel von Rosenhof.

Ammonia, Gaseous, first isolated 1774 by Joseph Priestley, b. 1733, d. 1804.

Amoy, former Chinese treaty-port, captured by British 1841.

Ampère, André Marie, French physicist, b. 1775, d. 1836.

Ampleforth College, British public school, exiled at the Reformation, revived 1802.

Amritsar, Indian city, founded 1577 by Ram Das as the holy city of the Sikhs. Riots, 10 to 15 April 1919.

Amsterdam, began to develop from a fishing village into a city about 1204.

Amundsen, Roald, Norwegian explorer (reached South Pole 14 Dec. 1911), b. 1872, d. 1928.

Amyot, Jacques, French translator of Plutarch, b. 1513, d. 1593.

Anabaptists, religious movement, began in Münster, Germany, 1521 ; first reached England 1549.

Anabasis, march of Cyrus the Younger against Artaxerxes, 401 B.C.

Anacletus (Anencletus), St, Pope 76–78.

Anacletus II, Anti-Pope 1130–1138.

Anacreon, Greek poet, b. about 550, d. about 465 B.C.

Anæsthesia, General, nitrous oxide used 1799 by Humphry Davy, 1844 by Horace Wells (U.S.A.) ; ethyl chloride used 1848 by Heyfelder ; ether used 1846 by William Morton (U.S.A.) ; chloroform demonstrated 1847 by Robert Simpson, administered to

Queen Victoria 1853 by John Snow. Local freezing used 1812 by Baron Larrey (in Napoleon's army) ; cocaine used 1884 by Carl Koller ; procaine used 1905 by Einhorn.

Anastasia, Grand Duchess of Russia, b. 1901.

Anastasius I, St, Pope 399–401.

Anastasius II, St, Pope 496–498.

Anastasius, Anti-Pope, 855–858.

Anastasius III, Pope, 911–913.

Anastasius IV, Pope 1153–1154.

Anastasius I, Roman emperor (from 491), b. about 430, d. 518.

Anastasius II, Roman emperor (from 713), executed 721.

Anaxagoras, Greek philosopher, b. about 500, d. about 428 B.C.

Anaximander, first world map designer, b. 611, d. 546 B.C.

Anaximenes, Greek philosopher, lived during 6th century B.C.

Anchor Escapement, Clock-making, invented by the English clockmaker Robert Hooke, b. 1635, d. 1703.

Ancon, Treaty of, almost ending the War of the Pacific (1879–1884), signed 20 Oct. 1883.

Andaman Islands, used as penal settlement at intervals from 1858–1942 ; occupied by Japanese 1942–1945 ; administered, together with the Nicobar Islands by the Government of India.

Andersen, Hans Christian, Danish writer of fairy stories, b. 1805, d. 1875.

Anderson, Elizabeth Garrett, first British woman doctor, qualified 1856, b. 1836, d. 1917.

Andhra Pradesh, India : constituted separate State 1953 ; on enlarging boundaries assumed present name 1956.

Andorra, traditionally granted independence by Charlemagne about 778 ; created a principality 1278.

Andrássy, Julius, Count, Hungarian statesman, b. 1823, d. 1890.

André, Major John, British spy in America, b. 1751, hanged 1780.

Andrea del Sarto, Italian painter, b. 1487, d. 1531.

Andrée, Salomon August, Swedish polar explorer, b. 1854, d. 1897.

Andrew, St, martyred 30 Nov. 69.

Andrew I, King of Hungary 1047–1061.

Andrew II, King of Hungary (from 1205), b. 1175, d. 1235.

Andrew III, King of Hungary 1290–1301.

Andrewes, Lancelot, Bishop of Winchester, b. 1555, d. 1626.

Andreyev, Leonid Nikolaievich, Russian playwright (*He Who Gets Slapped*, 1916), b. 1871, d. 1919.

Andronicus I, Comnenus, Byzantine emperor (from 1183), murdered 1185.

Andronicus II, Palæologus, Byzantine emperor (1282–1328), b. 1260, d. 1332.

Andronicus III, Palæologus, Byzantine emperor (from 1325), b. about 1296, d. 1341.

Andronicus IV, Palæologus, Byzantine emperor (1376–1379), d. 1385.

Angas, George Fife, South Australian pioneer, b. 1789, d. 1879.

Angel, gold coin first used in France 1340 ; in England 1465.

Angelico, Fra (Guido di Pietri), Italian painter, b. 1387, d. 1455.

Angell, Sir Norman (Lane), British economist (*The Great Illusion*, 1910), b. 1874.

Angelo, Domenico, fencing-master (*L'École d'armes*, 1763), b. 1716, d. 1802.

Angelo, Henry, fencing-master (son of Domenico), b. 1760, d. about 1839.

Angerstein, John Julius, important figure in the development of Lloyds, b. 1735, d. 1823.

Angiosperms, plants whose seeds ripen in a container, first defined by Paul Hermann 1690.

Angkor Vat, Cambodia, constructed about the period 1112–1152.

Anglesey, conquered by the Romans 61; by the English 1295.

Anglican Church (Church of England), established by Augustine 597, separated from Catholic Church 1534.

Anglo-Afghan Treaty, concluded by the Dobbs Mission in Kabul, 22 Nov. 1921.

Anglo-Irish Treaty, setting up the Irish Free State, signed 6 Dec. 1921.

Anglo-Persian Oil Company, now British Petroleum Company, formed Apr. 1909.

Anglo-Saxons, first landed in Britain about 449.

Angola, discovered by the Portuguese navigator Diogo Cão 1482–1485.

Ångström Unit (1-millionth of 1 mm.), named after the Swedish physicist Anders Jöns Ångström, b. 1814, d. 1874.

Anhydrite, discovered 1794 ; named 1804 by Abraham Gottleb Werner, b. 1750, d. 1817.

Anicetus, St, Pope 155–166.

Aniline, discovered by O. Unverdorben 1826, present name given by C. J. Fritzsche 1841.

Aniline Dyes, discovered 1856 by Sir William Henry Perkin, b. 1838, d. 1907.

Animism, philosophical doctrine propounded in the 18th century by Georg Ernst Stahl, b. 1660, d. 1734.

Ankara, capital of Turkey since 1920.

Ann Arbor, Michigan, first settled 1824 ; incorporated 1851.

Anna Comnena, Byzantine princess, b. 1083, d. 1148.

Annam, finally freed from the Chinese 1428 ; French influence began with treaty between Louis XVI and the ruler Gia-long 1787.

Annapolis, Maryland, first settled (under the name Providence) 1649 ; assumed present name 1694 ; incorporated 1708.

Anne, Queen of England (from 1702), b. 1665, d. 1714.

Anne, Russian empress (from 1730), b. 1693, d. 1740.

Anne, Queen of Richard III, b. 1456, d. 1485.

Anne Boleyn, 2nd wife of Henry VIII, b. about 1507, beheaded 1536.

Anne of Austria, Queen of France, b. 1601, d. 1666.

Anne of Bohemia, first Queen of Richard II, b. 1366, d. 1394.

Anne of Brittany, wife successively of Maximilian of Austria and of Louis XII, b. 1477, d. 1514.

Anne of Cleves, 4th wife of Henry VIII,

b. 1515, m. 1540, divorced 1540, d. 1557.

Anne of Denmark, Queen of James I, b. 1574, d. 1619.

Anning, Mary, English discoverer 1811 onwards of saurian remains, b. 1799, d. 1847.

Annual Register, first issued 1759.

Annunciation, Feast of the, celebrated in the Christian Church 25 Mar. each year.

d'Annunzio, Gabriele, Italian writer (*Francesca da Rimini*, 1901), b. 1863, d. 1938.

Anselm, St, Archbishop of Canterbury, b. about 1033, d. 1109.

Anson, George, Baron Anson, explorer, sailed round the world 1740–1744, b. 1697, d. 1762.

Ansermet, Ernest, Swiss conductor, b. 1883.

Anstey, Christopher, English writer (*The New Bath Guide*, 1766), b. 1724, d. 1806.

' Anstey, F.' (Thomas Anstey Guthrie), writer (*Vice-versa*, 1882), b. 1856, d. 1934.

Anterus, St, Pope 235–236.

Antheil, George, American composer, b. 1900.

Anthesteria, Athenian festival in honour of Dionysus, 11–13 month of Anthesterion (Feb.–Mar.).

Anthony, St, the Great, first Christian monk, b. about 250, d. 356.

Anthony of Padua, St, b. 1197, d. 1231.

Anthrax Bacteria, first discovered independently by Pollender and Brauell, 1849.

Anthropometry, first so named 1872 by Cesare Lombroso, b. 1836, d. 1909.

Anthroposophy, form of theosophy founded by Rudolf Steiner, b. 1861, d. 1925.

Anti-aircraft Defence, first used in siege of Paris, 1870.

Anticosti, Canadian island, first sighted 1534 by the French explorer Jacques Cartier, b. 1491, d. 1557.

Anti-Corn-Law League, founded 1838 by Richard Cobden, b. 1804, d. 1865.

Antietam, Battle of, American Civil War, fought 16–17 Sept. 1862.

Antigua, discovered by Christopher Columbus 1493.

Antimony, discovered (according to tradition) by 'Basilius Valentinus' (possibly a 16th-century monk).

Antinomian Controversy, between Agricola and the Lutherans, 1527–1540.

Antioch, founded by Seleucus 300 B.C.

Anti-proton, discovered 1955 by the American scientists Dr Owen Chamberlain and Dr Emilio Segre of the University of California (awarded Nobel Prize 1959).

Antisepsis, founded 1847 by the Austrian physician Semmelweiss ; introduced in England 1860 by Lord Lister, b. 1827, d. 1912 ; in Vienna 1847 by Ignatz Philipp Semmelweiss, b. 1818, d. 1865.

Antislavery Society, U.S.A., founded about 1833 by William Lloyd Garrison, b. 1805, d. 1879.

Antisthenes, Greek philosopher, b. about 444, d. about 365 B.C.

Antitoxins, study initiated by the French scientist Pierre Paul Emile Roux, b. 1853, d. 1933.

Antofagasta, Chile, founded 1870.

Antonello Da Messina, Italian painter, b. about 1430, d. 1479.

Antoninus, St, b. 1389, d. 1459.

Antoninus Pius, Roman emperor (from 138), b. 86, d. 161.

Antonius, Marcus (Mark Antony), b. about 83, committed suicide 30 B.C.

d'Antraigues, Comte Emanuel, French diplomat, b. 1755, murdered 1812.

Anzac Day, first celebrated in London 25 Apr. 1916.

Anzio Landings, World War II, 22–25 Jan. 1944.

Apache Tribe, North American Indians, finally surrendered 1886.

Apartheid, South African theory of separate political and cultural development for white and black races, first so named by the Rev. J. C. du Plessis at Kroonstad 1929 ; official policy of the government of the Union of South Africa since 1948.

Apollinaire, Guillaume (Wilhelm Appolinaris Kostrowicki), French poet, b. 1880, d. 1918.

Apollinaris, the Younger, bishop of Laodicea, d. about 390.

Apothecaries Company, London, incorporated 1606 and 1617.

Apperley, Charles James, 'Nimrod' the sporting writer, b. 1779, d. 1843.

Appian Way, Roman road, constructed 312–308 B.C.

'Appleseed, Johnny' (John Chapman), American pioneer, b. about 1775, d. 1847.

Apponyi, Albert, Count, Hungarian statesman, b. 1846, d. 1933.

Apraksin, Feodor Matveievich, founder of the Russian Navy, b. 1671, d. 1728.

Apricots, first planted in England about 1540.

April-Fools' Day (All Fools' Day), 1 Apr ; similar Indian custom, The Feast of Huli, 31 Mar.

Apsley, Sir Allen, royalist leader, b. 1616, d. 1683.

Apuleius, Lucius, writer of *The Golden Ass*, b. about 125.

Aquatint, invented in France 1768.

Aquinas, Thomas, Italian theologian and philosopher, b. about 1227, d. 1274.

Arab Federation of Iraq and Jordan, proclaimed 14 Feb. 1958.

Arab League, founded at Cairo 1945 ; Libya joined 1953 ; Sudan 1956.

Arabella Stuart, heir to English throne, b. 1575, d. in prison 1615.

Arachnidæ, family to which spiders belong, first distinguished 1815 by the French naturalist Jean Lamarck, b. 1744, d. 1829.

Arago, Dominique François Jean, French scientist, b. 1786, d. 1853.

Aragon, Louis, French writer, b. 1897.

Aram, Eugene, murderer, b. 1704, hanged 1759.

Ararat, Mt., reputed resting-place of Noah's Ark, first climbed 1829 by the German Dr Johann Jacob Parrot, b. 1792, d. 1840.

Arber, Edward, English bibliographer and scholar, b. 1836, d. 1912.

d'Arblay, Madame (Frances Burney), English novelist (*Evelina*, 1778), b. 1752, d. 1840.

Arbuthnot, Alexander, printer of the first Bible issued 1575 in Scotland, d. 1585.

Arbuthnot, John, Scottish writer (*Martin Scriblerus*), b. 1667, d. 1735.

Arc de Triomphe, Paris, constructed in honour of the Grande Armée 1806–1836.

Arcadius, Roman emperor (from 395), b. 378, d. 408.

Arcesilaus, Greek philosopher, b. about 316 ; d. about 241 B.C.

Archangel, Russia, founded 1584.

Archangel Passage, discovered 1553 by the English navigator Richard Chancellor, d. 1556.

Archbishop Holgate's Grammar School, York, British public school founded 1546 by Robert Holgate, Archbishop of York, b. about 1481, d. 1551.

Archer, Frederick, outstanding English jockey, b. 1857, committed suicide 1886.

Archer, William, dramatic critic, b. 1856, d. 1924.

Archibald, Sir Adams George, Canadian statesman, b. 1814, d. 1892.

Archimedes, Greek mathematician, b. about 287, killed 212 B.C.

Archipenko, Aleksandr, Russian sculptor, b. 1887.

Arden, Edward, English High Sheriff, b. about 1542, hanged 1583.

Arderne, John, English pioneer surgeon, lived in the 14th century.

Arditi, Luigi, Italian composer (*Il Bacio*), b. 1822, d. 1903.

Ardingly College, Sussex, English public school, founded 1858, moved to present site 1870.

Arensky, Anton Stepanovich, Russian composer (*Raphael*, 1894), b. 1861, d. 1906.

Areopagus, Greek tribunal, founded about 1507 B.C.

Arequipa, Peru, founded 1539 by the Spanish conquistador Francisco Pizarro, b. 1478, murdered 1541.

Aretino, Pietro, Italian poet and playwright, b. 1492, d. 1556.

d'Argenson, Marc, Comte, French army reformer, b. 1696, d. 1764.

Argentina, discovered by the Spanish explorer Don Juan Díaz de Solis 1516 ; ruled by Spain until 1816 ; independent series of governments from 1816 ; constitutional republic since 1853.

Argon, inert gas, discovered 1894 by the British scientists Lord Lister (1827–1912) and Sir William Ramsay (1852–1916).

Arian Movement, heretical Christian movement, founded about 314 by the Libyan theologian Arius, d. 336.

Ariosto, Lodovico, Italian poet (*Orlando furioso*, 1516), b. 1474, d. 1533.

Ariovistus, German chieftain, lived in the 1st century B.C.

Aristarchus of Samos, Greek astronomer at Alexandria, b. about 310, d. about 250 B.C.

Aristarchus of Samothrace, Greek man of letters, b. about 214, d. 143 B.C.

Aristides, Athenian general, d. about 468 B.C.

Aristippus, Greek philosopher, lived in the 5th and 4th centuries B.C.

Aristophanes, Greek playwright (*The Wasps*), b. about 450, d. about 380 B.C.

Aristotle, Greek philosopher, b. 384, d. 322 B.C.

Arithmetic of Cardinal Numbers, axiomatised by the Italian mathematician Giuseppe Peano 1899.

Arius, Libyan theologian and leader of the Arian Movement, d. 336.

Arizona, U.S.A., settled 1732 ; created a Territory 1863 ; admitted to the Union 1912.

Arkansas, U.S.A., settled 1686 ; created a Territory 1819 ; admitted to the Union 1836.

Arkhangelsky, Aleksandr, Russian composer (*Mass for the Dead*), b. 1846, d. 1924.

Arkwright, Sir Richard, English inventor 1768 of the spinning frame, b. 1732, d. 1792.

' Arlen, Michael **'** (Dikran Kou-youmdjian), Armenian-born novelist (*The Green Hat*, 1924), b. 1895, d. 1956.

Arles, Synod of, convened by the Emperor Constantine 314.

Armada, Spanish, assembled 1587 ; defeated by the English 1588.

Armaments, Limitation of, Conference held Washington, D.C., 1921–1922.

Armenia (Haiastan), created a Soviet Socialist Republic 1920 ; proclaimed a constituent Republic of the U.S.S.R. 1936.

Armenian Church, separate since 451.

Arminianism, religious movement, founded by the Dutch theologian Jacobus Arminius (Hermandzoon), b. 1560, d. 1609.

Arminius, German leader (17 B.C.–A.D. 21), routed Roman army under Varus A.D. 9.

Armistice Day (Day of Remembrance), World War I, 11 Nov. 1918.

Armour Plate, first proposed for ships of war 1805 by the English scientist and politician Sir William Congreve, b. 1772, d. 1828.

Armstrong, Henry Edward, English chemist and educationist, b. 1848, d. 1937.

Armstrong, William George, Baron, English engineer and inventor, b. 1810, d. 1900.

Armstrong-Jones, Anthony, husband of Princess Margaret since 1960, b. 1930.

Arne, Thomas Augustine, English composer (*Rule, Britannia*, 1740), b. 1710, d. 1778.

Arnhem, Battle of, World War II, 19–28 Sept. 1944.

Arnold, Benedict, American soldier, b. 1741, d. 1801.

Arnold, Bion Joseph, American electrical engineer and inventor 1900 of the magnetic clutch, b. 1861, d. 1942.

Arnold, Sir Edwin, English writer (*The Light of Asia*, 1879), b. 1832, d. 1904.

Arnold, Matthew, English educationist and poet (*Sohrab and Rustum*, 1853), b. 1822, d. 1888.

Arnold, Thomas, Headmaster of Rugby (1828–1842), b. 1795, d. 1842.

Arnold School, Blackpool, English public school, founded by the first headmaster F. T. Pennington 1896 at South Shore ; transferred to the present site 1901 ; reconstituted 1937.

Arnolfo di Cambio, Italian architect, b. about 1232, d. about 1310.

Arnulf, Bishop of Rochester, b. 1040, d. 1124.

Aroostook ' War ', American boundary dispute between Maine and New Brunswick, 1839.

Arp, Hans, French artist, b. 1888.

Árpád, Magyar leader, d. 907 ; dynasty ruled Hungary until 1301.

Arras, Treaty of, between Charles VII and Philip the Good, signed 1435.

Arrau, Claudio, Chilean pianist, b. 1904.

Arrhenius, Svante August, Swedish chemist, b. 1859, d. 1927.

Arrian, Greek historian (*Indica*), lived in the 1st and 2nd centuries.

Arrol, Sir William, British bridge builder, b. 1839, d. 1913.

Arrowsmith, Aaron, English geographer and map-publisher, b. 1750, d. 1823.

Arsacid Dynasty, ruled Persia 227 B.C. to A.D. 224.

d'Artagnan, Charles de Baatz, French captain of the Musketeers, b. 1611, d. 1673.

Artaxerxes I, Persian king, reigned 465–425 B.C.

Artaxerxes II, Persian king, reigned 404–358 B.C.

Artaxerxes III, Persian king, reigned 358–338 B.C.

Artevelde, Jacob van, Governor of Flanders, killed 1345.

Arthur, King, possibly real 5th- or 6th-century British chieftain.

Arthur, Duke of Brittany, b. 1187, murdered 1203.

Arthur, Chester Alan, U.S. President (1881–1885), b. 1830, d. 1886.

Arthur, Sir George, Governor of Bombay (1842–1846), b. 1784, d. 1854.

Artichokes, first grown in England in the 16th century.

Articles of Religion, 6 published by King Henry VIII 1536 ; 42 published without Parliamentary consent 1552 ; reduced to 39 1563, and received Parliamentary authority 1571.

Artificial Radioactivity, discovered 1934 by the French physicist Frédéric Joliot-Curie, d. 1958.

Artificial Silk, made 1883 by the English electro-chemist Sir Joseph Wilson Swan (1828–1914). Industry founded about 1885 by the French scientist Hilaire, Comte de Chardonnet (1839–1924).

Artigas, José Gervasio, Uruguayan revolutionary leader, b. 1774, d. 1850.

Arts Council of Great Britain, London, founded as the Council for the Encouragement of Music and the Arts (C.E.M.A.) 1940 ; incorporated under present name 1946.

Artsybashev, Mikhail Petrovich, Russian-born writer (*Sanine*, 1907), b. 1878, d. 1927.

Arundel, Thomas, Archbishop of Canterbury (1396–1414), b. 1353, d. 1414.

Asaph, St, d. about 596.

Asbury, Francis, English-born Methodist leader in America, b. 1745, d. 1816.

Ascalon, Battle of, fought between the Crusaders and the Moslems, 15 Aug. 1099.

Ascension, Feast of the, held on a Thursday each year 40 days after Easter Sunday.

Ascension Island, discovered by the Portuguese navigator João da Nova on Ascension Day 1501.

Asch, Sholem, Yiddish writer (*Dos Shtelt*, 1904), b. 1880.

Ascham, Roger, English writer (*The Schoolmaster*, 1570), b. about 1515, d. 1568.

Asclepiades, Greek physician, lived in the 2nd century B.C.

Ascot Gold Cup, instituted 1807.

Ascot Race Meeting, first held 11 Aug. 1711.

Asen Dynasty, ruled Bulgaria, 1185–1258.

Ash Wednesday, the first day of Lent.

Ashanti, West Africa, placed under British protection 1896 ; formally annexed by Britain 1901.

Ashanti Wars, 1863–1864, 1873–1874 and 1895–1900.

Ashdown, Battle of, between the Saxons and the Danes, 6 Jan. 871.

Ashendene Press, private press, founded and operated by C. H. St John Hornby 1895–1923.

' Ashes, The ', instituted 1882.

Ashford, Daisy, English writer (*The Young Visiters*, 1919), b. about 1891.

Ashmolean Museum, Oxford, founded about 1677 by the English antiquary Elias Ashmole (1617–1692) ; opened 1682.

Ashmun, Jehudi, American reformer in Liberia, b. 1794, d. 1828.

Aske, Robert, English leader 1536 of the Pilgrimage of Grace, executed 1537.

Aslib, London, founded as the Association of Special Libraries and Information Bureaux 1924.

Asoka, Indian Emperor, b. 273 d. 232 B.C.

Aspasia, mistress of Pericles, lived in 5th century B.C.

Aspdin, Joseph, English stonemason and inventor (1824) of Portland cement, b. 1779, d. 1855.

Asquith, Herbert Henry, Earl of Oxford and Asquith, British statesman (Prime Minister 1908–1916), b. 1852, d. 1928.

Assam, made a British Protectorate 1826 ; separately governed since 1874 (except 1905–1912).

Asser, English historian and Bishop of Sherborne, d. about 909.

Assignats, French Revolutionary paper money used 1789–1797.

Assumption of the Blessed Virgin Mary, Feast of the, celebrated each year 15 Aug. ; Catholic dogma defined 195.

Assur-Bani-Pal, Assyrian King (about 669–626 B.C.), d. 626 B.C.

Asteroid, First (Ceres), discovered 1801 by the Italian astronomer Giuseppe Piazzi, b. 1746, d. 1826.

Astley's Circus, founded 1770 by the

English equestrian Philip Astley, b. 1742, d. 1814.

Aston, Francis William, English inventor of the mass spectograph, b. 1877, d. 1945.

Astor, John Jacob, American millionaire, b. 1763, d. 1848.

Astor, Nancy Witcher Langhorne, Viscountess, American-born, first woman to sit (1919) in the House of Commons, b. 1879.

Astrolabe, Mariner's, adapted from the astronomer's astrolabe about 1480 by the German Martin Behaim, b. about 1459, d. 1507.

Astrophysics, study founded 1855 by the English scientist Sir William Huggins, b. 1824, d. 1910.

Aswan Dam, Upper Egypt, completed 1902.

Atahualpa, last Inca of Peru (1532–1533), executed 1533.

Atatürk, Kemal, Turkish soldier and statesman (Prime Minister 1923–1938), b. 1880, d. 1938.

Athanasius, St, Patriarch of Alexandria, b. about 298, d. 373.

Athelstan, King (924) of Wessex and Mercia, b. about 895, d. 939.

Athenæum, British periodical, began publication 1828 ; absorbed into *The Nation* 1921.

Athenæum Club, London, founded 1824.

Athens, schools closed 529 ; ruled by Turks 1456–1832.

Atkinson, Sir Harry, New Zealand Prime Minister (1876–1877, 1883–1884, 1887–1891), b. 1831, d. 1892.

Atlantic Charter, signed 1941.

Atlantic Flight, First solo Trans-, New York to Paris, made 1927 by the American aviator Colonel Lindbergh, b. 1902.

Atlantic Ocean, crossed by Christopher Columbus 1492.

Atlantic Telephone Cable, first opened for traffic 1956.

Atlantic Telegraph Cable, first successfully laid by the S.S. *Great Eastern* 1866.

Atlantic Treaty, North, signed in Washington, D.C., 1949.

Atmosphere, composition determined by the British scientist Henry Cavendish, b. 1731, d. 1810.

Atom, split 1919 by the New Zealand-born scientist Lord Rutherford, b. 1871, d. 1937.

Atom Bomb, first used in warfare at Hiroshima and Nagasaki August 1945.

Atomic Bomb Explosion, first carried out by the U.S.A. at New Mexico 1945.

Atomic Central Heating Plant, First, started operating at Harwell 1951.

Atomic Energy Research Establishment, British, set up at Harwell 1945.

Atomic Nucleus, first split (and the atom's energy released) by Sir John Cockcroft and Dr Walton 1932.

Atomic Numbers, of elements, determined by the British scientist Henry Gwyn Jeffreys Moseley, b. 1887, killed in battle 1915.

Atomic Pile, First, started operating in Chicago 2 Dec. 1942.

Atomic-powered Surface Ship, World's first, the Russian ice-breaker *Lenin,* launched 1957, put to sea 1958.

Atomic Shell, First, fired in Nevada, U.S.A., 1953.

Atomic Theory, classical version postulated by Leucippus of Miletus about 475 B.C. ; modern version developed by the English chemist John Dalton, b. 1766, d. 1844.

Atomic Weights, pioneer work done by the Swedish chemist Baron Berzelius, b. 1779, d. 1848.

Atropine, drug extracted from Belladonna, discovered by the German scientist Philipp Lorenz Geiger 1833.

Atticus, Titus Pomponius, Roman scholar, b. 109, d. 32 B.C.

Attila, ' Scourge of God ', King of the Huns, b. about 406, d. 453.

Attlee, Clement Richard, British statesman (Prime Minister 1945–1951), b. 1883.

Attorney-General, First English, William Bonneville 1277.

Auber, Daniel François Esprit, French composer (*Fra Diavolo,* 1830), b. 1782, d. 1871.

Aubrey, John, English antiquary and writer (*Minutes for Lives*), b. 1626, d. 1697.

Auchinleck, Sir Claude, British soldier, b. 1884.

Auden, Wystan Hugh, English-born poet (*The Orators*, 1932), b. 1907.

Audenarde (Oudenarde), Battle of, fought between the English and the French 30 June–11 July 1708.

Audubon, John James, American naturalist, b. 1785, d. 1851.

Auer von Welsbach, Karl, inventor 1885 of gas-mantle, b. 1858, d. 1929.

Auckland, William Eden, Baron, British statesman, b. 1744, d. 1814.

Augsburg, The Confession of, Lutheran creed, prepared 1530.

Augustine, St, Bishop of Hippo, N. African philosopher and theologian (*De Civitate Dei*), b. 354, d. 430.

Augustine, St, first Archbishop of Canterbury, d. about 604.

Augustus, first Roman Emperor (27 B.C.–A.D. 14), b. 63 B.C., d. A.D. 14.

Augustus II, King (1697–1733) of Poland, b. 1670, d. 1733.

Augustus III, King (1736–1763) of Poland, b. 1696, d. 1763.

Aulus Vitellius, Roman Emperor (69), b. 15, murdered 69.

Aurangzeb, Mogul Emperor of India (1659–1707), b. 1618, d. 1707.

Aurelian, Roman Emperor (270–275), b. about 212, assassinated 275.

Aurelius, Marcus, Roman Emperor (161–180), and author of *The Meditations*, b. 121, d. 180.

Auric, Georges, French composer (*Les Matelots*, 1925), b. 1899.

Auscultation by Stethoscope, medical examination, introduced by the French physician René Théophile Hyacinthe Laënnec, b. 1781, d. 1826.

Austen, Jane, English novelist (*Pride and Prejudice*, 1813), b. 1775, d. 1817.

Austerlitz, Battle of, between the French, and the Austrians and Russians, 2 Dec. 1805.

Australia, circumnavigated 1642–1643 by the Dutch navigator Abel Janszoon Tasman (about 1603–1659). Reached by air from England by Ross and Keith Smith 1919.

Australia, The Commonwealth of, created 1 Jan. 1901.

Austria, ruled by Hapsburgs 1278–1918 ; republic 1918–1938 ; annexed by Germany 1938 ; occupied 1943–1955 ; regained sovereignty and independence 1955.

Austrian Succession, War of the, 1740–1748.

Authorised Version of the Bible, made at order of James I, first published 1611.

Autogyro, invented by La Cierra 1920.

Automatic Calculating Engine (Ace), initiated 1945, completed at the British National Physical Laboratory 1950.

Avars, entered Europe about 555 ; defeated by Franks in 8th and 9th centuries.

Averroes (Ibn Rushd), Arabian philosopher, b. 1126, d. 1198.

Avicenna (Ibn Sina), Persian philosopher, b. about 980, d. 1037.

Avignon, ceded to the Papacy 1274 ; seat of Papacy 1309–1418 ; annexed to France 1791.

Avoirdupois, generally superseded the merchants' pound in England 1303.

Axminster Carpet, introduced into Britain from the U.S.A. about 1878.

Azañay Diaz, Manuel de, Spanish statesman (last Republican President), b. 1880, d. 1940.

Azerbaijan, freed 1918 ; created a Soviet Socialist Republic 1920 ; made a constituent Republic of the U.S.S.R. 1936.

Aztec Empire, Mexico, established in the 14th century, destroyed by Spaniards in early 16th century.

B

Baader, Franz Xaver von, German theologian, b. 1765, d. 1841.

Baalbek, Syrian city, destroyed by earthquake 1759.

Baal-Shem-Tov (Israel ben Eliezer), Russian founder of the modern Hasidim (Jewish sect), b. 1700, d. 1760.

Babbage, Charles, English mathematician and founder of the Royal Astronomical Society, b. 1792, d. 1871. Designed an ' analytical engine ' (1827–1847), the prototype for modern computers.

Babbitt Metal, anti-friction alloy, invented 1839 by the American Isaac Babbitt, b. 1799, d. 1862.

Babcock Test, for butterfat content in milk, invented 1890 by the American Stephen Moulton Babcock, b. 1843, d. 1931.

Babel, Isaac Emmanuilovich, Russian writer (*Red Cavalry*, 1926), b. 1894.

Baber, Mogul dynasty founder and conqueror of North India, b. about 1483, d. 1530.

Babeuf, François Noël, French revolutionary leader, b. 1760, prepared Babouvist conspiracy 1796, guillotined 1797.

Babi, Persian religious sect, founded 1844 by Mirza Ali Mohammed, b. 1821, killed 1850.

Babington Plot, to murder Queen Elizabeth in 1585, devised by Anthony Babington, b. 1561, executed 1586.

Bablake School, Coventry, British public school, founded by Queen Isabella 1344 ; refounded 1560.

Babur, Mogul Emperor of India (1526–1530), b. 1483, d. 1530.

Babylon, Babylonian capital, chosen as capital about 2100 B.C., declined in importance after 538 B.C.

Babylonian Captivity, of the Jews, 586–516 B.C.

' Babylonish Captivity ', of the Popes, 1309–1377.

Baccarat Case, in which future Edward VII gave evidence concerning gambling at Tranby Croft, tried June 1891.

Bacchelli, Riccardo, Italian novelist (*Il Diavolo al Pontelungo*, 1927), b. 1891.

Bach, Carl Philipp Emmanuel, German composer, b. 1714, d. 1788.

Bach, Johann Christian, German composer, b. 1725, d. 1782.

Bach, Johann Sebastian, German composer, b. 1685, d. 1750.

Bache, Alexander Dallas, American founder 1863 of the National Academy of Sciences, b. 1806, d. 1867.

Bacon, Francis, Baron Verulam, English statesman and writer, b. 1561, d. 1626.

Bacon's Authorship of Shakespeare, first suggested 1769 by H. Laurence.

Bacon, Francis, British artist, b. 1910.

Bacon, Roger, English philosopher, b. about 1214, d. about 1294.

Bacon's Rebellion, American revolt 1676 in Virginia, led by Nathanie Bacon, b. 1647, d. 1676.

Bacteria, discovered 1680 by the Dutch scientist A. van Leeuwenhoek, b. 1632, d. 1723 ; classified by F. J. Cohn 1872.

Badajoz, Battle of, Peninsular war, between Wellington and the French, 1812.

Baden-Powell, Robert, Lord, founder 1908 of the Boy Scouts, b. 1857, d. 1941.

Badminton, game played with shuttlecock, first played in England about 1873.

Badoglio, Pietro, Italian Field-Marshal, b. 1871, d. 1956.

Badon, Mount, legendary battle between British and Saxons, about 500.

Baedeker, Karl, German guide book compiler and publisher, b. 1801, d. 1859.

Baer, Karl Ernst von, Esthonian scientist and discoverer 1827 of the mammalian ovum, b. 1792, d. 1876.

Baer, Max, world heavy-weight boxing champion 1934, b. 1910, d. 1959.

Baeyer, Johann Friedrich Wilhelm Adolf von, German scientist and Nobel Prize winner (1905), b. 1835, d. 1917.

Baffin Bay, discovered 1616 by William Baffin, b. about 1584, d. 1622.

Bagehot, Walter, English sociologist and editor of the *Economist*, b. 1826, d. 1877.

Baghdad Pact, mutual defence treaty between Turkey, Iraq, Pakistan and Great Britain, signed 1955. Baghdad Pact Organisation set up on permanent footing Apr. 1956. Now Central Treaty Organisation (since 1958), known as CENTO.

Baghdad Railway, started 1888, completed 1940.

Bagration, Piotr Ivanovich, Russian general who fought (1812) Napoleon at Borodino, b. 1765, d. 1812.

Baha'i, religious sect developed from Babi by Mirza Hozain Ali, b. 1817, d. 1892, and his son Abbas Effendi, b. 1844, d. 1921.

Bahamas, West Indian islands, discovered 1492 by Christopher Columbus ; finally ceded to British 1783.

Bahia Blanca, Argentine port, founded 1828.

Bahrein Islands, Persian Gulf, made British Protectorate 1861.

Baïf, Jean Antoine de, French poet, b. 1532, d. 1589.

Baikie, William Balfour, Scottish explorer of West Africa, b. 1825, d. 1864.

Bailey Bridge, invented 1941 by Donald Bailey.

Baillie, Joanna, Scottish dramatist and poet, b. 1762, d. 1851.

Bain, Alexander, Scottish philosopher, b. 1818, d. 1903.

Baird, John Logie, Scottish inventor (1926) of television, b. 1888, d. 1946.

Bairnsfather, Bruce, English cartoonist and creator of the character ' Old Bill ', b. 1888.

Bajazet I, Turkish sultan, b. 1347, d. 1403.

Bajazet II, Turkish sultan, b. 1446, d. 1513.

Bakelite, invented 1907 by the American Leo Hendrik Baekeland, b. 1863, d. 1944.

Baker, Sir Benjamin, English designer of the Forth Bridge, b. 1840, d. 1907.

Baker, Sir Samuel White, English explorer of Africa, discoverer (1864) of Albert Nyanza, b. 1821, d. 1893.

Bakerloo Tube, London, opened 1906.

Bakewell, Robert, English agricultural pioneer, b. 1725, d. 1795.

Bakst, Leon, Russian-born stage designer, b. 1866, d. 1924.

Bakunin, Mikhail, Russian anarchist leader, b. 1814, d. 1876.

Balakirev, Mili Alexeivich, Russian composer, b. 1836, d. 1910.

Balaklava, Battle of, scene of the

Charge of the Light Brigade, fought 25 Oct. 1854.

Balanchine, George, Russian-born ballet dancer, b. 1904.

Balboa, Vasco Núñez de, Spanish discoverer (1513) of the Pacific Ocean, b. 1475, beheaded 1517.

Balbus, Lucius Cornelius, Roman consul defended by Cicero, fl. 56–40 B.C.

Balchin, Nigel, English writer (*The Small Back Room*, 1943), b. 1908.

Baldovinetti, Alessio, Italian painter, b. about 1425, d. 1499.

Baldwin I, Emperor at Constantinople, b. 1171, killed 1205.

Baldwin II, Emperor at Constantinople, b. 1217, d. 1273.

Baldwin I, first King of Jerusalem, b. 1058, d. 1118.

Baldwin II, King of Jerusalem, succeeded to the throne 1118, d. 1131.

Baldwin III, King of Jerusalem, b. 1130, d. 1162.

Baldwin IV, King of Jerusalem, b. about 1161, d. 1185.

Baldwin V, King of Jerusalem, b. 1178, d. 1186.

Baldwin, Robert, Canadian statesman, b. 1804, d. 1858.

Baldwin, Stanley, British statesman (Prime Minister, 1935–1937), b. 1867, d. 1947.

Bale, John, English dramatist, b. 1495, d. 1563.

Balearic Islands, finally ceded to Spain by the British 1803.

Balfe, Michael William, British composer (*The Bohemian Girl*), b. 1808, d. 1870.

Balfour, Arthur James, Earl Balfour, British statesman (Prime Minister 1902–1905), b. 1848, d. 1930.

Balfour Declaration, favouring the creation of a Jewish national home in Palestine, made by the British Government 2 Nov. 1917.

Bali, Indonesian island, first reached by the Dutch 1597.

Balliol College, Oxford University, founded about 1263 by John de Baliol, d. 1269.

Balliol, John de, King of Scots (1295–1296), b. 1249, d. 1313.

Balkan Wars, fought by the Balkan powers over the division of the Turkish empire in Europe 1912–1913.

Ball, John, English priest and peasants' leader, executed 1381.

Ballantyne, Robert Michael, Scottish writer of boys' stories, b. 1825, d. 1894.

Ballarat, Victoria, founded through discovery of gold nearby, in 1851.

Ballistite, smokeless powder, invented 1888 by the Swedish chemist Alfred Nobel, b. 1833, d. 1896.

Ballot, voting by, made compulsory in Britain 1872.

Balloons, invented by the brothers Joseph and Etienne Montgolfier 1783, first ascent by Montgolfier and Pilâtre de Roziers 21 Nov. 1783 ; first ascent in hydrogen balloon made by the physicist J. A. C. Charles 1 Dec. 1783 ; first ascents in Britain made 1784.

Balmoral Castle, Aberdeenshire, British Royal residence, completed 1855.

Balsamo, Giuseppe, ' Count Alessandro di Cagliostro ', Italian charlatan and alchemist, b. 1743, d. 1795.

Baltic Exchange (The Baltic Mercantile and Shipping Exchange), London, developed from informal 17th-century coffee-house transactions to the formal establishment of the Baltic Club 1823.

Baltimore, Maryland : formally founded 1729 ; settled about fifty years earlier.

Baluchistan, merged in West Pakistan 14 Oct. 1955.

Balzac, Honoré de, French novelist (*La Comédie Humaine,* 1829–1850), b. 1799, d. 1850.

Bampton Lectures, delivered annually at Oxford University since 1780, founded by John Bampton, b. about 1690, d. 1751.

Banat, ruled by Austria 1718–1779 ; ceded by Hungary to Rumania and Yugoslavia 1918.

Bancroft, George, American historian, b. 1800, d. 1891.

Bancroft, Sir Squire, English actor-manager, b. 1841, d. 1926.

Bancroft's School, Essex, British public school, founded by will of Francis Bancroft 1727.

Bandung Conference, First, of Asian-African countries, held 18–27 Apr. 1955.

Bangalore, Mysore capital, founded 1537.

Bangkok, made capital of Siam (Thailand) by Paya Tak 1782.

Bangorian Controversy, begun 1717 by Benjamin Hoadly, Bishop of Bangor.

Bank for International Settlements, founded 13 Nov. 1929.

Bank for Reconstruction and Development, International, proposed at Bretton Woods Conference 1944, constituted Dec. 1945, started operations 27 June 1946.

Bank Holidays : Act passed 1871 establishing present English holidays—Good Friday, Easter Monday, Whit Monday, first Monday in August, Christmas and Boxing Days.

Bank of England, founded 1694 by William Paterson, b. 1658, d. 1719 ; nationalised 1946.

Bank of France, founded by Napoleon 1800.

Bank of Scotland, founded by the Scottish Parliament 1695.

Bank of the United States : 1st, founded by the Federalists 1791, ended 1811 ; 2nd, founded 1816, ended 1836.

Bank Robbery, First American, carried out by rebel soldiers at St Albans, Vermont, 1864 ; first by the James-Younger gang 1866.

Bankhead, Tallulah, American actress, b. 1903.

Bankruptcy Act, abolished imprisonment for debt 1870.

Banks, Sir Joseph, English naturalist, founder of the African Association, b. 1744, d. 1820.

Bannockburn, Battle of, fought between Scots and English, 24 June 1314.

Banting, Sir Frederick Grant, Canadian scientist, b. 1891, killed in an air crash 1941.

Banting, William, English undertaker and pioneer in slimming by diet, b. 1797, d. 1878.

Bantock, Sir Granville, English composer (*The Great God Pan*, 1903), b. 1868, d. 1946.

Bantry Bay, Battle of, when French attempted the invasion of Ireland 1689—and again in 1796.

Baptist Church, First English, formed 1609 at Amsterdam, and 1611 in London. The Baptist Union of Great Britain and Ireland formed 1891. In U.S.A., first Baptist Church formed at the Providence settlement of Narragansett Bay 1639.

Bara, Theda, actress, b. 1857, d. 1934.

Barbados, visited by the English 1605, formally occupied by the English 1625, became part of the British Caribbean Federation 1956.

Barbarossa Brothers, Turkish pirates who terrorised Christian shipping in the Mediterranean in early 16th century.

Barbarossa (Frederick I), Holy Roman Emperor, b. about 1123, d. 1190.

Barbed Wire, invented 1873 by the American Joseph Farwell Glidden, b. 1813, d. 1906.

'Barbellion, W. N. P.' (Bruce Frederick Cummings), English writer (*The Journal of a Disappointed Man*, 1919), b. 1889, d. 1919.

Barber, Samuel, American composer (*Essay for Orchestra*, 1938), b. 1910.

Barbey d'Aurevilly, Jules, French writer, b. 1808, d. 1889.

Barbirolli, Sir John, conductor of the Hallé Orchestra from 1943, b. 1899.

Barbizon School, French art movement 1830–1870.

Barbon, Nicolas (son of Praise-God Barebone), English pioneer of fire insurance, b. 1640, d. 1698.

Barbusse, Henri, French writer (*Le Feu*, 1916), b. 1873, d. 1935.

Barcelona Cathedral, erected 1298–1448.

Barcelona University, founded 1430.

Bard College, Annandale-on-Hudson, N.Y., founded 1860, chartered in its present form and name 1935.

Barebone's Parliament, called by Cromwell during the Commonwealth, sat 4 July to 12 Dec. 1653. Named from one of its members, Praise-God Barebone, b. about 1596, d. 1679.

Barents Sea, named after William Barents, d. 1597, Dutch explorer.

Barham, Richard Harris, English writer (*The Ingoldsby Legends*, 1837–1840), b. 1788, d. 1845.

Barhebraeus (Abulfaraj), Armenian writer and Bishop of Aleppo, b. 1226, d. 1286.

Baring, Maurice, English writer (*In My End is My Beginning*, 1931), b. 1874, d. 1945.

Baring Brothers, English merchant bankers, founded by John Baring, b. 1730, d. 1816, and Francis Baring, b. 1740, d. 1810.

Baring-Gould, Sabine, English writer and hymn-writer ('Onward, Christian soldiers', 1865), b. 1834, d. 1924.

Barium, first investigated by V. Casciorolus of Bologna 1602, discovered 1808 by Sir Humphry Davy, b. 1778, d. 1829.

Barker, Granville, English poet and novelist (*Alanna Autumnal*, 1933), b. 1913.

Barker, Sir Herbert Atkinson, English specialist in manipulative surgery, b. 1869, d. 1950.

Bar-Kochba, Simon, Jewish leader in revolt against Romans (131–135), killed fighting 135.

Barlach, Ernst, German artist, b. 1870, d. 1937.

Barnabites, Catholic religious order, founded 1537 by St Antony Mary Zaccaria, d. 1539.

Barnard Castle School, Co. Durham, British public school, founded 1883.

Barnardo's Homes, Dr, founded 1867 by Dr Thomas Barnardo, b. 1845, d. 1905.

Barnato, Barnett, English-born South African financier, b. 1852, committed suicide 1897.

Barnes, Barnabe, English poet, b. about 1569, d. 1609.

Barnes, Thomas, English journalist (edited *The Times*, 1817–1841), b. 1785, d. 1841.

Barnes, William, English dialect poet, b. 1800, d. 1886.

Barnet, Battle of, Wars of the Roses, 14 Apr. 1471.

Barnet Fair, Hertfordshire, held during first week in Sept.

Barnfield, Richard, English pastoral poet, b. 1574, d. 1627.

Barnstaple Fair, Devon, held during Sept. (Wednesday, Thursday, Friday preceding 20 Sept.).

Barnum's Show, founded 1871 by the American Phineas Taylor Barnum, b. 1810, d. 1891.

Baroja, Pio, Spanish novelist, b. 1872.

Barometers, invented 1644 by Evangelista Torricelli, b. 1608, d. 1647.

Baronet, title created by King James I of England, 1611.

Barr, Robert, Scottish writer (*In the Midst of Alarms*, 1894), b. 1850, d. 1912.

Barren Grounds, Canada, first crossed 1770–1772 by the English explorer Samuel Hearne, b. 1745, d. 1792.

Barrès, Maurice, French politician and writer (*Le jardin de Bérénice*, 1891), b. 1862, d. 1923.

Barrie, Sir James Matthew, Scottish writer (*Peter Pan*, 1904), b. 1860, d. 1937.

Barrington, George, Irish pickpocket who became an Australian chief constable, b. 1755, d. 1804.

Barrister, first English woman, qualified 25 May 1921.

Barrow, Sir John, English explorer and founder (1830) of the Royal Geographical Society, b. 1764, d. 1848.

Barry, Sir Charles, English architect of the House of Commons, b. 1795, d. 1860.

Barrymore, John, American actor, b. 1882, d. 1942.

Barrymore, Lionel, American actor, b. 1878.

Bart, Jean, French admiral, b. 1650, d. 1702.

Barth, Hans, German composer, b. 1897.

Barth, Heinrich, German traveller and scientist, b. 1821, d. 1865.

Barth, Karl, German pianist, b. 1847, d. 1922.

Barth, Karl, Swiss theologian, b. 1886.

Bartholdi, Frédéric Auguste, French sculptor (*Statue of Liberty*), b. 1834, d. 1904.

Bartholomew, John George, Scottish cartographer, b. 1860, d. 1920.

Bartholomew Fair, held at West Smithfield, London, on St Bartholomew's Day (24 Aug. O.S.) from 1133–1855.

Bartholomew, Massacre of St, of Protestants by Catholics in Paris, 24 Aug. 1572.

Barthou, Jean, French statesman, b. 1862, assassinated 1934.

Bartlett, John, compiler of standard collection of *Familiar Quotations* (first issued 1855), b. 1820, d. 1905.

Bartók, Bela, Hungarian composer (*The Castle of Duke Bluebeard*, 1918), b. 1881, d. 1945.

Bartolommeo, Fra, Italian painter (*The Marriage of St Catherine*), b. about 1470, d. 1517.

Bartolozzi, Francesco, Italian engraver, b. 1727, d. 1815.

Bartram, John, first American botanist, b. 1739, d. 1823.

Baruch, Bernard Mannes, American financier, b. 1870.

Barye, Antoine Louis, French sculptor, b. 1795, d. 1875.

Baseball, invention attributed to Abner Doubleday, b. 1819, d. 1883, of Cooperstown, New York.

Basevi, George, English architect of the Fitzwilliam Museum, Cambridge (1837), b. 1794, d. 1845.

Bashkirtsev, Marie, Russian painter and writer (*Journal*, 1887), b. 1860, d. 1884.

Basic English, produced 1930 by C. K. Ogden.

Basil, St, known as Basil the Great, b. about 330, d. 379.

Basil I, Byzantine Emperor (867–886), b. about 813, d. 886.

Basil II, Byzantine Emperor (963–1025), b. about 958, d. 1025.

Baskerville, John, British printer and type-founder, b. 1706, d. 1775.

Basket-ball, invented by James Naismith at Springfield, Mass., 1891.

Basle University, founded by Pope Pius II 1460.

Bass & Co., British brewers, founded 1777 by William Bass, b. 1720.

Bassano, Jacopo, Italian painter, b. 1510, d. 1592.

Bassompierre, François de, French Field-Marshal at the siege of La Rochelle (1628–1629), b. 1579, d. 1646.

Bass Strait, between Australia and Tasmania, discovered 1798 by George Bass, English naval surgeon, d. about 1812.

Bastien-Lepage, Jules, French painter, b. 1848, d. 1884.

Bastille, The, Paris, built by Hugues Aubriot 1369–1383 ; destroyed 14 July 1789.

Basutoland, South Africa, made British Protectorate 1868.

Bataille, Henri, French writer, b. 1872, d. 1922.

Batavia, Java, founded by the Dutch Governor-General Pieter Roth 1619.

Bates, Herbert Ernest, English writer (*My Uncle Silas*, 1939), b. 1905.

Bath, Order of the (custom in existence by 1127), founded by George I in 1725.

Bathurst, New South Wales, founded by Governor Macquarie 1815.

Batoni, Pompeo Girolamo, Italian painter, b. 1708, d. 1787.

Battaan, World War II, occupied 14 Apr. 1945 by the Allies.

Battenberg, title conferred on Julia von Hanke in 1851 on the occasion of her morganatic marriage with Prince Alexander of Hesse ; their son Louis changed the name to Mountbatten in 1917.

Battle, Ordeal by, valid in English law until 1818.

'Battle Hymn of the Republic, The ',

written 1862 by the American poet Mrs Julia Ward Howe, b. 1819, d. 1910.

Battle of Britain, fought 8 Aug. to 5 Oct. 1940.

Battle of the Bulge, World War II, fought in France Dec. 1944 to Jan. 1945.

Battle of the Spurs, fought between Henry VIII and the French 16 Aug. 1513.

Baudelaire, Charles, French poet (*Les Fleurs du Mal*, 1857), b. 1821, d. 1867.

Bauxite, discovered by the Belgian P. Berthier 1821.

Bauhaus, architectural movement founded 1919 by Walter Gropius.

Bavaria, ruled by Wittelsbachs 1180–1918.

Bavarian Succession, War of the, fought 1778–1779.

Bax, Sir Arnold, composer (*The Poisoned Fountain*, 1920), b. 1883, d. 1953.

Baxter, George, English engraver and colour printer, b. 1804, d. 1867.

Baxter, Richard, English nonconformist writer (*The Saints' Everlasting Rest*, 1650), b. 1615, d. 1691.

Bay Bridge, San Francisco, built 1936.

Bay Psalm Book, earliest American printed book, published at Cambridge, Mass., 1640.

Bayard, Chevalier de, French general, b. about 1474, killed 1524.

Bayeux Tapestry, probably embroidered in the 12th century ; first recorded mention 1476.

Bayle, Pierre, French dictionary-compiler, b. 1647, d. 1707.

Baylis, Lilian, British theatre manager, b. 1874, d. 1937.

Bayreuth, Bavaria, founded 1194.

Bayreuth Theatre, Germany, home of Wagnerian opera, built 1872, opened 1876.

Bazin, René, French writer (*Les Oberté*, 1901), b. 1853, d. 1932.

Beale, Dorothea, principal of Cheltenham Ladies' College, b. 1831, d. 1906.

Bear-Baiting, prohibited in Britain by Act of Parliament 1835.

Beardsley, Aubrey, English artist

(illustrated *The Yellow Book*, 1894–1895), b. 1872, d. 1898.

Beattie, James, Scottish poet (*The Minstrel*, 1771–1774), b. 1735, d. 1803.

Beatty, David, 1st Earl Beatty, British First Sea Lord, b. 1871, d. 1936.

Beaufort, Margaret, Countess of Richmond and Derby, philanthropist, b. 1443, d. 1509.

Beauharnais, Eugène de, Prince of Venice, b. 1781, d. 1824.

Beaumarchais, Pierre Augustine Caron de, French playwright (*The Barber of Seville*, 1775), b. 1732, d. 1799.

Beaumont, Sir Francis, English dramatist (with John Fletcher, 1579–1625, *The Knight of the Burning Pestle*), b. 1584, d. 1616.

Beaumont College, Old Windsor, British public school, founded by the Society of Jesus 1861.

Beaverbrook, William Maxwell Aitken, 1st Baron, Canadian-born newspaper publisher, b. 1879.

Bebop, dance movement began developing as distinct phenomenon 1941.

Bechuanaland, South Africa, made British Protectorate 1885.

Becket, Thomas à, Archbishop of Canterbury, b. about 1118, murdered 1170.

Beckett, Gilbert Abbott à, English humorous writer and contributor to *Punch*, b. 1811, d. 1856.

Beckett, Samuel, Irish-born writer (*Waiting for Godot*, 1952), b. 1906.

Beckford, William, English writer (*Vathek*, 1787), b. 1760, d. 1844.

Becquer, Gustavo Adolfo, Spanish writer, b. 1836, d. 1870.

Becquerel, Antoine Henri, French scientist and discoverer (1896) of radioactivity in uranium, b. 1852, d. 1908.

Bedales, Hampshire, British co-educational school founded 1893.

Beddoes, Thomas Lovell, English writer (*The Bride's Tragedy*, 1822), b. 1803, committed suicide 1849.

Bede, The Venerable, English writer, b. about 672, d. 735.

Bedford Modern School, British public school, founded through funds left

1566 by Sir William Harper, b. about 1496, d. 1573.

Bedford School, British public school, founded before the Norman Conquest.

Bedlam (Bethlehem Hospital), London, founded by Simon Fitzmary 1247.

Beecham, Sir Thomas, English conductor and composer, b. 1879, d. 1961.

Beecher, Henry Ward, American writer, preacher and social reformer, b. 1813, d. 1887.

Beerbohm, Sir Max, English writer (*Zuleika Dobson*, 1911), b. 1872, d. 1956.

Beethoven, Ludwig van, German composer, b. 1770, d. 1827.

Beeton, Mrs (Isabella Mary Beeton), pioneer arbitor of British housekeeping, b. 1836, d. 1865.

Beet Sugar, discovered 1747 by the German chemist Andreas Sigismund Maggraf, b. 1709, d. 1782.

Beguines, lay sisterhoods founded about 1180 at Liège by Lambert le Bègue, d. about 1187.

Behn, Mrs Aphra, English writer (*Oronooko*, 1688), b. 1640, d. 1689.

Behring Strait, discovered 1725 by Vitus Bering, b. 1681, d. 1741.

Beilby Enamel Glass, introduced 1760.

Beira, Mozambique port, founded 1884 on site of Arab settlement.

Beit, Alfred, German-born British South African financier and philanthropist, b. 1853, d. 1906.

Belasco, David, American actor-manager, b. 1853, d. 1931.

Belfast Royal Academical Institution, British public school, founded 1810.

Belgian Congo, created Free State 1885; annexed to Belgium 1908; achieved independence 30 June 1960.

Belgium, part of Burgundian and Spanish Netherlands until 1572; Spanish rule until 1700; Austrian rule 1713–1794; part of Netherlands 1815–1830; became independent Kingdom 1830.

Belisarius, Byzantine general and defeater of Persians, Vandals and Ostrogoths, b. 505, d. 565.

Bell, Alexander Graham, Scottish-born inventor (1876) of the telephone, b. 1847, d. 1922.

Bell, Gertrude, English explorer in Arabia, b. 1868, d. 1926.

Bell, John, English bookseller and introducer about 1788 of ' modern face ' type, b. 1745, d. 1831.

Bellarmine, Robert, Italian Jesuit writer (*Disputations*, 1581), b. 1542, d. 1621.

Belleau Wood, Battle of, World War I, fought between U.S. Marines and Germans 6–10 June 1918.

Belle Sauvage, London, one of England's oldest coaching inns, first mentioned 1453.

Bellini, Giovanni, Italian painter (*Agony in the Garden*), b. about 1426, d. 1516.

Belloc, Hilaire, Anglo-French writer (*The Path to Rome*, 1902), b. 1870, d. 1953.

Bell Rock Lighthouse, North Sea, completed 1812.

Belo Horizonte, capital of Minas Gerais, Brazil, founded 1895.

Belvoir Hunt, Leicestershire and Lincolnshire, dates from 1750 ; became a fox pack 1762.

Belzoni, Giovanni Battista, Italian archæologist in Middle East, b. 1778, d. 1823.

Bembo, Cardinal Pietro, Italian poet, b. 1470, d. 1547.

Ben Day Process, illustrative method in printing, invented by the American Benjamin Day, b. 1838, d. 1916.

Benavente, Jacinto, Spanish playwright, b. 1866, d. 1954.

Benbow, John, English admiral, b. 1653, d. 1702.

Benchley, Robert, American humorous writer, b. 1889, d. 1945.

Benedict of Nursia, St, b. about 480, d. about 544.

Benedict I, Pope, 575–579.

Benedict II, Pope, 684–685.

Benedict III, Pope, 855–858.

Benedict IV, Pope, 900–903.

Benedict V, Pope, 964–965.

Benedict VI, Pope, 973–974 (murdered).

Benedict VII, Pope, 974–983

Benedict VIII (Theophylactus), Pope, 1012–1024.

Benedict IX (Theophylactus), Pope, 1032–1048, b. about 1021, d. 1056.

Benedict X (Johannes Mincius), Anti-Pope, 1058–1059.

Benedict XI (Niccolo Boccasini), Pope, 1303–1304, b. 1240, d. 1304.

Benedict XII (Jacques Fournier), Pope, 1334–1342.

Benedict XIII (Pedro de Luna), Anti-Pope, 1394–1417, b. about 1328, d. about 1423.

Benedict XIII (Piero Francesco Orsini), Pope, 1724–1730, b. 1649, d. 1730.

Benedict XIV (Prospero Lorenzo Lambertini), Pope, 1740–1758, b. 1675, d. 1758.

Benedict XV (Giacomo della Chiesa), Pope, 1914–1922, b. 1854, d. 1922.

Benedict Biscop, English churchman and founder of monastery at Wearmouth, b. about 628, d. 690.

Benedictine Order, founded 529 by St Benedict of Nursia, b. about 480, d. about 544.

Beneš, Eduard, Czech statesman, b. 1884, d. 1948.

Benét, Stephen Vincent, American writer (*John Brown's Body*, 1928), b. 1898, d. 1943.

Bengal, became English settlement about 1652 ; made Chief Presidency 1773 ; divided between India and Pakistan 1947.

Benghazi, World War II, captured by British 7 Feb. 1941 ; by Rommel 3 Apr. 1941 ; recaptured by British 24 Dec. 1941, and again 20 Nov. 1942.

Bennett, Arnold, English novelist (*The Old Wives' Tale*, 1908), b. 1867, d. 1931.

Benno, St, Bishop of Meissen, b. 1010, d. 1106. Canonised 1523.

Bentham, Jeremy, English philosopher and social reformer, b. 1748, d. 1832.

Bentley, Richard, English literary critic (*Dissertation on the Epistles of Phalaris*, 1699), b. 1662, d. 1742.

Benzole, discovered 1825 by Michael Faraday, b. 1791, d. 1867.

' Beowulf ', Anglo-Saxon epic poem, written about 1000.

Béranger, Pierre Jean de, French songwriter (*Chansons Nouvelles,* 1830), b. 1780, d. 1857.

Bérard, Christian, French painter (*Seated Acrobat*), b. 1902.

Berchtold's Day, Swiss annual festival held 2 Jan.

Berdyaev, Nicholas, Russian-born philosopher, b. 1874, d. 1948.

Berenson, Bernhard, Lithuanian-born American art critic, b. 1865, d. 1959.

Berg, Alban, Austrian composer (*Wozzeck,* 1922), b. 1885, d. 1935.

Bergerac, Cyrano de, French writer and soldier, b. 1619, d. 1655.

Bergh, Henry, founder (1866) of the American Society for the Prevention of Cruelty to Animals, b. 1811, d. 1888.

Bergson, Henri, French philosopher, b. 1859, d. 1942.

Bering, Vitus, Danish-born Russian explorer, b. 1681, d. 1741.

Berkeley, George, Irish philosopher, b. 1685, d. 1753.

Berkhamsted School, Hertfordshire, British public school, founded by Dr John Incent, Dean of St Paul's in Henry VIII's reign ; refounded 1841.

Berkman, Alexander, Russian-born anarchist, b. 1870, imprisoned 1892–1906, committed suicide 1936.

Berlin, Irving, American composer (*Alexander's Ragtime Band,* 1911), b. 1888.

Berlin, captured by the French 1806. Decree of Berlin, 21 Nov. 1806. Congress of Berlin 1878 ; Treaty of Berlin signed 13 July 1878. Berlin Blockade began 28 June 1948 ; lifted 12 May 1949 ; airlift ended 6 Oct. 1949.

Berlioz, Hector, French composer (*The Damnation of Faust*), b. 1803, d. 1869.

Bermuda, discovered by the Spaniard Juan Bermúdez 1503 ; settled by the English 1609, and formally taken over 1684.

Bernadette (Soubirous), St, of Lourdes (visions 1858), b. 1844, d. 1879.

Bernadotte, Count Folke, Swedish humanitarian, b. 1895, assassinated 1948.

Bernadotte, Jean Baptiste, French

general and Swedish king from 1818, b. 1763, d. 1844.

Bernanos, Georges, French writer (*Diary of a Country Parson,* 1936), b. 1888, d. 1948.

Bernard, St, Abbot of Clairvaux, b. 1091, d. 1153.

Bernardin de St Pierre, Jacques-Henri, French writer (*Paul et Virginie,* 1787), b. 1737, d. 1814.

Bernhardt, Sarah, French actress, b. 1844, d. 1923.

Bernini, Giovanni Lorenzo, Italian sculptor and architect, b. 1598, d. 1680.

Bernoulli's Principle, of the flow of liquids, formulated by Daniel Bernoulli, b. 1700, d. 1782.

Bernoulli's Numbers, mathematics, discovered by Jacques Bernoulli, b. 1654, d. 1705.

Berruguete, Alonso, Spanish artist, b. about 1480, d. 1561.

Berthelot, Marcelin, French organic chemist, b. 1827, d. 1907.

Bertillon System, criminal investigation by anthropometry, devised 1880 by the Frenchman Alphonse Bertillon, b. 1853, d. 1914.

Berwick, Peace of, signed (between England and Scotland) 1639.

Beryllium, isolated 1828 by the German scientist Friedrich Wöhler, b. 1800, d. 1882.

Berzelius, Baron Jöns Jakob, Swedish chemist, b. 1779, d. 1848.

Besant, Mrs Annie, British theosophist and reformer, b. 1847, d. 1933.

Bessel Functions, invented 1817, fully developed 1824, by the German astronomer Wilhelm Bessel, b. 1784, d. 1846.

Bessemer Converter, invented 1856 by the English engineer Sir Henry Bessemer, b. 1813, d. 1898.

Bessemer Steel Process, first used in U.S.A. at Phillipsburg 1856.

Beta Rays, discovered 1896 by Lord Rutherford, b. 1871, d. 1937.

Betatron, instrument for producing very high-speed electrons, invented 1940 by the American scientist D. W. Kerst.

Bethlen, Gábor, Hungarian leader, b. 1580, d. 1629.

Bethmann-Hollweg, Theobald von, German Chancellor, b. 1856, d. 1921.

Betterton, Thomas, English actor-manager, b. 1635, d. 1710.

Betting Houses and Lists, abolished 1853 by an Act of Parliament introduced by Sir Alexander Cockburn, b. 1802, d. 1880.

Bevan, Aneurin, British statesman, b. 1897, d. 1960.

Beveridge Plan, national insurance scheme for Britain conceived by Lord Beveridge, b. 1879 ; published 20 Nov. 1942.

Bevin, Ernest, British trade-union leader and statesman, b. 1881, d. 1951.

Bewick, Thomas, English wood engraver, b. 1753, d. 1828.

Béza, Theodore, French religious reformer, b. 1519, d. 1605.

Bhave, Vinobha, Indian social reformer and spiritual leader, b. 1895.

Bhopal, India, founded 1728 ; amalgamated with the State of Madhya Pradesh 1956.

Bhutan, Himalayan State, concluded treaty with East India Company 1774 ; subsidised by British from 1865, by Indian government from 1942 ; new treaty with Government of India, 1949.

Bibliographical Society, London, founded 1892.

Bibliothèque Nationale, Paris, founded 1721.

Bicycles : pedal-operated model invented by the British inventor Kirkpatrick Macmillan 1838 ; ' Penny-farthings ' popular 1870s ; Rover ' safety ' bicycle 1885 ; inflated tyres invented 1888.

Bifocal Lens, invented 1780 by Benjamin Franklin, b. 1706, d. 1790.

Big Ben, London, hour bell cast 10 Apr. 1858. Clock went into service 31 May 1859. Chimes first broadcast 31 Dec. 1923.

Big Bertha, German long-range gun that shelled Paris Mar. 1918.

Big Brother Movement, scheme for emigration of boys from Britain to Australia founded by New Zealand-born Sir Richard Linton, b. 1879, d. 1959.

Bihar, Indian State, treaty made with East India Company 1765. Separated from Bengal Province 1912 and united with Orissa. Made separate province 1936.

Bikaner, capital of Bikaner State, India, founded 1488.

Bikini Atoll, Marshall Islands, scene of atom-bomb tests started by U.S. navy 1946.

Bill of Rights, English, based on Declaration of Rights (Feb.) and passed by Parliament Oct. 1689.

Billiards, believed to have been invented by Henrique Devigne, French artist, about 1571.

Bimetallism, use of gold and silver for currency, first so termed 1869 by Henri Cernuschi, Italian economist, b. 1821, d. 1896.

Binomial Theorem, invented before 1676 by Sir Isaac Newton, b. 1642, d. 1727.

Binyon, Laurence, English poet (*For the Fallen*), b. 1869, d. 1943.

Birkbeck College, London University, founded (as the London Mechanics' Institution) 1823 by Dr George Birkbeck, b. 1776, d. 1841.

Birkenhead, Frederick Edwin Smith, 1st Earl of, British statesman, b. 1872, d. 1930.

Birkenhead School, Cheshire, English public school founded 1860.

Birmingham Repertory Theatre, England, founded 1913 by Sir Barry Jackson, b. 1879, d. 1961.

Birmingham University, founded 1875 as Mason College by Sir Josiah Mason, b. 1795, d. 1881. Charter granted 1900.

Birrell, Augustine, English writer and statesman, b. 1850, d. 1933.

Birth Control Clinics : 1st in world at Amsterdam 1881 ; 1st English opened London 1921 ; 1st American opened New York 1923 (previously opened 1916 and closed by police).

Bischof, Werner, Swiss photographer, b. 1916, killed in car accident 1954.

Bishop Wordsworth's School, Salisbury, British public school, founded 1890 by John Wordsworth, Bishop of Salisbury, b. 1843, d. 1911.

Bishop's Stortford College, Hertfordshire, British public school, founded 1868, reconstituted 1904.

Bisley, National Rifle Association first met at Bisley 1890. First woman (Miss M. E. Foster) to win King's Prize 19 July 1930.

Bismarck, World War II naval battle, 24–27 Mar. 1941.

Bismarck Sea, Battle of the World War II, 2–4 Mar. 1943.

Bismarck, Otto Eduard Leopold, Prinz von, German Chancellor (1861–1890), b. 1815, d. 1898.

Bismuth, chemical element, identified 1530 by the German scientist Georg Agricola, b. 1490, d. 1555.

Bizet, Georges, French composer (*Carmen,* 1875), b. 1838, d. 1875.

Björnson, Björnstjerne, Norwegian writer (*Synnöve Solbakken,* 1857), b. 1832, d. 1910.

Black, Joseph, British scientist who developed (about 1765) the theory of latent heat, b. 1728, d. 1799.

' Black and Tans ', auxiliary police used against Irish republicans 1920–1921.

Black Death, The plague pandemic affecting Asia and N. Africa, Italy 1340, England 1348–1349.

Black Friday, American financial disaster, 24 Sept. 1869.

Black Hawk, North American Indian chief, b. 1767, d. 1838.

Black Hole of Calcutta, scene of imprisonment of English by rebels 20–21 June 1756.

Black Letter, for English newspaper titles, first used 1679.

Black Phosphorus, first prepared by the American physicist Percy Williams Bridgman, b. 1882.

Black Prince, The, Edward, son of Edward III, b. 1330, d. 1376.

Black Rod, House of Lords, first appointed 1350.

Black Watch, Highland regiment, formed 1725, became Royal Highland Black Watch 1739.

Blackfriars, Dominican convent, established in London 1276.

Blackfriars Bridge, London, erected 1865–1869.

Blackmore, Richard Doddridge, English novelist (*Lorna Doone,* 1869), b. 1825, d. 1900.

Blackstone's Commentaries (1765–1769), legal guide, written by Sir William Blackstone, English jurist, b. 1723, d. 1780.

Blackwell, Dr Elizabeth, first (1859) British registered woman doctor, b. 1821, d. 1910.

Blackwood's Magazine, founded 1817 by William Blackwood, b. 1776, d. 1834, of Edinburgh.

Blades, William, London printer, b. 1824, d. 1890.

Blaeu, Willem Janszoon, founder of Dutch firm of map-makers, b. 1571, d. 1638.

Blair, Robert, Scottish poet (*The Grave,* 1743), b. 1699, d. 1746.

Blake, Robert, English admiral, b. 1599, d. 1657.

Blake, William, English painter and poet (*The Marriage of Heaven and Hell,* 1790), b. 1757, d. 1827.

Blanc, Mont (15,782 ft.), first climbed by Jacques Balmat and Michel Paccard 1786.

Blanche of Castile, wife of Louis VIII, b. 1188, d. 1252.

Blanqui, Louis, French revolutionary leader, b. 1805, d. 1881.

Blatchford, Robert, British socialist writer, b. 1851, d. 1943.

Blavatsky, Madame Helena, Russian-born founder of the Theosophical Society, b. 1831, d. 1891.

Bleaching Powder, discovered 1798 by the English scientist Smithson Tennant, b. 1761, d. 1815.

Blenheim, Battle of, fought between the English and the French, 13 Aug. 1704; Palace, Oxfordshire, built 1705–1722.

Blériot, Louis, French aviator, inventor of monoplane which he flew across the English Channel 27 July 1909, b. 1872, d. 1936.

Blessed Virgin Mary, The Assumption of The, celebrated 15 Aug.

Blew-Coat School, London, founded by Edward VI 1553.

Bligh, Admiral William of *The Bounty*, b. 1754, d. 1817. Mutiny of the Bounty 28 Apr. 1789.

Blind Books, letters first printed in relief 1771 by the French philanthropist Valentin Haüy.

Bliss, Sir Arthur, Master of the Queen's Musick since 1953, b. 1891.

Blitz (from German *Blitzkrieg*, ' lightning war '), military technique of surprise attack, 1939–1941 ; applied in England to heavy bombing 1940–1941.

Bloch, Ernst, Swiss-born composer (*America*, 1926), b. 1880, d. 1959.

Bloch, Jean Richard, French novelist (*—et Cie*, 1918), b. 1884, d. 1947.

Blok, Alexander Alexandrovich, Russian poet, b. 1880, d. 1921.

Blom, Eric, English music critic and historian, b. 1888, d. 1959.

Blomfield, Sir Arthur William, English architect of the London Law Courts in Fleet Street, b. 1829, d. 1899.

Blondin, Charles, French acrobat, b. 1824, d. 1897. Crossed Niagara Falls on a tightrope 1859.

Blood, Col. Thomas, Irish malcontent, attempted to steal the Crown Jewels 9 May 1671, b. about 1618, d. 1680.

Blood, Circulation of the, discovered 1615 by William Harvey, b. 1578, d. 1657.

Blood Groups, defined 1901 by Landsteiner.

Bloody Assizes, held 1685 by Judge Jeffreys, b. about 1644, d. 1689.

Bloody Sunday, massacre of St Petersburg workers, 22 Jan. 1905.

Bloomer, Amelia Jenks, American dress reformer, b. 1818, d. 1894.

Bloomfield, Robert, English poet (*The Farmer's Boy*, 1800), b. 1766, d. 1823.

Blow, John, English composer, b. about 1648, d. 1708.

Bloxham School (All Saints School, Bloxham), English public school,

founded by the Rev. P. R. Egerton 1860.

Blücher, Gebhard Leberecht von, German Field-Marshal, b. 1742, d. 1819.

Blueprint Process, for copying plans etc., first used 1842 by the English astronomer Sir John Herschel, b. 1792, d. 1871.

Blum, Léon, French statesman (Premier 1936, 1938, 1946), b. 1872, d. 1950.

Blundell's School, Tiverton, English public school, built and endowed by the clothier Peter Blundell 1604.

Blunden, Edmund, English poet and writer (*Undertones of War*, 1928), b. 1896.

Blunt, Wilfrid Scawen, English writer, b. 1840, d. 1922.

Boadicea, British queen of the Iceni, committed suicide 62.

Board of Trade, London, founded 1661.

Boccaccio, Giovanni, Italian writer (*The Decameron*, 1348–1353), b. 1313, d. 1375.

Boccherini, Luigi, Italian composer, b. 1743, d. 1805.

Bodichon, Mrs Barbara, English founder 1869 of Girton College, Cambridge University, b. 1827, d. 1890.

Bodin, Jean, French political thinker (*Six Livres de la République*, 1576), b. about 1530, d. 1596.

Bodleian Library, Oxford, founded 1598, opened 1602, by Sir Thomas Bodley, b. 1545, d. 1613 ; New Library opened 1946.

Bodoni, Giambattista, Italian printer and typographer, b. 1740, d. 1813.

Boece, Hector, Scottish historian, b. about 1465, d. 1536.

Boecklin, Arnold, Swiss painter, b. 1827, d. 1901.

Boehme, Jakob, German theosophist, b. 1575, d. 1624.

Boer War, South Africa, began 11 Oct. 1899, ended 31 May 1902.

Boethius, Roman statesman and philosopher (*De Consolatione Philosophiae*), b. about 473, executed 525.

Bogotá, Colombian capital, founded by Gonzalo Jiménez de Quesada 1538.

Bohemia, ruled by Hapsburgs 1526–1918 ; part of Czechoslovakia since 1918.

Bohemian Brethren, Christian sect, founded among followers of Hus by Peter Chelčicky in early 15th century.

Bohn, Henry George, English publisher of popular series of classics, b. 1796, d. 1884.

Bohr, Niels, Danish atomic scientist, b. 1885.

Boileau, Nicolas, French writer and critic, b. 1636, d. 1711.

Boito, Arrigo, Italian composer (*Mefistofele*, 1868), b. 1842, d. 1918.

Bojer, Johan, Norwegian novelist (*Troens Magt,* 1903), b. 1872, d. 1959.

'Boldrewood, Rolf' (Thomas Alexander Browne), English-born Australian writer (*Robbery under Arms,* 1888), b. 1826, d. 1915.

Boleslaus I, Polish King (992–1025), d. 1025.

Boleslaus II, Polish King (1058–1079), b. 1039, d. about 1081.

Boleslaus III, Polish King (1102–1139), b. 1086, d. 1139.

Boleyn, Anne, English Queen, b. about 1507, m. Henry VIII 1533, beheaded 1536.

Bolingbroke, Henry St John, Viscount Bolingbroke, English statesman and writer (*The Idea of a Patriot King*), b. 1678, d. 1751.

Bolívar, Simón, liberator of South America (1810–1824), b. 1783, d. 1830.

Bolivia, proclaimed a republic 1825 ; boundary with Chile fixed after war 1879–1882 ; with Paraguay after war 1932–1935 ; with Peru after war 1935–1938.

Bologna, Giovanni da, Flemish sculptor, b. 1524, d. 1608.

Bolometer, thermometer for measuring small differences of temperature, invented 1880 by the American scientist Samuel Pierpont Langley, b. 1834, d. 1906.

Bolsheviks, majority faction of Russian Social-Democrat Party at Congress in Brussels and London, 1903 ; became Communist Party 1918.

Bolton School, English public school, founded 1524 by William Haighe ; rebuilt and endowed by Robert Lever 1641.

Boltzmann, Ludwig, Austrian physicist, b. 1844, committed suicide 1906.

Bombay University, founded 1857.

Bonaparte (Buonaparte until 1796), Napoléon, Emperor of France (1804–1813), b. 1769, d. 1821 ; Jerome, King of Westphalia (1807–1813), b. 1784, d. 1860 ; Joseph, King of Naples (1806–1807) and Spain (1808–1813), b. 1768, d. 1844 ; Louis, King of Holland (1806–1810), b. 1778, d. 1846 ; Louis Napoléon, Emperor of France (1851–1870), b. 1808, d. 1873.

Bonar Law, Andrew, British statesman (Prime Minister 1922–1923), b. 1858, d. 1923.

Bonaventura, St, b. 1221, d. 1274.

Bond, Sir Edward Augustus, head librarian of the British Museum, b. 1815, d. 1898.

Bondfield, Miss Margaret, first (1929) woman Privy Councillor, b. 1873, d. 1953.

Bone, Henry, English enamel-painter, b. 1755, d. 1834.

Bone, Muirhead, Scottish artist, b. 1876, d. 1953.

Bone-setting (Osteopathy), practice founded 1874 by the American surgeon Andrew Taylor Still, b. 1828, d. 1917.

Bonheur, Rosa, French painter, b. 1822, d. 1899.

Boniface, St, b. about 680, murdered 754.

Boniface I, St, Pope 418–422.

Boniface II, Pope 530–532.

Boniface III, Pope 607.

Boniface IV, Pope 608–615.

Boniface V, Pope 619–625.

Boniface VI, Pope 896.

Boniface VII, Anti-Pope 974.

Boniface VIII (Benedetto Gaetano), Pope 1294–1303, b. 1235, d. 1303.

Boniface IX (Piero Tomacelli), Pope 1389–1404, b. about 1345, d. 1404.

Bonington, Richard Parkes, English painter (*Grand Canal, Venice*), b. 1802, d. 1828.

Bonn, capital of German Federal Republic since 1949.

Book Auction, First, the sale of George Dousa's library, held in Leyden 1604.

Book Jackets, or dust-wrappers, first used in England 1832 ; came into general use about 1890.

Book of Common Prayer, Church of England, *First* published 1549, *Second* 1552, *Elizabethan* 1559, *revised* 1661.

Book-plates, to mark ownership, first introduced in Germany about 1450.

Booksellers Association, of Great Britain and Ireland, founded as the Associated Booksellers 1895 ; assumed present name 1948.

Boole, George, English mathematician and originator of Boolean algebra, b. 1815, d. 1864.

Boone, Daniel, American explorer, b. 1734, d. 1820.

Booth, Edwin Thomas, American actor, b. 1833, d. 1893.

Booth, John Wilkes, murderer (1865) of Abraham Lincoln, b. 1838, shot 1865.

Booth, William, English founder (1865) of the Salvation Army, b. 1829, d. 1912.

Booth, William Bramwell, who succeeded (1912) his father William Booth as General of the Salvation Army, b. 1856, d. 1929.

Bootham School, York, English public school, founded 1823.

Bordeaux, Henri, French novelist (*Le Feu*), b. 1870.

Borgia, Cesare, Italian statesman and general, b. 1476, killed in battle 1507.

Borgia, Lucrezia, Duchess of Ferrara, b. 1479, d. 1519.

Borgia, Rodrigo, elected Pope Alexander VI 1492, b. 1431, poisoned 1503.

Boric Acid, first prepared 1702 by the Dutch chemist Willem Homberg, b. 1652, d. 1715.

Boring Machine, The first practical, invented 1769 by the English engineer John Smeaton, b. 1724, d. 1792.

Boris II, Bulgarian Tsar, b. 1894, d. 1943.

Boris Godunov, Russian Tsar, b. about 1551, d. 1605.

Borneo, discovered by the Portuguese 1521. North Borneo made British Protectorate 1881.

Borodin, Alexander, Russian composer (*Prince Igor*, 1869–91), b. 1833, d. 1887.

Borodino, Battle of, fought between Napoleon and the Russians 7 Sept. 1812.

Boron, chemical element isolated 1808 by Sir Humphry Davy, b. 1778, d. 1829.

Borromeo, St Charles, b. 1538, d. 1584.

Borromini, Francesco, Italian architect, b. 1599, d. 1667.

Borrow, George Henry, English writer (*Lavengro*, 1851), b. 1803, d. 1881.

Borstal system of imprisonment for young criminals, began in England 1902.

Bosanquet, Bernard, English philosopher, b. 1848, d. 1923.

Bosch, Hieronymus, Flemish painter (*The Temptation of St Anthony*), b. about 1462, d. 1516.

Boscobel, Shropshire, scene of the hiding-place (in an oak) of Charles II in 1651.

Bose, Sir Jagadis Chandra, Indian plant expert, b. 1858, d. 1937.

Bosnia–Hercegovina, ruled by Austria 1878–1918 ; part of Yugoslavia since 1918.

Bossuet, Jacques Bénigne, French theologian, b. 1627, d. 1704.

Boston, Massachusetts, settled by John Winthrop 1630.

Boston Massacre, occurred 1770.

Boston Symphony Orchestra, founded 1381 by the American philanthropist Henry Lee Higginson, b. 1834, d. 1919.

Boston Tea Party, American revolutionary incident, 16 Dec. 1773.

Boswell, James, Scottish biographer of Dr Samuel Johnson, b. 1740, d. 1795.

Bosworth Field, Battle of, fought between Henry VII and Richard III, 22 Aug. 1485.

Botany Bay, New South Wales, discovered 28 Apr. 1770 by Captain James Cook, b. 1728, d. 1779 ; became British penal settlement 1786 ; transportation ceased 1840.

Botha, General Louis, Boer leader (Prime Minister of South Africa, 1910–1919), b. 1863, d. 1919.

Bothwell, James Hepburn, Earl of, husband of Mary, Queen of Scots, b. about 1537, d. 1578.

Bothwell Bridge, Battle of, fought between the English and the Scottish Covenanters 1679.

Botticelli, Sandro, Italian painter (*The Birth of Venus*), b. 1444, d. 1510.

Bottomley, Horatio, English politician, financier and founder (1906) of *John Bull* ; in prison for fraud 1920–1927 ; b. 1860, d. 1933.

Boucher, François, French painter (*The Toilet of Venus*), b. 1703, d. 1770.

Boucicault, Dion, Irish-born playwright (*The Colleen Bawn,* 1860), b. 1822, d. 1890.

Bougainville, Louis Antoine de, French explorer, b. 1729, d. 1811.

Boughton, Rutland, English composer (*The Immortal Hour,* 1913), b. 1878, d. 1960.

Boulanger, George Ernest Jean Marie, French general and politician, b. 1837, committed suicide 1891.

Boulder Dam, harnessing the Colorado River, project initiated 1928.

Boulsover, Thomas, English inventor (1743) of Sheffield plate.

Boulton, Matthew, English engineer and inventor, b. 1728, d. 1809.

Bounty, Mutiny of the, 28 Apr. 1789.

Bourbon Dynasty, ruled France 1589–1792, 1814–1848 ; Spain 1700–1808, 1814–1868, 1874–1930 ; Naples 1759–1799, 1799–1806, 1815–1860 ; Parma 1748–1815, 1847–1860.

Bourges Cathedral, constructed between 1220 and 1260.

Bourne, Francis, English Cardinal, b. 1861, d. 1935.

Bourse, The Paris, French Stock Exchange, founded 1724.

Bouts, Dirk, Dutch painter, b. about 1410, d. 1475.

Bouvet Island, South Atlantic, discovered 1739 by the French navigator Jean Baptiste Lozier Bouvet ; annexed by Norway 1927–1930.

Bow Porcelain, manufactured 1745–1776.

Bow Street Runners, London, superseded by the Police 1829.

Bowdler, Thomas, English self-appointed censor of the classics, b. 1754, d. 1825.

Bowdoin College, Maine, founded 1794.

Bowen, Elizabeth, Anglo-Irish writer (*The Death of the Heart,* 1938), b. 1889.

Bowen, York, English composer (*The Lament of Tasso,* 1903), b. 1884.

Boxer Rising, Peking, in which the Chinese rose against foreigners in China, June and July 1900.

Boxing, legalised in England 1901.

Boy Scout Movement, began with camp for 20 boys in 1907 held by Lord Baden-Powell, b. 1857, d. 1941. First Rally and Conference, Crystal Palace, London, 4 Sept. 1909. Incorporated in U.S.A. 1910.

Boyce, William, English organist and composer, b. 1710, d. 1779.

Boycott, Captain Charles Cunningham, Lord Erne's English land agent in Co. Mayo, who was ' boycotted ' from 24 Sept. 1880, b. 1832, d. 1897.

Boyd-Orr, John, Baron, Scottish nutritionist, b. 1880.

Boyle, Richard, Earl of Cork, British Lord High Treasurer, b. 1566, d. 1643.

Boyle, Robert, Irish-born scientist and discoverer (1662) of Boyle's Law, b. 1627, d. 1691.

Boyne, Battle of the, fought between William III and James II, 1 July 1690.

Boys' Brigade, The, founded 1883 by Sir William Alexander Smith, b. 1854, d. 1914.

Boys' Brigade of America, United, founded 1887.

Brabançonne, La, Belgian national anthem, composed by François van Campenhout, b. 1779, d. 1849.

Brabazon of Tara, John Theodore Cuthbert Moore-Brabazon, Baron, awarded Royal Aero Club Pilot Certificate No. I, 8 Mar. 1910, b. 1884.

Bracegirdle, Mistress Anne, English actress, b. about 1664, d. 1748.

Bradfield College (St Andrew's College, Bradfield), English public school, founded by the Rev. Thomas Stevens 1850.

Bradford Grammar School, English public school, founded before 1548 ; incorporated in 1662.

Bradlaugh, Charles, English politician and social reformer, b. 1833, d. 1891.

Bradley, Andrew Cecil, English critic, b. 1851, d. 1935.

Bradley, Francis Herbert, English philosopher, b. 1846, d. 1924.

Bradley, Henry, one of the editors of the *New (Oxford) English Dictionary,* b. 1845, d. 1923.

Bradshaw, John, English regicide, President of Court that condemned Charles I, 1649 ; b. 1602, d. 1659.

Bradshaw's Railway Guide, Great Britain, first published 1839 by George Bradshaw, b. 1801, d. 1853; discontinued 1961. Continental Bradshaw established 1848.

Brady, Matthew B., ' Lincoln's cameraman ', American pioneer photographer, b. about 1823, d. 1896.

Bragg, Sir William Henry, English scientist, b. 1862, d. 1942.

Brahe, Tycho, Danish astronomer, b. 1546, d. 1601.

Brahms, Johannes, German composer (*Hungarian Dances,* 1852–1869), b. 1833, d. 1897.

Braid, James, Scottish pioneer in study of hypnotism, b. about 1796, d. 1860.

Braille Alphabet for the Blind, invented 1834 by the blind Frenchman Louis Braille, b. 1809, d. 1852.

Braine, John, English novelist (*Room at the Top,* 1957), b. 1922.

Bramalea, near Toronto, Canada's first satellite city, founded 1959.

Bramante, Donato, Italian architect, b. 1444, d. 1514.

Brancusi, Constantin, Rumanian-born sculptor, b. 1876, d. 1957.

Brandeis, Louis Dembitz, American chief justice, b. 1856, d. 1941.

Brandywine, Battle of, Delaware, fought between the English and the Americans 11 Sept. 1777.

Brangwyn, Frank, British artist, b. 1867, d. 1935.

Brant, Sebastian, German writer (*Das Narrenschiff,* 1494), b. 1457, d. 1521.

Braque, Georges, French painter, b. 1882.

Brassey's Naval Annual, founded 1886 by Lord Brassey, b. 1836, d. 1918.

Bratby, John, English painter, b. 1928.

Braun, Wernher von, German-born scientist and developer of ballistic missiles and satellites, b. 1912.

Bray, The Rev. Thomas, English pioneer in the provision of libraries, b. 1656, d. 1730.

Brazil, discovered 1500 by Vicente Yáñez Pinzón, b. about 1460, d. about 1524 ; independent empire 1822–1889, republic since 1889.

Breakspear, Nicolas (Adrian IV), only English Pope (1154–1159).

Breasted, James Henry, American Egyptologist, b. 1865, d. 1935.

Brecht, Bertolt, German dramatist (*Dreigroschenoper,* 1928), b. 1898, d. 1956.

Breda, Peace of, between England and the United Netherlands, 1667.

Breech-loading Cartridge Case, first adopted in principle by the Prussians about 1841.

' Breeches ' Bible, published by the Calvinists at Geneva, 1558.

Bremen, belonged to Hanseatic League 1260–1285, 1358–1422, 1433–1646 ; became free city 1646 ; became German 1867.

Brendan, St, b. 484, d. 577.

Brenner Pass, Swiss Alps : road built 1772, railway 1864–67.

Brentwood School, Essex, English public school, founded by Sir Antony Browne 1557 ; chartered 1558.

Breslau, capital of Silesia, founded about 1000 ; since 1945 included in Poland and called Wroclaw.

Brest (France), Blockade of, by the English 1794.

Brest-Litovsk, Treaty of, World War I, confirming Russian Armistice with the Central Powers, signed 3 Mar. 1918.

Breton, Nicholas, English writer, b. about 1545, d. about 1626.

Bretton Woods Conference, on international monetary policy, held July 1944.

Breughel, Pieter, the Elder, Dutch painter (*The Harvesters*), b. about 1525, d. 1569.

Breuil, Henri, French priest and archæologist and expert in cave-paintings, b. 1877, d. 1961.

Brewster, Sir David, Scottish scientist, b. 1781, d. 1868.

Brian Boru, Irish King, b. 926, killed 1014.

Briand, Aristide, French statesman, b. 1862, d. 1932.

Bricks, size standardised in England about 1625 ; taxed in England 1784 to 1850.

Bride, St, b. 453, d. 523.

Bridge, first iron, built 1779 by Wilkinson and Darby at Ironbridge, Shropshire.

Bridge, card game, first recorded mention in England 1886.

Bridge of Sighs, Venice, built 1597.

Bridges, Robert, English poet (*The Testament of Beauty*, 1929), b. 1844, d. 1930.

Bridget, St, Swedish visionary, b. about 1303, d. 1373.

Bridgewater Canal, Worsley to Manchester, constructed 1756–1761 by the Duke of Bridgewater, b. 1736, d. 1806 ; engineer James Brindley, b. 1716, d. 1772.

Bridie, James (Osborne Henry Mavor), Scottish playwright, b. 1888, d. 1951.

Brieux, Eugène, French playwright (*Les Avariés*, 1901), b. 1858, d. 1932.

Briggs, Henry, English mathematician and pioneer in the study of logarithms, b. 1561, d. 1631.

Bright, John, English statesman, b. 1811, d. 1889.

Brighton College, English public school, founded by prominent Brighton residents 1845.

Bright's Disease, identified 1827 by Dr Richard Bright, b. 1789, d. 1858.

Brillat-Savarin, Anthelme, French gastronome, b. 1755, d. 1826.

Brindley, James, English engineer, b. 1716, d. 1772.

Brisbane, Queensland capital, founded by the English explorer John Oxley 1824 ; named after General Sir Thomas Brisbane (1773–1860), Governor of New South Wales, 1821–1825.

Bristol Grammar School, English public school, founded earlier, but chartered 1532.

Bristol Porcelain, manufactured 1750–1780.

Bristol University, England, founded as University College 1876 ; granted Royal Charter 24 May 1909.

Britannia Royal Naval College, Dartmouth, founded 1857 at Portland ; transferred to Dartmouth 1863.

British Academy, London, granted charter 8 Aug. 1902.

British and Foreign Bible Society, London, founded 1804.

British Association for the Advancement of Science, founded 1831.

British Broadcasting Corporation (preceded by British Broadcasting Company, formed 1922), constituted under Royal Charter 1 Jan. 1927.

British Cameroons, West Africa, British-administered U.N. trust territory since 1919.

British Columbia, Canada, constituted British Crown Colony 2 Aug. 1858. Became a Province of the Dominion of Canada 1871.

British Council, London, established 1935 ; chartered 1940.

British Drama League, London, founded by Geoffrey Whitworth 1919.

British Empire, Order of, founded by George V in 1917.

British Empire Exhibition, Wembley, London, opened 23 Apr., closed 1 Nov. 1924.

British Film Institute, London, founded 1933.

British Guiana, first settled by the Dutch West Indian Company 1620 ; captured by the English 1796 ; formally ceded to Britain 1814.

British Guiana issued the most valuable postage stamp (only one copy known) Feb. 1856.

British Honduras (Belize), settled by British colonists 1662 ; formally proclaimed British colony 1862.

British Interplanetary Society, founded at Liverpool 1933.

British Legion, founded in London by Earl Haig 24 May 1921.

British Museum, London, founded 1753 ; opened 16 Jan. 1759.

British North American Act, by which the Dominion of Canada was created, proclaimed 1 July 1867.

British Pharmacopœia, first published 1864.

British Railways, amalgamating existing regional railway companies under national ownership, inaugurated 1 Jan. 1948.

British Red Cross Society, founded 1905. Received Royal Charter 1908.

British Somaliland, British protectorate, established 1887.

British Standards Institution, founded 1901 as the Engineering Standards Committee ; incorporated by Royal Charter 1929.

Brittany, united with France 1488.

Britten, Benjamin, English composer (*Billy Budd*, 1951), b. 1913.

Britton, John, English topographical writer (*The Beauties of England and Wales*, 1803–1814), b. 1771, d. 1857.

Broadcasting, American daily, began from KDKA 2 November 1920 ; British daily, began from 2LO 14 Nov. 1922.

Broadcasting Licences, British : 10s., introduced 1 Nov. 1922 ; increased to £1, and £2 for combined television and sound licence, 1 June 1946. Combined licence increased to £3, 1 June 1954 ; increased to £4 per annum from 1 Aug. 1957.

Broadcasts, from Britain to the Continent, first began on a weekly basis 16 Oct. 1925.

Broadmoor, England, criminal lunatic asylum, opened 1863.

Brod, Max, Czech writer (*Tycho Brahe,* 1914) and literary executor of Kafka, b. 1884.

Brockhaus Conversations-Lexikon, German national encyclopedia, first published 1810–1811 by Friedrich Arnold Brockhaus, b. 1772, d. 1823.

Broglie, Louis de, French physicist, b. 1892.

Broken Hill, New South Wales, silver lode discovered 1883.

Bromine, discovered 1826 by Antoine Jérôme Balard, b. 1802, d. 1876.

Bromsgrove School, English public school, founded earlier, reorganised by King Edward VI 1553.

Brontë, Anne, English novelist (*Agnes Grey*, 1850), b. 1820, d. 1849.

Brontë, Charlotte, English novelist (*Jane Eyre*, 1847), b. 1816, d. 1855.

Brontë, Emily, English novelist (*Wuthering Heights*, 1847), b. 1818, d. 1848.

Brooke, Henry, Irish writer (*The Fool of Quality*, 1766), b. 1708, d. 1783.

Brooke, Sir James, India-born Rajah of Sarawak, b. 1803, d. 1868.

Brooke, Rupert, English poet, b. 1887, d. 1915.

Brookings Institution, Washington, founded 1922 for research in administration and economics by Robert Somers Brookings, American philanthropist, b. 1850, d. 1932.

Brooklands Motor Racecourse, opened 6 July 1907.

Brooklyn Bridge, New York, built 1870–1883 by the German-born engineer John Augustus Roebling, b. 1806, d. 1869.

Brooks's Club, London, established 1778. Formerly known as Almack's founded 1763.

Brougham, Henry, Lord Brougham and Vaux, British statesman, b. 1778, d. 1868.

Brouwer, Adriaen, Dutch painter, b. about 1605, d. 1638.

Brown, Ford Maddox, French-born painter (*Romeo and Juliet*), b. 1821, d. 1893.

Brown, George Douglas 'George Douglas', Scottish writer (*The House* *with the Green Shutters*, 1901), b. 1869, d. 1902.

Brown, John, Scottish medical pioneer, b. 1736, d. 1788.

Brown, John, American abolitionist, b. 1800, hanged 1859.

Brown, Tom, English poet and pamphleteer, b. 1663, d. 1704.

Brown University, Providence, Rhode Island, founded 1764 as Rhode Island College.

Browne, Hablot Knight ('Phiz'), English artist and illustrator, b. 1815, d. 1882.

Browne, Robert, English religious leader (founded Brownist sect—later Congregationalists—1582), b. about 1550, d. 1633.

Browne, Sir Thomas, English writer (*Hydriotaphia*, 1658), b. 1605, d. 1682.

Brownian Motion (physics), discovered 1828 by the Scottish botanist Robert Brown, b. 1773, d. 1858.

Browning, Elizabeth Barrett, English poetess and wife of Robert Browning (*Aurora Leigh*, 1856), b. 1806, d. 1861.

Browning, Robert, English poet (*Andrea del Sarto*, 1855), b. 1812, d. 1889.

Browning Machine Gun, invented by the American John Moses Browning, b. 1855, d. 1926.

Bruce, Robert, Scottish King, b. 1274, d. 1329.

Bruce, Sir David, British pioneer in tropical medicine, b. 1855, d. 1932.

Bruce, James, Scottish explorer of Abyssinia, b. 1730, d. 1794.

Bruce, William Speirs, Scottish polar explorer, b. 1867, d. 1921.

Bruch, Max, German composer (*Violin concerto*, 1865–1867), b. 1838, d. 1920.

Brucine, alkaloid, discovered 1819 by the French scientist Pierre Joseph Pelletier, b. 1788, d. 1842.

Bruckner, Anton, Austrian composer (*Missa Solemnis*, 1854), b. 1824, d. 1896.

Brulé, Etienne, French explorer of North America, b. about 1592, murdered 1632.

Brumaire, 2nd month (mid-Oct. to mid-Nov.) in the French Revolutionary calendar established 1793.

Brummell, 'Beau' (George Bryan Brummell), English dandy, b. 1778, d. 1840.

Brunei, N.W. Borneo state, placed under British protection 1888.

Brunel, Isambard Kingdom, English civil engineer, b. 1806, d. 1859.

Brunel, Sir Marc Isambard, French-born engineer, b. 1769, d. 1849.

Brunelleschi, Filippo, Italian architect, b. 1377, d. 1446.

Brunet, Jacques Charles, French bibliographer (*Manuel du libraire*, 1810), b. 1780, d. 1867.

Brüning, Heinrich, German statesman (Chancellor 1930–1932), b. 1885.

Brunner, Heinrich, German historian, b. 1840, d. 1915.

Brunner, Thomas, English explorer in New Zealand, b. 1821, d. 1874.

Bruno, St, German-born founder (1084) of the Carthusian Order, b. about 1030, d. 1101.

Bruno, Giordano, Italian philosopher, b. 1548, burnt at the stake 1600.

Brussels, Belgian capital, founded by St Géry of Cambrai in the 7th century.

Brussels Treaty, concerning Western Union, signed 17 Mar. 1948 ; came into force 25 July 1948.

Brutus, Marcus Junius, Roman patriot, b. 85, committed suicide 42 B.C.

Bryan, William Jennings, American statesman, b. 1860, d. 1925.

Bryanston School, Dorset, English public school, founded 1928.

Bryce, James, Viscount Bryce, British statesman, b. 1838, d. 1922.

Bryn Mawr College, Philadelphia, American women's college, founded 1880.

Bubonic Plague, bacillus discovered 1894 by the French scientist Alexandre Emile John Yersin, b. 1863, d. 1943.

Buccaneers, French and English pirates active in Caribbean between 1625 and 1700.

Bucer, Martin, German religious reformer, b. 1491, d. 1551.

Buchan, John, 1st Baron Tweedsmuir, Scottish statesman and writer (*Greenmantle*, 1916), b. 1875, d. 1940.

Buchan's Days, weather predictions defined 1869 by Alexander Buchan, b. 1829, d. 1907.

Buchanan, George, Scottish scholar, b. 1506, d. 1582.

Buchanan, James, U.S. President (1857–1861), b. 1791, d. 1868.

Buchanites, Scottish religious sect, founded by Elspeth Buchan, b. 1738, d. 1791.

Buchman, Frank, American evangelist and founder (1921) of Moral Re-Armament, b. 1878, d. 1961.

Buchner, Eduard, German scientist and discoverer 1903 of zymose, b. 1860, d. 1917.

Büchner, Georg, German playwright (*Dantons Tod*, 1835), b. 1813, d. 1837.

Buckingham, George Villiers, Duke of, favourite of James I, b. 1592, assassinated 1628.

Buckingham, George Villiers, 2nd Duke of, favourite of Charles II, b. 1627, d. 1687.

Buckingham Palace, built by the Duke of Buckingham 1703 ; rebuilt 1825–1837.

Buckle, Henry Thomas, English historian, b. 1821, d. 1862.

Buddha, Gautama Siddharta, the Indian founder of Buddhism, b. about 568, d. about 488 B.C.

Budé, Guillaume, French classicist, b. 1467, d. 1540.

Budge, Sir Ernest Alfred Wallis, English Egyptologist, b. 1857, d. 1934.

Buell, Abel, American map-engraver, silversmith and inventor, b. 1742, d. 1822.

Buenos Aires, founded 1536 by Don Pedro de Mendoza, b. about 1487, d. 1537.

Buenos Aires Standard, first English-language South American daily newspaper, founded 1861 by the Irish-born economist Michael George Mulhall, b. 1836, d. 1900.

'Buffalo Bill' (William Frederick Cody), American frontiersman and showman, b. 1846, d. 1917.

Buffon, Georges Louis Leclere, Comte de, French naturalist, b. 1707, d. 1788.

Buhl Cabinets, style introduced by the French furniture maker André Charles Boulle, b. 1642, d. 1732.

Bukharin, Nikolai Ivanovich, Russian Communist leader, b. 1888, tried and shot 1938.

Bulawayo, Southern Rhodesian mining city, founded 1893.

Bulganin, Nikolai Aleksandrovich, Soviet leader, b. 1895.

Bulgaria, established in 7th century, conquered by Byzantines in 10th century, revived in 12th century, conquered by Turks in 14th century ; constituted Principality under Turkish suzerainty 1878 ; became independent kingdom 1908 ; became a Communist republic 1946.

Bull-baiting, prohibited in England by Act of Parliament 1835.

Bull-fighting, padding for horses made compulsory in Spain in 1926.

Bull Run, Battles of, American Civil War : 1st, 21 July 1861 ; 2nd, 30 Aug. 1862.

Buller, Sir Redvers Henry, British military hero, b. 1839, d. 1908.

Bullinger, Heinrich, Swiss Reformation leader, b. 1504, d. 1575.

Bülow, Prince Bernhard von, German Chancellor, b. 1849, d. 1929.

Bunin, Ivan Alexeyevich, Russian writer in exile, b. 1870, d. 1954.

Bunker Hill, Battle of American Revolution, fought between Americans and English 17 June 1775.

Bunsen, Christian Karl Josias, Baron, German diplomat, b. 1791, d. 1860.

Bunsen Burner, invented for use in laboratories by the German scientist Robert Wilhelm Bunsen, b. 1811, d. 1899.

Bunyan, John, English religious leader and writer (*Pilgrim's Progress*, 1678–1684), b. 1628, d. 1688.

Buonarroti, Philippe, French revolutionary leader, b. 1761, d. 1837.

Buononcini, Giovanni Battista, Italian composer (*Muzio Scevola*, 1710), b. 1672, d. about 1750.

Burbage, Richard, English actor, b. about 1567, d. 1619.

Burbank, Luther, American horti-culturalist, b. 1849, d. 1926.

Burchell, William John, English explorer, b. about 1782, d. 1863.

Burckhardt, Jacob, Swiss historian, b. 1818, d. 1897.

Burdett, Francis, English politician, b. 1770, d. 1844.

Burghley, William Cecil, Lord, English statesman, b. 1520, d. 1598.

Burgkmair, Hans, German artist, b. 1473, d. 1531.

Burgoyne, John, English general in American Revolution, b. 1723, d. 1792.

Burke, Edmund, Irish-born statesman and writer, b. 1729, d. 1797.

Burke, Robert O'Hara, Australian pioneer, b. 1820, d. 1861.

Burke, William, Irish criminal (with William Hare), b. 1792, hanged 1829.

Burke's Peerage, founded 1826 by Sir John Bernard Burke, b. 1814, d. 1892.

Burlington Arcade, Piccadilly, London, opened 20 Mar. 1819.

Burlington House, Piccadilly, London, built by Sir John Denham (b. 1615, d. 1669) about 1664 ; rebuilt 1731.

Burma, gained independence as a Republic 4 Jan. 1948.

Burne-Jones, Sir Edward, English painter (*Cophetua and the Beggar-maid*), b. 1833, d. 1898.

Burnet, Gilbert, British writer and divine, b. 1643, d. 1715.

Burnett, Mrs Frances Hodgson, English-born writer (*Little Lord Fauntleroy*, 1886), b. 1849, d. 1924.

Burney, Charles, English music historian, b. 1726, d. 1814.

Burney, Fanny (Madame d'Arblay), English writer (*Evelina*, 1778), b. 1752, d. 1840.

Burning to Death, British punishment for women, last inflicted 1729 ; legally abolished 1790.

Burns, John, British socialist leader, b. 1858, d. 1943.

Burns, Robert, Scottish poet, b. 1759, d. 1796.

Burr, Aaron, American statesman, b. 1756, d. 1836.

Burton, Decimus, English architect, b. 1800, d. 1881.

Burton, Sir Richard Francis, English explorer and translator of *The Arabian Nights*, b. 1821, d. 1890.

Burton, Robert, English writer (*The Anatomy of Melancholy*, 1621), b. 1577, d. 1640.

Bus, First London, ran from Marylebone Road to the Bank 4 July 1829.

Busch, Wilhelm, German humorous artist, b. 1832, d. 1908.

Bushell, Edward, English champion of juries, *fl.* 1670–1671.

Busoni, Ferruccio, Italian composer (*Die Brautwahl*, 1912), b. 1866, d. 1924.

Buss, Frances Mary, English pioneer of high schools for girls, b. 1827, d. 1894.

Butcher, Samuel Henry, Irish classicist, b. 1850, d. 1910.

Bute, John Stuart, Earl of, British statesman, b. 1713, d. 1792.

Butler, Joseph, Bishop of Durham, b. 1692, d. 1752.

Butler, Mrs Josephine, social reformer b. 1828, d. 1906.

Butler, Samuel, English poet (*Hudibras* 1663–1678), b. 1612, d. 1680.

Butler, Samuel, English writer (*Erewhon*, 1872), b. 1835, d. 1902.

Butlin, William E. (' Billy ' Butlin), South African-born pioneer of holida camps, b. 1900.

Butt, Dame Clara, English contralto, b. 1873, d. 1936.

Butt, Isaac, Irish nationalist politician b. 1813, d. 1879.

Buxtehude, Dietrich, Danish-born organist and composer, b. 1637, d. 1707.

Byng, George, Viscount Torrington, English admiral, b. 1663, d. 1733.

Byng, John, English admiral, b. 1704, shot 1757.

Byrd, Richard Evelyn, American polar aviator, b. 1888, d. 1957.

Byrd, William, English composer, b. about 1542, d. 1623.

Byrom, John, English shorthand pioneer, b. 1692, d. 1763.

Byron, George Gordon, Lord, English poet (*Don Juan*), b. 1788, d. 1824.

Byzantine Empire, existed 330–1453.

Byzantium, founded 658 B.C. ; rebuilt as Constantinople, A.D. 330 ; conquered by the Turks 1453 and renamed Istanbul.

C

Ça Ira, French revolutionary song written by Ladré 1789.

Cabal Ministry, formed 1668 by King Charles II of England ; ended 1673 (from names of members : Clifford Ashley, Buckingham, Arlington, Lauderdale).

Cabell, James Branch, American novelist (*Jurgen,* 1919), b. 1879, d. 1958.

Cabinet, form of British government, introduced by Charles II, formally instituted by William III 1693, principles developed by Sir Robert Walpole, b. 1676, d. 1745.

Cabinet Noir, French postal censorship, instituted in reign of Louis XI, formally constituted in reign of Louis XV, abolished 1868.

Cable, First Atlantic, completed 5 Aug. 1858 by Sir Charles Tilston Bright (1832–1888) ; first successful cable laid completed 7 Sept. 1866.

Cabochiens, Parisian rioters led by Simon ' Caboche ' (real name Lecoustellier) active 1413–1414.

Cabot, John, Italian-born explorer (discovered Newfoundland 1497), b. 1451, d. 1498.

Cabral, Pedro, Portuguese explorer, b. about 1467, d. about 1520.

Cabrillo, Juan Rodríguez, Spanish explorer, d. 1543.

Cadbury, George, English cocoa manufacturer and newspaper owner, b. 1839, d. 1922.

Cade, Jack, English revolutionary leader, killed 1450.

Cadets, Russian political party, formed 1905 by Paul Milyukov.

Cadillac, Antoine de la Mothe, Sieur, Governor of Louisiana (1713–1716), b. about 1656, d. 1730.

Cadiz, Naval Battle of, fought between Sir Francis Drake and the Spaniards 1587.

Cadmium, chemical element, first isolated by the German scientist F. Stromeyer 1817.

Cadogan, William, 1st Earl Cadogan, Irish general, b. 1675, d. 1726.

Cadwalladr, Welsh prince, d. 1172.

Caedmon, English poet, d. about 680.

Caen, French city, captured by the English 1346 and 1417 ; finally retaken by the French 1450.

Cæsar, Caius Julius, Roman dictator, b. 100 B.C., assassinated 44 B.C.

Cæsarian Section, performed on living woman as early as 1500.

Cæsium, chemical element first isolated 1860 by the German scientist Robert Wilhelm Bunsen (1811–1899).

Café Royal, London, founded 1864, bombed 1940.

' Cagliostro, Alessandro ' (Giuseppe Balsamo), Italian alchemist, b. 1743, d. 1795.

Cahiers, statements of local grievances submitted to the French States-General 1789.

Caicos Islands, British West Indies, discovered about 1512.

Caine, Sir Hall, British novelist (*The Deemster,* 1887), b. 1853, d. 1931.

Caius, John, English physician to the Royal family, b. 1510, d. 1593.

Caius, St, Pope 283–296.

Caius College, Gonville and, Cambridge University, founded as Gonville Hall by Edmund Gonville (d. 1351) in 1348 ; assumed present name under Royal Charter 1557.

Cajetan, Cardinal Thomas, Italian theologian, b. 1469, d. 1534.

Calais, English siege of, 1346–1347 ; finally recovered by the French 1558.

' Calamity Jane ' (Martha Jane Burke), American pioneer, b. about 1852, d. 1903.

Calamy, Edmund, English historian of nonconformity (*Account of the Ejected Ministers,* 1702), b. 1671, d. 1732.

Calas, Jean, French Calvinist, b. 1698, tortured to death 1752.

Calcium, discovered 1808 by Sir Humphry Davy (1778–1829).

Calculating Machine, first model built 1694 by the German scientist Gottfried Wilhelm Leibniz (1646–1716).

Calculus, *Infinitesimal,* invented 1675 by the German scientist Gottfried Wilhelm Leibniz (1646–1716) ; *Integral and Differential,* invented independently by Leibniz and Isaac Newton (1642–1727).

Calcutta, founded 1686–1690 by the English official Job Charnock (d. 1693) ; Black Hole of, episode occurred 20 June 1756.

Calder Hall, British atomic station, construction begun 1953, commissioning trials started 1956. Power station opened Oct. 1956.

Calderon de la Barca, Pedro, Spanish playwright (*La Vida es Sueño*), b. 1600, d. 1681.

Caledonian Canal, Scotland, constructed 1804–1822 by the Scottish engineer Thomas Telford (1757–1834).

Calendar, French Revolutionary, instituted 1793, abolished 1806.

Calendar, Gregorian, reformed version of Julian Calendar, introduced by Pope Gregory XIII 1582 ; adopted in Britain Sept. 1752.

Calendar, Hebrew, calculated from 3761 B.C. ; system adopted A.D. 358.

Calendar, Julian, reformed version of Roman Calendar, introduced by Julius Cæsar 46 B.C.

Calendar, Mohammedan, calculated from the Hegira 622.

Calendar, Roman, calculated from the supposed date of the foundation of Rome 754 B.C.

Calhoun, John Caldwell, American statesman, b. 1782, d. 1850.

California, U.S.A., first settled 1769 ; ceded by Mexico to the U.S.A. 1848 ; admitted to the Union 1850.

California, University of, founded at Berkeley 1868.

Californian Gold Fields, discovered Dec. 1847.

Caligula, Roman emperor (37–41), b. 12, assassinated 41.

Caliphate, Egyptian, extinguished by Ottoman conquest 1517.

Caliphate of the Islamic Empire, Umayyad, 661–750 ; Abbasid, established 750, extinguished by the Mongols 1258.

Caliphate, Ottoman, extinguished by the Kemalist Revolution 1923.

Callimachus, Greek poet who lived in the 3rd century B.C.

Callisthenes, Greek historian, b. about 360, executed 328 B.C.

Callistus I, St, Pope 217–222.

Callistus II (Guido), Pope 1119–1124.

Callistus III (Alfonso de Borja), Pope 1455–1458.

Callistus III, Anti-Pope 1168–1179.

Callot, Jacques, French engraver, b. 1592, d. 1635.

Calorimeters, invented 1865 by the French scientist Pierre Eugène Marcelin Berthelot (1827–1907).

Calorimeters, Steam, perfected 1886 by the French scientist John Joly.

Calpurnia, wife of Julius Cæsar, *fl.* 50–40 B.C.

Calvin, John (Jean Cauvin), French theologian (*Institutes,* 1535), and leader of the Reformation at Geneva, b. 1509, d. 1564.

Camargo, Marie Anne, French dancer, b. 1710, d. 1770.

Cambodia, Indo-China, made French Protectorate 1863 ; granted independence as an Associate State of the French Union 1949 ; granted complete independence 1955.

Cambrai, Treaty of (The Ladies' Peace), renewing Treaty of Madrid, signed 1529.

Cambrian Period, Earth history, 520 million years ago.

Cambridge University, founded in 13th century, granted Royal Charter 1231.

Cambridge University Observatory, opened 1820.

Cambridge University Press, founded 1583 by Thomas Thomas, b. 1553, d. 1588.

Cambridgeshire Stakes, Newmarket, first run 1839.

Cambyses, King of the Medes and Persians (529–522 B.C.), committed suicide 521.

Camden, Battle of, American War of Independence, fought between the British and the Americans 16 Aug. 1780.

Camden, Charles Pratt, Earl, English reforming judge, b. 1713, d. 1794.

Camden, William, English antiquary (*Britannia*, 1586), b. 1551, d. 1623.

Camera, First roll-film, marketed 1888 by the American inventor George Eastman (1854–1932).

Camera Lucida, invented by English scientist William Hyde Wollaston, b. 1766, d. 1828.

Camera Obscura, described 1569.

Cameron, Basil, English conductor, b. 1884.

Cameron, Sir David Young, Scottish artist, b. 1865, d. 1945.

Cameroons, British, West Africa, trusteeship territory since 1919 ; captured from the Germans 1916.

Cameroons, French, West African trusteeship territory, occupied by the French 1916 ; placed under French administration 1919.

Cameroons Republic (formerly French Cameroons), independent republic outside the French Community since 1 Jan. 1960.

Camisards, French Protestant rebels in the Cevennes active from 1685 to 1705.

Cammaerts, Emile, Belgian poet, b. 1878.

Camões, Luís de, Portuguese poet (*Os Lusiadas*, 1572), b. about 1524, d. 1579.

Camorra, The, Neapolitan secret society, formed in the 16th century, suppressed in the late 19th century.

Camouflage, Thayer's Law of, defined 1910 by the American painter Abbott Henderson Thayer, b. 1849, d. 1921.

Campagnola, Domenico, Italian painter (*The Holy Family*), b. about 1490, d. about 1565.

Campanella, Tommaso, Italian philosopher (*Città del Sole*), b. 1568, d. 1639.

Campbell, Sir Colin, British Field-Marshal, b. 1792, d. 1863.

Campbell, Mrs Patrick, English actress, b. 1865, d. 1940.

Campbell, Robert, Scottish explorer of Canada, b. 1808, d. 1894.

Campbell, Thomas, Scottish poet (*Ye Mariners of England*), b. 1777, d. 1844.

Campbell-Bannerman, Sir Henry, British statesman (Prime Minister 1905–1908), b. 1836, d. 1908.

Campbell College, Belfast, public school founded by Henry James Campbell of Craigavad ; opened 1894.

Campeggio, Cardinal Lorenzo, Italian divine, b. 1472, d. 1539.

Camperdown, Battle of, naval engagement fought between the British and the Dutch fleets 11 Oct. 1797.

Campion, Edmund, Jesuit missionary to England, b. 1540, hanged 1581, beatified 1886

Campo Formio, Treaty of, between Napoleon I and Austria, signed 1797.

Camus, Albert, French novelist (*La Peste*, 1947), b. 1913, killed in car accident 1960.

Canada, granted constitution as a Dominion 1867 ; defined as an autonomous community freely associated as a member of the British Commonwealth of Nations 1926.

Canadian-Pacific Railway, completed 1886.

Canadian-U.S.A. Frontiers, defined 9 Aug. 1842.

Canal, chief period of construction in England, 1755–1827.

Canaletto, Antonio, Italian painter (*S. Maria della Salute*), b. 1697, d. 1768.

Canary Islands, Spanish territory in the Atlantic, occupation completed by Spain 1496.

Canberra, Australian federal capital, founded 1923.

Cancer, first associated virus agent discovered by Ellerman and Bang 1908.

Cancer Research Institute, London, founded 1902.

Candlemas, Festival of the Purification of the Virgin, 2 Feb.

Canford School, Wimborne, British public school, founded 1923.

Cannæ, Italy, battle between Romans and Carthaginians 216 B.C.

Canning, Elizabeth, English perjurer, b. 1734, tried 1754, d. 1773.

Canning, George, British statesman (Prime Minister 1827), b. 1770, d. 1827.

Canning, to preserve food, pioneered by François Appert 1809 ; patented in England by Durand 1810.

Canon Law, study developed by the 12th-century Italian monk Gratian, in his *Decretum* published about 1140.

Canossa, Italy, scene of penance of the Emperor Henry IV 1077.

Canova, Antonio, Italian sculptor (*Perseus*), b. 1757, d. 1822.

Canterbury, ecclesiastical centre of England since 597.

Canterbury Cathedral, England, built 1070–1495.

Cantor, Georg, German mathematician, b. 1845, d. 1918.

Canute, Danish King of England (1016–1035), b. about 994, d. 1035.

Capablanca, Josè Raoul, Cuban chess champion, b. 1888.

Cape to Cairo Railway, first proposed 1874 by Sir Edwin Arnold (1832–1904).

Cape of Good Hope, South Africa, first doubled 1488 by the Portuguese navigator Bartolomeu Diaz, d. 1500.

Cape of Good Hope Triangular Postage Stamps, first issued 1 Sept. 1853.

Cape Horn, South America, discovered by the Dutch navigator Willem Cornelis Schouten 1616.

Cape Province, settled by Dutch 1652, bought by Britain 1814.

Cape Verde Islands, Atlantic, Portuguese overseas province, discovered by the Portuguese navigator Diogo Gomes 1460.

Cape St Vincent, Naval Battle of, fought between British and Spanish fleets 14 Feb. 1797.

Čapek, Karel, Czech writer (*R.U.R.*, 1920), b. 1890, d. 1938.

Capet Dynasty, ruled France 987–1328, Naples 1265–1435, Hungary 1308–1382.

Capgrave, John, English theologian, b. 1393, d. 1464.

Capone, Alphonso, Italian-born gangster, b. 1895, d. 1947.

Caporetto, Battle of, World War I, fought between Austrians and Italians 24 Oct. 1917.

Capuchin Order, founded 1528 by Matteo di Bassi.

Caracalla, Roman emperor (211–217), b. 188, assassinated 217.

Caractacus, English king, d. in captivity in Rome about 54.

' Caran d'Ache ' (Emmanuel Poiré), Russian-born humorous artist, b. 1858, d. 1909.

Carausius, Marcus Aurelius Mausaeus, British leader in 3rd century.

Caravaggio, Michelangelo Amerighi, Italian painter (*The Supper at Emmaus*), b. 1569, d. 1609.

Carbolic, first used 1863 as a disinfectant by Lord Lister (1827–1912).

Carbon Disulphide, solvent and insecticide, discovered about 1796 by the German scientist Wilhelm August Lampadius (1772–1842).

Carbonari, Italian secret revolutionary society, formed about 1810.

Carboniferous Period, Earth history, 275 million years ago.

Carducci, Giosuè, Italian poet, b. 1835, d. 1907.

Carew, Thomas, English poet, b. about 1598, d. 1639.

Carey, Henry, English poet (*Sally in our alley*), b. about 1690, d. 1743.

Carinus, Roman emperor (283–285), murdered 285.

Carl Rosa Opera Company, founded by Carl Rosa, b. 1843, d. 1889.

Carleton, William, Irish writer (*Traits and Stories of the Irish Peasantry*, 1830), b. 1794, d. 1869.

Carlile, Richard, English radical, b. 1799, d. 1843.

Carlile, The Rev. Wilson, English founder of the Church Army (1882), b. 1847, d. 1942.

Carlisle, Cumberland, English city, granted charter 1158 by King Henry II.

Carlisle Grammar School, British public school, probably founded by Henry I in 1122 ; refounded by Henry VIII 1541.

Carlists, supporters of the claims of Don Carlos (1788–1855) and his heirs to the Spanish throne, formed early in 19th century, suppressed 1875.

Carlos, Don, heir of Philip II of Spain, b. 1545, d. 1568.

Carlotta, Empress of Mexico (1863–1867), b. 1840, d. 1927.

Carlowitz, Treaty of, between the Turks and the Allies, signed 1699.

Carlsbad Decrees, repressing growth of German democratic movements, signed by the German states 1819.

Carlyle, Jane Welsh, wife of Thomas Carlyle, b. 1801, d. 1866.

Carlyle, Thomas, Scottish writer (*The French Revolution,* 1837), b. 1795, d. 1881.

Carmelite Order, founded about 1150 by the Crusader Berthold ; monastic order recognised 1224.

‘ Carmagnole, La ’, French revolutionary song (possibly of Italian origin), composed 1792, suppressed 1799.

‘ Carmen Sylva ’, Elizabeth, Queen of Rumania, b. 1843, d. 1916.

Carnarvon, Henry Howard Molyneux Herbert, Earl of, British statesman, b. 1831, d. 1890.

Carnegie, Andrew, Scottish-born philanthropist, b. 1835, d. 1919.

Carnegie Endowment for International Peace, Washington, founded 1910.

Carnot, Lazare Nicolas Marguérite, French revolutionary leader, b. 1753, d. 1823.

Carol I, Rumanian king (1866–1914), b. 1839, d. 1914.

Carol II, Rumanian king (1930–1940), b. 1893.

Caroline of Anspach, Queen of England, wife of George II, b. 1683, d. 1737.

Caroline, Queen, wife of George IV, b. 1768, d. 1821.

Carolingian Dynasty, ruled the Franks 751–887.

Carpaccio, Vittore, Italian painter (*The Presentation in the Temple*), b. about 1455, d. 1522.

Carpenter, Edward, English writer and social reformer (*Towards Democracy,* 1905), b. 1844, d. 1929.

‘ Carpet Baggers ’, Northern businessmen who ‘ invaded ’ the Southern States of the U.S.A. after the American Civil War 1865.

Carpet Sweepers, invented 1876 by the American businessman Melville R. Bissell.

Carracci, Ludovico, Italian painter (*Transfiguration*), b. 1555, d. 1619.

‘ Carroll, Lewis ’ (Charles Lutwidge Dodgson), English mathematician and writer (*Alice's Adventures in Wonderland,* 1865), b. 1832, d. 1898.

Carson, Edward, Baron, British politician, b. 1854, d. 1935.

Carson, Kit, American pioneer, b. 1809, d. 1878.

Cartagena, Colombia, founded 1533 by Pedro de Heredia ; captured by Sir Francis Drake 1585.

Carteret, Sir George, Jersey-born English administrator, b. about 1610, d. 1680.

Carteret, John, Baron, British politician, b. 1690, d. 1763.

Cartesian Co-ordinates, theory first propounded 1637 by the French philosopher René Descartes, b. 1596, d. 1650.

Carthage, Phœnician city on north African coast, traditionally founded 814–813 B.C., finally destroyed by the Arabs A.D. 648.

Carthusian Order, founded 1084 by St Bruno, b. about 1030, d. 1101.

Cartier, Jacques, French discoverer 1534 of the St Lawrence River, b. 1491, d. 1557.

Cartwright, Edmund, English inventor 1785 of the power loom, b. 1743, d. 1823.

Cartwright, Thomas, English religious leader, b. 1535, d. 1600.

Carus, Roman Emperor (282–283), d. 283.

Caruso, Enrico, Italian opera singer, b. 1873, d. 1921.

Carver, John, English leader of the Pilgrim Fathers, b. about 1576, d. 1621.

Cary, Joyce, Anglo-Irish writer (*The Horse's Mouth,* 1945), b. 1888, d. 1957.

Casabianca, Louis, French naval captain, b. about 1755, d. 1798.

Casablanca, Moroccan port, founded 1468.

Casablanca Conference, World War II, meeting between Franklin D. Roosevelt and Winston Churchill at which ' unconditional surrender' formula was agreed, held 14–20 Jan. 1943.

Casals, Pablo, Catalan 'cellist, b. 1876.

Casanova, Giovanni Giacomo, Italian adventurer and writer (*Memoirs*), b. 1725, d. 1798.

Casaubon, Isaac, Swiss-born classical scholar, b. 1559, d. 1614.

Casca, Publius Servilius, Roman conspirator and assassin of Julius Cæsar, d. about 42 B.C.

Casement, Sir Roger, Irish leader, b. 1864, hanged 1916.

Cash Registers, invented by the American John Ritty of Ohio 1879.

Casimir I, Polish king (1040–1058), b. 1015, d. 1058.

Casimir II, Polish king (1177–1194).

Casimir III, Polish king (1333–1370), b. 1310, d. 1370.

Casimir IV, Polish king (1447–1492), b. 1427, d. 1492.

Casimir V (John II Casimir), Polish king (1648–1668), b. 1609, d. 1672.

Caslon, William, English typefounder, b. 1692, d. 1766.

Cassatt, Mary, American painter, b. about 1845, d. 1926.

Cassel, Gustav, Swedish economist, b. 1866, d. 1945.

Cassell, John, English publisher, b. 1817, d. 1865.

Cassianus, Joannes, French-born pioneer founder of monasteries, b. 365, d. 435.

Cassini, Giovanni Domenico, Italian astronomer, b. 1625, d. 1712.

Cassino, Monte, monastery founded by St Benedict 529, destroyed by Allies May 1944.

Cassiodorus, Roman statesman and scholar, b. about 478, d. 570.

Cassius, Roman conspirator against Julius Cæsar, committed suicide 42 B.C.

Castagno, Andrea del, Italian painter, b. 1390, d. 1457.

Castelnau, Michel de, French soldier and ambassador to English court, b. about 1520, d. 1592.

Castiglione, Giovanni Benedetto, Italian painter, b. 1616, d. 1670.

Castillon, Battle of, fought between French and English, and ending the Hundred Years' War, 17 July 1453.

Castlereagh, Robert Stewart, Viscount, Ulster-born statesman, b. 1769, committed suicide 1822.

Castro Ruz, Fidel, ruler of Cuba since 1959, b. 1926.

Catalysis, chemical action, discovered 1836 by the Swedish scientist Baron Berzelius, b. 1779, d. 1848.

Caterham School, Surrey, British public school, founded 1811.

Catesby, Robert, English conspirator, b. 1573, killed 1605.

Catherine I, Russian empress (1725–1727), b. 1684, d. 1727.

Catherine II, ' The Great', Russian empress (1762–1795), b. 1729, d. 1796.

Catherine de Médicis, Queen of France and Regent (1560–1572), b. 1519, d. 1589.

Catherine of Aragon, 1st wife of Henry VIII, b. 1485, d. 1536.

Catherine of Siena, St, b. 1347, d. 1380. Feast : 30 Apr.

Catherine Howard, 5th wife of Henry VIII, beheaded 1542.

Catherine Parr, 6th wife of Henry VIII, b. 1512, d. 1548.

Cathode Rays, discovered by the English scientist Sir William Crookes, b. 1832, d. 1919.

Catholic Emancipation in Britain, Apr. 1829.

Catholic Hierarchy, restored in Britain 29 Sept. 1850.

Catholic and Apostolic Church (Irvingites), founded 1829 by the Scottish preacher Edward Irving, b. 1792, d. 1834.

Catholic Reform, commenced about 1522, completed 1590.

Catilina, Lucius Sergius, Roman conspirator, b. about 108, killed in battle 62 B.C.

Catlin, George, American artist famous for his depiction of North American Indians and their life, b. 1796, d. 1872.

Cato the Elder (Marcus Portius Cato), Roman statesman, b. 234, d. 149 B.C.

Cato the Younger (Marcius Portius Uticensis), Roman statesman, b. 95, committed suicide 46 B.C.

Cato Street Conspiracy, unsuccessful plot to assassinate members of the British Cabinet 1820, planned by Arthur Thistlewood, b. 1770, executed 1820.

Catt, Mrs Carrie Chapman, American suffragette and peace crusader, b. 1859, d. 1947.

Cattermole, George, English painter, b. 1800, d. 1868.

Catullus, Valerius, Roman poet, b. about 84, d. about 54 B.C.

Caudine Forks, Battle of the, fought between the Samnites and the Romans, 321 B.C.

Caughley Porcelain, manufactured 1772–1799.

Caulaincourt, Armand, Marquis de, French statesman, b. 1772, d. 1827.

Cavalcanti, Guido, Italian poet, b. about 1230, d. 1300.

Cavell, Nurse Edith, English patriot, b. 1866, executed by the Germans 12 Oct. 1915.

Cavendish, Henry, English scientist and eccentric, b. 1731, d. 1810.

Cavour, Count Camillo, Italian statesman, b. 1810, d. 1861.

Cawnpore (Kanpur), Mutiny of, in which rioters murdered the English garrison and their families, 6 June 1857.

Caxton, William, first English printer, b. about 1422, d. about 1491.

Cayenne, French Guiana, founded 1664.

Cecil, Robert, first Earl of Salisbury, statesman, b. about 1563, d. 1612.

Cecil, William, Baron Burghley, English Elizabethan statesman, b. 1520, d. 1598.

Cecilia, St, martyred 230. Feast : 22 Nov.

Cedar Creek, Battle of, American Civil War, 17 Oct. 1864.

Celebes (Sulawesi), Indonesian island, discovered by the Portuguese 1512.

Celestine I, St, Pope 422–432.

Celestine II, Anti-Pope 1124–1130.

Celestine II, Pope 1143–1144.

Celestine III (Giacinto Bobo), Pope 1191–1198.

Celestine IV (Godfrey Castiglione), Pope 1241–1243.

Celestine V (St Peter Celestine), Pope 1294, b. 1215, d. 1296.

Cell Theory, botany, developed about 1850 by the German botanist Hugo von Mohl, b. 1805, d. 1872.

Cellini, Benvenuto, Italian artist and writer (*Autobiography*), b. 1500, d. 1571.

Cellular Composition of Plant Tissue, proved 1838 by the German botanist Matthias Jakob.

Cellophane, invented about 1900 by the Swiss scientist J. E. Brandenberger.

Celluloid, patented 1855 by the English chemist Alexander Parkes ; successfully invented 1870 by the American chemist John Wesley Hyatt, b. 1837, d. 1920.

Cellulose Nitrate, first synthetic plastic material, invented 1855 by the British chemist Alexander Parkes, b. 1813, d. 1890.

Celsius, Anders, Swedish astronomer and inventor (1742) of the Centigrade thermometer, b. 1701, d. 1744.

Celsus, Aulus Cornelius, Roman medical writer (*De Medecina*) in 1st century.

Cenci, Beatrice, Italian heroine and possibly murderess, b. 1577, executed 1599.

Cennini, Cennino, Italian painter, b. about 1365, d. 1440.

Cenozoic Era, Earth history, between 1 and 70 million years ago.

Centigrade Thermometer, invented 1742 by the Swedish scientist Anders Celsius, b. 1701, d. 1744.

Cenotaph, Whitehall, London, memorial to the dead of both World Wars, unveiled 11 Nov. 1920.

Censorship, of printed books, begun in Mainz in 1486.

Census, first in Britain made 1801.

Centlivre, Mrs Susannah, English dramatist and actress, b. about 1667, d. 1723.

Central African Republic, autonomous republic within the French Community, since 1958.

Central London Electric Railway, opened 27 June 1900.

Central Treaty Organisation (CENTO), set up as the Baghdad Pact Organisation 1956 (Treaty signed 1955). Adopted present title 1958.

Ceres, first planetoid sighted by man, discovered 1801 by the Italian astronomer Giuseppe Piazzi, b. 1746, d. 1826.

Cerium, chemical element, isolated 1803 by the Swedish chemist Baron Berzelius, b. 1779, d. 1848.

Cerularius, Michael, Byzantine divine in 11th century.

Cervantes, Miguel de, Spanish writer (*Don Quixote*, 1605–1615), b. 1547, d. 1616.

Cesarewitch Stakes, Newmarket, first run in 1839.

Cetewayo, Zulu king, b. about 1836, d. 1884.

Ceylon, settled by the Portuguese 1505 ; constituted British Crown Colony 1802 ; achieved self-government within the British Commonwealth 4 Feb. 1948.

Cézanne, Paul, French painter, b. 1839, d. 1906.

Chabrier, Emmanuel, French composer (*España*), b. 1841, d. 1894.

Chad, Equatorial Africa, autonomous republic within the French Community since 1960.

Chadwick, Sir Edwin, English pioneer in public health, b. 1800, d. 1890.

Chæronea, Battle of, fought between the Macedonians and the Athenians 338 B.C.

Chæronea, Battle of, fought between the Roman general Sulla and Mithridates' army 86 B.C.

Chagall, Marc, Russian-born painter, b. 1889.

Chalcedon, Council of, Fourth Ecumenical Council, held 451.

Chalgrove Field (Oxfordshire), Battle of, fought between the Royalists and the Parliamentarians 1643.

Chaliapin, Fyodor Ivanovich, Russian operatic singer, b. 1873, d. 1938.

Châlons, Battle of, fought between the Romans and the Goths and Huns 451.

Chamber of Commerce, First British, founded at Glasgow 1783.

Chamberlain, Austen, British statesman, b. 1863, d. 1937.

Chamberlain, Houston Stewart, English-born racialist, b. 1855, d. 1926.

Chamberlain, Joseph, British statesman, b. 1836, d. 1914.

Chamberlain, Neville, British statesman (Prime Minister 1937–1940), b. 1869, d. 1940.

Chamberlain Porcelain, manufactured 1786–1840.

Chambers's Encyclopædia, founded 1859–1868 by the Scottish publisher William Chambers, b. 1800, d. 1883.

Chambre Ardente, French special court for trial of heretics, etc., instituted 1535, abolished 1682.

Chamisso, Adalbert von, German poet, b. 1781, d. 1838.

Champaigne, Philippe de, Flemish painter, b. 1602, d. 1674.

Champion Hurdle, Cheltenham, first run 1927.

Champlain, Samuel de, Lieutenant of Canada (1612–1629), b. 1567, d. 1635.

Champlain, Battle of, fought between the Americans and the British 1814.

Champney, Benjamin, American painter, b. 1817, d. 1907.

Champollion, Jean François, French Egyptologist and decipherer of the Rosetta Stone, b. 1790, d. 1832.

Chancellor, Richard, English navigator and instigator of the Muscovy Company, d. in shipwreck 1556.

Chandernagor, Bengal, town settled by the French 1688 ; incorporated in India 9 June 1952.

Channel, English : submarine cable first laid 1850 ; first crossed by balloon 1785 by Blanchard and Jeffries ;

first swum 1875 by Matthew Webb ; first flown by aeroplane 1909 by Louis Blériot ; first woman flier Miss Harriet Quimby 1912 ; tunnel scheme abandoned by British Government 1924.

Channel Islands, under German occupation June 1940–May 1945.

Channing, William Ellery, American Unitarian leader, b. 1780, d. 1842.

Chantrey Bequest, to Royal Academy (and now at Tate Gallery, London), made by Sir Francis Legatt Chantrey, b. 1781, d. 1841.

Chaplin, Charles Spencer, English-born film actor, b. 1889.

Chapman, George, English poet and dramatist (*Bussy d'Ambois,* 1607), b. about 1559, d. 1634.

Chapman, John Jay, American man of letters, b. 1862, d. 1933.

Chapter of Mitton, battle fought between Scots and English 1319.

Chardin, Jean Baptiste Siméon, French painter (*La Bénédicité*), b. 1699, d. 1779.

Charge of the Light Brigade, Balaklava, Crimean War, 25 Oct. 1854.

Charlemagne, King of Franks (768–814), King of Lombards (774–814), Holy Roman Emperor (800–814), b. 742, d. 814.

Charles II, the Bald, French king, Holy Roman Emperor (875–881), b. 823, d. 881.

Charles III, the Fat, Holy Roman Emperor (881–891), b. 839, d. 891.

Charles IV, Holy Roman Emperor (1347–1378), b. 1316, d. 1378.

Charles V, King of Spain, Holy Roman Emperor (1519–1555), b. 1500, d. 1558.

Charles VI, Holy Roman Emperor (1711–1742), b. 1697, d. 1745.

Charles VII, Holy Roman Emperor (1742–1745), b. 1697, d. 1745.

Charles I, Austrian Emperor (1916–1918), b. 1887, d. 1922.

Charles I, English king (1625–1649), b. 1600, beheaded 1649.

Charles II, English king (1660–1685), b. 1630, crowned at Scone 1651, d. 1685.

Charles Edward, the Young Pretender to the English throne, b. 1720, d. 1788.

Charles, Prince of Wales, b. 14 Nov. 1948.

Charles III, the Simple, French king, b. 879, d. 929.

Charles IV, the Fair, French king (1322–1328), b. 1294, d. 1328.

Charles V, the Wise, French king (1364–1380), b. 1337, d. 1380.

Charles VI, the Foolish, French king (1380–1422), b. 1368, d. 1422.

Charles VII, French king (1422–1461), b. 1403, d. 1461.

Charles VIII, French king (1483–1498), b. 1470, d. 1498.

Charles IX, French king (1560–1574), b. 1550, d. 1574.

Charles X, French king (1822–1830), b. 1757, d. 1836.

Charles II, Spanish king (1665–1700), b. 1661, d. 1700.

Charles III, Spanish king (1759–1788), b. 1716, d. 1788.

Charles IV, Spanish king (1788–1808), b. 1748, d. 1819.

Charles I to **Charles VI,** legendary Swedish kings.

Charles VII, Swedish king (1160–1167), d. 1167.

Charles VIII, Swedish king (1436–1441, 1448–1470), d. 1470.

Charles IX, Swedish king (1600–1611), b. 1550, d. 1611.

Charles X, Swedish king (1654–1660), b. 1622, d. 1660.

Charles XI, Swedish king (1660–1697), b. 1655, d. 1697.

Charles XII, Swedish king (1697–1718), b. 1682, killed 1718.

Charles XIII, Swedish king (1809–1818), b. 1748, d. 1818.

Charles XIV, Swedish king (1818–1844), b. 1763, d. 1844.

Charles XV, Swedish king (1859–1872), b. 1826, d. 1872.

Charles the Bold, Duke of Burgundy, b. 1433, killed 1477.

Charles Borromeo, St, b. 1538, d. 1584.

Charles Martel, ruler of the Franks, b. about 689, d. 741.

Charleston, South Carolina, founded 1670, by the Englishman William Sayle, d. 1671.

Charlotte Sophia, wife of George III, b. 1744, d. 1818.

Charter, Great (Magna Carta) 1215 ; People's (Chartist) 1836.

Charterhouse School, British public school, founded 1611 by Thomas Sutton, b. 1532, d. 1611.

Chartist Movement, English social reform, begun 1836, ended about 1858 ; petitions rejected by Parliament 1839, 1842 and 1848.

Chartres Cathedral, constructed 1194 to 1260.

Chartreuse Liqueur, manufactured at La Grande Chartreuse Monastery near Grenoble 1607–1901, when the monks left France for Tarragona in Spain.

Chastelard, Pierre de, French poet, b. 1540, hanged 1564.

Chateaubriand, François René, Vicomte de, French statesman, b. 1768, d. 1848.

Chatham, William Pitt, Earl of, British statesman (Prime Minister 1766–1767), b. 1708, d. 1778.

Chattanooga, Battle of, American Civil War, 23 to 25 Nov. 1863.

Chatterton, Thomas, English forger and poet (*The Rowley Poems*), b. 1752, committed suicide 1770.

Chaucer, Geoffrey, English poet (*The Canterbury Tales*, 1387–1400), b. about 1340, d. 1400.

Chausson, Ernest, French composer, b. 1855, d. 1899.

Cheka, Soviet secret police, U.S.S.R., established 1917, superseded 1921 by N.K.V.D.

Chekhov, Anton, Russian writer (*The Cherry Orchard*, 1903), b. 1860, d. 1904.

Chelcicky, Peter, Bohemian religious leader in 15th century.

Chelsea-Derby Porcelain, manufactured 1770–1784.

Cheltenham College, British public school, founded 1840.

Cheltenham Gold Cup, first run 1924.

Cheltenham Ladies' College, British public school for girls, opened 1854. Miss Dorothea Beale, principal, 1858–1906.

Chemical Wood Pulp, for paper manufacture, invented 1857.

Cheng-hua Period, China, 1465–1487.

Cheng-têh Period, China, 1506–1521.

Chenier, André, French poet, b. 1762, guillotined 1794.

Cheops, Egyptian king, *fl.* about 2900 B.C.

Cheques, first printed by the English banker Lawrence Childs about 1762.

Cherepnin, Nikolai, Russian-born composer (*Le Pavillon d'Armide*, 1903), b. 1873, d. 1945.

Cherokee Tribe, North American Indians, disbanded 1906.

Cherubini, Luigi, Italian composer, b. 1760, d. 1842.

Chesapeake Bay, battle between French and British fleets, 5 Sept. 1781.

Chess, played in India by 7th century A.D., brought to Spain between 8th and 10th centuries, to England in late 13th century.

Chester Cathedral, England, founded 1093 ; created cathedral by Henry VIII 1541.

Chesterfield, Philip Dormer Stanhope, Earl of, British statesman and writer of the *Letters*, b. 1694, d. 1773.

Chesterton, Gilbert Keith, English writer (The *Father Brown* Stories), b. 1874, d. 1936.

' Chevalier sans peur et sans reproche ' (Pierre du Terrail, Chevalier de Bayard), French soldier, b. 1474, d. in battle 1524.

Chetham's Library, Manchester, founded 1653 by the English manufacturer Humfrey Chetham, b. 1580, d. 1653.

Chevalier, Albert, English music-hall artist, b. 1861, d. 1923.

Chevalier, Maurice, French actor, b. 1888.

Chevy Chase, Battle of, fought between Scots and English 1388.

Chia Ching Period, China, 1522–1566.

Chiang Kai-shek, Chairman of the Chinese Republic since 1935 and President since 1948, b. 1887.

Chicago, Illinois, settled at the beginning of the nineteenth century ; partly destroyed by fire 1871.

' **Chicago Anarchists** ', hanged 1886.

Chicago University, founded 1890.

Chickamauga, Battle of, American Civil War, fought 19–20 Sept. 1863.

Ch'ien-Lung Period, China, 1736–1795.

Chigwell School, Essex, British public school, founded 1629 by Samuel Harsnett, Archbishop of York, b. 1561, d. 1631.

Childermas, Holy Innocents' Day, 28 Dec.

Childers, Erskine, Irish Republican and writer (*The Riddle of the Sands*, 1903), b. 1870, executed 1922.

Children's Crusade, set out from France and Germany to the Holy Land 1212.

Chile, South America, settled by the Spaniards 1540–1565 ; national government set up 1810 ; complete independence from Spanish rule achieved 1818.

Chiltern Hundreds, first granted to an M.P. as grounds for resignation, 1750.

Chimborazo, volcanic mountain in Ecuador, first climbed 1880 by the English mountaineer Edward Whymper, b. 1840, d. 1911.

China, empire from at least the 23rd century B.C. until 1912 ; republic since 1912 ; the Communist People's Republic of China, governing the whole of China except Taiwan, proclaimed 21 Sept. 1949 ; Constitution adopted 20 Sept. 1954.

Chinese Law, first codified about 950 B.C.

Chinese Newspapers, first appeared with characters printed horizontally and reading from left to right 1956. Roman characters began to be introduced 1958.

Ch'ing Dynasty, China, 1644–1912.

Chippendale, Thomas, English furniture designer, b. 1718, d. 1779.

Chirico, Giorgio de, Italian painter, b. 1888.

Chiswick Press, London, founded 1810 by the English printer Charles Whittingham, b. 1767, d. 1840.

Chladni Figures, accoustic phenomenon discovered 1787 by the German physicist Ernst Chladni, b. 1756, d. 1827.

Chlorine, first isolated 1774 by the Swedish chemist Karl Wilhelm Scheele, b. 1742, d. 1786.

Chloroform, discovered 1831 by the German scientist Justus Liebig, b. 1803, d. 1873. (Rival claimants for the discovery : Guthrie and Soubeiran.) First used as an anæsthetic 1847.

Chmielnicki, Bogdan, Cossack leader, b. about 1593, d. 1657.

Chocolate (Cocoa), brought to Europe during 16th century.

Chodowiecki, Daniel Nikolaus, Polish artist, b. 1726, d. 1801.

Choiseul, Etienne François, Duc de, French statesman, b. 1719, d. 1785.

Cholera, bacillus, discovered 1883 by the German scientist Robert Koch, b. 1843, d. 1910 ; last major epidemic in England 1866.

Chopin, Frédéric, Polish-born composer, b. 1810, d. 1849.

Chosroes I, Persian ruler (from 531), d. 579.

Chosroes II, Persian ruler (from 591), murdered 628.

Chou Dynasty, China, 1122 to 255 B.C.

Chouans, Breton royalists, formed 1792, suppressed 1800.

Chrétien de Troyes, French poet (*Conte del Graal*), lived in the 12th century.

Christ, title of Jesus of Nazareth, founder of Christianity, b. between 5 B.C. and A.D. 2, crucified between 30 and 33.

Christ Church, Oxford University, founded 1525.

Christ College, Brecon (The College of Christ of Brecknock), British public school, founded 1541 by King Henry VIII ; reconstituted 1853.

Christ's College, Cambridge University, founded as God's-House 1448 by King Henry VI ; refounded and enlarged by the Lady Margaret Beaufort, Countess of Richmond and Derby, 1505.

Christ's Hospital, Sussex, English public school, founded in London 1552 by King Edward VI ; moved to present site 1902.

Christadelphians, religious movement, founded by John Thomas, b. 1805, d. 1871.

Christian I, Danish king (1448–1481), b. 1426, d. 1481.

Christian II, Danish king (1513–1523), b. 1481, died in prison 1559.

Christian III, Danish king (1535–1559), b. 1503, d. 1559.

Christian IV, Danish king (1588–1648), b. 1577, d. 1648.

Christian V, Danish king (1670–1699), b. 1646, d. 1699.

Christian VI, Danish king (1730–1746), d. 1746.

Christian VII, Danish king (1766–1808), b. 1749, d. 1808.

Christian VIII, Danish king (1839–1848), b. 1786, d. 1848.

Christian IX, Danish king (1863–1906), b. 1818, d. 1906.

Christian X, Danish king (1912–1947), b. 1870, d. 1947.

Christian Era, calculated from ostensible date of Incarnation, adopted in Italy in 6th century.

Christian, Fletcher, leader of the 1789 mutiny on the *Bounty* ; may have lived until after 1810.

Christian Science, religious movement, founded 1879 by the American Mrs Mary Baker Eddy, b. 1821, d. 1910.

Christian Socialism, founded 1850 by John Ludlau, b. 1821, d. 1911.

Christian Tract Society, London, founded 1809 by the Unitarian minister Robert Aspland, b. 1782, d. 1845.

Christianity, religious movement founded by Jesus of Nazareth in 1st century.

Christie, Agatha, English detective-story writer and playwright, b. 1891.

Christie, John Reginald Halliday, English murderer, b. 1898, hanged 1953.

Christie's, London auctioneers, founded 1766 by James Christie, b. 1730, d. 1803.

Christina, Swedish queen (1632–1654), b. 1626, d. 1689.

Christmas Cards, first examples designed in Britain 1843.

Christmas Day : 25 Dec. (Spain : 6 Jan. ; Russia and Greece : 7 Jan.).

Christmas Island, Western Pacific, discovered 1777 by Captain James Cook ; annexed 1888 by Britain ; included in the Gilbert and Ellice Islands Colony since 1919.

Christophe, Henry, King of Haiti, b. 1767, committed suicide 1820.

Christopher, Anti-Pope 903.

Chrome Tanning, process invented by Augustus Schultz 1884.

Chromium, first isolated 1797 by the French chemist Louis Nicolas Vauquelin, b. 1763, d. 1829.

Chromosphere, layer of the sun's atmosphere, so named by the English astronomer Sir Joseph Norman Lockyer, b. 1836, d. 1920.

Chronometers, invented 1726 by the English inventor John Harrison, b. 1693, d. 1776.

Church Army, founded in London 1882 by the English Rev. Wilson Carlile, b. 1847, d. 1942.

Church of England, established by St Augustine 597, separated from the Catholic Church by the Act of Supremacy 1534.

Church of Ireland (Anglican), disestablished 1869.

Church of Scotland, The Reformed, established 1560.

Church of Wales (Anglican), disestablished 1919.

Churchill, Charles, English satirical writer (*The Rosciad*, 1761), b. 1731, d. 1764.

Churchill, Lord Randolph, British statesman, b. 1849, d. 1894.

Churchill, Sarah, Duchess of Marlborough, b. 1660, d. 1744.

Churchill, Sir Winston, British states-man (Prime Minister 1940–1945, 1951–1955), b. 30 Nov. 1874.

Churchill College, Cambridge University, opened 1960.

Churriguera, José de, Spanish architect, b. about 1650, d. 1725.

Ciano, Galeazzo, Italian politician, b. 1903, shot 1944.

Cibber, Colley, English poet laureate (appointed 1730), b. 1671, d. 1757.

Cicero, Marcus Tullius, Roman statesman and writer, b. 106, d. 43 B.C.

Cigarettes, introduced into Britain 1854.

Cid, The (Rodrigo Diaz), Spanish hero, b. about 1026, d. 1099.

Cigars, introduced into Britain from Cuba 1762.

Cimabue, Giovanni (Cenni di Pepi), Italian painter (*St Francis*), b. about 1240, d. 1302.

Cimarosa, Domenico, Italian composer (*Il Matrimonio Segreto*, 1792), b. 1749, d. 1801.

Cinchona, introduced 1860 to India from South America by the explorer Sir Clements Robert Markham, b. 1830, d. 1916.

Cinchonine, an alkaloid, discovered by the French scientist Pierre Joseph Pelletier, b. 1788, d. 1842.

Cincinnatus, Lucius Quinctius, Roman patriot, b. 519, d. 438 B.C.

Cinema Projector, first model constructed by the French inventor Etienne J. Marey 1893.

Cinematograph, first model constructed by the French brothers Auguste and Louis Lumière 1895.

Cinerama (and other 3-dimensional film processes), came into general use 1952.

Cinna, Roman consul, murdered 84 B.C.

Cinq-Mars, Henri, Marquis de, French conspirator, b. 1620, executed 1642.

Cintra, Treaty of, concerning the French evacuation of Portugal, signed Aug. 1808.

Circumcision, Christian Feast of the, celebrated 1 Jan.

Circulation of the Blood, discovered 1615 by the English physician William Harvey, b. 1578, d. 1657.

Cisalpine Republic, existed in N. Italy 1797–1802.

Cistercian Order, founded 1098 by St Stephen Harding, d. 1134.

Cîteaux, French monastery, founded by St Robert of Molesme 1098.

City and South London Railway, first electric underground line, opened 18 Dec. 1890 between King William St. and Stockwell.

City of London School, English public school, founded 1442 by the English Member of Parliament John Carpenter, b. about 1370, d. about 1442.

Civil Engineers, Institution of, London, founded 1818 ; granted Royal Charter 1828.

Civil List, instituted by Parliament in 1697.

Civil War, American, 1861–1865.

Civil War, English. First, 1642–1646 ; second, 1648.

Civil War, Spanish, 1936–1939.

Clair, René, French film producer, b. 1898.

Clairvaux, French abbey, founded 1115 by St Bernard, b. 1091, d. 1153.

Claque, existed in the Théâtre Français until 1878.

Clare, John, English poet (*Shepherd's Calendar*, 1827), b. 1793, d. 1864.

Clare College, Cambridge University, founded 1326 as Union Hall by Richard Badew, Chancellor of Cambridge ; refounded 1336 by Lady Elizabeth de Clare, b. about 1291, d. 1360.

Clarendon, Edward Hyde, Earl of, British statesman (chief minister 1660–1667), b. 1608, d. 1674.

Clarendon, Constitutions of, royal proclamation, issued 1164.

Clark, William George, Shakespearean editor, b. 1821, d. 1878.

Clarke, John, pioneer settler 1638 in Rhode Island, b. 1609, d. 1676.

Clarkson, Thomas, English opponent of slavery, b. 1760, d. 1846.

Claudel, Paul, French writer and diplomat, b. 1868, d. 1955.

Claudius I, Roman Emperor (41–54), b. 10 B.C., poisoned A.D. 54.

Claudius II, Roman Emperor (268–270), d. 270.

Clausewitz, Karl von, Prussian strategist (*On War*), b. 1780, d. 1831.

Claverhouse, John Graham of, Scottish soldier, b. about 1649, d. in battle 1689.

Clay, Henry, American statesman, b. 1777, d. 1852.

Clayesmore School, Dorset, English public school, founded 1896.

Clemenceau, Georges, French statesman (Premier 1906–1909, 1917–1920), b. 1841, d. 1929.

Clement I, St, Pope 88–97.

Clement II (Suidger), Pope 1046–1047.

Clement III (Paolo Scolari), Pope 1187–1191.

Clement IV (Gui Foulques), Pope 1268–1271.

Clement V (Bertrand de Gouth), Pope 1305–1314, b. about 1264, d. 1314.

Clement VI (Pierre Roger), Pope 1342–1352, b. 1291, d. 1352.

Clement VII (Robert of Geneva), Anti-Pope 1378–1394, d. 1394.

Clement VII (Giulio dei Medici), Pope 1523–1534, d. 1534.

Clement VIII (Aegidius Muñoz), Anti-Pope 1425–1429, d. 1446.

Clement VIII (Ippolito Aldobrandini), Pope 1592–1605, b. 1535, d. 1605.

Clement IX (Giulio Respigliosi), Pope 1667–1669, b. 1600, d. 1669.

Clement X (Emilio Altieri), Pope 1670–1676, b. 1590, d. 1676.

Clement XI (Gian Francesco Albani), Pope 1700–1721, b. 1649, d. 1721.

Clement XII (Lorenzo Corsini), Pope 1730–1740, b. about 1652, d. 1740.

Clement XIII (Carlo della Torre Rezzonico), Pope 1758–1769, b. 1693, d. 1769.

Clement XIV (Lorenzo Ganganelli), Pope 1769–1774, b. 1705, d. 1774.

Clement of Alexandria, Greek theologian in 2nd century.

Clementi, Muzio, Italian composer (*Gradus ad Parnassum,* 1817), b. 1752, d. 1832.

Cleopatra, Egyptian Queen, b. 69, committed suicide 30 B.C.

Cleopatra's Needle, transferred from Egypt to London 1877 by the English surgeon Sir Erasmus Wilson, b. 1809, d. 1884.

Clerk-Maxwell, James, Scottish physicist, b. 1831, d. 1879.

Clermont, the first steamship, built 1807 by the American engineer Robert Fulton, b. 1765, d. 1815.

Cleve, Joos van, Flemish artist, b. about 1518, d. 1556.

Cleveland, Stephen Grover, U.S. President (1885–1889), b. 1837, d. 1908.

Clifton College, Bristol, English public school, founded 1862.

Clifton Suspension Bridge, opened 1864.

Clive, Robert, Baron Clive, Indian Empire pioneer, b. 1725, d. 1774.

Clodion (Michel Claude), French sculptor, b. 1738, d. 1814.

Clontarf, Battle of, between the Irish and the Danes, 1014.

Clotaire I, King of the Franks 558–561.

Clotaire II, King of the Franks 584–628.

Cloth of Gold, Field of the, nr. Calais, Conference between Henry VIII and Francis I, 6 June 1520.

Clothworkers, Livery Company, London, founded before 1480 ; incorporated 1528.

Cloud, St, b. about 520, d. 560.

Cloud Chamber, expansion chamber, invented by the Scottish scientist Charles Thomson Rees Wilson, b. 1869, d. 1959.

Clouet, Jean, French miniaturist, b. about 1485, d. about 1541.

Clovis, first Merovingian King of the Franks, b. 465, d. 511.

Cluny Abbey, founded 910.

Clynes, John Robert, British politician, b. 1869, d. 1949.

Cnossos Excavations, started 1900 by the English archæologist Sir John Evans, b. 1851, d. 1941.

Coal Gas, invented 1792–1796 by the Scottish engineer William Murdock (1754–1839). First used for lighting in Soho 1803.

Coal Industry, in Britain, taken over by State 1938, nationalised 1947.

Coalitions, in Britain, 1757, 1782, 1852, 1915, 1931, 1940.

Coalport Porcelain, manufactured from 1790 to present day.

Cobalt, first isolated by the German scientist Georg Brandt 1735.

Cobbett, William, English politician, writer (*Rural Rides*, 1830), b. 1763, d. 1835.

Cobden, Richard, English political reformer, b. 1804, d. 1865.

Cock-fighting, made illegal in England 1849.

Cocos Islands, Indian Ocean, discovered by Captain William Keeling of the East India Company 1609 ; settled 1826 ; annexed by Britain 1857 ; placed under the authority of the Commonwealth of Australia 1955.

Cocteau, Jean, French writer, b. 1891.

Code Napoléon, promulgated as the French civil law code 1804 ; assumed its present name 1807.

Codex Sinaiticus, purchased from the Soviet Government by Britain 1933.

Cody, Colonel Samuel Franklin, American aviation pioneer, b. 1862, killed in flying accident 1913.

Cody, William Frederick ('Buffalo Bill'), American frontiersman and showman, b. 1846, d. 1917.

Coello, Alonzo Sánchez, Spanish painter, b. 1515, d. 1590.

Coello, Claudio, Spanish painter, b. about 1621, d. 1693.

Coffee, brought to England about 1650.

Coimbra, University of, founded 1288 in Lisbon and transferred to Coimbra 1537.

Coke, Sir Edward, English statesman and jurist, b. 1552, d. 1634.

Coke, manufacture of, patented 1621 by Dud Dudley, the ironmaster, b. 1599, d. 1684.

Coke Ovens, invented by Friedrich Hoffmann 1893.

Colbert, Jean Baptiste, French statesman, b. 1619, d. 1683.

Colburn, Zerah, American calculating prodigy, b. 1804, d. 1840.

Coldstream Guards, raised 1659.

Cole, Douglas, English political writer, b. 1889, d. 1959.

Colenso, William, English missionary and explorer in New Zealand, b. 1811, d. 1899.

Coleridge, Samuel Taylor, English poet (*The Ancient Mariner*, 1798), b. 1772, d. 1834.

Coleridge-Taylor, Samuel, English composer (*The Song of Hiawatha*, 1898–1900), b. 1875, d. 1912.

Colet, John, English divine and scholar, b. about 1467, d. 1519.

'Colette' (Sidonie Gabrielle Colette), French novelist, b. 1873, d. 1954.

Coligny, Gaspard de, French statesman, b. 1519, murdered 1572.

College Postal Stamps, first used by Keble College, Oxford University, 1871 ; suppressed by the Postmaster-General Dec. 1885.

Collingwood, Cuthbert Collingwood, Baron, English admiral, b. 1750, d. 1810.

Collingwood, Robin George, English historian and philosopher, b. 1889, d. 1943.

Collins, Michael, Irish leader, b. 1890, killed 1922.

Collins, Wilkie, English novelist (*The Moonstone*, 1868), b. 1824, d. 1889.

Collins, William, English poet (*How sleep the brave*, 1746), b. 1721, d. 1759.

Collodion Process, invented 1850 by the English photographer Frederick Scott Archer, b. 1813, d. 1857.

Colloidal Chemistry, study initiated 1861 by the Scottish chemist Thomas Graham, b. 1805, d. 1869.

Collotype, illustrations printing process, invented by the French inventors Tessie du Motay and C. R. Maréchal 1865.

Colman, George, the elder, English dramatist (*The Jealous Wife*, 1761), b. 1732, d. 1794.

Colman, George, the younger, English dramatist (*The Heir at Law*, 1797), b. 1762, d. 1836.

Cologne University, founded 1388.

Colombia, achieved freedom from Spanish rule 1819 ; formed part of the State of Greater Colombia 1819–1830 ; became the Republic of New Granada 1830 ; transformed into the Confederación Granadina 1858 ; adopted the name of the United States of Colombia 1863 ; became the Republic of Colombia 1886.

Colon, Cristobal, Italian-born explorer, b. 1451, d. 1506.

Colonial Office, London, founded as the Council of Foreign Plantations 1660.

Colorado, U.S.A., first settled 1858 ; made a Territory 1861 ; admitted to the Union 1876.

Colorado Beetle, reached Europe 1922.

Colosseum, Roman amphitheatre, built 75–80.

Colossus of Rhodes, statue built about 285 B.C. ; destroyed by an earthquake 224 B.C.

Colour Photography, invented 1907 by the French pioneer in cinematography Auguste Lumière, b. 1862.

Colour Television, first experimental transmission to include ' live ' pictures made from Alexandra Palace, London, 1956.

Colt Revolver, invented 1835 by the American manufacturer Samuel Colt, b. 1814, d. 1862.

Colum, Padraic, Irish poet, b. 1881.

Columba, St, b. 521, d. 597.

Columban, St, b. about 540, d. 615.

Columbia River, discovered 1792 by the American explorer Robert Gray, b. 1755, d. 1806.

Columbia University, New York, founded 1754 as King's College ; reopened with present name 1784.

Columbium (Niobium), isolated 1801 by the English chemist Charles Hatchett, b. about 1765, d. 1847.

Columbus, Christopher, Italian-born explorer, b. 1451, d. 1506.

Columbus Day, commemorating the discovery of America : 12 Oct.

Combe, William, English writer (*Dr Syntax*, 1812–1821), b. 1741, d. 1823.

Combine Harvester-Thresher, invented in California 1875.

Comédie-Française, Paris, instituted 1658 ; assumed present name 1680.

Comenius (John Amos Komensky), Moravian scholar, b. 1592, d. 1671.

Comets, studied 1698–1705 by Edmund Halley, b. 1656, d. 1742.

Comic Strips, originated by the German artist Wilhelm Busch, b. 1832, d. 1908.

Cominform, international Communist body, founded 1947.

Comintern, international Communist body, founded 1919 ; dissolved 1943.

Commedia dell' Arte, came into being in Italy 1567.

Commodus, Roman Emperor (180–192), b. 161, murdered 192.

Commonwealth, Republican régime in England, 1649–1653.

Commonwealth Day, British, founded as Empire Day, 24 May 1902.

Commonwealth of Nations, British, title first used during First World War 1914–1918.

Commonwealth Relations Office, founded 1925 as the Dominions Office ; assumed present name 1947.

Commune of Paris, revolutionary régime March–May 1871.

Communism, origins in the Parisian secret societies of the 1830s. Karl Marx's *Communist Manifesto* issued by Communist League 1848.

Communist Party, *Russian :* Bolshevik fraction of Social-Democrat Party, re-named Communist Party 1918. *German :* formed from Spartakusbund 1918. *British :* formed from Socialist Party 1919.

Commynes, Philippe de, French historian, b. 1445, d. 1509.

Comoro Islands, a Protectorate of France until 1912 ; proclaimed a French colony 1912 ; attached to the Government-General of Madagascar 1914.

Compass, Magnetic, described 1269 by Peter Peregrinus of Picardy.

Compensated Pendulum, invented 1722 by the English mechanician George Graham, b. 1675, d. 1751.

Complutensian Bible, first polyglot Bible, prepared 1514–1522

Compressibility of Water, first demonstrated 1762 by the English scientist John Canton, b. 1718, d. 1772.

Comptometers, invented 1884 by the American inventor Dorr Eugene Felt, b. 1862, d. 1930.

Computer, First complete (the Harvard Mark I), built by the American Professor Howard Aiken and the I.B.M. Company 1939–1944.

Computer, first mechanical model discussed in Italy 1840–1841 by the British mathematician Dr. Charles Babbage, b. 1792, d. 1871.

Comstock, Anthony, American pioneer in censorship, b. 1844, d. 1915.

Comstock Silver Lode, Nevada, discovered about 1856 by the American trapper Henry Tompkins Paige Comstock, b. 1820, d. 1870.

Comte, Auguste (Isidore Xavier), French positivist philosopher, b. 1798, d. 1857.

Concentration Camps, common in Nazi Germany (1933–1945).

Concepción, Chilean city, founded 1541 by the Spanish conquistador Pedro de Valdivia, b. about 1510, d. 1554.

Concert Hall, London's first public, Hickford's Room, The Haymarket, opened 1697.

Concertina, invented 1829 by Charles Wheatstone.

Conclave of Cardinals, to elect a Pope (Gregory X), first held at Viterbo 1268–1271.

Condé, Louis II de Bourbon, Prince de, French general, b. 1621, d. 1686.

Condell, Henry, first Shakespearean editor, d. 1627.

Condensed Milk, process invented 1856 by the American inventor Gail Borden, b. 1801, d. 1874.

Conder, Charles, English painter, b. 1868, d. 1909.

Condillac, Etienne Bonnot de, French philosopher, b. 1715, d. 1780.

Condorcet, Marie Jean Antoine Nicolas Caritat, Marquis de, French philosopher, b. 1743, committed suicide 1794.

Confederate States of America, formed 4 Feb. 1861 ; defeated by Union 1865.

Confederation of the Rhine, Napoleonic organisation of German states, formed 1806 ; ended 1813.

Confession of Augsburg, Lutheran creed, prepared 1530.

Confucianism, religious movement, founded about 531 B.C. by the Chinese sage Confucius, b. 551, d. 478 B.C.

Congo River, discovered by the Portuguese navigator Diogo Cão 1482.

Congregational Movement, founded about 1580 by the English leader Robert Browne, b. about 1550, d. about 1633.

Congress of Industrial Organisations, U.S.A., founded 1936.

Congress of the United States of America, instituted 1787.

Congreve, William, English playwright (*The Way of the World*, 1700), b. 1670, d. 1729.

Connecticut, U.S.A., first settled 1635 ; organised commonwealth since 1637 ; one of the original states of the Union.

Connelly, Marc, American playwright (*Green Pastures*, 1930), b. 1890.

Connor, Patrick Edward, Irish-born American soldier, b. 1820, d. 1891.

Conon, Pope 686.

Conrad I, German king (911–918), d. 918.

Conrad II, German king (1024–39), b. about 990, d. 1039.

Conrad III, German king (1138–1152), b. about 1093, d. 1152.

Conrad IV, German king (1250–1254), b. 1228, d. 1254.

Conrad, Joseph (Teodor Josef Konrad Korzeniowski), Polish-born writer (*Lord Jim*, 1900), b. 1857, d. 1924.

Conscription, in England 1916–1918, 1939–1960 (women 1941–1947).

Conservation of Energy, principles defined 1847 by the German physicist Hermann von Helmholtz, b. 1821, d. 1894.

Conservation of Matter, principle defined 1789 by Lavoisier.

Conservative Party, British, origins about 1680 in the Tories ; present name began to be adopted 1824–1832.

Consols, British consolidated annuities, first consolidated between 1750 and 1757.

Constable, John, English painter (*The Hay Wain*), b. 1776, d. 1837.

Constans I, Roman Emperor (337–350), b. about 320, assassinated 350.

Constans II, Byzantine Emperor (641–668), b. 630, murdered 668.

Constant, Benjamin, French painter (*Samson et Délilah*), b. 1845, d. 1902.

Constantine, Pope 708–715.

Constantine, Anti-Pope 767.

Constantine I, Byzantine Emperor (309–337), b. about 288, d. 337.

Constantine II, Byzantine Emperor (337–340), b. 316, killed in battle 340.

Constantine III, Byzantine Emperor (641), d. 641.

Constantine IV, Byzantine Emperor (668–685), d. 685.

Constantine V, Byzantine Emperor (740–775), b. 718, d. 775.

Constantine VI, Byzantine Emperor (780–797), b. about 770.

Constantine VII, Byzantine Emperor (913–919, 944–959), b. 905, d. 959.

Constantine VIII, Byzantine Emperor (1025–1028).

Constantine IX, Byzantine Emperor (1042–1055).

Constantine X, Byzantine Emperor (1059–1067), d. 1067.

Constantine XI, last Byzantine Emperor (1448–1453), killed 1453.

Constantine I, King of the Hellenes (1913–1917, 1920–1922), b. 1868, d. 1923.

Constantinople, founded as Byzantium 658 B.C. ; rebuilt as Constantinople A.D. 330 ; captured by the Turks 1453 and renamed Istanbul.

Constantius I, Roman Emperor (305–306), b. about 250, d. 306.

Constantius II, Roman Emperor (337–361), b. 317, d. 361.

Constantius III, Roman Emperor (421), d. 421.

Consulate, The, French Napoleonic government, established 1799 ; abolished 1804.

Contact Lenses, first suggested 1827 by the English astronomer Sir John Herschel (1792–1871) ; first made by the German lens-maker F. E. Müller 1887.

Contemporary Art Society, London, founded 1910.

Continental Congress, American Federal legislative body, established 1774 ; ended 1789.

Continental Drift, theory developed 1910 by the German geologist Alfred Wegener, b. 1880, d. 1930.

Continental System, blockade carried out by Napoleon 1804–1812.

Conventicle Acts, to suppress nonconformist worship in Britain, enacted 1593 and 1664 ; repealed 1689.

Convulsionaries, Jansenist group in Paris who venerated François de Paris, d. 1727.

Cook, James, English explorer and mariner, b. 1728, murdered 1779. First voyage 1768–1771 ; second, 1772–1775 ; third, 1776–1779.

Cook, Thomas, English pioneer travel agent, b. 1808, d. 1892.

Cook Strait, New Zealand, discovered by Captain James Cook 1770.

Cooke, Jay, American financier, b. 1821, d. 1905.

Coolidge, Susan, American writer (*What Katy Did*), b. 1845, d. 1905.

Coolidge, Calvin, U.S. President (1923–1929), b. 1872, d. 1933.

Coombes, Robert, English champion sculler, b. 1808, d. 1860.

Cooper, James Fenimore, American writer (*The Last of the Mohicans*, 1826), b. 1789, d. 1851.

Cooper, Samuel, English miniaturist, b. 1609, d. 1672.

Co-operative Congress, First, held London 1869.

Co-operative Party, Great Britain, formed 1917 ; first M.P. elected 1919.

Co-operative Societies, origins in England in the Rochdale Society, founded 1844.

Copeland, William Taylor, English potter, b. 1797, d. 1868.

Copenhagen, Battle of, between the British and Danish fleets, 2 Apr. 1801.

Copenhagen University, founded 1479.

Copernicus, Nicolas (Mikdaj Kopernik), Polish astronomer, b. 1473, d. 1543.

Copland, Aaron, American composer (*Billy the Kid*, 1938), b. 1900.

Copley, John Singleton, American painter (*The Death of Chatham*), b. 1737, d. 1815.

Coppard, Alfred Edgar, English writer (*Adam and Eve and Pinch Me*, 1921), b. 1878, d. 1957.

Coppée, François, French writer (*Le Réliquaire*, 1866), b. 1842, d. 1908.

Coptic Church, separated from Orthodox Church 451.

Coptic Era, began 29 Aug. 284.

Copyright, first Act passed in England 1709 ; law consolidated by Act of 1911.

Coquelin, Benoît Constant, French actor, b. 1841, d. 1909.

Coral Sea, Battle of the, World War II, 7–9 May 1942.

Coram, Thomas, English philanthropist, b. 1668, d. 1751.

Corday, Charlotte, French murderer of Marat, b. 1768, guillotined 1793.

Cordite, invented by Sir Frank Augustus Abel (1827–1902) and Sir James Dewar (1842–1923), and adopted by the British Government 1891.

Corelli, Arcangelo, Italian composer (*La Follia*), b. 1653, d. 1713.

Corelli, Marie, English popular novelist (*Sorrows of Satan*, 1895), b. 1854, d. 1924.

Corinth, Lovis, German painter, b. 1858, d. 1925.

' Corn Law Rhymer, The ' (Ebenezer Elliott), English poet (*Battle Song*), b. 1781, d. 1849.

Corn Laws, enacted in Britain 1815 and 1828 and 1842 ; repealed 1844 and 1869.

Corneille, Pierre, French playwright (*Le Cid*, 1636), b. 1606, d. 1684.

Cornelius. St, Pope 251–253.

Cornell University, Ithaca, N.Y., founded 1865 by the American financier Ezra Cornell, b. 1807, d. 1874.

Cornet, cavalry rank, abolished 1871.

Cornford, Frances, English poetess, b. 1886, d. 1960.

Cornish Languages, spoken until 18th century.

Cornwallis, Charles, Marquis, Governor-General of India, b. 1738, d. 1805.

Coronado, Francisco Vásquez de, Spanish explorer of south-western U.S.A., b. about 1510, d. 1554.

Coronation Cup, Epsom, first run 1902.

Coronation Stone (Stone of Scone), placed in Westminster Abbey 1296 by King Edward I. Stolen by the Scottish Nationalists 1950 ; returned to Westminster 1952.

Corot, Jean Baptiste Camille, French painter, b. 1796, d. 1875.

Corps of Commissionaires, founded 1859 by the English soldier Sir Edward Walter, b. 1823, d. 1904.

Corpus Christi, feast day, founded 1264 by Pope Urban IV, celebrated on the Thursday after Trinity Sunday.

Corpus Christi College, Cambridge University, founded by the united Guilds of Corpus Christi and of the Blessed Virgin Mary 1352.

Corpus Christi College, Oxford University, founded 1516 by the statesman Richard Foxe, b. 1448, d. 1528.

Corpus Juris Civilis, Roman legal code, compiled at the Emperor Justinian I's orders 528–533.

Corpuscles, Red, first discovered by the Dutch naturalist Jan Swammerdam, b. 1637, d. 1680.

Correggio, Antonio Allegri da, Italian painter (*The Assumption of the Virgin*), b. 1494, d. 1534.

Corsica, finally taken over by France 1796.

Cort, Cornelis, Dutch engraver, b. about 1536, d. 1578.

Cortés, Hernando, Spanish *conquistador* of Mexico (1519–1521), b. 1485, d. 1547.

Cortisone, discovered 1936 by the English chemist James Kendall, b. 1889.

Cortona, Pietro da, Italian artist, b. 1596, d. 1669.

Cortot, Alfred, Swiss pianist, b. 1877.

' Corvo, Baron ' (Frederick Rolfe), English novelist (*Hadrian the Seventh*, 1904), b. 1860, d. 1913.

Coryate, Thomas, English traveller and writer (*Crudities*, 1611), b. about 1577, d. 1617.

Cosgrave, William, Irish politician, b. 1880.

Cosmic Rays, discovered 1925 by the American scientist Robert Andrews Millikan, b. 1868, d. 1953.

Costa, Lorenzo, Italian painter (*Madonna and Child Enthroned*), b. 1460, d. 1535.

Costa Rica, Central America, discovered 1502 by Christopher Columbus ; achieved independence from Spanish rule 1822.

Cosway, Richard, English miniaturist, b. about 1742, d. 1821.

Cotman, John Sell, English painter, b. 1782, d. 1842.

Cotton, Charles, English poet (*New Year Poem*), b. 1630, d. 1687.

Cotton, Sir Robert Bruce, English collector of the Cottonian Collection (now in the British Museum), b. 1571, d. 1631.

Coué, Emile, French founder of auto-suggestion, b. 1857, d. 1926.

Coulomb, Charles Augustin de, French physicist, b. 1736, d. 1806.

Council of Chalcedon, 4th Ecumenical Council, 451.

Council of Constance, Catholic general council, 1414–1418.

Councils of Constantinople, 2nd Ecumenical Council, 381 ; 5th Ecumenical Council, 533 ; 6th Ecumenical Council, 680.

Council of Elders, French revolutionary government, 1795–1799.

Council of Ephesus, 3rd Ecumenical Council, convened 431.

Council of Europe, Statute signed 1949 at 10-Power London Conference ; came into effect 1949.

Council of Five Hundred, French Revolutionary government, 1795–1799.

Councils of Nicaea, 1st Ecumenical Council, 325 ; 7th Ecumenical Council, 787.

Council of Ten, Venetian cabal, set up 1310 ; abolished about 1797.

Council of Trent, Catholic General Council, began 1545 ; ended 1563.

Council, Vatican, Catholic General Council, 1869–1870.

Counter Reformation, within the Catholic Church, began 1513 ; completed 1563.

Countess of Huntingdon's Connection, Calvinist Methodist sect, founded in the 1740s.

Couperin, François, French composer (*Les Nations*, 1726), b. 1668, d. 1733.

Couperus, Louis, Dutch writer, b. 1863, d. 1923.

Coupon Election, held 1918.

Courbet, Gustave, French painter, b. 1819, d. 1877.

Courtauld, Samuel, British silk manufacturer, b. 1793, d. 1881.

Courtauld Institute of Art, London, established 1930.

Courtrai, Battle of (The Battle of the Golden Spurs), between the Flemish and the French, 1302.

Cousin, Jean, French painter (*The Last Judgment*), b. about 1500, d. about 1590.

Cousins, Samuel, English engraver, b. 1801, d. 1887.

Coutts & Co., British bankers, founded by the Scottish banker Thomas Coutts, b. 1735, d. 1822.

Covent Garden Theatre, London, opera house built 1858.

Coventry Cathedral, built in the 15th century ; destroyed in World War II 1940.

Coverdale's Bible, translated into English by the English divine Miles Coverdale (1488–1568) ; published 1535.

Coward, Noël, English playwright (*Bitter Sweet*, 1929), b. 1899.

Cowley, Abraham, English writer (*The Mistress*, 1647), b. 1618, d. 1667.

Cowper, William, English poet (*The Task*, 1785), b. 1731, d. 1800.

Cox, David, English painter, b. 1783, d. 1859.

Coxwell, Henry Tracey, English balloonist, b. 1819, d. 1900.

Coypel, Noël, French painter, b. 1628, d. 1707.

Cozens, John Robert, English water-colour artist, b. 1752, d. 1799.

Crabbe, George, English poet (*The Borough,* 1810), b. 1754, d. 1832.

Craig, Edward Gordon, English man of the theatre, b. 1872.

Craigavon, James Craig, Viscount, first Prime Minister of Northern Ireland, b. 1871.

Craik, Mrs (Dinah Maria Mulock), English writer (*John Halifax, Gentleman,* 1857) b. 1826, d. 1887.

Cramer, Johann Baptist, German-born pianist and music teacher, b. 1771, d. 1858.

Cranach, Lucas, German painter (*The Judgment of Paris*), b. 1472, d. 1553.

Cranbrook School, Kent, English public school, founded about 1520 by John Blubery ; granted a Royal Charter 1574.

Crane, Hart, American poet, b. 1899, d. 1932.

Crane, Stephen, American writer (*The Red Badge of Courage,* 1896), b. 1871, d. 1900.

Crane, Walter, English artist, b. 1845, d. 1915.

Crane, Hydraulic, invented about 1845 by William George Armstrong (later Baron Armstrong), b. 1810, d. 1900.

Cranleigh School, Surrey, English public school, founded 1863 ; incorporated by Royal Charter 1898.

Cranmer, Thomas, Archbishop of Canterbury, b. 1489, burnt at the stake 1556.

Crashaw, Richard, English poet (*Steps to the Temple,* 1646), b. about 1613, d. 1649.

Crassus, Marcus Licinius, Roman triumvir, b. about 114, murdered 53 B.C.

Crawford, Francis Marion, American expatriate novelist (*Via Crucis,* 1898), b. 1854, d. 1909.

Cream, Thomas Neill, Canadian-born murderer, b. 1850, hanged 1892.

Cream Separator, first centrifugal model invented 1877 by the Swedish engineer Carl Gustaf de Laval, b. 1845, d. 1913.

Crébillon, Claude Prosper Jolyot de, French writer (*Le Sofa,* 1742), b. 1707, d. 1777.

Crébillon, Prosper Jolyot de, French playwright (*Catilina,* 1748), b. 1674, d. 1762.

Crécy, Battle of, between the English and the French, 26 Aug. 1346.

Creevey, Thomas, English diarist, b. 1768, d. 1838.

Cremona Cathedral, Italy, built 1107–1606.

Creosote, discovered 1833 by the German manufacturer Baron von Reichenbach, b. 1788, d. 1869.

Crespi, Giuseppe Maria ('Lo Spagnuolo'), Italian painter, b. 1665, d. 1747.

Crete, ruled by Venetians 1204–1645, by Turks 1645–1898 ; part of Greece since 1913.

Crewe, Robert Offley Ashburton Crewe Milnes, Marquess of, British statesman, b. 1858, d. 1945.

'Crichton, The Admirable' (James Crichton), Scottish scholar, b. 1560, killed 1582.

Cricket, played in England since 13th century ; M.C.C. founded 1787.

Crimean War, between the Allies and Russia, 1854–1856.

Criminology, study founded by the Italian Cesare Lombroso, b. 1836, d. 1909.

Crippen, Dr Hawley Harvey, American murderer in England, b. 1861, hanged 1910.

Cripps, Richard Stafford, British statesman, b. 1889, d. 1952.

Crivelli, Carlo, Italian painter, b. about 1434, d. 1493.

Croatia, independent 925–1102 ; part of Hungary 1102–1918, of Yugoslavia since 1918.

Croce, Benedetto, Italian philosopher, b. 1866, d. 1952.

Crockett, David, American pioneer, b. 1786, killed in battle 1836.

Crockett, Samuel Rutherford, Scottish novelist (*The Stickit Minister*, 1893), b. 1860, d. 1914.

Crœsus, King of Lydia (560–546 B.C.).

Crome, John, English painter, b. 1768, d. 1821.

Cromer, Evelyn Baring, Earl of, British agent and Consul-General in Egypt (1883–1907), b. 1841, d. 1917.

Crompton, Richmal (Richmal Crompton Lamburn), English writer (*Just William*, 1922), b. 1890.

Croker, John Wilson, Irish politician, b. 1780, d. 1857.

Crompton's Mule, spinning machine, invented 1779 by the English weaver Samuel Crompton, b. 1753, d. 1827.

Cromwell, Oliver, Puritan general, Lord Protector (1653–1658), b. 1599, d. 1658.

Cromwell, Richard, Lord Protector (1658–1659), b. 1626, d. 1712.

Cromwell, Thomas, Earl of Essex, English statesman (chief minister 1533–1540), b. about 1485, beheaded 1540.

Cronin, Archibald Joseph, Scottish novelist (*Hatter's Castle*, 1931), b. 1896.

Crookes Tube, high vacuum tube, invented by the English scientist Sir William Crookes, b. 1832, d. 1919.

Cross-bow, first used in Europe about 1090.

Crossword Puzzles, first introduced in England at the beginning of 19th century.

Cruden's Concordance, published 1737, compiled by Alexander Cruden, b. 1701, d. 1770.

Cruikshank, George, English artist, b. 1792, d. 1878.

Crusades, in Eastern Mediterranean, 1095–1291.

Crusoe, Robinson, story founded on the experiences of Scottish sailor Alexander Selkirk, b. 1676, d. 1721.

Cryolite, translucent mineral, discovered 1794.

Crystal Palace, designed by Sir Joseph Paxton, b. 1801, d. 1865 ; erected in Hyde Park 1851, moved to Penge 1854, destroyed by fire 1936.

Cuba, discovered 1492 by Christopher Columbus ; achieved independence from Spanish rule 1898.

Cube Sugar, manufacturing process invented by Sir Henry Tate, b. 1819, d. 1899.

Cubism, art movement, founded in France about 1909.

Cui, César, Russian-born composer (*The Saracen*, 1899), b. 1835, d. 1918.

Culford School, Suffolk, British public school founded as the East Anglian School 1881.

Cullen, Countée, American negro poet, b. 1903.

Cullinan Diamond, found at Pretoria 1905, presented to Edward VII on behalf of the people of Transvaal 9 Nov. 1907.

Culloden, Battle of, fought between the Duke of Cumberland and the Young Pretender 16 Apr. 1746 (last battle fought in Britain).

Culpeper's Herbal, published 1653, compiled by Nicholas Culpeper, b. 1616, d. 1654.

Cumberland, William Augustus, Duke of, British military commander, b. 1721, d. 1765.

Cumberland, Richard, Bishop of Peterborough and philanthropist, b. 1631, d. 1718.

Cummings, Edward Estlin, American writer (*The Enormous Room*, 1922), b. 1894.

Cunard, Sir Samuel, Nova Scotia manufacturer, founder of the first regular Atlantic steamship service, b. 1787, d. 1865.

Cunard Company, founded by Samuel Cunard, George Burns and David MacIver 4 May 1839 ; merger of Cunard and White Star Lines 1934.

Cuneiform, writing first deciphered 1835 by Sir Henry Rawlinson.

Cunha, Tristão da, Portuguese explorer, b. about 1460, d. about 1540.

Cunningham, Alexander, Earl of Glencairn, Scottish reformer, d. 1574.

Cunninghame Graham, Robert Bontine, Scottish writer, b. 1852, d. 1936.

Curaçao, island in Netherlands Antilles, discovered, became Dutch colony 1634.

Curare, discovered about 1740 by the Frenchman Charles Marie de Lacondamine, b. 1701, d. 1774.

'Curé d'Ars', The (Jean-Marie Vianney), patron saint of parish priests, b. 1787, d. 1859.

Curfew, introduced at Oxford by King Alfred to reduce fire risks 872.

Curie, Professor Frédéric Joliot-, French physicist, b. 1900, d. 1958.

Curie, Marie (Marie Sklodowska), wife of Pierre Curie, Polish scientist and discoverer of radium, b. 1867, d. 1934.

Curie, Pierre, French scientist and discoverer of radium, b. 1859, d. 1906.

Curll, Edmund, English bookseller, b. 1675, d. 1747.

Curragh, Meeting of the, Ireland, Mar. 1914.

Curran, John Philpot, Irish judge and patriot, b. 1750, d. 1817.

Currier, Nathaniel, American lithographer, b. 1813, d. 1888.

Curtiss, Glenn Hammond, American aviation pioneer, b. 1878, d. 1930.

Curzon, George Nathaniel, Marquess, British statesman and Viceroy of India (1899–1905), b. 1859, d. 1925.

Curzon Line, dividing Poland on linguistic lines, 1919.

Cust, Sir Lionel Henry, English art historian and critic, b. 1859, d. 1929.

'Custer's Last Stand', made 25 June 1876 at Little Big Horn, Montana, by George Armstrong Custer, b. 1839, d. 1876.

Cuthbert, St, b. about 635, d. 687.

Cuyp, Albert, Dutch painter (*Piper with Cows*), b. 1620, d. 1691.

Cyanide, invented 1905 by the German chemist Heinrich Caro, b. 1834, d. 1910.

Cyanogen, first isolated 1815 by the French scientist Joseph Louis Gay-Lussac, b. 1778, d. 1850.

Cyclotron, invented 1929 by the American physicist Ernest Lawrence, b. 1901, d. 1958.

Cymbeline (Cunobelinus), British king, d. about 43.

Cynewulf, Anglo-Saxon poet (*The Dream of the Cross*), lived in the 8th century.

Cyprian, St, b. about 200, martyred 14 Sept. 258.

Cyprus, taken from the Venetians by the Turks 1571 ; ceded to Britain 1878 ; made British Crown Colony 1925 ; became Republic 1960.

Cyrano de Bergerac, Savinien, French writer and duellist, b. 1619, d. 1655.

Cyril, St, of Alexandria, d. 444.

Cyril, St, of Jerusalem, b. about 315, d. 386.

Cyrillic Alphabet, invention attributed to Saint Cyril, b. 827, d. 869.

Cyrus the Great, Persian Emperor (563–529 B.C.), d. 529 B.C.

Cyrus the Younger, Persian satrap, b. 424, killed in battle 401 B.C.

Cyzicus, Naval Battle of, between Alcibiades and the Lacedæmonians 410 B.C.

Czechoslovakia, Republic founded 28 Oct. 1918 ; annexed by Germany 1939 ; liberated 1944–1945 ; Communist régime since 1948.

Czermak, Jaroslav, Bohemian artist, b. 1831, d. 1878.

Czerny, Carl, Austrian pianist and composer (*Daily Studies*), b. 1791, d. 1857.

D

D-Day, World War II, Allies landed in Normandy, 6 June 1944.

D.D.T., Dichloro - Diphenyl - Trichloroethane), insecticide, invented by the German scientist Zeidler 1874. First used as insecticide 1939.

Dabrowski, Jan Henryk, Polish military leader and national hero, b. 1755, d. 1818.

Dadaism, art movement founded about 1915 in Zürich ; ended about 1922.

Dagobert I, King of the Franks (629–639), d. 639.

Daguerrotype Process, invented between 1826 and 1839 by the French artist Louis Jacques Mandé Daguerre, b. 1789, d. 1851.

Dahl, Michael, Swedish painter (*Queen Christina*), b. 1656, d. 1743.

Dahlgren, John Adolf, American ordnance specialist and inventor, b. 1809, d. 1870.

Dahomey, West Africa, first settled by the French 1851 and completely annexed 1894 ; autonomous republic within the French Community since 1958.

Dáil Eireann, Irish Free State Chamber of Deputies, formed in Dublin Jan. 1919.

Daily Courant, The, first English daily newspaper, founded 1702, ran until 1735.

Daily Express, The, British newspaper, founded 1900 by C. Arthur Pearson.

Daily Graphic, The, British newspaper, founded 1890 by W. L. Thomas ; absorbed by *Daily Sketch* 1925.

Daily Herald, The, British newspaper, began publication 16 Apr. 1912 ; placed under joint control of Odhams and the T.U.C. in 1929.

Daily Mail, The, British newspaper, founded 1896 by Lord Northcliffe, b. 1865, d. 1922.

Daily Mirror, The, British newspaper, founded 1903 by Lord Northcliffe, b. 1865, d. 1922.

Daily News, The, British newspaper, founded 1846, merged in *News Chronicle* 1930.

Daily Sketch, The, British newspaper, founded 1909 by Edward Hulton.

Daily Telegraph, The, British newspaper, re-founded 1855 by Joseph Moses Levy, d. 1888.

Daimler, Gottlieb, German automobile manufacturer, b. 1834, d. 1900.

Daladier, Edouard, French statesman, b. 1884.

Dalai Lama, highest ecclesiastical and secular official of Tibet since 15th century ; present incumbent b. about 1928, installed 1940, assumed full power 1950, escaped to India 1959.

Dalcroze Eurhythmics, music educational system, invented by the Swiss composer Emile Jaques-Dalcroze, b. 1865, d. 1950.

Dale, Sir Thomas, English governor of Virginia (1611, 1614-1616), d. 1619.

Dalhousie, James Andrew Brown Ramsay, Marquis of, Governor-General of India (1848-1856), b. 1812, d. 1860.

Dallas, Texas, first settled 1841, assumed present name 1845, in honour of the American statesman George Mifflin Dallas, b. 1792, d. 1864.

Dalmatia, ruled by Venice 1718-1797, by Austria 1797-1918 ; part of Yugoslavia since 1918 (occupied by Italians 1941-1945).

Dalton's Law, defined 1803 by the English scientist John Dalton, b. 1766, d. 1844.

Dalton Plan, educational system, introduced at Dalton, Mass., by Helen Parkhurst in about 1920.

Damasus I, St, Pope 366-384.

Damasus II, Pope July-Aug. 1048.

Dame Allan's School, Newcastle-upon-Tyne, British public school, founded by Dame Eleanor Allan 1705.

Damão, Portuguese India, discovered by Vasco da Gama 1498 ; taken under Portuguese rule 1595.

Damian, St, martyred 303.

Damiani, Pietro, Italian papal legate and reformer, b. about 1007, d. 1072.

Damien, Father Joseph (Joseph de Veuster), French leper missionary in Hawaii, b. 1840, d. 1889.

Dampier, William, English navigator, b. 1652, d. 1715.

Damrosch, Leopold, German composer and conductor, b. 1832, d. 1885.

Damrosch, Walter Johannes, German-born composer and conductor, b. 1862, d. 1950.

Dana, Charles Anderson, American writer and editor, b. 1819, d. 1897.

Dana, Richard Henry, American writer (*Two Years Before the Mast*, 1840), b. 1815, d. 1882.

Dance, George, English architect (Mansion House, London), b. 1700, d. 1768.

Dance, George, son of George Dance (1700-1768), English architect (College of Surgeons), b. 1741, d. 1825.

Danegeld, tax first levied in England 991 ; finally abolished 1163.

Danelaw, name applied in 11th century to area of eastern England settled by Danes in 9th and 10th centuries.

Daniel, Samuel, English writer (*Defence of Rhyme,* 1602), b. 1562, d. 1619.

Daniel Stewart's College, Edinburgh, Scottish public day school, founded by Daniel Stewart, d. 1814.

Daniell Cell, invented by the English scientist John Frederick Daniell, b. 1790, d. 1845.

Danish Invasion of England, began about 835.

Dantan, Joseph Edouard, French painter, b. 1848, d. 1897.

Dante Alighieri, Italian poet (*The Divine Comedy*), b. 1265, d. 1321.

Danton, Georges Jacques, French revolutionary leader, b. 1759, guillotined 1794.

Danube Navigation European Commission appointed under the Treaty of Paris 1856 ; Statute 2 Dec. 1861 ; International Commission appointed 1904.

Danzig (Gdańsk), Poland, made capital of the Dukes of Pomerania 1230 ; Free City 1466–1793, 1807–1814, 1919–1939.

Dardanelles Expedition, World War I, Feb.–Mar. 1915.

Darien, Central America, discovered 1501 by the Spanish explorer Rodrigo de Bastidas.

Darien Scheme, Scottish overseas trading venture, conceived 1684 by the Scottish merchant William Paterson, b. 1658, d. 1719. Darien expedition set out for Panama 1698.

Darius I, Persian king (521–486), b. 548, d. 486 B.C.

Darius II, Persian king (423–404), d. 404 B.C.

Darius III, Persian king (336–330), assassinated 330 B.C

Darling, Grace, English heroine of the rescue of the *Forfarshire's* survivors on 7 Sept. 1838, b. 1815, d. 1842.

Darling River, Australia, discovered 1828 by the English explorer Charles Sturt, b. 1795, d. 1869.

Darnley, Henry, husband of Mary Queen of Scots, b. 1545, murdered 1567.

Dartmoor Prison, foundation stone laid 20 Mar. 1806 ; opened 24 May 1809.

Dartmouth College, New Hampshire, founded 1769.

Dartmouth College (Britannia Royal Naval College), opened 1905.

Darwin, Charles, English biologist (*The Origin of Species,* 1859), b. 1809, d. 1882.

Darwin, Erasmus, English physician and writer (*The Botanic Garden,* 1789–1792), b. 1731, d. 1802.

Dasent, Sir George Webbe, British Nordic scholar (*Burnt Njal,* 1861), b. 1817, d. 1896.

Daubigné, Théodore Agrippa, French historian, b. 1552, d. 1630.

Daudet, Alphonse, French writer (*Tartarin de Tarascon,* 1872), b. 1840, d. 1897.

Daughters of the American Revolution, Washington, D.C., founded as a national society 1890.

Daumier, Honoré, French painter (*The Good Samaritan*), b. 1808, d. 1879.

Dauntsey's School, Wiltshire, British public school, founded by Alderman William Dauntsey 1543.

D'Avenant, Sir William, English writer (*The Wits,* 1633), b. 1606, d. 1668.

Davenant Porcelain, manufactured 1793–1882.

David, St (Dewi), lived in Wales in 6th century.

David I, Scottish king (1124–1153), b. about 1080, d. 1153.

David II, Scottish king (1329–1371), b. 1324, d. 1371.

David, Gerhard, Flemish painter (*Pietà*), b. about 1450, d. 1523.

David, Jacques Louis, French painter (*Madame Recamier*), b. 1748, d. 1825.

'David, Pierre' (David d'Angers), French sculptor (*Lafayette*), b. 1789, d. 1856.

Davidson, Jo, American sculptor, b. 1883.

Davidson, Randall, Archbishop of Canterbury (1903–1928), b. 1848, d. 1930.

Davies, Emily, English founder 1866–1869 of Girton College, Cambridge, b. 1830, d. 1921.

Davies, Sir John, English poet (*Nosce teipsum*, 1599), b. 1569, d. 1626.

Davies, Sir Walford, English composer (*Everyman*, 1904), b. 1869, d. 1941.

Davies, William Henry, English poet (*The Autobiography of a Super-tramp*, 1906), b. 1871, d. 1940.

Davis, Jefferson, President (1861–1865) of the Southern Confederacy, b. 1808, d. 1889.

Davis, John, English explorer and discoverer (1587) of Davis Strait, b. about 1550, killed 1605.

Davis, Richard Harding, American writer (*Soldiers of Fortune*, 1897), b. 1864, d. 1916.

Davis Strait, Greenland, discovered 1587 by the English navigator John Davis.

Davitt, Michael, Irish patriot, b. 1846, d. 1906.

Davy, Sir Humphry, English chemist, b. 1778, d. 1829.

Dawes Plan, concerning reparations for World War I, devised by the American statesman Charles Gates Dawes, b. 1865, d. 1951.

Dawson, Henry, English painter (*The Wooden Walls of Old England*), b. 1811, d. 1878.

Day, mean terrestrial, 23 h., 56 m., 4.1 s. ; mean solar, 24 h., 3 m., 56.6 s. ; mean sidereal, 23 h., 56 m., 4.091 s.

Day, John, English printer, b. 1522, d. 1584.

Day, Thomas, English writer (*Sandford and Merton*, 1783–1789), b. 1748, d. 1789.

Day of Atonement (*Yom Kippur*), Jewish holy day, falls during last fortnight of Sept. and first fortnight of Oct. (10th day of Tishri).

Daye, Stephen, English-born first New England printer, b. about 1600, d. 1668.

Daylight Saving, pioneered in Britain by William Willett, b. 1856, d. 1915. Officially adopted 1916.

De Grey, Walter, Archbishop of York (1215–1255) and Chancellor of England (1205–1214), d. 1255.

De La Mare, Walter, English poet (*Peacock Pie*, 1913), b. 1873, d. 1958.

De La Rue, Thomas, British printer and founder of the playing-card publishing firm, b. 1793, d. 1866.

De La Rue, Warren, British scientist and inventor, b. 1815, d. 1889.

De La Warr, Thomas West, Baron, governor of Virginia (1610–1618), b. 1577, d. 1618.

De Mille, Cecil B., American film producer, b. 1881, d. 1959.

De Morgan, Augustus, English logician (*Budget of Paradoxes*, 1872), b. 1806, d. 1871.

De Morgan, William Frend, English writer (*Joseph Vance*, 1906), b. 1839, d. 1917.

De Paul University, Chicago, founded 1898.

De Pauw University, Indiana, founded 1837 as the Indiana Asbury College ; assumed present name 1884.

De Quincey, Thomas, English writer (*Confessions of an English Opium-Eater*, 1821), b. 1785, d. 1859.

De Soto, Hernando, Spanish explorer of North America, b. about 1498, d. 1542.

De Valera, Eamon, Irish statesman (Prime Minister 1927–1948, 1951–1954, 1957–1959), b. 1882.

De Valois, Dame Ninette, director of The Royal Ballet, b. 1898.

De Vere, Aubrey, British poet, b. 1814, d. 1902.

De Vinne, Theodore Low, American printer, b. 1828, d. 1914.

De Vries, David Pietersen, Dutch pioneer in America, b. about 1593, d. in the middle or late 17th century.

De Wet, Christian Rudolf, Boer patriot, b. 1854, d. 1922.

De Wint, Peter, English painter (*A Cornfield*), b. 1784, d. 1849.

De Witt, Johan, Dutch statesman, b. 1625, lynched 1672.

'**Deadwood Dick**' (Richard W. Clarke), American pioneer, b. 1825, d. 1930.

Deaf and Dumb School, First British, set up 1760 at Edinburgh by the Scottish teacher Thomas Braidwood, b. 1715, d. 1798.

Dean Close School, Cheltenham, British public school, founded 1886 in memory of Dean Francis Close, b. 1797, d. 1882.

Death Duties, revived in England 1894.

Debrett's Peerage, first published 1802 by the English publisher John Debrett, d. 1822.

Debs, Eugene, American socialist leader, b. 1855, d. 1926.

Debussy, Claude, French composer (*L'Après-midi d'un Faune*, 1892–1894), b. 1862, d. 1918.

Decatur, Stephen, American naval commander, b. 1779, killed 1820.

December Rising, Russian revolt concerning the succession of Tsar Nicolas I 1825.

Decimal Classification, for books, invented 1876 by the American Melvil Dewey, b. 1851, d. 1931.

Decimal Numbers, first used extensively by Simon Stevin b. 1548, d. 1620.

Decius, Roman Emperor (249–251), b. 201, killed in battle 251.

Decker, Sir Matthew, Dutch-born economist, b. 1679, d. 1749.

Declaration of Independence, American Revolution, adopted 4 July 1776.

Declaration of Right, England, Feb. 1689.

Decree of Union (Laetentur caeli), uniting the Latin and Greek Churches, issued 6 July 1439.

Dee, John, English alchemist, b. 1527, d. 1608.

Defender of the Faith, English royal title first bestowed by Pope Leo X on Henry VIII in 1521 ; continued by Parliament 1544.

Deffand, Marie de Vichy-Chamrond, Marquise du, French writer, b. 1697, d. 1780.

Defoe, Daniel, English writer (*Robinson Crusoe*, 1719), b. about 1661, d. 1731.

Degas, Edgar Hilaire Germain, French painter (*The Rehearsal*), b. 1834, d. 1917.

Dehydration, of food, first extensively employed during the American Civil War, 1861–1865.

Dekker, Thomas, English playwright (*The Shoemaker's Holiday*, 1599), b. about 1570, d. about 1640.

Delacroix, Eugène, French painter (*The Triumph of Apollo*), b. 1798, d. 1863.

Delane, John Thadeus, English editor of *The Times* (1841–1877), b. 1817, d. 1879.

Delaroche, 'Paul' (Hippolyte Delaroche), French painter (*The Finding of Moses*), b. 1797, d. 1856.

Delaware, U.S.A., first settled 1638 ; entered the Union 1787.

Deledda, Grazia, Italian novelist (*Cenere*), b. 1875, d. 1936.

Delibes, Léo, French composer (*Lakmé,* 1883), b. 1836, d. 1891.

Delius, Frederick, English composer (*Brigg Fair*, 1907), b. 1862, d. 1934.

Della Robbia, Luca, Italian sculptor, b. about 1400, d. 1482.

Delorme, Philibert, French architect, b. about 1512, d. 1570.

Delphin Classics, published by the French printer François Ambroise Didot, b. 1730, d. 1804.

Demarcation, Bull of, of Pope Alexander VI, dividing discoveries in the known world between Spain and Portugal, issued 1493.

Demetrius I, King of Macedon, b. 337 d. 283 B.C.

Demetrius II, King of Macedon, d. 229 B.C.

Demetrius I, Syrian King, b. about 187, d. 150 B.C.

Demetrius II, Syrian King, killed in battle 125 B.C.

Demetrius III, Syrian King, d. 88 B.C.

Democratic Party, U.S.A., developed from Republican Party during 1820s.

Democritus, Greek philosopher, d. 370 B.C.

Demosthenes, Greek orator, b. about 384, committed suicide 322 B.C.

Dengue, disease first described 1780 by the American physician Benjamin Rush, b. 1745, d. 1813.

Denmark, kingdom since the 10th century ; new constitution granted 1953.

Dennis, John, English playwright (*Appius and Virginia,* 1709), b. 1657, d. 1734.

Denny, Sir Archibald, Scottish shipbuilder, b. 1860, d. 1936.

Denstone College, Staffordshire, English public school founded by Canon Woodard 1868.

Dental Forceps, invented by the English dental surgeon Sir John Tomes, b. 1815, d. 1895.

d'Eon, Chevalier, French secret agent and transvestist, b. 1728, d. 1810.

Deposition, Bull of, first issued by Pope Paul III excommunicating King Henry VIII 1535 ; second issued by Pope Pius V excommunicating Queen Elizabeth I, 1570.

Depression, The, began in U.S.A. in Oct. 1929.

Derain, André, French painter, b. 1880, d. 1954.

'Derby, The ', Epsom Downs, first run 4 May 1780.

Derby Porcelain, manufactured 1750 to present day.

Derby-Chelsea Porcelain, manufactured 1770–1784.

Descartes, René, French philosopher, b. 1596, d. 1650.

Desmoulins, Camille, French Revolutionary leader, b. 1760, guillotined 1794.

Despard's Plot, against the British Government, devised by the English officer Edward Marcus Despard, b. 1751, executed 1803.

Determinants, mathematical theory developed 1851 by the English scientist William Spottiswoode, b. 1825, d. 1883.

Detroit University, Michigan, founded 1877.

Deusdedit I, St, Pope 615–619.

Deusdedit II, Pope 672–676.

Devil's Island (Cayenne), French Guiana, used as a penal settlement 1854–1938.

Devolution, War of, enforcing the Queen of France's claim to parts of the Spanish Netherlands, 1667–1668.

Dew, nature discovered by the American-born physician William Charles Wells, b. 1757, d. 1817.

Dewey, John, American philosopher, b. 1859, d. 1952.

Dewey, Melvil, American inventor (1876) of the Decimal Classification for printed material, b. 1851, d. 1931.

Diagnosis, Medical, established as an exact science by the English physician Thomas Sydenham, b. 1624, d. 1689.

Diabelli, Anton, Austrian music publisher and composer, b. 1781, d. 1858.

Diaghilev, Sergei, Russian impresario and ballet master, b. 1872, d. 1929.

Diamonds, carbon composition demonstrated 1796 by the English scientist Smithson Tennant, b. 1761, d. 1815.

Diamond Necklace Affair, involving Queen Marie Antoinette, took place 1784–1785 ; tried 1786.

Diamonds, first discovered in South Africa 1867.

Diaz, Bartolomeu, Portuguese explorer, d. 1500.

Dickens, Charles, English novelist (*Pickwick Papers,* 1836–1838), b. 1812, d. 1870.

Dickinson, Emily, American poet, b. 1830, d. 1886.

Dictaphone, invented by the American electrician Charles Sumner Tainter, b. 1854, d. 1940.

Dictionary of American Biography, published 1872 ; compiled by Francis Samuel Drake, b. 1828, d. 1885.

Dictionary of National Biography, British, founded 1882 by George Smith (1824–1901) ; published 1885–1900.

Diderot, Denis, French encyclopædist, writer and philosopher, b. 1713, d. 1784.

Didius Julianus, Roman Emperor (193), murdered 193.

Diemen, Antony van, Governor-General of Batavia, b. 1593, d. 1645.

Diesel Engines, invented 1893 by the German engineer Rudolf Diesel, b. 1858, d. 1913.

Diesel-driven Vessel, first model—the m.s. *Selandia*—launched at Copenhagen 1912.

Dieskau, Dietrich Fischer-, German lieder-singer, b. 1925

Diet of Worms, concerning Martin Luther's actions and writings, held 1521.

Differential Motor Gear, invented 1885 by the German engineer Karl Benz, b. 1844, d. 1929.

Digby, Sir Kenelm, English writer (*Private Memoirs*), b. 1603, d. 1665.

Diggers, group of English communists led by Gerrard Winstanley, active 1648–1652.

Digital Computer, idea conceived 1812 by the English mathematician Dr Charles Babbage, b. 1792, d. 1871.

Dilke, Sir Charles, British statesman, b. 1843, b. 1911.

Dimitrov, Georgi, Bulgarian communist leader (Prime Minister 1945–1949), b. 1882, d. 1949.

Dingaan's Day, South African anniversary commemorating the rout of the Zulu chief Dingaan 16 Dec. 1838.

Diocletian, Roman Emperor (284–305), b. 245, d. 313.

Diode Valve, invented 1904 by the English electrical engineer Sir John Ambrose Fleming, b. 1849, d. 1945.

Diodorus Siculus, Greek historian, lived in the 1st century B.C.

Diogenes, Greek cynic philosopher, b. about 412, d. 323 B.C.

Dion Cassius, Roman historian, b. about 155, d. about 235.

Dionysius, St, Pope 259–269.

Diophantine Equations, invented by the Greek mathematician Diophantus of Alexandria, lived in the 3rd century.

Dioscorus, Anti-Pope 530.

Disney, Walter, American film-maker, b. 1901.

Dispensing, in the U.S.A., first dispensary opened 1785 in Philadelphia

by the American physician Benjamin Rush, b. 1745, d. 1813.

Disraeli, Benjamin, Earl of Beaconsfield, British writer (*Coningsby*, 1844) and statesman (Prime Minister 1868, 1874–1880), b. 1804, d. 1881.

d'Israeli, Isaac, English writer (*Curiosities of Literature*, 1791–1793, 1823), b. 1766, d. 1848.

Dissolution of the Monasteries, England, 1536–1540.

District Line, London—see **Metropolitan District Railway.**

District Nursing Movement, introduced in Britain 1859 by the English philanthropist William Rathbone, b. 1819, d. 1902.

Dittersdorf, Karl Ditters von, Austrian violinist and composer, b. 1739, d. 1799.

Divorce, for grounds other than adultery, made legal in England 1937.

Dobson, Austin, English poet (*At the Sign of the Lyre*, 1885), b. 1840, d. 1921.

Docking of Horses' Tails, prohibited by law in Britain since 1950.

Doctor Wall (Worcester) Porcelain, manufactured 1751–1783.

Doctor's Commons, founded 1568, incorporated 1768, dissolved 1857.

Dodo, became extinct about 1680.

Dod's *Parliamentary Companion*, founded 1832 by the English journalist Charles Roger Phipps Dod, b. 1793, d. 1855.

Dodsley, Robert, English publisher, b. 1703, d. 1764.

Dog Licence, fixed in Britain at 7s. 6d. by Act of Parliament 1878.

Doggett's Coat and Badge Prize, Thames rowing competition, founded 1715 by the English actor Thomas Doggett, d. 1721.

Dohnanyi, Ernst von, Hungarian composer (*Ruralia Hungarica*, 1924), b. 1877, d. 1960.

Dolabella, Roman general, b. about 70, d. 43 B.C

Dolci, Danilo, Italian social reformer, b. 1924.

Dole, British unemployment payments, first so named by the *Daily Mail* 1919.

Dollar, first issued in U.S.A. 1794, in England 1804.

Dollfuss, Engelbert, Austrian Chancellor (1932–1934), b. 1892, assassinated 1934.

Döllinger, Johann, German theologian, b. 1799, d. 1890.

Dolomite Rock, nature first studied 1791 by the French geologist Déodat de Gratet de Dolomieu, b. 1750, d. 1801.

Domagk, Gerhard, German pathologist, b. 1895, awarded a Nobel Prize 1938.

Domesday Book, William the Conqueror's survey of England, prepared 1085–1086.

Dominic, St, b. about 1170, d. 1221.

Dominican Order, founded by St Dominic 1216.

Dominican Republic, discovered 1492 by Christopher Columbus ; achieved independence from Spanish rule 1821 ; the Republic founded 1844 ; new constitution granted 1924.

Dominion Day, Canada, celebrated 1 July.

Domitian, Roman Emperor (81–96), b. 51, assassinated 96.

Donatello (Donato di Niccolò), Italian sculptor (*St George*), b. about 1386, d. 1466.

Dongan, Thomas, Earl of Limerick, Irish-born Governor (1682–1688) of New York, b. 1634, d. 1715.

Dönitz, Karl, German admiral (Reichsführer in May 1945), b. 1892.

Donizetti, Gaetano, Italian composer (*Lucia di Lammermoor*, 1835), b. 1797, d. 1848.

Donne, John, English poet and divine, b. 1573, d. 1631.

Donnybrook Fair, Ireland, licensed by King John 1204 ; suppressed 1855.

Donus, Pope 676–678.

Doolittle, Hilda ('H. D.'), American poet (*Hymen*, 1921), b. 1886.

Doppler Effect, physics, predicted 1842 by the Austrian scientist Christian Doppler, b. 1803, d. 1853.

Dorchester Grammar School (Hardye's School), English public school, refounded and endowed by Thomas Hardye 1569.

Doré, Gustave, French artist and illustrator (Dante's *Inferno*), b. 1833, d. 1883.

Dorr's Rebellion, to extend the suffrage to Rhode Island, led (1841) by the American politician Thomas Wilson Dorr, b. 1805, d. 1854.

Dort, Synod of, held to discuss the Arminian heresy, 1618–1619.

Dortmund-Ems Canal, Germany, constructed 1892–1899.

Dos Passos, John, American novelist (*U.S.A.*), b. 1896.

Dostoyevsky, Fyodor Mikhailovich, Russian novelist (*The Brothers Karamazov*, 1880), b. 1821, d. 1881.

Douai Bible, first English Catholic translation, published 1609–1610.

Douai School, Woolhampton, English public school, refounded at Douai 1818 ; transferred to Woolhampton 1903.

Double Refraction, theory developed by the French physicist Etienne Louis Malus, b. 1775, d. 1812.

Double Valency, study (contributing to the study of Isomerism) developed 1893 by the Swiss chemist Alfred Werner, b. 1866, d. 1919.

Doughty, Charles Montagu, English explorer and writer (*Arabia Deserta*, 1888), b. 1843, d. 1926.

Douglas, Sir James, of Douglas, Scottish patriot, b. about 1286, killed in battle 1330.

Douglas, Norman, Scottish writer (*South Wind*, 1917), b. 1868, d. 1952.

Dounreay, Scotland, world's largest atomic reactor, opened 1959.

Dover, Treaty of, to re-establish Catholicism in England, signed between Charles II and Louis XIV 1670.

Dover College, English public school, opened 1871.

Downing College, Cambridge University, founded by Sir George Downing (1634–1749) ; built 1807.

Dowland, John, English poet and composer, b. 1563, d. 1626.

Downside School, Bath, English public school, founded at Douai about 1605 ; transferred to Britain 1790, and to Downside 1814.

Doyle, Sir Arthur Conan, Scottish writer of the Sherlock Holmes stories, b. 1859, d. 1930.

Doyle, Richard, English caricaturist, b. 1824, d. 1883.

D'Oyly Carte, Richard, English impresario (the Gilbert and Sullivan operas), b. 1844, d. 1901.

Draft Riots, U.S.A., against conscription for the Northern cause, 1863

Dragonades, expeditions by French soldiers to persecute the Huguenots in the provinces, 1685.

Drake, Sir Francis, English sailor (circumnavigated the world 1577–1580), b. about 1540, d. 1596.

Draper, Ruth, American actress and diseuse, b. 1889, d. 1959.

Drayton, Michael, English poet, b. 1563, d. 1631.

Dreadnoughts, heavily armed warships, introduced in Britain by Lord Fisher 1905.

Dresden China, originated by the German Johann Friedrich Böttger, b. 1628, d. 1719.

Dreyfus, Alfred, French artillery officer, b. 1859 ; first trial for treason 1894 ; rehabilitated 1906 ; d. 1935.

Drinkwater, John, English writer (*Abraham Lincoln,* 1918), b. 1882, d. 1937.

Drive-in Bank, First British (Westminster), opened at Liverpool Jan. 1959.

Drogheda, Ireland, sacked by Cromwell 10 Sept. 1649.

Drummond, Thomas, Scottish engineer and inventor, b. 1797, d. 1840.

Drummond, William, of Hawthornden, Scottish writer (*The Cypresse Grove,* 1623), b. 1585, d. 1649.

Drury Lane, Theatres in London, opened 1663, 1674, 1794, 1812.

Druses, heretical Muslim sect, followers of Egyptian Caliph al Hakim (996–1020).

Dryden, John, English poet and playwright (*All for Love,* 1678), b. 1631, d. 1700.

Du Barry, Madame, mistress of King Louis XV of France, b. 1741, guillotined 1793.

Du Bartas, Guillaume de Sallust, Huguenot poet, b. 1544, d. 1590.

Du Bellay, Joachim, French poet, b. 1522, d. 1560.

Du Guesclin, Bertrand, French general, b. about 1320, d. 1380.

Du Maurier, George, French-born novelist (*Trilby,* 1894), b. 1834, d. 1896.

Duel, last fought in England at Priest Hill, Egham, Surrey, 1852.

Dufy, Raoul, French painter, b. 1877, d. 1953.

Dugdale, Sir William, English antiquarian writer (*Monasticon Anglicanum,* 1655–1673), b. 1605, d. 1686.

Duhamel, Georges, French writer (*Civilisation*), b. 1884.

Dukas, Paul, French composer (*L'Apprenti-Sorcier,* 1897), b. 1865, d. 1935.

Duke University, North Carolina, founded 1838 ; assumed present name 1930.

Dulles, John Foster, American statesman, b. 1888, d. 1959.

Dulwich College, English public school, founded 1619 as ' The College of God's Gift ' by the Elizabethan actor-manager Edward Alleyn, b. 1566, d. 1626.

Dumas, Alexandre, *père,* French writer (*Les Trois Mousquetaires,* 1844), b. 1802, d. 1870.

Dumas, Alexandre, *fils,* French writer (*La Dame aux Camélias,* 1848), b. 1824, d. 1895.

Dumbarton Oaks Conference, at which the foundations of the United Nations were laid, held Washington, D.C., 1944.

Dumdum Bullets, use banned by the Hague Conference 1907.

Dunant, Henri, Swiss founder (1864) of the International Red Cross, b. 1828, d. 1910.

Dunbar, Battle of, between the English and the Scots, 3 Sept. 1650.

Dunbar, William, Scottish poet (*Lament for the Makaris*), b. about 1460, d. about 1522.

Duncan, Isadora, American dancer, b. 1878, d. 1927.

Duncan-Rubbra, Edmund, English composer and conductor, b. 1901.

Dunes, Battle of, Dunkirk, between French and Spanish, 4 June 1658.

Dunkirk, sold to France by King Charles II 1662 ; Battle of, World War II, 22 May to 4 June 1940.

Dunmow Flitch Trial, held at Great Dunmow, Essex, every second August Bank Holiday Monday.

Duns Scotus, Scottish philosopher, b. about 1266, d. 1308.

Dunstan, St, Archbishop of Canterbury (961–988), b. about 910, d. 988.

Dupes, Day of, dissembling the triumph of the Spanish policy in France, 12 Nov. 1630.

Dupleix, Joseph, Governor-General of India under the French, b. 1697, d. 1763.

Durand Line, defining the frontier between India and Afghanistan, determined 1893.

Dürer, Albrecht, German artist (*St Jerome*), b. 1471, d. 1528.

Durham, John, Earl of, British statesman, b. 1792, d. 1840.

Durham School, English public school, reconstituted 1414 by Cardinal Thomas Langley (d. 1437), and by King Henry VIII 1541.

Durham University, founded by William Van Mildert, Bishop of Durham, and the Dean and Chapter of Durham 1832.

Durkheim, Emile, French sociologist, b. 1858, d. 1917.

Durrell, Lawrence, Anglo-Irish writer (*Bitter Lemons*, 1957), b. 1912.

Duse, Eleanora, Italian actress, b. 1859, d. 1924.

Dussek, Johann Ladislaus (Jan Ladislav Dušek), Bohemian composer (*Elégie Harmonique*), b. 1760, d. 1812.

Dust Wrappers, for books, first used in Britain 1832 ; came into general use there about 1890.

Duveen, Sir Joseph Joel, Dutch-born art-dealer, b. 1843, d. 1908.

Dvořák, Antonín, Czech composer (*From the New World*, 1893), b. 1841, d. 1904.

Dynamite, discovered 1867 by the Swedish manufacturer Alfred Nobel, b. 1833, d. 1896.

Dynamo, invented 1823 by the English electrician William Sturgeon, b. 1783, d. 1850.

Dynamometer, Electrical, invented 1840 by the German physicist Wilhelm Eduard Weber, b. 1804, d. 1891.

Dysentery, bacillus first isolated by the Danish scientist C. Sonne 1915.

Dysprosium, chemical element, first isolated 1886 by the French scientist Paul Emile Lecoq de Boisbaudran, b. 1838, d. 1912.

E

E.D.S.A.C. (Electronic Delayed Storage Automatic Computer), completed at Cambridge University's Mathematical Laboratory 1949.

E.N.I.A.C. (Electronic Numerical Integrator and Calculator), first electronic computer, planned by the American scientists Dr J. W. Mauchly and Dr J. P. Eckert, first publicly demonstrated at Aberdeen, Md., Feb. 1946.

EOKA (National Organisation of Cypriot Combatants), guerrilla and terrorist group organised in Cyprus 1954.

Eagles, Solomon (Solomon Eccles), Quaker missionary, b. 1618, d. 1683.

Earhart, Amelia, American aviator, b. 1898, d. 1937.

Earle, John, English divine and writer (*Microcosmographie*, 1628), b. about 1601, d. 1665.

Earth, Circumference of the, first calculated by Eratosthenes about 230 B.C.

Earth, Circumnavigation of the, by Magellan's sailors Sept. 1519–Sept. 1522.

Earth, Density of the, calculated by the English mathematician Charles Hutton, b. 1737, d. 1823. Sir George Airy, b. 1801, d. 1892, Astronomer-Royal, calculated the mean density of the earth to be 6.566 in 1954.

Earth, Magnetism of the, described 1600 by William Gilbert.

Earth, Mass of the, first calculated 1797 by Henry Cavendish.

Earth Current, discovered 1862 by the Scottish-born astronomer Johann von Lamont, b. 1805, d. 1879.

Earthquakes, Lisbon 1755, Assam 1896, San Francisco 1906, Tokyo 1923, Hawkes Bay 1931, Agadir 1960.

East, Sir Alfred, English painter, b. 1849, d. 1913.

East Africa High Commission, founded 1948 to administer services common to Kenya, Uganda and Tanganyika.

East India Company, first chartered 1600, dissolved 1858.

East London, South African port, founded 1848.

East Prussia, German *land,* absorbed into Russia and Poland in 1945.

Eastbourne College, English public school, founded 1867 by the seventh Duke of Devonshire.

Easter, Christian Feast of the Resurrection, celebrated on the first Sunday after the first full moon after the Vernal Equinox.

Easter Island, Pacific, discovered by the Dutch navigator Jakob Roggeveen 1722.

Eastlake, Sir Charles Lock, English painter and President of the Royal Academy (1850–1865), b. 1793, d. 1865.

Eastman, George, American pioneer developer of photographic equipment, b. 1854, d. 1932.

Eau de Cologne, traditionally invented by the Italian Johann Maria Farina, b. 1685, d. 1766.

Eberlein, Gustav, German sculptor (*Boy Extracting a Thorn*), b. 1847, d. 1926.

Ebers, Georg, German novelist (*Kleopatra,* 1894), b. 1837, d. 1898.

Ebert, Friedrich, German statesman (President 1919–1925), b. 1871, d. 1925.

Ebonite (vulcanised rubber), invented 1849 by the American inventor Charles Goodyear, b. 1800, d. 1860.

Echegaray, José, Spanish playwright (Nobel Prize 1904), b. 1833, d. 1916.

Echeverria, Esteban, Argentine poet, b. about 1805, d. 1851.

Echo, The, British newspaper founded 1876 by John Passmore Edwards, b. 1823, d. 1911.

Eckermann, Johann Peter, German friend of Goethe, b. 1792, d. 1854.

Eckhardt, Meister Jean, German theologian and mystic, b. about 1260, d. 1327.

Eclipse Stakes, Sandown Park, first run 1883.

Ecole des Beaux Arts, Paris, founded 1648 ; adopted present name 1793.

Economist, The, British periodical founded 1843 by the Scottish economist James Wilson, b. 1805, d. 1860.

Ecuador, achieved independence by secession from Republic of Colombia 1830. Granted new constitution 1945.

Eddington, Sir Arthur Stanley, British astronomer and writer (*The Expanding Universe,* 1933), b. 1882, d. 1944.

Eddy, Mrs Mary Baker, American founder of Christian Science, b. 1821, d. 1910.

Eddystone Lighthouse, first structure erected by Henry Winstanley 1696–1700 and swept away 1703 ; second, by John Rudyerd, completed 1709 and burnt Dec. 1755 ; third, by John Smeaton, completed 1759 ; fourth, by J. N. Douglass, completed 1882.

Edelinck, Gérard, French engraver, b. 1640, d. 1707.

Eden, Anthony, Lord Avon, British statesman (Prime Minister 1955–1957), b. 1897.

Edgar, King of the English (959–975), b. 944, d. 975.

Edgar Atheling, English prince, b. about 1050, d. about 1125.

Edgehill, Battle of, between King Charles I and the Parliamentary forces 23 Oct. 1642.

Edgeworth, Maria, Irish novelist (*Castle Rackrent,* 1800), b. 1767, d. 1849.

Edict of Diocletian, Roman measure to check speculation, issued 301.

Edict of Nantes, granting religious freedom to the Huguenots, signed by Henri IV 1598 ; revoked by Louis XIV 1685.

Edinburgh, founded about 617 by Edwin, King of Northumbria.

Edinburgh, Treaty of, enacting peace between England and Scotland, signed 1560.

Edinburgh Academy, Scottish public school, opened by Sir Walter Scott 1824.

Edinburgh Festival, founded 1947.

Edinburgh Review, British periodical, began publication Oct. 1802.

Edinburgh University, founded 1583.

Edison, Thomas Alva, American inventor, b. 1847, d. 1931.

Edmund, St, (Edmund Rich), d. 1240.

Edmund, St, King of East Anglia (855–870), b. 841, killed 870.

Edmund, King of the English (940–946), b. about 922, d. 946.

Edmund Crouchback, Earl of Lancaster, b. 1245, d. 1296.

Edmund Ironside, King of the English (1016), b. about 981, d. 1016.

Edred, King of the English (946–955), d. 955.

Education, Ministry of, founded as the Board of Education 1899.

Education Acts, 1870, 1944.

Edward The Confessor, King of the English (1043–1066), d. 1066.

Edward The Elder, King of the Angles and Saxons (901–924), d. 924.

Edward, the Black Prince, b. 1330, d. 1376.

Edward, Prince of Wales (now Duke of Windsor), b. 1894 ; proclaimed King 21 Jan. 1936 ; abdicated 10 Dec. 1936.

Edward I, King of England (1272–1307), b. 1239, d. 1307.

Edward II, King of England (1307–1327), b. 1284, murdered 1327.

Edward III, King of England (1327–1377), b. 1312, d. 1377.

Edward IV, King of England (1461–1483), b. 1442, d. 1483.

Edward V, King of England (1483), b. 1470, murdered 1483.

Edward VI, King of England (1547–1553), b. 1537, d. 1553.

Edward VII, King of England (1901–1910), b. 1841, d. 1910.

Edward VIII, King of England (Jan.–Dec. 1936), b. 1894.

Edward, Lake Uganda, discovered 1889 by Sir Henry Morton Stanley, b. 1841, d. 1904.

Edwards, Edward, English library pioneer, b. 1812, d. 1886.

Edwards, Jonathan, American theologian (*Freedom of Will,* 1754), b. 1703, d. 1758.

Edwin, King of Northumbria (617–633), b. about 585, killed 633.

Edwy, King of the English (955–959), b. about 940, d. 959.

Egan, Pierce, English writer (*Life in London,* 1821), b. 1772, d. 1849.

Egbert, King of the West Saxons (802–839), d. 839.

Egerton, Francis, Earl of Ellesmere, statesman and poet, b. 1800, d. 1857.

Egerton, Francis, Duke of Bridgewater, pioneer canal builder, b. 1736, d. 1803.

Egmont, Lamoral, Count of, Flemish statesman, b. 1522, executed 1568.

Egypt, approximate extent of ancient history (1st to 31st dynasties), 3188–332 B.C. ; Arab conquest A.D. 640 ; Turkish conquest 1517 ; proclaimed an independent kingdom 1922, an independent republic 1956 ; joined Syria in the United Arab Republic 1958.

Egyptian Era (Cycle of Sothis), began 19 July 4241 B.C.

Ehrenburg, Ilya Grigoryevich, Russian writer (*Julio Jurenito*), b. 1891.

Ehrlich, Paul, German bacteriologist, b. 1854, d. 1915.

Eiffel Tower, opened 1889, built by the French engineer Gustave Eiffel, b. 1832, d. 1923.

Eimmart, G. C., German mathematician and designer and engraver of terrestrial and celestial globes, b. 1638, d. 1705.

Einstein, Albert, German-born physicist, b. 1879, d. 1955.

Eire, established as Irish Free State 1921 ; renamed ' Eire ' 1937 ; became Irish Republic (*Poblacht na h'Eireann*) and left British Commonwealth 1949.

Eisenhower, Dwight D., U.S. General and President (1953–1961), b. 1890.

Eisenstein, Sergei, Russian film director (*The Battleship Potemkin,* 1925), b. 1898, d. 1948.

Eisner, Kurt, German statesman, b. 1867, assassinated 1919.

Eisteddfod, Welsh national festival with a history of at least fourteen centuries, first so named in the twelfth century.

Eitler, Esteban, Austrian-born composer (*Policromia*, 1950) in Chile, b. 1913, d. 1960.

Eitner, Robert, German musicologist (*Quellenlexikon der Musiker*, 1899–1904), b. 1832, d. 1905.

El Alamein, World War II, 8th Army offensive begun 23 Oct. 1942; victorious 4 Nov. 1942.

El Paso, Texas, first settled 1659.

El Salvador, became an independent Republic 1839 ; new constitution granted 1950.

Elastic, first British patent issued 1832 to J. V. Desgrand.

Eldon, John Scott, Lord, English jurist, b. 1751, d. 1838.

Eleanor of Aquitaine, wife of Henry II of England, b. 1122, d. 1204.

Eleanor of Castile, wife of Edward I of England, d. 1290.

Eleanor of Provence, wife of Henry III of England, d. 1291.

Electors (*Kurfürsten*), of Holy Roman Empire, system established in 13th century, revised 1356 ; ended with Empire 1806.

Electric Batteries, invented 1800 by Italian scientist Alessandro Volta, b. 1745, d. 1827.

Electric Lamps, first publicly demonstrated by Sir Joseph Swan, b. 1828, d. 1914 ; invented simultaneously by Thomas Edison, b. 1847, d. 1931.

Electric Light, first produced 1800 by Sir Humphry Davy, b. 1778, d. 1829. First used domestically in Britain 1881.

Electric Locomotives, invented 1851 by American inventor Alfred Vail, b. 1807, d. 1859.

Electric Power Station, First English, opened at Godalming, Surrey, 1881.

Electric Recording of Sound, introduced 1925 by Maxfield and Harrison.

Electrical Engineers, Institution of, founded as The Society of Telegraph Engineers 1871.

Electrified Railway, first commercial line (City & South London Railway) opened 1890.

Electrocardiography, study of heart action, first developed by the Dutch physiologist Willem Einthoven, b. 1860, d. 1927.

Electrodynamics, theory developed 1822 by French scientist André Marie Ampère, b. 1775, d. 1836.

Electroencephalography, pioneered 1929 by the German neurologist H. Berger.

Electrolysis, investigated 1833 by Michael Faraday, b. 1791, d. 1867.

Electromagnet, invented 1825 by the English electrician William Sturgeon, b. 1783, d. 1850.

Electromagnetic Induction, laws defined 1831 by the English chemist Michael Faraday, b. 1791, d. 1867.

Electromagnetic Waves, existence established 1864 by the Scottish physicist James Clerk Maxwell, b. 1831, d. 1879.

Electromagnetism, discovered 1819 by the Danish physicist Hans Christian Oersted, b. 1777, d. 1851.

Electron Microscope, constituted 1932 by Knoll and Ruska.

Electrons, discovered 1897, by Sir Joseph John Thomson, b. 1856, d. 1940 ; first isolated about 1920 by the American physicist Robert Andrews Millikan, b. 1868, d. 1953.

Electroplating, invented 1832 by the English manufacturer George Richards Elkington, b. 1801, d. 1865.

Eleutherius, St, Pope 175–189.

Elevated Railway, world's first, opened at Liverpool 1893.

Elgar, Sir Edward, English composer (*The Dream of Gerontius*, 1900), b. 1857, d. 1934.

Elgin Marbles, brought from the Parthenon to London 1801–1803 by Lord Elgin, b. 1766, d. 1841.

' Eliot, George ' (Mary Ann Evans), English novelist (*The Mill on the Floss*, 1860), b. 1819, d. 1880.

Eliot, Sir John, English Parliamentarian, b. 1592, died in prison 1632.

Eliot, John, English missionary to the North American Indians, b. 1604, d. 1690.

Eliot, Thomas Stearns, American-born critic and poet (*The Waste Land*, 1922), b. 1888.

Elizabeth, St, b. 1207, d. 1231.

Elizabeth I, Queen of England, b. 1533, succeeded Mary 1558, d. 1603.

Elizabeth II, Queen of Great Britain, b. 21 Apr. 1926, married 20 Nov. 1947, succeeded her father King George VI 6 Feb. 1952.

Elizabeth, Queen, the Queen Mother, b. 1900.

Elizabeth, Empress of Austria, b. 1837, d. 1898.

Elizabeth, Empress of Russia, b. 1709, d. 1761.

Elizabeth, English Queen of Bohemia, b. 1596, d. 1662.

Elizabeth College, Guernsey, public school, founded by Queen Elizabeth 1563.

Elizabethville, Belgian Congo, founded 1910.

Ellenborough, Edward Law, Baron, Lord Chief Justice, b. 1750, d. 1818.

Ellesmere College, English public school, opened 1884.

Elliott, George Augustus, Baron Heathfield, governor of Gibraltar, b. 1717, d. 1790.

Elliptical Functions, discovered 1829 by Karl Gustav Jakob Jacobi, b. 1804, d. 1851.

Ellis, Havelock, English scientist (*The Psychology of Sex*, 1901–1910), b. 1859, d. 1939.

Elphinstone, William, Scottish bishop, b. 1431, d. 1514.

Elssler, Fanny, Austrian dancer, b. 1810, d. 1884.

Elssler, Thérèse, Austrian dancer (and sister of Fanny), b. 1808, d. 1878.

Eltham College, English public school, founded as ' The School for the Sons of Missionaries ' 1842.

Ely Cathedral, built 11th to 14th centuries.

Elyot, Sir Thomas, diplomatist and writer, b. about 1490, d. 1546.

Elzevir, Louis, Dutch publisher of the classics, b. 1540, d. 1617.

Emancipation of Catholics, in Britain, enacted 1829.

Emancipation of Slaves, in the U.S.A., proclaimed 1863.

Emanuel School, English public school, founded by the will of Anne Sackville, wife of Gregory Fiennes, Lord Dacre of the South, 1595.

Ember Days (in W. Christendom), fasts on Wednesday, Friday and Saturday after first Sunday in Lent, after Pentecost, after 14 Sept. and after 13 Dec.

Emerson, Ralph Waldo, American writer (*Essays*, 1841–1844), b. 1803, d. 1882.

Emin Pasha (Eduard Schnitzer), German explorer, b. 1840, d. 1892.

Emmet, Robert, Irish leader, b. 1778, hanged 1803.

Emmett, Daniel Decatur, American composer (*Dixie*, 1859), b. 1815, d. 1904.

Empedocles, Greek philosopher, b. about 494, d. about 434 B.C.

Empire, French. First 1804–1814, Second 1852–1870.

Empire, German. First 962–1806, Second 1871–1918, Third 1933–1945.

Empire State Building, New York, built 1930–1931.

Encyclopædia Americana, first published 1829–1833.

Encyclopædia Britannica, first produced and published by Andrew Bell, Colin Macfarquhar and William Smellie 1768–1771.

Enderby Land, Antarctic, discovered 1831 by the British navigator John Biscoe, d. 1848.

Enesco, Georges, Rumanian violinist, b. 1881.

Engels, Friedrich, German Marxist, b. 1820, d. 1895.

d'Enghien, Louis, Duc, French Royalist, b. 1772, shot 1804.

Engleheart, George, English miniaturist, b. 1752, d. 1829.

English Folk Dance Society, founded 1911 by Cecil Sharp, b. 1859, d. 1924.

Eniwetok Atoll, Marshall Islands, scene of atom bomb tests started by the U.S. Navy 1946.

Ennius, Quintus, Latin poet, b. 239, d. 170 B.C.

Enosis, movement for the union of Cyprus with Greece, had its origins in the Greek Government's demand of 1912.

Ensenada, Zenón, Marqués de la, Spanish statesman, b. 1702, d. 1781.

Ensign, infantry rank, abolished 1871.

Entente, Triple, between England, France and Russia, 1904–1917 ; Little, between Czechoslovakia, Yugoslavia and Rumania, 1920–1938.

Entropy, the relation between the total amount of heat and temperature, discovered by the German physicist Rudolf Clausius, b. 1822, d. 1888.

Envelope-making Machine, First, invented 1851 by the British scientist Warren de la Rue, b. 1815, d. 1889.

Enver Pasha, Turkish leader, b. 1881, killed in action 1922.

Eocene Epoch, Earth history, 60 million years ago.

d'Eon, Chevalier, French secret agent and transvestist, b. 1728, d. 1810.

Epaminondas, Greek general, b. about 418, d. 326 B.C.

l'Epée, Charles Michel, Abbé de, French priest and benefactor of the deaf and mute, b. 1712, d. 1789.

d'Epernon, Jean Louis de Nogaret, Duc, French governor, b. 1554, d. 1642.

Epictetus, Greek philosopher, b. about 55, d. about 120.

Epicurus, Greek philosopher, b. 341, d. 270 B.C.

d'Epinay, Louise, Marquise, French writer, b. 1726, d. 1783.

Epiphany, Christian Feast of the Manifestation of Christ to the Gentiles (connected with both the Nativity and the Baptism), celebrated 6 Jan.

Epsom, races first run about 1620.

Epsom College, English public school, founded 1853 by John Propert ; opened 1855.

Epsom Salts, discovered 1618.

Epstein, Sir Jacob, American-born sculptor (*Rima*, 1925), b. 1880, d. 1959.

Equinox, time at which day and night are of equal length ; Vernal Equinox, 21–22 Mar. ; Autumnal Equinox, 21–22 Sept.

Erasmus, Desiderius, Dutch religious reformer and theologian, b. 1467, d. 1536.

Erastus, Thomas (Thomas Lüber), German-Swiss theologian, b. 1524, d. 1583.

Eratosthenes, Alexandrian philosopher, b. about 276, d. about 194 B.C.

Erbium, chemical element, first isolated 1843 by the Swedish chemist Karl Gustav Mosander, b. 1797, d. 1858.

Erckmann-Chatrian, pen-name of the French writers, Émile Erckmann (1822–1899) and Alexandre Chatrian (1826–1890), who worked in collaboration between 1847 and 1889.

Erebus, Mt., volcanic mountain in the Antarctic, discovered 1841 by Sir James Ross, b. 1800, d. 1862.

Eric, King of Denmark, reigned 814 to 854.

Eric Eiggod, King of Denmark (1095–1101), b. about 1056, d. 1101.

Eric Emune, King of Denmark (1131–1137), assassinated 1137.

Eric Lam, King of Denmark (1137–1146), d. 1146.

Eric Plogpenning, King of Denmark (1241–1250), b. 1216, beheaded 1250.

Eric Klipping, King of Denmark (1259–1286), b. about 1249, assassinated 1286.

Eric Menved, King of Denmark (1286–1319), b. 1274, d. 1319.

Eric VII of Denmark (1396–1438), and XIII of Sweden, b. 1382, d. 1459.

Eric I to V, legendary Kings of Sweden.

Eric VI, King of Sweden, reigned from about 850 till his death about 880.

Eric VII, King of Sweden, d. about 994.

Eric VIII, King of Sweden, reigned towards the end of the 11th century.

Eric IX, St, King of Sweden and Denmark, beheaded 1160.

Eric X, King of Sweden (1210–1216), d. 1216.

Eric XI, King of Sweden (1222–1252), b. 1216, d. 1252.

Eric XII, King of Sweden, b. 1339, d. 1359.

Eric XIII, King of Sweden (1396–1438), b. 1382, d. 1459.

Eric XIV, King of Sweden (1560–1577), b. 1533, d. 1577.

Eric the Red, Norwegian discoverer (about 981) of Greenland, b. about 949.

Ericsson, John, Swedish-born inventor, b. 1803, d. 1889.

Ericsson, Leif, Scandinavian discoverer (about 1000) of North America, b. about 971.

Erie Canal, New York State, begun 1817, completed 1825.

Erie, Battle of Lake, between Americans and British, Sept. 1813.

Erigena, Johannes Scotus, Irish philosopher and theologian in 9th century.

Eritrea, conquered by Italy 1885–1889 ; invaded by British forces 1941 ; sovereignty handed over by the British to Ethiopia 1952.

Erivan, Ivan Fyodorovich Paskevich, Count of, Russian Field-Marshal, b. 1782, d. 1856.

Erkel, Franz, Hungarian composer (*Bánk Bán*, 1861), b. 1810, d. 1893.

Ernle, Rowland Edmund Prothero, Baron, English agricultural historian, b. 1851, d. 1937.

Ernst, Max, German painter, b. 1891.

Erskine, Ebenezer, Scottish church reformer, b. 1680, d. 1754.

Erskine, John, Scottish reformer, b. 1509, d. 1591.

Erskine, John, Earl of Mar, Jacobite supporter, b. 1675, d. 1732.

Erskine, Thomas, Baron Erskine, Scottish lawyer, b. 1750, d. 1823.

Ervine, St John, Ulster-born playwright (*Jane Clegg*, 1911), b. 1883.

Escalator, first in England installed at Earls Court Station, London, in 1911.

Escorial, The, Spain, palace built by King Philip II 1563–1584.

Esher, Reginald Baliol Brett, Viscount, English historian, b. 1852, d. 1930.

Esparto Grass, first used for the manufacture of paper about 1855.

Esperanto, universal language, produced 1887 by the Polish scholar Lazarus Ludovic Zamenhof, b. 1859, d. 1917.

Essad Pasha, Albanian leader, b. 1863, d. 1920.

Essex, Robert Devereux, Earl of, English statesman and rebel, b. 1566, executed 1601.

Essex, Robert Devereux, Earl of, English statesman and general, b. 1591, d. 1646.

d'Este, Beatrice, Italian diplomat and patron of the arts, b. 1475, d. 1497.

Esterházy, Prince Pál Antal, Austro-Hungarian diplomat, b. 1786, d. 1866.

Estienne, Henri, French printer and publisher, b. about 1531, d. 1598.

Estienne, Robert, French printer and publisher, b. 1503, d. 1559.

Estonia, proclaimed an independent Republic 1918 ; incorporated in the Soviet Union 1940.

d'Estrées, Gabrielle, mistress of King Henri IV of France, b. 1573, d. 1599.

Ethelred the Unready, King of England (from 978), b. about 968, d. 1016.

Ethelreda, St, b. 630, d. 679.

Ether, soporific qualities discovered 1818 by the English chemist Michael Faraday, b. 1791, d. 1867 ; first used as an anæsthetic 1846 by the American physician Crawford Williamson Long, b. 1815, d. 1878.

Etherege, Sir George, English playwright (*She Would If She Could*, 1667), b. about 1635, d. 1692.

Ethiopia, independence established 1906 ; conquered by Italy 1935–1937 ; independence regained 1941.

Etna (Mongibello), Sicilian volcano : main eruptions 125, 121 and 43 B.C. ; A.D. 1169, 1444, 1537, 1553, 1666, 1669, 1830, 1852, 1865, 1879, 1886, 1892, 1899, 1910, 1923, and 1928.

Eton College, founded 1440 by King Henry VI, b. 1421, d. 1471.

'Ettrick Shepherd', The (James Hogg), Scottish poet, b. 1770, d. 1835.

Etty, William, English painter (*Youth at the Prow and Pleasure at the Helm*), b. 1787, d. 1849.

Euclid, Greek mathematician, *fl.* 300 B.C.

Eudocia, Byzantine Empress, b. about 400, d. about 459.

Eudoxia, Byzantine Empress, d. 404.

Eugéne I, St, Pope 654–657.

Eugene II, Pope 824–827.

Eugene III (Bernardo Paganelli), Pope 1145–1153.

Eugene IV (Gabriel Condulmieri), Pope 1431–1447.

Eugene of Savoy, Prince, b. 1663, d. 1736.

Eugénie, wife of the Emperor Napoleon III, b. 1826, d. 1920.

Eulalius, Anti-Pope 418.

Euler, Leonhard, Swiss mathematician, b. 1707, d. 1783.

Eumenes, Greek general, b. about 360, killed 316 B.C.

Euratom, established by Treaty signed at Rome 25 Mar. 1957. Came into force 1 Jan. 1958.

Eurhythmics, Dalcroze, music educational system, invented by the Swiss composer Emile Jaques-Dalcroze, b. 1865, d. 1950.

Euripides, Greek dramatist (*The Trojan Women*, 413 B.C.), b. about 480, d. about 406 B.C.

European Defence Community, set up 27 May 1952.

European Economic Community, established by Treaty signed at Rome 25 Mar. 1957. Came into force 1 Jan. 1958.

European Monetary Agreement, signed 5 Aug. 1955.

European Nuclear Energy Agency, founded within O.E.E.C. 1 Feb. 1958.

European Payments Union Agreement, retroactive to 1 July 1950, signed 19 Sept. 1950.

European Productivity Agency, created 1 May 1953.

European Steel and Coal Community, established by Treaty 18 Apr. 1951 ; came into force 25 July 1952 ; High Authority, Luxemburg, inaugurated 10 Aug. 1952.

Eurovision, television link-up between European countries, first carried out on a large scale by the B.B.C. 1954.

Eusebius, St, Pope 309–311.

Eusebius of Cæsarea, theologian, b. about 264, d. 340.

Eustachian Tube, anatomy, first described by the Italian anatomist Bartolommeo Eustachio, d. 1574.

Eustathius, Greek literary critic, d. about 1198.

Euston Station, London, opened 1838.

Eutyches, Byzantine theologian, d. after 452.

Eutychian, St, Pope 275–283.

Evacuation of civilians from British towns, Sept. 1939.

Evans, Sir Arthur John, English archæologist, b. 1851, d. 1941.

Evans, Edwin, English musicologist, b. 1874, d. 1945.

Evans, Sir John, English archæologist, b. 1823, d. 1908.

Evans, Oliver, American inventor of milling machinery, b. 1755, d. 1819.

Evaporated Milk, invented 1856 by the American surveyor Gail Borden, b. 1801, d. 1874.

Evaristus, St, Pope 97–105.

Evelyn, John, English diarist, b. 1620, d. 1706.

Evening News, The, British newspaper. founded 1881 ; absorbed the *Star* 1960.

Evening Standard, The, British newspaper, founded 1827 ; absorbed the *St James's Gazette* 1905.

Everest, Mt, summit reached 29 May 1953 by the New Zealander Sir Edmund Hillary, b. 1919, and the Sherpa Tensing.

Everlasting League, The Swiss patriotic pact made 1291 between Schwyz, Uri and Unterwalden.

Evolution, by natural selection, Darwinian theory first communicated to the Linnean Society of London 1 July 1858 ; Charles Darwin's *Origin of the Species* first published 1859.

Ewart, William, English library pioneer, b. 1798, d. 1869.

Ewing, Sir James Alfred, Scottish scientist, b 1855, d. 1935.

Ewing, Mrs Juliana Horatia, English writer (*Jackanapes*, 1884), b. 1841, d. 1885.

Exclusion Struggle, against the succession of James, Duke of York (later James II), 1678–1681.

Excursion Train, World's first (Leicester-Loughborough return), organised by the English pioneer travel-agent Thomas Cook, b. 1808, d. 1892.

Exeter Cathedral, constructed 1285–1367.

Exeter College, Oxford University, founded 1314 by Walter de Stapeldon, Bishop of Exeter, b. 1261, d. 1326.

Exeter School, English public school, founded 1633.

Exmouth, Edward Pellew, Viscount, English admiral, b. 1757, d. 1833.

Expanding Universe, theory developed by the Dutch scientist William de Sitter, b. 1872, d. 1934.

Eyck, Hubert van, Flemish painter, b. about 1370, d. 1426.

Eyck, Jan van, Flemish painter, b. about 1389, d. 1440.

Eyre, Edward John, English explorer and statesman, b. 1815, d. 1901.

Eyre, Sir James, English lawyer, b. 1734, d. 1799.

Eyre, Lake, South Australia, discovered 1840 by the English explorer Edward John Eyre, b. 1815, d. 1901.

F

F.I.D.O., airfield fog clearance method, developed 1942 by the British engineer Arthur Clifford Hartley, b. 1889, d. 1960.

Faber, Frederick William, English theologian and poet, b. 1814, d. 1863.

Faber, Jacobus (Jacques Lefèvre d'Etaples), French reformer, b. about 1455, d. 1536.

Fabian, St, Pope 236–250.

Fabian Society, London, founded 1883 by the English writers Edward R. Pease and Frank Podmore, b. 1855, d. 1910.

Fabius Maximus, Quintus, Roman statesman, d. 203 B.C.

Fabre, Jean Henri, French entomologist (*Souvenirs entomologiques,* 1879–1907), b. 1823, d. 1915.

Fabriano, Gentile da, Italian painter, b. about 1370, d. 1427.

Fabricius, Hieronymus, Italian anatomist, b. 1533, d. 1619.

Fabricius, Johann Christian, Danish entomologist, b. 1745, d. 1808.

Fabritius, Carel, Dutch painter, b. 1622, d. 1654.

Fabyan, Robert, English historian, d. 1513.

Factory Act, first in England passed 1802.

Fahrenheit Scale, temperature, invented about 1714 by the German physicist Gabriel Daniel Fahrenheit, b. 1686, d. 1736.

Fairbairn, Sir William, Scottish engineer and inventor, b. 1789, d. 1874.

Fairbanks, Douglas, American film actor, b. 1883, d. 1939.

Fairbanks, Thaddeus, American inventor, b. 1796, d. 1886.

Fairey, Sir Charles Richard, British aviation pioneer, b. 1887, d. 1956.

Fairfax, Thomas, English puritan general, b. 1612, d. 1671.

Faithful, Emily, English champion of rights for women, b. 1832, d. 1895.

Falange, Spanish Fascist Party, founded 1933 by José Antonio Primo de Rivera ; completed control of Spain in 1939.

Faliero, Marino, Doge of Venice (1354–1355), b. 1274, executed 1355.

Falkirk, Battle of, 22 July 1298, between the English and the Scots.

Falkirk, Battle of, 17 Jan. 1746, between the Young Pretender and General Hawley.

Falkland Islands, Naval Battle of the, between the British and German fleets 8 Dec. 1914.

Falla, Manuel de, Spanish composer (*The Three-cornered Hat,* 1919), b. 1876, d. 1946.

Fallopian Tubes, physiological function first described by the Italian anatomist Gabriello Fallopio, b. about 1523, d. 1562.

Family Allowances, introduced into Britain 1945 ; general in France by 1932.

Fanshawe, Sir Richard, English diplomat and translator, b. 1608, d. 1666.

Fantin-Latour, Ignace Henri Jean Théodore, French painter (*Homage à Delacroix*), b. 1836, d. 1904.

Faraday, Michael, English physicist, b. 1791, d. 1867.

Farel, Guillaume, Swiss religious reformer, b. 1489, d. 1565.

Fargo, William George, American partner in the Wells Fargo express company, b. 1818, d. 1881.

Farinelli (Carlo Broschi), Italian *castrato* singer, b. 1705, d. 1782.

Farington, Joseph, English artist and art historian, b. 1747, d. 1821.

Farnese, Alessandro, Italian cardinal, b. 1520, d. 1589.

Farnese, Alessandro, Italian diplomat and soldier, b. 1545, d. 1592.

Farnese Palace, Rome, built about 1513–1515.

Faroe Islands, Atlantic, came under Danish rule 1380 ; granted separate legislature and executive 1948.

Farouk, King of Egypt (1936–1952), b. 1920.

Farquhar, George, Irish-born dramatist (*The Beaux' Stratagem*, 1707), b. 1678, d. 1707.

Farr, William, English pioneer in the study of vital statistics, b. 1807, d. 1883.

Farragut, David Glasgow, American admiral, b. 1801, d. 1870.

Farrar, Dean Frederick William, English theologian, b. 1831, d. 1903.

Fascist Party, Italian, founded Mar. 1919 by Mussolini ; seized power 20 Oct. 1922 ; dissolved 28 July 1943. Spanish (Falange), founded 1933 ; gained control of Spain 1936–1939. English (British Union of Fascists), founded 1932 by Sir Oswald Mosley ; revived (British Union Movement) in 1948.

Fashoda Incident, Egypt, between British and French 1898.

Fast Breeder Reactor, First Experimental, set up by the United Kingdom Atomic Energy Authority at Dounreay, Scotland, 1957. Reactor became critical 1959.

Fast of Ab, Jewish fast, Ab 9th.

Fastolf, Sir John, English soldier, b. about 1378, d. 1459.

Father's Day : U.S.A., 3rd Sunday in June.

Fatima, daughter of Mahomet, born about 605, d. 632.

Fatima, Miracle of (Portugal), occurred 13 Oct. 1917.

Fatimids, Caliphs in North Africa 909–1171.

Faulkner, William, American novelist (*Sanctuary*, 1931), b. 1897.

Fauré, Gabriel, French composer (*Messe basse*, 1907), b. 1845, d. 1924.

Faust, Johann or Georg, German magician, b. about 1480, d. about 1540.

Faustin I (Faustin Elie Souloque), Emperor of Haiti (1849–1851), b. about 1785, d. 1867.

Fauvist Movement, French art group, first recognised 1905 ; disintegrated 1908.

Fawcett, Henry, English economist, b. 1833, d. 1884.

Fawcett, Mrs Millicent Garrett, English champion of women's rights, b. 1847, d. 1929.

Fawcett, Sir William, English soldier and statesman, b. 1728, d. 1804.

Fawkes, Guy, English conspirator, b. 1570, hanged 1606.

Feast of Tabernacles (*Sukkoth*), Jewish festival, 15th to 22nd Tishri inclusive.

Feast of Weeks (*Sharuoth*), Jewish festival, Sivan 6th.

Federal Reserve Bank, Washington, D.C., founded 23 Dec. 1913.

Federation of Arab Amirates of the South (West Aden Protectorate Federation), inaugurated 11 Feb. 1959.

Federation of British Industries, founded 1916.

Feisal I, first king of Iraq (1921–1933), b. 1883, d. 1933.

Feisal II, third and last king (from 1939) of modern Iraq, b. 1935, assassinated 1958.

Fejervary, Geza, Baron, Hungarian soldier and statesman, b. 1833, d. 1914.

Félibien, André, French architect, b. 1619, d. 1695.

Felix I, St, Pope 269–275.

Felix II, Anti-Pope 355–357, d. 365.

Felix III, Pope 483–492.

Felix IV, Pope 526–530.

Felix V (Amadeus), Anti-Pope 1440–1449, b. 1383, d. 1451.

Fell, Dr John, bishop of Oxford (from 1675), b. 1625, d. 1686.

Fellowes, Edmund, English musicologist, b. 1870.

Felsted School, English public school, founded 1564 by Richard, Lord Riche, Lord Chancellor of England, b. about 1496, d. 1567.

Felton, John, English assassin of the Duke of Buckingham, b. about 1595, hanged 1628.

Fénelon, François de Salignac de la Mothe, French theologian (*Télémaque,* 1699), b. 1651, d. 1715.

Fenians (Irish Republican Brotherhood), Irish-American revolutionary movement founded 1858 in the U.S.A. by John O'Mahony, b. 1816, d. 1877.

Feodor I, Tsar of Russia (1584–1598), b. 1557, d. 1598.

Feodor II, Tsar of Russia (1605), b. 1589, assassinated 1605.

Feodor III, Tsar of Russia (1676–1682) b. 1656, d. 1682.

Ferber, Edna, American writer (*Cimarron,* 1929), b. 1887.

Ferdinand I, Holy Roman Emperor (1558–1564), b. 1503, d. 1564.

Ferdinand II, Holy Roman Emperor (1619–1637), b. 1578, d. 1637.

Ferdinand III, Holy Roman Emperor (1637–1658), b. 1608, d. 1658.

Ferdinand I, King of Portugal (1367–83), b. 1345, d. 1383.

Ferdinand II, consort of Maria II (1826–1853) of Portugal, b. 1816, d. 1885.

Ferdinand I, King of Castile and Leon, d. 1065.

Ferdinand II, King of Leon (1157–1188), **Ferdinand III,** King of Castile and Leon, b. 1199, d. 1252.

Ferdinand IV, King of Castile and Leon (1296–1312), d. 1312.

Ferdinand V, King of Castile and Leon (1474–1516), b. 1452, d. 1516.

Ferdinand VI, King of Spain (1746–1759), b. 1713, d. 1759.

Ferdinand VII, King of Spain (1813–1833), b. 1784, d. 1833.

Ferdinand I, King of Naples (1458–1494), b. 1423, d. 1494.

Ferdinand II, King of Naples (1495–1496), b. 1469, d. 1496.

Ferguson, James, Scottish astronomer, b. 1710, d. 1776.

Ferguson, Patrick, Scottish inventor, b. 1744, killed in action 1780.

Fergusson, Sir James, Scottish-born statesman, b. 1832, d. 1907.

Fermat, Pierre de, French mathematician, b. 1601, d. 1665.

Fermi, Enrico, Italian-born atomic physicist, b. 1901.

Fernandel (Fernand Contandin), French comedian, b. 1903.

Fernandez, Juan, Spanish explorer, b. about 1537, d. about 1603.

Fernando Po, Spanish Guinea, island of West Africa, discovered by the Portuguese navigator Fernão de Po about 1470.

Fernel, Jean François, French scientist, b. 1497, d. 1558.

Ferrar, Nicholas, English religious leader, b. 1592, d. 1637.

Ferrara, Andrea, Italian sword-maker, active in the second half of the 16th century.

Ferraris, Galileo, Italian scientist, b. 1847, d. 1897.

Ferrer, Francisco, Spanish educationist, b. 1859, shot 1909.

Ferrers, Laurence, Earl, last nobleman who was executed in Britain, b. 1720, hanged 1760.

Ferrier, Kathleen, English singer, b. 1912, d. 1953.

Ferrier, Susan, Scottish novelist (*Marriage,* 1818), b. 1782, d. 1854.

Ferris Wheel, invented for the World's Columbian Exposition 1892 by the American engineer George Washington Gale Ferris, b. 1859, d. 1896.

Ferro

Ferro, Canary Isles, prime meridian adopted by French in 17th century (after Arab usage) ; superseded by Paris and in 1911 by Greenwich.

Fersen, Hans Axel, Count, Swedish diplomat, b. 1755, murdered 1810.

Fervidor, French Revolutionary Calendar month, 19 July to 17 Aug.

Festival of Britain, opened 3 May, closed 30 Sept. 1951.

Festival of Lights (Chanucah), Jewish festival, Kislev 25th.

Festival of the Purification of the Virgin (Candlemas), 2 Feb.

Fettes College, Scottish public school, founded 1830 by Sir William Fettes, b. 1750, d. 1836.

Feuchtwanger, Lion, German novelist (*Jud Süss*, 1924), b. 1884, d. 1958.

Feuerbach, Ludwig Andreas, German philosopher, b. 1804, d. 1872.

Feuillère, Edwige, French actress, b. 1907.

Feuillet, Octave, French novelist (*Sibylle*, 1862), b. 1821, d. 1890.

Féval, Paul, French novelist (*Les Mystères de Londres*, 1844), b. 1817, d. 1887.

Feydeau, Georges, French playwright, b. 1862, d. 1921.

Fez, Treaty of, concerning the establishment of a French protectorate (1912–1956) in Morocco, concluded 30 Mar. 1912 ; terminated 2 Mar. 1956.

Fianna Fail ('Soldiers of destiny'), Irish political party founded 1927 by statesman Eamon de Valera, b. 1882.

Fichte, Johann Gottlieb, German philosopher, b. 1762, d. 1814.

Fido, airfield clearance method, developed 1942 by the British engineer Arthur Clifford Hartley, b. 1889, d. 1960.

Field, John, Irish-born composer of nocturnes, b. 1782, d. 1837.

Field, Marshall, American department store pioneer, b. 1834, d. 1906.

Field-Marshal, military rank, introduced into Britain in 1736.

Field of the Cloth of Gold, scene of the meeting between Henry VIII and François I, 6 June 1520.

Firewatching

Fielding, Henry, English novelist (*Tom Jones*, 1748), b. 1707, d. 1754.

Fields, Gracie, British singer, b. 1898.

Fifth Dimension, existence affirmed 1929 by Sir Owen Williams Richardson, b. 1879, d. 1959.

Fifth Monarchy Men, English religious movement, active 1642 to 1661.

Fifth Republic, France, constitution came into force 5 Oct. 1958.

Figueroa, Francisco de, Spanish poet, b. about 1535, d. about 1618.

Fiji, Polynesia, discovered 1643 by Abel Janszoon Tasman, b. about 1603, d. 1659.

Fillmore, Millard, U.S. President (1850–1853), b. 1800, d. 1874.

Film, First flexible transparent, suitable for motion pictures, invented 1889 by the American inventor George Eastman, b. 1854, d. 1932.

Filmer, Sir Robert, English political writer (*Patriarcha*, 1680), d. 1653.

Films on Colour (Kinemacolour), first shown 1906.

Finland, ruled by Sweden until 1808, by Russia 1808–1918 ; independent republic since 1918.

Firdausi, Persian poet, b. about 940, d. 1020.

Fire-arms, used in Europe in late 14th century ; wheel-lock introduced in early 16th century, flint-lock in late 16th century ; percussion detonator invented 1805 by the Scottish minister Alexander Forsyth, b. 1768, d. 1843.

Fire Engines, first acquired by a London insurance company 1722.

Fire Extinguisher, First portable, invented 1816 by the English barrack-master, George William Manby, b. 1765, d. 1854.

Fire Insurance, pioneered by Nicholas Barbon 1666.

Fire Rules, drawn up by the City of London 1189.

Fireplaces, in Britain, removed from the centre of the hall to the side wall in the 14th century.

Fire Plugs, put into water mains in Britain 1667.

Firewatching, made compulsory in Britain 31 Dec. 1940.

First of June, sea battle between French and British, 1794.

First Republic, France, proclaimed 22 Sept. 1792, ended 1804.

Fischer von Erlach, Johann Bernhard, Austrian architect, b. about 1657, d. 1723.

Fischer-Dieskau, Dietrich, German Lieder-singer, b. 1925.

Fish Harvest Festival, held at St Dunstan's-in-the-East, London, on Sunday nearest All Souls' Day.

Fisher, John, Admiral Lord, British sailor, b. 1841, d. 1920.

Fishmongers Company, London, origins uncertain, first extant Charter granted by King Edward III 1364.

Fisk University, Nashville, Tennessee, American negro university founded 1866.

Fiske, John, American philosopher, b. 1842, d. 1901.

Fitzgerald, Edward, English poet (*The Rubaiyat of Omar Khayyam*, 1859), b. 1809, d. 1883.

Fitzgerald, Lord Edward, Irish patriot, b. 1763, d. 1798.

Fitzherbert, Mrs Maria, wife of King George IV, b. 1756, m. 1785, d. 1837.

Fitzwilliam Collection, bequeathed to the University of Cambridge by Viscount Richard Fitzwilliam, b. 1745, d. 1816.

Fiume (Rijeka), seized by d'Annunzio 1919 ; ruled by Italy 1924–1947 ; by Yugoslavia since 1947.

Flag Day (U.S.A.), celebrated 14 June.

Flagstad, Kirsten, Norwegian operatic singer, b. 1895.

Flambard, Ranulf, English statesman, d. 1128.

Flaminian Way, from north of Rome to Ariminum on Adriatic coast, built 220 B.C. by the tribune Flaminius Gaius.

Flamininus, Titus Quinctus, Roman military tribune, d. 174 B.C.

Flaminius, Gaius, Roman democratic leader, killed 217 B.C.

Flammarion, Camille, French astronomer, b. 1842, d. 1925.

Flamsteed, John, first English Astronomer Royal, b. 1646, d. 1719.

Flatman, Thomas, English artist and poet, b. 1637, d. 1688.

Flaubert, Gustave, French novelist (*Madame Bovary*, 1857), b. 1821, d. 1880.

Flavian I, St, Patriarch of Antioch, b. about 320, d. 404.

Flavian II, St, Patriarch of Antioch, d. 518.

Flaxman, John, English sculptor (*St Michael*), b. 1755, d. 1826.

Flecker, James Elroy, English poet (*Hassan*, 1922), b. 1884, d. 1915.

Fleet Prison, London, founded in Norman times ; burnt down 1666 ; rebuilt, but again destroyed 1780 ; rebuilt 1782 ; pulled down 1844.

Fleming, Sir Alexander, British biologist (discovered penicillin 1928), b. 1881, d. 1955.

Fleming, Sir John Ambrose, English electrical engineer, b. 1849, d. 1945.

Fleming, Marjorie, Scottish child prodigy, b. 1803, d. 1811.

Fleming, Sir Sandford, Scottish-born Canadian engineer, b. 1827, d. 1915.

Fletcher, John, English dramatist (with Francis Beaumont, *The Knight of the Burning Pestle,* 1607), b. 1579, d. 1625.

Fleury, André Hercule, Cardinal, French statesman, b. 1653, d. 1743.

Flight and Barr (Worcester) **Porcelain,** manufactured 1792–1807 ; Flight period 1783–1792.

Flint-locks, invented about 1635.

Flodden, Battle of, between English and Scots, 9 Sept. 1513.

Flogging in the British Navy abolished through the efforts of the Irish politician John Gordon Swift Macneill, b. 1849, d. 1926.

Floral Games, first held at Toulouse May 1324.

Floréal, French Revolutionary calendar month, 20 Apr. to 19 May.

Florence of Worcester, English historian (*Chronicon*), d. 1118.

Florida, discovered Mar. 1512 by Juan Ponce de Leon, b. 1460, d. 1521. Ceded by Spain to U.S.A. 1819 ; granted Statehood 1845.

Florio, John, English translator (Montaigne's *Essays*, 1603), b. about 1553, d. 1625.

Flotow, Friedrich, Freiherr von, German composer (*Martha*, 1847), b. 1812, d. 1883.

Flour-mill, First steam, erected by the Scottish engineer John Rennie at Blackfriars, London, 1784–1788 ; burnt down 1791.

Fluorescence, nature discovered by the Irish-born scientist Sir George Gabriel Stokes, b. 1819, d. 1903.

Fluorescent Lighting, Low voltage, first marketed 1938.

Fluorine, first isolated 1886 by the French chemist Henri Moissan, b. 1852, d. 1907.

Fluorine in Drinking Water, beneficial effects in preventing tooth decay first demonstrated by the American doctor Frederick S. McKay, b. 1874, d. 1959.

Flying Boats, invented 1912 by the American aviator Glenn Hammond Curtiss, b. 1878, d. 1930.

Flying Bombs, first used by the Germans against the Allies 12 June 1944.

Flying Doctor Service, Australia, founded by the Australian Inland Mission of the Presbyterian Church of Australia 1928.

' Flying Saucers ', first so-named by the American Kenneth Arnold June 1947.

Foch, Ferdinand, French Commander-in-Chief Allied Forces during World War I, b. 1851, d. 1929.

Fogazzaro, Antonio, Italian novelist (*Il Santo*, 1905), b. 1842, d. 1911.

Fokine, Michael, Russian ballet-dancer, b. 1880, d. 1942.

Fokker, Anton Hermann Gerard, Dutch aviation pioneer, b. 1890, d. 1939.

Folger, Henry Clay, American collector of Shakespeareana, b. 1857, d. 1930.

Folger Shakespeare Memorial Library, Washington, D.C., opened 1932.

Fontainebleau, Palace of, France, origins unknown, oldest building erected in 12th century, additions being made up to 19th century.

Fontana, Domenico, Italian architect, b. 1543, d. 1607.

Fontane, Theodor, German writer (*Stine*, 1890), b. 1819, d. 1898.

Fontanne, Lynn, English-born American actress, b. about 1890.

Fontenelle, Bernard le Bouvier de, French writer (*La Pluralité des mondes*, 1686), b. 1657, d. 1757.

Fontenoy, Battle of, between French and English, 11 May 1745.

Football Association, formed 1863.

Foote, Samuel, English playwright (*The Nabob*, 1772), b. 1720, d. 1777.

Footlights, in British theatres, first used 1672.

Foppa, Vincenzo, Italian painter, b. about 1429, d. about 1516.

Forbes-Robertson, Sir Johnston, English actor, b. 1853, d. 1937.

Ford, Ford Madox, English novelist (*No More Parades*, 1925), b. 1873, d. 1939.

Ford, John, English dramatist ('*Tis Pity She's a Whore*, 1633), b. 1586, d. about 1639.

Ford Motor Works, U.S.A., founded 1903 by Henry Ford, b. 1863, d. 1947.

Forefathers' Day (U.S.A.), celebrating the landing (1620) of the Pilgrim Fathers at Plymouth Rock. Celebrated 21 Dec.

Forest School, London, English public school, founded 1834.

Forli, Melozzo da, Italian painter, b. 1438, d. 1494.

Formosa (Taiwan), ceded by China to Japan 1895 ; seized by Chiang Kai-shek 1945.

Formosus, Pope 891–896.

Forster, Edward Morgan, English writer (*A Passage to India*, 1924), b. 1879.

Forsyth, Rev. Alexander John, British inventor 1805 of the percussion lock, b. 1768, d. 1843.

Fort Duquesne, Pennsylvania, built 1754, burnt 1758.

Fort Sumter, Battle of, America Civil War, fought 12 to 14 Apr. 1861.

Forte, Charles, Italian-born British caterer, b. 1908.

Fortescue, Sir John, Lord Chief Justice, b. about 1394, d. about 1476.

Forth and Clyde Canal, begun 1768 by John Smeaton, b. 1724, d. 1792 ; completed 1790.

Forth Bridge, Scotland, designed by Sir John Fowler, b. 1817, d. 1898, and Sir Benjamin Baker, b. 1840, d. 1907 ; constructed 1883–1890 by Sir William Arrol, b. 1839, d. 1913.

Forth Road Bridge, construction begun 21 Nov. 1958 ; to be completed 1963.

Foscolo, Ugo, Italian writer (*Sepolcri,* 1807), b. 1778, d. 1827.

Fosse Way, Lincoln to Exeter, Roman road begun as frontier line against raiding forces by Publius Ostórius Scapula 47.

Foster, Birket, English artist, b. 1825, d. 1899.

Foster, Stephen Collins, American song-writer (*Old Folks at Home*), b. 1826, d. 1864.

Foucault Pendulum, to measure rotation of the Earth, constructed 1851 by the French scientist, Jean Foucault, b. 1819, d. 1868.

Foulis, Andrew, Scottish printer, b. 1712, d. 1775.

Foulis, Robert, Scottish printer, b. 1707, d. 1776.

Fountains Abbey, Cistercian house in Yorkshire, founded 1132 ; building completed 1526.

Fouquet, Jean, French painter (miniatures in *Book of Hours*), b. about 1415, d. about 1481.

Fouquier-Tinville, Antoine Quentin, French revolutionary leader, b. 1747, guillotined 1795.

Fourier, François Marie Charles, French socialist, b. 1772, d. 1837.

Fourier, Jean Baptiste Joseph, Baron, French mathematician, b. 1768, d. 1830.

' Fournier, Alain ' (Henri Fournier), French writer (*Le Grand Meaulnes,* 1913), b. 1886, killed in action 1914.

Fourth Republic, France, constitution came into force 1946 ; collapsed 1958.

Fowler, Henry Watson, expert on English usage, b. 1858, d. 1933.

Fowler, Sir John, English engineer, b. 1817, d. 1898.

Fowler, John, English engineer and inventor, b. 1826, d. 1864.

Fox, Charles James, British statesman, b. 1749, d. 1806.

Fox, George, English founder (1647) of the Society of Friends (Quakers), b. 1624, d. 1690.

Foxe's *Book of Martyrs* (1554–1559), written by the English historian John Foxe, b. 1516, d. 1587.

Fra Angelico (Fra Giovanni da Fiesole), Italian painter, b. about 1387, d. 1455.

Fracastoro, Girolamo, Italian physician, b. 1483, d. 1553.

Fragonard, Jean Honoré, French painter (*The Swing*), b. 1732, d. 1806.

Framlingham College, English public school, founded 1864 by public subscription as the Suffolk County Memorial to the Prince Consort.

Frampton, Sir George, English sculptor (*Peter Pan*), b. 1860, d. 1928.

' France, Anatole ' (Jacques Anatole Thibault), French novelist (*Penguin Island,* 1908), b. 1844, d. 1924.

France : monarchy, Merovingian (481–751), Carolingian (751–987), Capetian (987–1328), Valois (1328–1589), (Bourbon (1589–1792) ; 1st republic, 1793–1804 ; 1st empire, 1804–1814 ; restored monarchy, 1814–1848 ; 2nd republic, 1848–1852 ; 2nd empire, 1852–1870 ; 3rd republic, 1871–1940 ; German occupation and Vichy régime, 1940–1944 ; 4th republic, 1946–1958 ; 5th republic since 1958.

Francesca, Piero della, Italian painter (*Battista Sforza*), b. about 1415, d. 1492.

Francesca da Rimini, Italian heroine, wife of Giovanni Malatesta, murdered about 1285.

Franceschini, Baldassare, Italian painter, b. 1611, d. 1689.

Francis Borgia, St, General of the Society of Jesus, b. 1510, d. 1572.

Francis de Sales, St, b. 1567, d. 1622.

Francis of Assisi, St, b. about 1182, d. 1226.

Francis Xavier, St, b. 1506, d. 1552.

Francis I, Holy Roman Emperor (1745–1765), b. 1708, d. 1765.

Francis II, Holy Roman Emperor (1792–1806), b. 1768, d. 1835.

Francis I, King of France (1515–1547), b. 1494, d. 1547.

Francis II, King of France (1559–1560), b. 1544, d. 1560.

Franciscan Order, founded 1208 by St Francis of Assisi ; constitution established 1209.

Franck, César, Belgian-born composer (*Le Chasseur Maudit*, 1882), b. 1822, d. 1890.

Franco (Francisco Franco Bahamonde), dictator of Spain since 1939, b. 1892.

Franco-Prussian War, began July 1870, ended Feb. 1871.

Frank, Anna, Jewish diarist (Diary published 1947), b. 1929, d. in Belsen 1945.

Frank, Bruno, German novelist (*Trenck*, 1926), b. 1887, d. 1945.

Frank, Leonhard, German novelist (*Karl und Anna*, 1928), b. 1882.

Frankenstein, word derived from book by Mary Shelley, written 1816–1818.

Frankfurter, Felix, American Supreme Court judge, b. 1882.

Franklin, Benjamin, American statesman, b. 1706, d. 1790.

Franklin, Sir John, Arctic explorer, b. 1786, d. 1847.

Franz, Robert, German composer, b. 1815, d. 1892.

Franz Ferdinand, Austrian archduke, b. 1863, assassinated 1914.

Franz Joseph, Austrian Emperor (1848–1916), b. 1830, d. 1916.

Franz Joseph Land, Arctic archipelago, discovered 1873 by the German explorer Karl Weyprecht, b. 1838, d. 1881.

Fraser, Claud Lovat, English artist and stage designer, b. 1890, d. 1921.

Fraser, Simon, American-born explorer of Canada, b. about 1776, d. 1862.

Fraser River, British Columbia, discovered 1793 by the explorer Sir Alexander Mackenzie.

Fraunhofer Lines, in solar spectrum, discovered by the English scientist William Wollaston, b. 1766, d. 1828 ; studied by German physicist Joseph von Fraunhofer, b. 1787, d. 1826.

Frazer, Sir James George, Scottish writer (*The Golden Bough*, 1890), b. 1854, d. 1941.

Frechette, Louis Honoré, French-Canadian writer, b. 1839, d. 1908.

Fredegunde, Frankish queen, b. about 546, d. about 598.

Frederick I (Barbarossa), Holy Roman Emperor, b. about 1123, d. 1190.

Frederick II, Holy Roman Emperor (1212–1250), b. 1194, d. 1250.

Frederick III, Holy Roman Emperor (1440–1493), b. 1415, d. 1493.

Frederick I, King of Denmark (1523–1533), d. 1533.

Frederick II, King of Denmark (1559–1588), b. 1534, d. 1588.

Frederick III, King of Denmark (1648–1670), b. 1609, d. 1670.

Frederick IV, King of Denmark (1699–1730), b. 1671, d. 1730.

Frederick V, King of Denmark (1746–1766), b. 1723, d. 1766.

Frederick VI, King of Denmark (1808–1839), b. 1768, d. 1839.

Frederick VII, King of Denmark (1848–1863), b. 1808, d. 1863.

Frederick VIII, King of Denmark (1906–1912), b. 1843, d. 1912.

Frederick IX, King of Denmark (1947–), b. 1899.

Frederick I, King of Prussia (1701–1713), b. 1657, d. 1713.

Frederick II, the Great, King of Prussia (1740–1786), b. 1712, d. 1786.

Frederick III, Emperor of Germany, b. 1831, d. 1888.

Frederick William I, King of Prussia (1713–1740), b. 1688, d. 1740.

Frederick William II, King of Prussia (1786–1797), b. 1744, d. 1797.

Frederick William III, King of Prussia (1797–1840), b. 1770, d. 1840.

Frederick William IV, King of Prussia (1840–1861), b. 1795, d. 1861.

Frederick William the Great Elector, of Brandenburg, b. 1620, d. 1688.

Fredericksburg, Battle of, American Civil War, 13 Dec. 1862.

Free Church of Scotland, formed 1843.

Freedom, British periodical, began publication 1886.

Freeman, Edward Augustus, English historian, b. 1823, d. 1892.

Freemasonry, derived from Lodges of English and Scottish masons in the 17th century ; Mother Grand Lodge inaugurated in London 1717.

Freetown, Sierra Leone capital, first settled 1787.

Freiligrath, Ferdinand, German poet, b. 1810, d. 1876.

Fremont, John Charles, American explorer, b. 1813, d. 1890.

French, John, Earl of Ypres, English Field-Marshal, b. 1852, d. 1925.

French Equatorial Africa, first settled 1839 ; assumed present name 1910.

French Foreign Legion, first formed 1831.

French Guiana, South America, first settled 1604–1643.

French Language, earliest known document, the ' Strasbourg Oaths ', dated 842.

French Revolution, began June 1789 ; Consulate established Nov. 1799.

French Revolutionary Calendar, began 21–22 Sept. 1792, ended 31 Dec. 1805.

French Revolutionary Era, First 1792–1804.

French Revolutionary Wars, 1792–1802.

French Somaliland, overseas territory of the French Republic, acquired by the French Government between 1856 and 1883.

French West Africa, mainly acquired in the second half of the 19th century, and organised on modern lines 1904.

Freneau, Philip, American poet, b. 1752, d. 1832.

Frenssen, Gustav, German novelist (*Jörn Uhl*, 1901), b. 1863, d. 1945.

Frere, Sir Bartle, Scottish-born statesman, b. 1815, d. 1884.

Frescobaldi, Girolamo, Italian organist and composer, b. 1583, d. 1643.

Freud, Sigmund, Austrian pioneer psychoanalyst (*The Interpretation of Dreams*, 1900), b. 1856, d. 1939.

Freytag, Gustav, German writer (*Soll und Haben*, 1855), b. 1816, d. 1895.

Frick, Henry Clay, American industrialist, b. 1849, d. 1919.

Fricker, Racine, English composer (*Rapsodia concertante*, 1954), b. 1920.

Friends, Society of (Quakers), founded 1647 by the Englishman George Fox, b. 1624, d. 1690.

Frimaire, French revolutionary calendar month, 21 Nov. to 20 Dec.

Friml, Rudolf, Czech composer (*Katinka*, 1915), b. 1879.

Frith, William, English painter (*Derby Day*), b. 1819, d. 1909.

Froben, Johannes, German pioneer printer, b. 1460, d. 1527.

Frobisher, Sir Martin, English navigator, b. about 1535, d. 1594.

Froebel System, of *Kindergarten* education, founded 1816 by the German educationalist Friedrich Wilhelm August Froebel, b. 1782, d. 1852.

Froissart, Jean, French historian (*Chroniques*), b. about 1337, d. 1410.

Fromentin, Eugène, French artist and writer, b. 1820, d. 1876.

Fronde, The, French civil war, begun 1648, ended 1653.

Frontenac, Louis de Buade, Comte de, French statesman, b. 1620, d. 1698.

Fronto, Marcus Cornelius, Roman orator, b. about 100, d. about 166.

Frost, Robert, American poet, b. 1875.

Froude, James Anthony, English historian (*History of England*, 1856–1870). b. 1818, d. 1894.

Fructidor, French revolutionary calendar month, 18 Aug. to 16 Sept.

Frumentius, St, apostle of Ethiopia in 4th century ; feast celebrated 27 Oct.

Fry, Christopher, English playwright (*The Lady's not for Burning*, 1948), b. 1907.

Fry, Elizabeth, English Quaker social reformer, b. 1780, d. 1845.

Fry, Joseph, English Quaker business man, b. 1728, d. 1787.

Fry, Roger, English painter and art critic, b. 1866, d. 1934.

Fuad I, King of Egypt (1922–1936), b. 1868, d. 1936.

Fuad II, Ahmed, King of Egypt (1952–1954), b. 1950.

Fuel Cell, World's first, successfully demonstrated 1959 by the English engineer F. T. Bacon, b. 1905.

Fugger, Jakob, German merchant, b. 1459, d. 1525.

Fulk, Count of Anjou and King of Jerusalem, b. 1092, d. 1143.

Fuller, Thomas, English religious historian, b. 1608, d. 1661.

Fuller, William, English criminal, b. 1670, d. about 1717.

Fulton, Robert, American inventor of the steamship, b. 1765, d. 1815.

Fulvia, wife of Marc Antony, d. 40 B.C.

Furfural, solvent, discovered by the German scientist Johann Wolfgang Döbereiner, b. 1780, d. 1849.

Furness, Christopher, Baron Furness, British shipowner, b. 1852, d. 1912.

Furniss, Harry, Irish-born humorous artist, b. 1854, d. 1925.

Furry Day, festival held at Helston, Cornwall, on St Michael's Day, 8 May (except when this is a Saturday or Monday).

Furtwängler, Wilhelm, German conductor, b. 1886, d. 1954.

Fuseli, Henry, Swiss-born painter and illustrator, b. 1741, d. 1825.

Fustel de Coulanges, Numa Denis, French historian, b. 1830, d. 1889.

Futurism, art movement, identified 1909 by the Italian poet Filippo Tommaso Marinetti, b. 1878 ; movement disintegrated about 1915.

G

G.A.T.T. (General Agreement on Tariffs and Trade), signed 1947.

Gabin, Jean (Alexis Montgorge), French actor, b. 1904.

Gabon, Equatorial Africa, autonomous republic within the French Community, first settled by the French 1839.

Gabinius, Aulus, Roman statesman, b. 100, d. 47 B.C.

Gaboriau, Emile, French novelist (*Monsieur Lecoq*, 1869), b. 1835, d. 1873.

Gabriel, Jacques Ange, French architect, b. about 1698, d. 1782.

Gaddi, Taddeo, Italian painter (*Life of the Virgin*), d. 1366.

Gadolinium, chemical element, first isolated 1880 by the Swiss chemist Jean Charles Galissard de Marignac, b. 1817, d. 1894.

Gaelic League, founded in Dublin 1893.

Gage, Thomas, English general, b. 1721, d. 1787.

Gainsborough, Thomas, English painter (*Mrs Siddons*), b. 1727, d. 1788.

Gaitskell, Hugh, British statesman, b. 1906.

Galapagos Islands, archipelago in the Pacific, annexed by Ecuador 1832.

Galba, Roman Emperor (68–69), b. 3 B.C., assassinated A.D. 69.

Galen, Claudius, Greek physician, b. about 130, d. about 201.

Galerius, Roman Emperor (305–311), d. 311.

Galiani, Ferdinando, Italian economist, b. 1728, d. 1787.

Galicia, ruled by Poland 1372–1772, by Austria 1772–1919, by Poland 1919–1939, by Russia since 1945.

Galileo Galilei, Italian astronomer, b. 1564, d. 1642.

Galla Placidia, Roman Empress, d. 450.

Galle, Johann, German astronomer (observed the planet Neptune, 23 Sept. 1846), b. 1812, d. 1910.

Gallegos, Romulo, Venezuelan writer (*Dona Barbara*, 1929), b. 1884.

Galli-Curci, Amelita, Italian operatic singer, b. 1889.

Gallieni, Joseph Simon, French statesman, b. 1849, d. 1916.

Gallienus, Roman Emperor (253–268), assassinated 268.

Gallipoli (Turkey), World War I, first Allied landings 25 Apr. 1915 ; withdrawal 8 Jan. 1916.

Gallitzin, Dmitri Augustin, Russian-born missionary in America, b. 1770, d. 1840.

Gallium, chemical element, first isolated 1875, by the French scientist Paul Emile Lecoq de Boisbaudran, b. 1838, d. 1912.

Gallon, Imperial standard, measure legalised in Britain 1824.

Gallus, Roman Emperor (251–253), murdered 253.

Galsworthy, John, English novelist (*The Forsyte Saga*, 1906–1922), b. 1867, d. 1933.

Galt, Sir Alexander Tilloch, British-born statesman in Canada, b. 1817, d. 1893.

Galt, John, Scottish novelist (*Annals of the Parish*, 1821), b. 1779, d. 1839.

Galton, Sir Francis, English scientist, b. 1822, d. 1911.

Galvani, Luigi, Italian scientist, b. 1737, d. 1798.

Galvanometer, Mirror, invented by Lord Kelvin, b. 1824, d. 1907.

Gama, Vasco da, Portuguese explorer and navigator, reached Calicut (India) 23 May 1498, b. about 1460, d. 1525.

Gambetta, Léon, French statesman, b. 1838, d. 1882.

Gambia, made 1843 an independent British Crown Colony ; incorporated in the West African settlements 1866 ; again made separate Crown Colony 1888.

Gamma Rays, discovered 1900 by Paul Villard.

Gandhi, Mohandas Karamchand, Indian leader, b. 1869, started civil disobedience campaign in India 1 Aug. 1920, and was assassinated after Independence 30 Jan. 1948.

Gantt Chart, industrial management, devised by the American engineer Henry Lawrence Gantt, b. 1861, d. 1919.

Gaon, The (Elijah ben Solomon Wilna), Jewish scholar and leader in Lithuania, b. 1720, d. 1797.

Gapon, Georgy Apollonovich, Russian priest and politician, b. 1870, murdered 1906.

Garamond, Claude, French type-designer, d. 1561.

Garbo, Greta, Swedish-born film actress, b. 1906.

Garden Cities, idea introduced into England (1898) by Sir Ebenezer Howard, b. 1850, d. 1928 ; Letchworth begun 1903.

Gardiner, Alfred George, English journalist, b. 1865, d. 1946.

Gardiner, Samuel Rawson, English historian, b. 1829, d. 1902.

Gardiner, Stephen, Bishop of Winchester, b. about 1483, d. 1555.

Gardner, Erle Stanley, American detective-story writer (the Perry Mason series), b. 1889.

Garfield, James Abram, U.S. President (1881), b. 1831, murdered 1881.

Garibaldi, Giuseppe, Italian leader, b. 1807, march to Rome 1862, d. 1882.

Garnett, David, English novelist (*Lady into Fox*, 1922), b. 1892.

Garnett, Edward, English man of letters, b. 1868, d. 1937.

Garnier, Francis, French explorer, b. 1839, killed 1873.

' Garofalo, Il ', Italian painter, b. 1481, d. 1559.

Garrick, David, English actor, b. 1717, d. 1779.

Garrison, William Lloyd, American abolitionist, b. 1805, d. 1879.

Garter, Order of the, founded by Edward III about 1348.

Garth, Sir Samuel, English poet (*The Dispensary*, 1699), b. 1661, d. 1719.

Garvin, James Louis, Irish-born journalist (edited *The Observer* 1908–1942), b. 1868, d. 1947.

Gary, Indiana, founded 1905 by the U.S. Steel Corporation, and named after Elbert Henry Gary, b. 1846, d. 1927.

Gas, Coal, first produced in quantity by the Scottish inventor William Murdock, b. 1754, d. 1839.

Gas Light and Coke Company, first gas company, granted Charter 1812.

Gas Masks, issued to civilians in Britain 1939.

Gas, Poison, first used in World War I by Germans 22 Apr. 1915 ; first used by British 25 Sept. 1915.

Gas-turbined Powered Car, First, built by the British Rover Company 1950.

Gascoigne, George, English poet (*Jocasta*, 1575), b. about 1525, d. 1577.

Gaskell, Mrs Elizabeth, English novelist (*Cranford*, 1853), b. 1810, d. 1865.

Gasparri, Cardinal Pietro, Italian codifier of canon law, b. 1852, d. 1934.

Gassendi, Pierre, French scientist, b. 1592, d. 1655.

Gatling Gun, invented 1861–1862 by the American engineer Richard Jordan Gatling, b. 1818, d. 1903.

Gatty, Harold, American pioneer aviator, b. 1903.

Gauden, John, Bishop of Worcester, theologian and probable author of *Eikon Basilike* (1649), b. 1605, d. 1662.

Gaudi, Antoni, Catalan architect, b. 1852, d. 1926.

Gaudier-Brzeska, Henri, French sculptor, b. 1891, killed in action 1915.

Gauguin, Paul, French painter, b. 1848, d. 1903.

Gaul (Ancient France), Roman conquest completed 51 B.C.

Gaulle, Charles de, French general and statesman (ruler since 1958), b. 1890.

Gaunt, John of, Duke of Lancaster, b. 1340, d. 1399.

Gauss, Karl Friedrich, German mathematician, b. 1777, d. 1855.

Gautier, Théophile, French writer (*Mlle. de Maupin*, 1835), b. 1811, d. 1872.

'Gavarni, Paul' (Hippolyte Chevalier), French humorous artist, b. 1804, d. 1866.

Gaveston, Piers, Earl of Cornwall, favourite of Edward II, executed 1312.

Gay, John, English writer (*The Beggar's Opera*, 1728), b. 1685, d. 1732.

Gay-Lussac, Joseph Louis, French scientist, b. 1778, d. 1850.

Ged, William, Scottish inventor 1725 of stereotyping, b. 1690, d. 1749.

Geddes, Andrew, Scottish painter, b. 1783, d. 1839.

Geddes, Sir Eric, British statesman, b. 1875, d. 1937.

Geertgen Van Haarlem (Geertgen tot Sint Jans), Dutch painter (*The Bones of St John the Baptist*), b. about 1462, d. about 1490.

Geiger Counter, invented 1908 by the scientists Hans Geiger and Lord Rutherford, b. 1871, d. 1937.

Geikie, Sir Archibald, Scottish geologist, b. 1835, d. 1924.

Geissler's Tube, invented by the German scientist Heinrich Geissler, b. 1814, d. 1879.

Gelasius, St, Pope 492–496, d. 496.

Gelasius II (John of Gaeta), Pope 1118–1119, d. 1119.

Geminiani, Francesco, Italian violinist and instructor, b. 1687, d. 1762.

General Medical Council, London, held first meeting 23 Nov. 1858.

General Strike, United Kingdom, began 3, ended 13 May 1926.

Genet, Jean, French writer (*Les Bonnes*), b. 1910.

Geneva Convention, establishing the International Red Cross, held 1864.

Geneviève, St, patron saint of Paris, d. 512.

Genghis Khan (Temujin), Mongol ruler, b. 1162, d. 1227.

Genlis, Stéphanie Félicité Ducrest de St Aubin, Comtesse de, French writer (*Mémoires*, 1825), b. 1746, d. 1830.

Genovesi, Antonio, Italian philosopher, b. 1712, d. 1769.

Gentile da Fabriano, Italian painter, b. about 1370, d. 1427.

Gentleman's Magazine, The, founded 1731 by 'Sylvanus Urban' (Edward Cave, 1691–1754).

Gentlemen-at-Arms, the Sovereign's personal bodyguard, established by King Henry VIII 1509.

Geoffrey of Monmouth, British divine and historian, b. about 1100, d. 1154.

Geographical Society, Royal, London, founded 1830 by Sir John Barrow, b. 1764, d. 1848.

Geologists' Association, London, founded 17 Dec. 1858.

Geometry, Descriptive, study founded 1771 by the French mathematician Gaspard Monge, b. 1746, d. 1818.

George I, Elector of Hanover (1698–1727) and King of Great Britain (1714–1727), b. 1660, d. 1727.

George II, Elector of Hanover and King of Great Britain (1727–1760), b. 1683, d. 1760.

George III, Elector of Hanover (1760–1815), King of Hanover (1815–1820) and King of Great Britain (1760–1820), b. 1738, d. 1820.

George IV, Prince Regent (1812–1820), King of Hanover and King of Great Britain (1820–1830), b. 1762, d. 1830.

George V, King of Great Britain (1910–1936), b. 1865, d. 1936.

George VI, King of Great Britain (1936–1952), b. 1895, d. 1952.

George I, King of Greece (1863–1913), b. 1845, assassinated 1913.

George II, King of Greece (1922–1923), b. 1890.

George, Henry, American propounder of the 'single-tax' system (*Progress and Poverty*, 1879), b. 1839, d. 1897.

George, Stefan, German poet, b. 1868, d. 1933.

George Cross and George Medal, British order instituted 23 Sept. 1940.

George Heriot's School, Edinburgh, Scottish public school, founded 1628 under an endowment of the Scottish goldsmith and royal banker, George Heriot, b. 1563, d. 1624.

George Washington Bridge, New York–New Jersey, constructed 1927–1931.

George Watson's College, Edinburgh, Scottish public day school, founded by the Scottish accountant George Watson, d. 1723.

Georgia, U.S.A., founded as a colony 1733 ; entered Union 1788.

Georgia (Gruzia, in Caucasus), acknowledged Russian suzerainty 1783 ; Soviet Socialist Republic, U.S.S.R., declared independent 1918 ; became a constituent republic of the U.S.S.R. 1936.

Gerard, Archbishop of York (1100–1108), d. 1108.

Gerard, John, English herbalist, b. 1545, d. 1612.

Gerard, John, English Jesuit, b. 1564, d. 1637.

Gerhardi, William, English writer (*The Polyglots*, 1925), b. 1895.

Géricault, Théodore, French artist, b. 1791, d. 1824.

German, Sir Edward, English composer (*Merrie England*, 1902), b. 1862, d. 1936.

German Silver, alloy, discovered by the German scientist Ernst Augustus Geitner, b. 1783, d. 1852.

Germanicus, Roman soldier, b. 15 B.C., d. A.D. 19.

Germanium, chemical element, first isolated 1886 by the German chemist Clemens Alexander Winkler, b. 1838, d. 1904.

Germany, separated from France by Treaty of Verdun (843) ; ruled by Emperors, Saxon (919–1024), Salian (1024–1125), Welf and Hohenstaufen (1125–1254), Hapsburg and Luxemburg (1273–1457), Hapsburg (1457–1806) ; Confederation of Rhine (1806–1812) ; German Confederation (1812–1866) ; North German Confederation (1867–1871) ; German Empire (Hohenzollern) (1871–1918) ; Weimar Republic (1919–1933) ; 'Third Empire' (Nazi Régime) (1933–1945) ; Allied Occupation after 1945 ; Bizonia 1946 and Trizonia 1947 became German Federal Republic 1949 ; Russian Zone became German Democratic Republic 1949.

Gerry, Elbridge Thomas, American founder 1874 of the American Society for the Prevention of Cruelty to Children, b. 1837, d. 1927.

Gershwin, George, American composer (*Rhapsody in Blue*, 1924), b. 1898, d. 1937.

Gerson, Jean Charlier de, French theologian, b. 1363, d. 1429.

Gerstäcker, Friedrich, German travel-writer, b. 1816, d. 1872.

Gertrude, St, b. 1256, d. about 1301.

Gervase of Canterbury, English historian, lived in the second half of the 12th century.

Gesenius, Friedrich Heinrich Wilhelm, Hebrew lexicographer, b. 1786, d. 1842.

Gesner, Konrad von, Swiss bibliographer and naturalist, b. 1516, d. 1565.

Gettysburg, Battle of, American Civil War, 1 to 3 July 1863 ; Address of, delivered by Abraham Lincoln 19 Nov. 1863.

Ghana (formerly Gold Coast), West Africa, state established 6 May 1957 ; became a Republic 1960.

Ghazali, Abu Hamid Mohammed al (Algazel), Muslim theologian, b. 1058, d. 1111.

Ghent, Treaty of, between the U.S.A. and Great Britain (ending the War of 1812), signed 24 Dec. 1814.

Ghent, University of, founded by King William of Württemberg 1816.

Ghent Cathedral, built 1274–1554 (Crypt 941).

Ghiberti, Lorenzo, Italian sculptor, b. about 1378, d. 1455.

Ghirlandaio (Domenico Curradi), Italian painter (*Adoration of the Shepherds*), b. 1449, d. 1494.

Gibbon, Edward, English historian (*The Decline and Fall of the Roman Empire*, 1766–1788), b. 1737, d. 1794.

Gibbons, Grinling, Dutch-born sculptor, b. 1648, d. 1720.

Gibbons, Orlando, English composer (*Fantasies*, 1610), b. 1583, d. 1625.

Gibbs, James, Scottish architect, b. 1682, d. 1754.

Gibbs, Sir Vicary, English judge, b. 1751, d. 1820.

Gibraltar, settled 711 ; conquered by Spain 1462 ; captured by British 1704 and ceded by Spain to Britain 1713.

Gibson, John, Welsh sculptor, b. 1790, d. 1866.

Gide, André, French writer (*Les Faux-Monnayeurs*, 1926), b. 1869, d. 1951.

Gielgud, Sir John, English actor, b. 1904.

Gierke, Otto von, German legal and political thinker, b. 1841, d. 1921.

Gieseking, Walter, French pianist, b. 1895, d. 1956.

Gifford, William, English writer and editor, b. 1756, d. 1826.

Gigantosaurus Africanus, largest-known saurian, remains discovered by the Cutler Mission in Tanganyika 1924.

Giggleswick School, Yorkshire, English public school, founded 1512.

Gigli, Beniamino, Italian operatic singer, b. 1890, d. 1957.

Gilbert, Sir Alfred, English sculptor (*Eros*, in Piccadilly Circus), b. 1854, d. 1934.

Gilbert, Sir Humphrey, English explorer, b. about 1539, drowned at sea 1583.

Gilbert, William, English pioneer in magnetism (*De Magnete*, 1600), b. about 1540, d. 1603.

Gilbert, Sir William Schwenk, English playwright (*Trial by Jury*, 1875), b. 1836, d. 1911.

Gilbert and Ellice Islands, Western Pacific, proclaimed a British protectorate 1892 ; annexed by Britain 1915.

Gilbertines, English religious order, founded at Sempringham (Lincs.) 1135 by St Gilbert, b. 1083, d. 1139.

Gildas, St, British historian, b. about 500, d. 570.

Gill, Eric, English artist, b. 1882, d. 1940.

Gillow, Robert, English cabinetmaker, d. 1773.

Gillray, James, English political caricaturist, b. 1757, d. 1815.

Gilmore, Patrick Sarsfield, Irish-born bandmaster and composer (*When Johnny Comes Marching Home*, 1863), b. 1829, d. 1892.

Gilpin, Bernard, English divine, b. 1517, d. 1583.

Gilson, Paul, Belgian composer (*Alvar*, 1895), b. 1865, d. 1942.

Ginkgo Tree, found in Japan (1690) by Kaempfer, introduced into Europe 1730.

Gioia, Melchiorre, Italian economist, b. 1767, d. 1829.

Giordano, Luca, Italian painter, b. 1632, d. 1705.

Giordano, Umberto, Italian composer (*Andrea Chénier*, 1896), b. 1867, d. 1948.

Giorgione, Italian painter, b. about 1478, d. 1510.

Giotto di Bondone, Italian painter, b. about 1267, d. 1337.

Giraldus Cambrensis, Welsh historian, b. about 1146, d. about 1220.

Giraudoux, Jean, French writer (*Amphitryon* 38, 1929), b. 1882, d. 1944.

Girl Guides and Girl Scouts, World Association of, formed in London 1928.

Girl Guides Association, movement formed in Britain 1910.

Girl Scouts, U.S.A., founded 1912 by Mrs Juliette Gordon Low, b. 1860, d. 1927.

Girondins, group in French Revolution 1791–1794.

Girtin, Thomas, English artist (*Bolton Bridge*, 1801), b. 1775, d. 1802.

Girton College, Cambridge University, founded by Miss Emily Davies and others 1866 ; College opened 16 Oct. 1869, as the College for Women. Acquired present name and site 1872.

Gissing, George, English novelist (*The Private Papers of Henry Ryecroft*, 1903), b. 1857, d. 1903.

Giulio Romano, Italian artist, b. about 1496, d. 1546.

Gjellerup, Karl Adolf, Danish writer (*Romulus*, 1884), b. 1857, d. 1919.

Gladstone, Herbert John, Viscount, British statesman, b. 1854, d. 1930.

Gladstone, William Ewart, British statesman (Prime Minister 1868–1874, 1880–1885, 1886, 1892–1894), b. 1809, d. 1898.

Gland Secretion, discovered 1889 by Mauritius-born Charles Edouard Brown-Séquard, b. 1817, d. 1894.

Glanvill, Joseph, English theologian (*The Vanity of Dogmatising*, 1661), b. 1636, d. 1680.

Glanvill, Ranulf, English statesman, d. 1190.

Glasgow Academy, Scottish public day school, founded 1845.

Glasgow Chamber of Commerce, oldest British chamber of commerce, founded 1783.

Glasgow University, founded 1450.

Glass, blown glass discovered about 30 B.C. ; English glass industry established about 1226 ; plate-glass first made commercially in France 1668.

Glauber's Salts, discovered by the German scientist Johann Rudolf Glauber, b. 1604, d. 1668.

Glazunov, Aleksandr Konstantinovich, Russian composer (*Raymonda*, 1898), b. 1865, d. 1936.

Glencoe, Massacre of, Scotland, 13 Feb. 1692.

Glidden, Joseph Farwell, American inventor 1873 of barbed wire, b. 1813, d. 1906.

Glinka, Mikhail Ivanovich, Russian composer (*A Life for the Tsar*, 1836), b. 1804, d. 1857.

' Glorious First of June ', naval battle between English and French fought off Ushant 1794.

Gloucester, Humphrey, Duke of, statesman and soldier, b. 1391, d. 1447.

Gloucester, Statute of, decreeing necessity of trial before the granting of the Royal pardon, 1278.

Gloucester Cathedral, built 1072–1104.

Glover, George, English engraver, b. before 1625, d. after 1650.

Glover, Sarah Ann, English inventor about 1845 of the Tonic Sol-fa system, b. 1785, d. 1867.

Glucinum, chemical element, first isolated 1828 by the German scientist Friedrich Wöhler, b. 1800, d. 1882.

Gluck, Christoph Willibald, German composer (*Alceste*, 1767), b. 1714, d. 1787.

Glycerine, discovered by the French chemist Charles Adolphe Wurtz, b. 1817, d. 1884.

Glycogen, discovered by Claude Bernard in 1857.

Glyndebourne Festival Opera founded 1934 by John Christie, b. 1882.

Glyndwr, Owain (Owen Glendower), Welsh rebel leader, b. about 1350, d. about 1416.

Gmelin, Leopold, German scientist, b. 1788, d. 1853.

Gneisenau, August Wilhelm Anton, Graf Neithardt von, Prussian military commander, b. 1760, d. 1831.

Gnosticism, philosophy founded by the philosopher Valentinus, d. about 160.

Goa, Portuguese India, discovered by Vasco da Gama 1498 ; annexed by Portugal 1510.

Gobelins, The, tapestry works near Paris, founded 1601. First Director (1662), Charles Le Brun, the painter, b. 1619, d. 1690.

Gobineau, Joseph Arthur, Comte de, French diplomat and writer, b. 1816, d. 1862.

Godefroy, Jacques, French jurist, b. 1587, d. 1622.

Gödel's Theory, mathematical philosophy, propounded 1931 by the German-born mathematician Kurt Gödel, b. 1906.

Godfrey of Bouillon, crusader and conqueror of Jerusalem, b. about 1060, d. 1100.

Godfrey, Sir Edmund Berry, English justice of the peace, b. 1621, murdered 1678.

Godfrey, Thomas, America's first playwright (*The Prince of Parthia*, 1765), b. 1736, d. 1763.

Godiva, Lady, wife of Leofric, Earl of Mercia, traditionally rode naked through the streets of Coventry 1040, fl. 1040–1085.

Godolphin, Sidney, Earl of Godolphin, British statesman, b. 1645, d. 1712.

Godunov, Boris, Tsar of Russia (1598–1605), b. 1552, d. 1605.

Godwin, Earl of the West Saxons, d. 1053.

Godwin, William, English writer and reformer (*Political Justice*, 1793), b. 1756, d. 1836.

Godwin-Austen, Robert Alfred Cloyne, English geologist, b. 1808, d. 1884.

Godwin-Austen, Mt (K 2), Himalayas, climbed by an Italian expedition 31 July 1954.

Goebbels, Paul Joseph, German Nazi leader, b. 1897, committed suicide 1945.

Goering, Hermann Wilhelm, German Nazi leader, b. 1893, committed suicide 1946.

Goes, Hugo van der, Flemish painter (The Portinari Alterpiece), d. 1482.

Goethals, George Washington, American builder (1907–1914) of the Panama Canal and first Governor (1914–1917) of the Canal Zone, b. 1858, d. 1928.

Goethe, Johann Wolfgang von, German scientist and writer (*Werther*, 1774), b. 1749, d. 1832.

Gogh, Vincent van, Dutch painter (*Sunflowers*), b. 1853, committed suicide 1890.

Gogol, Nikolai, Russian writer (*Dead Souls*, 1837), b. 1809, d. 1852.

Gold, found in New Granada (S. America) 1537 ; near Sacramento (California) 1847 ; on the Blue Hills (New South Wales) 12 Feb. 1851, by Edmund Hammond Hargraves (1815–1891) ; in Otago (New Zealand) June 1861 ; at Barberton (S. Africa) 1882 and Witwatersrand (S. Africa) 1884 ; in Rabbit Creek (Klondike) 16 Aug. 1896 by George Washington Carmack.

Gold Coast, West Africa, settled by the Portuguese by 1482 ; became a British colony 1898 ; became the State of Ghana 1957.

Gold Rush : California 1848 ; Australia 1851 ; S. Africa 1886 ; Klondike 1897.

Gold Standard, abandoned by Great Britain 21 Sept. 1931.

Golden Bull, on German Government, promulgated by the Emperor Charles IV 1356.

Golden Gate Bridge, San Francisco, opened 1937.

Golden Spurs, Battle of the (Battle of Courtrai), between Flemish and French 1302.

Golding, Louis, English writer (*Magnolia Street*), b. 1895, d. 1958.

Goldman, Emma, Russian-born anarchist, b. 1869, d. 1940.

Goldoni, Carlo, Italian dramatist (*The Mistress of the Inn*, 1753), b. 1707, d. 1793.

Goldsmith, Oliver, Irish-born writer (*The Vicar of Wakefield*, 1766), b. 1728 d. 1774.

Golf, origins uncertain, earliest recorded allusion Scotland 1457. Introduced in the U.S.A. 1779.

Golf Club, Earliest, the Honourable Company of Edinburgh Golfers founded 1754.

Gollancz, Victor, English publisher and writer (*My Dear Timothy*), b. 1893.

Goltzius, Hendrik, Dutch artist, b. 1558 d. 1617.

Golytsin, Vasily Vasilievich, Russian statesman, b. 1643, d. 1714.

Gompers, Samuel, English-born American labour leader, b. 1850, d. 1924.

Gomulka, Wladyslaw, ruler of Poland since 1956, b. 1905.

Goncharov, Ivan, Russian novelist (*Oblomov*, 1857), b. 1812, d. 1891.

Goncourt, Edmond de, French writer (*La Fille Elisa*, 1878), b. 1822, d. 1896.

Goncourt, Jules de, French writer (with Edmond, *Germinie Lacerteux*, 1865), b. 1830, d. 1870.

Gondomar, Diego Sarmiento de Acuña, Count of, Spanish diplomat (English ambassador 1613–1622), b. 1567, d. 1626.

Gongora (Luis de Gongora y Argote), Spanish poet, b. 1561, d. 1627.

Gonville and Caius College, Cambridge University, founded as Gonville Hall 1348 by Edmund Gonville. Assumed present name by Royal Charter 1557.

Gonzaga, Federigo, Duke of Mantua (1530–1540), b. 1500, d. 1540.

Gooch, Sir Daniel, English railway pioneer, b. 1816, d. 1889.

Good Friday, Christian commemoration of the Crucifixion, the Friday before Easter.

Goodwin Sands, off S.E. coast of England, first mapped by the Dutch cartographer Lucas Janszon Waghenaer 1585.

Goodwood Cup, Goodwood, first run 1812.

Googe, Barnabe, English poet, b. 1540, d. 1594.

Goossens, Eugène, English composer (*Judith*, 1925), b. 1893.

Goossens, Leon, English oboe player, b. 1896.

Gorchakov, Prince Aleksandr Mikhailovich, Russian statesman, b. 1798, d. 1883.

Gordian I, Roman Emperor (238), b. about 158, committed suicide 238.

Gordian II, Roman Emperor (238), b. 192, killed 238.

Gordian III, Roman Emperor (238–244), b. about 224, murdered 244.

Gordon, Adam Lindsay, British poet, b. 1833, committed suicide 1870.

Gordon, General Charles George, Governor of the Sudan (1877–1880), b. 1833, killed 1885.

Gordon, Lord George, leader of the Gordon Riots (1770), b. 1751, d. 1793.

Gordon Highlanders, raised by the Marquis of Huntly (later Duke of Gordon) 1794.

Gordonstoun School, Elgin, Scottish public school, founded 1935 by the German educationalist Kurt Hahn, b. 1886.

Gorges, Sir Ferdinando, pioneer in North America, b. about 1566, d. 1647.

Gorgias, Greek philosopher, b. about 485 d. 380 B.C.

Gorki, Maxim (Alexei Maximovich Peshkov), Russian novelist (*My Universities*, 1923), b. 1868, d. 1936.

Gort, John, Viscount, British soldier and administrator, b. 1886, d. 1946.

Goschen, George Joachim, Viscount Goschen, British statesman, b. 1831, d. 1907.

Gosse, Sir Edmund, English writer (*Father and Son*, 1907), b. 1845, d. 1928.

Gothic Language, first written by Bishop Wulfila (311–383) ; spoken in Crimea up to 1560.

Goths, first attacked Romans 214, defeated Decius 251, became Christian about 340, attacked by Huns 363 ; **Visigoths** crossed Danube 376, defeated Valens 378, became *foederati* 382, attacked Greece 396, invaded Italy 401, sacked Rome 410, invaded Gaul 412–470, defeated by Arabs 711 ; **Ostrogoths** crossed Danube and became *foederati* 380, attacked Italy 405, occupied Italy 489–493, defeated by Byzantines 536–562.

Gottfried von Strassburg, German poet (*Tristan und Isolde*), lived in the late 12th and early 13th centuries.

Gottschalk, German theologian, b. about 804, d. 868.

Gottsched, Johann Christoph, German critic and writer, b. 1700, d. 1766.

Götz von Berlichingen, German leader, b. 1480, d. 1562.

Goucher College, Baltimore, Md., American women's college, founded 1885 ; assumed present name 1910.

Goudy, Frederick William, American type designer, b. 1865, d. 1947.

Gough Island, probably discovered by the Portuguese navigator Pero d'Anhaya 1505.

Goujon, Jean, French sculptor, flourished during the middle of 16th century.

Gould, Sir Francis Carruthers, humorous artist, b. 1844, d. 1925.

Gould, Jay, American financier, b. 1836, d. 1892.

Gounod, Charles, French composer (*Faust,* 1859), b. 1818, d. 1893.

Gourmont, Remy de, French writer (*Sixtine,* 1890), b. 1858, d. 1915.

Gower, John, English poet (*Speculum Meditantis*), b. about 1325, d. 1408.

Goya y Lucientes, Francisco de, Spanish painter (*Charles IV*), b. 1746, d. 1828.

Gozzi, Count Carlo, Italian playwright (*Love for Three Oranges,* 1761), b. 1720, d. 1806.

Gozzoli, Benozzo, Italian painter (*The Medici Family as the Magi*), b. about 1421, d. 1497.

Gracchus, Tiberius Sempronius, Roman reformer, b. about 169, murdered 133 B.C.

Gracchus, Caius Sempronius, b. about 160, killed 121 B.C.

Grace, Princess (Grace Kelly), married to Prince Rainier of Monaco 19 Apr. 1956.

Grace, Dr William Gilbert, English cricketer, b. 1848, d. 1915.

Graetz, Heinrich, German historian (*History of the Jews,* 1853–1876), b. 1817, d. 1891.

Graf, Urs, Swiss artist, b. about 1485, d. 1528.

Graf Spee, German warship, trapped by the British in a naval action 13–17 Dec. 1939 ; scuttled 17 Dec.

Graf Zeppelin, German airship, completed first transatlantic flight 15 Oct. 1928. Circumnavigated the world 15–29 Aug. 1929.

Grafton, Augustus, Duke of, English statesman, b. 1735, d. 1811.

Graham, Billy, American evangelist, b. 1918.

Graham, John, of Claverhouse, Viscount Dundee, soldier, b. about 1649, killed in battle 1689.

Graham, Thomas, Baron Lynedoch, Scottish soldier, b. 1748, d. 1843.

Graham's Law, concerning the diffusion of gas, formulated by the Scottish chemist Thomas Graham, b. 1805, d. 1869.

Grahame, Kenneth, Scottish writer (*The Wind in the Willows,* 1908), b. 1859, d. 1931.

Grahame-White, Claude, pioneer British aviator, b. 1879, d. 1959.

Grainger, Percy Aldridge, Australian composer (*Spoon River,* 1930), b. 1882, d. 1961.

Gramont, Philibert, Comte de, French courtier, b. 1621, d. 1707.

Gramophone (phonograph), invented 1876 by the American Thomas Alva Edison, b. 1847, d. 1931.

Granados, Enrique, Spanish composer (*Goyescas,* 1916), b. 1867, d. 1916.

Grand Alliance, war of, between France and the Allies, 1688–1697.

Grand Canyon National Park, Arizona, established 1919.

Grand Central Terminal, New York, opened 1913.

Grand Junction Canal, England, built 1793–1805.

Grand National, Liverpool, first run 1837.

Grand Prix, motor race, first held at Le Mans 1906 (and won by M. Szisz in a Renault). First held in Britain at Brooklands Aug. 1926.

Grand Trunk Canal, England, built 1766 onwards by the English engineer James Brindley, b. 1716, d. 1772.

Grand Trunk Herald, first newspaper to be printed in a train, published by the American inventor Thomas Alva Edison, b. 1847, d. 1931.

Granjon, Robert, French type designer, lived in the middle of the 16th century.

Grant, Duncan, Scottish painter, b. 1885.

Grant, Ulysses S., U.S. President (1869–1877), b. 1822, d. 1885.

Granville, George, Baron Lansdowne, English writer (*Heroick Love,* 1698), b. 1667, d. 1735.

Granville, George, Earl, English statesman, b. 1815, d. 1891,

Granville-Barker, Harley, English playwright and critic (*Waste*, 1907), b. 1877, d. 1946.

Grape Sugar, discovered 1799 by the French scientist Joseph Louis Proust, b. 1754, d. 1826.

Grasse, François Joseph Paul, Comte de, French admiral in the West Indies, b. 1722, d. 1788.

Gratian, Roman Emperor (375–383), b. 359, assassinated 383.

Grattan, Henry, Irish reformer, b. 1746, d. 1820.

Graves, Robert, English writer (*I, Claudius*, 1934), b. 1895.

Gravity, Law of, established 1684 by Sir Isaac Newton, b. 1642, d. 1727.

Gray, Elisha, American inventor, b. 1835, d. 1901.

' Gray, Maxwell ' (Mary Glied Tuttiet), English writer (*The Silence of Dean Maitland*, 1886), b. 1847, d. 1923.

Gray, Thomas, English poet (*Elegy*, 1750), b. 1716, d. 1771.

Great Australian Basin, largest artesian basin in the world, resources discovered in north-western New South Wales 1878.

Great Exhibition, Crystal Palace, London, held 1 May to 15 Oct. 1851.

Great Fire of London, 2–6 Sept. 1666.

Great Schism, between Catholic and orthodox churches 1054–1439 and since 1472.

Great Schism, within Catholic Church, 1378–1417.

Great Trek, of Boers from Cape Colony to the Orange Free State area 1836.

Great Yarmouth, granted first charter by King John 18 Mar. 1208.

Greco, El (Domenico Theotocopuli), Cretan-born painter (*El Espolio*), b. 1541, d. 1614.

Greece, Ancient, Greek-speaking peoples entered Greece about 2000 B.C. Persians crossed Bosphorus 512 ; campaign of Xerxes 480 ; Confederacy of Delos 477 ; Peloponnesian wars 431–404 ; Macedonian conquest completed 338 ; Roman conquest completed 133 ; Constantinople founded A.D. 330.

Greece, Modern, Turkish conquest completed 1466 ; achieved independence from Turkey 1821–1827 ; monarchy 1833–1922 ; republic 1922–1935 ; monarchy since 1935 ; German occupation 1941–1944.

Greek Orthodox Era, began 5509 B.C.

Greeley, Horace, American editor and politician, b. 1811, d. 1872.

Green, Charles, English balloonist, b. 1785, d. 1870.

Green, John Richard, English historian, b. 1837, d. 1883.

Green, Thomas Hill, English philosopher, b. 1836, d. 1882.

Green Belt Scheme, approved by the London County Council 29 Jan. 1935; came into operation 1 Apr. 1935.

Greenaway, Kate, English illustrator of children's books (*Mother Goose*), b. 1846, d. 1901.

' Greenbacks ', American legal tender notes, first issued by Abraham Lincoln 5 Feb. 1862.

Greene, Graham, English writer (*Brighton Rock*, 1938), b. 1904.

Greene, Hugh Carleton, Director-General of the B.B.C. since 1959, b. 1910.

Greene, Maurice, English organist and composer (*Jephthah*, 1737), b. about 1695, d. 1755.

Greene, Robert, English writer (*Friar Bacon and Friar Bungay*, 1594), b. about 1560, d. 1592.

Greenland, discovered about 982 by the Norwegian explorer Eric the Red (b. about 949) ; re-settled 1721 ; first crossed 1888 by the Norwegian explorer Fridtjof Nansen, b. 1861, d. 1930 ; declared a dependency of Denmark 1933.

Greenwood, Thomas, British library pioneer, b. 1851, d. 1908.

Greenwich Mean Time, made legal time for Great Britain 1880 ; made prime meridian of world 1884.

Greenwich Observatory, established by Charles II 1675 ; moved to Herstmonceaux during 1950s.

Greg, Sir Walter Wilson, English bibliographer, b. 1875, d. 1959.

Gregg, Sir Cornelius, introducer (1944) of P.A.Y.E. in Britain, b. 1888, d. 1959.

Gregg, John Robert, Irish-born inventor 1888 of Gregg's shorthand, b. 1867, d. 1948.

Gregorovius, Ferdinand, German historian, b. 1821, d. 1891.

Gregory I, St, Pope 590–604, b. about 540, d. 604.

Gregory II, St, Pope 715–731, d. 731.

Gregory III, St, Pope 731–741, d. 741.

Gregory IV, Pope 827–844, d. 844.

Gregory V (Bruno), Pope 996–999, b. about 971, d. 999.

Gregory VI (Johannes Gratianus), Pope 1045–1046, d. 1047.

Gregory VII, St (Hildebrand), Pope 1073–1085, b. about 1035, d. 1085.

Gregory VIII (Mauritius Burdinus), Anti-Pope 1118–1121.

Gregory VIII (Alberto de Mora), Pope 1187, d. 1187.

Gregory IX (Ugolino Conti de Segno), Pope 1227–1241, d. 1241.

Gregory X (Tebaldo Visconti), Pope 1271–1276, b. 1208, d. 1276.

Gregory XI (Pierre Roger de Beaufort), Pope 1371–1378, b. 1330, d. 1378.

Gregory XII (Angelo Coriaro), Pope 1406–1415, b. about 1326, d. 1417.

Gregory XIII (Ugo Buoncompagno), Pope 1572–1585, b. 1502, d. 1585.

Gregory XIV (Nicolo Sfondrato), Pope 1590–1591, b. 1535, d. 1591.

Gregory XV (Alessandro Ludovisi), Pope 1621–1623, b. 1554, d. 1623.

Gregory XVI (Bartolommeo Alberto Cappellari), Pope 1831–1846, b. 1765, d. 1846.

Gregory, Lady Augusta, Irish patroness and playwright (*Hyacinthe Halevy*, 1909), b. 1852, d. 1932.

Gregory, Sir Augustus Charles, English explorer of Australia, b. 1819, d. 1905.

Gregory Nazianzen, St, b. about 330, d. about 390.

Gregory of Tours, St, historian, b. about 540, d. 594.

Grenadier Guards, organised on a permanent basis 1740.

Grenfell, Sir Wilfred, English medical missionary, b. 1865, d. 1940.

Grenville, George, English statesman, b. 1712, d. 1770.

Grenville, Sir Richard, Captain of *The Revenge*, b. about 1541, d. of wounds 1591.

Gresham's Law, on the question of coinage, propounded by Sir Thomas Gresham, b. about 1519, d. 1579.

Gresham's School, Holt, English public school, founded 1555 by Sir John Gresham, d. 1556.

Gretchaninov, Aleksandr, Russian-born composer (*Missa festiva*, 1939), b. 1864, d. 1956.

Gretna Green, Scotland, scene of runaway marriages, particularly 1754 to 1856.

Grétry, André Ernest Modeste, Belgian composer (*Andromaque*, 1780), b. 1741, d. 1813.

Greuze, Jean Baptiste, French painter (*The Broken Pitcher*), b. 1725, d. 1805.

Greville, Sir Fulke, English poet, b. 1554, murdered 1628.

Greville, Charles Cavendish Fulke, English political diarist (*Memoirs*, 1875–1887), b. 1794, d. 1865.

Grey, Charles, Earl, British statesman (Prime Minister 1831–1834), b. 1764, d. 1845.

Grey, Edward, Viscount Grey of Fallodon, British statesman, b. 1862, d. 1933.

Grey, Lady Jane, claimant to the English throne, b. about 1537, proclaimed Queen July 1553, beheaded 1554.

Grey, Zane, American writer (*The Last of the Plainsmen*, 1908), b. 1875, d. 1939.

Greyhound Racing, in Britain, began at White City 20 June 1927.

Grieg, Edvard, Norwegian composer (*Peer Gynt*, 1874), b. 1843, d. 1907.

Grierson, Sir Robert (prototype of Scott's Sir Robert Redgauntlet), b. about 1655, d. 1733.

Griffith, Arthur, Irish patriot, b. 1872, d. 1922.

Griffith, David Wark, American film producer (*The Birth of a Nation*, 1915), b. 1875, d. 1948.

Griffiths, Ernest Howard, Welsh physicist, b. 1851, d. 1932.

Grignard Reagents, organo-magnesium compounds, discovered by the French scientist Victor Grignard, b. 1871, d. 1935.

Grillparzer, Frans, Austrian poet (*Sappho*, 1819), b. 1791, d. 1872.

Grimald, Nicholas, English writer (*Christus Redivivus*, 1543), b. 1519, d. 1562.

Grimaldi, Joseph, English clown, b. 1779, d. 1837.

Grimbald, St, Flemish-born abbot at Winchester, b. about 820, d. 903.

Grimm, Jakob, German writer (*Fairy Tales*), b. 1785, d. 1863.

Grimm, Wilhelm Karl, German writer, b. 1786, d. 1859.

Grimmelshausen, Hans Jacob Christoph von, German writer (*Simplicissimus*, 1669), b. about 1625, d. 1676.

Grimond, Joseph, British statesman, b. 1913.

Grimthorpe, Edmund Beckett, Baron, inventor and lawyer, b. 1816, d. 1905.

Grindal, Edmund, English divine, b. 1519, d. 1583.

Gringoire, Pierre, French poet, b. about 1475, d. 1538.

Gris, Juan, Spanish-born painter, b. 1887, d. 1927.

Grisi, Giulia, Italian operatic singer, b. 1811, d. 1869.

Grocers Company, London, origins uncertain but at least as early as 1231 ; Hall built 1427 ; first Charter granted by King Edward III 1345.

'Grock' (Adrien Wettach), Swiss clown, b. 1880, d. 1959.

Grocyn, William, English scholar, b. about 1446, d. 1519.

Grolier, Jean, French diplomat and book-collector, b. 1479, d. 1565.

Gropius, Walter, German-born architect, b. 1883.

Gros, Baron Antoine Jean, French painter (particularly of Napoleon), b. 1771, committed suicide 1835.

Grosseteste, Robert, English theologian, b. about 1175, d. 1253.

Grossmith, George, English actor and writer (*Diary of a Nobody*, 1892), b. 1847, d. 1912.

Grosz, Georg, German-born painter, b. 1893, d. 1959.

Grote, George, English historian, b. 1794, d. 1871.

Grotius, Hugo, Dutch jurist (*De jure belli et pacis*, 1625), b. 1583, d. 1645.

Groton, American boys' preparatory school, originally founded 1793.

Grouchy, Emmanuel, Marquis de, French general, b. 1766, d. 1847.

Groundnut Scheme, in Tanganyika, begun 1947.

Grove, Sir George, English compiler of the *Dictionary of Music and Musicians* (first published 1879–1889), b. 1820, d. 1900.

Grove Cell, electric battery, invented 1839 by Sir William Robert Grove, b. 1811, d. 1896.

Gruber, Franz Xaver, Austrian composer (*Silent Night*, 1818), b. 1787, d. 1863.

Grünewald, Matthias (Mathis Nithart), German painter (the Isenheim altarpiece), b. about 1480, d. 1528.

Guadalcanal Islands, World War II, evacuated by the Japanese 9 Feb. 1943.

Guam, World War II, occupied by the Americans 21 July 1944.

Guardi, Francesco, Italian painter, b. 1712, d. 1793.

Guarneri, Giuseppe Antonio, Italian violin-maker, b. 1687, d. about 1745.

Guatemala, Central American republic, independence proclaimed 1822, established 17 Apr. 1839.

Guelphs, German family founded by Welf, d. about 825.

Guericke, Otto, German scientist, b. 1602, d. 1686.

Guérin, Maurice de, French poet (*Le Centaurel*, about 1835), b. 1810, d. 1839.

Guernica, Spanish Civil War, bombed 26 Apr. 1937.

Guernsey, Channel Islands, acquired 933 by William Duke of Normandy (d. 943), and attached to England since 1066.

Guesclin, Bertrand du, French leader, b. about 1320, d. 1380.

Guest, Lady Charlotte (*later* Lady Charlotte Schreiber), translator of the *Mabinogion*, b. 1812, d. 1895.

Guggenheim, Meyer, American financier, b. 1828, d. 1905.

Guiana, British, settled by the Dutch about 1620 ; ceded to Britain 1814.

Guiana, French, settled by the French 1604 ; raised to the status of a Department of France 1947.

Guiana, Netherlands (Surinam), assigned to the Netherlands 1667.

Guicciardini, Francesco, Italian diplomat and historian, b. 1483, d. 1540.

Guido d'Avezzo, pioneer in musical instruction and notation, b. about 995, d. 1050.

Guido Reni, Italian painter (*Deeds of Hercules*), b. 1575, d. 1642.

Guilbert, Yvette, French actress, b. 1869, d. 1944.

Guild Socialism, in Britain : National Guilds League formed 1915 ; movement collapsed by 1924.

Guillaume de Lorris, French poet (part of the *Roman de la rose*), lived in the first half of the 13th century.

Guillotine, introduced 1792 by the French doctor Joseph Guillotin, b. 1738, d. 1814.

Guinea, left the French Union 28 Sept., proclaimed independent republic 2 Oct. 1958.

Guinea, Portuguese, discovered 1446 by Nuno Tristão ; made a separate colony of Portugal 1879.

Guinea, Spanish, settled by the Spanish at the end of the 18th century.

Guinness, Sir Alec, English actor, b. 1914.

Guinness, Sir Benjamin Lee, Irish brewer, b. 1798, d. 1868.

Guise, François de Lorraine, Duc de, French soldier and politician, b. 1519, assassinated 1563.

Guise, Henri de Lorraine, Duc de, French soldier, b. 1550, assassinated 1588.

Guitry, Sacha, French actor and playwright (*Le Veilleur de nuit*, 1911), b. 1885, d. 1957.

Guizot, François Pierre Guillaume, French statesman and historian, b. 1787, d. 1874.

Gun, traditionally invented 1313 by Berthold Schwartz.

Gunpowder, introduced into Europe by 1300.

Gunpowder Plot, against the Houses of Parliament 5 Nov. 1605.

Gunter, Edmund, English mathematician, b. 1581, d. 1626.

Gurney, Sir Goldsworthy, English inventor, b. 1793, d. 1875.

Gustavus I, King of Sweden (1523–1560), b. 1496, d. 1560.

Gustavus II, King of Sweden (1611–1632), b. 1594, killed in battle 1632.

Gustavus III, King of Sweden (1771–1792), b. 1746, assassinated 1792.

Gustavus IV, King of Sweden (1792–1809), b. 1778, d. 1837.

Gustavus V, King of Sweden (1907–1950), b. 1858, d. 1950.

Gustavus VI, King of Sweden (1950–) b. 1882.

Gutenberg, Johannes, German founder about 1440 of Western printing, b. about 1397, d. 1468.

Guthrie, Thomas, Scottish reformer, b. 1803, d. 1873.

Guy Fawkes Day : 5 Nov., commemorating the attempt on the Houses of Parliament by the English conspirator Guy Fawkes, b. 1570, executed 1606.

Guy's Hospital, London, founded 1722 by the English Thomas Guy, b. about 1644, d. 1724.

Guy de Lusignan, King of Jerusalem (1186–1192), d. 1194.

Guyon, Jeanne, French mystic, b. 1648, d. 1717.

Guyot, Arnold, Swiss geographer, b. 1807, d. 1884.

Guys, Constantin, French artist, b. 1802, d. 1892.

Gwinnett, Button, American patriot, b. 1735, d. 1777.

Gwyn, Nell, mistress of King Charles II, b. 1650, d. 1687.

Gypsies, known in Greece by 810, in Rumania 1370 ; reached Germany 1417, France and Italy 1418–1422, Spain and Portugal 1447, Poland and Russia 1501, Scotland 1505, Sweden 1512, England 1514.

Gyrocompass, invented 1915 by the American inventor Elmer Ambrose Sperry, b. 1860, d. 1930.

Gyroscope, invented 1852 by the French scientist Jean Bernard Léon Foucault, b. 1819, d. 1868.

H

H-Bomb, first exploded by the Americans in the Pacific 21 Nov. 1952 ; first Russian explosion (U.S.S.R.) 12 Aug. 1953.

Haakon I, the Good, King of Norway (935–961), killed in battle 961.

Haakon II, the Broadshouldered, King of Norway (1161–1162), b. 1047, d. 1162.

Haakon III, King of Norway (1202–1204).

Haakon IV, The Old, King of Norway (1217–1263), b. 1204, d. 1263.

Haakon V, King of Norway (1299–1319).

Haakon VI, King of Norway (1343–1380), b. 1340, d. 1386.

Haakon VII, King of Norway (1905–1957), b. 1872, d. 1957.

Habberton, John, American writer (*Helen's Babies*, 1876), b. 1842, d. 1921.

Habeas Corpus Act, principle stated in Magna Carta 1215, confirmed by Petition of Right 1627 ; became law in England 27 May 1679.

Haberdashers' Aske's Hampstead School, London, English public school, founded 1690 by bequest of Robert Aske.

Haberdashers' Company, London, origins uncertain ; bye-laws drawn up 1371 ; granted first Charter by Henry VI 1448.

Hackney Carriages, used at least as early as 1636 in London ; regularised by the Carriage Act 1831.

Haden, Sir Francis Seymour, English surgeon and etcher, b. 1818, d. 1910.

Hadow, Sir William Henry, English musicologist (*William Byrd*, 1923), b. 1859, d. 1937.

Hadrian, Roman Emperor (117–138), b. 76, d. 138.

Hadrian's Wall, Roman wall across northern England, built under the Governorship of Aulus Platorius Nepos, 122–126.

Haeckel, Ernst Heinrich, German naturalist, b. 1834, d. 1919.

Hafiz (Shams ad-Din Mohammed), Persian poet, b. about 1320, d. about 1389.

Hafnium, a metal, first isolated by the Norwegian scientist Dirk Coster and the Hungarian scientist Georg von Hevesy 1922.

Hagedorn, Friedrich von, German poet, b. 1708, d. 1754.

Haggard, Sir Rider, English novelist (*King Solomon's Mines*, 1885), b. 1856, d. 1925.

Hahn, Otto, German nuclear physicist, b. 1879.

Hahn, Reynaldo, Venezuelan composer (*Concerto provençal*, 1930), b. 1875, d. 1947.

Haidar Ali, Indian leader, b. about 1728, d. 1782.

Haig, Douglas, Earl Haig, Field-Marshal, b. 1861, d. 1928.

Haile Selassie (Ras Tafari), Emperor of Ethiopia from 1930 (King 1928–1930 ; in exile 1936–1941), b. 1892.

Haileybury and Imperial Service College, Hertford, English public school formed 1942 by the union of Haileybury College (founded 1862) and Imperial Service College (founded 1912).

Haiti, discovered by Christopher Columbus 6 Dec. 1492 ; ruled by French 1697–1792 independence proclaimed 1803 ; ruled by U.S.A. 1915–1934.

Hakluyt, Richard, English historian (*Voyages*, 1598–1600), b. about 1552, d. 1616.

Haldane, John Burdon Sanderson, British scientist, b. 1892.

Haldane, John Scott, Scottish physiologist, b. 1860, d. 1936.

Haldane, Richard Burdon, Viscount Haldane of Cloan, British statesman and reformer, b. 1856, d. 1928.

Hale, Edward Everett, American storyteller (*The Man Without a Country*, 1863), poet and Unitarian minister, b. 1822, d. 1909.

Hale, Sir Matthew, English jurist and writer, b. 1609, d. 1676.

Hale, Nathan, American patriot, b. 1755, hanged 1776.

Halévy, Jacques François Fromental Élie, French composer (*La Juive*, 1835), b. 1799, d. 1862.

Halfpenny Postage, introduced in Britain 1 Oct. 1870.

Halftone Engraving, first practical process invented 1878 by the American pioneer in photography Frederick Eugene Ives, b. 1856, d. 1937.

Halifax, Earl of, Viceroy and Governor-General of India (1926–1931), b. 1881, d. 1959.

Halifax, Charles Montagu, Earl of, British statesman and writer, b. 1661, d. 1715.

Halifax, Nova Scotia, founded 1749.

Hall, Sir Edward Marshall, English lawyer, b. 1858, d. 1929.

Hall, Joseph, English theologian and writer, b. 1574, d. 1656.

Hall, Marshall, English physiologist, b. 1790, d. 1857.

Hall of Fame, New York, U.S. national shrine, established 1900.

Hall's Effect, electromagnetism, discovered 1879 by the American scientist Edwin Herbert Hall, b. 1853, d. 1921.

Hallam, Henry, English historian, b. 1777, d. 1859.

Halle, Adam de la, French troubadour, b. about 1240, d. 1287.

Hallé Orchestra, Manchester, established 1857 by Sir Charles Hallé, b. 1819, d. 1895. First regular public concert 30 Jan. 1858.

Halley, Edmond, English astronomer, b. 1656, d. 1742.

Halley's Comet, named after Edmund Halley ; appeared 1456, 1531, 1607, 1682, 1758, 1835, 1910. First photographed by astronomers 1910. Next appearance 1986.

Hallowe'en (All-Hallows Eve), celebrated 31 Oct.

Hals, Frans, Dutch painter (*Laughing Cavalier,* 1624), b. about 1580, d. 1666.

Hambourg, Mark, Russian-born pianist, b. 1879, d. 1960.

Hamburg-Amerika Line, founded 1847.

Hamilcar Barca, Carthaginian general, d. 228 B.C.

Hamilton, Alexander, American statesman, b. 1757, killed in a duel 1804.

Hamilton, Emma, Lady, mistress of Lord Nelson, b. about 1765, d. 1815.

Hamilton, Patrick, Scottish martyr, b. about 1504, burnt at the stake 1528.

Hamilton, Sir Robert, Governor of Tasmania (1886–1893), b. 1836, d. 1895.

Hamilton, Sir William, diplomat and archæologist (purchaser of the Portland Vase), b. 1730, d. 1803.

Hamlet, Story of, in existence in 12th century.

Hammarskjöld, Dag, Swedish-born Secretary-General of the United Nations (1953–   ), b. 1905.

Hammer Action, in modern pianos, invented about 1710 by the Italian harpsichord-maker Bartolommeo Cristofori, b. 1655, d. 1731.

Hammerstein, Oscar, American impresario, b. 1848, d. 1919.

Hammett, Dashiel, American detective story writer (*Red Harvest,* 1929), b. 1894.

Hammond, Joan, Australian operatic singer, b. 1912.

Hammond, John, English social historian, b. 1872, d. 1949.

Hammurabi, King of Babylonia, reigned in the 21st century B.C.

Hampden, John, English parliamentarian, refused 1636–1637 to pay ship-money ; b. about 1594, killed in battle 1643.

Hampton Court, Treaty of, alliance between Queen Elizabeth I and the Prince de Condé, signed 21 Sept. 1562.

Hampton Court Conference, of English clergy, held 1604.

Hamsun, Knut, Norwegian writer (*Hunger*, 1888), b. 1859, d. 1952.

Han Dynasty, China, 206 B.C. to 220 A.D.

Handel, George Frideric, German-born composer (*The Messiah*, 1742), b. 1685, d. 1759.

Hannibal, Carthaginian general, b. 247, invaded Italy 218–203, committed suicide about 182 B.C.

Hannington, James, first Bishop of Eastern Equatorial Africa, b. 1847, murdered 1885.

Hanno, Carthaginian navigator, explored W. African coast about 450 B.C.

Hansard, record of parliamentary debates, begun 1774 by Luke Hansard, b. 1752, d. 1828 ; present series founded 1803 by William Cobbett, b. 1763, d. 1835.

Hanseatic League, N. German and Baltic commercial alliance, origins about 1140 ; formal alliance 1241 ; last meeting 1669.

Hansen, Gerhard, Norwegian scientist, b. 1841, d. 1912.

Hansom Cab, idea patented 1834 by the English architect Joseph Aloysius Hansom, b. 1803, d. 1882.

Hapsburg Dynasty, ruled Austria 1278–1918, Netherlands 1482–1700 (and Belgium 1713–1794), Spain 1516–1700, Bohemia 1526–1918.

Hara-kiri, Japanese obligatory suicide, abolished officially 1868.

Harald I, Haarfager, King of Norway (860–933), b. 850, d. 933.

Harald II, Graafeld, King of Norway (961–969), murdered 969.

Harald III, Haardraade, King of Norway (1048–1066), killed in battle 1066.

Harald IV, Gylle, King of Norway (1134–1136), murdered 1136.

Harcourt, Sir William, British statesman, b. 1827, d. 1904.

Harde Canute, King of England (1040–1042), b. about 1019, d. 1042.

Hardie, James Keir, Scottish socialist leader, b. 1856, d. 1915.

Harding, Warren Gamaliel, U.S. President (1921–1923), b. 1865, d. 1923.

Harding, St Stephen, d. 1134.

Hardinge, Henry, Viscount Hardinge, statesman and soldier, b. 1785, d. 1856.

Hardwicke, Sir Cedric, English actor, b. 1893.

Hardwicke, Philip Yorke, Earl of Lord Chancellor, b. 1690, d. 1764.

Hardy, Thomas, English writer (*Tess of the D'Urbevilles*, 1891), b. 1840, d. 1928.

Hardye's School, Dorchester, English public school, refounded 1569 by Thomas Hardye.

Hare, Augustus, English writer (*The Story of My Life*, 1896–1900), b. 1834, d. 1903.

Hare, William, Irish murderer in the Burke and Hare case, d. about 1865.

Harewood, Henry George Charles Lascelles, Earl of, diplomat and soldier, b. 1882, d. 1947.

Harewood, George Henry Hubert Lascelles, Earl of, b. 1923.

Hargreaves' Spinning Jenny, invented about 1764 by the English weaver James Hargreaves, d. 1778.

Harington, Sir John, English writer (*Metamorphosis of Ajax*, 1596), b. 1561, d. 1612.

Harleian Library, British Museum, formed by Robert Harley, Earl of Oxford, b. 1661, d. 1724.

Harley, Robert, Earl of Oxford, English statesman and book-collector, b. 1661, d. 1724.

Harmonium, invented 1840 by the French organ manufacturer Alexandre François Debain, b. 1809, d. 1877.

Harold, King of the English (1066), b. about 1022, killed in battle 1066.

Harold Harefoot, King of the English (1037–1040), d. 1040.

Haroun-al-Rashid, Abbasid, caliph, b. about 763, d. 809.

Harper's Ferry, Virginia, captured by John Brown, 16 Oct. 1859.

Harpignies, Henri, French painter (*View of Capri*), b. 1819, d. 1916.

Harris, Frank, Irish-born writer (*My Life and Loves*, 1923–1927), b. 1856, d. 1931.

Harris, Joel Chandler, American writer (*Uncle Remus*, 1880), b. 1848, d. 1908.

Harris, Thomas Lake, British-born founder of the Brotherhood of the New Life, b. 1823, d. 1906.

Harrison, Benjamin, U.S. President (1889–1893), b. 1833, d. 1901.

Harrison, William Henry, U.S. President (1841), b. 1773, d. 1841.

Harrison, William, English topographer (*Description of England*, 1577), b. 1534, d. 1593.

Harrow School, English public school, founded 1572 by the yeoman John Lyon, b. about 1514, d. 1592.

Hart, Lorenz, American song-writer (*With a Song in My Heart*), b. 1895.

Harte, Bret, American writer (*The Luck of Roaring Camp*, 1870), b. 1839, d. 1902.

Hartley, Arthur Clifford, British inventor of ' Pluto ' and ' Fido ', b. 1889, d. 1960.

Hartley, Leslie Poles, English writer (*The Shrimp and the Anemone*), b. 1895.

Hartmann von Aue, German minnesinger, b. about 1168, d. about 1217.

Harty, Sir Hamilton, English conductor, b. 1879, d. 1941.

Harun-al-Rashid, Caliph, b. about 763, d. 809.

Harunobu, Suzuki, Japanese artist (*The Broken Shoestring*), b. about 1720, d. about 1770.

Harvard University, founded 1636 ; named after the Puritan minister John Harvard, b. 1607, d. 1638.

Harvard University Observatory, built 1843–1847.

Harvest Moon, the full moon within a fortnight of 22 or 23 Sept.

Harvester, Mechanical, invented 1831 by the American manufacturer Cyrus Hall McCormick, b. 1809, d. 1884.

Harvey, Gabriel, English poet, b. about 1545, d. 1630.

Harvey, Thomas, Quaker relief worker and theologian, b. 1812, d. 1884.

Harvey, William, English discoverer of the circulation of the blood (*De Motu Cordis*, 1628), b. 1578, d. 1657.

Hasdrubal, Carthaginian general (brother of Hannibal), killed in battle 207 B.C.

Hastings, Warren, first English Governor-General of Bengal (1774–1785), tried (1788–1794), b. 1732, d. 1818.

Hastings, Battle of, fought at Battle between the Normans and the English 14 Oct. 1066.

Hathaway, Anne, wife of William Shakespeare, b. about 1556, d. 1623.

Hatton, Sir Christopher, Lord Chancellor, b. 1540, d. 1591.

Hauptmann, Gerhart, German playwright (*Rose Bernd*, 1903), b. 1862, d. 1946.

Haussmann, Georges Eugène, Baron, French town planner, b. 1809, d. 1891.

Havas Agency, French press agency, founded 1835 by the Frenchman Charles Havas, d. 1850.

Havelock the Dane, early 14th century Anglo-Danish epic.

Havelock, Sir Henry, General in India, b. 1795, d. 1857.

Haverford West Grammar School, Welsh public school, founded before 1488.

Hawaii, Pacific, discovered 1778 by Captain James Cook ; formally annexed by the U.S.A. 1898 ; admitted to the Union 1959.

Hawes, Stephen, English poet (*Passetyme of Pleasure*, 1509), d. about 1523.

Hawker, Robert Stephen, English poet (' And shall Trelawny die ? '), b. 1803, d. 1875.

Hawkins, Sir John, English naval reformer and slave-trader, b. 1532, d. 1595.

Hawkins, Sir Richard, English admiral, b. about 1562, d. 1622.

Hawksmoor, Nicholas, English architect, b. 1661, d. 1736.

Hawthorne, Nathaniel, American writer (*The Scarlet Letter*, 1850), b. 1804, d. 1864.

Haydn, Franz Josef, Austrian composer (*The Creation*, 1798), b. 1732, d. 1809.

Haydn, Joseph, English compiler of the *Dictionary of Dates* (1841), d. 1856.

Haydon, Benjamin Robert, English painter (*Lazarus*), b. 1786, committed suicide 1846.

Hayes, Rutherford Birchard, U.S. President (1877–1881), b. 1822, d. 1893.

Hays, William Harrison, American film administrator, b. 1879, d. 1954.

Hazlitt, William, English essayist (*Table Talk*, 1821), b. 1778, d. 1830.

Healy, Timothy Michael, Irish Free State Governor-General (1922–1928), b. 1855, d. 1931.

Heaphy, Charles, explorer in New Zealand and New Zealand's first (1867) V.C., b. 1820, d. 1881.

Hearn, Lafcadio, naturalised Japanese writer (*Japan*, 1904), b. 1850, d. 1904.

Hearst, William Randolph, American newspaper publisher, b. 1863, d. 1951.

Heart, Surgery of, pioneered by Rehn of Frankfurt in 1896.

Heat, Latent, existence established about 1765 by the British scientist Joseph Black, b 1728, d. 1799 ; Dynamical theory of, suggested by experiments of Count Rumford at Munich in 1798, and postulated 1841 by James Joule, b. 1818, d. 1889.

Heath, Neville, English murderer, b. 1917, hanged 1946.

Heavier-than-Air Machine, First flight by, made by the American brothers Orville and Wilbur Wright 17 Dec. 1903.

Heaviside, Oliver, English scientist, b. 1850, d. 1925.

Heavy Hydrogen (Deuterium), discovered 1931 by the American chemist Harold Clayton Urey, b. 1893.

Heavy Oil Engine, first used in Britain, invented by William Priestman 1885.

Heavy Water, discovered 1931 by the American chemist Harold Clayton Urey, b. 1893.

Hebbel, Friedrich, German writer (*Agnes Bernauer*, 1852), b. 1813, d. 1863.

Heber, Reginald, English hymn-writer (' From Greenland's icy mountains '), b. 1783, d. 1826.

Hebert, Jacques René, French revolutionary leader, b. 1757, guillotined 1794.

Hectograph, duplicating process, invented 1780 by the Scottish engineer James Watt, b. 1736, d. 1819.

Hedin, Sven, Swedish explorer, b. 1865, d. 1952.

Hegel, Georg Wilhelm Friedrich, German philosopher, b. 1770, d. 1831.

Hegira, Mahomet's flight from Mecca to Medina, 13 Sept. 622.

Heidegger, Martin, German philosopher, b. 1889.

Heidelberg Catechism, instigated by the Elector Frederick III ; published 19 Jan. 1563 by Zacharias Ursinus, b. 1536, d. 1583, and Caspar Olevianus, b. 1536, d. 1587.

Heidelberg University, Germany, founded 1385.

Heifetz, Jascha, Russian-born violinist, b. 1901.

Heine, Heinrich, German poet (*Atta Troll*, 1843), b. 1797, d. 1856.

Heinsius, Daniel, Dutch classical scholar, b. 1580, d. 1655.

Hejaz, proclaimed independent kingdom 1916 ; conquered by and annexed to the Kingdom of Saudi Arabia 1925–1926.

Helena, St, b. about 248, d. about 328.

Helena, St, South Atlantic, discovered by the Portuguese navigator João de Nova 1502 ; appropriated by the British East India Company 1661 ; vested in the Crown 1833.

Helicopter, first successful model built 1918 by the Americans Peter Cooper Hewitt, b. 1861, d. 1921, and F. B. Crocker.

Heliogabalus (Elagabalus), Roman Emperor (218–222), b. about 204, assassinated 222.

Heliograph, invented by the German mathematician and astronomer Johann Karl Friedrich Gauss, b. 1777, d. 1855.

Heliometer, modern form invented 1754 by the English optician John Dollond, b. 1706, d. 1761.

Helioscope, instrument for observing the sun, invented by the American engineer Herschel Clifford Parker, b. 1867.

Heliport, Britain's first, opened in London 23 Apr. 1959.

Helium, discovered spectroscopically in sun 1868 by Sir Joseph Norman Lockyer, b. 1836, d. 1920 ; obtained 1895 by Sir William Ramsay, b. 1852, d. 1916.

Helium, Liquid, obtained 1913 by the Dutch scientist Heike Kamerlingh Onnes, b. 1853, d. 1926.

Hellgate Bridge, New York, built 1902–1903 by Austrian-born engineer Gustav Lindenthal, b. 1850, d. 1935.

Helmholtz, Hermann von, German scientist, b. 1821, d. 1894.

Helsinki, capital of Finland since 1812.

Helvetius, Claude Adrien, French writer (*De l'Esprit*, 1758), b. 1715, d. 1771.

Hemans, Mrs Felicia Dorothea, English hymn-writer and poet (*Casabianca*, 1829), b. 1793, d. 1835.

Hematin, artificial blood pigment, discovered 1928 by the German scientist Hans Fischer, b. 1881, d. 1945.

Heming, John, English actor-manager, d. 1630.

Hemingway, Ernest, American writer (*A Farewell to Arms*, 1929), b. 1898, d. 1961.

Hémon, Louis, French-Canadian novelist (*Marie Chapdelaine*, 1913), b. 1880, d. 1913.

Henderson, Alexander, Scottish religious leader, b. about 1583, d. 1646.

Henderson, Arthur, British statesman, b. 1863, d. 1935.

Henley, William Ernest, English poet (*For England's Sake*, 1900), b. 1849, d. 1903.

Henley Regatta, Henley-on-Thames, founded 1839.

Henri I, King of France (1031–1060), b. about 1008, d. 1060.

Henri II, King of France (1547–1559), b. 1519, d. 1559.

Henri III, King of France (1574–1589), b. 1551, assassinated 1589.

Henri IV, King of France (1589–1610), b. 1553, assassinated 1610.

Henri V ' (Henri, Comte de Chambord), claimant to the French throne, b. 1820, d. 1883.

Henrietta, daughter of King Charles I, 2nd Duchess of Orleans, b. 1644, d. 1670.

Henrietta Maria, wife of King Charles I, b. 1609, d. 1669.

Henry I, King of England (1100–1135), b. 1068, d. 1135.

Henry II, King of England (1154–1189), b. 1133, d. 1189.

Henry III, King of England (1216–1272), b. 1207, d. 1272.

Henry IV, King of England (1399–1413), b. 1367, d. 1413.

Henry V, King of England (1413–1422), b. 1387, d. 1422.

Henry VI, King of England (1422–1461, 1470–1471), b. 1421, murdered 1471.

Henry VII, King of England (1485–1509), b. 1457, d. 1509.

Henry VIII, King of England (1509–1547), b. 1491, d. 1547.

Henry II, Holy Roman Emperor (1002–1024), b. 973, d. 1024.

Henry III, Holy Roman Emperor (1039–1056), b. 1017, d. 1056.

Henry IV, Holy Roman Emperor (1056–1106), b. 1050, d. 1106.

Henry V, Holy Roman Emperor (1106–1125), b. 1081, d. 1125.

Henry VI, Holy Roman Emperor (1190–1197), b. 1165, d. 1197.

Henry VII, Holy Roman Emperor (1308–1313), b. 1269, d. 1313.

Henry the Fowler, German King (919–936), b. about 875, d. 936.

Henry the Navigator, Portuguese Prince, b. 1394, d. 1460.

Henry Christophe, King of Haiti, b. 1767, committed suicide 1820.

' Henry, O ' (William Sydney Porter), American writer (*Cabbages and Kings*, 1904), b. 1862, d. 1910.

Henry, Patrick, Governor of Virginia, b. 1736, d. 1799.

Henry, William, English chemist, b. 1774, d. 1836.

Henryson, Robert, Scottish poet (*Testament of Cresseid*), b. about 1430, d. about 1506.

Henschel, Sir George, German-born composer and conductor, b. 1850, d. 1934.

Henslowe, Philip, English theatre manager, d. 1616.

Henty, George Alfred, English writer for boys, b. 1832, d. 1902.

Hepplewhite, George, English cabinet-maker, d. 1786.

Hepworth, Barbara, English sculptor, b. 1903.

Heraclitus, Greek philosopher, b. about 540, d. 475 B.C.

Heraclius, Byzantine Emperor (610–641), b. about 575, d. 641.

Heralds College, London, founded 1461 by King Edward IV. Chartered 1483.

Herbart, Johann Friedrich, German philosopher, b. 1776, d. 1841.

Herbert, George, Welsh-born poet (*The Temple*, 1633), b. 1593, d. 1633.

Herbert, Victor, American composer (*Princess Pat*, 1915), b. 1859, d. 1924.

Herbert of Cherbury, Edward Herbert, Baron, English philosopher and historian, b. 1583, d. 1648.

Herder, Johann Gottfried, German writer (*Der Cid*, 1805), b. 1744, d. 1803.

Heredia, José Maria de, Cuba-born poet (*Les Trophées*, 1893), b. 1842, d. 1905.

Heredity, principles of, postulated 1865 by the Austrian biologist and monk Gregor Johann Mendel, b. 1822, d. 1884.

Hereford Cathedral, England, constructed 1079–1148 (crypt Anglo-Saxon).

Hereford Cathedral School, English public school, founded before 1381 ; reconstituted 1894.

Hereward the Wake, English outlaw, lived in second half of 11th century.

Herford, William Henry, British educational reformer, b. 1820, d. 1908.

Hergesheimer, Joseph, American novelist (*Java Head*, 1919), b. 1880, d. 1954.

Heriot, George, Scottish goldsmith and royal banker, b. 1563, d. 1624.

Herkomer, Sir Hubert von, German-born painter, b. 1849, d. 1914.

Hero of Alexandria, Greek mathematician in 1st century.

Herod Agrippa, Tetrarch of Galilee and Peræa, later of Judea and Samaria, b. 10 B.C., d. A.D. 44.

Herod Antipas, Tetrarch of Galilee and Peræa, d. about 39.

Herod the Great, King of Judea, b. about 68, d. 4 B.C.

Herodotus, Greek historian, b. about 485, d. about 425 B.C.

Hérold, Louis Joseph Ferdinand, French composer (*Zampa*, 1831), b. 1791, d. 1833.

Herrara, Ferdinando, Spanish poet, b. about 1534, d. 1597.

Herrick, Robert, English poet (*Hesperides*, 1648), b. 1591, d. 1674.

Herrings, Battle of the (Battle of Rouvray), between the English and the French, 1429.

Herriot, Edouard, French statesman, b. 1872, d. 1957.

Herschel, Sir John Frederick William, English astronomer, b. 1792, d. 1871.

Herschel, Sir William, German-born astronomer, b. 1738, d. 1822.

Hertford College, Oxford University, founded as Hertford Hall 1282 by Elias de Hertford ; incorporated as Hertford College 1740 ; reincorporated 1874.

Hertslet, Lewis, English compiler of collections of treaties, b. 1787, d. 1870.

Hertzog, James Barry Munnik, South African statesman, b. 1866, d. 1942.

Herzen, Aleksandr, Russian revolutionary leader, b. 1812, d. 1870.

Herzl, Theodor, Hungarian-born founder of Zionism (*Der Judenstaat*, 1896), b. 1860, d. 1904.

Heseltine, Philip ('Peter Warlock'), English composer (*Capriol Suite*, 1926), b. 1894, committed suicide 1930.

Hesiod, Greek poet of the 8th century B.C.

Hesperia, an asteroid, discovered 1861 by the Italian astronomer Giovanni Virginio Schiaparelli, b. 1835, d. 1910.

Hess, Dame Myra, English pianist, b. 1890.

Hess, Rudolf, German Nazi leader, b. 1894, flew to Britain 1941.

Hesse, Hermann, German writer (*Peter Camenzind*, 1904), b. 1877.

Hesychasts, Greek mystic movement in 14th century.

Hetton (Co. Durham) **Line,** oldest mineral railway in Britain and first real railway on a prepared surface, built 1819–1822 by George Stephenson, b. 1781, d. 1848, opened 1822, closed 1959.

Heuristic Method, of education, suggested 1884 by Professor Meiklejohn.

Heuss, Dr Theodor, President (1949–1959) of West Germany, b. 1884.

Hevelius, Johannes, Polish astronomer, b. 1611, d. 1687.

Hewlett, Maurice, English writer (*The Forest Lovers*, 1897), b. 1861, d. 1923.

Heyward, Dubose, American writer (*Porgy*, 1925), b. 1885, d. 1940.

Heywood, John, English writer (*The Four P's*, 1569), b. about 1497, d. about 1580.

Heywood, Thomas, English writer (*A Woman Killed with Kindness*), b. about 1574, d. 1641.

Hibbert Trust, originally for the elevation of the Unitarian ministry, founded 1847 by the British merchant Robert Hibbert, b. 1770, d. 1849.

'**Hickok,** Wild Bill' (James Butler Hickok), American pioneer, b. 1837, murdered 1876.

Hiero I, King of Syracuse (478–467 B.C.), d. 467 B.C.

Hiero II, King of Syracuse (270–215 B.C.), d. 215 B.C.

Higden, Ranulf, English historian (*Polychronicon*), d. 1364.

High Pressure Steam, pioneered 1800 by the English engineer Richard Trevithick, b. 1771, d. 1833.

Highgate School, English public school, founded 1565 by Roger Cholmley, d. 1565.

Hilarius, St, b. about 300, d. 367.

Hilary, St, Pope, 461–467, d. 467.

Hilary Term, legal term beginning 11 Jan., ending Wednesday before Easter.

Hilda, St, b. 614, d. 680.

Hildebert, French ecclesiastic and writer, b. about 1055, d. 1133.

Hildebrand, Adolf von, German sculptor, b. 1847, d. 1921.

Hildegard, St, b. 1098, d. 1179.

Hill, Octavia, English social reformer, b. 1838, d. 1912.

Hill, Sir Rowland, English pioneer in postal services, b. 1795, d. 1879.

Hilliard, Nicholas, English painter (particularly of miniatures), b. about 1547, d. 1619.

Himmler, Heinrich, German Nazi leader, b. 1900, committed suicide 1945.

Hindemith, Paul, German composer (*Mathis der Maler*, 1938), b. 1895.

Hindenburg, Paul von, German General and President (1925–1934), b. 1847, d. 1934.

Hinton, Dr William Augustus, first American negro to hold a professorship, Harvard University, b. 1884, d. 1959.

Hipparchus, Greek astronomer, b. about 160, d. about 125 B.C.

Hippocrates, Greek physician, b. about 460, d. about 370 B.C.

Hippolytus, Roman heretical leader in 3rd century.

Hire Purchase Holidays, started in England at Eastbourne 1960.

Hirohito, Emperor of Japan from 1926, b. 1901.

Hiroshige, Ando, Japanese artist, b. 1797, d. 1858.

Hiroshima, Japanese city, destroyed by an atom bomb 6 Aug. 1945.

Hirsch, Samson Raphael, German-Jewish scholar, b. 1808, d. 1888.

Hirsch Music Library, British Museum, founded by Paul Adolf Hirsch, b. 1881, d. 1951.

Hispanic and Luso-Brazilian Councils, London, incorporated 1943.

Hispanic Society of America, New York, founded 1904.

Hitchcock, Alfred, English-born film director, b. 1899.

Hitler, Adolf, German Nazi Leader : b. 1889 ; German Chancellor 1933 ; Reichsführer 1934 ; attempted assassination 1944 ; committed suicide 1945.

Hoadly, Benjamin, English theologian, b. 1676, d. 1761.

Hoban, James, Irish-born architect who designed the White House in Washington, b. about 1762, d. 1831.

Hobart, capital of Tasmania, founded 1804.

Hobbema, Meindert, Dutch painter (*The Water Mill*), b. 1638, d. 1709.

Hobbes, Thomas, English philosopher and historian (*The Leviathan*, 1651), b. 1588, d. 1679.

Hobhouse, Leonard Trelawney, English sociologist, b. 1864, d. 1929.

Hoccleve, Thomas, English poet (*De Regimine Principum*, 1411–1412), b. about 1369, d. about 1450.

Hoche, Lazare, French revolutionary general, b. 1768, d. 1797.

Hockey Association, present body formed 1886.

Hodgson, Ralph, English poet (*The Last Blackbird*, 1907), b. 1877.

Hodler, Ferdinand, Swiss artist, b. 1853, d. 1918.

Hodograph, curve demonstrating acceleration, invented by the astronomer Sir William Rowan Hamilton, b. 1805, d. 1865.

Hoe, Horse-drawn, invented 1731 by the English farmer Jethro Tull, b. 1674, d. 1741.

Hoe, Richard Marsh, American inventor (1846) of the rotary printing press, b. 1812, d. 1886.

Hoefnagel, Joris, Flemish artist, b. 1545, d. 1600.

Hofer, Andreas, Tyrolese patriot, b. 1767, executed 1810.

Hoffmann, Ernst Theodor Amadeus, German poet, b. 1776, d. 1822.

Hoffmann, Heinrich, German humorous writer (*Struwwelpeter*, 1847), b. 1809, d. 1894.

Hoffnung, Gerard, English caricaturist, musician and social reformer, b. 1925, d. 1959.

Hofmannsthal, Hugo von, Austrian poet (*Ariadne auf Naxos*, 1912), b. 1874, d. 1929.

Hofmeyr, Jan Hendrik, South African statesman, b. 1845, d. 1909.

Hogarth, David George, English archaeologist, b. 1862, d. 1927.

Hogarth, William, English painter (*Rake's Progress*, 1735), b. 1697, d. 1764.

Hogg, James, the Ettrick Shepherd, Scottish poet, b. 1770, d. 1835.

Hogg, Quintin, English founder (1882) of The (London) Polytechnic, b. 1845, d. 1903.

Hohenlinden, Battle of, Wars of the French Revolution, between the French and the Austrians 3 Dec. 1800.

Hohenstaufen Dynasty, Emperors of Germany 1138–1254.

Hohenzollern Dynasty, ruled Brandenburg 1411–1701, Prussia 1701–1871, Germany 1871–1918.

Hokusai, Japanese painter, b. 1760, d. 1849.

Holbach, Paul Heinrich Dietrich, Baron d', French philosopher (*Système de la Nature*, 1770), b. 1723, d. 1789.

Holbein, Hans, the elder, German painter, b. about 1465, d. 1524.

Holbein, Hans, the younger, German painter (*The Ambassadors*, 1533), b. 1497, d. 1543.

Holbrooke, Josef, English composer (*Queen Mab*, 1904), b. 1878, d. 1958.

Holcombe, Henry, English composer, b. about 1690, d. about 1750.

Holcroft, Thomas, English playwright *The Road to Ruin*, 1792), b. 1745, d. 1809.

Hölderlin, Johann Christian Friedrich, German poet, b. 1770, d. 1843.

Holgate, Robert, Archbishop of York (1545–1554), b. about 1481, d. 1555.

Holidays with Pay, enforced by law in Britain since 1938.

Holinshed, Raphael, English historian (*Chronicles*, 1578), d. about 1580.

Holl, Frank, English painter, b. 1845, d. 1888.

Holland, Henry, English architect (Battersea Bridge, 1771–1772), b. about 1746, d. 1806.

Holland, Henry Richard Vassal Fox, Baron, British statesman, b. 1773, d. 1840.

Holland, John, founder and first Governor (1695) of the Bank of Scotland, d. 1722.

Hollar, Wenceslaus, Bohemian artist, b. 1607, d. 1677.

Holles, Denzil, Baron, Puritan leader, b. 1599, d. 1680.

Hollywood, California, founded 1887 ; incorporated 1903.

Holman Hunt, William, English painter (*The Light of the World*, 1854), b. 1827, d. 1910.

Holmes, Oliver Wendell, American writer (*The Autocrat of the Breakfast-table*, 1831-1858), b. 1809, d. 1894.

Holmes, Oliver Wendell, U.S. Supreme Court judge, b. 1841, d. 1935.

Holmium, chemical element, discovered 1879 by Per Teodor Cleve.

Holocene Epoch, the time from about 8000 B.C. to the present day.

Holst, Gustav, English composer (*The Perfect Fool*, 1923), b. 1874, d. 1934.

Holstein, Friedrich von, German statesman, b. 1837, d. 1909.

Holy Alliance, made between the Emperors of Russia and Austria and the King of Prussia, 26 Sept. 1815.

Holy Island (Lindisfarne), England, chosen for the site of his church and monastery by St Aidan 635.

Holy Roman Empire, crown first held 800 by Charlemagne ; renounced by Francis II 1806.

Holy Spirit, dogma of procession from the Father *and the Son* (' Filioque ') added to Catholic doctrine 589.

Holy Thursday (Ascension Day), 40th day after Easter Sunday.

Holy Week, the week from Palm Sunday to Easter Saturday.

Holyoake, George Jacob, English pioneer in co-operation, b. 1817, d. 1906.

Holyoke, Samuel, American hymn-writer (*Arnheim*, 1778), b. 1762, d. 1820.

Holyrood Abbey, Scotland, founded by King David I 1128 ; Palace begun 1498.

Homberg, Willem, Dutch chemist, b 1652, d. 1715.

Home, John, Scottish playwright (*Douglas*, 1756), b. 1722, d. 1808.

Home Guard, founded May 1940 as L.D.V., adopted new name July 1940, disbanded Dec. 1945.

Home Office, Great Britain, founded by 1785.

Home Rule for Ireland League founded 1870 by Isaac Butt ; first Bill 1886, second Bill 1893, third Bill 1912–1914 ; Government of Ireland Bill 1919–1920.

Home Service, B.B.C., began 1 Sept. 1939.

Homer, Greek poet (*The Iliad* and *The Odyssey*), probably lived in the 10th century B.C.

Homer, Winslow, American painter, b. 1836, d. 1910.

Homoeopathic Physician, first to practice in England, Dr Frederic Hervey Foster Quin, b. 1799, d. 1878.

Homoeopathy, principles first enunciated 1796 by the German physician Samuel Hahnemann, b. 1755, d. 1843.

Homology, principle declared 1818 by the French naturalist Étienne St Hilaire.

Honduras, discovered by Christopher Columbus 1502 ; proclaimed independent sovereign state 1838.

Honduras, British, settled by the English about 1638 ; declared a British colony 1862 ; became an independent colony 1884.

Honegger, Arthur, Swiss composer (*King David*, 1921), b. 1892, d. 1955.

Hong Kong, ceded to Britain by China 1842 ; occupied by the Japanese 1941–1945.

Honorius I, Pope 625–638.

Honorius II (Pietro Cadalo), Anti-Pope 1061–1064, d. 1072.

Honorius II (Lamberto Scannabecchi), Pope 1124–1130, d. 1130.

Honorius III (Cencio Savelli), Pope 1216–1227, d. 1227.

Honorius IV (Giacomo Savelli), Pope 1285–1287, d. 1287.

Honourable Corps of Gentlemen at Arms, the Queen's personal bodyguard, founded 1559.

Honthorst, Gerard van, Dutch painter (*Christ before Pilate*), b. 1590, d. 1656.

Hooch, Pieter de, Dutch painter (*Scene in a Courtyard*), b. 1629, d. about 1685.

Hood, Samuel, Viscount Hood, admiral, b. 1724, d. 1816.

Hood, Thomas, English poet (*Eugene Aram's Dream*, 1829), b. 1799, d. 1845.

Hook, Theodore, English writer (*Maxwell*, 1830), b. 1788, d. 1841.

Hooke, Robert, English clockmaker and inventor of the anchor escapement, b. 1635, d. 1703.

Hooker, Richard, English theologian (*Ecclesiasticall Politie*, 1594–1648), b. about 1554, d. 1600.

Hooker, Sir William Jackson, English botanist, b. 1785, d. 1865.

Hooper, John, English religious reformer, burnt at the stake 1555.

Hoover, Herbert, U.S. President (1929–1933), b. 1874.

Hoover Moratorium, proposed by President Hoover in the U.S.A. 1931.

' Hope, Anthony ' (Sir Anthony Hope Hawkins), English novelist (*The Prisoner of Zenda*, 1894), b. 1863, d. 1933.

Hope, Thomas, English designer (*Household Furniture*, 1807), b. 1709, d. 1831.

Hopkins, Gerard Manley, English poet (*Poems*, 1918), b. 1844, d. 1889.

Hopkins, Johns, American merchant and philanthropist, b. 1795, d. 1873.

Hopkins, Stephen, Governor of Rhode Island, b. 1707, d. 1785.

Hopkinson, Joseph, American lawyer and writer 1798 of ' Hail, Columbia ', b. 1770, d. 1842.

Hoppner, John, English painter (*The Countess of Oxford*), b. 1758, d. 1810.

Horace, Latin poet (*Odes*, about 24 B.C.), b. 65, d. 8 B.C.

Hormisdas, St, Pope 514–523.

Hormones, internal secretions, discovered 1902–1903 by the English physiologists Sir William Bayliss, b. 1866, d. 1924, and Ernest Henry Starling, b. 1866, d. 1927.

Hornung, Ernest William, English author of the *Raffles* stories, b. 1866, d. 1921.

Horowitz, Vladimir, Russian-born pianist, b. 1904.

Horrocks, Jeremiah, English astronomer, b. about 1617, d. 1641.

Horsley, Samuel, English theologian, b. 1733, d. 1806.

Hortensius, Quintus, Roman orator, 114, d. 50 B.C.

Horthy of Nagybanya, Admiral Miklos, Regent of Hungary (1920–1944), b. 1868, d. 1957.

Hot-blast, in smelting process, invented 1825–1828 by the Scottish engineer James Beaumont Neilson, b. 1792, d. 1865.

Hot-Springs Conference, World War II, held 18 May–1 June 1943.

Hotchkiss Machine-gun, invented 1872 by the American Benjamin Berkeley Hotchkiss, b. 1826, d. 1885.

' Hotspur ' (Sir Henry Percy), b. 1364, killed in battle 1403.

' Houdini, Harry '** (Erich Weiss), Hungarian-born magician and conjurer, b. 1874, d. 1926.

Houdon, Jean Antoine, French sculptor (*Morpheus*, 1777), b. 1741, d. 1828.

House, Colonel Edward Mandell, American statesman, b. 1858, d. 1938.

House of Commons, Great Britain, origins in 13th century.

House of Lords, Great Britain, origins in 13th century.

House of Representatives, U.S. Congress, instituted 1787.

Housman, Alfred Edward, English poet (*A Shropshire Lad*, 1896), b. 1859, d. 1936.

Housman, Laurence, English writer (*Palace Plays*, 1930), b. 1865, d. 1959.

Houston, Samuel, first Texas President (1836–1844), b. 1793, d. 1863.

Hovercraft, started as a private venture 1953 by its English inventor Christopher S. Cockerell ; development and manufacture undertaken 1958.

Howard, Catherine, fifth wife of Henry VIII, b. 1521, m. 1540, beheaded 1542.

Howard, Sir Ebenezer, English garden-city pioneer, b. 1850, d. 1928.

Howard, Henry, Earl of Surrey, English politician and poet, b. 1517, beheaded 1547.

Howard, John, English prison reformer, b. 1726, d. 1790.

Howard, Sidney, American playwright (*Alien Corn*, 1933), b. 1891, d. 1939.

Howard League for Penal Reform, founded 1866.

Howe, Elias, American inventor 1846 of the sewing-machine, b. 1819, d. 1867.

Howe, Admiral Richard, of 'The Glorious First of June' 1794, b. 1726, d. 1799.

Howe, Samuel Gridley, American philanthropist, b. 1801, d. 1876.

Howell, James, Welsh writer (*Epistolae Ho-Elianae*, 1655), b. about 1594 d. 1666.

Howells, Herbert, English composer, b. 1892.

Howells, William Dean, American writer and editor, b. 1837, d. 1920.

Howrah Bridge, Calcutta, opened 1943.

Hoyle, Edmond, English whist expert, b. 1672, d. 1769.

Hsüan Tê Period, China, 1426–1435.

Huber, François, Swiss agriculturist, b. 1750, d. 1830.

Huber, Wolf, Tyrolese painter (*Abschied Christi*), b. about 1485, d. 1553.

Hubert, St, b. about 656, d. about 727.

Hubert de Burgh, Chief Justiciar of England, d. 1243.

Huc, Evariste Régis, French missionary to Tibet, b. 1813, d. 1860.

Huch, Ricarda, German writer (*Ludolf Urslev*, 1883), b. 1864, d. 1947.

Hudson, Henry, English navigator, d. about 1611.

Hudson, William Henry, Argentine-born naturalist (*Green Mansions*, 1904), b. 1841, d. 1922.

Hudson's Bay, discovered 1610 by the English navigator Henry Hudson, d. 1611.

Hudson's Bay Company, formed by Prince Rupert, chartered by King Charles II 1670.

Huggins, Godfrey, Viscount Malvern, Prime Minister (1953–1956) of the Federation of Rhodesia and Nyasaland, b. 1883.

Hughes, Thomas, English writer (*Tom Brown's Schooldays*, 1856), b. 1822, d. 1896.

Hugo, Victor, French writer (*Les Misérables*, 1862), b. 1802, d. 1885.

Huguenots, French Protestants, so called from the middle of 16th century.

Hugues Capet, King of France (987–996), b. about 938, d. 996.

Huli, Feast of, Indian custom similar to April Fools' Day, celebrated 31 Mar.

Hull, Cordell, American statesman, b. 1871, d. 1955.

Hulme Grammar School, Oldham, English public school, founded 1611 by James Assheton.

Hulme, Thomas Ernest, English writer (*Speculations*, 1924), b. 1883, d. 1917.

Human Experiment, First planned, to test an hypothesis based on observation, undertaken 1798 by the English physician Edward Jenner, b. 1749, d. 1823.

Human Rights, Declaration of, adopted by the United Nations General Assembly 10 Dec. 1948.

Humboldt, Alexander von, German naturalist and explorer, b. 1769, d. 1859.

Hume, David, Scottish philosopher (*Political Discourses*, 1752), b. 1711, d. 1776.

Humperdinck, Engelbert, German composer (*Hansel and Gretel*, 1893), b. 1854, d. 1921.

Hundred Days, The, Napoleon's return from Elba, 20 Mar. 1815 to 28 June 1815.

Hundred Years' War, The, between England and France, 1337–1453.

Hung Chih Period, China, 1488–1505.

Hung Wu Period, China, 1368–1398.

Hungary, traditionally conquered by Magyars 896 ; independent kingdom from 1001 ; Hapsburg rule 1526–1918 ; republic and Communist régime 1918–1919 ; Horthy's dictatorship 1920–1944 ; republic proclaimed 1946 ; Communist régime since 1949 ; revolution Oct.–Nov. 1956.

Huns, invaded Europe 363 ; defeated 454.

Hunt, Leigh, English essayist (*Imagination and Fancy*, 1844), b. 1784, d. 1859.

Hunt, William Holman, English painter (*The Light of the World*, 1854), b. 1827, d. 1910.

Hunt, Wilson Price, American explorer, b. about 1782, d. 1842.

Hunter, John, Scottish surgeon, b. 1728, d. 1793.

Hunter, William, Scottish anatomist, b. 1718, d. 1783.

Hunter, Sir William Wilson, Scottish administrator in India, b. 1840, d. 1900.

Hunters' Moon, the first full moon after the Harvest Moon.

Huntingdon, Selina Hastings, Countess of, founder of the Calvinist-Methodist ' Countess of Huntingdon's Connexion ', b. 1707, d. 1791.

Huntington, Henry Edwards, American railway promoter, b. 1850, d. 1927.

Huntley, Sir Henry Vere, British colonial administrator, b. 1795, d. 1864.

Hunyadi, János, Hungarian patriot, b. about 1387, d. 1456.

Hurricane, last fly-past over London commemorating the Battle of Britain, Sunday, 20 Sept. 1959.

Hurst, Fannie, American novelist (*Back Street*, 1931), b. 1889.

Hurstpierpoint College, Sussex, English public school, founded 1849 by Canon Nathaniel Woodard, b. 1811, d. 1891.

Hus, Jan, Bohemian religious reformer, b. about 1369, burnt at the stake 1415.

Huskisson, William, British statesman, b. 1770, d. 1830.

Hussein, King of Jordan, b. 1935.

Hussein ibn Ali, King of the Hejaz (1916–1924), b. 1856, d. 1931.

Husserl, Edmund, Austrian philosopher, b. 1859, d. 1938.

Hutcheson, Francis, Irish philosopher (*System of Moral Philosophy*, 1755), b. 1694, d. 1746.

Hutchinson, Anne, English-born religious leader, b. 1590, killed 1643.

Hutchinson, Thomas, Governor of Massachusetts Bay, b. 1711, d. 1780.

Hutton, James, Scottish pioneer in the study of geology, b. 1726, d. 1797.

Huxley, Aldous, English writer (*Point Counter Point*, 1928), b. 1894.

Huxley, Sir Julian, English biologist, b. 1887.

Huxley, Thomas Henry, English scientist and educationist (*Lay Sermons*, 1870), b. 1825, d. 1895.

Huygens, Christiaan, Dutch scientist, b. 1629, d. 1695.

Huysmans, Cornelis, Flemish painter, b. 1648, d. 1727.

Huysmans, Joris Karl, French novelist (*A Rebours*, 1884), b. 1848, d. 1907.

Huysum, Jan van, Dutch painter (particularly of flower-pieces), b. 1682, d. 1749.

Hyder Ali, Indian leader, b. about 1728, d. 1782.

Hyderabad, India, founded 1589 ; forcibly absorbed into India 1948.

Hydraulic Crane, invented about 1845 by William George Armstrong (later Baron Armstrong), b. 1810, d. 1900.

Hydraulic Press, invented 1796 by the English inventor Joseph Bramah, b. 1748, d. 1814.

Hydraulic Pressure Accumulator, invented 1850 by William George Armstrong (later Baron Armstrong), b. 1810, d. 1900.

Hydro-Electric Station, first example begun in Northern Ireland 1883.

Hydro-Electricity, discovered 1843 by the English scientist Michael Faraday, b. 1791, d. 1867.

Hydrogen, properties discovered 1776 by the British scientist Henry Cavendish, b. 1731, d. 1810.

Hydrogen Bomb, First American, exploded over Bikini Atoll 1 Mar. 1954.

Hydrogen Bomb, First Russian, exploded in the Pacific, 12 Aug. 1953.

Hydrogen Peroxide, obtained 1810 by the French chemist Louis Jacques Thénard, b. 1777, d. 1857.

Hydrophobia, effective vaccine treatment developed 1885 by the French scientist Louis Pasteur, b. 1822, d. 1895.

Hygiene, modern practice developed by the English physician Edmund Alexander Parkes, b. 1819, d. 1876.

Hyginus, St, Pope 136–140.

Hygrometer, invented 1783 by the Swiss scientist Horace Bénédict de Saussure, b. 1740, d. 1799.

Hymers College, Hull, English public school, founded 1889 in accordance with the wishes of the Rev. John Hymers, b. 1803, d. 1887.

Hyndman, Henry Mayers, English socialist leader, b. 1842, d. 1921.

Hypatia, Alexandrian scholar, murdered 415.

Hypnotism, term first introduced 1841, by the Scottish scholar James Braid, b. 1796, d. 1860.

Hyppolytus, St, Anti-Pope 217.

Hysterisis, Law of, discovered by the German-born engineer Charles Proteus Steinmetz, b. 1865, d. 1923.

I

I.C.A.O. (International Civil Aviation Organisation), Montreal, proposed at an international conference at Chicago 1944 ; came into being 1947.

Ibáñez, Vicente Blasco, Spanish novelist (*The Four Horsemen of the Apocalypse*), b. 1867, d. 1928.

Ibn Batuta, Arab traveller, b. 1304, d. 1378.

Ibn Khaldun, Arab historian (*Kitab al 'Ibar*), b. 1332, d. 1406.

Ibn Sa'ud, King of Saudi Arabia, b. about 1880, d. 1953.

Ibrahim Pasha, Viceroy of Egypt (1844), b. 1789, d. 1848.

Ibsen, Henrik, Norwegian dramatist (*Peer Gynt*, 1867), b. 1828, d. 1906.

Iceland, first settled 874 ; independent Republic 930-1262 ; ruled by Denmark 1381-1918 ; sovereign state 1918-1944 ; independent Republic since 1944.

Ichthyosaurus, first brought to scientific notice 1811 by the English fossil-collector Mary Anning, b. 1799, d. 1847.

Icknield Way, from Berkshire Down to the Fens, England, natural road of Celtic origin, first recorded mention 45.

Iconoclast Controversy, in Byzantine Empire, 726-843.

Idaho, U.S.A., first permanently settled 1860 ; organised as a Territory 1863 ; admitted to the Union 1890.

Identity Cards, introduced in Britain 1939 ; abolished 21 Feb. 1952.

Ido, revision of Esperanto, produced 1907 by Marquis de Beaufront.

Idrisi, Arab geographer, b. about 1099, d. about 1155.

Ifni, northern litteral of Africa, Spanish province administered from Madrid, ceded by Morocco to Spain 1860.

Ignatius of Antioch, St, lived in the 1st century.

Ignatius of Constantinople, St, b. about 800, d. about 878.

Ignatius Loyola, St, founder 1534 of the Society of Jesus, b. 1491, d. 1556.

Ikhnaton, Pharaoh of Egypt, d. about 1357 B.C.

Illinium, chemical element, discovered 1926 by the American scientist B. Smith Hopkins, b. 1873, d. 1952.

Illinois, U.S.A., discovered by the French 1673 ; settled 1720 ; ceded by France to Britain 1763 ; organised as a Territory 1809 ; admitted to the Union 1818.

Illinois University, Urbana, founded 1867.

Illium, alloy, discovered by the American chemist Samuel Wilson Parr, b. 1857, d. 1931.

Illuminati, German rationalist society founded 1776 by the German philosopher Adam Weishaupt (1748-1830) ; officially proscribed and dissolved 1785.

Illustrated London News, British periodical, began publication 1842.

Immaculate Conception, of the Virgin Mary, Catholic dogma defined 1854.

Imperial Defence College, London, for senior army, navy and air force officers, founded 1926.

Inauguration Day, U.S.A., on which American Presidents take the oath of office every four years ; 20 Jan.

Incandescent Electric Lamp, invented 1878 by Thomas Alva Edison (1847-1931) and Sir Joseph Wilson Swan (1828-1914).

Incandescent Gas Mantles, invented 1886 by the Austrian chemist Baron Auer von Welsbach, b. 1858, d. 1929.

Inchbald, Mrs Elizabeth, English actress and novelist, b. 1753, d. 1821.

Income Tax, introduced in Britain 1799.

Incunabula, books printed in Europe before the year 1500.

Independence Day, commemorating the Declaration of Independence, 4 July 1776 ; celebrated in the U.S.A. 4 July each year.

Independent Labour Party, founded 1893 by the Scottish socialist James Keir Hardie, b. 1856, d. 1915 ; seceded from Labour Party 1932 under James Maxton, b. 1885, d. 1946 ; ceased to have parliamentary representation 1948.

Index Vaticanus (*Index librorum prohibitorum*), the list of books condemned by the Catholic Church, first issued 1559.

India : Government of India transferred from East India Company to British Government 1858 ; Indian Empire proclaimed 1877 ; established as a Dominion 1947.

India Office Library, London, founded by the East India Company 1801.

India Rubber, discovered about 1740 by the French traveller Charles Marie de la Condamine, b. 1701, d. 1774.

Indian Mutiny, against the British, 1857–1858.

Indian National Congress, founded 1885 by Wedderburn and Hume.

Indian Post Office, established 24 July 1837.

Indiana, U.S.A., first settled 1732 ; organised as a Territory 1800 ; admitted to the Union 1816.

Indianapolis, Indiana, state capital, first settled 1819.

Indium, metallic element, discovered by the German scientists F. Reich and Th. Richter 1863.

Indo-China, occupied by French 1859–1885 ; Japanese occupation 1945.

Indo-European Language, existence postulated 1786 by Sir William Jones.

Indonesia, settled by the Portuguese about 1545 ; ruled by the Netherlands East India Company 1602–1798 ; governed by the Netherlands 1816–1949 ; independent republic since 1949.

Induction, principles discovered 1830 by the English scientist Michael Faraday, b. 1791, d. 1867.

Industrial Revolution, in Britain, occurred roughly 1760–1840 ; name first applied 1884 by Arnold Toynbee.

Industrial Workers of the World, Labour organisation, founded in U.S.A. in 1905.

d'Indy, Vincent, French composer (*Istar*, 1896), b. 1851, d. 1931.

Infallibility, of the Pope, Catholic dogma defined 1870.

Influenza, pandemics 1889–1890, 1918–1919.

Information, Ministry of, existed in Britain 1939–1946.

Inge, Dean Ralph, English writer and divine, b. 1880, d. 1945.

Inglis, James, Abbot of Culross, murdered 1531.

Ingoldsby, Thomas (Richard Harris Barham), English writer, b. 1788, d. 1845.

Ingres, Jean Auguste Dominique, French painter (*Apotheosis of Homer*), b. 1780, d. 1867.

Inkerman, Battle of, between the Russians and British in the Crimean War, 5 Nov. 1854.

Inman, Henry, American painter (*William Penn*), b. 1801, d. 1846.

Inness, George, American painter (*Georgia Pines*), b. 1825, d. 1894.

Innocent I, St, Pope 401–417, d. 417.

Innocent II (Gregorio Papareschi dei Guideni), Pope 1130–1143, d. 1143.

Innocent III (Lando da Sezza), Anti-Pope 1179–1180.

Innocent III (Lotario de' Conti di Segni), Pope 1198–1216, b. about 1160, d. 1216.

Innocent IV (Sinibaldo Fiesco), Pope 1243–1254, d. 1254.

Innocent V (Pierre de Champagni), Pope 1276, b. about 1225, d. 1276.

Innocent VI (Etienne Aubert), Pope 1352–1362, d. 1362.

Innocent VII (Cosimo dei Migliorati), Pope 1404–1406, b. 1339, d. 1406.

Innocent VIII (Giovanni Battista Cibo), Pope 1484–1492, b. 1432, d. 1492.

Innocent IX (Giovanni Antonio Fachinetti), Pope 1591, b. 1519, d. 1591.

Innocent X (Giovanni Battista Pamfili), Pope 1644–1655, b. 1574, d. 1655.

Innocent XI (Benedetto Odescalchi), Pope 1676–1689, b. 1611, d. 1689.

Innocent XII (Antonio Pignatelli), Pope 1691–1700, b. 1615, d. 1700.

Innocent XIII (Michele Angelo Conti), Pope 1721–1724, b. 1655, d. 1724.

Inoculation, for smallpox, introduced about 1718 into England from Constantinople by Lady Mary Wortley Montagu, b. 1689, d. 1762.

Inquisition, Holy office of the, founded 1231 ; Spanish Inquisition reorganised 1478, abolished 1820.

Institute of Contemporary Arts, London, founded 1948.

Institute of International Law, Ghent, founded 1873 by the Swiss jurist Johann Kaspar Bluntschli, b. 1808, d. 1881.

Insulin, isolated 1921 by the Canadian scientists Sir Frederick Grant Banting (1891–1941) and Charles Herbert Best, b. 1899.

Insurance, earliest recorded policy 1523 ; fire insurance pioneered 1666 by Nicolas Barbon ; earliest recorded life assurance bond 1228.

Intelligence Test, IQ scale devised by Binet and Simon in 1905 ; Stanford-Binet scale introduced 1916.

Interdict, Papal, on England 1208–1213.

Interferometry, study pioneered 1861 by the French physicist Armand Fizeau, b. 1819, d. 1896.

Internal Combustion Engine, first constructed 1860 by Lenoir.

International : *First* (' International Working Men's Association ', Marxist and Anarchist), 1864–1876 ; *Second* (Socialist), 1889–1914, revived 1918–1946 (as so-called ' 2½th International ') and again in 1948 (as ' Comisco ') ; *Third* (' Comintern ', Communist), 1919–1943, revived in 1947 (as ' Cominform ') ; *Fourth* (Trotskyist), formed in 1928.

International Atomic Energy Agency (I.A.E.A.), Vienna, established 1956.

International Broadcasting Union, formed 1925.

International Civil Aviation Organisation (I.C.A.O.), Montreal, proposed at an international conference at Chicago 1944 ; came into being 1947.

International Code of Signals, devised by the British Government 1857 ; amended 1901.

International Criminal Police Commission (Interpol), formed in Vienna 1923.

International Date Line, in Pacific Ocean, represented by the meridian of 180°, for the convenience of adjusting the loss or gain of one day ; established 1883.

International Institute of Agriculture Rome, set up 1905.

International Labour Organisation, Geneva, set up 1919.

International Monetary Fund, established 27 Dec. 1945.

International Postal Union, founded at Berne 9 Oct. 1875.

International Power Conference, first session held Wembley 30 June 1924.

International Red Cross, founded at Geneva 22 Aug. 1864.

International Statistical Congress, first convened 1853 at Brussels by the Belgian scientist Lambert Adolphe Jacques Quetelet, b. 1796, d. 1874.

International Telecommunication Union, founded 1865, reorganised 1947.

Intertype, printing machine invented in the U.S.A. 1912.

Invar, alloy discovered 1920 by the Swiss scientist Charles Edouard Guillaume, b. 1861, d. 1938.

Iodine, discovered 1811 in the ashes of seaweed by the French chemist Bernard Courtois, b. 1777, d. 1838.

Iona, home of St Columba from 563 A.D.

Iona Community, founded 1938 by the Rev. George Macleod, b. 1895.

Ionisation, theory developed 1887 by Swedish chemist Svante August Arrhenius, b. 1859, d. 1927.

Ionium, discovered 1907 by the American chemist Bertram Borden Boltwood, b. 1870, d. 1927.

Iowa, U.S.A., first settled 1788 ; organised as a Territory 1838 ; admitted to the Union 1846.

Ipswich School, English public school, founded before 1400 ; first Charter granted by Henry VIII ; status of independent school adopted 1945.

Iran, *see* **Persia.**

Iraq, conquered by British from Turkey 1914–1918 ; British mandate 1919–1921 ; Hashemite kingdom 1921–1958 ; military republic since 1958.

Iraq—Mediterranean Oil Pipeline, Kirkuk to Haifa, inaugurated 14 Jan. 1935.

Ireland, first invaded by Norsemen 795, by English 1167 ; Act of Union 1800 ; Easter Rising 1916 ; Irish Free State recognised 1921 (*see* **Eire**).

Ireland, John, English composer (*The Forgotten Rite,* 1915), b. 1879.

Ireland, William Henry, English literary forger, b. 1777, d. 1835.

Irenaeus, St, Bishop of Lyons, lived in the 2nd century.

Irene, Byzantine Empress (797–802), b. 752, d. 803.

Ireton, Henry, English Puritan leader, b. 1611, d. 1651.

Iriarte, Ignacio, Spanish painter, b. 1620, d. 1685.

Iridium, discovered 1804 by the English chemist Smithson Tennant, b. 1761, d. 1815.

Irish Free State, title of Southern Ireland 1922–1937.

Irish Land League, founded 1879 by Michael Davitt, b. 1846, d. 1906.

Irish Republican Army, formed 1919.

Irish Volunteers, first formed 1779 ; second formed 1913, and merged with I.R.A. in 1919.

Iron Bridge, first example constructed at Coalbrookdale 1773–1779.

'Iron Curtain' as term describing barrier between the U.S.S.R. and Western Europe, first popularised by Sir Winston Churchill 5 Mar. 1946 ; had been used earlier in the sense of protection by *Pravda* 11 Oct. 1939.

Ironclad Ships, First battle of, took place in the American Civil War between *Monitor* and *Merrimac* 9 Mar. 1862.

Ironmongers Company, London origins uncertain ; first recorded mention 1300 ; grant of arms 1455 ; Royal Charter 1463.

Irving, Sir Henry (John Henry Brodribb), English actor, b. 1838, d. 1905.

Irving, Washington, American writer (*Rip Van Winkle,* 1819), b. 1783, d. 1859.

Irvingites, Catholic Apostolic Church, founded 1829, by the Scottish preacher Edward Irving, b. 1792, d. 1834.

Isaac I, Byzantine Emperor (1057–1059), d. 1061.

Isaac II, Byzantine Emperor (1185–1195, 1203–1204), executed 1204.

Isabella, wife of the Emperor Frederick II, b. 1214, d. 1241.

Isabella of Angoulême, Queen of England, d. 1246.

Isabella, of France, Queen of England, b. 1292, d. 1358.

Isabella I, Queen of Castile and Leon, b. 1451, d. 1504.

Isabella II, Queen of Spain, b. 1830, d. 1904.

Isabey, Jean Baptiste, French painter (*The Empress Josephine*), b. 1767, d. 1855.

Isidore, St, Bishop of Seville (*Etymologies*), b. about 560, d. 636.

Islam, religious movement, founded about 610 by Mahomet, b. about 570, d. 632.

Ismail Pasha, Khedive of Egypt, b. 1830, d. 1895.

Ismailis, Muslim sect, formed in 8th century.

Isocrates, Greek orator, b. 436, d. 338 B.C.

Isomorphism, chemical relationship, principle defined 1820 by the German scientist Eilhard Mitscherlich, b. 1794, d. 1863.

Isotopes, theory developed 1912 by the English scientist Frederick Soddy (b. 1877) ; first identified 1910 by Sir Joseph John Thomson (1856–1940).

Israel, State of, proclaimed 14 May 1948.

Israels, Jozef, Dutch painter (*Toilers of the Sea*), b. 1824, d. 1911.

Isserlis, Julius, Bessarabian pianist, b. 1888.

Istanbul, founded (as Byzantium) 658 B.C. ; capital of Byzantine Empire (as Constantinople) 330–1453 ; of Ottoman Empire (as Istanbul) 1453–1923.

Isthmian Games, held in Ancient Greece, began 581 B.C.

Italian Language, earliest known document, the *Placito Capuano*, dated Mar. 960.

Italian Parliament, opened 18 Feb. 1861.

Italian Somaliland (Somalia), Italian protectorate 1899–1941 ; British military administration 1941–1949 ; U.N. trusteeship 1950–1960 ; granted independence 1960.

Italy, Kingdom 1861–1946 ; Fascist régime 1922–1943 ; democratic republic since 1946.

Ito, Prince Hirobumi, Japanese statesman and reformer, b. 1841, assassinated 1909.

Iturbi, José, Spanish pianist and conductor, b. 1895.

Iturbide, Agustin de, Emperor of Mexico (1822–1823), b. 1783, shot 1824.

Iturrigaray, Jose de, Spanish Viceroy of New Spain, b. 1742, d. 1815.

Ivan I, Grand Duke of Vladimir, d. 1341.

Ivan II, Grand Duke of Vladimir (1353–1359), b. 1326, d. 1359.

Ivan III, the Great, Grand Duke of Muscovy (1462–1505), b. 1440, d. 1505.

Ivan IV, the Terrible, Tsar of Muscovy (1547–1584), b. 1530, d. 1584.

Ivan V, Tsar of Russia (1682–1696), b. 1666, d. 1696.

Ivan VI, Emperor of Russia (1740–1741), b. 1740, murdered 1764.

Ives, St, b. 1253, d. 1303.

Ives, Burl, American singer, actor and collector of American folk-songs, b. 1909.

Ivo, St, Bishop of Chartres, b. about 1040, d. 1116.

Ivory Coast, West Africa, autonomous republic within the French Community since 1960.

J

' Jack of Tilbury ' (Sir John Arundell), b. 1495, d. 1561.

' Jack the Ripper ', perpetrator of series of unsolved murders of women in London 1888.

Jackson, Andrew, U.S. President (1829–1837), b. 1767, d. 1845.

Jackson, Sir Barry, English theatre manager and director, b. 1879, d. 1961.

Jackson, Frederick George, British Arctic explorer, b. 1860, d. 1938.

Jackson, ' Stonewall ' (Thomas Jonathan Jackson), American Confederate General, b. 1824, killed 1863.

Jacob, Sir Ian, Director-General of the BBC (1952–1959), b. 1899.

Jacobin Club, founded in France 1789. Movement ended 1794, but was revived during the 1848 Revolution.

Jacobites, supporters of James II and his descendants 1688–1760.

Jacobite Glass, manufactured mainly 1745–1765.

Jacobs, William Wymark English writer (*The Skipper's Wooing*, 1897), b. 1863, d. 1943.

Jacobus de Voragine, Italian writer (*The Golden Legend*), lived in the 13th century.

Jacopone da Todi, Italian poet (*Stabat Mater*), b. about 1240, d. 1306.

Jacquard Loom, first to weave patterns, invented 1801 by the French inventor Joseph Marie Jacquard, b. 1752, d. 1834.

Jacquerie, The, insurrection of French peasants, May 1358.

Jadassohn, Solomon, German composer, b. 1831, d. 1902.

Jadwiga, Polish Queen, b. about 1372, d. 1399.

Jaggard, William, English publisher of Shakespeare, b. about 1568. d. 1623.

Jagiellon Dynasty, Lithuanian dynasty, ruled Poland 1386–1572.

Jahangir, Mogul Emperor of India (1605–1627), b. 1569, d. 1627.

Jainism, Indian religious movement, had its beginnings in the 6th century B.C.

Jalal Ad-din Rumi, Mohammed, Persian mystical poet, b. 1207, d. 1273.

Jalalian (or Seljuk) Era, began 15 Mar. 1079.

Jamaica, Discovered by Christopher Columbus 1494 ; under Spanish rule until 1655 ; British annexation confirmed 1670 ; included in the British Caribbean Federation 1956.

Jamboree, World, of Boy Scouts, first held London 1920.

James I, King of Great Britain (1603–1625), b. 1566, d. 1625. Proclaimed King of Scotland 1567.

James II, King of Great Britain (1685–1688), b. 1633, d. 1701.

James, the Old Pretender (James Francis Edward Stewart), b. 1688, d. 1766.

James I, King of Scotland (1406–1437), b. 1394, assassinated 1437.

James II, King of Scotland (1437–1460), b. 1430, killed 1460.

James III, King of Scotland (1460–1488), b. 1451, assassinated 1488.

James IV, King of Scotland (1488–1513), b. 1473, killed in battle 1513.

James V, King of Scotland (1513–1542), b. 1512, d. 1542.

James VI, King of Scotland (1567–1603) see **James I,** King of Great Britain.

James, Henry, American theologian, b. 1811, d. 1882.

James, Henry, American-born novelist (*The Ambassadors,* 1903), b. 1843, d. 1916.

James, Jesse, American outlaw, b. 1847, killed 1882.

James, William, American philosopher and psychologist, b. 1842, d. 1910.

Jameson, Mrs Anna, Irish-born popular writer (*Legend of the Madonna,* 1852), b. 1794, d. 1860.

Jameson Raid, Transvaal, led 29 Dec. 1895 to 2 Jan. 1896 by the Scottish pioneer in South Africa Sir Leander Starr Jameson, b. 1853, d. 1917.

Jammes, Francis, French writer (*Le Roman du lièvre,* 1903), b. 1868, d. 1938.

Jan Mayen Island, Arctic, discovered 1607 by the English explorer Henry Hudson (d. about 1611) ; annexed by Norway 1929.

Janacek, Leos, Czech composer (*Jenufa,* 1902), b. 1854, d. 1928.

Jane, Queen (Lady Jane Grey), b. about 1537, proclaimed queen 1553, beheaded 1554.

Janin, Jules Gabriel, French writer (*L'Ane mort et la femme guillotiné,* 1829), b. 1804, d. 1874.

Janissaries, Turkish troops, first levied 1330, abolished 1826.

Jansen, Dr Ernest George, Governor-General of the Union of South Africa (1951–1959), b. 1881, d. 1959.

Jansenism, religious movement deriving from the posthumous publication 1640 of *Augustinus* by the Dutch theologian Cornelis Jansen, b. 1585, d. 1638.

Janssens Van Nuyssen, Abraham, Flemish painter (*Ecce Homo !*), b. about 1575, d. 1632.

Japan, empire for at least 2000 years ; Togukawa Shogunate 1600–1867 ; feudal system abolished 1867 ; American occupation 1945–1952 ; new Constitution granted 1947.

Jaques-Dalcroze, Emile, Swiss composer, b. 1865, d. 1950.

Jarry, Alfred, French writer (*Ubu Roi,* 1896), b. 1873, d. 1907.

Jarvis, John Wesley, English-born painter (*Alexander Anderson*), b. about 1781, d. 1839.

Jasper National Park, Canada, established 1907.

Jaurès, Jean Léon, French socialist leader, b. 1859, assassinated 1914.

Jay, John, American statesman, b. 1745, d. 1829.

Jazz, began to develop in New Orleans about 1893–1895 ; first so named 1910.

Jean de Meung, French writer of the second part of the *Roman de la rose,* d. about 1305.

Jeanne d'Albret, Queen of Navarre b. 1528, d. 1572.

Jeanne d'Arc, Ste, b. about 1412, burnt at the stake 1431.

Jeans, Sir James, English scientist (*The Stars in Their Courses*, 1931), b. 1877, d. 1946.

Jefferies, Richard, English writer (*The Story of My Heart*, 1883), b. 1848, d. 1887.

Jeffers, Robinson, American poet (*Flagons and Apples*, 1912), b. 1887.

Jefferson, Thomas, U.S. President (1801–1809), b. 1743, d. 1826.

Jeffreys, George, Baron, Judge of the ' Bloody Assizes ', b. 1648, d. 1689.

Jehovah's Witnesses, founded 1872 in Pennsylvania by Charles Taze Russell, b. 1852, d. 1916.

Jellicoe, Admiral John, Earl Jellicoe, Governor-General of New Zealand (1920–1924), b. 1859, d. 1935.

Jemison, Mrs Mary (' The White Woman of the Genesee '), b. 1743, d. 1833.

Jena, Battle of, between Napoleon and the Prussians, 14 Oct. 1806.

Jena University, Germany, founded 1558.

Jenghiz Khan (Temujin), Mongol ruler, b. 1162, d. 1227.

Jenkin's Ear, War of, between Britain and Spain, 1739 to 1741.

Jenner, Edward, English physician and discoverer 1796 of vaccination, b. 1749, d. 1823.

Jenson, Nicolas, French pioneer printer in Italy, d. about 1480.

Jenyns, Soame, English writer (*Free Enquiry into the Nature and Origin of Evil*, 1756), b. 1704, d. 1787.

Jerome, St (produced *Vulgate*, 382–405), b. about 340, d. 420.

Jerome of Prague, Czech religious reformer, b. about 1365, d. 1416.

Jerome, Jerome Klapka, English humorous writer (*Three Men in a Boat*, 1889), b. 1859, d. 1927.

Jerrold, Douglas, English writer (*Mrs Caudle's Curtain Lectures*, 1846), b. 1803, d. 1857.

Jerusalem, destroyed by Nebuchadnezzar 587–586 B.C. ; rebuilt 536–516 B.C. ; razed 168 B.C. by Antiochus Epiphanes ; destroyed A.D. 70 by Titus ; sacked by the Persians 615 ; captured by the Crusaders 1099 ; recovered by Saladin 1187 ; taken by the British 1918 ; divided between Jordan and Israel since 1949.

Jervis, John, Earl of St Vincent, Admiral of the Fleet, b. 1735, d. 1823.

Jesus of Nazareth, founder of Christianity, b. between 5 B.C. and A.D. 2, crucified between 30 and 33.

Jesus, Society of, founded 1534 by St Ignatius Loyola (1491–1556) ; dissolved 1773 by Pope Clement XIV ; re-established by Pope Pius VII 1814.

Jesus College, Cambridge University, founded 1496 by John Alcock, Bishop of Ely, b. 1430, d. 1500.

Jesus College, Oxford University, founded by Queen Elizabeth I 1571.

Jet Aircraft Engine, developed by Sir Frank Whittle (b. 1907), first ran on test-bed 1937.

Jewel, John, English divine and writer (*Apologia Ecclesiae Anglicanae*, 1562), b. 1522, d. 1571.

Jewett, Sarah Orne, American writer (*The Country of the Painted Firs*, 1896), b. 1849, d. 1909.

Jewish Calendar, calculated from 3761 B.C. ; fixed A.D. 358.

Jewish Diaspora, dispersal of the Jews, began with deportations by Assyrians 721 B.C.

Jewish Disabilities Removal Act, Great Britain, passed 1858.

Jewish Era, began 7 Oct. 3761 B.C.

Jewish Member of Parliament, First, Baron Lionel de Rothschild (1808–1879), took his seat in the House of Commons 26 July 1858.

Jews, expelled from England 1290, from Spain 1492, from Portugal 1497 ; emancipated in France 1790, in Russia 1917.

Jex-Blake, Sophia Louisa, English physician, mathematician and champion of women's right, b. 1840, d. 1912.

Jimenes de Cisneros, Francisco, Spanish divine and statesman, b. 1436, d. 1517.

Jinnah, Mohammed Ali, Indian Muslim leader and founder of Pakistan, b. 1876, d. 1948.

Joachim, Joseph, Bohemian violinist, b. 1831, d. 1907.

Joan of Arc, St, born about 1412, burnt at the stake 30 May 1431 ; canonised 1920.

Joan, Fair Maid of Kent, wife of the Black Prince, b. 1328, d. 1385.

Joan, Pope, mythical female Pope, about 855–858.

Joanna I, Queen of Naples (1343–1382), b. about 1327, executed 1382.

Joanna II, Queen of Naples (1414–1435), b. 1371, d. 1435.

Jocelin de Brakelond, English historian, lived at the end of the 12th and the beginning of the 13th centuries.

Jodelle, Etienne, French playwright (*Cléopatre captive,* 1552), b. 1532, d. 1573.

Jodrell Bank Radio Telescope, largest in the world, completed 1958.

Joffre, Joseph Jacques Césaire, French soldier, b. 1852, d. 1931.

Johannesburg, South Africa, founded 1886.

John I, St, Pope 523–526, d. in prison 526.

John II, Pope 533–535.

John III, Pope 561–574.

John IV, Pope 640–642.

John V, Pope 685–686.

John VI, Pope 701–705.

John VII, Pope 705–707.

John VIII, Pope 872–882, murdered 882.

John IX, Pope 898–900.

John X, Pope 914–928.

John XI, Pope 931–935.

John XII (Octavian), Pope 955–963, b. about 938, d. 963.

John XIII, Pope 965–972.

John XIV, Pope 983–984, d. in prison 984.

John XV, Pope 985–996.

John XVI (Philagathus), Anti-Pope 997–998.

John XVII (Sicco), Pope 1003.

John XVIII, Pope 1004–1009.

John XIX, Pope 1024–1032.

John XX (non-existent : a fault in numbering).

John XXI (Pedro Giuliamo Rebulo), Pope 1276–1277.

John XXII (Jacques Duèse), Pope 1316–1334, b. 1249, d. 1334.

John XXIII (Baldassare Cossa), Anti-Pope 1410–1415, d. 1419.

John XXIII (Angelo Boncalli), Pope since 1958, b. 1881.

John I, Tzimisces, Byzantine Emperor (969–976), b. 925, d. 976.

John II, Comnenus, Byzantine Emperor (1118–1143), b. 1088, d. 1143.

John III, Vatatzes, Byzantine Emperor (1222–1254), b. 1193, d. 1254.

John IV, Lascaris, Byzantine Emperor (1258–1261), b. about 1250, d. about 1300.

John V, Palaeologus, Byzantine Emperor (1341–1347), b. 1332, d. 1391.

John VI, Cantacuzene, Byzantine Emperor (1347–1355), b. about 1292, d. 1383.

John VII, Byzantine Emperor 1390.

John VIII, Byzantine Emperor (1425–1448), b. 1390, d. 1448.

John, King of England (1199–1216), b. 1167, d. 1216.

John I, King of Poland, 1492–1501.

John II, Casimir, King of Poland (1648–1668), b. 1609, d. 1672.

John III, Sobieski, King of Poland (1674–1696), b. 1624, d. 1696.

John I, King of Portugal (1385–1433), b. 1357, d. 1433.

John II, King of Portugal (1481–1495), b. 1455, d. 1495.

John III, King of Portugal (1521–1557), b. 1502, d. 1557.

John IV, King of Portugal (1640–1656), b. 1603, d. 1656.

John V, King of Portugal (1706–1750), b. 1689, d. 1750.

John VI, King of Portugal (1816–1826), b. 1769, d. 1826.

John Chrysostom, St, b. about 357, d. 407.

John of Austria, Don, Austrian soldier and administrator, b. 1545, d. 1578.

John of Beverley, St, b. 687, d. 721.

John of Damascus, St, theologian, lived during late 7th and first half of 8th centuries.

John of Fornsete, English monk and reputed composer of *Sumer is icumen in*, d. 1239.

John of Gaunt, Duke of Lancaster, b. 1340, d. 1399.

John of Lancaster, Duke of Bedford, b. 1389, d. 1435.

John of Leyden (John Beuckelszoon), Dutch anabaptist, b. 1509, killed 1536.

John of Nepomuk, St, national saint of Bohemia, killed 1393.

John of the Cross, St, b. 1542, d. 1591.

John of Salisbury, English scholar and divine, b. about 1115, d. 1180.

John of Trevisa, English translator (of Higden's *Polychronicon*, 1387), b. 1326, d. 1412.

John Rylands Library, Manchester, founded 1899 by his widow in memory of John Rylands, b. 1801, d. 1888.

John, Augustus, Welsh painter (*Bella*), b. 1878.

John O'London's Weekly, British periodical, published 1919–1954, revived 1959.

Johns Hopkins University, Baltimore, founded 1867 by bequest of the American philanthropist Johns Hopkins, b. 1795, d. 1873. Opened 1876.

Johnson, Amy, English aviator, b. 1903, d. 1941.

Johnson, Andrew, U.S. President (1865–1869), b. 1808, d. 1875.

Johnson, Dr John, first Colonial-Surgeon in New Zealand, b. 1794, d. 1848.

Johnson, Dr Samuel, English writer (*Dictionary*, 1755), b. 1709, d. 1784.

Johnston, Joseph, American soldier, b. 1807, d. 1891.

Joinville, Jean, Sire de, crusader and historian, b. about 1224, d. 1319.

Joliot-Curie, Professor Frédéric, French physicist, b. 1900, d. 1958.

Jolliet, Louis, French explorer, b. 1645, d. 1700.

Jones, Ernest, first British psychoanalyst, b. 1879, d. 1958.

Jones, Henry Arthur, English playwright (*Judah*, 1890), b. 1851, d. 1929.

Jones, Inigo, English architect, b. 1573, d. 1652.

Jones, John Luther ('Casey'), American railway hero, b. 1864, killed 1900.

Jones, John Paul, American naval adventurer, b. 1747, d. 1792.

Jones, Owen, British architect (*Grammar of Ornament*, 1856), b. 1809, d. 1874.

Jonson, Ben, English dramatist (*The Alchemist*, 1610), b. about 1573, d. 1637.

Jonson, Cornelis, English painter (*Charles I*), b. 1593, d. 1661.

Jooss, Kurt, German-born choreographer, b. 1901.

Jordaens, Jacob, Flemish painter (*Triumph of Bacchus*), b. 1593, d. 1678.

Jordan : Transjordan declared independent 25 May 1923. Name of territory changed to the Hashimite Kingdom of Jordan 17 June 1946, and came into general use 1949. Jordan united with Iraq in the Arab Federation 14 Feb. 1958 (Federation dissolved July 1958).

Jordan, Mrs Dorothy, Irish actress and mistress of William IV, b. 1762, d. 1816.

Joseph I, Holy Roman Emperor (1705–1711), b. 1678, d. 1711.

Joseph II, Holy Roman Emperor (1765–1790), b. 1741, d. 1790.

Joseph, Chief, American Indian leader, d. 1904.

Josephine, Empress of the French, wife of Napoleon I, b. 1763, d. 1814.

Josephus, Flavius, Jewish historian, b. about 37, d. about 95.

Joubert, Barthélemy Catherine, French general, b. 1769, killed in battle 1799.

Joubert, Joseph, French writer, b. 1754, d. 1824.

Joule's Law of Electrical Energy, pronounced 1841 by the English scientist James Prescott Joule, b. 1818, d. 1889.

Jouvenet, Jean, French painter, b. 1647, d. 1717.

Jovian, Roman Emperor (363–364), b. about 331, d. 364.

Jowett, Benjamin, English scholar and educationist, b. 1817, d. 1893.

Joyce, James, Irish-born writer (*Ulysses*, 1922), b. 1882, d. 1941.

Joyce, William ('Lord Haw-Haw'), British traitor, b. 1906, hanged 1946.

Juan Fernandez, archipelago, discovered about 1564 by the navigator Juan Fernandez, d. about 1603.

Juarez, Benito, Mexican President (1861–1862, 1867–1872), b. 1806, d. 1872.

Jugurtha, King of Numidia (113–106), d. in prison 104 B.C.

Julian the Apostate, Roman Emperor (361–363), b. about 331, d. 363.

Julian Calendar, introduced in Rome by Julius Cæsar 46 B.C.

Juliana of Norwich, English mystic, b. 1343, d. 1443.

Juliana, Queen of the Netherlands, b. 1909 ; married 1937 ; succeeded to the throne 1948.

Jülich-Cleves, dispute over succession 1609–1614.

Julius I, St, Pope 337–352.

Julius II (Giuliano della Rovere), Pope 1503–1513, b. 1443, d. 1513.

Julius III (Giovanni Maria del Monte), Pope 1550–1555, b. 1487, d. 1555.

Julius Cæsar, Caius, Roman dictator, b. 100, assassinated 44 B.C.

July Revolution, provoked by the reactionary measures of Charles X of France, 27 July to Aug. 1830.

Juneau, Solomon Laurent, French-American founder 1846 of Milwaukee, b. 1793, d. 1856.

Jung, Carl Gustav, Swiss psychoanalyst, b. 1875.

Jungfrau, Swiss mountain (13,699 ft.), first climbed 1811 on the east side by the Swiss brothers Meyer of Aaravi, first climbed on the west side by Sir George Young and the Rev. H. B. George 1865.

Jungfrau Railway, highest in Europe, constructed 1896–1912.

'Junius', writer of political letters published 1769–1772. Pseudonym believed to conceal the authorship of Sir Philip Francis, b. 1740, d. 1818.

Jupiter, satellites first discovered 1610 by Galileo ; Red Spot first observed 1831.

Jurassic Period, 170 million years ago.

Jusserand, Jean Antoine Jules, French diplomat and historian, b. 1855, d. 1932.

Justice of the Peace, English judicial and administrative post, first recorded reference 1264.

Justiciar, official of Anglo-Norman kings until 1234.

Justin, St, b. about 100, martyred about 165.

Justin I, Byzantine Emperor (518–527), b. 450, d. 527.

Justin II, Byzantine Emperor (565–578), d. 578.

Justinian I, Byzantine Emperor (527–565), b. 483, d. 565.

Justinian II, Byzantine Emperor (685–695, 704–711), b. 669, assassinated 711.

Jutland, Naval Battle of, between the British and German fleets, 31 May 1916.

Juvenal, Roman satirical poet, b. about 55, d. about 140.

Juvenile Courts, set up in Britain under the Children Act 1908.

Juxon, William, English divine, b. 1582, d. 1663.

K

K-2 (Mt. Godwin-Austen), Himalayas, climbed by an Italian expedition 31 July 1954.

Kabalevsky, Dimitri, Russian composer (*Master of Clamecy*, 1937), b. 1904.

Kabul, capital of Afghanistan since 1774.

Kafka, Franz, Austrian novelist (*Der Prozess*), b. 1883, d. 1924.

Kagawa, Toyohiko, Japanese writer (*The Psychology of the Poor*, 1915), b. 1888, d. 1960.

Kaiser, Georg, German dramatist (*Die Bürger von Calais*, 1913), b. 1878, d. 1945.

Kaiser Wilhelm II Land, Antarctica, discovered 1903 by the German explorer Erich von Drygalski, b. 1865 d. 1949.

Kaleidoscopes, invented 1816 by Sir David Brewster, b. 1781, d. 1868.

Kalevala, Finnish folk epic, first published 1822 onwards.

Kalidasa, Indian writer (*The Sakuntala*), probably lived in the 4th century.

Kalinin, Mikhail Ivanovich, Russian Bolshevik leader, b. 1875, d. 1946.

Kalium (Potassium), discovered 1817 by the English chemist Sir Humphrey Davy, b. 1778, d. 1829.

Kamenev, Lev Borisovich (Rosenfeld), Russian Bolshevik leader, b. 1883, executed 1936.

Kamerlingh Onnes, Heike, Dutch scientist, b. 1853, d. 1926.

Kanchenjunga, Himalayas, climbed by a British expedition 25 May 1955.

Kandinsky, Wassily, Russian-born painter, b. 1866, d. 1944.

K'ang Hsi Period, China, 1662–1722.

Kansas, U.S.A., formed into a Territory 1854 ; admitted to the Union 1861.

Kansas University, Lawrence, Kansas, founded 1864.

Kant, Immanuel, German philosopher (*Critique of Pure Reason*, 1781), b. 1724, d. 1804.

Kapitza, Pyotr, Russian physicist, b. 1894.

Karg-Elert, Siegfried, German composer, b. 1877, d. 1933.

Kariba Hydro-Electric Project High Dam, Zambezi River, construction began 6 Nov. 1956, opened 18 May 1960.

Karlsefni, Thorfinn, Icelandic navigator, lived in the late 10th and first half of the 11th centuries.

Karolyi, Count Michael, Hungarian statesman, b. 1875.

Karsavina, Tamara, Russian-born ballet dancer, b. 1885.

Karsh, Yousuf, Armenian-born photographer (*Sir Winston Churchill*), b. 1908.

Kashmir, Jammu and, became part of the Mogul Empire 1586 ; British supremacy recognised 1846 ; the Maharajah acceded to the Dominion of India 1947.

Kassem, Abdul Karim, ruler of Iraq since July 1958, b. 1914.

Kate Greenaway Medal, British award for the most distinguished work in the illustration of children's books, awarded annually by the British Library Association since 1956.

Katherine of Aragon, Queen of England, b. 1485, m. Prince Arthur, m. Henry VIII, d. 1536.

Kauffmann, Angelica, Swiss-born painter, b. 1741, d. 1807.

Kaufman, George Simon, American writer (*Of Thee I Sing*, 1931), b. 1889.

Kaulbach, Wilhelm von, German painter (*Narrenhaus*), b. 1805, d. 1874.

Kautsky, Karl, German socialist b. 1854, d. 1938.

Kay's Flying Shuttle, invented 1733 by the English clockmaker John Kay, b. 1704, d. 1764.

Kaye, Danny (Daniel Kominski), American comedian, b. 1913.

Kean, Charles John, English actor, b. about 1811, d. 1868.

Kean, Edmund, English actor, b. 1787, d. 1833.

Keats, John, English poet (*Endymion*, 1818), b. 1795, d. 1821.

Keble, John, English divine (*Christian Year*, 1827), b. 1792, d. 1866.

Keble College, Oxford University, erected 1870 as a memorial to the English divine John Keble, b. 1792, d. 1866.

Keene, Charles, English artist and illustrator, b. 1823, d. 1891.

Keir Hardie, James, Scottish socialist leader, b. 1856, d. 1915.

Keller, Gottfried, Swiss novelist (*Der grüne Heinrich*, 1851–1853), b. 1819, d. 1890.

Keller, Helen, American deaf-mute and blind writer *The Story of My Life*, 1903), b. 1880.

Kellogg-Briand Pact (The Pact of Paris), renouncing war, signed 27 Aug. 1928.

Kelly College, Devon, English public school, founded by Admiral Benedictus Marwood Kelly, 1867 ; opened 1877.

Kelmscott Press, private press, founded and operated by William Morris, 1891–1898.

Kelvin, William Thomson, Baron, British physicist, b. 1824, d. 1907.

Kemal Atatürk (Mustafa Kemal), Turkish soldier and statesman (President 1923–1938), b. about 1880, d. 1938.

Kemble, Fanny, English actress, b. 1809, d. 1893.

Kemény, Zsigmond, Baron, Hungarian politician and writer, b. 1814, d. 1875.

Ken, Thomas, Bishop of Bath and Wells and hymn-writer (' Praise God from Whom all blessings flow '), b. 1637, d. 1711.

Kennedy, John Fitzgerald, U.S. President since 1961, b. 1917.

Kenneth I, first King of Scotland, d. about 860.

Kenneth II, King of Scotland (971–995), assassinated 995.

Kensington Gardens, London, became generally accessible to the public at the beginning of the 19th century.

Kensington Palace, London, acquired 1661 by the Earl of Nottingham (1621–1682), purchased by King William III, 1689.

Kent, Rockwell, American artist writer (*Salamina*, 1935), b. 1882.

Kent, William, English architect, b. 1684, d. 1748.

Kentucky, U.S.A., first settled 1765 ; admitted to the Union 1792.

Kentucky Derby, U.S.A., first run 17 May 1875.

Kenya, annexed to the British Crown as a colony 1920.

Keokuk, American Indian chief, b. about 1780, d. 1848.

Kepler, Johannes, German mathematician and astronomer, b. 1571, d. 1630.

Ker, William Paton, Scottish literary critic (*Epic and Romance*, 1897), b. 1855, d. 1923.

Kerensky, Aleksandr, Russian socialist (head of government July–Nov. 1917), b. 1881.

Kerguelen Archipelago, Southern Indian Ocean, discovered 1772 by the French explorer Yves Kerguélen-Trémarec, b. 1745, d. 1797.

Kern, Jerome, American composer (*Sally*, 1920), b. 1885, d. 1945.

Kerosene Oil, discovered 1852 by the Canadian geologist Abraham Gesner, b. 1797, d. 1864.

Kerschensteiner, Georg, German educationist, b. 1854, d. 1932.

Keswick Convention, Cumberland, annual religious reunion held since 1875.

Ketch, Jack, official executioner (1663–1686), d. 1686.

Ketelby, Albert William, English composer (*In a Monastery Garden*, 1912), b. 1880, d. 1959.

Kett's Rebellion, 1549, led by the English landowner Robert Kett, hanged 1549.

Kew Gardens, established by Princess Augusta, Dowager Princess of Wales, 1759.

Kew Palace, the Dutch House, purchased King George III, 1781.

Key, Francis Scott, American lawyer and poet (*The Star-spangled Banner*, 1814), b. 1779, d. 1843.

Keyes, Roger, Baron of Zeebrugge, sailor and politician, b. 1872, d. 1945.

Keynes, John Maynard, English economist (*General Theory of Employment, Interest and Money*, 1936), b. 1883, d. 1946.

Khachaturiyan, Aram, Armenian composer (*Masquerade Suite*, 1944), b. 1903.

Khaki, first worn 1843, introduced by Colonel Sir Harry Burnett Lumsden (1821–1896) of the Queen's Own Corps of Scouts and Guides, became general in the 2nd Afghan War.

Khaki Election, Gt. Britain, won by Conservatives, 28 Sept. to 16 Oct. 1900.

Khartoum, Capital of the Sudan, founded about 1823.

Khayyam, Omar, Persian poet (*The Rubaiyat*), lived in the 11th century.

Khedive of Egypt, The last, Abbas Hilmi II, deposed 1914.

Khosru I, Persian ruler from 531, d. 579.

Khosru II, Persian ruler from 591, murdered 628.

Khrushchev, Nikita Sergeyevich, Russian statesman, b. 1894.

Khufu (Cheops), Egyptian king, *fl.* about 2900 B.C.

Kidd, Captain William, Scottish pirate, b. about 1645, hanged 1701.

Kiel Canal, first opened 1784 ; second opened 21 June 1895.

Kiel Mutiny, of the German Navy, World War I, 3 Nov. 1918.

Kiepura, Jan, Polish-born operatic singer, b. 1902.

Kierkegaard, Søren, Danish philosopher, b. 1813, d. 1855.

Kilimanjaro, highest African mountain (19,710 ft.) first climbed 1889 by the German geographer Hans Meyer, b. 1858, d. 1929.

Killiecrankie, Battle of, between the Jacobites and the Royal force, 27 July 1689.

Killigrew, Thomas, English playwright (*The Parson's Wedding*, 1637), b. 1612, d. 1683.

' Kilmainham Treaty ', between Gladstone and Parnell, May 1882.

Kilogram, National Standard, established in Britain 1897.

Kindergarten, First American, opened by the American educationalist Elizabeth Peabody (1804–1894) at Boston 1860.

Kindergarten, First English, opened about 1850 by Johannes Ronge.

Kindergarten, First Froebel, started at Blankenburg, Switzerland, 1837–1845, by the German educationalist Friedrich Wilhelm August Froebel, b. 1782, d. 1852.

Kinetic Theory of Gases, postulated 1859 by the Scottish physicist James Clerk Maxwell, b. 1831, d. 1879.

Kinetoscope, invented 1887 by the American inventor Thomas Alva Edison, b. 1847, d. 1931.

King Charles the Martyr, Anniversary of, commemorating his execution 1649, held 30 Jan.

King Edward VII Land, Antarctica, sighted 1842 by Sir James Clark Ross (1800–1862) ; identified 1902 by the English explorer Robert Scott (1868–1912).

King Edward VII School, Lytham, English public school, opened 1908.

King Edward's School, Birmingham, English public school, founded 1552.

King George V Dock, Glasgow, opened 10 July 1931.

King George V Dock, London, opened 1921.

King George V Land, Antarctica, discovered 1912–1913 by the Australian explorer Sir Douglas Mawson, b. 1882, d. 1958.

King George's War, waged by Britain and France in North America 1745–1754.

King, Henry, English divine and poet, b. 1592, d. 1669.

King Philip's War, waged 1675–1676 by the American Indian chief Philip (killed 1676).

King, Sir Frederick Truby, New Zealand mothercraft pioneer, b. 1858, d. 1938.

King, William Mackenzie, Canadian Prime Minister, 1921–1930, 1935–1948, b. 1874, d. 1950.

King William Island, Arctic, discovered 1831 by the Scottish explorer Sir James Clark Ross, b. 1800, d. 1862.

King's College, Cambridge University, founded by King Henry VI, 1441.

King's College, London University, founded 1829 ; reincorporated 1882.

King's College, New York (now Columbia University), founded by grant of King George II, 1754.

King's College, Taunton, English public school, founded 1293 ; rebuilt 1522.

King's College School, Wimbledon, London, English public school founded 1829.

King's Police Medal, instituted by Royal Warrant 1909.

King's School, Bruton, English public school founded by Richard Fitzjames, Bishop of London, 1519 ; refounded by King Edward VI 1550.

King's School, Canterbury, English public school, founded about 600, reconstituted by King Henry VIII 1541, Royal Charter 1946.

King's School, Chester, English public school, founded by King Henry VIII 1541.

King's School, Ely, English public school, founded in 11th century ; reconstituted by King Henry VIII, 1541.

King's School, Macclesfield, English public school, founded by the Will of Sir John Percyvale 1502 ; re-established by Charter of Edward VI 1552.

King's School, Rochester, English public school, origins uncertain, reconstituted and endowed by King Henry VIII, 1542.

King's School, Worcester, English public school, established and endowed by King Henry VIII 1541 ; re-organised 1884.

Kinglake, Alexander William, English traveller (*Eothen,* 1844) and historian, b. 1809, d. 1891.

Kingsley, Charles, English writer (*Westward Ho !* 1855), b. 1819, d. 1875.

Kingsley, Henry, English writer (*Raven-shoe,* 1861), b. 1830, d. 1876.

Kingsley, Mary, English traveller and writer (*Travels in West Africa,* 1897), b. 1862, d. 1900.

Kingsway, London, opened 18 Oct. 1905.

Kingswood School, Bath, English public school founded by John Wesley, 1748.

Kinsey, Alfred, American sexologist (the Kinsey Reports), b. 1894, d. 1956.

Kipling, John Lockwood, British artist, b. 1837, d. 1911.

Kipling, Rudyard, British writer (*Kim,* 1911), b. 1865, d. 1936.

Kipnis, Alexander, Russian operatic singer, b. 1891.

Kircher, Athanasius, German inventor of the magic lantern (1646), b. 1601, d. 1680.

'Kirke's Lambs ', British soldiers led at the Battle of Sedgemoor (1685) by the English brigadier Percy Kirke, b. about 1646, d. 1691.

Kit-Cat Club, London, anti-Jacobite dining-club of writers, politicians, etc., existed roughly 1700–1720.

Kitchener of Khartoum, Herbert, Viscount, British soldier, b. 1850, drowned 1916.

Kléber, Jean Baptiste, French general, b. 1755, assassinated 1800.

Klee, Paul, Swiss painter (*High Spirits,* 1939), b. 1879, d. 1940.

Kleist, Heinrich von, German poet and playwright (*Prinz Friedrich von Hom-burg,* 1811), b. 1777, d. 1811.

Klemperer, Otto, German conductor, b. 1885.

Klondike Gold Rush, gold discovered 1896 ; rush began 1897.

Klopstock, Friedrich Gottlieb, German poet (*Messias,* 1748–1773), b. 1724, d. 1803.

Kneller, Sir Godfrey, German-born portrait painter, b. about 1648, d. 1723.

Knight, Dame Laura, English painter, b. 1877.

Knight, William Angus, Scottish philosopher, b. 1836, d. 1916.

Knights Hospitallers of St John of Jerusalem, Order founded during the First Crusade, recognised by Papacy 1113.

Knights of Malta, Order of St John of Jerusalem, 1529–1798.

Knights of Rhodes, Order of St John of Jerusalem, 1309–1522.

Knights Templars, Order formed about 1118, recognised by Papacy 1128, abolished 1314.

Knights, Teutonic, Order formed 1190, recognised by Papacy 1191, went to Prussia about 1225.

Knitting Frame, Cotton's, invented 1864 by the merchant William Cotton, b. 1786, d. 1866.

Knowles, James, English architect and founder (1877) of the *Nineteenth Century,* b. 1831, d. 1908.

Knowles, Sir James Sheridan, Irish-born playwright (*Virginius,* 1820), b. 1784, d. 1862.

Knox, John, Scottish religious reformer, b. about 1505, d. 1572.

Knox, Ronald, English writer, b. 1888, d. 1958.

Knut II, the Great (Canute), King of Denmark and England, b. about 995, d. 1035.

Knut III, Hardeknut, King of Denmark (1035–1042) and England, d. 1042.

Knut IV, St, King of Denmark (1080–1086), killed 1086.

Knut V, King of Denmark (1147–1157), assassinated 1157.

Knut VI, King of Denmark (1182–1202), b. 1163, d. 1202.

Koberger, Anton, German pioneer printer and publisher, b. about 1445, d. 1513.

Koch, Charles Henri Emmanuel, German traveller and naturalist, b. 1809, d. 1879.

Koch, Robert, German bacteriologist and discoverer 1882 of the T.B. bacillus, b. 1843, d. 1910.

'Kodak' Folding Cameras, first marketed 1898 by the American inventor George Eastman, b. 1854, d. 1932.

Kodály, Zoltán, Hungarian composer (*Háry János*, 1926), b. 1882.

Kodiak Island, Alaska, discovered 1764 by the Russian fur-trader Stephen Glotov.

Koh-I-Noor, Indian diamond, known since 1304 ; acquired by East India Company, and presented to British regalia 1850.

Kokoschka, Oskar, Austrian painter, b. 1886.

Kollwitz, Käthe, German artist, b. 1867, d. 1945.

Königsmark, Otto Wilhelm, Freiherr von, German General, b. 1639, d. 1688.

Koninck, Laurent Guillaume de, Belgian palæontologist, b. 1809, d. 1887.

Konrad von Würzburg, German poet (*Trojanerkrieg*, 1280–1287), d. 1287.

Koran, sacred book of Islam, written approximately 620 to 632.

Korda, Sir Alexander, Hungarian-born film producer, b. 1893, d. 1956.

Korea, occupied by Japan 1905 and formally annexed to that country 22 Aug. 1910 ; occupied and partitioned by U.S.A. and U.S.S.R. 1945.

Korea, North, liberated 1945, became the Korean People's Republic 1948.

Korea, South, liberated 1945, became the Republic of Korea 1948.

Korean Truce, between the United Nations and North Korea, signed 27 July 1953.

Korean War, between the United Nations and North Korean and Chinese forces, June 1950 to June 1951.

Koreshchenko, Arsen Nikolaievich, Russian composer (*Belshazzar*, 1891), b. 1870, d. 1918.

Kościuszko, Tadeusz, Polish leader b. 1746, d. 1817.

Kossuth, Lajos, Hungarian patriot, b. 1802, d. 1894.

Kotzebue, August Friedrich Ferdinand von, German playwright (*Adelheid von Wulfingen*, 1789), b. 1761, killed 1819.

Koussevitsky, Sergei, Russian-born conductor, b. 1874, d. 1951.

Krafft-Ebing, Richard, Freiherr von, German expert in mental disorders, b. 1840, d. 1902.

Kreisler, Fritz, Austrian-born violinist, b. 1875.

Kreuger, Nils Edvard, Swedish painter, b. 1858, d. 1930.

Kreutzer, Rodolphe, French-born violinist, b. 1766, d. 1831.

Krishnamurti, Jiddu, Indian mystic, b. 1895.

Kronstadt, Russian naval base, founded 1710 ; scene of mutiny Mar. 1921.

Kropotkin, Prince Peter, Russian scientist and anarchist (*Mutual Aid*, 1902), b. 1842, d. 1921.

Kruger, Stephanus Johannes Paulus, Boer leader and President of South Africa (1883–1900), b. 1825, d. 1904.

Krupp Works, founded 1810 at Essen, Germany, by Friedrich Krupp (1787–1826) and developed by his son Alfred Krupp (1812–1887).

Krusenstern, Adam Ivan, Russian circumnavigator (1803–1806) of the world, b. 1770, d. 1846.

Krylov, Ivan Andreievich, Russian writer of fables, b. 1786, d. 1844.

Krypton, inert gas, first obtained 1898 from the atmosphere by the British scientists Sir William Ramsay (1852–1916) and Morris William Travers.

Ku-Klux-Klan, American secret society, founded 1865 at Polask, Tennessee ; revived 1915 by William J. Simmons, and again in 1945 by Dr Samuel Green.

Kubelik, Jan, Czech violinist, b. 1880, d. 1940.

Kublai Khan, Mongolian Emperor (1276–1294), b. 1216, d. 1294.

Kulturkampf, Bismarck's struggle with Catholic Church in Germany 1871-1887.

Kun, Bela, Communist leader in Hungary Mar.–Aug. 1919, b. 1886, disappeared in Russia after 1919.

Kuomintang, Chinese national republic party, founded at the beginning of 20th century.

Kuprin, Aleksandr, Russian novelist (*Yama, the Pit,* 1909), b. 1870, d. 1938.

Kuropatkin, Alexei Nikolaievich, Russian general, b. 1848, d. 1925.

Kut, Mesopotamia, World War I, captured by the British 1915 ; surrendered to the Turks 1916, retaken by the British 1917.

Kutuzov, Mikhael Ilarionovich, Russian diplomat, administrator and soldier, b. 1743, d. 1813.

Kuwait, Persian Gulf state, became British protectorate 1899 ; recognised as an independent government under British protection 1914; complete independence, 1961.

Kyd, Thomas, English playwright (*The Spanish Tragedy,* 1586), b. about 1558, d. 1594.

Kynaston, Edward, English actor (possibly the last to take female parts), b. about 1640, d. 1706.

Kyoto, capital of Japan until 1868.

L

L.D.V. (Local Defence Volunteers), formed May 1940, became Home Guard July 1940.

La Bruyère, Jean de, French writer (*Characters,* 1688), b. 1645, d. 1696.

La Calprenède, Gauthier de Costes de, French writer (*Cassandre,* 1642–1650), b. 1614, d. 1663.

La Chaise, François de, father-confessor to Louis XIV, b. 1624, d. 1709.

La Fayette, Marie Joseph Paul Yves Roch Gilbert du Motier, Marquis de, French political reformer, b. 1757, d. 1834.

La Fayette, Marie Madeleine, Comtesse de, French writer, b. 1634, d. 1693.

La Follette, Robert, American senator, b. 1855, d. 1925.

La Fontaine, Jean de, French writer (*Fables,* 1668–1690), b. 1621, d. 1695.

La Motte-Fouqué, Friedrich, Freiherr de, German writer (*Undine,* 1811), b. 1777, d. 1843.

La Paz, Capital of Bolivia, founded 1548 by the 16th century Spanish explorer Alfonso de Mendoza.

La Pérouse, Jean François de Galaup, Comte de, French navigator, b. 1741, probably shipwrecked 1788.

La Rochefoucald, François de, French writer (*Maxims,* 1665), b. 1613, d. 1680.

La Salle, Robert Cavelier, Sieur de, French explorer and navigator (the Mississippi, 1682), b. 1643, assassinated 1687.

La Tour, Maurice Quentin de, French artist (*Louis XV*), b. 1704, d. 1788.

La Vallière, Louise de, mistress of Louis XIV, b. 1644, d. 1710.

Labé, Louise (La Belle Cordière), French poet (*Sonnets,* 1555), b. about 1525, d. 1566.

Labiche, Eugène Marin, French playwright (*Le Voyage de M. Perrichon,* 1860), b. 1815, d. 1888.

Labienus, Titus, Roman tribune, killed 45.

Labor Day, U.S.A. and Canada, first Monday in Sept. Inaugurated 1882 ; officially adopted 1894.

Labouchere, Henry, English politician and journalist (founded *Truth,* 1877), b. 1831, d. 1912.

Labour and National Service, Ministry of, created as the Ministry of Labour 1916 ; assumed present title and functions 1939.

Labour Day, 1 May.

Labour Exchanges, First British state, opened 1 Feb. 1910 ; first recorded local office opened at Egham, Feb. 1885.

Labour Party, origins in the Labour Representation League, organised 1869, and the Labour Electoral Association, formed by the T.U.C. in 1887 ; founded (as Labour Representation Committee) at a conference in London 27–28 Feb. 1900 ; present name adopted 1906 ; constitution adopted 1918.

Labuan, Malay Archipelago, island off N.W. Borneo, ceded to Britain by the Sultan of Brunei 1846.

Laccadive Islands, Indian Ocean, discovered by the Portuguese 1498 ; sequestrated by Britain 1877 ; now a territory of the Republic of India.

Lace-making, Pillow, introduced 1561 into Germany by the German Barbara Uttman, b. 1514, d. 1575.

Lactantius Firmianus, early Christian Father, b. about 260, d. about 340.

Ladies' Automobile Club, London, first met at Carlton House Terrace, 9 June 1904.

'Ladies of Llangollen ', Lady Eleanor Butler (1778–1829) and Sarah Ponsonby (1778–1831).

'Ladies' Peace ', the Treaty of Cambrai, renewing the Treaty of Madrid, signed 1529.

Ladislaus I, St (Laszlo), King of Hungary (1077–1095), b. 1040, d. 1095.

Ladislaus II, King of Hungary (1161), b. about 1134, d. 1162.

Ladislaus III, King of Hungary (1204–1205), b. 1199, d. 1205.

Ladislaus IV, King of Hungary (1272–1290), b. 1262, murdered 1290.

Ladislaus V, King of Hungary (1444–1457), b. 1440, d. 1457.

Lady Day (Annunciation of the Virgin), 25 Mar.

Lady Margaret Hall, Oxford University, founded 1879.

Ladysmith, Siege of, Boer War, Oct. 1899, relieved 28 Feb. 1900.

Laetare Sunday, the fourth Sunday in Lent.

Laffitte, Jacques, French financier, b. 1767, d. 1844.

Laforgue, Jules, French poet (*Complaintes*, 1885), b. 1860, d. 1887.

Lagerlöf, Selma, Swedish novelist (*Gösta Berling*, 1894), b. 1858, d. 1940.

Lagrange, Joseph Louis, Italian-born scientist, b. 1736, d. 1813.

Lalande, Joseph Jérome Lefrançais de, French astronomer, b. 1732, d. 1807.

Lalo, Edouard, French composer (*Symphonie espagnole*, 1875), b. 1823, d. 1892.

Lamarck, Jean Baptiste Pierre Antoine de Monet, Chevalier de, French naturalist, b. 1744, d. 1829.

Lamartine, Alphonse Marie Louis de, French writer (*Méditation*, 1820), b. 1790, d. 1869.

Lamb, Charles, English essayist (*Elia*, 1823), b. 1775, d. 1834.

Lamb, John, British pioneer in the development of gas turbine propulsion, b. 1890, d. 1958.

Lambert, Constant, English composer (*Rio Grande*, 1929), b. 1905, d. 1951.

Lambert, Daniel, English fat man, b. 1770, d. 1809.

Lambert, John, English Puritan general, b. 1619, d. 1684.

Lambeth Articles, concerning predestination and election, drawn up 1595 by John Whitgift, Archbishop of Canterbury, b. about 1530, d. 1604.

Lambeth Bridge, London, opened 1862, pulled down 1929, new bridge opened 1932.

Lambeth Conference, Anglican bishops' assembly, first convened 1867.

Lambeth Palace, origin uncertain, chapel built 1245–1270, Water Tower built about 1430.

Lamennais, Fèlicité Robert de, French church reformer (*Paroles d'un croyant*, 1834), b. 1782, d. 1854.

Lammas Day, 1 Aug.

Lamond, Frederick, Scottish pianist, b. 1868, d. 1948.

Lamp, Electric, first public demonstration 1879 by the inventor Sir Joseph Swan, b. 1828, d. 1914.

Lancashire Witch, the last, Mary Nutter, b. 1856, d. 1928.

Lancaster, Duchy of, established 1265 ; attached to the Crown since 1399.

Lancaster Royal Grammar School, English public school, origins uncertain, first recorded mention 1469.

Lancers, form of quadrille, came into fashion in Britain about 1850.

Lancet, The, British medical journal, founded 1823 by the English surgeon Thomas Wakley, b. 1795, d. 1862.

Lancing College, Sussex, English public school, founded by the Rev. Nathaniel Woodard, 1848.

Lancret, Nicolas, French painter (*Les cinq sens*), b. 1660, d. 1743.

Land Registry, British, established 1862, reformed 1875.

Landon, Pope 913–914.

Landor, Walter Savage, English writer (*Imaginary Conversation*, 1824–1846), b. 1775, d. 1864.

Landowska, Wanda, Polish-born harpsichord player, b. 1877, d. 1959.

Landseer, Sir Edwin, English painter (*Suspense*, 1834), b. 1804, d. 1875.

Lane, Sir Hugh, Irish art collector, b. 1875, drowned at sea 1915.

Lane Bequest, of modern paintings, bequeathed by Sir Hugh Lane, shared by Britain with Eire 1959.

Lanfranc, Archbishop of Canterbury (1070–1089), b. about 1005, d. 1089.

Lang, Andrew, Scottish writer and translator (*Myth, Ritual and Religion,* 1887), b. 1844, d. 1912.

Langham, Simon, Archbishop of Canterbury (1366–1368), d. 1376.

Langland, William, English poet (*Piers Plowman,* 1362), lived during the second half of the 14th century.

Langton, Stephen, Archbishop of Canterbury (1207–1228), b. about 1150, d. 1228.

Langtry, Lillie, ' The Jersey Lily ', actress, b. 1852, d. 1929.

Lanier, Sidney, American poet (*Florida,* 1875), b. 1842, d. 1881.

Lansbury, George, British socialist leader, b. 1859, d. 1940.

Lansdowne, William Petty Fitzmaurice, Marquess of, Irish-born Secretary of State, b. 1737, d. 1805.

Lanthanum, metallic element, discovered 1839 by Swedish scientist Karl Gustav Mosander, b. 1797, d. 1858.

Lâo-tse, Chinese founder of Taoism, b. about 604 B.C.

Laos, French protectorate 1893, became independent sovereign state, within the French Union, 1949.

Laplace, Pierre Simon, Marquis de, French astronomer, b. 1749, d. 1827.

Laporte, Pierre de, valet to Louis XIV and intriguer, b. 1603, d. 1650.

Larbaud, Valéry, French writer (*Enfantines,* 1918), b. 1881, d. 1957.

Lardner, Ring (Ringgold Wilmer Lardner), American humorous writer (*Gullible's Travels,* 1917), b. 1885, d. 1933.

Largillière, Nicolas de, French painter (*Mlle Duclos*), b. 1656, d. 1746.

Laroche, Raymonde, Baronne de, French aviator, first woman in the world (1910) to qualify for a pilot's certificate.

Larousse, Pierre Athanase, French encyclopædist, b. 1817, d. 1875.

Laryngoscope, use introduced 1861 by the American physician Louis Elsberg, b. 1836, d. 1885.

Layrngoscopy, study founded by the Bohemian scientist Johann Nepomuk Czermak, b. 1828, d. 1873.

Las Casas, Bartolomé de, Spanish prelate, b. 1474, d. 1566.

Lascaux Caves, S.W. France, painted caves discovered by five boys from Montignac 1940.

Lasker, Emanuel, German chess player, b. 1868, d. 1941.

Laski, Harold, English politician and economist, b. 1893, d. 1950.

Lassalle, Ferdinand, German socialist (*System of Acquired Rights,* 1860), b. 1825, killed 1864.

Lasso, Orlando di, Dutch composer (*Psalma Davidis poenitentiale*), b. about 1531, d. 1594.

Laszlo, Philip, Hungarian painter, b. 1869, d. 1937.

Latent Heat, nature defined about 1765 by the British scientist Joseph Black, b. 1728, d. 1799.

Lateran Council, First, 18 Mar. 1123 onwards.

Lateran Council, Second, Apr. 1139.

Lateran Council, Third, Mar. 1179.

Lateran Council, Fourth, 1215.

Lateran Council, Fifth, 3 May 1512 to 16 Mar. 1517.

Lateran Treaty, between the Holy See and the Kingdom of Italy, 1929.

Latimer, Hugh, English religious reformer, b. about 1485, burnt at the stake 1555.

Latrobe, Charles Joseph, Lt.-Governor of Victoria, Australia, b. 1801, d. 1875.

Latter-day Saints, Church of Jesus Christ of the, (Mormons), founded 1827 by the American Joseph Smith, b. 1805, d. 1844.

Latvia, ruled by Russia 1795–1918 ; independence declared 1919 ; occupied by the Russians June 1940 and admitted to the Soviet Union Aug. 1940.

Latvian Language, earliest known text dated 1585.

Latymer Upper School, London, English public day school, founded 1624.

Laud, William, Archbishop of Canterbury (1633–1645), b. 1573, beheaded 1645.

Laudanum, alcoholic tincture of opium, formula developed about 1660 by the English physician Thomas Sydenham, b. 1624, d. 1689.

Lauder, Sir Harry, Scottish comedian and singer, b. 1870, d. 1950.

Lauderdale, John Maitland, Duke of, Scottish statesman, b. 1616, d. 1682.

Laughing Gas (Nitrous Oxide), discovered 1772 by the English scientist Joseph Priestley, b. 1733, d. 1804. First used 1844 as an anæsthetic in dentistry by the American dentist Horace Wells, b. 1815, d. 1848.

Laughton, Charles, English-born actor, b. 1899.

Laurie, Annie (Mrs Alexander Ferguson), b. 1682, d. 1764.

Laurier, Sir Wilfrid, first French-Canadian Premier of Canada (1896–1911), b. 1841, d. 1919.

Lausanne Pact, between the Allies and Germany, signed 1932.

Lausanne, Treaty of, concerning Turkey, signed 24 July 1923.

Lautréamont, Isidore Lucien Ducasse, self-styled Comte de, French writer (*Chants de Maldoror*, 1868–1870), b. 1846, d. 1870.

Lautrec, Henri Marie Raymond de Toulouse, French painter (*Attablés*), b. 1864, d. 1901.

Laval, Pierre, French statesman, b. 1883, executed 1945.

Lavater, Johann Kaspar, Swiss theologian and physiognomist, b. 1741, d. 1801.

Lavery, Sir John, Ulster painter, b. 1856, d. 1941.

Lavoisier, Antoine Laurent, French scientist, b. 1743, guillotined 1794.

Law, John, Scottish Controller-General of Finance in France, b. 1671, d. 1729.

Law, William, English theologian (*Serious Call*, 1729), b. 1686, d. 1761.

Lawes, William, English composer (' Gather ye rosebuds while ye may '), b. 1582, killed 1645.

Lawrence, Anti-pope 498.

Lawrence, David Herbert, English writer (*Lady Chatterley's Lover*, 1928), b. 1885, d. 1930.

Lawrence, Dr Ernest Orlando, American physicist, b. 1901, d. 1958.

Lawrence, John Laird Mair, Baron Lawrence, Viceroy and Governor-General of India (1864–1869), b. 1811, d. 1879.

Lawrence, Sir Thomas, English painter (*Mrs Siddons*), b. 1769, d. 1830.

Lawrence, Thomas Edward, ' Lawrence of Arabia ', British explorer and writer (*Seven Pillars of Wisdom*, 1926), b. 1888, d. 1935.

Lawrence, Kansas, sacked by Quantrill Gang, 1863.

Layamon, English priest and historian (*The Brut*), lived in the late 12th and early 13th centuries.

Layard, Sir Austen Henry, archæologist and diplomat, b. 1817, d. 1894.

Le Brun, Charles, French painter, (*La Famille de Darius*), b. 1619, d. 1690.

Le Brun, Marie Anne Elisabeth Vigé-, French painter (*Le Comte Orloff*), b. 1755, d. 1842.

' Le Corbusier ' (Charles Edouard Jeanneret), Swiss architect, b. 1887.

Le Despenser, Hugh, Earl of Winchester, Royal favourite, b. 1262, hanged 1326.

L'Enfant, Pierre Charles, French architect and town planner in the U.S.A., b. 1754, d. 1825.

Le Fanu, Sheridan, Irish writer (*In a Glass Darkly*, 1872), b. 1814, d. 1873.

Le Gallienne, Richard, English poet *English Poems*, 1892), b. 1866, d. 1947.

Le Moine, François, French painter *Ruth et Boaz*, 1711), b. 1688, committed suicide 1737.

Le Nain, The brothers, French painters : Antoine (1588–1648), Louis (1593–1648) and Mathieu (1607–1677).

Le Nôtre, André, French landscape architect, b. 1613 d. 1700 (St James's Park, London).

Le Play, Pierre Guillaume Frédéric, French engineer and economist, b. 1806, d. 1882.

Le Sage, Alain René, French writer (*Gil Blas*, 1715–1735), b. 1668, d. 1747.

Le Sueur, Jean François, French composer (*Paul et Virginie*, 1794), b. 1760, d. 1837.

Le Vau, Louis, French architect, b. 1612, d. 1670.

Leacock, Stephen, English-born humorist (*Nonsense Novels*, 1911), b. 1869, d. 1944.

League of Nations, founded 28 Apr. 1919 ; superseded by U.N.O. 8 Apr. 1946.

Leaning Tower of Pisa, built 1174–1350.

Leap Year, the system by which every fourth year comprises 366 days, the extra day being 29 Feb.

Lear, Edward, English artist and humorist (*Book of Nonsense*, 1846), b. 1812, d. 1888.

Lease-Lend, U.S. aid to Britain programme, proposed by President Roosevelt 1940 ; put into action 1941 ; made reciprocal 1942.

Leather, Artificial, first manufactured in Britain 1884.

Leather Hose, for fire fighting, invented 1672.

Léautaud, Paul, French writer (*Le Petit ami*, 1903), b. 1872, d. 1956.

Lebanon, under French mandatory rule 1920–1941 ; independence proclaimed 1941 ; French evacuation completed 1946.

Leblanc, Nicolas, French chemist, b. 1742, d. 1806.

Lecky, William Edward Hartpole, Irish historian, b. 1838, d. 1903.

Lecocq, Charles, French composer (*Giroflé-Girofla*, 1874), b. 1832, d. 1918.

Leconte de Lisle, Charles Marie, French poet (*Poèmes antiques*, 1852), b. 1818, d. 1894.

Lecouvreur, Adrienne, French actress, b. 1692, d. 1730.

Lee, Ann, English founder (1758) of the religious movement the Society of Shakers, b. 1736, d. 1784.

Lee, Nathaniel, English playwright (*The Rival Queens*, 1677), b. about 1653, d. 1692.

Lee, Robert Edward, American Confederate General, b. 1807, d. 1870.

Lee, Sir Sidney, English Editor of the *Dictionary of National Biography*, b. 1859, d. 1926.

Leech, John, English engraver, b. 1817, d. 1864.

Leeds Grammar School, English public school, founded by Sir W. Sheafield, 1552, enlarged by John Harrison 1663.

Leeds University, England, founded 1874, granted university status 1904.

Leeuwenhoek, Anton van, Dutch microscopist, b. 1632, d. 1723.

Legal Memory, in England, dates back to accession of Richard I, 1 Sept. 1189.

Legion of Honour (La Légion d'Honneur), created by the French Consular law of 19 May 1802.

Legitimacy, by marriage of parents, made legal in England 1926.

Legros, Alphonse, French artist (*Ex voto*, 1861), b. 1837, d. 1911.

Lehár, Franz, Hungarian composer (*The Merry Widow*, 1905), b. 1870, d. 1948.

Lehmann, Beatrix, English actress, b. 1903.

Lehmann, John, English writer and editor, b. 1907.

Lehmann, Lilli, German operatic singer, b. 1848, d. 1929.

Lehmann, Lotte, German operatic singer, b. 1888.

Lehmann, Rosamund, English novelist (*Dusty Answer*, 1927), b. 1903.

Leibniz, Gottfried Wilhelm, German philosopher, b. 1646, d. 1716.

Leicester, Robert Dudley, Earl of, Elizabethan courtier, b. about 1531, d. 1588.

Leicester University, England, founded 1918 as the Leicester, Leicestershire and Rutland College ; became University College, Leicester, 1927 ; gained University status 1957.

Leif Ericsson, Icelandic discoverer of North America about 1000.

Leigh, Vivien, English actress, b. 1913.

Leighton, Frederick, Lord, English painter (*Andromache*, 1888), b. 1830, d. 1896.

Leighton Park School, Reading. English public school, founded under the direction of the Yearly Meeting of the Society of Friends, 1890.

Leipzig University, Germany, founded 1409.

Lekeu, Guillaume, French composer (*Andromède*, 1891), b. 1870, d. 1894.

Leland, John, English antiquary (*Itinerary*, 1710), b. about 1506, d. 1552.

Lely, Cornelis, Dutch statesman, engineer and planner of the Zuider Zee, b. 1854, d. 1929.

Lely, Sir Peter, German-born painter (*Nell Gwynn*), b. 1618, d. 1680.

Lemon, Mark, English writer and editor of *Punch*, b. 1809, d. 1870.

Lemonnier, Pierre Charles, French astronomer, b. 1715, d. 1799.

Lenbach, Franz, German painter (*Bismarck*), b. 1836, d. 1904.

'**Lenclos,** Ninon de ' (Anne Lenclos), French courtesan, b. 1620, d. 1705.

Lenin, Nikolai (Vladimir Ilyich Ulianov), Russian Bolshevik leader, b. 1870, d. 1924.

Leningrad (previously Petrograd), named after Lenin 1924.

Leningrad, Siege of, by the Germans, relieved after 16 months by the Russians 18 Jan. 1943.

Lennox, Charlotte, American-born writer (*The Female Quixote*, 1752), b. 1720, d. 1804.

'**Leno,** Dan ' (George Galvin), English comedian, b. 1861, d. 1904.

Le Normand, Henri René, French playwright (*Le Lâche*, 1925), b. 1882.

Lens, first referred to by Meisner in 13th century.

Lent, period of 40 days of fasting preceding Easter.

Leo I, the Great, St, Pope 440–461.

Leo II, St, Pope 682–683.

Leo III, St, Pope 795–816.

Leo IV, St, Pope 847–855.

Leo V, Pope 903.

Leo VI, Pope 928.

Leo VII, Pope 936–939.

Leo VIII, Pope 963–964.

Leo IX (Bruno), Pope 1049–1054, b. 1002, d. 1054.

Leo X (Giovanni de Medici), Pope 1513–1521, b. 1475, d. 1521.

Leo XI (Alessandro de Medici), Pope 1605, b. about 1535, d. 1605.

Leo XII (Annibale della Genga), Pope 1823–1829, b. 1760, d. 1829.

Leo XIII (Gioacchino Pecci), Pope 1878–1903, b. 1810, d. 1903.

Leon, Juan Ponce de, Spanish colonial administrator, b. 1460, killed 1521.

Leon, Luis Ponce de, Spanish poet, b. about 1527, d. 1591.

Leonardo da Vinci, Italian engineer and artist (*Mona Lisa*), b. 1452, d. 1519.

Leopardi, Giacomo, Italian poet (*Operette Morali*, 1827), b. 1798, d. 1837.

Leopold I, Holy Roman Emperor (1658–1705), b. 1640, d. 1705.

Leopold II, Holy Roman Emperor (1790–1792), b. 1747, d. 1792.

Leopold I, first King of the Belgians (1831–1865), b. 1790, d. 1865.

Leopold II, King of the Belgians (1865–1909), b. 1835, d. 1909.

Leopold III, King of the Belgians (1934–1951), b. 1901.

Leopoldville, Belgian Congo, capital, founded 1881 by the Welsh explorer Sir Henry Morton Stanley, b. 1841, d. 1904.

Lepanto, Naval Battle of, fought between the Holy League under Don John and the Turks, 7 Oct. 1571.

Lepidus, Marcus Æmilius, Roman triumvir, d. 13.

Leprosy, mentioned in India 1400 B.C. and in Egypt 1350 B.C. ; bacillus discovered 1872 by the Norwegian physician Gerhard Hansen, b. 1841, d. 1912.

Lermontov, Mikhail Yurevich, Russian writer (*A Hero of Our Times*, 1839), b. 1814, killed in a duel 1841.

Leschetizky, Theodor, Polish-born pianist, b. 1830, d. 1915.

Lespinasse, Jeanne Julie Eléonore de, French writer (*Lettres*, 1809), b. 1732, d. 1776.

Lesseps, Ferdinand de, French canal builder, b. 1805, d. 1894.

Lessing, Mrs Doris, Rhodesian writer (*Martha Quest*, 1952), b. 1919.

Lessing, Gotthold Ephraim, German writer (*Laokoon*, 1766), b. 1729, d. 1781.

Lesueur, Eustache, French painter (*Vie de St Bruno*, 1645–1648), b. 1617, d. 1655.

L'Estrange, Sir Roger, English pamphleteer, journalist and translator, b. 1616, d. 1704.

Letchworth, England's first garden city, founded 1903.

Letter Office, General, first established in England by Act of Parliament 1660.

Letters of Marque, Licences granted to private persons to fit out armed ships in time of war, abolished by the Declaration of Paris, 1855.

Leukæmia, disease of the blood, treatment developed by the American physician Edward Gamaliel Janeway, b. 1841, d. 1911.

Levant Company, English trading venture, founded 1581 ; chartered 1592.

Levellers, English republican and democratic group ; appeared 1647, crushed by Cromwell 1649, disappeared after Restoration 1660.

Lever, Charles, Irish-born novelist (*Harry Lorrequer*, 1837), b. 1806, d. 1872.

Leverhulme, William Lever, Viscount, English manufacturer, b. 1851, d. 1925.

Leverrier, Urbain, French astronomer (predicted position of the planet Neptune 1846), b. 1811, d. 1877.

Lewes, Battle of, between Henry III and barons, 1265.

Lewis, Clive Staples, English scholar and writer (*The Screwtape Letters*, 1942), b. 1898.

Lewis, Meriwether, American explorer of the Far West, b. 1774, committed suicide 1809.

Lewis, ' Monk ' (Mathew Gregory Lewis), English writer (*The Monk*, 1796), b. 1775, d. 1818.

Lewis, Samuel, American song-writer (*In a Little Spanish Town*), b. 1883, d. 1959.

Lewis, Sinclair, American novelist (*Babbitt*, 1922), b. 1885, d. 1951.

Lewis, Percy Wyndham, English writer (*Childermass*) and painter, b. 1884, d. 1957.

Lewis Machine-gun, invented 1911 by the American Isaac Newton Lewis, b. 1858, d. 1931.

Lewisite, poison gas, invented 1916 by the American chemist Gilbert Newton Lewis, b. 1875, d. 1946.

Leyden Jar, electric condenser first made 1746 by the Dutch scientist Pieter van Musschenbroek, b. 1692, d. 1761, and his pupil Cunaeus in Leyden ; and simultaneously by the German divine Ewald von Kleist at Cammin in Pomerania.

Leyden University, Netherlands, founded 1575.

Leys School, Cambridge, English public school, founded 1875 ; incorporated 1878.

Li Po, Chinese poet, b. about 700, d. 762.

Liadov, Anatol Constantinovich, Russian composer (*Danse de l'Amazone*), b. 1855, d. 1914.

Liao Dynasty, China, 907–1125.

Liberal Party, British origins in the Whigs (so named about 1679) ; present name used from about 1816, adopted officially during 1830s.

Liberals, Spanish supporters of 1812 constitution ; French opponents of ' Ultras ' in 1815 and from 1820–1830 ; Italian opponents of Austrian rule after 1815 ; European supporters of 1848 revolts.

Liberia, West Africa ; group of freed slaves brought (1820) from the U.S.A. to Liberia on board the *Elizabeth* ; became a Commonwealth 1838, declared independent 26 July 1847.

Liberius, Pope 352–366.

Liberty Bell, Independence Hall, Philadelphia, hung 1753, replaced 1781, cracked 1835.

Library, first public, built in Rome by C. Asinius Pollio 39 B.C. ; Vatican, begun by Pope Nicolas V 1447 ; Bodleian opened 1602 ; British Museum, founded 1753 ; Congress, established 1800 ; London, founded 1840.

Library Act, First British Public, passed 1850 ; after several amendments, superseded by the Act of 1919.

Library Association, American, established 1876.

Library Association of the United Kingdom, established 1877.

Libreville, capital of Gabon, founded 1848.

Libya, North Africa, conquered by Italians 1911–1930 ; became an independent state 24 Dec. 1951.

Lichfield Cathedral, England, constructed 13th–14th centuries.

Licinius, Roman Emperor (307–323), b. about 250, executed 324.

Lick Observatory, Mt. Hamilton, U.S.A. founded 1876–1888 by the legacy of James Lick, b. 1796, d. 1876.

Lie, Jonas, Norwegian novelist (*The Pilot and His Wife,* 1874), b. 1833, d. 1908.

Lie, Trygve, Norwegian-born Secretary-General of the United Nations (1946–1953), b. 1896.

Lie-Detector, principle stated and first apparatus constructed by the Italian criminologist Cesare Lombroso, b. 1836, d. 1909.

Lieber, Francis, German-born founder (1829–1833) of the *Encyclopædia Americana,* b. 1800, d. 1872.

Liebermann, Max, German painter (*Knöpflerinnen*), b. 1848, d. 1935.

Liebig, Justus Frieherr von, German chemist, b. 1803, d. 1873.

Liebknecht, Karl, German socialist leader, b. 1871, killed 1919.

Liebknecht, Wilhelm, German socialist leader, b. 1826, d. 1900.

Liechtenstein, formed (as the Principality of Vaduz) 1342 ; enlarged to present size 1434 ; constituted as the

Principality of Liechtenstein 1719 ; independent since 1866.

Liège Cathedral, Belgium ; first cathedral destroyed 1794, second, constructed 10th century, rebuilt 13th century.

Lifeboat, First, designed by the English coachbuilder Lionel Lukin 1785.

Life-line, fired by mortar from shore to ship, invented 1807 by the English barrack-master George William Manby, b. 1765, d. 1854.

Lift, First hydraulic passenger, installed in New York, 1857, by the American inventor Elisha Graves Otis, b. 1811, d. 1861 ; electric lifts developed in U.S.A. and Britain during 1880s.

Ligature, use in amputations introduced by the French surgeon Ambroise Paré, b. about 1510, d. 1590.

Light, Composition of, discovered 1660 by Sir Isaac Newton, b. 1642, d. 1727.

Light, Refraction of, law postulated 1621 by the Dutch scientist Willebrord Snell, b. 1591, d. 1626.

Light, Velocity of, first calculated 1675 by Olaus Roemer (1644–1710) ; also measured by Jean Bernard Léon Foucault (1819–1868).

Light Brigade, Charge of the, Balaklava, 25 Oct. 1854.

Light Programme, B.B.C., began 29 July 1945.

Light Year, distance (nearly 6 million million miles) travelled by light in one year.

Lightfoot, Joseph Barber, English theologian, b. 1828, d. 1889.

Lighthouse, Pharos, Alexandria, built about 280 B.C. ; Eddystone, built 1698, 1708, 1759, 1879–1881 ; Bell Rock, 1807–1810 ; Bishop Rock, 1858.

Lightning Conductor, principle discovered 1747 by the American statesman Benjamin Franklin, b. 1706, d. 1790.

Ligne, Charles Joseph, Prince de, Field Marshal, b. 1735, d. 1814.

Liguori, Alfonso Maria dei, St, Italian theologian, b. 1696, d. 1787.

Lilburne, John (' Freeborn John '), English pamphleteer and Leveller leader, b. about 1614, d. 1657.

Liliencron, Detlev von, German writer (*Krieg und Frieden*, 1891), b. 1844, d. 1909.

Lilienthal, Otto, German engineer, b. 1848, d. 1896.

Liliuokalani, last Queen of Hawaii (1891–1893), b. 1838, d. 1917.

Lilliput, British periodical, founded 1937 by the Hungarian journalist Stefan Lorant, b. 1901.

Lillo, George, English dramatist (*The London Merchant*, 1731), b. 1693, d. 1739.

Lilly, William, English astrologer, b. 1602, d. 1681.

Lima, Peru, founded about 1541 by the Spanish conquistador Francisco Pizarro b. 1478, d. 1541.

Lime-juice, made compulsory in the Royal Navy as a preventative of scurvy 1795. Its use introduced for this purpose by Sir Gilbert Blane, b. 1749, d. 1834.

Limelight (Drummond Light), invented by Sir Goldsworthy Gurney (1793–1875) ; introduced by Thomas Drummond (1797–1840).

Limitation of Armaments Conference, held at Washington 12 Nov. 1921 to 6 Feb. 1922.

Limousin, Léonard, French painter (*Marguérite de Valois*), b. about 1505, d. about 1577.

Linacre, Thomas, English founder 1518 of the (Royal) College of Physicians, b. about 1460, d. 1524.

Lincoln, Abraham, U.S. President (1861–1865), b. 1808, assassinated 14 Apr. 1865.

Lincoln Cathedral, England, construction began 1086, consecrated 1092.

Lincoln School, English public school, founded at least as early as 1090.

Lincolnshire Insurrection, largely against religious and fiscal oppression, arose 1536, suppressed 1536–1537.

Lind, Jenny, The ' Swedish Nightingale ', operatic singer, b. 1820, d. 1887.

Lindbergh, Charles, American aviator, b. 1902, crossed the Atlantic 20–21 May 1927.

Lindisfarne (Holy Island), chosen as the site of his church and monastery by St Aidan 635.

Lindley, John, English botanist, b. 1799, d. 1865.

Lindsay, Lady Anne, Scottish poet (*Auld Robin Gray*, 1771), b. 1750, d. 1825.

Lindsay, Vachel, American poet (*The Congo*, 1914), b. 1879, d. 1931.

Line Co-ordinates, geometry, introduced 1868–1869 by the German mathematician and physician Julius Plücker, b. 1801, d. 1868.

Ling, Pehr Henrik, Swedish pioneer in gymnastics, b. 1776, d. 1839.

Lingard, John, English historian, b. 1771, d. 1851.

Linklater, Eric, British writer (*Poet's Pub*, 1929), b. 1899.

Linnaeus, Carl, Swedish botanist, b. 1707, d. 1778.

Linnean Society, London, founded 1788 by the botanist Sir James Edward Smith, b. 1759, d. 1828.

Linoleum, Cork, invented by the Englishman Frederick Walton, 1860.

Linotype, invented 1884 by the German-born Ottmar Mergenthaler (1854–1899). First made in England 1892.

Linton, Sir Richard, New Zealand-born founder of the Big Brother Movement (scheme for migration of boys from Britain to Australia), b. 1879, d. 1959.

Linus, St, Pope 67–76.

Liotard, Jean Etienne, French painter (*Général Hérault*), b. 1702, d. 1789.

Lippi, Fra Lippo, Italian painter (*St Margaret*), b. about 1406, d. 1469.

Lippershey, Hans, Dutch optician and inventor, 1608, of the telescope, d. 1619.

Lippmann, Walter, American political commentator and writer, b. 1889.

Lipton, Sir Thomas, Scottish-born merchant and sportsman, b. 1850, d. 1931.

Liquefaction of Gas, principle discovered 1878 by the French chemist Louis Paul Cailletet, b. 1832, d. 1913.

Lisbon Earthquake (greatest of many suffered by the city), 1. Nov. 1755.

List, Friedrich, German economist, b. 1789, committed suicide 1846.

Listener, The, first published 16 Jan. 1929.

Lister, Joseph Lister, Baron, English surgeon, b. 1827, d. 1912.

Liszt, Franz, Hungarian-born composer (*Piano concertos,* 1857 and 1863), b. 1811, d. 1886.

Lithium, an alkali metal, discovered 1817 by the Swedish chemist Johann August Arfvedson, b. 1792, d. 1841.

Lithography, invented 1798 by the German inventor Alois Senefelder, b. 1771, d. 1834.

Lithuania, ruled by Russia 1795–1918 ; proclaimed an independent republic 16 Feb. 1918 ; occupied by the Russians and admitted to the Soviet Union 1940.

Lithuanian Language, earliest known text dated 1547.

Litolff, Henry Charles, English pioneer 1851 in the publication of cheap editions of music, b. 1818, d. 1891.

Littell, Frank Bowers, American astronomer, b. 1869.

Little Entente Permanent Council, founded on Czech-Yugoslav Treaty of 14 Aug. 1920, created 16 Feb. 1933.

Little Rock, Arkansas, U.S.A., scene of racial conflict 1957.

Littleton, Sir Thomas, English jurist, b. 1422, d. 1481.

Littré, Maximilien Paul Emile, French compiler of a French dictionary, b. 1801, d. 1881.

Litvinov, Maksim Maksimovich, Russian diplomat, b. 1876, d. 1951.

Liutprand, Lombard divine and chronicler, b. about 921, d. 972.

Liverpool, Robert Banks Jenkinson, Earl, British statesman (Prime Minister 1812–1827), b. 1770, d. 1828.

Liverpool Cathedral, first stone laid 19 July 1904, consecrated 19 July 1924.

Liverpool College, English public school, founded 1840.

Liverpool University, civic inauguration 7 Nov. 1903.

Livery Companies, London, see under individual names—*Skinners, Vintners,* etc.

Livia Drusilla, Roman Empress, b. about 55 B.C., d. A.D. 29.

Livingston, Edward, American statesman, b. 1764, d. 1836.

Livingston, Robert, Scottish-born administrator in New York, b. 1654, d. 1728.

Livingstone, David, Scottish explorer and missionary, b. 1813, d. 1873.

Livius Andronicus, Roman poet, lived in the 3rd century B.C.

Livonia, ruled by Russia 1710–1918 ; absorbed into Latvia 1918.

Livy (Titus Livius), Roman historian, b. 59 B.C., d. A.D. 17.

Llandaff Cathedral, original building opened 1120, second, 18th century, third, built 1844–1869.

Llandovery College, Welsh public school, founded by Thomas Phillips, 1848.

'**Llangollen, Ladies of** ', Lady Eleanor Butler (1778–1829) and Sarah Ponsonby (1778–1831).

Llewelyn I, Prince of North Wales (1194–1229), d. 1240.

Llewelyn II, Prince of North Wales (1246–1282), killed in battle 1282.

'**Lloyd, Marie** ' (Matilda Alice Victoria Wood), English music-hall comedian, b. 1870, d. 1922.

Lloyd George, David, British statesman (Prime Minister 1916–1922), b. 1863, d. 1945.

Lloyd's of London, first known allusion as Edward Lloyd's Coffee House, Tower St, London, Feb. 1688.

'**Lloyd's List and Shipping Gazette** ', London, founded 1734.

'**Lloyd's Register** ', of shipping, first prepared about 1764.

Loanda, capital of Angola, oldest extant European settlement in Africa, founded 1576.

Lobachevsky, Nikolai Ivanovich, Russian mathematician, b. 1793, d. 1856.

Lobel, Matthias de, French botanist and physician, lived early in the 17th century.

Locard, Edward, French criminologist, b. 1877.

Locarno Pact, guaranteeing peace and frontiers in Europe, signed 16 Oct. 1925.

Loch Lomond, Scotland, first swum (22 miles) by Commander Gerald Forsberg (b. 1912) in 1959.

Lochner, Stephen, German painter (*The Last Judgment*), b. about 1401, d. 1451.

Locke, Joseph, English civil engineer, b. 1805, d. 1860.

Locke, John, English philosopher (*Essay Concerning Human Understanding*, 1690), b. 1632, d. 1704.

Lockhart, John Gibson, Scottish writer (*Ancient Spanish Ballads*, 1823), b. 1794, d. 1854.

Lockwood, James Booth, American Polar explorer, b. 1852, d. 1884.

Lockyer, Sir Joseph Norman, English astronomer, b. 1836, d. 1920.

Locomotives, early models constructed 1803 by the English engineer Richard Trevithick and 1814 by the English civil engineer George Stephenson, b. 1781, d. 1848.

Lodge, Sir Oliver, British physicist, b. 1851, d. 1940.

Lodge, Thomas, English writer (*Rosalynde*, 1590), b. about 1558, d. 1625.

Loeb, James, American banker and philanthropist, b. 1867, d. 1933.

Loeb Classical Library, authoritative texts and translations, series founded by James Loeb, 1912.

Loeffler, Charles Martin, American composer (*A Pagan Poem*, 1909), b. 1861, d. 1935.

Loewe, Carl, German composer (*Erlkönig*), b. 1796, d. 1869.

Löffler, Friedrich, German bacteriologist, b. 1852, d. 1915.

Lofting, Hugh, English-born writer (*Dr Dolittle*, 1920), b. 1896, d. 1947.

Logan, Benjamin, American pioneer, b. about 1743, d. 1802.

Logarithms, invented 1614 by the Scottish inventor John Napier, b. 1550, d. 1617.

Logic, study founded by the Greek philosopher Aristotle, b. 384, d. 322 B.C.

Logical Positivism, philosophical movement originating in Vienna in 1920s.

Logue, Cardinal Michael, Archbishop of Armagh, b. 1840, d. 1924.

Lollards, English church reformers (followers of John Wyclif) after 1382, active during early 15th century.

Lombard, Peter, Italian theologian (*Sententiae*, 1145–1150), b. about 1100, d. about 1160.

Lombard League, of cities in Lombardy, founded 1167.

Lombardo, Pietro, Italian sculptor, b. about 1435, d. 1515.

Lombards, invaded Italy 568 ; conquered by Franks 774.

Lombroso, Cesare, Italian pioneer criminologist, b. 1836, d. 1909.

Lomonosov, Mikhail Vasilievich, Russian scientist and writer, b. 1711, d. 1765.

London, Jack (John Griffith), American novelist (*The Call of the Wild*, 1903), b. 1876, d. 1916.

London, Metropolitan Police Force set up 1829 ; London divided into postal districts 1858 ; Port of London Authority established 1909.

London, Declaration of, concerning maritime law, signed 1909.

London, Tower of, built mainly at the end of the 11th century, additions made in the late 17th century.

London Airport, opened 1946 ; new terminal and buildings opened 1955.

London Bridge, Old, built by Peter, Chaplain of St Mary's Colechurch, 1176–1209.

London Bridge, New, constructed 1824–1831 by Sir John Rennie, b. 1794, d. 1874.

London Company, formed to colonise part of Virginia, chartered 1606.

London County Council, formed 1888.

London County Hall, foundation stone laid 9 Mar. 1912.

London Gazette founded 1665.

London Irish Volunteer Rifles, now the only Irish territorial infantry regiment in Britain, formed 25 Nov. 1859.

London Library, London subscription library, founded 1840, opened 1841.

London Naval Conference, concerning war at sea, held 1908–1909.

London Naval Treaty, ratified 1930.

London Oratory, established 1849 by the English theologian and poet Frederick William Faber, b. 1814, d. 1863.

London—Paris Daily Air Service, inaugurated 25 Aug. 1919.

London—Paris Phone Service, opened 1891.

London Passenger Transport Board, took control of most of London's transport service 1 July 1933. Replaced by London Transport Executive 1948.

London Symphony Orchestra, first concert given 9 June 1904.

London Salvage Corps, founded 1866.

London Transport Executive, replacing London Passenger Transport Board, established 1948.

London University, founded 1828, chartered 1836.

Londonderry, Edith Helen, Marchioness of, founder and Director of the Women's Legion, first to be created (1917) a D.B.E. (Military), b. 1879, d. 1959.

Long, Huey, U.S. Senator and Governor of Louisiana, b. 1893, shot 1935.

Long, John Luther, American writer (*Madame Butterfly*, 1898), b. 1861, d. 1927.

Long Island, first settled about 1640 ; annexed to New York 1664.

Long Parliament, called 1640, purged 1648, expelled 1653, recalled 1659, dissolved 1660.

Longchamp, William of, Bishop of Ely and statesman, d. 1197.

Longfellow, Henry Wadsworth, American poet (*Hiawatha*, 1855), b. 1807, d. 1882.

Longhi, Pietro, Italian painter (*Exhibition of a Rhinoceros*), b. 1702, d. 1785.

Longinus, Greek philosopher, b. about 213, beheaded 273.

Longman, Thomas, English publisher, b. 1699, d. 1755.

Longomontanus, Christian Sorensen, Dutch astronomer, b. 1562, d. 1647.

Longueuil, Charles le Moyne, Sieur de, French pioneer in Canada, b. 1626, d. 1685.

Longus, Greek writer in 4th or 5th century (*Daphnis and Chloë*).

Longworth, Nicholas, American pioneer in viticulture, b. 1782, d. 1863.

Lönnrot, Elias, Finnish collector of folk material, b. 1802, d. 1884.

Löns, Hermann, German writer (*Mein grunes Buch*), b. 1866, killed in battle 1914.

Lonsdale Boxing Belt, founded 1909 by the English sportsman Lord Lonsdale, b. 1857, d. 1944.

Loomis, Mahlon, American radio pioneer, b. 1826, d. 1886.

Loop, first aeronautic, performed 27 Aug. 1913, by the Russian pilot Peter Nesterov.

Lope de Vega, Spanish playwright (*Pedro en Madrid*), b. 1562, d. 1635.

Lopez, Carlos Antonio, President of Paraguay (1844–1862), b. 1790, d. 1862.

Lopez, Francisco Solano, President of Paraguay (1862–1870), b. 1827, killed in battle 1870.

Lorca, Federico García, Spanish writer (*Bodas de sangre*, 1933), b. 1899, shot 1936.

Lord Howe Island, Southern Pacific, discovered by Lt. H. L. Ball 1778.

Lord Mayor of London, office traditionally held to have been founded 1189.

Lord Mayor's Show, London, First held 1215, first organised Sir Christopher Draper's pageant 1566.

Lords, House of, absolute power of veto abolished by Act of Parliament 1911.

Lords Appellants, group of English nobles, held power 1388–1397.

Lords Ordainers, group of English nobles, held power 1310–1316.

Lorentz, Hendrik Antoon, Dutch physicist, b. 1853, d. 1928.

Lorenz, Adolf, Austrian surgeon, b. 1854, d. 1946.

Lorenzetti, Ambrogio, Italian painter, b. before 1319, d. after 1347.

Lorenzetti, Pietro, Italian painter, b. before 1320, d. after 1345.

Lorenzo de' Medici, ' the Magnificent ', Florentine leader, b. 1449, d. 1492.

Lorenzo di Pietro, Italian artist, b. about 1412, d. 1480.

Loreto, Italy, reputed site of the house of the Virgin Mary, miraculously deposited in 1295.

Loretto School, Scottish public school, founded 1862 by Dr Hely Hutchinson Almond, b. 1832, d. 1903.

Lorimer, George Horace, American writer (*Letters from a Self-made Merchant*, 1902), b. 1868, d. 1937.

Loring, William Wing, American military commander and adviser, b. 1818, d. 1886.

Lorne, John Douglas Sutherland Campbell, Marquess of, Governor General of Canada (1878–1883), b. 1845, d. 1914.

Lorrain, Claude, French painter (*Liber veritatis*), b. about 1600, d. 1682.

Lorraine, ruled by France 1766–1870, by Germany 1871–1918, by France 1918–1940, by Germany 1940–1944, by France since 1944.

Lorris, Guillaume de, French poet (part of the *Roman de la Rose*) lived in the first half of the 13th century.

Lortzing, Albert, German composer (*Der Wildschütz*, 1842), b. 1801, d. 1851.

Los Angeles, California, founded 1781.

Lothair I, Holy Roman Emperor (817–855), b. 795, d. 855.

Lothair II, Holy Roman Emperor (1075–1137), b. about 1070, d. 1137.

Lothair III, King of France (954–986), b. 941, d. 986.

Lotharingia, created by Treaty of Verdun, 843.

' Loti,' Pierre ' (Julian Viaud), French writer (*Pécheur d' Islande*, 1886), b. 1850, d. 1923.

Lotto, Lorenzo, Italian painter (*St Jerome*), b. about 1480, d. 1556.

Lotze, Rudolf Hermann, German philosopher, b. 1817, d. 1881.

Loudon, John Claudius, Scottish horticulturist, b. 1783, d. 1843.

Louis I, Emperor and King of France, b. 778, d. 840.

Louis II, King of France (877–879), b. 846, d. 879.

Louis III, King of France (879–882), b. about 863, d. 882.

Louis IV, King of France (936–954), b. 921, d. 954.

Louis V, King of France (986–987), b. 967, d. 987.

Louis VI, King of France (1108–1137), b. 1081, d. 1137.

Louis VII, King of France (1137–1180), b. about 1121, d. 1180.

Louis VIII, King of France (1223–1226), b. 1187, d. 1226.

Louis IX, King of France (St Louis), b. 1214, reigned 1226–1270, d. 1270. Canonised 1297.

Louis X, King of France (1314–1316), b. 1289, d. 1316.

Louis XI, King of France (1461–1483), b. 1423, d. 1483.

Louis XII, King of France (1499–1515), b. 1462, d. 1515.

Louis XIII, King of France (1610–1643), b. 1601, d. 1643.

Louis XIV, King of France (1643–1715 b. 1638, d. 1715.

Louis XV, King of France (1715–1774), b. 1710, d. 1774.

Louis XVI, King of France (1774–1792), b. 1754, guillotined 1793.

Louis XVII, titular King of France (1793–1795), b. 1785, said to have died 1795.

Louis XVIII, King of France (1814–1824), b. 1755, d. 1824.

Louis Ferdinand, Prince of Prussia, b. 1772, killed in battle 1806.

Louis Napoleon (Napoleon III), Emperor of the French (1852–1870), b. 1808, d. 1873.

Louis Philippe, King of France (1830–1848), b. 1773, d. 1850.

Louisiana, U.S.A., first settled 1699 ; admitted to the Union 1812.

Louisiana Purchase from France, of territory west of the Mississippi, completed by the U.S.A. 1803.

Lourdes, First visions of Bernadette Soubirous at, 1858. Festival of Our Lady at Lourdes celebrated 11th Feb.

Loutherbourg, Philip James, French-born artist, b. 1740, d. 1812.

Louvre, Paris, designed 1546–1578 by the French architect, Pierre Lescot, b. about 1510, d. 1578.

Louÿs, Pierre, French writer (*Aphrodite*, 1896), b. 1870, d. 1925.

Lovejoy, Owen, American abolitionist, b. 1811, d. 1864.

Lovelace, Richard, Cavalier poet (*Lucasta*, 1649), b. 1618, d. 1658.

Loveless, George, British trade union pioneer (' Tolpuddle martyr ' 1834), b. 1792, d. 1874.

Lover, Samuel, Irish novelist (*Rory O'More*, 1836), b. 1797, d. 1868.

Low, David, New Zealand-born cartoonist, b. 1891.

Low, Juliette Gordon, founder of the Girl Scouts in America, b. 1860, d. 1927.

Low, Sampson, English publisher, b. 1797, d. 1886.

Low Sunday, first Sunday after Easter.

Lowe, Sir Hudson, Irish-born Governor of St Helena (1815–1821), b. 1769, d. 1844.

Lowell, Amy, American poet, b. 1874, d. 1925.

Lowell, James Russell, American writer (*Biglow Papers*, 1848 and 1867), b. 1819, d. 1891.

Lowell Observatory, Arizona, founded 1894 by the American astronomer Percival Lowell, b. 1855, d. 1916.

Lowestoft, Naval battle of, between the English and the Dutch, 3 June 1665.

Lowie, Robert Heinrich, American anthropologist, b. 1883.

Lowndes, William Thomas, English bibliographer, b. about 1798, d. 1843.

Loyalty Islands, South Pacific, formally annexed 1864 by France.

Loyola, Ignatius, St, Spanish founder 1534 of the Society of Jesus, b. 1491, d. 1556.

Loyola University, Chicago, founded as St Ignatius College 1870 ; established with present status and title 1907.

Lubbock, Sir John, Baron Avebury, English writer and naturalist, b. 1834, d. 1913.

Lubin, David, American merchant and founder of the International Institute of Agriculture, b. 1849, d. 1919.

Lubitsch, Ernst, German film director, b. 1892, d. 1947.

Lucan, Marcus Annaeus, Roman poet (*Pharsalia*), b. 39, committed suicide 65.

Lucaris, Cyril, Greek theologian, b. 1572, d. 1637.

Lucas, Edward Verrall, English writer (*Over Bemerton's*, 1908), b. 1868, d. 1938.

Lucas, Frank Laurence, English writer (*Poems*, 1935), b. 1894.

Lucas van Leyden, Dutch painter (*The Last Judgment*), b. about 1494, d. 1533.

Luce, Henry Robinson, American publisher, b. 1898.

Lucian, Greek writer (*Dialogues*), b. about 120, d. 180.

Lucifer Matches, invented 1827 by the English chemist John Walker, b. about 1781, d. 1859.

Lucius I, St, Pope 253–254.

Lucius II (Gherardo Caccianemici dal Orso), Pope 1144–1145.

Lucius III (Ubaldo Allucingoli), Pope 1181–1185.

Luckner, Felix, Graf von (The ' Sea Devil '), German naval commander, b. 1886.

Lucknow Residency, defended by the Duke of Cornwall's Light Infantry, 1857.

Lucrece (Lucretia), victim of Tarquinius Superbus, committed suicide 510 B.C.

Lucretius, Roman poet (*De Rerum Natura*), b. about 96, d. about 55 B.C.

Lucullus, Roman general, b. about 110, d. 57 B.C.

Lucy, St, martyred about 305.

Lucy, Sir Thomas, prototype of Shakespeare's Justice Shallow, b. 1532, d. 1600.

Luddites, English machine wreckers, active 1810–1818.

Ludendorff, Erich von, German general, b. 1865, d. 1937.

Ludlow, Edmund, English Puritan soldier and regicide, b. about 1617, d. 1692.

Ludwig I, King of Bavaria (1825–1848), b. 1786, d. 1868.

Ludwig II, King of Bavaria (1864–1886), b. 1845, d. 1886.

Ludwig III, King of Bavaria (1913–1918), b. 1845, d. 1921.

Ludwig, Emil, German writer (*Napoleon*, 1924), b. 1881.

Lugard, Frederick John Dealtry Lugard, Baron, pioneer administrator in East Africa, b. 1858, d. 1945.

Luini, Bernardino, Italian painter (*Madonna*), b. about 1481, d. 1532.

Lull, Ramón, Catalan mystic, b. about 1236, d. 1315.

Lully, Jean-Baptiste, Italian-born composer (*Alceste*, 1674), b. 1632, d. 1687.

Lumière, Auguste, French pioneer in cinematography, b. 1862, d. 1954.

Lumière, Louis, French pioneer in cinematography, b. 1864, d. 1948.

Lumsden, Sir Harry Burnett, Indian Army reformer, b. 1821, d. 1896.

Luna, Alvaro de, Constable of Castile, executed 1453.

Lunacharsky, Anatoli Vasilievich, Russian writer and Bolshevik leader, b. 1875, d. 1933.

Lundy, Benjamin, American abolitionist, b. 1789, d. 1839.

Luneville, Peace of, between France and Austria, signed 1801.

Lunik I, Russian lunar rocket, launched 11 Oct. 1958.

Lunik II, Russian lunar rocket, hit the moon 10.00 hrs. B.S.T. 13 Sept. 1959.

Lusaka, chosen as capital of Northern Rhodesia, 1935.

Lusitania, Atlantic passenger liner, launched 7 June 1906 ; torpedoed by the Germans 7 May 1915.

Lutecium, rare earth metal discovered independently 1907 by the Austrian chemist Baron von Welsbach (1858–1929) and 1906 by Georges Urbain.

Luther, Martin, German church reformer, b. 1483, excommunicated 1521, d. 1546.

Lutheran Church, organised 1522.

Luttrell Psalter, illuminated manuscript in the British Museum, is dated about 1340.

Lutyens, Sir Edwin Landseer, English architect, b. 1869, d. 1944.

Lützen, Battle of, between the Swedes and the Imperialists in the Thirty Years' War, 16 Nov. 1632.

Lützow, Adolf, Freiherr von, German military leader, b. 1782, d. 1834.

Luxemburg, Grand Duchy, created by the Congress of Vienna, 1814–1815 ; neutrality guaranteed 1817 ; Constitution granted 1868 and revised 1919 and 1948.

Luxembourg, Palace of, Paris, built 1615–1620.

Luxemburg, Rosa, German socialist leader, b. 1870, killed 1919.

Luxorius, Roman epigrammatist, lived in the early 6th century.

Luynes, Charles d'Albert, Duc de, Constable of France, b. 1578, d. 1621.

Lvov, Alexis von, composer of the Russian national anthem (' God save the Czar ', 1833), b. 1798, d. 1870.

' Lyall, Edna ' (Ada Ellen Bayly), English novelist (*Donovan*, 1882), b. 1857, d. 1903.

Lyautey, Louis Hubert Gonsalve, French Commissary-General in Morocco (1912–1925), b. 1854, d. 1934.

Lycurgus, Spartan reformer believed to have lived in the 7th or 8th century B.C.

Lydekker, Richard, English naturalist, b. 1849, d. 1915.

Lydgate, John, English poet (*Troy Book*, 1412–1420), b. about 1370, d. about 1451.

Lyell, Sir Charles, Scottish geologist, b. 1797, d. 1875.

Lyly, John, English writer (*Euphues*, 1578), b. about 1554, d. 1606.

Lyman, Theodore, American naturalist, b. 1833, d. 1897.

Lynching, term believed to derive from the American military leader Charles Lynch, b. 1736, d. 1796.

Lyndhurst, John Singleton Copley, Baron, statesman, b. 1772, d. 1863.

Lyndsay, Sir David, Scottish poet (*The Three Estaits*, 1540), b. 1490, d. 1555.

Lyon, Mary, American advocate of advanced education for women, b. 1797, d. 1849.

Lyon, Nathaniel, American military commander, b. 1818, killed in battle 1861.

Lyons, Joseph Aloysius, Australian statesman (Prime Minister 1932–1939), b. 1879, d. 1939.

Lyons, France, founded 43 B.C. by Lucius Plancus.

Lyons, Ecumenical Councils of, 1st, 1245 ; 2nd, 1274.

Lysander, Spartan commander, lived at the end of the 5th and beginning of the 4th century B.C.

Lysenko, Trofim Denisovich, Russian scientist, b. 1898.

Lysimachus, Greek general, b. about 355, killed in battle 281 B.C.

Lysippus, Greek sculptor, lived in the 4th century B.C.

Lysistratus, Greek sculptor, lived in the 4th century B.C.

Lyte, Henry Francis, British hymn-writer (*Abide with me*, 1833), b. 1793, d. 1847.

Lytle, William Haines, American poet, b. 1826, killed in battle 1863.

Lyttleton, George Lyttleton, Baron, English politician and writer, b. 1709, d. 1773.

Lytton, Bulwer, Lord Lytton, English novelist (*The Last Days of Pompeii*, 1834), b. 1803, d. 1873.

Lytton, Edward Robert Bulwer, Earl Lytton, Viceroy of India (1876–1880) and writer, b. 1831, d. 1891.

M

M1, London–Birmingham motorway, main section officially opened 2 Nov. 1959.

M & B 693 (Sulphapyridine), produced 1938.

M.C.C., Marylebone Cricket Club, founded 1787 ; first match 1788 ; present ground opened 1814.

M.I.T., Massachusetts Institute of Technology, founded Boston 1859, moved to Cambridge, Mass., 1915.

M.V.D., Ministry of Internal Affairs. U.S.S.R., succeeded the N.K.V.D, 1934.

' Maartens, Maarten ' (Joost Marius William van der Poerten-Schwartz), Dutch-born novelist (*God's Fool*, 1893), b. 1858, d. 1915.

Mabillon, Jean, French monk and writer, b. 1632, d. 1707.

Mabinogion, Welsh epic collection, compiled 14th–15th centuries.

Mabuse, Jan de, Flemish painter (*Madonna and Child*), b. about 1470, d. about 1533.

Macadamised Roads, invented 1816 by the Scottish surveyor John Loudon Macadam, b. 1756, d. 1836.

McAdoo, William Gibbs, American politician, b. 1863, d. 1941.

Macao, China, first settled by the Portuguese 1557 ; Portuguese suzerainty recognised by China by treaty of 1887.

MacArthur, Douglas, American general, b. 1880.

McArthur, John, English pioneer in New South Wales, b. 1767, d. 1834.

Macaulay, Dame Rose, English novelist (*Potterism*, 1920), b. 1887, d. 1958.

Macaulay, Thomas Babington, Lord, historian (*History of England*, 1849–1861), b. 1800, d. 1859.

Macbeth, King of the Scots (1040–1054), killed in battle 1057.

Maccabees, Jewish leaders from about 170 B.C. and rulers until 63 B.C.

McCarthy, Joseph Raymond, American lawyer and politician (prominent as a demagogue 1950–1954), b. 1909, d. 1957.

McCarthy, Justin, Irish politician and historian, b. 1830, d. 1912.

McClellan, George Brinton, American general, b. 1826, d. 1885.

M'Clintock, Admiral Sir Francis Leopold, Irish-born explorer, b. 1819, d. 1907.

McClure, Sir John David, Scottish headmaster of Mill Hill School, b. 1860, d. 1922.

McClure, Sir Robert John le Mesurier, British navigator, b. 1807, d. 1873.

McCook, Alexander McDowell, American general, b. 1831, d. 1903.

McCormack, Count John, Irish tenor, b. 1884, d. 1945.

McCormick, Cyrus Hall, American inventor 1831 of the reaper, b. 1809, d. 1884.

McCoy, Sir Frederick, Irish-born palæontologist, b. 1823, d. 1899.

McCulloch, Ben, American pioneer, b. 1811, killed in battle 1862.

MacCunn, Hamish, Scottish composer (*Cior Mhor*, 1887), b. 1868, d. 1916.

Macdonald, Flora, Scottish rescuer 1746 of the Young Pretender, b. 1722, d. 1790.

MacDonald, George, Scottish writer (*At the Back of the North Wind*, 1871), b. 1824, d. 1905.

MacDonald, James Ramsay, British statesman (Prime Minister 1924, 1929–1935), b. 1866, d. 1937.

Macdonell, Alastair, ' Pickle the Spy ', b. about 1725, d. 1761.

Macdonnell, Alexander, British champion chess-player, b. 1798, d. 1835.

Macdonough, Thomas, American naval officer, b. 1786, d. 1825.

McDougall, William, English-born psychologist (*Introduction to Social Psychology*, 1908), b. 1871, d. 1938.

MacDowell, Edward Alexander, American composer (*Sea Pieces*, 1898), b. 1861, d. 1908.

MacDuff, Earl of Fife, possibly mythical 11th century Scottish patriot.

Macedonians, ruled Greece 338–306 B.C.

McEntee, Jervis, American painter (*Clouds*), b. 1828, d. 1891.

McEvoy, Ambrose, English painter (*The Ear-Ring*, 1911), b. 1878, d. 1927.

MacEwen, Sir William, Scottish surgeon, b. 1848, d. 1924.

McGill University, Montreal, chartered 1821, opened 1829. Named after the Scottish benefactor James McGill, b. 1744, d. 1813.

McGillivray, Alexander, American Indian chief, b. about 1739, d. 1793.

Macgregor, Robert (' Rob Roy '), Scottish rebel, b. 1671, d. 1734.

Machado, Bernardino, Portuguese statesman, b. 1851, d. 1944.

Machaut, Guillaume de, French poet, b. about 1300, d. 1377.

Machen, Arthur, English writer (*The Great Return*, 1915), b. 1863, d. 1947.

Machiavelli, Niccolò di Bernardo dei, Italian political reformer (*The Prince*, 1532), b. 1469, d. 1527.

Machine-gun, orgues used 1467 and 1512 ; models made by Drummond 1626, Palmer 1663, Puckle 1718, Gatling 1862, Nordenfeldt 1873, Hotchkiss 1878, Maxim 1884.

Macintosh, Charles, Scottish chemist and inventor (1823) of waterproofs, b. 1766, d. 1843.

McKay, Charles, Scottish singer (*Cheer, Boys, Cheer*), b. 1814, d. 1889.

McKaye, Steele, American playwright (*Hazel Kirke*, 1880), b. 1842, d. 1894.

Macke, August, German painter (*Franz Marc*), b. 1887, killed 1914.

Mackensen, August von, German Field-Marshal, b. 1849, d. 1945.

Mackenzie, Sir Compton, British novelist (*Sinister Street*, 1913–1914), b. 1883.

Mackenzie, Henry, Scottish writer (*The Man of Feeling*, 1771), b. 1745, d. 1831.

Mackenzie, William Lyon, Canadian politician and lawyer, b. 1795, d. 1861.

McKinley, William, U.S. President (1897–1901), b. 1843, assassinated 1901.

McKinley, Mt., Alaska, first climbed 1913 by the American missionary Hudson Stock, b. 1863, d. 1920.

Mackintosh, Sir James, Scottish historian and lawyer, b. 1765, d. 1832.

Macklin, Charles, British actor, b. about 1697, d. 1797.

' **Maclaren,** Ian ' (John Watson), Scottish novelist (*Beside the Bonnie Brier Bush*, 1894), b. 1850, d. 1907.

McLean, Sir Donald, New Zealand statesman, b. 1820, d. 1877.

MacLeish, Archibald, American poet (*Conquistador*, 1932), b. 1892.

' **Macleod,** Fiona ' (William Sharp) Scottish novelist (*The Immortal Hour*, 1900), b. 1855, d. 1905.

Maclise, Daniel, Irish-born painter (*The Death of Nelson,* 1857–1866), b. 1806, d. 1870.

McLoughlin, John, American fur trader and explorer, b. 1784, d. 1857.

Maclure, William, American geologist, b. 1763, d. 1840.

McMahon Line, delineating the North-East frontier of India, agreed by British, Chinese and Tibetan representatives at the 1914 Simla Conference. Named after the British representative Sir Henry McMahon, b. 1862, d. 1949.

Macmanus, Terence Bellew, Irish patriot, b. about 1823, d. 1860.

McMaster, John Bach, American historian, b. 1852, d. 1932.

Macmillan, Daniel, Scottish publisher, b. 1813, d. 1857.

Macmillan, Harold, British statesman (Prime Minister since 1957), b. 1894.

McMillan, Margaret, American-born pioneer in British school clinics, b. 1860, d. 1931.

McMillan, Rachel, American-born pioneer in British nursery school work, b. 1859, d. 1917.

MacNaghten Rules, legal definition of insanity, formulated after the trial for murder of Daniel MacNaghten, 1843.

Macon, Nathaniel, American statesman, b. about 1757, d. 1837.

Maconchy, Elizabeth, English composer (*Great Agrippa,* 1935), b. 1907.

Maconochie, Captain Alexander, Scottish geographer and prison reformer, first secretary of the Royal Geographical Society, b. 1787, d. 1860.

McPherson, Aimée Semple, American evangelist, b. 1890, d. 1944.

Macpherson, James, Scottish ' editor ' of Ossian, b. 1736, d. 1796.

Macpherson, Samuel Charters, Scottish administrator in India, b. 1806, d. 1860.

Macready, William Charles, English actor, b. 1793, d. 1873.

Macrinus, Roman Emperor (217–218), b. 164, killed 218.

MacSwiney, Terence James, Irish patriot, b. 1880, starved himself to death in prison 1920.

M'Taggart, John M'Taggart Ellis, English philosopher, b. 1866, d. 1925.

MacVeagh, Wayne, American lawyer and diplomat, b. 1833, d. 1917.

Macy, Mrs Anne Sullivan American teacher of Helen Keller, b. 1866, d. 1936.

Mad Mullah of Somaliland (Mohammed bin Abdullah), active 1899–1904.

Mad Parliament, held in Oxford 1256.

Madagascar, autonomous federal republic within the French Community, discovered by the Portuguese navigator Diego Diaz 1500 ; annexed by France 1885.

Madame Tussaud's Waxworks, London, founded by the Swiss showman Mme Marie Tussaud (1760–1850) ; new building opened 1928.

Madariaga, Don Salvador de, Spanish-born writer (*Don Quixote,* 1934), b. 1886.

Madden, Sir Frederic, English antiquary and palæographer, b. 1801, d. 1873.

Madeira Islands, discovered 1418 by pupils of Prince Henry the Navigator, b. 1394, d. 1460.

Madeira Pet, British-owned ship, made first voyage (51 days) from Liverpool to Chicago, arriving 14 July 1857.

Madeleine, Paris, construction begun 1764, completed 1842.

Madison, James, U.S. President (1809–1817), b. 1751, d. 1836.

Madog, reputed Welsh discoverer of America, lived in the second half of 12th century.

Madras State, India : trading begun by the British 1611 ; brought under British rule by 1801.

Madrid University, Spain, founded 1508.

Mæcenas, Gaius Cilnius, Roman statesman and patron of letters, b. about 70, d. 8 B.C.

Maes, Nicolas, Dutch painter (*The Card Players*), b. 1632, d. 1693.

Maeterlinck, Maurice, Belgian writer (*The Blue Bird,* 1909), b. 1862, d. 1949.

Mafeking, Cape Province, besieged by the Boers 12 Oct. 1899 ; relieved by the British 17 May 1900. Mafeking Night 18 May.

Magdalen College, Oxford University, founded 1458 by William of Wayneflete, b. 1395, d. 1486.

Magdalen College School, Oxford, English public school, founded by William of Wayneflete about 1478.

Magdalene College, Cambridge University, founded by Thomas, Baron Audley of Walden, 1542.

Magellan, Ferdinand (Ferñao Magalhães), Portuguese navigator, whose ship first circumnavigated the World (1519–1522), b. about 1480, killed 1521.

Magdeburg Hemispheres, demonstrating air pressure, invented 1654 by the German scientist Otto von Guericke, b. 1602, d. 1686.

Magendie, François, French scientist, b. 1783, d. 1855.

Magenta, Battle of, between the Italian and the Austrians, 4 June 1859.

Maggraf, Andreas Sigismund, German scientist, b. 1709, d. 1782.

Magic Lantern, invented 1646 by the German scientist Athanasius Kircher, b. 1601, d. 1680.

Maginn, William, Irish writer (*Homeric Ballads,* 1849), b. 1793, d. 1842.

Maginot Line, French defence system, construction began 1928, handed over to the Germans 1940.

Magistrate, First British stipendiary, Henry Fielding, appointed 1748 ; First British woman, Miss Emily Duncan, appointed 26 May 1913.

Magliabechi, Antonio, Italian librarian, b. 1633, d. 1714.

Magna Charta, sealed by King John at Runnymede 15 June 1215.

Magnesium, discovered 1808 by the English chemist Sir Humphry Davy, b. 1778, d. 1829.

Magnetic Clutch, eliminating spring action, invented 1900 by the American engineer Bion Joseph Arnold, b. 1861, d. 1942.

Magnetic Compass, used by Chinese before 1200 ; Variations of the, discovered 1622 by the English scientist Edmund Gunter, b. 1581, d. 1626.

Magnetic Pole, North, located 1831 by Sir James Clark Ross, b. 1800, d. 1862.

Magnetic Pole, South, reached by the Shackleton Expedition 16 Jan. 1909.

Magnetism, defined 1600 by the English physician, William Gilbert, b. 1540, d. 1603.

Magnetism by Electricity, achieved 1820 by the French physicist Dominique François Arago, b. 1786, d. 1853.

Magnus I, the Good, King of Norway (1035–1047), b. 1024, d. 1047.

Magnus II, King of Norway (1067–1069), d. 1069.

Magnus III, King of Norway (1093–1103), d. 1103.

Magnus IV, King of Norway (1130–1135), d. 1135.

Magnus V, King of Norway (1162–1184), killed in battle 1184.

Magnus VI, King of Norway (1263–1280), b. 1238, d. 1280.

Magnus VII, King of Norway (1319–1343), b. 1316, d. 1374.

Magnusson, Finnur, Icelandic archæologist, b. 1781, d. 1847.

Magrath, William, Irish-born painter, b. 1838, d. 1918.

Magritte, René, Belgian painter, b. 1898.

Magsaysay, Ramón, Philippine statesman, b. 1907, d. 1957.

' Mahabharata ', Indian epic, composed about the 6th century B.C.

Mahan, Alfred Thayer, American naval historian, b. 1840, d. 1914.

' Mahdi, The ', name applied to several fanatical Muslim leaders, especially the Sudanese rebel, Mohammed Ahmed, b. about 1843, rose against Anglo-Egyptian government, d. 1885.

Mahler, Gustav, Bohemian composer (Symphonies, 1891–1913), b. 1860, d. 1911.

Mahmud I, Sultan of Turkey (1730–1754), b. 1696, d. 1754.

Mahmud II, Sultan of Turkey (1808–1839), b. 1785, d. 1839.

Mahomet, the Prophet, founder of Islam, b. about 570, d. 632.

Mahon, Charles James Patrick (' The O'Gorman Mahon '), Irish politician, b. 1800, d. 1891.

Maiden Castle, Dorset, developed in the Iron Age, turned into a camp 250 B.C., destroyed about A.D. 70 ; excavated 1934.

Maidstone Grammar School, Kent, English public school, founded 1549 ; origin before 1348.

Mail Coaches, first ran between Bristol and London, 1784.

Maillol, Aristide, French sculptor, b. 1861, d. 1944.

Maimonides (Moses ben Maimon), Jewish theologian (*Mishna Torah*), b. 1135, d. 1204.

Maine, Sir Henry James Sumner, English jurist and historian, b. 1822, d. 1888.

Maine, U.S. battleship, blown up in Havana Harbour 1898.

Maine, U.S.A., first successful settlement 1623, admitted to the Union 1820.

Maintenon, Françoise d'Aubigné, Mme, de, wife of Louis XIV, b. 1635, d. 1719.

Maitland, Frederick William, English jurist, b. 1850, d. 1906.

Maitland, William, Scottish statesman, b. about 1528, d. 1575.

Majorca (Mallorca), conquered by James I of Aragon, 1229.

Majorian, Roman Emperor (457–461), d. 461.

Makarios III, Cypriot archbishop and statesman, b. 1913.

Makhno, Nestor, Ukrainian anarchist leader, b. 1889, d. 1935.

Malacca, Federation of Malaya, settled by the Portuguese 1511, came finally under British rule 1824 ; incorporated in the Malayan Union 1946.

Malachy, St, b. about 1094, d. 1148.

Malaria Parasite, discovered 1895–1898 by the India-born physician Sir Ronald Ross, b. 1857, d. 1932.

Malatesta, Enrico, Italian anarchist, b. 1853, d. 1932.

Malatesta, Sigismonde, Italian tyrant and soldier, b. 1417, d. 1468.

Malaya, Straits Settlements formed 1826 ; Federation of Malaya formed 1895, occupied by Japanese 1942–

1945, became a sovereign member-state of the British Commonwealth 1957.

Malcolm I, King of the Scots, 942–954.

Malcolm II, King of the Scots, 1005–1034.

Malcolm III, King of the Scots (1054–1093), killed 1093.

Malcolm IV, King of the Scots (1153–1165), b. about 1141, d. 1165.

Malcontents, Treaty of the, signed with the Prince of Parma, 19 May 1579.

Maldive Islands, Indian Ocean, came under British protection 1887.

Maldon, Battle of, between the Danes and the East Saxons, 991.

Mâle, Emile, French art critic and historian (*L'An Mil*), b. 1862, d. 1954.

Malebranche, Nicolas, French philosopher, b. 1638, d. 1715.

Malesherbes, Chrétien Guillaume de Lamoignon, French statesman, b. 1721, guillotined 1794.

Malherbe, François de, French poet (*Larmes de St Pierre* 1587), b. 1555, d. 1628.

Mali, Federation of, formed from the French territories of Senegal and Sudan, 4 Apr. 1959.

Malinowski, Bronisław, Polish-born anthropologist, b. 1884, d. 1942.

Malipiero, Francesco, Italian composer (*I Corvi di San Marco*, 1932), b. 1882.

Mallarmé, Stéphane, French poet (*L'Après-midi d'un faune*, 1876), b. 1842, d. 1898.

Mallet, David, Scottish poet (*William and Margaret*, 1723), b. about 1705, d. 1765.

Mallorca (Majorca), conquered by James I of Aragon 1229.

Malmö, Treaty of, between Gustavus Vasa and the Danes, signed 1523.

Malone, Edmond, Irish literary critic, b. 1741, d. 1812.

Malory, Sir Thomas, English writer (*Le Morte Darthur*, printed 1485), d. about 1471.

Malpighi, Marcello, Italian biologist, b. 1628, d. 1694.

Malplaquet, Battle of, between the Allies and the French, 11 Sept. 1709.

Malraux, André, French writer (*La Condition humaine*, 1933), b. 1902.

Malta, ruled by Knights of St John of Jerusalem (1530–1798) ; conquered from French by English 1800 ; annexed to the British Crown by the Treaty of Paris 1814. Awarded the George Cross by King George VI 15 Apr. 1942.

Malta, Knights of, Order of St John of Jerusalem, 1529–1798.

Malthus, Thomas Robert, English economist and population expert (*Essay on the Principle of Population*, 1798), b. 1766, d. 1834.

Malvern, Godfrey Huggins, Viscount, Prime Minister (1953–1956) of the Federation of Rhodesia and Nyasaland, b. 1883.

Malvern Hill, Battle of, American Civil War, 1 July 1862.

Malvern College, English public school, founded 1862, opened 1865.

Malvern Festival, of English drama, instituted 1928.

Mamluks, ruled Egypt 1250–1517, Iraq 1749–1831.

Man, Isle of, ceded to Scotland 1266 ; came under English government 1290 ; ruled by Stanley family 1405–1651, 1660–1736 ; by Duke of Atholl 1736–1766 ; Crown colony 1766–1866 ; home rule since 1866.

Man-made Fibres, industry established about 1885 by the French scientist Hilaire, Comte de Chardonnet, b. 1839, d. 1924.

Manasseh ben Israel, Portuguese-born Jewish scholar, who successfully interceded with Cromwell for the re-admission of Jews to England, b. 1604, d. 1657.

Manchester Grammar School, English public school, founded by Hugh Oldham, Bishop of Exeter, 1515.

Manchester Guardian, founded 1821, changed its name to the *Guardian* 1959.

Manchester November Handicap, first run 1876.

Manchester-Liverpool Railway, opened 15 Sept. 1830.

Manchester Ship Canal, construction began 1887 ; opened 1894.

Manchester University, founded 1846 as Owens College by the English philanthropist John Owens (1790–1846) ; first session formally opened 6 Oct. 1903.

Manchu Dynasty, China, 1644–1912.

Mancini, Pasquale Stanislao, Italian statesman, b. 1817, d. 1888.

Mandate, system of governing a people not qualified for independence, introduced by the League of Nations 1920.

Mandeville, Bernard de, Dutch-born physician and writer (*A Fable of the Bees*, 1714), b. 1670, d. 1733.

Manet, Edouard, French painter (*Olympia*, 1865), b. 1832, d. 1883.

Manetho, Egyptian historian, lived in the 4th century B.C.

Manfred, King of Sicily (1255–1266), b. about 1232, killed in battle 1266.

Manganese, metallic chemical element, isolated by J. G. Gahn 1774.

Manganese Steel, discovered 1885 by the British metallurgist Sir Robert Abbott Hadfield, b. 1859, d. 1940.

Manhattan Bridge, N.Y., construction began 1901 ; officially opened 1909.

Manhattan Island, bought (1626) from the Indians by Peter Minuit, b. about 1580, d. 1638.

Mani, Persian founder of Manichæism, b. about 215, crucified about 276.

Manila Conference, on South East Asia defence, held 6–8 Sept. 1954.

Manilius, Roman poet in 1st century.

Manin, Daniele, Italian statesman, b. 1804, d. 1857.

Manitoba, organised as the Red River Settlement 1812, admitted to the Dominion of Canada 1870.

Manley, Mary de la Riviere, English writer (*Secret Memoirs*, 1709), b. about 1663, d. 1724.

Manley, Norman, Jamaican statesman, b. 1893.

Manlius, Titus, Roman statesman, *fl.* 363–340 B.C.

Mann, Heinrich, German novelist (*Professor Unrat*, 1904), b. 1871, d. 1950.

Mann, Thomas, German novelist (*Buddenbrooks*, 1901), b. 1875, d. 1955.

Mann Act (White Slave Act) brought 1910 into being by the American politician James Robert Mann, b. 1856, d. 1922.

Manning, Cardinal Henry Edward, English convert (6 Apr. 1851) to Catholicism, b. 1808, d. 1892.

Mannyng, Robert, English poet (*Handlyng Synne*), b. about 1264, d. about 1340.

Manoel I, King of Portugal (1495–1521), b. 1469, d. 1521.

Manoel II, King of Portugal (1908–1910), b. 1889, d. 1932.

Mansard, François Nicolas, French architect, b. 1598, d. 1666.

Mansard, Jules Hardouin, French architect, b. 1645, d. 1708.

Mansell, Sir Robert, English pioneer 1615–1636 in manufacture of looking-glasses, b. 1573, d. 1656.

'Mansfield, Katherine ' (Katherine Beauchamp), New Zealand short-story writer (*The Dove's Nest*, 1923), b. 1888, d. 1923.

Mansfield College, Oxford University (formerly Spring Hill College, Birmingham), refounded at Oxford 1886.

Manship, Paul, American sculptor, b. 1885.

Mansion House, London, designed 1739 by the English architect George Dance, b. 1700, d. 1768.

Mansur, Caliph, founder (762) of Baghdad, d. 775.

Mantegna, Andrea, Italian painter (*St Euphemia*), b. 1431, d. 1506.

Mantell, Gideon Algernon, English geologist, b. 1790, d. 1852.

Manu, Laws of, Brahman code, composed before 3rd century B.C.

Manuel I, Commenus, Byzantine Emperor (1143–1180), b. about 1120, d. 1180.

Manuel II, Palæologus, Byzantine Emperor (1391–1425), b. 1350, d. 1425.

Manutius, Aldus, Venetian printer, b. 1449, d. 1515.

Manzoni, Alessandro, Italian writer (*I Promessi sposi*, 1825–1827), b. 1785, d. 1873.

Maori Wars, New Zealand, began 1860, ended 1870.

Maoris, New Zealand, pioneer studies carried out by Stephenson Percy Smith, b. 1840, d. 1922.

Map, Walter, Welsh writer (*De nugis curialium*), b. about 1138, d. 1209.

Mapungubwe, Southern Rhodesia, ruins of remarkable buildings erected 12th to 16th centuries.

Mar, John, Earl of, Jacobite leader, b. 1675, d. 1732.

Marat, Jean Paul, French revolutionary leader, b. 1743, assassinated 1793.

Marathon, Battle of, between Greeks and Persians, 29 Sept. 490 B.C.

Marbeck, John, English composer and organist, b. 1523, d. 1585.

Marble Arch, London, built 1828 ; re-erected at Cumberland Gate, Hyde Park, 1851.

Marbling, printing process came into use in England late in the 17th century.

Marburg Colloquy, Protestant conference, held 1529.

Marc Antony (Marcus Antonius), Roman leader, b. about 83, committed suicide 30 B.C.

Marc, Franz, German painter (*La Tour des chevaux bleux*), b. 1880, killed in battle 1916.

Marcellinus, St, Pope 296–308.

Marcellus, St, Pope 308–309.

Marcellus II, Pope 1555.

March, Roger de Mortimer, Earl of, statesman, b. about 1287, hanged 1330.

March, Roger de Mortimer, Earl of, Lieutenant of Ireland, b. 1374, killed in battle 1398.

Marchesi, Mathilde, German singer and music teacher, b. 1826, d. 1913.

Marchmont, Patrick Hume, Earl of, statesman, b. 1641, d. 1724.

Marcian, (Martianus Capella), 5th century North African writer.

Marcion of Sinope, shipowner and founder of the Sect of Marcionites, b. about 100, d. about 165.

Marco Polo, Italian explorer, b. 1254, d. 1324.

Marconi, Guglielmo, Italian radio pioneer, b. 1874, d. 1937.

Marconi Transatlantic Wireless Service, inaugurated 1907.

Marcus Aurelius, Roman Emperor (161–180), author of the *Meditations*, b. 121, d. 180.

Mardi Gras, the last day of carnival, celebrated on Shrove Tuesday.

Maréchal, Charles Laurent, French painter, b. 1801, d. 1887.

Marees, Hans von, German painter (*St George*), b. 1837, d. 1887.

Marengo, Battle of, between Napoleon and the Austrians, 4 June 1800.

Margaret, St, Queen of Scotland, b. about 1045, d. about 1093.

Margaret, Mary Alacoque, St, French visionary (Sacred Heart 1673–1675), b. 1647, d. 1690.

Margaret, Queen of Navarre, and writer (*The Heptameron,* 1558), b. 1492, d. 1549.

Margaret, Maid of Norway, b. 1283, drowned 1290.

Margaret Tudor, Queen of Scotland, b. 1489, d. 1541.

Margaret, Princess, b. 21 Aug. 1930, m. 6 May 1960.

Margarine, invented by the French chemist Hippolyte Mège-Mouriés, b. 1817, d. 1880.

Marggraf, Andreas, German chemist, b. 1709, d. 1782.

Maria I, Queen of Portugal (1777–1786), b. 1734, d. 1816.

Maria Stella, Lady Newborough, pretender, b. 1773, d. 1843.

Maria Theresa, Austrian Empress, b. 1717, d. 1780.

Marianas, Pacific Islands, passed into U.S. trusteeship 1947 ; except Guam, which was ceded by Spain to the U.S.A. 1898.

Marianus Scotus, Irish historian, b. 1028, d. 1082.

Marie Amélie, Queen of France, b. 1782, d. 1866.

Marie Antoinette, Queen of France, b. 1755, guillotined 1793.

Marie de Médicis (Maria de' Medici), Queen of France (Regent 1610–1617), b. 1573, d. 1642.

Marie Leszczynska, Queen of France, b. 1703, d. 1768.

Marie Byrd Land, Antarctica, discovered 1929 by the American Admiral Richard Evelyn Byrd, b. 1888, d. 1957.

Mariette, Auguste Ferdinand François, French Egyptologist, b. 1821, d. 1881.

Marignan, Battle of, between the French and the Swiss, 13–14 Sept. 1515.

Marine Steam Turbines, first installed in the *Turbinia* 1894.

Marini, Marino, Italian sculptor, b. 1901.

Marinus I, Pope 882–884.

Marinus II, Pope 942–946.

'Mario, Giuseppe' (Giovanni de Candia), Italian operatic singer, b. 1810, d. 1883.

Marion, Francis, American Brigadier-General, b. 1732, d. 1795.

Mariotte, Edme, French physician, b. about 1620, d. 1684.

Maris, William, Dutch painter (principally landscapes and animals), b. 1844, d. 1910.

Marischal College, Aberdeen, founded 1593 by George Keith, Earl Marischal, b. about 1553, d. 1623.

Marisco, Geoffrey de, Viceroy of Ireland, d. 1245.

Marists, Catholic orders, Fathers founded 1816, Brothers founded 1817, Sisters founded 1834.

Maritain, Jacques, French philosopher, b. 1882.

Marius, Caius, Roman consul, b. about 155, d. 86 B.C.

Marivaux, Pierre Carlet de, French writer (*L'Amour et la Vérité,* 1720), b. 1688, d. 1763.

Mark, St, Pope 336–337.

Markham, Sir Clements Robert, English geographer and historian, b. 1830, d. 1916.

Markham, Gervase, English scholar and agricultural reformer, b. about 1568, d. 1637.

Markova, Alicia, English dancer, b. 1910.

Marlborough, John Churchill, Duke of, victor (1704) at Blenheim, b. 1650, d. 1722.

Marlborough, Sarah, Duchess of, b. 1660, d. 1744.

Marlborough College, English public school, founded 1843 ; incorporated by Royal Charter 1845.

Marlowe, Christopher, English poet and dramatist (*Doctor Faustus,* 1588), b. 1564, killed 1593.

Marmont, August Viesse de, Duc de Raguse, Marshal of France, b. 1774, d. 1852.

Marmontel, Jean François, French writer (*Aristomène,* 1749), b. 1723, d. 1799.

Marne, Battle of the, World War I, 6–12 Sept. 1914.

Maronites, Christian heretical sect, appeared in the Lebanon about 681, reconciled to Rome 1182 ; massacre by Druses 1860.

'Marprelate, Martin', unidentified writer of Puritan pamphlets issued 1588–1589.

Marquesas Islands, French Polynesia, formally annexed by France 1842.

Marquette, Jacques, French missionary and explorer in America, b. 1637, d. 1675.

Marquis, Don, American humorous writer (*Archy and Mehitabel,* 1927), b. 1878, d. 1937.

Marriages, clandestine, abolished in England 1754 ; non-religious, made legal 1836.

Married Women's Property Act, Britain, became law 1883.

Marryat, Frederick, English sailor and novelist (*Mr Midshipman Easy,* 1836), b. 1792, d. 1848.

Mars, 'Canals' observed 1877 by the Italian astronomer Giovanni Schiaparelli, b. 1835, d. 1910.

'Marseillaise, La', composed and written 1792 by the French Claude Joseph Rouget de l'Isle, b. 1760, d. 1836.

Marsh, Charles Wesley, American inventor, b. 1834, d. 1918.

Marsh, James, English pioneer in electromagnetism, b. 1794, d. 1846.

Marshall, William, Earl of Pembroke, Regent of England, d. 1219.

Marshall Islands, Pacific, passed into U.S. trusteeship 1947.

Marshall Plan, concerning European post-war recovery, proposed 1947 by the American General George Catlett Marshall, b. 1880, d. 1959.

Marshalsea Prison, London, established by King Edward II's reign ; abolished 1849.

Marsilius of Padua, Italian writer (*Defensor Pacis,* 1324), lived in the 2nd half of the 13th and the 1st half of the 14th centuries.

Marston, John, English playwright (*Antonio and Mellida,* 1602), b. about 1575, d. 1634.

Marston Moor, Battle of, between the Parliamentarians and the Royalists 2 July 1644.

Martello Towers, English coastal defences, built at the turn of the 18th century.

Marten, Maria, murdered 1827 by William Corder, b. 1804, executed 1828.

Martha's Vineyard, Mass., discovered 1602 by the English navigator Captain Bartholomew Gosnold, d. 1607.

Marti, Jose Maria, Cuban patriot, b. 1853, killed in battle 1895.

Martial, Latin poet (*Epigrams*), b. about 40, d. 104.

Martin, St, Bishop of Tours, b. about 316, d. 397.

Martin I, St, Pope 649–653, d. 655.

Martin II ⎧ (non-existent ; numbering
Martin III ⎨ confused with Popes
　　　　　　 ⎩ Marinus I and II).

Martin IV (Simon Monpitié de Brion), Pope 1281–1285, b. about 1210, d. 1285.

Martin V (Otto Colonna), Pope 1417–1431, d. 1431.

Martin, John, English painter (*Belshazzar's Feast,* 1821), b. 1789, d. 1854.

Martin du Gard, Roger, French writer (*Les Thibault,* 1922–   ), b. 1881.

Martineau, Harriet, English writer (*Feats on the Fjord,* 1841), b. 1802, d. 1876.

Martini, Padre (Giambattista Martini), Italian composer, b. 1706, d. 1784.

Martinique, discovered 1502 by Christopher Columbus ; colonised by the French from 1625.

Martinmas, Feast of St Martin, celebrated 11th Nov.

Martinu, Bohuslav, Czech composer (*The Judgment of Paris*, 1935), b. 1890.

Martyn, Henry, English missionary, b. 1781, d. 1812.

Marvell, Andrew, English poet (*Appleton House*), b. 1621, d. 1678.

Marx, Karl, German socialist (*Das Kapital*, 1867–1883), b. 1818, d. 1883.

Mary I, Queen of England (1553–1558), b. 1516, d. 1558.

Mary II, Queen of England, Scotland and Ireland, b. 1662, d. 1694.

Mary, Queen of Scots, b. 1542, beheaded 1587.

Mary, Queen, wife of King George V, b. 1867, d. 1953.

Mary Celeste, derelict ship, found 5 Dec. 1872.

Mary of Modena, Queen of King James II, b. 1658, d. 1718.

Maryland, U.S.A., first settled 1634 ; one of the 13 original States of the Union.

Maryland University, Baltimore, founded 1807.

Marylebone Cricket Club, founded 1787 ; first match 1788 ; present ground opened 1814.

Masaccio (Tommaso di Ser Giovanni di Mone), Italian painter (*Madonna and Child*), b. 1401, d. about 1428.

Masaniello (Tommaso Aniello), Italian patriot, b. 1623, murdered 1647.

Masaryk, Jan, Czech statesman, b. 1886, d. 1948.

Masaryk, Thomas Garrigue, Czech President (1918–1935), b. 1850, d. 1937.

Mascagni, Pietro, Italian composer (*Cavalleria rusticana*, 1890), b. 1863, d. 1945.

Masefield, John, English poet (*The Everlasting Mercy*, 1911), b. 1878 ; Poet Laureate from 1930.

Masham, Abigail, Lady Masham, Court favourite, d. 1734.

Maskelyne, John Nevil, English conjuror, b. 1839, d. 1917.

Masolino, Italian painter (*Madonna*), b. about 1383, d. about 1447.

Mason, John, English founder 1631 of New Hampshire, U.S.A., b. 1586, d. 1635.

Mason, Lowell, American composer (*From Greenland's Icy Mountains*), b. 1792, d. 1872.

Mason and Dixon's Line, boundary between Pennsylvania and Maryland (and so between free and slave regions), fixed 1763–1767.

Maspero, Gaston, French Egyptologist, b. 1846, d. 1916.

Massachusetts, U.S.A., first settled 1620 ; one of the 13 original states of the Union.

Massachusetts Bay Company, granted territory 1628 by the Council of New England ; grant ratified by Royal Charter 1629.

Massachusetts Institute of Technology, founded Boston 1859 ; moved to Cambridge, Mass., 1915.

Masséna, Marshal André, Italian-born French army leader, b. 1756, d. 1817.

Massenet, Jules, French composer (*Manon Lescaut*, 1884), b. 1842, d. 1912.

Massey, Vincent, first Canadian Governor-General of Canada (1952–59), b. 1887.

Massinger, Philip, English dramatist (*The City Madam*, 1632), b. 1583, d. 1640.

Massingham, Henry William, English journalist, b. 1860, d. 1924.

Masson, David, Scottish historian, b. 1822, d. 1907.

Master-Gunner of England, office last held (from 1709) by Colonel James Pendlebury, d. about 1758.

Master of the King's Musick, title originated about 1625 ; first Master Nicholas Lanier, b. 1588, d. 1666.

Masters, Edgar Lee, American poet (*Spoon River Anthology*, 1915), b. 1869, d. 1950.

Mastoid, operation first successfully performed in 1774 by the French surgeon Jean Louis Petit.

Masurian Lakes, Battles of the, World War I, between the German and the Russians, 1914–1915.

Masurium (Technetium), chemical element, discovered 1925 by I. and W. Noddack. Confirmed by C. Perrier and E. Segré 1937.

Matapan, Battle of, World War II, 28 Mar. 1941.

Matches, Book, invented 1892 by the American attorney John Pusey.

Matches, Friction wooden, invented 1827 by the English chemist John Walker, b. about 1781, d. 1859.

Matches, Safety, invented 1855 by the Swedish inventor Johan Edvard Lundström.

Mather, Cotton, American witch-hunting writer (*Memorable Providences Relating to Witchcraft*, 1685), b. 1663, d. 1728.

Mather, Increase, American President of Harvard College, b. 1639, d. 1723.

Mathews, Charles James, English actor and playwright, b. 1803, d. 1878.

Matilda, Queen of England, d. 1083.

Matisse, Henri, French painter (*Odalisque*, 1910), b. 1869, d. 1954.

Matsys, Quentin, Flemish painter (*Burial of Christ*), b. about 1466, d. 1530.

Matterhorn, Swiss-Italian frontier, first climbed 1865 by the English mountaineer Edward Whymper, b. 1840, d. 1911.

Matthay, Tobias, English musician, b. 1858, d. 1945.

Matthew of Paris, English historian (*Chronica majora*), d. 1259.

Matthew, Tobie, Archbishop of York (1606–1628), b. 1546, d. 1628.

Matthias, Holy Roman Emperor (1612–1619), b. 1557, d. 1619.

Matthias Corvinus, King of Hungary (1458–1490), b. 1440, d. 1490.

Maturin, Charles Robert, Irish writer (*Melmoth*, 1820), b. 1782, d. 1824.

Mau Mau, terrorist movement in Kenya 1952–1957.

Maud, wife of King Henry I of England, b. 1080, d. 1118.

Maugham, William Somerset, British writer (*Of Human Bondage*, 1916), and playwright, b. 1874.

Maundy Thursday, commemoration on the Thursday before Easter of Christ's washing the Apostles' feet.

Maupassant, Guy de, French writer (*Boule de suif*, 1880), b. 1850, d. 1893.

Maupeou, René Nicolas Charles Augustin de, French statesman, b. 1714, d. 1792.

Maupertuis, Pierre Louis, French mathematician, b. 1698, d. 1759.

Maurepas, Jean Frédéric Phélipeaux, Comte de, French statesman, b. 1701, d. 1781.

Mauretania, Atlantic passenger liner, launched 20 Sept. 1906.

Mauriac, François, French novelist (*Le Baiser aux Lépreux*, 1922), b. 1885.

Maurice, Byzantine Emperor (582–602), b. about 540, assassinated 602.

Mauritania, West Africa, autonomous Islamic republic within the French Community since 1960.

Mauritius, British colony, discovered 1507 by the Portuguese ; ceded by France to Britain 1814.

Maurois, André (Emile Herzog), French writer (*Vie de Disraeli*, 1927), b. 1885.

Maurras, Charles, French writer (*Les Amants de Venise*, 1902), b. 1868, d. 1952.

Maury, Jean Siffrein, French Cardinal and political writer, b. 1746, d. 1817.

Mauve, Anton, Dutch painter (*Watering Horses*), b. 1838, d. 1888.

Mauveine, first synthetic organic dye, discovered 1856 by the English chemist Sir William Henry Perkin, b. 1838, d. 1907.

Mavrocordato, Prince Alexander, Greek statesman, b. 1791, d. 1865.

Mawson, Professor Sir Douglas, Antarctic explorer, b. 1882, d. 1958.

Max, Gabriel, Czech painter (*The Widow*, 1872), b. 1840, d. 1915.

Maxentius, Roman Emperor (306–312), drowned 312.

Maxim Machine Gun, invented 1884 by the American-born inventor Sir Hiram Stevens Maxim, b. 1840, d. 1916.

Maximian, Roman Emperor (286–305), committed suicide 310.

Maximilian I, King of Bavaria (1806–1825), b. 1756, d. 1825.

Maximilian II, King of Bavaria (1848–1864), b. 1811, d. 1864.

Maximilian I, Holy Roman Emperor (1493–1519), b. 1459, d. 1519.

Maximilian II, Holy Roman Emperor (1564–1576), b. 1527, d. 1576.

Maximilian, Austrian-born Emperor of Mexico (1864–1867), b. 1832, shot 1867.

Maximin, Roman Emperor (235–238), murdered 238.

Maximin, Roman Emperor (308–313), d. 313.

Maximus, St, the Confessor, b. about 580, d. 662.

Maximus, Roman Emperor (383–388), executed 388.

Max-Müller, Friedrich, German-born philologist and orientalist, b. 1823, d. 1900.

Maxton, James, Scottish socialist, b. 1885, d. 1946.

Maxwell, James Clerk-, Scottish physicist, b. 1831, d. 1879.

Maxwell, John, Earl of Morton, Warden of the West Marches, b. 1553, killed 1593.

May, Phil, humorous artist, b. 1864, d. 1903.

May, Thomas, English writer (*History of the Long Parliament*, 1647), b. 1595, d. 1650.

May Day, day of celebration connected with vegetation and labour.

Mayakovsky, Vladimir Vladimirovich, Russian poet, b. 1894, committed suicide 1930.

Mayan Calendar, interpreted 1920 by the American anthropologist Herbert Joseph Spinden, b. 1879.

Mayan Empire, Mexico, flourished 3rd to 15th centuries A.D.

Mayenne, Charles de Lorraine, Duc de, French king-maker, b. 1554, d. 1611.

Mayer, Joseph, English antiquary and philanthropist, b. 1803, d. 1886.

Mayerling Tragedy, in which the Crown Prince Rudolf of Austria and Mary Vetsera committed suicide 30 Jan. 1889.

Mayflower Pilgrims, set sail from Plymouth for New England 6 Sept. 1620 ; arrived Plymouth Rock, Massachusetts, 16 Dec. 1620 (O.S.).

Mayhew, Henry, English writer on social subjects (particularly London), b. 1812, d. 1887.

Maynard, François, French poet (*Philandre*, 1619), b. 1582, d. 1646.

Maynooth, Irish seminary for Catholic priesthood, founded 1795.

Mayo Clinic and **Mayo Foundation for Medical Education,** founded respectively 1889 and 1912 in Rochester, Minnesota, by the American surgeons Charles (b. 1865, d. 1939) and William (b. 1861, d. 1939) Mayo.

Mayor, First English woman, Elizabeth Garrett Anderson, b. 1836, d. 1917, elected Mayor of Aldeburgh 1908.

Mayow, John, English physiologist, b. 1640, d. 1679.

Mazarin, Jules, Cardinal, Italian-born French statesman (Regent 1642–1661), b. 1602, d. 1661.

Mazarine, public library of Paris, opened 1643 ; absorbed by the Bibliothèque Nationale 1930.

Mazeppa, Ivan Stepanovich, Cossack leader, b. about 1644, d. 1709.

Mazzini, Giuseppe, Italian leader, b. 1805, d. 1872.

Mazzuchelli, Samuel Charles, Italian missionary in N. America, b. 1806, d. 1864.

Mead, Richard, English Royal physician, b. 1673, d. 1754.

Meade, Richard James, Earl of Clanwilliam, Admiral of the Fleet, b. 1832, d. 1907.

Meagher, Thomas Francis, Irish patriot, b. 1823, drowned 1867.

Meal Tub Plot, 1679, conceived by the English adventurer Thomas Dangerfield, b. 1650, d. 1685.

Mecca, Muslim holy city ; captured by Mohammed 630 ; by Ibn Sa'ud 1924.

Mechnikov, Ilya (see **Metchnikoff** Elie).

Mecklenburg Declaration, of American independence, made 1775.

Medal, First English, struck by King Charles I 1643. The first medal given to all ranks : King George II's 1745–1746.

Medical Inspection of School-children, First British, held at Bradford 1899.

Medical Profession, British, opened 1876 to women by the efforts of the English physician and mathematician Sophia Louisa Jex-Blake, b. 1840, d. 1912.

Medici Family, ruled Florence 1434–1494, 1512–1527, 1530–1737.

Medici, Catherine de', Queen of France and Regent (1560–1572), b. 1519, d. 1589.

Medici, Cosimo de', Florentine leader, b. 1389, d. 1464.

Medici, Ferdinand de', Grand Duke of Tuscany (1587–1609), b. 1549, d. 1609.

Medici, Giovanni de', Italian military commander, b. 1498, mortally wounded 1526.

Medici, Lorenzo de', the Magnificent, Florentine leader, b. 1449, d. 1492.

Medici, Maria de', Queen of France, b. 1573, d. 1642.

Medina, Arabian city, home of Mohammed after *hegira* 622.

Medina-Sidonia, Alonso Pérez de Guzman el Bueno, Duke of, Spanish Armada commander, b. 1550, d. 1615.

Medtner, Nikolai, Russian-born composer (*Märchen*), b. 1880, d. 1951.

Meer, Jan van der, Dutch painter (*The Astronomer*), b. 1628, d. 1691.

Meerut, place of outbreak of Indian Mutiny 10 May 1857.

Mège-Mouries, Hippolyte, French chemist and inventor 1869 of margarine, b. 1817, d. 1880.

Mèhul, Etienne Nicolas, French composer (*Joseph*, 1807), b. 1763, d. 1817.

Meigs, Return Jonathan, American military commander, b. 1740, d. 1823.

Meiklejohn, John Miller Dow, Scottish textbook writer, b. 1836, d. 1902.

Meilhac, Henri, French playwright (with Halévy, *Barbe-Bleue*, 1866), b. 1831, d. 1897.

Meillet, Antoine, French philologist, b. 1866.

Meissonier, Jean Ernest, French painter (*Napoleon with His Staff*), b. 1815, d. 1891.

Melanchthon, Philipp (Schwartzerd), German religious reformer, b. 1497, d. 1560.

Melba, Dame Nellie (Helen Porter Mitchell), Australian singer, b. 1861, d. 1931.

Melbourne, William Lamb, Viscount, British statesman (Prime Minister 1834–1841), b. 1779, d. 1848.

Melbourne University, Victoria, Australia, founded 1854 ; opened 1855.

Melchers, Gari, American painter, b. 1860, d. 1932.

Melchett, Alfred Moritz Mond, Baron, English industrialist, b. 1868, d. 1930.

Melchiades, St, Pope 311–314.

Melchior, Lauritz, Danish operatic singer, b. 1890.

Meletius, St, Patriarch of Antioch, b. about 310, d. 381.

Melkites, name given to orthodox Christians after 451, and again to Catholics after 1724, in the Levant.

Mellon, Andrew William, American financier, b. 1855, d. 1937.

'Melmoth, Sebastian' (Oscar Wilde), Irish writer, b. 1856, d. 1900.

Melozzo da Forli, Italian painter, b. about 1438, d. 1494.

Melrose Abbey, Scotland, founded by King David I 1136.

Melville, Herman, American novelist (*Moby Dick*, 1852), b. 1819, d. 1891.

Melville, James, Scottish reformer, b. 1556, d. 1614.

Member of Parliament, First Quaker (1833) ; First Jewish (1858), Baron Lionel de Rothschild, b. 1808, d. 1879. First atheist (1886), Charles Bradlaugh, b. 1833, d. 1891.

Member of Parliament, First woman, Lady Astor, took her seat in the House of Commons 1 Dec. 1919.

Memling, Hans, Flemish painter (*The Marriage of St Catherine*), b. about 1435, d. about 1494.

Memorial Day (Decoration Day), U.S.A., 30 May ; first observed 1869.

Menai Suspension Bridge, built 1818–1826 by the Scottish engineer Thomas Telford, b. 1757, d. 1834.

Menander, Greek playwright (*Diskolos*), b. 342, d. about 291 B.C.

Mencius, Chinese philosopher, b. 372, d. about 289 B.C.

Mencken, Henry Louis, first editor (1924–1933) of the *American Mercury*, b. 1880, d. 1956.

Mendel, Gregor, Austrian monk and pioneer student of heredity, b. 1822, d. 1884.

'Mendele Moichersforim' (Shalom Abramovich), Yiddish writer, b. 1835, d. 1917.

Mendeleieff, Dmitri Ivanovich, Russian chemist, b. 1834, d. 1907.

Mendelian Principles of Heredity, postulated 1865 by the Austrian scientist and monk Gregor Johann Mendel, b. 1822, d. 1884.

Mendelsohn, Erich, German-born architect, b. 1887, d. 1953.

Mendelssohn, Felix, German composer (*Fingal's Cave*, 1830), b. 1809, d. 1847.

Mendelssohn, Moses, German Jewish philosopher, b. 1729, d. 1786.

Mendès, Catulle, French poet (*Philomela*, 1864), b. 1841, killed in an accident 1909.

Mendès-France, Pierre, French statesman (Prime Minister 1954–1955), b. 1907.

Mendoza, Antonio de, Spanish poet (*La Celestina*), b. about 1590, d. 1644.

Menelik I, Emperor of Ethiopia, son of Solomon and Sheba, lived in 13th century B.C.

Menelik II, Emperor of Ethiopia (1889–1913), b. 1844, d. 1913.

Menendez Pidal, Ramón, Spanish philologist, b. 1869.

Mengelberg, Willem, Dutch conductor, b. 1871, d. 1951.

Mengs, Anton Raffael, German painter (*Mount Parnassus*, 1861), b. 1728, d. 1779.

Menin Gate, Belgium, memorial to the British who fell in the Ypres salient, World War I, unveiled 1927.

Meninsky, Bernard, Russian-born painter, b. 1891.

Menken, Adah Isaacs, American actress, b. 1835, d. 1868.

Mennonites, religious movement, originating among Anabaptists 1525, founded 1537 by the Dutch religious leader Menno Simons, b. 1492, d. 1559.

Menorca (Minorca), captured by British 1708, returned to Spain 1802.

Menotti, Gian-Carlo, Italian-born composer (*The Medium*, 1946), b. 1911.

Menpes, Mortimer, Australian-born painter (*Head of Cecil Rhodes*), b. 1859, d. 1938.

Mensheviks, minority fraction of Russian Social-Democrat Party at Congress in Brussels and London, 1903 ; expelled from Party by Bolsheviks in 1912.

Menshikov, Prince Aleksandr Danilovich, Russian statesman, b. 1672, d. 1729.

Mental Hygiene, modern study founded by the Swiss-born psychiatrist Adolf Meyer, b. 1866, d. 1950.

Menton, elected by plebiscite to be annexed to France 1860.

Menuhin, Hepzibah, American pianist, b. 1920.

Menuhin, Yehudi, American-born violinist, b. 1916.

Menzies, Robert, Australian statesman (Prime Minister 1939–1941 ; 1949–), b. 1894.

Merbecke, John, English composer and organist, b. 1523, d. 1585.

Mercator, Gerardus, Flemish geographer (first world map 1538 ; first atlas published 1595), b. 1512, d. 1594.

Mercer, John, English chemist and inventor 1850 of mercerising, b. 1791, d. 1866.

Mercers' Company, London livery company, first recorded reference 1172 ; Chartered 1393.

Mercers' School, London, English public school, founded by the Mercers' Company 1542.

Merchant Taylors Company, London livery company, origins uncertain ; first Chartered by King Edward III 1327 ; again Chartered by King Henry VII 1503.

Merchant Taylors' School, Middlesex, English public school founded by the Company of Merchant Taylors 1561.

Merchant Taylors' School, Crosby, English public school, founded by the merchant tailor John Harrison of London 1620.

Merchiston Castle School, Edinburgh, Scottish public school, established 1833.

Mercier, Sébastien, French writer (*Tableau de Paris,* 1781–1790), b. 1740, d. 1814.

Merciless Parliament, which condemned friends of Richard II to death, Feb.-May 1388.

Mercury, planet, transit first observed 1631 by the French scientist Pierre Gassendi, b. 1592, d. 1655.

Mercury Vapour Lamp, invented 1901 by the American scientist Peter Cooper-Hewitt, b. 1861, d. 1921.

Meredith, George, English writer (*The Egoist,* 1879), b. 1828, d. 1909.

'Meredith, Owen' (Edward Robert Bulwer Lytton, Earl Lytton), English poet (*The Wanderer,* 1857), b. 1831, d. 1891.

Merezhkovsky, Dmitri Sergeivich, Russian writer (*Leonardo da Vinci,* 1901), b. 1865, d. 1941.

Mergenthaler, Ottmar, German-born inventor of Linotype, b. 1854, d. 1899.

Meridian, first measured 1735–1736 by the Frenchmen Charles Marie la Condamine, b. 1701, d. 1774, and Pierre Louis Moreau de Maupertuis, b. 1698, d. 1759.

Merimée, Prosper, French novelist (*Carmen,* 1845), b. 1803, d. 1870.

Merit, Order of, Great Britain, founded 1902.

Merlin (Medium Energy Research Light-water moderated Industrial Nuclear reactor), Britain's first privately owned research reactor, started operating at Aldermaston 16 July 1959.

Mermaid Theatre, first English theatre opened in the City of London since The Restoration, opened 1959.

Merovingian Dynasty, ruled France 481–751.

'Merriman, Henry Seton' (Hugh Stowell Scott), British novelist (*In Kedar's Tents,* 1897), b. 1862, d. 1903.

Merry del Val, Cardinal Rafael, diplomat and administrator, b. 1865, d. 1930.

Mersen, Treaty of, dividing the kingdom of Lothair II between Charles the Bald and Louis the German, signed 8 Aug. 870.

Mersey Tunnel, Liverpool–Birkenhead, construction began 1925 ; opened 1934.

Merton, Walter de, Bishop of Rochester (1274–1277), d. 1277.

Merton College, Oxford University, founded 1264–1274 by Walter de Merton.

Meryon, Charles, French engraver (*La Vieille Morgue*), b. 1821, d. 1868.

Mesmerism, founded 1776 by the German physician Friedrich Franz Mesmer, b. 1734, d. 1815.

Mesozoic Era, Earth history, between 70 and 200 million years ago.

Messager, André, French composer (*Véronique,* 1898), b. 1853, d. 1929.

Messala, Roman consul, b. 64 B.C., d. A.D. 8.

Messalina, Valeria, Roman Empress, executed 48.

Messiaen, Olivier, French composer (*L'Ascension,* 1933), b. 1908.

Meštrović, Ivan, Yugoslav sculptor, b. 1883.

Metaphysical Society, London, founded 1869 by the English architect Sir James Knowles, b. 1831, d. 1908.

Metastasio, Pietro, Italian writer (*Olimpiade,* 1733), b. 1698, d. 1782.

Metaurus, Battle of, between the Romans and the Carthaginians, 207 B.C.

Metcalf, John, ' Blind Jack of Knaresborough ', English horse dealer and racer, athlete, soldier, road and bridge builder, b. 1717, d. 1810.

Metchnikoff, Elie, Russian-born bacteriologist (Nobel Prize 1908), b. 1845, d. 1916.

Metellus Macedonicus, Quintus Cæcilius, Roman prætor, d. 115 B.C.

Meteors, Leonid, great shower recorded 12 Nov. 1833.

Meteorological Office, London, founded 1850 by the English meteorologist James Glaisher, b. 1809, d. 1903.

Methodism : John Wesley, b. 1703, d. 1791, founded the first Methodist association May 1738. First General Conference of Methodists 1744. The Methodist Church of Great Britain and Ireland, uniting the Wesleyan, Primitive and United Methodist Churches, came into being 20 Sept. 1932.

Methodists, Primitive, Methodist sect, appeared 1811.

Methodists, United, group of Methodist sects, merged 1857, joined by other sects 1907.

Methuen Treaty, concerning British trade with Portugal, negotiated 1703 by the British statesman and diplomat John Methuen, b. about 1650, d. 1706.

Meton, Greek astronomer, lived in the 5th century B.C.

Metre, National standard, established in Britain 1897.

Metric System, introduced and legally adopted in France 1 Aug. 1793 ; new standards adopted 1889.

Metronome, invented 1812 by the mechanician Winkel of Amsterdam.

Metropolitan Board of Works, London, precursor of the London County Council, inaugurated 1885.

Metropolitan District Railway, London, opened 24 Dec. 1868 between Mansion House and S. Kensington.

Metropolitan Drainage System, London, planned and carried out 1855–1865 by the English engineer Sir Joseph William Bazalgette, b. 1819, d. 1891.

Metropolitan Museum of Art, New York, opened 1871.

Metropolitan Opera Company, New York, founded as Abbey's Italian Opera Company 1883.

Metropolitan Opera House, New York, opened 22 Oct. 1883 ; gold curtain installed 1905.

Metropolitan Police, London, established 1829.

Metropolitan Railway, London, opened 10 Jan. 1863 between Paddington and Farringdon Street ; electrified between Baker Street and Harrow 1904 ; Paris, opened 1900.

Metropolite, The, London's oldest music-hall, opened 1861 ; renamed London's Irish Music Hall 1959.

Metsu, Gabriel, Dutch painter (*The Music Lesson*), b. 1629, d. 1667.

Metternich, Clemens, Prince, Austrian diplomat and statesman, b. 1773, d. 1859.

Metz, Siege of, Franco-Prussian War, 27 Aug.–Oct. 1870.

Meulen, Adams Frans van der, Flemish painter (*Nancy and Arras*), b. 1632, d. 1690.

Meung, Jean de, French writer (part of the *Roman de la Rose*), b. about 1250, d. about 1305.

Mexican War, between the U.S.A. and Mexico, 1846–1848.

Mexico, conquered by the Spanish 1520 ; Spanish Viceroyalty 1535–1821 ; war of independence 1810–1821 ; period of national formation 1810–1910 ; social revolution 1911–1921.

Meyer, George W., American composer (*For Me and My Girl*), b. 1884, d. 1959.

Meyer, Lothar, German chemist, b. 1830, d. 1895.

Meyer-Förster, Wilhelm, German writer (*Karl Heinrich*, 1899), b. 1862, d. 1934.

Meyerbeer, Giacomo (Jakob Beer), German-born composer (*The Huguenots*, 1836), b. 1791, d. 1864.

Meyerhof, Otto, German physiologist, b. 1884, d. 1951.

Meyerling Tragedy : Crown Prince Rudolf and Mary Vetsera committed suicide 30 Jan. 1889.

Meynell, Alice, English writer (*The Children*, 1896), b. 1847, d. 1922.

Meyrink, Gustav, Austrian writer (*The Golem*, 1915), b. 1868, d. 1932.

Mezzotint Process, invented 1642 by the Dutch-born engraver Ludwig von Siegen, b. about 1609, d. 1680.

Miami, University of, Florida, founded 1925 ; opened 1926.

Michael I, Byzantine Emperor (811–813), d. 845.

Michael II, Byzantine Emperor (820–829), d. 829.

Michael III, Byzantine Emperor (842–867), assassinated 867.

Michael IV, Byzantine Emperor (1034–1041), d. 1041.

Michael V, Byzantine Emperor (1041–1042).

Michael VI, Byzantine Emperor (1056–1057).

Michael VII, Byzantine Emperor (1071–1078).

Michael VIII, Byzantine Emperor (1260–1282), b. 1234, d. 1282.

Michael, Tsar of Russia (1613–1645), b. 1596, d. 1645.

Michael, King of Rumania (1927–1930), b. 1921.

Michaelis, Johann David, German theologian, b. 1717, d. 1791.

Michaelmas (Feast of St Michael the Archangel), celebrated 29 Sept.

Michaud, Joseph François, French historian (*Biographie Universelle*, 1811–1828), b. 1767, d. 1839.

Michael, Sir John, British Field Marshal, b. 1804, d. 1886.

Michelangelo, Italian artist (*Pietà*), b. 1475, d. 1564.

Michelet, Jules, French historian, b. 1798, d. 1874.

Michelozzi, Michelozzo, Italian artist, b. 1396, d. 1472.

Michelson, Albert Abraham, American scientist, b. 1852, d. 1931.

Michigan, U.S.A., first settled 1668 ; admitted to the Union 1837.

Michigan University, Ann Arbor, founded 1839 ; opened 1841.

Mickiewicz, Adam, Polish poet (*Konrad Wallenrod*, 1827), b. 1798, d. 1855.

Microbes, as agents of disease, postulated 1546 by the Italian physician Fracastoro, b. 1483, d. 1553.

Microphone, invented 1877 by the German-born inventor Emile Berliner, b. 1851, d. 1929 ; and 1878 by the American inventor David Edward Hughes, b. 1831, d. 1900.

Microscope, Compound, traditionally invented by the Dutch opticians Johann and Zacharias Janssen about

1590 ; used by Galileo 1610 and Hooke 1665.

Microwave Telecommunication System, first publicly demonstrated 1931 ; first commercial service 1934.

Middle Ages, in W. Europe, roughly 5th century to 15th century ; in E. Europe 330–1453 ; in Arab world 622–1517.

Middle English, in use from the 12th century to about 1500.

Middleton, Conyers, English scholar (*Life of Cicero*, 1741), b. 1683, d. 1750.

Middleton, Thomas, English playwright (*A Game of Chesse*, 1624), b. about 1570, d. 1627.

Midrash, Rabbinical commentary on the Holy Scriptures, compiled 1st to 12th centuries.

Midsummer Day (Feast of the Nativity of St John the Baptist), 24 June ; Summer Solstice, 21 or 22 June.

Midsummer Night : 23 June.

Midway, Battle of, World War II, between the Americans and the Japanese, 5–6 June 1942.

Midwinter, Winter Solstice, 21 or 22 Dec.

Mieris, Frans van, Dutch painter (*The Lute Player*), b. 1635, d. 1681.

Miës van der Rohe, Ludwig, German-born architect, b. 1886.

Mignard, Pierre, French painter (*Le Printemps*), b. 1612, d. 1695.

Migne, Jacques Paul, French theologian (*De la Liberté*), b. 1800, d. 1875.

Mignet, François Auguste Marie, French historian (*Charles-Quint*, 1854), b. 1796, d. 1884.

Migraine, described by Aretæus of Cappadocia in about 131.

Milan Cathedral, Italy, constructed 1386–1813 ; consecrated 1577.

Milan Decree, extending ban on British goods, issued by Napoleon 1807.

Mildenhall Treasure, Roman silver tableware, discovered near Mildenhall, Suffolk, 1942–1943.

Mile, British Statute, established by law 1593.

Miles, Nelson Appleton, Commanding General of the U.S.A., b. 1839, d. 1925.

Milhaud, Darius, French composer (*David*, 1954), b. 1892.

Military Cross, Gt. Britain, instituted 1 Jan. 1915.

Milk, Evaporated, process invented 1856 by the American Gail Borden, b. 1801, d. 1874.

Milk Bar, First British, opened in London by the Australian Hugh McIntosh 1935.

Milky Way, constitution discovered by the German-born astronomer Sir William Herschel, b. 1738, d. 1822.

Mill, James, British philosopher, b. 1773, d. 1836.

Mill, John Stuart, English philosopher (*On Liberty*, 1859), b. 1806, d. 1873.

Mill Hill School, Middlesex, English public school, founded 1807 ; reconstituted 1869.

Millais, Sir John, English painter (*Eve of St Agnes*, 1862), b. 1829, d. 1896.

Millay, Edna St Vincent, American writer (*Poems*, 1929), b. 1892.

Millennium, period of 1,000 years, particularly that of Christ's reign in person on Earth.

Miller, Arthur, American playwright (*Death of a Salesman*, 1949), b. 1915.

Miller, Henry, American writer (*Tropic of Cancer*, 1931), b. 1891.

Miller, Joe, English comedian, b. 1684, d. 1738.

Millerand, Alexandre, French statesman, b. 1859, d. 1943.

Millet, Jean François, French painter (*The Gleaners*, 1857), b. 1814, d. 1875.

Millikan, Robert Andrews, American scientist, b. 1868, d. 1953.

Millin, Sarah Gertrude, South African writer (*God's Stepchildren*, 1924), b. 1889.

Mills, Sir Charles, first Agent-General for Cape Colony, b. 1825, d. 1895.

Mills, George, British shipbuilder, b. 1808, d. 1881.

Milman, Henry Hart, Dean of St Paul's and historian, b. 1791, d. 1868.

Milne, Alan Alexander, Scottish writer (*Winnie the Pooh*, 1926), b. 1882, d. 1956.

Milner, Alfred, Lord, Colonial Secretary (1919–1921), b. 1854, d. 1925.

Milner, Samuel Roslington, English physicist, b. 1875, d. 1958.

Milo, Roman leader, b. 95, killed 47 B.C.

Milovanovich, Milovan, Serbian statesman, b. 1863, d. 1912.

Miltiades, Greek general, d. 489 B.C.

Milton, John, English pamphleteer (*Areopagitica*, 1644) and poet (*Paradise Lost*, 1667), b. 1608, d. 1674.

Milwaukee, Wisconsin, founded by the French-American fur-trader Solomon Laurent Juneau, b. 1793, d. 1856.

Milyukov, Paul Nikdayevich, Russian politician and historian, b. 1859, d. 1943.

Mindanao, World War II, reconquered by the Americans 23 June 1945.

Minden, Battle of, between the English and the French, 1 Aug. 1759.

Mines, explosive, first used by Russians at Kronstadt between 1853 and 1856.

Ming Dynasty, China, 1368–1644.

Ministries : *see under significant word of title :* **Agriculture,** etc.

Minnesota, U.S.A., organised as a Territory 1849 ; granted Statehood 1858.

Minoan Age, Crete, dating from the late Neolithic age to 1200 B.C.

Minoan Civilisation, discovered 1900 by the English archæologist Sir John Evans, b. 1851, d. 1941.

Minoan Script B, Mycenæan Greek, first deciphered 1952 by the English architect Michael Ventris, b. 1922, d. 1956.

Minorca (see **Menorca**).

Minot, Laurence, English poet, lived in the 14th century.

Mint, The Royal, London, origins uncertain ; first recorded mention 1229.

Minto, Gilbert John Elliot-Murray-Kynynmond, Earl of, Governor-General of Canada (1898–1904) and Viceroy of India (1905–1910), b. 1845, d. 1914.

Minuit, Peter, purchaser 1626 of Manhattan Island, b. about 1580, d. 1638.

Miocene Epoch, Earth history, 35 million years ago.

Mirabeau, Honoré Gabriel Riquetti, Comte de, French political writer, b. 1749, d. 1791.

Miracle Plays, originated in France ; first played in England about the beginning of the 14th century and continued into the 16th century.

Mirage of Hastings, occurred July 1798.

Miranda, Francisco de, South American revolutionary leader and dictator, b. 1750, d. 1816.

Miro, Joan, Spanish painter (*The Horse*), b. 1893.

Missionary Ridge, Battle of, American Civil War, 24–25 Nov. 1863.

Mississippi River, navigated 1682 by Robert Cavelier, Sieur de La Salle, b. 1643, assassinated 1687.

Mississippi Scheme, inaugurated as the ' Western Company ' 1717 by the Scottish financier John Law, b. 1671, d. 1729.

Missouri, U.S.A., first settled 1735 ; made a Territory 1812 ; admitted to the Union 1821.

Mistral, Frédéric, Provençal poet (*Mirèio*, 1859), b. 1830, d. 1914.

' Mistral, Gabriela ' (Lucila Gedoy Alcayaga), Chilean poetess (*Tala*, 1938), b. 1889.

Mitchel, John, Irish patriot, b. 1818, d. 1875.

Mitchell, Peter, Canadian statesman, b. 1821, d. 1899.

Mitchell, Sir Thomas Livingston, Australian explorer, b. 1792, d. 1855.

Mitford, Mary Russell, English writer (*Our Village*, 1824–1832), b. 1787, d. 1855.

Mithridates I, Satrap of Pontus 402–363 B.C.

Mithridates II, King of Pontus, d. 302 B.C.

Mithridates III, King of Pontus, 302–266 B.C.

Mithridates IV, King of Pontus, d. about 222 B.C.

Mithridates V, King of Pontus 222–184 B.C.

Mithridates VI, King of Pontus, assassinated 123 B.C.

Mithridates VII, King of Pontus (122–63 B.C.), b. about 131, d. 63 B.C.

Mitre, Bartolomé, Argentine statesman, b. 1821, d. 1906.

Mitropoulos, Dimitri, Greek-born conductor, b. 1896.

Mitscherlich, Eilhard, German scientist, b. 1794, d. 1863.

Mivart, St George Jackson, English biologist, b. 1827, d. 1900.

Mixed Bathing, in the Serpentine, London, began 16 June 1930.

Moabite Stone, discovered at Dibon by the German missionary F. Klein, 1868.

Modern Face, type design, introduced about 1788 by the English bookseller John Bell, b. 1745, d. 1831.

Modigliani, Amadeo, Italian-born artist (*Woman with Cigarette*, 1911), b. 1884, d. 1920.

Modjeska, Helena, Polish actress, b. 1844, d. 1909.

Moe, Jörgen Engebretsen, Norwegian poet, b. 1813, d. 1882.

Moeran, Ernest John, English composer (*Rhapsody*, 1924), b. 1894, d. 1950.

Moguls, ruled India 1525–1707.

Mohammed, the Prophet, founder about 610 of Islam, b. about 570, d. 632.

Mohammed I, Ottoman Emperor (1413–1421), b. 1387, d. 1421.

Mohammed II, Sultan of Turkey (1451–1481), b. 1430, d. 1481.

Mohammed III, Sultan of Turkey (1595–1603), b. 1566, d. 1603.

Mohammed IV, Sultan of Turkey (1648–1687), b. 1638, d. 1692.

Mohammed V, Sultan of Turkey (1909–1918), b. 1844, d. 1918.

Mohammed VI, Sultan of Turkey (1918–1922), b. 1861, d. 1926.

Mohammed Ali, Viceroy of Egypt (1805–49), b. 1769, d. 1849.

Mohl, Hugo von, German botanist, b. 1805, d. 1872.

Mohr, Charles Theodor, German-born botanist, b. 1824, d. 1901.

Moir, David Macbeth, Scottish physician and writer, b. 1798, d. 1851.

Moiseiwitsch, Benno, Russian-born pianist, b. 1890.

Moissan, Henri, French scientist, b. 1852, d. 1907.

Moivre, Abraham de, French-born mathematician, b. 1667, d. 1754.

Molay, Jacques Bernhard de, last Grand Master of the Knights Templars, b. about 1243, burnt at the stake 1319.

Moldavian S.S.R., formed 1940 from Moldavian Autonomous Republic and Bessarabia.

Molesworth, Sir Guilford Lindsey, engineer and economist, b. 1828, d. 1925.

Molesworth, Mrs (Mary Louisa Stewart), British writer (*Robin Redbreast*, 1892), b. 1839, d. 1921.

Molière, Jean Baptiste Poquelin, French playwright (*Le Malade Imaginaire*, 1673), b. 1622, d. 1673.

Molinism, Jesuit reconciliation of predestination and free will, postulated in his *Concordia* (1588) by Luís de Molina, b. 1535, d. 1600.

Molinos, Miguel de, Spanish founder (in his *Guida Spirituale*, 1675) of the Quietist movement, b. 1640, condemned by Inquisition 1687, d. 1697.

Mollison, James Allan, British aviator, b. 1906, d. 1959.

Molly Maguires, Irish-American secret labour organisation, flourished in Pennsylvania about the years 1865 to 1875 ; also Irish secret society of the 1840's.

Molnar, Ferenc, Hungarian writer (*Liliom*, 1909), b. 1878, d. 1952.

Molotov, Vyacheslav Mikhailovich Skryabin, Bolshevik leader, b. 1890.

Moltke, Helmut, Graf von, German Field Marshal, b. 1800, d. 1891.

Molybdenum, metal discovered 1778 by the Swedish chemist Carl Wilhelm Scheele, b. 1742, d. 1786.

Mommsen, Theodor, German historian, b. 1817, d. 1903.

Mompou, Federico, Spanish composer (*Dialogues*, 1923), b. 1893.

Monaco, independence recognised by Savoy 1489, by France 1512, by Papacy and Spain 1524 ; alliance with France since 1641 ; constitutional monarchy established 1911 ; reign of Prince Rainier since 1949.

Monasteries, English, dissolved 1536–1539.

Monastery, First Christian, founded about 315 by the Egyptian Pachomius on an island in the Nile.

Monck, Charles Stanley, Viscount Monck, Governor-General of Canada (1861–1868), b. 1819, d. 1894.

Monck, George, Duke of Albemarle, English soldier, Cromwellian governor of Scotland (1654–1660) and restorer of Charles II, b. 1608, d. 1670.

Monckton, Mary, Countess of Cork and Orrery, bluestocking, b. 1746, d. 1840.

Mond, Ludwig, German-born chemist and businessman, b. 1839, d. 1909.

Monday, the second day of the week.

Monet, Claude, French artist (*Waterloo Bridge*), b. 1840, d. 1926.

Monge, Gaspard, Comte de Péluse, French mathematician, b. 1746, d. 1818.

Mongolia, recognised Chinese suzerainty in 1636 (Inner) and 1688 (Outer) ; Outer Mongolia joined the U.S.S.R. in 1924.

Mongols, invaded China 1210, Transoxiana 1219, Caucasia 1221, Persia 1222, Russia 1224, Central Europe 1241, Mesopotamia 1258. Ruled China 1280–1368 ; Persia 1225–1386 ; Russia 1242–1380.

Monk, Maria, fraudulent exposer of convent life, b. about 1817, d. 1850

Monkey Gland, transplantation for rejuvenation introduced by the Russian-born surgeon Serge Voronov, b. 1866, d. 1951.

Monkton Combe School, Somerset, English public school, founded by the Rev. F. Pocock 1868.

Monmouth, Battle of (New Jersey), American War of Independence, 28 June 1778.

Monmouth School, British public school, founded by William Jones 1615.

Monmouth's Rebellion, led 11 June–6 July 1685 by James, Duke of Monmouth, b. 1649, beheaded 1685.

Monocacy, Battle of, American Civil War, 8 July 1864.

Monophysitism, Christian heresy, condemned at Council of Chalcedon 451.

Monotheletism, Christian heresy similar to monophysitism, condemned at Council of Constantinople 680.

Monotype, invented 1887 by the American inventor Tolbert Lanston, b. 1844, d. 1913.

Monro, Harold, English poet (*Trees,* 1915), b. 1879, d. 1932.

Monroe, James, U.S. President (1817–1825), b. 1758, d. 1831.

Monroe Doctrine, concerning American foreign policy, announced by President James Monroe 1823.

Mons, Retreat from, World War I, Aug. 1914.

Mont Blanc, first climbed June 1786 by the French mountaineer Jacques Balmat, b. 1762, d. 1834.

Mont Blanc Tunnel, construction began 1959 ; to be completed 1961.

Mont Cenis Pass, between France and Italy, completed 1806 ; Tunnel opened 1871.

Mont Saint Michel, France, monastery founded by Aubert, Bishop of Avranches 708.

Montagna, Bartolommeo, Italian painter (*Presentation of Christ in the Temple*), b. about 1450, d. 1523.

Montagu, Lady Mary Wortley, English writer and traveller, b. 1689, d. 1762.

Montague, Charles Edward, English writer (*Fiery Particles*), b. 1867, d. 1928.

Montaigne, Michel Eyquem de, French essayist, b. 1533, d. 1592.

Montalembert, Marc René, Marquis de, French engineer and soldier, b. 1714, d. 1800.

Montana, U.S.A., first settled 1809 ; made a Territory 1864 ; admitted to the Union 1889.

Montanism, Christian heresy, prominent in Asia Minor in 2nd century.

Montcalm, Louis Joseph, Marquis de, French general, b. 1712, mortally wounded in battle 1759.

Montefiore, Sir Moses Haim, Italian-born champion of Jewish freedom, b. 1784, d. 1885.

Montemayor, Jorge de, Spanish poet (*La Diana Enamorada,* c. 1550), b. about 1520, assassinated 1561.

Montenegro, independent since 14th century, monarchy since 1910 ; occupied by Austrians 1916–1918 ; part of Yugoslavia since 1919.

Montes, Ismael, Bolivian statesman, b. 1861, d. 1933.

Montespan, Françoise Athénaïs, Mme de, mistress of Louis XIV, b. 1641, d. 1707.

Montesquieu, Charles de Secondat, Baron de la Brède et de, French writer (*Lettres Persanes,* 1721), b. 1689, d. 1755.

Montessori Method, in education, founded about 1909 by the Italian educationalist Maria Montessori, b. 1870, d. 1952.

Monteverdi, Claudio, Italian composer (*Orfeo,* 1608), b. 1567, d. 1643.

Monteux, Pierre, French conductor, b. 1875.

'Montez, Lola' (Marie Dolores Eliza Rosanna Gilbert), adventuress, b. 1818, d. 1861.

Montezuma I, Aztec Emperor (1436–1464), b. 1390, d. 1464.

Montezuma II, Last Aztec Emperor (1502–1520), b. about 1480, killed 1520.

Montfort, Simon de, English crusader and baronial leader, b. about 1208, killed in battle 1265.

Montfort, Simon de, English soldier and rebel, b. 1240, d. 1271.

Montgolfier, Joseph Michel, French balloonist, b. 1740, d. 1810.

Montgomerie, Alexander, Scottish poet (*The Cherry and the Slae*), b. about 1556, d. about 1610.

Montgomery, Bernard Law Montgomery, Viscount, British soldier, b. 1887 ; appointed Field Marshal 1944.

Month, in astronomy, 29.53 days ; in calendar 28, 29, 30 or 31 days ; in law, 28 days.

Montholon, Charles Tristan, Comte de, French general, b. 1783, d. 1853.

Monticelli, Adolphe, French painter (*Baigneuses*), b. 1824, d. 1886.

Montmorency, Anne, Duc de, French statesman and soldier, b. 1493, d. 1567.

Montpensier, Anne Marie Louise d'Orléans, Duchesse de, the ' Grande Mademoiselle ', b. 1627, d. 1693.

Montreal, Canada, founded 1642.

Montreal University, founded 1876 ; opened 1878.

Montreuil, Pierre de, French architect, b. about 1201, d. 1266.

Montrose, James Graham, Marquis of, Royalist supporter, b. 1612, hanged 1650.

Montt, Jorge, Chilean statesman, b. 1846, d. 1922.

Montt, Manuel, Chilean statesman, b. 1809, d. 1880.

Monvel, Jacques-Marie Boutet de, French actor and playwright (*L'Amant Bourru,* 1777), b. 1745, d. 1812.

Moody, Richard Clement, first Governor (1841–1849) of the Falkland Islands, b. 1813, d. 1887.

Moody, Dwight Lyman, American revivalist, b. 1837, d. 1899.

Moon Alphabet, for the blind, invented 1845 by the English Dr William Moon, b. 1818, d. 1894.

Moon Rockets, Russian, first launched 11 Oct. 1958 ; second hit the moon 10 p.m. B.S.T. 13 Sept. 1959.

Moorcroft, William, English veterinary surgeon and explorer, b. 1765, d. 1825.

Moore, George, Irish writer (*Esther Waters,* 1894), b. 1852, d. 1933.

Moore, Grace, American operatic singer, b. 1901, died in an air-crash 1947.

Moore, Henry, English sculptor (*Madonna*), b. 1898.

Moore, Sir John, Scottish soldier, b. 1761, died of wounds 1809.

Moore, Thomas, Irish poet (*Lalla Rookh,* 1817), b. 1779, d. 1852.

Moræs Barros, Prudente de, President of Brazil (1894–1898), b. 1841, d. 1902.

Morales, Luis de, Spanish painter, d. 1586.

Morality Plays, played mainly in the 15th and 16th centuries.

Moral Re-armament, religious movement founded 1921 by the American religious leader Frank Buchman, b. 1878, d. 1961.

Moran, Edward, English-born painter (*Outward Bound*), b. 1829, d. 1901.

Morand, Paul, French novelist (*Fermé la Nuit,* 1922), b. 1888.

Moravian Brethren, Christian sect, appeared 1457 among followers of Hus, regathered 1722, began mission work 1732.

Moravian Church in America, founded 1739 by Bishop August Gottlieb Spangenberg, b. 1704, d. 1792.

More, Hannah, English writer (*Cœlebs in Search of a Wife,* 1809), b. 1745, d. 1833.

More, Paul Elmer, American writer (*Pages from an Oxford Diary,* 1937), b. 1864, d. 1937.

More, Sir Thomas, Lord Chancellor (1529–1532) and writer (*Utopia,* 1516), b. 1478, beheaded 1535.

Moreau, Gustave, French painter (*Œdipe et le Sphinx,* 1868), b. 1826, d. 1898.

Morgan, Charles, English novelist (*Portrait in a Mirror,* 1929), b. 1894, d. 1958.

Morgan, John Pierpont, American financier, b. 1837, d. 1913.

Morgan, Sir Henry, Welsh buccaneer, b. about 1635, d. 1688.

Morgan, William de, English writer (*Joseph Vance,* 1906), b. 1839, d. 1917.

Morgenstern, Christian, German poet, b. 1871, d. 1914.

Morgenthau, Henry, German-born financier, b. 1856, d. 1946.

Morier, James, British traveller and writer (*Hajji Baba,* 1824), b. about 1780, d. 1849.

Mörike, Eduard Friedrich, German poet, b. 1804, d. 1875.

Morison, James, Scottish founder 1843 of the Evangelical Union, b. 1816, d. 1893.

Morisot, Berthe, French painter (*Le Berceau*, 1873), b. 1841, d. 1895.

Morland, George, English painter (*The Angler's Repast*), b. 1763, d. 1804.

Morley, Henry, English writer and editor, b. 1822, d. 1894.

Morley, John, Viscount Morley, English statesman and writer (*Edmund Burke*, 1867), b. 1838, d. 1923.

Mormon Movement, founded 1827 in Fayette, N.Y., by the American religious leader Joseph Smith, b. 1805, murdered 1844.

Mornay, Philippe de (Duplessis-Mornay), ' the Pope of the Huguenots ', b. 1549, d. 1623.

Moro, Antonio, Flemish painter (*Mary Tudor*), b. about 1520, d. about 1576.

Morocco : arrival of the first Arabs under Okbar ben Nafi' 682 ; first invasion of Spain under Ibn Tariq 711 ; dynastic governments 788 to 1911 ; Protectorate régime 1912–1956 ; restoration of independence 2 Mar. 1956.

Moroni, Giambattista, Italian painter (*Ludovico di Terzi*), b. about 1525, d. 1578.

Moronobu, Hishikawa, Japanese painter, lived in the 2nd half of the 17th century.

Morphy, Paul Charles, American chess player, b. 1837, d. 1884.

Morris, Gouverneur, American diplomat and statesman, b. 1752, d. 1816.

Morris, William, English artist and writer (*News from Nowhere*, 1891), b. 1834, d. 1896. Founded the Kelmscott Press (1891–1898).

Morris Dancing, revived in England as a result of Cecil Sharp's first seeing Morris dancing under the leadership of William Kimber (b. 1873) at Headington, Oxford, 26 Dec. 1899.

Morrow, Dwight Whitney, American financier, b. 1873, d. 1931.

Morse, Henry, English Jesuit missionary in England, b. 1595, executed 1645.

Morse Code, invented about 1832 by the American inventor Samuel Finley Breese Morse, b. 1791, d. 1872.

Mortar, developed 1756 by the English architect John Smeaton, b. 1724 d. 1792.

Mortimer, Edmund, Earl of March, Lieutenant of Ireland, b. 1391, d. 1425.

Mortimer, Roger, Earl of March, Royal adviser, b. about 1287, hanged 1330.

Morton, Cardinal John, Archbishop of Canterbury (1486–1500), b. about 1420, d. 1500.

Morton, Thomas, Scottish shipwright and inventor, b. 1781, d. 1832.

Mosander, Karl, Gustav, Swedish scientist, b. 1797, d. 1858.

Moscheles, Ignaz, Austrian pianist and composer, b. 1794, d. 1870.

Moschus, Greek poet of Syracuse, lived in 2nd century B.C.

Moscow, Russian capital, burnt and pillaged by the Mongols 1382 ; taken and burnt by the French Sept. 1812 ; battle of Moscow 5–7 Sept. 1812.

Moscow Conference, World War II, 9–21 Nov. 1944.

Moseley, Henry Gwyn Jeffreys, British physicist, b. 1887, killed in battle 1915.

' Moses, Grandma ' (Mrs Anna Mary Robertson Moses), American primitive painter, b. 1860.

Moslem League, founded in India 1906.

Mosley, Sir Oswald, British political leader, b. 1896 ; Conservative, Independent and Labour M.P. (1918–1931), founded New Party 1931, British Union of Fascists 1932, British Union Movement 1948.

Most, Johann, German anarchist, b. 1846, d. 1906.

Moszkowski, Moritz, German-born pianist and composer (*Spanish Dances*), b. 1854, d. 1925.

Mother's Day : 2nd Sunday in May (U.S.A.) ; 2nd Sunday in Mar. (U.K.).

Motherwell, William, Scottish poet (*Jeannie Morrison*, 1832), b. 1797, d. 1835.

Motion, planetary, Kepler's Laws of, 1609 and 1619.

Motley, John Lothrop, American diplomat and historian (*The Rise of the Dutch Republic*, 1856), b. 1814, d. 1877.

Motor-cars, invented 1890–1895.

Motor Scooter, First, invented 1919 by Greville Bradshaw.

Motor Cycle, three-wheeled model built 1884 by Edward Butler ; two-wheeled model built in Paris 1900 by the Werner Frères.

Mott, Mrs Lucretia, American anti-slavery worker, b. 1793, d. 1880.

Mount Palomar, California, site of observatory selected 1934 ; observatory opened 1949.

Mount St Mary's College, Derbyshire, English public school, founded by the Society of Jesus 1842.

Mount Wilson Observatory, California, opened 1904.

Mountbatten of Burma, Louis Mountbatten, Earl, British sailor and administrator, b. 1900.

'Mounties', Royal Canadian Mounted Police, formed as the North-West Mounted Police 1873 ; assumed present title 1920.

Moussorgsky, Modest, Russian composer (*Boris Godunov,* 1874), b. 1839, d. 1881.

Mowat, Sir Oliver, Canadian statesman, b. 1820, d. 1903.

Mowbray, Thomas, Duke of Norfolk, Warden of the Scottish Marches, b. about 1366, d. 1399.

Mozambique (Portuguese East Africa), discovered by Vasco da Gama's fleet 1498 ; first colonised 1505 ; created an overseas territory of Portugal 1951.

Mozart, Wolfgang Amadeus, German composer (*Don Giovanni,* 1787), b. 1756, d. 1791.

Mudie, Charles Edward, founder of Mudie's library (1842–1937), b. 1818, d. 1890.

Muggletonians, religious sect, founded about 1651 by the English journeyman tailors Lodowicke Muggleton (b. 1609, d. 1698) and John Reeve (b. 1608, d. 1658).

Mühlenberg, Heinrich Melchior, German-born pioneer of American Lutheranism, b. 1711, d. 1787.

Muir, Sir Robert, Scottish pathologist, b. 1864, d. 1959.

Muir, William, British engineer, b. 1806, d. 1888.

Mukden, Battle of, between Russians and Japanese, fought Feb.–Mar. 1905.

'Mulberry', artificial harbour used at Arromanches, Normandy, in 1944.

Mulcahy, Richard, Irish statesman, b. 1886.

Mulhall, Michael George, Irish-born editor and statistician, b. 1836, d. 1900.

Mullah, Mad, of Somaliland (Mohammed bin Abdullah), active 1899–1904.

Mullan, John, American soldier and surveyor, b. 1830, d. 1909.

Müller, Friedrich Max-, German-born philologist and orientalist, b. 1823, d. 1900.

Müller, Fritz, German naturalist, b. 1827, d. 1897.

Müller, Wilhelm, German poet, b. 1794, d. 1827.

Mulock, Dinah Maria (Mrs Craik), English writer (*John Halifax, Gentleman,* 1857), b. 1826, d. 1887.

Mulready, William, Irish painter, b. 1786, d. 1863.

Mumbles Railway, Swansea, Britain's oldest passenger railway, first recorded journey 1807 ; closed 1 Jan. 1960.

Mumford, Lewis, American writer (*The Culture of Cities,* 1938), b. 1895.

Munch, Edvard, Norwegian painter, b. 1863, d. 1944.

Münchhausen, Karl Friedrich Hieronymus, Baron von, German cavalry officer, b. 1720, d. 1797.

Munday, Anthony, English writer and spy, b. 1553, d. 1633.

Munich Pact, determining the fate of Sudetenland, made 29 Sept. 1938.

Munich Putsch, unsuccessfully attempted by Hitler, 8 Nov. 1923.

Munkacsy, Michael, Hungarian painter (*The Blind Milton,* 1878), b. 1844, d. 1900.

Munnings, Sir Alfred, English painter (*The Prince of Wales on Forest Witch,* 1921), b. 1878, d. 1959.

Munro, Hector Hugh (' Saki '), British writer (*Chronicles of Clovis,* 1911), b. 1870, killed in battle 1916.

Munro, Sir Thomas, Governor of Madras, b. 1761, d. 1827.

Munroe, Charles Edward, American scientist, b. 1849, d. 1938.

Münster, Treaty of, concluding 30 Years' War, 1649.

Murad I, Turkish Sultan (1360–1389), b. 1319, assassinated 1389.

Murad II, Turkish Sultan (1421–1451), d. 1451.

Murad III, Turkish Sultan (1574–1596), d. 1596.

Murad IV, Turkish Sultan (1623–1640), b. about 1611, d. 1640.

Murad V, Turkish Sultan (1876), b. 1840, d. 1904.

Murasaki, Lady, Japanese novelist (*Tale of Genji*), lived in the 10th century.

Murat, Achille, Prince, French writer (*Letters of a United States Citizen*, 1830), b. 1801, d. 1841.

Murat, Joachim, French soldier and King of Naples, b. 1767, shot 1815.

Murchison, Sir Roderick Impey, Scottish geologist, b. 1792. d. 1871.

Murdoch, Iris, Anglo-Irish writer (*The Sand Castle*, 1957), b. 1919.

Murdock, William, Scottish engineer and inventor, 1792 of coal-gas lighting, b. 1754, d. 1839.

Murfreesboro, Battle of, American Civil War, 31 Dec. 1862–2 Jan. 1863.

Murger, Henri, French novelist (*Scènes de la vie de Bohème*, 1848), b. 1822, d. 1861.

Murillo, Bartolomé, Spanish painter (*Vision of St Anthony*), b. 1617, d. 1682.

Murmansk, Port of, U.S.S.R., founded 1915.

Murphy, Jeremiah Daniel, Irish boy linguist, b. 1806, d. 1824.

Murray, Gilbert, Australian-born classical scholar, b. 1866, d. 1957.

Murray, Sir James, British editor of the *Oxford English Dictionary* (1879–1928), b. 1837, d. 1915.

Murray, Sir John, Canadian oceanographer, b. 1841, d. 1914.

Murray, John, Scottish publisher, and founder 1809 of the *Quarterly Review*, b. 1778, d. 1843.

Murry, John Middleton, English critic (*Aspects of Literature,* 1920), b. 1889, d. 1957.

Museum Association, London, founded 1889 .

Museum of Modern Art, New York, established 1929.

Music Printing, first complete collection of part-songs printed from movable type issued about 1498 by Ottaviano dei Petrucci, b. 1466, d. 1539.

Musil, Robert, Austrian writer (*The Man Without Qualities*, 1930–1942), b. 1880, d. 1939.

Muslim Era, began 16 July 622.

Musset, Alfred de, French playwright (*Les Nuits*, 1835–1836), b. 1810, d. 1857.

Mussolini, Benito, Italian dictator, b. 1883 ; founded Fascist movement 1919 ; came to power 1923 ; fell and was arrested 1943 ; rescued by the Germans 1943 ; executed 1945.

Mussorgsky, Modest Petrovich, Russian composer (*Boris Godunov*, 1874), b. about 1835, d. 1881.

Mustafa Kemal (Kemal Atatürk), Turkish soldier and statesman (Prime Minister 1923–1938), b. 1880, d. 1938.

Mustapha I, Turkish Sultan (1617–1618 ; 1622–1623), b. 1591, strangled 1639.

Mustapha II, Turkish Sultan (1695–1703), b. 1664, d. 1703.

Mustapha III, Turkish Sultan (1757–1774), b. 1717, d. 1774.

Mustapha IV, Turkish Sultan (1807–1808), b. 1779, put to death, 1808.

Mustard Gas, first used by the Germans in World War I, July 1917.

Mutation, biological variation, study first developed 1901 by the Dutch botanist Hugo de Vries, b. 1848, d. 1935.

Mutiny, *Bounty* 1789, Nore 1797, *Danaë* 1800, Indian 1857–1858, Curragh 1914.

Muybridge, Eadweard, English pioneer in the study of human and animal movement, b. 1830, d. 1904.

Muzaffar-ed-Din, Shah of Persia (1896–1907), b. 1853, d. 1907.

Muziano, Girolamo, Italian painter (*St Jerome*), b. 1530, d. 1590.

Myddleton, Sir Hugh, English builder of 'New River', b. about 1560, d. 1631.

Myers, Frederick William Henry, English writer, and joint-founder 1882 of the Society for Psychical Research, b. 1843, d. 1901.

Mytens, Daniel, Dutch painter (*Duke of Hamilton*, 1629), b. about 1590, d. about 1647.

Myxomatosis, first used to destroy rabbits in Australia 1950 ; in Britain 1952.

N

N.A.T.O. (North Atlantic Treaty Organisation), Council first met 17 Sept. 1949.

Nato Allied Command, Europe, came into being 2 Apr. 1951.

Nato's Fifth Tactical Air Force, Allied Air Forces, Southern Europe, came into operation 1956.

N.K.V.D., Soviet Commissariat of Internal Affairs (including secret police), founded 1921 ; became M.V.D. 1934.

Nabokov, Vladimir, Russian-born writer (*Lolita*, 1955), b. 1899.

Nabonassar, Era of (Babylonian chronology), began 26 Feb. 747 B.C.

Nabonidus, King of Babylonia, d. about 539 B.C.

Nachtigal, Gustav, German explorer, b. 1834, d. 1885.

Nagasaki, Japan, bombed by the Allies' second atomic bomb 9 Aug. 1945.

Nagy, Imre, Hungarian Communist leader, b. 1895, executed 1958.

Naidu, Sarajini, Indian politician, b. 1879, d. 1949.

Nairne, Caroline, Baroness Nairne, Scottish ballad writer (*Charlie is My Darling*), b. 1766, d. 1845.

Namier, Lewis, Polish-born historian, b. 1888, d. 1960.

Nanak, Indian religious leader, founder of the Sikh religion, b. 1469, d. 1538.

Nancy, Battle of, between the Duke of Lorraine and Charles the Bold, 5 Jan. 1477.

Nanga Parbat, Himalayas, climbed by a German Austrian expedition 3 July 1953.

Nansen, Fridtjof, Norwegian explorer, b. 1861, expedition to Greenland 1888, d. 1930.

Nantes, Edict of, granting tolerance to French Protestants, signed by Henry IV 1598 ; revoked by Louis XIV 1685.

Nanteuil, Robert, French artist (*Louis XIV*), b. 1623, d. 1678.

Napier, Sir Charles, naval strategist and politician, b. 1786, d. 1860.

Napier, John, Scottish inventor 1614 of logarithms, b. 1550, d. 1617.

Napier, Sir William, Irish-born historian of the Peninsular War, b. 1785, d. 1860.

Naples, ruled by Normans 1139–1194, by Angevins 1265–1382, by Aragonese 1442–1501, by Spain 1503–1707, by Austria 1707–1734, by Bourbons 1734–1799, 1815–1860.

Napoleon Buonaparte, Emperor of France, b. 1769 ; Consul 1799 ; Emperor 1804 ; King of Italy 1805 ; abdicated 1814 ; at Elba 1814–1815 ; defeated at Waterloo and banished to St Helena 1815 ; d. 1821.

Napoleon II, King of Rome, Duke of Reichstadt, b. 1811, d. 1832.

Napoleon III, French President (1848–1851) and Emperor (1852–1870), b. 1808, d. 1873.

Napoleonic Wars, waged between the Allies and the French 1799 to 1815.

Narses, Byzantine General, b. about 478, d. about 573.

Narvik, Norway, scene of unsuccessful Allied expedition, World War II, 28 May–9 June 1940.

Naseby, Battle of, between Parliamentarians and Royalists, 14 June 1645.

Nash, 'Beau' (Richard Nash), master of ceremonies at Bath, b. 1674, d. 1762.

Nash, John, English architect, b. 1752, d. 1835.

Nash, Paul, English painter, b. 1889, d. 1946.

Nashe, Thomas, English writer (*Pierce Penilesse*, 1592), b. 1567, d. 1601.

Nasmyth, James, Scottish engineer, b. 1808, d. 1890.

Nasr-ed-Nir, Shah of Persia (1848–1896), b. about 1831, assassinated 1896.

Nassau-Siegen, Charles Henry Nicolas Othon, Prince de, French adventurer, b. 1745, d. 1808.

Nasser, Gamal Abdul, Egyptian ruler since 1954 (President since 1956) b. 1918.

Natal, annexed to Cape Colony 1844 ; made a British colony 1856 ; merged in the Union of South Africa 1910.

Nathan, George Jean, American dramatic critic, b. 1882.

Nathan's, theatrical costumiers, established in London 1790.

Nation, The, British periodical, founded 1907 ; absorbed into the *New Statesman* 1931.

Nation, Carry, American temperance advocate, b. 1846, d. 1911.

National Assembly, of France, formed 1789 ; renamed Constituent Assembly 1789 ; replaced by the Legislative Assembly 1791.

National Assistance, Act passed 1948.

National Bureau of Standards, U.S. Department of Commerce, Washington D.C., founded 1901.

National Debt, began definitely 1694.

National Farmer's Union, London, founded 10 Dec. 1908.

National Fire Service, Great Britain, formed 1941 ; dissolved 1948.

National Gallery, London, founded 1824.

National Guard, U.S.A. founded 1903.

National Health Service, Great Britain, White Paper published 1944 ; came into effect 5 July 1948.

National Insurance Act, Great Britain, came into force 15 July 1912 ; Ministry set up 1944.

National Loaf, introduced in Britain 24 Mar. 1942.

National Park, Britain's first, started by a gift of 300 acres near Snowdon 1935.

National Physical Laboratory, Great Britain, founded 1899.

National Playing Fields Association, Great Britain, granted Charter 3 Jan. 1933.

National Portrait Gallery, London, founded 1857 ; opened 1859.

National Savings Movement, Great Britain, founded 1916.

National Socialism, Germany, founded 1919.

National Socialist German Workers Party (Nazis), founded by Adolf Hitler 1919.

National Socialist Party, Germany, founded 1843.

National Society for the Prevention of Cruelty to Children, London, founded 1884.

National Sporting Club, Great Britain, founded 1891.

National Trust, for places of historic interest or natural beauty, Great Britain, founded 1895.

National Trust for Scotland, for places of historic interest or natural beauty, founded 1931.

National University of Ireland, Dublin, came into being 31 Oct. 1909. Previously Royal University of Ireland, founded 1882, superseding the Queen's University in Ireland, founded 1849.

Nationalisation of The Bank of England, 1946.

Nationalisation of Civil Aviation, Great Britain, 1946.

Nationalisation of the Coal Industry, Great Britain, 1946.

Nationalisation of the Electrical Industry, Great Britain, 1947.

Nationalisation of the Gas Industry, Great Britain, 1949.

Nationalisation of Health Services, Great Britain, 1948.

Nationalisation of the Railways, Great Britain, 1948.

Nationalisation of the Steel Industry, Great Britain, 1948 ; denationalisation 1953.

Nationalisation of Road Transport, Great Britain, 1947 ; denationalisation 1953.

Nattier, Jean Marc, French painter (*Portrait a Lady of in Blue*), b. 1685 d. 1766.

Nature, British periodical, began publication 1869 under the editorship of Sir Joseph Norman Lockyer, b. 1836, d. 1920.

Nature Conservancy, Great Britain, set up 1949.

Naundorff, Karl Wilhelm, pretender to the Throne of France, d. 1845.

' **Nautical Almanac** ', British, first published 1767.

Naval Architects, Institution of, London, founded 1860.

Naval Limitation Conference, Washington, D.C. held 1921-1922.

Navarino, Battle of, between the Allied and Egyptian fleets, 20 Oct. 1827.

Navarrete, Battle of, between the Black Prince and Spanish rebels, 13 Apr. 1367.

Nayler, James, English Quaker, b. about 1617, d. 1660.

Nazianzen, St Gregory, b. about 330, d. 390.

Nazis, German National Socialists, movement founded 1919.

Neal, Daniel, English historian of New England, b. 1678, d. 1743.

Neale, John Mason, English hymn-writer (*Jerusalem the Golden*, 1865), b. 1818, d. 1866.

Neander, Johnson August Wilhelm, German theologian, b. 1789, d. 1850.

Neanderthal Man, remains discovered near Dusseldorf 1856.

Nebraska, U.S.A., discovered by Francisco Vasquez de Coronado 1541 ; sold to the U.S.A. by France 1803 ; first settled 1847 ; admitted to the Union 1867.

Nebraska University, Lincoln, founded 1867 ; opened 1871.

Nebuchadnezzar, Babylonian king 605-562 B.C.

Nebula, in Andromeda, described by the Arab astronomer Al Sufi before 1000.

Necker, Jacques, French statesman and financier, b. 1732, d. 1804.

Needle and Thread Ceremony, Queen's College, Oxford University, 1st Jan. each year.

Negretti, Enrico, Italian-born optician and scientific instrument maker, b. 1817, d. 1879.

Negus, hot, sweet wine and water, invented 1704 by the English soldier Colonel Francis Negus, b. about 1665, d. 1732.

Negri, Pola, Polish-born film actress, b. 1899.

Nehru, Pandit Jawaharlal, Indian statesman (Prime Minister since 1947), b. 1889.

Neilson, Samuel, United Irishman, b. 1761, d. 1803.

Nekrasov, Nikolai Alekseievich, Russian poet, b. 1821, d. 1877.

Nelson, Horatio, Lord, English sailor, b. 1758, killed in action 1805.

Nemours, Louis, Duc de, French soldier, b. 1814, d. 1896.

Nennius, Welsh writer (*Historia Britonum*), lived in the 8th century.

Neodymium, metallic element, discovered 1885 by the Austrian chemist Baron von Welsbach, b. 1858, d. 1929.

Neon, gaseous element, discovered 1898 by the Scottish scientist Sir William Ramsay, b. 1852, d. 1916.

Nepal, independent kingdom, conquered by the Gurkhas 1768 ; constitutional monarchy since 1951.

Nepomuk, St John of, national hero of Bohemia, killed 1393.

Nepos, Cornelius, Roman biographer, b. about 100, d. about 25 B.C.

Nepos, Julius, Roman Emperor (474-475), d. 480.

Neptune, planet, position predicted 1845 by the English astronomer John Couch Adams (1819-1892) and 1846 by the French astronomer Urbain Leverrier (1811-1877) ; observed 23 Sept. 1846 by the German astronomer Johann Gottfried Galle (1812-1910).

Neri, St Filippo, b. 1515, d. 1595.

Nernst, Walther, German physicist, b. 1864, d. 1941.

Nero, Roman Emperor (54-68), b. 37, committed suicide 68.

Neruda, Jan, Czech writer (*Mala Strana*, 1878), b. 1834, d. 1891.

Nerva, Roman Emperor (96-98), b. about 30, d. 98.

Nerval, Gérard de, (Gérard Labrunie), French writer (*Voyage en Orient,* 1848–1850), b. 1808, d. 1855.

Nesbit, Edith, English children's writer (*The Treasure Seekers,* 1899), b. 1858, d. 1924.

Nesselrode, Karl Robert, Count, Russian statesman, b. 1780, d. 1862.

Nestorian Church, Middle Eastern religious movement dating from the deposition 431 of Nestorius, Patriarch of Constantinople (428–431), d. about 451.

Netherlands, The, Revolt against Spain (1572–1609), war with Spain (1621–1648) ; Republic 1650–1672, 1702–1747 ; French domination 1795—1813 ; restored as an independent monarchy 1814 ; Belgian provinces seceded 1830 ; new constitution granted 1848, revised Constitution granted 1917.

Neuhof, Theodor, Baron von, German King of Corsica (1736–1743), b. 1686, d. 1756.

Neuilly, Treaty of, between the Allies and Bulgaria, signed 1919.

Neumann, Alfred, German writer (*Alfred de Musset,* 1925), b. 1895.

Neumann, Theresa, German woman, b. 1898, exhibited the stigmata 1926.

Neutrons, nuclear particles, discovered 1932 by the English scientist Sir James Chadwick, b. 1891.

Nevada, U.S.A., first settled 1849 ; created a Territory 1861 ; admitted to the Union 1864.

Nevada University, Reno, founded 1873 ; opened 1874.

Neville, George, Archbishop of York and Chancellor of England, b. about 1433, d. 1476.

Neville's Cross, Battle of, between the Northern Levies and the Scottish armies, 17 Oct. 1346.

Nevin, Ethelbert Woodbridge, American composer (*Narcissus,* 1891), b. 1862, d. 1901.

Nevinson, Henry Woodd, English journalist, b. 1856, d. 1941.

New Amsterdam, early name of New York City until 1664.

New Caledonia, South Pacific, discovered by Captain James Cook 1774 ; annexed by France 1853.

New College, Oxford University, founded 1379 by William of Wykeham, b. 1324, d. 1404.

New Daily, The, British newspaper, founded 1960.

New Deal, U.S.A., President Roosevelt's legislative policy 1933 onwards.

New Delhi, Indian capital, construction began 1911 ; opened officially 10 Feb. 1931.

New England Confederation, formed 1643 ; dissolved 1684.

New Forest, England, named by William the Conqueror 1079 ; scheduled as a National Park 1877.

New Guinea, sighted by Antonio d'Abreu and Francisco Serrano 1512 ; part occupied by the Dutch East India Company 1793 ; part by the Government of Queensland 1883.

New Hampshire, U.S.A., first settled 1623 ; entered the Union 1788.

New Hebrides, South Pacific, discovered by the Portuguese navigator Pedro Fernandez de Queiras, b. about 1560, d. 1614.

New Jersey, U.S.A., first settled in the early 17th century ; entered the Union 1787.

New Mexico, U.S.A., first settled 1598 ; annexed to New Spain 1771 ; made a Territory 1850 ; admitted to the Union 1912.

New Orleans, Louisiana, founded about 1718 by the French Canadian explorer Jean Baptiste le Mayne, Sieur de Bienville, b. 1680, d. 1768.

'New River', London, built between 1609 and 1613 by the English goldsmith Sir Hugh Myddleton, b. about 1560, d. 1631.

New South Wales, Australia, declared British by Cook on 23 Aug. 1770, first free settlers arrived 1793.

New Statesman, British periodical, founded 1913 ; absorbed *The Nation* 1931.

New Stone Age, six to eight thousand years ago.

New Style, British calendar (Gregorian), introduced Sept. 1752.

New Year's Day, 1 Jan.

New York City, founded as New Amsterdam 1626.

New York Herald Tribune, American newspaper, founded as *The New York Tribune* 1841 by the American editor Horace Greeley, b 1811, d. 1872.

New York Public Library, founded 1895.

New York State, U.S.A., first settled by the Dutch 1614 ; came under English rule 1664 ; entered the Union 1788.

New York Times, American newspaper, founded 1851 by the American editor and politician Henry Jarvis Raymond (1820–1869), called the *New York Daily Times* 1851–1857.

New York University, founded 1831.

New Zealand, discovered 925 by the Polynesian explorer Kupe ; rediscovered 1642 by the Dutch navigator Abel Janszoon Tasman (1603–1659) ; declared a Dominion 1907 ; National Day, 6 Feb., celebrating the signing with the Maoris of the Treaty of Waitangi 1840.

Newberry, John Strong, American geologist, b. 1822, d. 1892.

Newberry Library, Chicago, founded by the will of the American financier Walter Loomis Newberry, b. 1804, d. 1868.

Newbolt, Sir Henry, English writer (*Drake's Drum,* 1914), b. 1862, d. 1938.

Newcastle, William Cavendish, Duke of, Royalist supporter, b. 1592, d. 1676.

Newcastle-under-Lyme High School, English public school, founded 1602.

Newcomen, Thomas, English engineer and inventor, b. 1663, d. 1729.

Newdigate Prize, Oxford University, for English verse, endowed 1805 by Sir Roger Newdigate, b. 1719, d. 1806.

Newfoundland, discovered by John Cabot 1497 ; annexed by England 1583 ; constituted a Dominion 1917 ; created a Province of Canada 1949.

Newgate, London prison, rebuilt 1770–1783 by the English architect George

Dance the younger, b. 1741, d. 1825 ; demolished 1902–1903.

Newman, Ernest, English music critic (*The Life of R. Wagner,* 1933–1937), b. 1868, d. 1959.

Newman, John Henry, English religious leader and writer (*Apologia Pro Vita Sua,* 1864), b. 1801, converted to Catholicism 1845, became Cardinal 1879, d. 1890.

Newmarch, Mrs Rosa, English music critic (Promenade Concert Notes), b. 1857, d. 1940.

Newmarket, English racing centre, first developed as such by King Charles I.

Newnes, Sir George, English newspaper and magazine publisher, b. 1851, d. 1910.

Newport, Rhode Island, U.S.A., first settled 1639.

News of the World, founded 1 Oct. 1843.

News Chronicle, formed by amalgamation of the *Daily News* and the *Daily Chronicle* 1930. Incorporated in the *Daily Mail* 1960.

Newsfilms introduced 1911 by the French photographer Charles Pathé, b. 1873, d. 1957.

Newspaper, First British daily, the *Daily Courant,* began 11 March 1702.

Newspaper Advertisement Duty, abolished in Britain 1853.

Newspaper Stamp Tax, introduced in Britain 1712 ; abolished 1855.

Newspapers, first printed on a train (the *Grand Trunk Herald*), produced by the American inventor Thomas Alva Edison, b. 1847, d. 1931.

Newton, Sir Isaac, English scientist (*Principia,* 1687), b. 1642, d. 1727.

Newton, Thomas, English divine, b. 1704, d. 1782.

Nexö, Martin Andersen, Danish novelist (*Ditte,* 1917–1921), b. 1869, d. 1954.

Ney, Michel, Duc d'Elchingen, Prince de la Moskova, Marshal of France, b. 1769, shot 1815.

Niagara Falls, first crossed on a tightrope 1859 by the French acrobat Charles Blondin, b. 1824, d. 1897.

Nibelungenlied, German epic poem, compiled about 1160.

Nicæa, First Council of, Ecumenical council, convened 325.

Nicæa, Second Council of, Ecumenical council, convened 787.

Nicaragua, achieved independence from Spain 1821 ; became an independent Republic 1838 ; new Constitution granted 1950.

Niccoli, Niccolo, Italian humanist and book collector, b. 1364, d. 1437.

Nice (Nizza), elected by plebiscite to be annexed to France 1860.

Nicene Creed, believed to be fundamentally the work of St Cyril of Jerusalem, b. about 315, d. 386 ; promulgated at Nicaea 325.

Nicephorus, St, b. 190, martyred 258.

Nicephorus I, Byzantine Emperor (802–811), killed in battle 811.

Nicephorus II (Phocas), Byzantine Emperor (963–969), b. about 912, assassinated 969.

Nicephorus III (Botaniates), Byzantine Emperor (1097–1081).

Nicholas I, St, Pope 858–867, d. 867.

Nicholas II (Gerard), Pope 1059–1061,

Nicholas III (Giovanni Guetano Orsini), Pope 1277–1280, d. 1280.

Nicholas IV (Girolamo Masci), Pope 1288–1293, d. 1293.

Nicholas IV (Pietro Rainalducci), Anti-Pope 1328–1330, d. 1333.

Nicholas V (Tomaso Parentucelli), Pope 1447–1455, b. 1398, d. 1455.

Nicholas I, Emperor of Russia (1825–1855), b. 1796, d. 1855.

Nicholas II, Emperor of Russia (1894–1919), b. 1868, murdered 1919.

Nicholson, Sir Francis, Governor of South Carolina (1719–1728), b. 1660, d. 1728.

Nicholson, John, Irish-born General in India, b. 1812, d. of wounds 1857.

Nicholson, Sir William, English artist (*W. E. Henley*), b. 1872, d. 1949.

Nicias, Peace of, effected 421 B.C. by the Greek statesman Nicias executed 413 B.C.

Nickel, discovered 1754 by the Swedish scientist Baron Cronstedt, b. 1722, d. 1765.

Nickel Carbonyl, a gas, discovered 1899 by the German-born chemist Ludwig Mond, b. 1839, d. 1909.

Nicobar Islands, Bay of Bengal, annexed by Britain 1869 ; centrally administered by the Government of India from 1956 to date.

Nicol Prism, polarisation of light, invented 1828 by the Scottish physicist William Nicol, b. about 1768, d. 1851.

Nicolai, Otto, German composer (*The Merry Wives of Windsor,* 1849), b. 1810, d. 1849.

Nicolls, Richard, first English Governor (1664–1667) of New York, b. 1624, killed 1672.

Nicot, Jean, French diplomat, b. about 1530 ; introduced tobacco into France; d. 1600.

Niebuhr, Reinhold, American theologian, b. 1892.

Niepce, Nicéphore, French physician and pioneer in photography, b. 1765, d. 1833.

Nietzsche, Friedrich, German philosopher (*Also Sprach Zarathustra,* 1883–1885), b. 1844, d. 1900.

Niger, navigated by Mungo Park 1795.

Niger, West Africa, automonous republic within the French Community, formed as a French Territory 1922–1926.

Nigeria, British colony, achieved independence 1960.

Nigeria, Northern, became self-governing 15 Mar. 1959.

' **Night of the Long Knives** ', Nazi purge in Germany, 30 June 1934.

Nightingale, Florence, English pioneer in the training of nurses, b. 1820, d. 1910.

Nightingale Training School, first British training school for nurses, founded by Florence Nightingale at St Thomas's Hospital, London, 1860.

Nihilism, Russian revolutionary movement, founded about 1860.

Nijinsky, Vladimir, Russian dancer, b. 1892, d. 1950.

Nikisch, Artur, Hungarian conductor, b. 1855, d. 1922.

Nikon, Russian Patriarch and church reformer, b. 1605, d. 1681.

Nile, Battle of the (Battle of Aboukir Bay), between the British and the French 1 Aug. 1798.

Nile, Source of the, discovered 1862 by the English explorer John Hanning Speke (1827–1864) and Colonel James Augustus Grant (1827–1892).

Nile Bridge, Cairo, built by the British engineer Sir William Arrol, b. 1839, d. 1913.

Niles, John Jacob, American collector of folk music, b. 1892.

Nineteenth Century, (now the *Twentieth Century*), founded 1877 by the English architect Sir James Knowles b. 1831, d. 1908.

Nine Lessons and Nine Carols, festival held at King's College Chapel, Cambridge, each year on Christmas Eve.

Nineveh, Assyrian capital, excavated 1845–1847 by the archæologist and diplomat Sir Austen Henry Layard, b. 1817, d. 1894.

Ninian, St, b. about 360, d. 432.

'**Ninon de Lenclos**' (Anne Lenclos), French courtesan, b. 1620, d. 1705.

Niobium (Columbium), chemical element, isolated 1801 by the English chemist Charles Hatchett, b. about 1765, d. 1847.

Nitrogen, discovered 1772 by the Scottish physician Daniel Rutherford, b. 1749, d. 1819.

Nitrogen Trichloride, discovered 1811 by the French scientist Pierre Louis Dulon, b. 1785, d. 1838.

Nitroglycerine, manufacture perfected about 1860 by the Swedish chemist Alfred Nobel, b. 1833, d. 1896.

Nitrous Oxide, first used 1844 as an anæsthetic in dentistry by the American dentist Horace Wells, b. 1815, d. 1848.

Nitroprussides, discovered 1841, by the Scottish chemist Lord Playfair, b. 1818, d. 1898.

Nixon, Richard Milhous, U.S. Vice-President (1953–61), b. 1913.

Nō Plays, Japanese traditional plays dating from 15th century.

Noailles, Adrien Maurice, Duc de, French soldier, b. 1678, d. 1766.

Nobel, Alfred, Swedish chemist and philanthropist, b. 1833, d. 1896.

Nobel Peace Prize, founded by Alfred Nobel 1895.

Nobile, Umberto, Italian explorer, b. 1885.

Noble, Sir Andrew, Scottish expert in ballistics, b. 1832, d. 1915.

Noguchi, Hideyo, Japanese bacteriologist, b. 1876, d. 1928.

Nollekens, Joseph, British sculptor (*King George III*), b. 1737, d. 1823.

Non-Euclidean Geometry, founded 1829 by the Russian mathematician Nicholas Lobachevsky, b. 1793, d. 1856.

Nonjurors, British clergymen who refused to take the oath of allegiance 1689–1805.

Nordenskjöld, Otto, Swedish explorer and scholar, b. 1869, d. 1928.

Nordraak, Rikard, Norwegian composer (National Anthem), b. 1842, d. 1866.

Norfolk, Hugh Bigod, Earl of Norfolk, Crusader, d. about 1177.

Norfolk, Roger Bigod, Earl of Norfolk, Marshal of England, d. 1270.

Norfolk Island, South Pacific, discovered by Captain James Cook 1774 ; settled 1856 ; made a Territory of the Commonwealth Government of Australia 1913.

Norham, Peace of, between Scotland England, held 1209.

Norman, Conolly, Irish alienist and reformer, b. 1853, d. 1908.

Norman, Montagu Collet, Baron Norman, Governor of the Bank of England (1920–44), b. 1871, d. 1950.

Norman Conquest, of England, by William the Conqueror 1066.

Normandy, founded 911.

Normandy, Alphonse René le Mire de, French-born chemist and inventor 1851, of a distiller for sea-water, b. 1809, d. 1864.

Normandy Offensive, World War II, began 6 June 1944.

Norris, Frank, American novelist (*The Pit*, 1903), b. 1870, d. 1902.

Norris, Sir Thomas, President of Munster, b. 1556, d. 1599.

Norroy King of Arms, post established in the 13th century.

'North, Christopher' (John Wilson), Scottish writer (*Recreations*, 1842), b. 1785, d. 1854.

North, Frederick, Earl of Guildford, British statesman (Prime Minister 1770–1782), b. 1732, d. 1792.

North, Sir Thomas, English translator (Plutarch's *Lives*, 1579), b. about 1525, d. about 1601.

North Atlantic Treaty, signed at Washington, D.C., 4 Apr. 1949 ; amended in London by protocol 17 Oct. 1951.

North Carolina, U.S.A., first settled 1585 ; permanently settled 1663 ; entered the Union 1789.

North Channel, between Scotland Northern Ireland, swum 1947 for the first (and, so far, the only) time, by Tom Blower of Nottingham.

North Dakota, U.S.A., first settled 1766 ; formed part of the Dakota Territory 1861 ; admitted to the Union 1889.

North-East Atlantic Fisheries Convention, international pact for the conservation of fish, signed 24 Jan. 1959, replacing a Convention.

North-East Passage, navigated 1878–1879 by the Swedish explorer Nils Adolf Erik Nordenskiöld, b. 1832, d. 1901.

North Pole, first reached 6 Apr. 1909 by the American explorer Robert Edwin Peary (1856–1920) ; first flown over 1926 by the American aviator Richard E. Byrd, b. 1888, d. 1957.

North Sea Fisheries Convention, held 1882.

North Staffordshire, University College of, Keele, founded 1949.

North-west Frontier Province, Pakistan, merged in West Pakistan Province 1955.

North-west Mounted Police, Canada, formed 1873 ; renamed the Royal Canadian Mounted Police, 1920.

North-west Passage, discovered 1850–1854 by the British navigator Sir Robert John le Mesurier McClure, b. 1807, d. 1873.

North-west Ordinance, for the government of U.S. Western territories, passed 1787.

North-west Territories, Canada, administered by a Commissioner since 1952.

North-western University, Illinois, founded 1851.

Northampton, Treaty of, recognising the independence of Scotland, signed 1328.

Northcliffe, Alfred Charles William Harmsworth, Viscount, Irish-born newspaper owner, b. 1865, d. 1922.

Northcote, Henry Stafford Northcote, Baron, Governor-General (1903–1907) of Australia, b. 1846, d. 1911.

Northern, Underground Line, London, opened 1904 as the Great Northern and City Railway.

Northern Ireland, administration by separate Parliament and executive government established by the Government of Ireland Act, 1920.

Northern Rhodesia, administered by the British South Africa Company until 1924 ; transferred to the Crown 1924 ; federated with Southern Rhodesia and Nyasaland, 1953.

Northern Territory, Australia, formerly part of New South Wales, annexed to South Australia 1863 ; finally placed under the control of a Commonwealth Administrator 1931.

Northern Wei Dynasty, China, 386–535.

Northumberland, Henry Percy, Earl of, Marshal of England, b. 1342, killed in battle 1408.

Northumberland, Thomas Percy, Earl of, rebel, b. 1528, beheaded 1572.

Norton, Charles Bowyer Adderley, Baron, statesman and town planning pioneer, b. 1814, d. 1905.

Norton, Thomas, English poet (with Sackville, *Gorboduc*, 1561), b. 1532, d. 1584.

Norway, united with Sweden 1319–1355, with Denmark 1380–1389, with Sweden and Denmark 1389–1450, with Denmark 1450–1814, with Sweden 1814–1905 ; independent kingdom since 1905 ; German occupation 1940–1945.

Norwich, granted first Charter by King Henry II 1158.

Norwich Cathedral, constructed 1096 to about 1150.

Norwich School, English public school, origins uncertain ; earliest recorded mention 1256 ; refounded 1547.

Nostradamus, French astrologer (*Centuries*, 1555), b. 1503, d. 1566.

Notke, Bernt, German artist (*St George and the Dragon*, 1489), b. about 1440, d. 1509.

Notre Dame de Paris, constructed 1163–1182.

Nottingham, Charles Howard, Earl of, Lord High Admiral, b. 1536, d. 1624.

Nottingham High School, English public school, founded by Agnes Mellers 1513.

Nottingham University, opened as University College 1881 ; achieved university status 1948.

Nova Scotia, Canada, first settled by the French in the early century ; ceded to Britain 1713 ; became a province of the Dominion of Canada 1867.

' Novalis ' (Friedrich von Hardenberg), German poet (*Hymnen an die Nacht*, 1798–1800), b. 1772, d. 1801.

Novatian, Anti-Pope 251.

Novello, Ivor, British actor and composer, b. 1893, d. 1951.

Novello, Vincent, English music publisher, b. 1781, d. 1861.

November, the eleventh month.

Noverre, Jean-Georges, French pioneer ballet-master at the Opéra-Comique, b. 1727, d. 1810.

Novi, Battle of, between the Allies and the French, 15 Aug. 1799.

Noyes, Alfred, English poet (*Drake*, 1908), b. 1880, d. 1958.

Noyes, John Humphrey, American founder 1848 of the Oneida Community, b. 1811, d. 1886.

Noyon, Treaty of, between France and Spain, signed 1516.

Nuclear Disintegration, in nitrogen atoms, first observed by Rutherford in 1919.

Nuclear Fission, in uranium atoms, first observed by Hahn and Strassman in 1939.

Nuclear Power Station, first British exported, built at Latina, near Rome, 1958.

Nuclear Reactor, First American, built at Chicago University Dec. 1942 by the Italian atomic physicist Enrico Fermi, b. 1901.

Nuclear Reactor, First British (GLEEP), built at Harwell 1947.

Nuffield, William Richard Morris, Viscount, motor manufacturer and philanthropist, b. 1877.

Nuffield College, Oxford University, founded 1937.

Nuffield Foundation, formed 1943.

Nunez, Alvar, Spanish navigator and discoverer 1528 of Florida, d. 1564.

Nunez, Pedro, Spanish painter (*Philip IV*), b. 1601, d. 1654.

Nuremberg, War Crimes Tribunal, World War II, held Nov. 1945–Oct. 1946.

Nuri-es-Said, Iraqi general and Prime Minister of the Arab Federation, b. 1888, assassinated 1958.

Nurses, Training of, organised by the English pioneer Florence Nightingale, b. 1820, d. 1910.

Nuttall, Enos, first Archbishop of the West Indies, b. 1842, d. 1916.

Nutter, Mary, the last Lancashire Witch, b. 1856, d. 1928.

Nyasa, Lake, discovered 1859 by the Scottish explorer David Livingstone, b. 1813, d. 1873.

Nyasaland, constituted 1891 as the British Central Africa Protectorate ; assumed present name 1907 ; federated with Southern and Northern Rhodesia 1953.

Nylon, discovered 1927 by research workers of the American firm Du Pont de Nemours.

Nylon Shirts, first introduced in the U.S.A. 1939.

Nymphenburg, Bavarian chateau, constructed 1664 ; Porcelain manufactured since 1747.

Nyon Conference, on the suppression of Mediterranean submarine piracy, held 1937.

O

O.E.E.C. (Organisation for European Economic Co-operation), set up 16 Apr. 1948.

O.G.P.U., Russian secret police, established 1922 ; abolished 1934.

Oak Apple Day, 29 May, celebrating the Restoration of King Charles II, 1660.

Oakham School, Rutland, English public school, founded by Archdeacon Johnson 1584.

' Oaks, The ', Epsom, first run 1779.

Oates, Titus, English conspirator (1678), b. 1649, d. 1705.

Oath of Strasbourg, sworn between Charles the Bold and Louis the German against Lothair I 842.

Oath of the Tennis Court, French Revolution, 20 June 1789.

Oberammergau, Germany, scene of the decennial presentation of the Passion Play since 1634.

Oberlin, Johann Friedrich, German reformer, b. 1740, d. 1826.

O'Brien, Murrough, Earl of Inchiquin, Royalist supporter, b. 1614, d. 1674.

O'Brien, William Smith, Irish patriot, b. 1803, d. 1864.

Observer, The, British newspaper, began publication 1791.

O'Casey, Sean, Irish-born dramatist (*Juno and the Paycock*, 1924), b. 1884.

Occleve, Thomas, English poet (*De Regimine Principum*), b. about 1369, d. about 1450.

Ockham, William of, English-born philosopher, b. about 1280, d. about 1349.

O'Clery, Michael, Irish historian (*Annals of the Four Masters*, 1632–1636), b. 1575, d. 1643.

O'Connell, Daniel, Irish nationalist leader, b. 1775, d. 1847.

O'Connor, Roderic, Irish king, b. 1116, d. 1198.

Octavia, wife of Marc Antony, d. 11 B.C.

Octavian (Augustus), first Roman Emperor (27 B.C.–A.D. 14), b. 63 B.C., d. A.D. 14.

Octavia, wife of the Roman Emperor Nero, killed 62 B.C.

October, the tenth month.

October Revolution, Russia, 7 Nov. 1917 (new style).

Oddfellows, Independent Order of, temperance society, founded in Manchester 1810 ; in the U.S.A. 1819.

Odo de Clugny, St, pioneer in the development of musical theory, d. 942.

Odovacar, Scirian King of Italy (476–493), killed 493.

Odyssey, Greek epic, attributed to Homer, believed to have lived in the 11th, 10th or 9th century B.C.

Oecolampadius, Johannes, German religious reformer, b. 1482, d. 1531.

Oersted, Hans Christian, Danish pioneer in electromagnetism, b. 1777, d. 1851.

Offa's Dyke, Welsh border defence, constructed 779 by Offa, King of Mercia, b. 747, d. 796.

Offenbach, Jacques (Jakdo Levy Eberst), German-born composer (*Tales of Hoffman*, 1881), b. 1819, d. 1880.

O'Flaherty, Liam, Irish novelist (*The Informer*, 1925), b. 1896.

Oglethorpe, James Edward, English founder 1732 of Georgia, U.S.A., b. 1696, d. 1785.

O'Higgins, Bernardo, Chilean leader, b. 1776, d. 1842.

Ohio, U.S.A., first settled 1788 ; entered the Union 1803.

Ohio Company, English colonising organisation, chartered 1749.

Ohm's Law, of electrical resistance, pronounced 1827 by the German physicist George Simon Ohm (1787–1854). His Law of Sound Vibrations : 1843.

Ohnet, Georges, French writer (*Serge Panine*, 1881), b. 1848, d. 1918.

Ohthered, Norse explorer, lived in the 9th century.

Oil, distilled from coal and shale 1847–1850 by the Scottish chemist James Young, b. 1811, d. 1883.

Oil, struck 1859 in Pennsylvania (first known drilling in the world), by the American oil prospector Colonel Edwin Laurentine Drake, b. 1819, d. 1880.

Oil Drilling, rotary method first adopted in Texas about 1900.

Oil Lighting, first used for London streets 1681.

Oil Pipeline, Kirkuk to Haifa, opened 14 Jan. 1935.

Oil Tanker, prototype (*The Gluckauf*), built on Tyneside 1886.

Oil Tanker, first 100,000 dead weight tonnage, built 1958.

Oil Tanker, World's first gas turbine powered, the British G.T.S. *Auris*, made maiden voyage 1959.

Oil Well, first drilled at Titusville, Pennsylvania, 1859.

Oireachtas, National Parliament of the Irish Republic, founded 1937.

Oistrakh, David, Russian violinist, b. 1908.

Oistrakh, Igor, Russian violinist, b. 1931.

Ojeda, Alonso de, Spanish explorer in Latin America, b. about 1466, d. about 1515.

Okapi, first noted 1878 by the Russian-born explorer Wilhelm Junker, b. 1840, d. 1892.

O'Keeffee, John, Irish playwright (*Tony Lumpkin in Town*, 1778), b. 1747, d. 1833.

Okhotsk, East Siberia, founded 1649.

Okinawa, Battle of, World War II, 1 Apr.–22 June 1945.

Oklahoma, U.S.A., first settled 1887 ; created a Territory 1890 ; admitted to the Union 1907.

Olaf I, King of Norway (995–1000), b. 969, drowned 1000.

Olaf II, St, King of Norway (1016–1029), b. 995, killed in battle 1030.

Olaf III, King of Norway (1067–1093), d. 1093.

Olaf IV, King of Norway (1103–1116), d. 1116.

Olaf V, King of Norway (1381–1387), d. 1387.

Olbers, Heinrich Wilhelm Mathias, German astronomer, b. 1758, d. 1840.

Olcott, Chauncey, American actor, b. 1860, d. 1932.

Old Age Pensions Act, Great Britain, came into force 1 Jan. 1909.

Old Catholics, religious movement, formed 1870–1871.

' Old Pretender, The ' (James Francis Edward Stewart), b. 1688, d. 1766.

Old Style, British calendar (Julian), superseded by New Style 1752.

Old Vic, London theatre, built 1818, assumed its present role 1914.

Oldcastle, Sir John, English leader of the Lollards, hung 1417.

Oldenbarneveldt, John van, Dutch statesman, b. 1547, executed 1619.

Oldham Hulme Grammar School, Lancashire, English public school, founded by James Assheton of Chadderton 1611 ; reconstituted 1887.

Oldys, William, English antiquary, b. 1696, d. 1761.

Oleic Acid, fat-forming acid, discovered 1815 by the French scientist Michel Eugene Chevreul, b. 1786, d. 1889.

Olga, St, d. about 969.

Oligocene Epoch, Earth history, 45 million years ago.

Oliphant, Laurence, South African-born writer and journalist, b. 1829, d. 1888.

Olivares, Gaspar, Spanish statesman, b. 1587, d. 1645.

Oliver, Isaac, French-born miniature painter (*James I*), b. about 1556, d. 1617.

Olivier, Sir Laurence, English actor, b. 1907.

Olmsted, Denison, American scientist, b. 1791, d. 1859.

Olympiad, ancient Greek 4-year period, calculated by the Olympian games.

Olympias, mother of Alexander the Great, killed 316 B.C.

Olympic Era, began 1 July 776 B.C.

Olympic Cup, instituted 1906 by Baron Pierre de Coubertin, b. 1863, d. 1937.

Olympic Games, Ancient, held 776 B.C. to A.D. 394.

Olympic Games, idea of revival introduced 1892 by Baron Pierre de Coubertin, b. 1863, d. 1937.

Olympic Games, Modern 1st, Athens 1896.

Olympic Games, Modern 2nd, Paris 1900.

Olympic Games, Modern 3rd, St Louis 1904.

Olympic Games, Modern 4th, London 1908.

Olympic Games, Modern 5th, Stockholm 1912.

Olympic Games, Modern 6th, Berlin 1916.

Olympic Games, Modern 7th, Antwerp 1920.

Olympic Games, Modern 8th, Paris 1924.

Olympic Games, Modern 9th, Amsterdam 1928.

Olympic Games, Modern 10th, Los Angeles 1932.

Olympic Games, Modern 11th, Berlin 1936.

Olympic Games, Modern 12th, Tokyo and Helsinki 1940. (Cancelled.)

Olympic Games, Modern 13th, London 1944. (Cancelled.)

Olympic Games, Modern 14th, London 1948.

Olympic Games, Modern 15th, Helsinki 1952.

Olympic Games, Modern 16th, Melbourne 1956 (Equestrian sports at Stockholm).

Olympic Games, Modern 17th, Rome 1960.

Olympic Winter Games, first unofficial, London 1908.

Olympic Winter Games, second unofficial, Antwerp 1920.

Olympic Winter Games, first official, Chamonix 1924.

Olympic Winter Games, second official, St Moritz 1928.

Olympic Winter Games, third official Lake Placid 1932.

Olympic Winter Games, fourth official, Garmisch-Partenkirchen 1936.

Olympic Winter Games, fifth official, St Moritz 1948.

Olympic Winter Games, sixth official, Oslo 1952.

Olympic Winter Games, seventh official, Cortina d'Ampezzo 1956.

Olympic Winter Games, eighth official, Squaw Valley 1960.

O'Mahony, John, Irish patriot, b. 1816, d. 1877.

Oman, Sir Charles, India-born historian, b. 1860, d. 1946.

Omar, second of the Mahommedan Caliphs, b. about 581, assassinated 644.

Omar Khayyam, Persian poet (*Rubaiyat*), lived in the 11th century.

Omayyad Dynasty, Of Arabian Caliphs, 661 to 750.

O'Meara, Barry Edward, Napoleon's surgeon at St Helena, b. 1786, d. 1836.

Omer Pasha, Turkish soldier and statesman, b. 1806, d. 1871.

Ompteda, Georg von, German novelist (*Herzeloyde*, 1905), b. 1863, d. 1931.

Onassis, Aristotle Socrates, Argentine ship-owner, b. 1906.

Oneida Community, N.Y., founded 1848 by the American reformer John Humphrey Noyes, b. 1811, d. 1886.

O'Neill, Eugene, American playwright (*Strange Interlude*, 1928), b. 1888, d. 1953.

'O'Neill, Peggy' (Margaret O'Neill), American, b. about 1796, d. 1879.

Onofri, Alessandro, Italian composer (*Assiuolo*, 1912), b. 1874, d. 1932.

Ontario, Canada, settled by the French; British territory from 1763; organised as Upper Canada 1791; made a province of the Dominion of Canada 1867.

Oost, Jacob van, Flemish painter (*Joueurs de cartes*), b. 1601, d. 1671.

Open-hearth Method, of making Bessemer steel invented about 1866 by the electrical engineers Sir William Siemens (1823–1883) and Ernst Werner von Siemens (1816–1892).

Opera, First real, *La Dafne* (1597) by Rinuccini and Peri.

Ophthalmoscope, invented 1851 by the German scientist Hermann von Helmholtz, b. 1821, d. 1894.

Opie, Mrs Amelia Alderson, English writer (*Father and Daughter*, 1801), b. 1769, d. 1853.

Opie, John, English painter (*The Assassination of Rizzio*, 1787), b. 1761, d. 1807.

Opium War, China, between Britain and China, waged 1840–1842.

Oppian, Greek poet (*Halieutica*), lived in the 2nd century.

Orange, William I, Prince of (William the Silent), b. 1533, d. 1584.

Orange, William II, Prince of, b. 1626, d. 1650.

Orange, William III, Prince of (William IV, King of England), b. 1650, d. 1702.

Orange Free State, South Africa, first settled about 1810 ; proclaimed British Territory 1848 ; independence recognised 1854 ; finally created a Province of the Union of South Africa 1910.

Orangemen, Irish Protestant association, formed by 1795.

Oratorians, religious order, founded 1575 by St Filippo Neri, b. 1515, d. 1595.

Oratorio, The first, deemed to have been composed 1600 by the Italian composer Emilio del Cavalieri, b. about 1550, d. 1602.

Oratory, The, Birmingham, founded 1847.

Oratory, The (Brompton Oratory), London, founded 1850.

Orcagna, Italian artist (*Life of the Virgin*), b. about 1308, d. 1368.

Orchardson, Sir William, Scottish painter (*Napoleon on board the Bellerophon*, 1880), b. 1832, d. 1910.

Ord, Sir Harry St George, first Colonial Governor of the Straits Settlements (1867–1873), b. 1819, d. 1885.

Ordericus Vitalis, English historian, b. 1075, d. about 1143.

Ordinance of 1787, for the government of U.S. western territories.

Ordnance Survey, of Great Britain, set up 1791.

Ordovician Period, Earth history, 420 million years ago.

Oregon, U.S.A., first settled about 1830 ; made a Territory 1848 ; admitted to the Union 1859.

Oregon University, founded 1876.

Oregon Trail, Missouri to Oregon, first travelled 1811.

Orford, Robert Walpole, Earl of, English statesman, b. 1676, d. 1745.

Organisation of American States, formed 1948.

Orgetorix, leader of the Helvetii against Julius Cæsar, d. about 60 B.C.

Oriel College, Oxford University, founded by King Edward II 1326.

Origen, Alexandrean theologian, b. 185, d. 254.

Orinoco, South American river, discovered 1498 by Christopher Columbus ; first explored by the Spaniard Diego de Ordaz 1531–1532.

Orissa, India, conquered by the British 1803 ; constituted a separate Province 1936 ; the independent princely states merged with the State of Orissa 1949.

Orkneys, passed (by default) from Danish to Scottish ownership 1468 ; formally annexed to the Scottish crown 1471.

Orlando, Vittorio Emanuele, Italian statesman, b. 1860, d. 1952.

Orleanists, French political party, arose about 1790 ; ceased to exist about 1874.

Orleans, relieved by Jeanne d'Arc 1429.

d'Orleans, Charles, Duc, French poet, b. 1391, d. 1465.

d'Orleans, Henri, Prince, explorer, b. 1867, d. 1901.

Orley, Bernard, Flemish painter (*Charles V*), b. about 1488, d. 1541.

Orlov, Aleksei Feodorovich, Prince, Russian statesman, b. 1787, d. 1862.

Ormandy, Eugène, Hungarian-born conductor, b. 1899.

Ormonde, Sir James, ' Black James ', Lord-Treasurer of Ireland, killed 1497.

Orm (or Ormin), English poet (*Ormulum*), lived in the 13th century.

Orosius, Spanish historian (*Historia adversus Paganos*), lived in the late 4th and early 5th centuries.

Orozco, Jose Clemente, Mexican painter, b. 1883, d. 1949.

Orpen, Sir William, Irish painter (*In the Wicklow Mountains*), b. 1878, d. 1931.

Orrery, Roger Boyle, Earl of, statesman and soldier, b. 1621, d. 1679.

Orsini, Felice, Italian patriot, b. 1819 ; unsuccessful attempt on the life of Napoleon III, 1858 ; executed 1858.

Ortega y Gasset, José, Spanish writer (*La Rebelión de las Masas*, 1930), b. 1883, d. 1955.

Orthodox Eastern Church, finally separated from the Western Church 1054.

Orton, Arthur, English pretender to the Tichbourne title, b. 1834, d. 1898.

Orwell, George (Eric Blair), British political writer (*Animal Farm*, 1945), b. 1903, d. 1950.

Osborne, Dorothy, Lady Temple, wife of Sir William Temple (1628–1699), b. 1627, d. 1695.

Osborne, John, English actor and playwright (*Look Back in Anger*, 1956), b. 1929.

Osborne, Ruth, last woman to be killed as a witch in England, b. 1680, d. 1751.

Oscar I, King of Sweden and Norway (1844–1859), b. 1799, d. 1859.

Oscar II, King of Sweden (1872–1907) and Norway (1872–1905), b. 1829, d. 1907.

Oscillograph, first devised (ondograph) by Hospitalier in 1903.

O'Shanassy, Sir John, Irish-born Australian statesman, b. 1818, d. 1883.

Osiander, Andreas, German religious reformer, b. 1498, d. 1552.

Osler, Sir William, Canadian professor of medicine, b. 1848, d. 1919.

Oslo, Convention of, electing the Norwegian King Magnus King of Sweden, 1319.

Osman Pasha, Turkish field-marshal, b. 1832, d. 1900.

Osmium, metallic element, discovered 1803 by the English chemist Smithson Tennant, b. 1761, d. 1815.

Ossendowski, Ferdynand Antoni, Polish writer (*Beasts, Men and Gods*, 1922), b. 1876, d. 1945.

' Ossian ' (James Macpherson), Scottish poet, b. 1736, d. 1796.

Ossory, Cearbhall, Lord of, King of Dublin 875, d. 888.

Ostade, Adriaan van, Dutch painter, b. 1610, d. 1685.

Ostend Manifesto, concerning the future of Cuba, drawn up 1854 (but was not implemented).

Ostenso, Martha, Norwegian-born novelist (*Wild Geese*, 1925), b. 1900.

Osteopathy, founded 1874 by the American surgeon Andrew Taylor Still, b. 1828, d. 1917.

Osterman, Andrei Ivanovich, Russian statesman, b. 1686, d. in exile 1747.

Ostrog Bible, first Russian Bible (printed in Church Slavonic), published by order of Konstantin, Prince of Ostrog, 1580–1581.

Ostwald Process, for the preparation of nitric acid, invented 1900 by the German scientist Wilhelm Ostwald, b. 1853, d. 1932.

Osuna, Pedro Tellez Girón, Duke of, Spanish Viceroy of Sicily and Naples, b. 1575, d. 1624.

Oswald, St, King of the Northumbrians, b. about 605, killed in battle 642.

Oswald, St, Archbishop of York (972–992), d. 992.

Otago, New Zealand province : Shore stations established 1832 ; first officially organised band of settlers landed 1848.

Othman, Caliph, b. about 574, assassinated 656.

Otho, Roman Emperor (69), b. 32, committed suicide 69.

Otis, Elisha Graves, American inventor (particularly of lift machinery), b. 1811, d. 1861.

Ottawa, Canada, founded 1827 as Bytown by the English engineer John By, b. 1781, d. 1836.

Ottawa Conference, Imperial Economic Conference held 21 July–20 Aug. 1932.

Otto I, the Great, Holy Roman Emperor (962–973), b. 912, d. 973.

Otto II, Holy Roman Emperor (973–983), b. 955, d. 983.

Otto III, Holy Roman Emperor (996–1002), b. 980, d. 1002.

Otto IV, Holy Roman Emperor (1209–1218), b. about 1182, d. 1218.

Otto I, King of Greece (1832–1862), b. 1815, d. 1867.

Ottocar I, King of Bohemia (1198–1230), d. 1230.

Ottocar II, King of Bohemia (1253–1278), b. about 1230, killed in battle 1278.

Ottoman Empire, began 1288 ; ended 1923 when Turkey became a Republic.

Otway, Thomas, English playwright (*Venice Preserved*, 1682), b. 1652, d. 1685.

Ouchy, Treaty of, by which Turkey recognised Italian sovereignty in Tripoli, signed 19 Oct. 1912.

Oudenarde, Battle of, between British and French, 11 July 1708.

' Ouida ' (Marie Louise de la Ramée), English novelist (*Under Two Flags*, 1867), b. 1839, d. 1908.

Ounce, Troy, for precious metals and stones, legalised in Britain 1853.

Oundle School, English public school, founded before the Reformation ; endowed 1566 by the will of Sir William Laxton, Lord Mayor of London ; taken over by the Grocers' Company 1573.

Outer Seven European Free Trade Association, agreement signed on behalf of the British Government 29 Dec. 1959.

Outlawry, abolished in Britain 1879.

Outram, Benjamin, English civil engineer, b. 1764, d. 1805.

Outward Bound Mountain School, Eskdale, opened 1950.

Outward Bound Sea School, Aberdovey, opened Autumn 1941.

Ovaries, Human, nature discovered 1672 by the Dutch naturalist Jan Swammerdam, b. 1637, d. 1680.

Overbeck, Johann Friedrich, German painter (*Pietà*, 1846), b. 1789, d. 1869.

Overbury, Sir Thomas, English courtier and writer (*Characters*), b. 1581, poisoned 1613.

Overland Mail, U.S.A., from the Mississippi River to California, authorised by Act of Congress 1857 ; inaugurated 15 Sept. 1858.

Overland Telegraph Line, completed from Darwin to Adelaide, 1872.

Ovid (Publius Ovidius Naso), Latin poet (*Metamorphoses*), b. 43 B.C., d. A.D. 17.

Owen, Sir Richard, English naturalist, b. 1804, d. 1892.

Owen, Robert, English social reformer, b. 1771, d. 1858.

Owen Falls Dam, Jinja, Uganda, opened 1954.

Owen Glendower (Owain Glyndwr),

Welsh rebel leader, b. about 1350, d. about 1416.

Owens College, now Manchester University, founded 1846 (opened 1851) by the bequest of the English merchant John Owens, b. 1790, d. 1846.

Oxenstierna, Count Axel Gustafsson, Chancellor of Sweden, b. 1583, d. 1654.

Oxford, Edward de Vere, Earl of, English poet (to whom Shakespeare's Works have been attributed), b. 1550, d. 1604.

Oxford, Robert de Vere, Earl of, Court favourite, b. 1362, d. 1392.

Oxford and Cambridge Boat Race, first held 10 June 1829. First broadcast 2 Apr. 1927.

Oxford Dictionary (New English Dictionary), published 1884–1928.

Oxford Group, religious movement founded 1921 by the American evangelist Frank Buchman (1878-1961) ; first so named 1929.

Oxford India Paper, first made at the O.U.P.'s Wolvercote Mill 1875 ; copied from an Indian paper brought to Oxford 1841.

Oxford Movement, launched by the English divine John Keble (1792–1866) on 14 July 1833.

Oxford Tracts, (*Tracts for the Times*), issued in defence of the Church of England as a Divine institution 1833 onwards.

Oxford Union Society, founded 1625.

Oxford University, in existence before 1200 ; granted Charter by King Henry III 1248 ; incorporated by Queen Elizabeth I 1570 ; religious tests abolished 1871 ; Rhodes Scholarships founded 1902 ; women admitted to degrees 1920.

Oxford University Observatory, founded 1873.

Oxford University Press, founded 1585.

Oxley, John, English explorer of Australia, b. 1781, d. 1828.

Oxygen, isolated 1773 by the Swedish scientist Karl Scheele, b. 1742, d. 1786 ; 1774 by the English scientist Joseph Priestley, b. 1733, d. 1804.

Oxyhydrogen Blow Pipe, invented 1801 by the American chemist Robert Hare, b. 1781, d. 1858.

Ozone, discovered 1840 by the German scientist Christian Friedrich Schönbein, b. 1799, d. 1868.

P

P.A.Y.E. (Pay As You Earn), British income-tax system, introduced 1944.

P.E.N., International, London, world association of writers, founded 1921.

P.E.P. (Political and Economic Planning), London, association formed 1931.

P.L.A. (Port of London Authority), constituted by Act of Parliament 1908 ; the Authority first met 16 March, 1909.

P.N.E.U. (Parents' National Educational Union), London, founded 1888.

Pablos, Juan, Italian-born first printer in the western hemisphere, d. about 1561.

Pachmann, Vladimir de, Russian pianist, b. 1848, d. 1953.

Pachomius, St, pioneer of cœnobitic monasticism, b. about 292, d. about 346.

Pacific, War of the, between Chile and Peru and Bolivia, 1879 to 1884.

Pacific Cable, completed at Suva 31 Oct. 1902.

Pacific Ocean, first sighted Sept. 1513 by the Spanish navigator Vasco Nuñez de Balboa, b. about 1475, d. about 1517.

Pacific Security Pact, between the U.S.A., Australia and New Zealand, signed 1 Sept. 1951.

Packard, Alpheus Spring, American scientist, b. 1839, d. 1905.

Paderewski, Ignace Jan, President of Poland (1940–1941), and pianist and composer, b. 1860, d. 1941.

Padua, University of, founded 1222.

Paganini, Nicolò, Italian violinist, b. 1782, d. 1840.

Page, Thomas, British bridge builder, b. 1803, d. 1877.

Paget, Francis, Bishop of Oxford (1901–1911), b. 1851, d. 1911.

Paget, Sir James, English surgeon, b. 1814, d. 1899.

Paget, William, Baron Paget, statesman and diplomat, b. 1505, d. 1563.

Pahang, Malay State, entered into treaty relations with Britain 1874–1895 ; agreed with three other States (1895) to form a federation ; federal council of these states constituted 1909.

Pain, Barry, English novelist and essayist, b. 1864, d. 1928.

Paine, Thomas, English-born radical (*The Rights of Man,* 1791–1792), b. 1737, d. 1809.

Painlevé, Paul, French statesman and pioneer in aviation, b. 1863, d. 1933.

Painter, William, English translator (*Palace of Pleasure,* 1566–1567), b. about 1540, d. 1594.

Pakenham, Francis Aungier Pakenham, Baron, British statesman, b. 1905.

Pakistan, established as a Dominion and separated from India 1947 ; proclaimed an Islamic Republic 1956.

Palafox y Melzi, José de, Duke of Saragossa, b. 1780, d. 1847.

Palæocene Epoch, Earth history, 70 million years ago.

Palæozoic Era, Earth history, between 200 and 520 million years ago.

Paléologue, Maurice, French diplomat, b. 1859, d. 1944.

Palestine, conquered from Turks by British 1917–1918 ; British Mandate proclaimed 1922, ended 1948 ; State of Israel proclaimed 14 May 1948.

Palestrina, Giovanni Pierluigi da, Italian composer, b. 1525, d. 1594.

Paley, William, English philosopher and theologian, b. 1743, d. 1805.

Palgrave, Francis Turner, English compiler of *The Golden Treasury* (1861), b. 1824, d. 1897.

Palissy, Bernard, French potter (invented Palissy Ware about 1545), b. 1509, d. 1589.

Palladio, Andrea, Italian architect, b. 1518, d. 1580.

Palladium, metallic element, discovered 1803 by the English scientist William Hyde Wollaston, b. 1766, d. 1828.

Pallavicino, Pietro Sforza, Italian Cardinal and writer, b. 1607, d. 1667.

Palm Sunday, the Sunday before Easter.

Palma, Jacopo, Italian painter (*Epiphany*), b. about 1480. d. 1528.

Palmer, Edward Henry, English expert in Middle East languages and politics, b. 1840, murdered 1882.

Palmer, George, English biscuit manufacturer, b. 1818, d. 1897.

Palmer, John, Comptroller-General (1786–1793) of the British post office, b. 1742, d. 1818.

Palmer, Samuel, English painter, b. 1805, d. 1881.

Palmer, William, English murderer, b. 1824, hanged 1856.

Palmerston, Henry John Temple, Viscount, British statesman (Prime Minister 1855–1858, 1859–1865), b. 1784, d. 1865.

Palmgren, Selim, Finnish composer (*Peter Schlemihl*), 1878, d. 1951.

Palomar, Mt., California, site of observatory selected 1934 ; observatory opened 1949.

Panama, proclaimed an independent republic 1903 ; new Constitution adopted 1946.

Panama Canal, preliminary work 1881–1889 ; construction began again 1904 ; opened 15 Aug. 1914.

Panama Canal and Canal Zone, treaty defining government and use signed by U.S.A. and Panama 18 Nov. 1903.

Pan-American Union, Washington, D.C., founded 1890.

Panchatantra, Sanskit collection of fables, assembled about 5th century.

Panchen Lama, deputy temporal and spiritual leader of Tibet, office dating from 1640.

Pancras, St, b. 290, martyred 304.

Pandulf, Italian-born Bishop of Norwich and Papal legate, d. 1226.

Paneth, Professor Friedrich Adolf, Austrian scientist, b. 1887, d. 1958.

Pan-German League (*Alldeutschen Verband*), German nationalist organisation, founded 1891, superseded by nationalist parties after 1918.

Panizzi, Sir Anthony, Italian-born Librarian (1856–1866) of the British Museum, b. 1797, d. 1879.

Pankhurst, Mrs Emmeline, English suffragette leader, b. 1858, d. 1928.

Pankhurst, Dame Christabel, English suffragette leader, b. 1880, d. 1958.

Pannartz, Arnold, German printer in Italy, lived in the 15th century.

Pannini, Giovanni Paolo, Italian painter (*The Roman Forum*), b. about 1691, d. 1765.

Pantheon, Rome, built by Agrippa about 25 B.C. ; rebuilt about 120 by Hadrian ; transformed into a Christian church 609.

Panthéon, Paris, designed by the French architect Jacques Germain Soufflot (1709–1780) ; built 1754–80 as a church ; secularised 1789.

Pantomimes, introduced into England by the English dancing-master John Weaver, b. 1673, d. 1760.

Panzini, Alfredo, Italian novelist (*Santippe*, 1914), b. 1863, d. 1939.

Paoli, Pascal, Corsican patriot, b. 1725, d. 1807.

Papagos, Alexander, Greek soldier, b. 1883, d. 1955.

Papal States, finally incorporated with the Italian kingdom 1859–1860 and 1870.

Papen, Franz von, German statesman (Chancellor, 1932), b. 1879.

Paper, traditionally invented by the Chinese Tsai-Lun 105.

Paper Duty, first imposed by Parliament 1643, cancelled at the Restoration. Reimposed 1712, repealed 1861. Act of 1794 allowed rebate on paper exported abroad, if watermarked with date of manufacture.

Papini, Giovanni, Italian writer (*Storia di Cristo*, 1921), b. 1881, d. 1956.

Papinian, Roman jurist, killed 212.

Papua, discovered 1526–1527 and named by the Portuguese navigator Don Jorge de Menezes ; annexed by the Government of Queensland 1883 ; created Territory 1906 ; placed under International Trusteeship 1949.

Paracelsus (Theophrastus Bombastus von Hohenheim), Swiss physician, b. 1493, d. 1541.

Parachutes, believed to have been invented 1785 by the French balloonist Jean Pierre Blanchard, b. 1753, d. 1809 ; first used 1802 by the Frenchman André Garnevin, b. 1769, d. 1823.

Paraffin, discovered 1830 by the German inventor Baron von Reichenbach, b. 1788, d. 1869.

Paraffin Industry, originated in England 1856 by the Scottish chemist James Young, b. 1811, d. 1883.

Paraguay, declared independent of Spanish rule, 1811.

Paratroops, first developed by the Russians about 1925 ; first used in war by the Germans in 1940.

Parcel Post, Inland, began in Britain 1883.

Parchment, traditionally invented by Eumenes II of Pergamon in the 2nd century B.C.

Paré, Ambroise, French surgeon, b. 1510, d. 1590.

Parents' National Educational Union, London, founded 1888.

Pareto, Vilfredo, Italian economist and sociologist, b. 1848, d. 1923.

Paris, Matthew, English historian (*Chronica Majora*), d. 1259.

Paris, Treaty of, adjusting the claims of King Henry III of England, ratified Dec. 1259 ; ending the Seven Years' War 1763 ; ending War of American Independence 1783 ; ending the Napoleonic Wars 1814 and 1815 ; ending Crimean War 1856.

Paris, University of, founded 1120.

Paris Observatory, founded 1667–1771.

Parish Magazine Insets, for insertion in local parish magazines, first issued in Britain 1859.

Park, Mungo, Scottish explorer (explored Niger 1796), b. 1771, d. about 1805.

Parker, Matthew, Archbishop of Canterbury (1559–1575), d. 1575.

Parker, Richard, leader of the mutineers (1797) at the Nore, b. about 1767, hanged 1797.

Parker, Sir Thomas, Earl of Macclesfield, Lord Chancellor, b. about 1666, d. 1732.

Parkes, Alexander, English scientist and inventor (1855) of celluloid, b. 1813, d. 1890.

Parkhurst, John, Bishop of Norwich (1560–1575), b. about 1512, d. 1575.

Parking Meters, first introduced in Britain in Westminster 1958.

Parkman, Francis, American historian, b. 1823, d. 1893.

'Parley, Peter', pseudonym adopted by both the English writers William Martin (1801–1867) and George Mogridge (1787–1854).

Parliament, first called as advisory body by King John in 1213.

Parliament, Addled, held 1614.

Parliament, Cavalier, held 1660 to 1678.

Parliament, Long, held 1640 to 1653, 1659 to 1660.

Parliament, Mad, held in Oxford 1256.

Parliament, Merciless, which condemned friends of Richard II to death, 1388.

Parliament, Rump, held 1648 to 1653, and 1659.

Parliament, Short, held 1640.

Parliament of Dunces, reign of King Henry IV, met at Coventry 1404.

Parmenides, Greek philosopher, lived in the 6th and 5th centuries B.C.

Parmigianino, Francesco, Italian painter (*St Jerome*), b. 1503, d. 1540.

Parnell, Charles Stewart, Irish nationalist leader, b. 1846, divorce case 1889, d. 1891.

Parr, Catherine, Queen of Henry VIII, b. 1512, d. 1548.

Parr, Thomas, ' Old Parr '—probably the longest-lived Englishman, b. about 1483, d. 1635.

Parrish, Maxfield, American artist, b. 1870.

Parry, Sir Charles Hubert Hastings, English composer (*De Profundis*, 1891) b. 1848, d. 1918.

Parsees, Indian followers of Zoroaster b. about 659, d. about 582 B.C.

Parsons, Elizabeth, ' the Cock Lane ghost ', b. 1749, d. 1807.

Parsons, Robert, Jesuit missionary in England, b. 1546, d. 1610.

Parthenogenesis, first recognised by the Greek philosopher Aristotle, b. 384, d. 322 B.C.

Parthenon, Athens, rebuilt by Pericles about 447–436 B.C. ; wrecked by an explosion 1687.

Parthian Empire, in existence 227 B.C. to A.D. 224.

Parton, James, English-born writer (*Aaron Burr*, 1857), b. 1822, d. 1891.

Partridge, John, English astrologer, b. 1644, d. 1715.

Pascal, Blaise, French philosopher, scientist and theologian (*Lettres Provinciales*, 1656–1657), b. 1623, d. 1662.

Paschal I, St, Pope 817–824, d. 824.

Paschal II (Ronieri), Pope 1099–1118, d. 1118.

Paschal III (Guido), Anti-Pope 1164–1168.

Pascin, Jules, Bulgarian-born painter (*Femme Assise*), b. 1885, committed suicide 1930.

Pasquier, Etienne, French writer (*Recherches de la France*, 1560–1615), b. 1529, d. 1615.

Passchendaele, Belgium, Battle of, World War I, 28 Sept. 1918.

Passion Play, Oberammergau, Germany, acted every ten years since 1634.

Passover (*Peisach*), Jewish feast, begins on evening of the 14th day of Nisan.

Passy, Frédéric, French economist, b. 1822, d. 1912.

Pasternak, Boris, Russian poet and novelist (*Dr Zhivago*, 1957), b. 1890, d. 1960.

Pasteur, Louis, French scientist, b. 1822, d. 1895.

Paston, John, English country gentleman, b. 1421, d. 1466.

Pastor, Ludwig, Freiherr von, German historian of the Popes, b. 1854, d. 1928.

Patent, World's first, granted in Venice to the German printer John of Speyer 1469.

Pater, Walter Horatio, English writer and critic (*Marius the Epicurean*, 1885), b. 1839, d. 1894.

Paterson, Mrs Emma Anne, first woman admitted (1875) to the Trade Union Congress, b. 1848, d. 1886.

Pathé, Charles, French pioneer film producer (*The Dancing Years*), b. 1873, d. 1957.

Pathé News Reel, founded by the French photographer Charles Pathé 1911.

Pathology, modern practice founded by Rudolf Virchow, b. 1821, d. 1902.

Pathology, Experimental, study founded by John Hunter, b. 1728, d. 1793.

Patmore, Coventry, English writer (*The Angel in the House*, 1854–1862), b. 1823, d. 1896.

Paton, John Brown, English founder of nonconformist social movements, b. 1830, d. 1911.

Patrick, St, b. about 372, d. about 463 ; Order of, founded by George III in 1783.

Patti, Adelina, operatic singer, b. 1843, d. 1919.

Pattinson, Hugh Lee, English metallurgical chemist and inventor, b. 1796 d. 1858.

Paul, St, the Apostle, beheaded about 67.

Paul I, Tsar of Russia (1799–1801), b. 1754, murdered 1801.

Paul I, St, Pope 757–767, d. 767.

Paul II (Pietro Barbo), Pope 1464–1471, b. 1417, d. 1471.

Paul III (Alessandro Farnese), Pope 1534–1549, b. 1468, d. 1549.

Paul IV (Giovanni Pietro Caraffa), Pope 1555–1559, b. 1476, d. 1559.

Paul V (Camillo Borghese), Pope 1605–1621, b. 1552, d. 1621.

Paul of the Cross, St, Italian founder (1720–1725) of the Passionists, b. 1694, d. 1775.

Paul the Deacon, Italian historian, lived in the 8th century.

' Paul, Jean ' (Johann Paul Friedrich Richter), German humorous writer (*Hesperus*, 1795), b. 1763, d. 1825.

Paulhan, Louis, French aviator and winner of the *Daily Mail* 1910 London-Manchester flight, b. 1883.

Pauli, Professor Wolfgang, Austrian physicist, b. 1900, d. 1958.

Paulinus, Roman bishop of York, d. 644.

Paulus Lucius Aemilius, Roman general, b. about 229, d. 160 B.C.

Pausanias, Spartan military commander, d. about 470 B.C.

Pausanias, Greek traveller and writer (*Description of Greece*), lived in the 2nd century.

Pavlov, Ivan Petrovich, Russian scientist, b. 1849, d. 1936.

Pavlova, Anna, Russian dancer, b. 1885, d. 1931.

Paxton, Sir Joseph, English designer (1850) of the Crystal Palace, b. 1801, d. 1865.

Pay As You Earn (P.A.Y.E.), British income tax system, introduced 1944.

Payne, Roger, English bookbinder, b. 1739, d. 1797.

Payne, John Howard, American writer (*Home, Sweet Home,* 1823), b. 1791, d. 1852.

Pazzi Assassination, of Giuliano de' Medici 26 Apr. 1478.

Peabody, Elizabeth Palmer, American pioneer in kindergarten provision, b. 1804, d. 1894.

Peabody, George, American merchant and philanthropist, b. 1795, d. 1869.

Peace, Charles, English murderer, b. about 1832, hanged 1879.

Peace Congress, First International, held in London 1843.

Peace Pledge, initiated 1934 by the Rev. Dick Sheppard, d. 1937.

Peacock, Thomas Love, English writer (*Headlong Hall,* 1816), b. 1785, d. 1866.

Peale, Charles Willson, American painter (*George Washington,* 1772), b. 1741, d. 1826.

Pearl Harbour Attack, World War II, made by the Japanese on the Honolulu naval base 7 Dec. 1941.

Pearse, Pádraic, Irish nationalist leader, b. 1879, shot 1916.

Pearson, Sir Arthur, English newspaper owner and philanthropist (founded *Pearson's Weekly,* 1890), b. 1866, d. 1921.

Pearson, John, English theologian (*Exposition of the Creed,* 1659), b. 1613, d. 1686.

Pearson, William, English astronomer, b. 1767, d. 1847.

Peary, Robert, American explorer in the Arctic, b. 1856, d. 1920.

Peasants' Revolt, led by the English rebel Wat Tyler 1381.

Peasants' War, South Germany, 1525.

Peck, Francis, English antiquary (*Desiderata Curiosa,* 1732–1735), b. 1692, d. 1743.

Peckham, John, Archbishop of Canterbury (1279–1292), d. 1292.

Pecock, Reginald, Welsh theologian (*Book of Faith,* 1466), b. about 1395, d. about 1460.

Peculiar People, religious movement, founded in London 1838 by John Banyard.

Pedal Bicycle, First, built 1838 by Kirkpatrick Macmillan.

Pedro the Cruel, King of Castile and Leon (1350–1369), b. 1334, killed in combat 1369.

Pedro I, Emperor of Brazil (1822–1831), b. 1798, d. 1834.

Pedro II, Emperor of Brazil (1831–1889), b. 1825, d. 1891.

Peel, Sir Robert, British statesman (Prime Minister 1834, 1841–1845) and reorganiser (1829) of London's police force, b. 1788, d. 1850.

Peele, George, English writer (*David and Bethsabe,* 1599), b. about 1558, d. about 1597.

Peep-of-Day Boys, Irish Protestant secret society, flourishing at the end of the 18th century.

Péguy, Charles, French writer (*Jeanne d'Arc,* 1897), b. 1873, d. 1914.

Peine Forte et Dure, used in England as late as 1741.

Peirce, Benjamin, American scientist, b. 1809, d. 1880.

Peisistratus, Greek statesman, b. about 605, d. 527 B.C.

Peking Man, early Pleistocene period remains discovered near Peking 1927.

Pelagius, I, Pope 555–561, d. 561.

Pelagius II, Pope 579–590, d. 590.

Pelagius, British theologian, b. about 360, d. about 420.

Pellegrini, Carlo, Italian-born caricaturist (' Ape ' in *Vanity Fair*), b. 1839, d. 1889.

Pelletier, Pierre Joseph, French chemist, b. 1788, d. 1842.

Pelopidas, Greek statesman and general, killed in battle 364 B.C.

Peloponnesian League, organised by Sparta about 550 B.C. ; ended in the 4th century B.C.

Peloponnesian War, between Sparta and Athens, 431 to 404 B.C.

Peltier Effect, heat properties of electric currents, discovered 1834 by the French scientist Jean Charles Athanase Peltier, b. 1785, d. 1845.

Pembroke, Mary Herbert, Countess of, patroness of poets, b. 1561, d. 1621.

Pembroke, William Herbert, Earl of, Governor of Calais, b. about 1501, d. 1570.

Pembroke College, Cambridge University, founded as the Hall or House of Valence-Mary by Mary de St Paul, widow of the Earl of Pembroke, 1347.

Pembroke College, Oxford University, founded 1624 ; previously known as Broadgates Hall.

Penang, (Prince of Wales' Island), first British settlement in the Malay Peninsula, ceded by the Sultan of Kedah to the East India Company 1786, Province Wellesley being added 1800 ; incorporated with Malacca and Singapore 1826 under a single government; known as the Straits Settlements 1867–1946.

Pencils, possibly invented much earlier, but certainly in use by the mid-16th century.

Pendleton, Edmund, Federalist Party leader in Virginia, b. 1721, d. 1803.

Pendulum, isochronism observed 1582 and time-keeping mechanism devised 1641 by Galileo Galilei ; pendulum clocks constructed 1649 by Vincenzio Galilei and 1658 by the Dutch scientist Christiaan Huygens (who described the principles in his *Horologium Oscillatorium*, 1673), b. 1629, d. 1695 ; compensated pendulum constructed 1722 by the English mechanician George Graham, b. 1675, d. 1751.

Penicillin, discovered 1928 by Sir Alexander Fleming, b. 1881, d. 1955.

Peninsular War, between the Allies and Napoleon, 1808 to 1814.

Penn, Sir William, Commander-in-Chief of the Fleet, b. 1621, d. 1670.

Penn, William, English Quaker, founder 1682 of Pennsylvania, b. 1644, d. 1718.

Pennell, Joseph, American artist, b. 1860, d. 1926.

Pen-nibs, Steel, manufacture perfected 1829 by the English industrialists Sir Josiah Mason (1795–1881) and Joseph Gillott (1797–1873).

Pennsylvania, U.S.A., first settled 1682 ; ratified U.S. Constitution 1787.

Pennsylvania University, Philadelphia, founded 1740.

'Penny Plain, Twopence Coloured', cut-out sheets of theatrical scenery and characters for model theatres, issued in England during the first half of the 19th century ; probable origins in the similar sheets issued in the late 18th century in France and Germany.

Penny Postage, invented 1837 and put into effect 1840 by Sir Rowland Hill, b. 1795, d. 1879.

Penrose, Francis Cranmer, English archæologist and astronomer, b. 1817, d. 1903.

Pentecost, Christian feast of the Holy Spirit, celebrated on Whit-Sunday.

Pepin I, Frankish ruler, d. 640.

Pepin II, Frankish ruler, d. 714.

Pepin III, King of the Franks (751–768), d. 768.

Pepper, John Henry, English illusionist (' Pepper's Ghost '), b. 1821, d. 1900.

Pepsin, first described 1836 by the German physiologist Theodor Schwann, b. 1810, d. 1882.

Pepusch, Dr John Christopher, German-born composer (*The Beggar's Opera*, 1728), b. 1667, d. 1752.

Pepys, Samuel, English statesman and diarist (1660–1669), b. 1633, d. 1703.

Perak, Malay State, entered into treaty relations 1874–1895 with Britain ; agreed 1895 with three other Malay states to form a federation ; federal council of these states formed 1909.

Perceval, Spencer, Prime Minister (1809–1812), b. 1762, assassinated 1812.

Percier, Charles, French architect, b. 1764, d. 1838.

Percussion Cap, gunmaking, introduced into the British Army 1842.

Percussion Lock, gunmaking, invented 1805 by the Scottish minister the Rev. Alexander John Forsyth, b. 1768, d. 1843.

Percy, Sir Henry (' Hotspur '), b. 1364, killed in battle 1403.

Percy, John, English physician and metallurgist, b. 1817, d. 1889.

Percy, Lord, of Newcastle, pioneer in English education, b. 1887, d. 1958.

Perdiccas, Regent of the Macedonian Empire (323–321 B.C.), assassinated 321 B.C.

Perdita ' (Mary Robinson), English actress and mistress of Prince of Wales, b. 1758, d. 1800.

Peretz, Isaac, Yiddish writer, b. 1852, d. 1915.

Perez de Ayala, Ramón, Spanish writer (*Belarmino y Apolonio* 1921), b. 1881.

Perez de Montalvan, Juan, Spanish playwright (*The Lovers of Teruel*), b. 1602, d. 1638.

Perez Galdos, Benito, Spanish novelist, (*Gloria*, 1877), b. 1843, d. 1920.

Pergolesi, Giovanni Battista, Italian composer (*La Serva Padrona*, 1733), b. 1710, d. 1736.

Pericles, Greek statesman, b. about 492 B.C.

Perim, island off Aden, permanently occupied by the British 1857.

Periodic Law, relating to chemical elements, developed 1869 from a paper published 1864 of the English chemist John Newlands (1837–1898) by the Russian chemist Dmitri Ivanovich Mendeleieff (1834–1907).

Periwig, use general in W. Europe approximately 1660–1800.

Perkin, Sir William Henry, English chemist and discoverer (1856) of mauveine, b. 1838, d. 1907.

Perkins, Loftus, English engineer and pioneer in refrigeration, b. 1834, d. 1891.

Perkins, William, English theologian (*Armilla Aurea*, 1590), b. 1558, d. 1602.

Permanent Court of Arbitration, The Hague, established 1899.

Permanganate Acid, first obtained 1830 by the German chemist Eilhard Mitscherlich, b. 1794, d. 1863.

Permian Period, Earth history, 220 million years ago.

Permindex, Permanent International Market, for the exhibition and sale of industrial products, opened in Rome 1960.

Perón, Juan, ruler of Argentina 1946–1955, b. 1895.

Perrault, Charles, French collector of fairy tales (*Contes de ma Mère l'Oie*, 1697), b. 1628, d. 1703.

Perrault, Claude, French architect, b. 1613, d. 1688.

Perrers, Alice, Royal mistress, d. 1400.

Perret, Auguste, French architect and pioneer in the use of modern concrete construction, b. 1874, d. 1954.

Perronet, Edward, English hymnwriter (*All Hail the Power of Jesu's Name*, 1780), b. 1721, d. 1792.

Perronneau, Jean Baptiste, French painter, b. 1715, d. 1783.

Perrot, Sir John, Lord-Deputy of Ireland (1584–1588), b. about 1527, d. 1592.

Perry, John, English traveller and canal-builder, b. 1670, d. 1732.

Perry, Stephen Joseph, English astronomer, b. 1833, d. 1889.

Perse School, Cambridge, founded by will of Stephen Perse, b. 1548, d. 1615.

Pershing, John Joseph, American general, b. 1860, d. 1948.

Persia, ruled by Achaemenids (about 550–330 B.C.), Arsacids (227 B.C.– A.D. 224), Sassanids (226–651), Muslims 651–1231), Mongols and Turks (1231–1502), Safavids (1502–1722), Turks (1722–1779), Kajars (1779–1925) ; by Pahlavis since 1925.

Persian Gulf States : see Bahrein ; Kuwait ; Qatar.

Persian Wars, with the Greek city-states, 500–449 B.C.

Persigny, Jean Gilbert Victor Fialin, Duc de, French diplomat and statesman, b. 1808, d. 1872.

Persius, Latin writer (*Satires*), b. 34, d. 62.

Perth, John Drummond, Duke of, Jacobite supporter, d. 1747.

Perthes, Justus, German publisher, b. 1749, d. 1816.

Pertinax, Roman emperor (193), b. 126, assassinated 193.

Peru, declared an independent Republic 1821.

Perugino (Pietro Vannucci), Italian painter (*The Assumption*), b. 1446, d. 1524.

Peruzzi, Baldassare, Italian architect, b. 1481, d. 1536.

Pervigilium Veneris, anonymous Latin poem written probably in the 2nd century.

Pestalozzi, Johann Heinrich, Swiss educationalist (opened his first orphan school 1798), b. 1746, d. 1827.

Pétain, Marshal Henri Philippe, French soldier and statesman (Prime Minister 1940–1944), b. 1856, d. 1951.

Peter, St, the Apostle, crucified about 67.

Peter I, the Great, Tsar of Russia (1689–1725), b. 1672, d. 1725.

Peter I Land, Antarctic island, discovered 1821 by the Russian Admiral von Bellingshausen ; annexed by Norway 1929–1931.

Peter II, Tsar of Russia (1728–1730), b. 1715, d. 1730.

Peter III, Tsar of Russia (1762), b. 1728, murdered 1762.

Peter Damian, St, Italian reformer, b. about 1007, d. 1072.

Peter des Roches, Bishop of Winchester, d. 1238.

Peter Lombard, Italian theologian (*Sententiæ*, 1145–1150), b. about 1100, d. about 1160.

Peter Martyr, St, Italian inquisitor, killed 1252.

Peter Martyr, Italian Protestant leader, b. 1500, d. 1555.

Peter Symonds School, Winchester, English public school founded by the London merchant Peter Symonds 1607.

Peter the Hermit, French Crusader, d. about 1115.

Peter the Wild Boy, b. about 1712, d. 1785.

Peter's Pence, annual English offering to the Pope, first sent 787 ; abolished 1534.

Peterborough, Charles Mordaunt, Earl of, admiral and diplomat, b. 1658, d. 1735.

Peterborough Cathedral, England, present building begun 1117 ; consecrated 1238.

Peterhouse, Cambridge, founded by Hugh de Balsham, Bishop of Ely, 1284.

Peterloo, massacre at reform meeting at St Peter's Field, Manchester 16 Aug. 1819.

Petermann, August Heinrich, German cartographer, b. 1822, committed suicide 1878.

Peters, Carl Friedrich, German music publisher, b. 1779, d. 1827.

Petersen, Wilhelm, Greek-born composer (*Grosse Messe*, 1930), b. 1890.

Petipa, Marius, French dancer and choreographer, b. 1822, d. 1910.

Petit Trianon, Versailles, constructed 1762–1768 by the French architect Jacques Ange Gabriel, b. about 1698, d. 1782.

Petition of Right, submitted by the House of Commons to King Charles I and accepted by him 1628.

Petitioners, political group (connected with Whigs) became prominent 1680.

Petlura, Semyon, Ukrainian leader, b. 1877, murdered 1926.

Petöfi, Sandor, Hungarian national poet, b. 1823, killed in battle 1849.

Petra, ruins of Nabatæan and Græco-Roman settlements in the present territory of Jordan, built mainly 6th century B.C. to 3rd century A.D.

Petrarch (Francesco Petrarca), Italian poet (*Rime in Vita e Morte*), b. 1304, d. 1374.

Petre, Edward, English Jesuit missionary to England, b. 1631, d. 1699.

Petri, Egon, German-born pianist, b. 1881.

Petrie, William Flinders, English archæologist, b. 1853, d. 1942.

Petrified Forest, Arizona, established a national monument 1906.

Petrol Engine, first constructed 1883 by the German engineer Gottlieb Daimler, b. 1834, d. 1900.

Petroleum, first transported in the brig *Elizabeth Watts* from the U.S.A. to Europe, arriving at the Port of London 1861.

Petroleum Flash-point, apparatus for its determination (the Abel close-test instrument) invented about 1879 by the English chemist Sir Frederick Augustus Abel, b. 1827, d. 1902.

Petronius 'Arbiter', Roman writer (*The Satyricon*), committed suicide about 66.

Petrucci, Ottaviano dei, Italian pioneer music printer, b. 1466, d. 1539.

Pettie, George, English writer (*A Petite Pallace*, 1576), b. 1548, d. 1589.

Petty, Sir William, English economist, b. 1623, d. 1687.

Petunia, Double, first grown (in France) about 1855.

Pfister, Albrecht, German pioneer printer, b. about 1420, d. about 1470.

Phædo, Greek philosopher, lived in the late 5th and early 4th centuries B.C.

Phalaris, tyrant of Acragas, b. about 570, killed about 554 B.C.

Pharmaceutical Society of Great Britain, founded 1841, incorporated by Royal Charter 1843.

Pharmacopeia, issue in Britain by the General Council of Medical Education and Registration, authorised by Acts of Parliament 1858 and 1862.

Pharnaces I, first King of Pontus 190–156 B.C.

Pharnaces II, King of Pontus, killed 47 B.C.

Pharos, near Alexandria, site of the world-famous lighthouse built about 280 B.C., and demolished in the 14th century.

Phelps, Samuel, English actor-manager, b. 1804, d. 1878.

Phelps, Thomas, English astronomer, b. 1694, d. after 1776.

Phidias, Greek sculptor, b. about 490, d. about 432 B.C.

Philadelphia, Pennsylvania, founded under a patent from King Charles II 1681.

Philemon, Greek playwright (*The Treasure*), b. about 360, d. 263 B.C.

Philidor, François André Danican, French chess champion, b. 1726, d. 1795.

Philip, Anti-Pope 768.

Philip I, possibly mythical early King of Macedonia.

Philip II, King of Macedonia, father of Alexander the Great, b. about 382, assassinated 336 B.C.

Philip III, King of Macedonia (323–317 B.C.) assassinated 317 B.C.

Philip IV, King of Macedonia (297–296 B.C.)

Philip V, King of Macedonia (220–179 B.C.), d. 179 B.C.

Philip I, King of France (1059–1108), b. 1052, d. 1108.

Philip II, King of France (1180–1223), b. 1165, d. 1223.

Philip III, the Bold, King of France (1270–1285), b. 1245, d. 1285.

Philip IV, the Fair, King of France (1285–1314), b. 1268, d. 1314.

Philip V, the Tall, King of France (1317–1322), b. about 1294, d. 1322.

Philip VI, King of France (1328–1350), b. 1293, d. 1350.

Philip I, the Handsome, King of Spain (1506), b. 1478, d. 1506.

Philip II, King of Spain (1556–1598), b. 1527, d. 1598.

Philip III, King of Spain (1598–1621), b. 1578, d. 1621.

Philip IV, King of Spain (1621–1665), b. 1605, d. 1665.

Philip V, King of Spain (1700–1746), b. 1683, d. 1746.

Philip Neri, St, b. 1515, d. 1595.

'Philippe Égalité' (Louis-Philippe, Duc d'Orléans), b. 1747, guillotined 1793.

Philippi, Battle of, between Octavius and Antony and the Senate party, 42 B.C.

Philippine Islands, discovered by the Portuguese navigator Ferdinand Magellan 1521 ; ceded by Spain to the U.S.A. 1898 ; became an independent Republic 1946.

Philippines, naval battle of the, World War II, 23–25 Oct. 1944.

Philips, John, English poet (*Cyder*, 1708), b. 1676, d. 1709.

Philips, Richard, Governor of Nova Scotia (1720–1749), b. 1661, d. 1751.

Phillimore, Greville, English divine and hymn-writer, b. 1821, d. 1884.

Phillipps, Sir Thomas, English book and MSS. collector, b. 1792, d. 1872.

Phillpotts, Eden, India-born writer (*The Girl and the Faun*, 1916), b. 1862, d. 1960.

Philo Judæus, Jewish philosopher of Alexandria, b. about 15 B.C., d. about A.D. 50.

Philopœmen, Greek general, b. about 253, executed 184 B.C.

Phipps, Charles John, English theatre architect, b. 1835, d. 1897.

'Phiz' (Hablot Knight Browne), English artist and illustrator, b. 1815, d. 1882.

Phlogiston Theory, propounded 1731 by the German scientist Georg Ernst Stahl, b. 1660, d. 1734.

Phocion, Greek statesman and general, b. about 402, d. 317 B.C.

Phœnix Park Murders, Dublin, the murder of Lord Frederick Cavendish and Thomas Henry Burke by Irish patriots 6 May 1882.

'Phoney War', at beginning of Second World War, Oct. 1939–Mar. 1940.

Phonograph, first sound recording machine, invented 1876 by the American inventor Thomas Alva Edison, b. 1847, d. 1931.

Phosphorus, discovered 1669 by the German alchemist Henning Brandt.

Photius, Patriarch of Constantinople, b. about 820, d. 891.

Photochromolithography, process invented 1868 by the British photo-lithographer William Griggs, b. 1832, d. 1911.

Photoelectric Property of Selenium, first observed 1875 by the English scientist Willoughby Smith, b. 1828, d. 1891.

Photoengraving, invented in France 1827.

Photograph, earliest surviving, taken 1835 by William Fox Talbot, b. 1800, d. 1877.

Photographer, the first, the English inventor Thomas Wedgwood, b. 1771, d. 1805.

Photographic Roll film, invented 1884 by the American inventor George Eastman, b. 1354, d. 1932.

Photography, principle discovered 1823 by the French physician Joseph Nicéphore Niepce, b. 1765, d. 1833.

Photography, Colour, invented 1907 by the French inventor Auguste Lumière, b. 1862, d. 1954.

Photogravure, invented 1895 by the Czech-born manufacturer Karl Klietsch (Karel Klič), b. 1841, d. 1926.

Phraates I, King of Parthia from 175 to 170 B.C.

Phraates II, King of Parthia (138–127 B.C.) killed 127 B.C.

Phraates III, King of Parthia (70–57 B.C.), murdered 57 B.C.

Phraates IV, King of Parthia (37 B.C.–A.D. 2), murdered A.D. 2.

Phraates V, King of Parthia (2–5), killed 5.

Phrenology, study founded by the German physician Franz Joseph Gall, b. 1758, d. 1828.

Phthisis, bacillus discovered 1890 by the German bacteriologist Robert Koch, b. 1843, d. 1910.

Phyfe, Duncan, American cabinet-maker, b. about 1768, d. 1854.

Physick, Philip Synge, American pioneer surgeon, b. 1768, d. 1837.

Pianoforte, first practical model invented about 1710 by the Italian harpsichord-maker Bartolommeo Cristofori, b. 1655, d. 1731.

Piatigorsky, Gregor, Russian 'cellist, b. 1903.

Piazzi, Giuseppe, Italian astronomer, b. 1746, d. 1826.

Picard, Jean, French astronomer, b. 1620, d. 1682.

Picasso, Pablo, Catalan artist (*Guernica*, 1937), b. 1881.

Piccadilly Circus, London, New underground station opened 1928. First lit by electricity 1932.

Piccard, Auguste, Belgian physicist and explorer of the stratosphere and the bathysphere, b. 1884.

Piccolomini, Prince Octavio, Military commander who brought to an end the Thirty Years' War, b. 1599, d. 1656.

Pickens, Andrew, American soldier and politician, b. 1739, d. 1817.

Pickering, John, leader in the Pilgrimage of Grace (1536), executed 1537.

Pickering, Timothy, American statesman, b. 1745, d. 1829.

Pickering, William, British publisher who introduced cloth bindings, b. 1796, d. 1854.

Pickford, Mary (Gladys Smith), American film star, b. 1893.

' Pickle the Spy ' (Alastair Macdonell), b. about 1725, d. 1761.

Pico della Mirandola, Count Giovanni, Italian philosopher (*Heptaplus*, 1490), b. 1463, d. 1494.

Picric Acid (Trinitrophenol), known since 1771 ; effective use dates from 1885 when Turpin patented its use as a bursting charge for shells.

Picture Post, British periodical, published 1938–1958.

Pierce, Franklin, U.S. President (1853–1857), b. 1804, d. 1869.

Pierné, Gabriel, French composer (*La Croisade des enfants*, 1902), b. 1863, d. 1937.

Piero della Francesca, Italian painter (*The Baptism of Christ*), b. about 1415, d. 1492.

Piero di Cosimo, Italian painter (*Death of Procris*), b. 1462, d. about 1521.

Pierrot, rôle created by the French actor Jean Gaspard Debureau, b. 1796, d. 1846.

Pietermaritzburg, Natal capital, founded 1839.

Pig-iron, process of production improved 1709 by the English ironmaster Abraham Darby, b. 1677, d. 1717.

Pigalle, Jean Baptiste, French sculptor (*Love and Friendship*), b. 1714, d. 1785.

Pike, Zebulon Montgomery, American soldier and explorer, b. 1779, killed in battle 1813.

Pilate, Pontius, Roman procurator in Judea 26–36.

Pilgrim Fathers, set sail in the *Mayflower* from Plymouth 6 Sept. 1620 ; arrived Plymouth Rock, Massachusetts, 16 Dec. 1620 (O.S.).

Pilgrim Trust, established 1930 by the American philanthropist Edward Stephen Harkness, b. 1874, d. 1940.

Pilgrimage of Grace, 1536, Yorkshire insurrection led by the English attorney Robert Aske, executed 1537.

Pillow Lace-making, introduced 1561 into Germany by the German woman Barbara Uttmann, b. 1514, d. 1575.

Pilsudski, Jozef, Polish statesman (Premier 1926–1928, 1930–1935), b. 1867, d. 1935.

Piltdown Skull, discovered 1912 ; exposed as a fraud 1955.

Pinchbeck, alloy of copper and zinc, invented 1732 by the English clockmaker Christopher Pinchbeck, b. 1670, d. 1732.

Pinckney, Charles Cotesworth, American statesman and diplomat, b. 1746, d. 1825.

Pindar, Greek poet (*Odes*), b. about 522, d. 443 B.C.

' Pindar, Peter ' (John Wolcot), English writer (*The Lousiad*, 1785), b. 1738, d. 1819.

Pinero, Sir Arthur, English playwright (*The Second Mrs Tanqueray*, 1893), b. 1855, d. 1934.

Pinkerton Detective Agency, U.S.A., founded about 1852 by the American detective Allan Pinkerton, b. 1819, d. 1884.

Pinkie, Battle of, between the English and the Scots, 10 Sept. 1547.

Pinturicchio, Bernardino, Italian painter (*Dispute of St Catherine*), b. 1454, d. 1513.

Pinza, Ezio, Italian opera singer, b. 1892, d. 1957.

Pinzon, Martin Alonso, Spanish navigator, b. about 1440, d. 1493.

Pinzon, Vicente Yañez, Spanish navigator, b. about 1460, d. about 1524.

Piozzi, Mrs Hester Lynch (Mrs Thrale), friend of Dr Samuel Johnson, b. 1741, d. 1821.

Pipe Rolls, of English Exchequer, annual rolls introduced 1110 by Roger, Bishop of Salisbury ; discontinued 1834.

Piper, John, English painter and designer for opera and ballet, b. 1903.

Pirandello, Luigi, Italian playwright (*Six Characters in Search of an Author*, 1921), b. 1867, d. 1936.

Piranesi, Giambattista, Italian artist (*Carceri d'Invenzione*), b. 1720, d. 1778.

Pisa, Council of, assembled 25 Mar. to unite Christendom under a new Pope, dissolved 7 Aug. 1409.

Pisa, Leaning Tower of, built 1174–1350.

Pisa, University of, founded 1343 by the Florentine leader Lorenzo de' Medici, b. 1449, d. 1492.

Pisanello, Vittore, Italian artist (*The Miraculous Stag Appearing to St Eustace*), b. about 1380, d. 1456.

Pisano, Andrea, Italian sculptor, b. about 1290, d. 1348.

Pisistratus, Greek statesman, b. about 605, d. 527 B.C.

Piso Cæsoninus, Lucius Calpurnius, Roman statesman, d. about 40 B.C.

Pissarro, Camille, French painter (*Paysanne Assise*), b. 1830, d. 1903.

Pissarro, Lucien, French-born painter (*Chrysanthèmes*), b. 1863, d. 1944.

Pistols, first manufactured by Camillo Vetelli, about 1540.

Piston, Walter, American composer (*Violin concerto*, 1939), b. 1894.

Pistrucci, Benedetto, Italian-born gem engraver and medallist, b. 1784, d. 1855.

Pitcairn Island, Pacific Ocean, discovered 1767 by the English navigator Philip Carteret (d. 1796) : settled by mutineers from H.M.S. *Bounty* 1790.

Pitman, Sir Isaac, English shorthand pioneer, b. 1813, d. 1897.

Pitt, William ' the Elder ', Earl of Chatham, British Statesman (Prime Minister 1756–1757, 1766–1767), b. 1708, d. 1778.

Pitt, William, ' The younger ', British statesman (Prime Minister 1783–1801, 1804–1805), b. 1759, d. 1806.

Pius I, St, Pope 141–154.

Pius II (Æneas Silvius), Pope (1458–1464), b. 1405, d. 1464.

Pius III (Francesco Nanni–Todeschini–Piccolomini), Pope (1503), b. 1439, d. 1503.

Pius IV (Giovanni Angelo Medici), Pope (1559–1565), b. 1499, d. 1565.

Pius V, St, (Michele Ghislieri), Pope (1566–1572), b. 1504, d. 1572.

Pius VI (Giovanni Angelo Braschi), Pope (1775–1799), b. 1717, d. 1799.

Pius VII (Luigi Barnaba Chiaramonti), Pope (1800–1823), b. 1740, d. 1823.

Pius VIII (Francesco Xaviero Castiglioni), Pope (1829–1830), b. 1761, d. 1830.

Pius IX (Giovanni Maria Mastai-Ferretti), Pope (1846–1878), b. 1792, d. 1878.

Pius X, St, (Giuseppe Sarto), Pope (1903–1914), b. 1835, d. 1914.

Pius XI (Achille Ratti), Pope (1922–1939), b. 1857, d. 1939.

Pius XII (Eugenio Pacelli), Pope (1939–1958), b. 1876, d. 1958.

Pizarro, Francisco, Spanish *conquistador* of Peru, b. about 1478, assassinated 1541.

Pizarro, Gonzalo, Spanish *conquistador*, executed 1548.

Place, Francis, English radical reformer, b. 1771, d. 1854.

Plague, bacillus discovered 1894 independently by the Swiss scientist, Alexander Emile John Yersin (1863–1943), and the Japanese doctor Shibasaburo Kitasato (1856–1931) ; last pandemic 1894–1901.

Plague of London, (The Great Plague), 1664–1665.

Planck, Max, German physicist (formulated quantum theory 1900), b. 1858, d. 1947.

Planetary Motion, Kepler's laws of, 1609, 1609 and 1619.

Plankton, term introduced 1886 by Henson.

Planquette, Robert, French composer (*Les Cloches de Corneville*, 1877), b. 1848, d. 1903.

Plantin, Christopher, French printer, b. 1514, d. 1589.

Plassey, Battle of, between Lord Clive and Indian rebel forces 23 June 1757.

Platform Scales, invented 1831 by the American engineer Thaddeus Fairbanks, b. 1796, d. 1886.

Platinite, alloy, discovered by the French scientist Charles Edouard Guillaume, b. 1861, d. 1938.

Platinum, found in Spain at least as early as 1538 ; discovered in England 1741 by the English chemist William Brownrigg, b. 1711, d. 1800.

Plato, Greek philosopher (*The Republic*), b. about 427, d. 347 B.C.

Platt Amendment, American measure concerning Cuba, framed 1901 by the American politician Orville Hitchcock Platt, b. 1827, d. 1905. Abolished 1934.

Plautus, Roman playwright (*Amphitruo*), b. about 254, d. 184 B.C.

Playfair, Sir Nigel, English actor-manager, b. 1874, d. 1934.

Playfair, William Henry, Scottish architect, b. 1789, d. 1857.

Playford, John, English music publisher, b. 1623, d. 1686.

Pléiade, The, French literary movement, launched 1549.

Pleistocene Epoch, The Great Ice Age, between 20,000 and one million years ago.

Plekhanov, Georgi Valentinovich, Russian socialist leader, b. 1857, d. 1918.

Plesiosaurus, remains first discovered 1821 by the English fossil-collector Mary Anning, b. 1799, d. 1847.

Plimsoll Line, limit to which a ship may be loaded, brought into force 1876 by the efforts of the coal merchant and politician Samuel Plimsoll, b. 1824, d. 1898.

Pliny, the Elder, Latin writer (*Historia Naturalis*, 77), b. 23, d. 79.

Pliny, the Younger, Latin writer (*Epistles*), b. 62, d. 114.

Pliocene Epoch, earth history, 15 million years ago.

Plotinus, Egypt-born philosopher, b. 205, d. 270.

Plücker, Julius, German scientist, b. 1801, d. 1868.

Plumptre, Edward Hayes, English

theologian and classical scholar, b. 1821, d. 1891.

Plunkett, Sir Horace, Irish statesman and pioneer in agricultural co-operation, b. 1854, d. 1932.

Plural Voting, discontinued in Britain by Act of Parliament 1948.

Plutarch, Greek philospher and historian, b. 50, d. about 120.

Pluto, planet, discovered 1930 by the American astronomer Clyde William Tombaugh, b. 1906.

Pluto, Channel underwater oil pipeline ('Pipe-line Under The Ocean'), first in action 12 Aug. 1944 ; proposed by the British engineer Arthur Clifford Hartley, b. 1889, d. 1960.

Plutonium, transuranic element, produced in the U.S.A. 1940.

Plymouth Breakwater, constructed 1811–1841 by the Scottish civil engineer John Rennie, b. 1761, d. 1821.

Plymouth Brethren, religious movement, founded 1830 by the Rev John Nelson Darby, b. 1800, d. 1882.

Plymouth College, English public school, formed 1896 by the amalgamation of Mannamead School (founded 1854) and Plymouth College (founded 1878).

Plymouth Colony, Massachusetts, first settled permanently by the Pilgrim Fathers 1620.

Pneumatic Tyres, invented 1845 by the Scottish engineer Robert William Thomson (1822–1873) ; perfected 1888 by the Scottish inventor John Boyd Dunlop (1840–1921).

Pocahontas, American Indian chieftain's daughter and wife of John Rolfe (1585–1622), b. 1595, brought to England 1616, d. 1617.

Pocklington School, Yorkshire, English public school, founded by Dr John Dolman 1514.

Pococke, Edward, English orientalist, b. 1604, d. 1691.

Poe, Edgar Allan, American writer (*The Gold Bug*, 1843), b. 1809, d. 1849.

Poel, William, English producer (particularly of Shakespeare's plays), b. 1852, d. 1934.

Pogany, Willy, Hungarian-born painter and illustrator, b. 1882, d. 1955.

Poggendorff, Johann Christian, German scientist, b. 1796, d. 1877.

Poggio, Gian Francesco, Italian scholar and writer (*Facetiae*), b. 1380, d. 1459.

Poincaré, Raymond, French statesman, b. 1860, d. 1934.

Poindexter, George, American politician, b. 1779, d. 1853.

Point Pleasant, Battle of, between the Virginia militia and the Indians, 10 Oct. 1774.

'Points' Rationing, World War II, introduced in Britain 1 Dec. 1941.

Poison Gas, first used in World War I by the Germans 22 Apr. 1915 ; first used by the British 25 Sept. 1915.

Poissy, Colloquy of, to reconcile French Catholics and Protestants, held 1561.

Poitiers, Battle of, between the English and the French 19 Sept. 1356.

Poland, independent kingdom since 1025 ; first partition (Prussia, Russia and Austria) 1772–1793 ; second (Prussia and Russia) 1793–1795 ; third (Prussia, Russia and Austria) 1795–1918 ; independent republic 1919–1939 ; German occupation 1939–1944 ; communist régime since 1947.

Polarisation of Heat, discovered 1837 by the Scottish scientist James David Forbes, b. 1809, d. 1868.

Polarisation of Light, discovered by the Dutch scientist Christiaan Huygens (1629–1695). Experiments on polarisation carried out 1845 by the English scientist Michale Faraday (1791–1867).

Polders, arable land, created in the Zuyder Zee ; first undertaken on a large scale 1930.

Poldini, Eduard, Hungarian composer (*Himfy*, 1938), b. 1869, d. 1957.

Pole, Margaret, Countess of Salisbury, b. 1473, beheaded 1541.

Pole, Cardinal Reginald, Archbishop of Canterbury, b. 1500, d. 1558.

Police, London, reorganised 1829 by the English statesman Sir Robert Peel, b. 1788, d. 1850.

Polignac, Prince Jules de, French diplomat and statesman, b. 1780, d. 1847.

Poliomyelitis, vaccine discovered 1934, by the American bacteriologist William Hallock Park (1863–1939) ; Salk vaccine developed 1954 by the American scientist Jonas Edward Salk, b. 1914.

Polish Succession, War of the, concerning the succession to the throne of Poland, 1733–1735.

Politian (Angelo Ambrogini), Italian scholar and poet (*La Giostra*), b. 1454, d. 1494.

Political and Economic Planning, (P.E.P.) London, association formed 1931.

Polk, James Knox, U.S. President (1845–1849), b. 1795, d. 1849.

Poll-tax, first levied in England 1380 ; abolished 1689.

Pollajuolo, Antonio, Italian artist, b. about 1432, d. 1498.

Pollard, Alfred Frederick, English historian, b. 1869, d. 1948.

Pollitt, Harry, English Communist leader, b. 1890, d. 1960.

Pollock, Sir Frederick, English jurist, b. 1845, d. 1937.

Polo, Marco, Italian explorer, b. 1254, d. 1324.

Polonium, radio-active element, discovered 1898 by the French scientists Pierre and Marie Curie.

Polybius, Greek historian, b. about 205, d. 123 B.C.

Polycarp, St, Bishop of Smyrna, martyred 155.

Polycrates, tyrant of Samos, crucified 522 B.C.

Polyglot Bible, Complutensian, first polyglot Bible, prepared 1514–1522.

Polythene, discovered by Imperial Chemical Industries chemists 1933.

Pombal, Sebastião José de Carvalho e Mello, Marquess of, Portuguese Statesman, b. 1699, d. 1782.

Pompadour, Mme de, mistress of Louis XV, b. 1721, d. 1764.

Pompeii, Italy, devasted by the eruptions of Mt. Vesuvius 63 and 79 ; ruins discovered 1748.

Pompey, Roman statesman, b. 106, murdered 48 B.C.

Ponce de Leon, Juan, Spanish colonial administrator, b. 1460, killed 1521.

Ponce de Leon, Luis, Spanish poet, b. about 1527, d. 1591.

Pond, John, English astronomer, b. 1767, d. 1836.

Pondicherry, India, settled by the French 1674 ; administration transferred to the Government of India 1954.

Pons, Lily, French operatic singer, b. 1904.

Ponsonby, George, Lord Chancellor of Ireland, b. 1755, d. 1817.

Ponsonby, William Brabazon Ponsonby, Baron, British politician, b. 1744, d. 1806.

Pontiac's Rebellion, 1763–1764, led by the American Indian chief Pontiac, b. about 1720, reputed murdered 1769.

Pontian, St, Pope 230–235.

Pontius Pilate, Roman procurator of Judea 26–36.

Pontormo, Jacopo, Italian painter (*The Deposition*), b. 1494, d. 1556.

Pony Express, U.S.A., began 1860, ended 1861.

Poole, William Frederick, American bibliographer and historian, b. 1821, d. 1894.

Poor Clares, order of Franciscan nuns organised by St Clare, b. about 1193, d. 1253.

Poor Law System, Modern, begun in Britain 1601, reformed 1834, abolished 1929.

Poore, Richard, English Bishop and builder of Salisbury Cathedral, d. 1237.

Pope, Alexander, English poet (*The Rape of the Lock*, 1714), b. 1698, d. 1744.

Pope, Sir Thomas, Privy Councillor and philanthropist, b. about 1507, d. 1559.

'Popish Plot ', to murder King Charles II, invented 1678 by Titus Oates, b. 1649, d. 1705 ; agitation 1678–1681.

Poppæa Sabina, wife of Nero, killed by Nero 65.

Popular Front, policy of co-operation of left-wing parties against Fascism, between 1933 and 1939.

Porcelain, Printing on, first achieved in Liverpool and Worcester 1756–1757 ; introduced into France 1789 by Christopher Potter, d. 1817.

Pordenone, Giovanni Antonio, Italian painter (*Le Mariage de Ste Catherine*), b. about 1483, d. 1539.

Porphyry, Greek philosopher, b. 233, d. about 304.

Porson, Richard, English classical scholar, b. 1759, d. 1808.

Port Arthur, surrendered to Japan by Russia, 1 Jan. 1905.

Port Elizabeth, South Africa, founded 1820.

Port of London Authority, constituted by Act of Parliament 1908 ; the Authority first met 16 Mar. 1909.

Port Radar System, World's first, opened at Gladstone Dock, Liverpool, 30 July 1948.

Port Royal, French abbey near Paris, founded 1204 ; transferred to Paris 1626 ; suppressed 1704.

Port Said, Egypt, founded 1859.

Porta, Giovanni Battista della, Italian sculptor, b. 1542, d. 1597.

Porteous Riots, Edinburgh, occasioned at a public execution by the hasty action of the Captain of the City Guard, John Porteous, hanged by the mob 1736.

Porter, Cole, American composer (*Anything Goes*, 1934), b. 1893.

Porter, William Sydney (' O Henry '), American writer (*The Gentle Grafter*, 1908), b. 1862, d. 1910.

Portland, Maine, first settled 1633 ; assumed present name 1786.

Portland, Oregon, founded 1845 ; chartered 1851.

Portland Cement, invented 1824 by the English stonemason Joseph Aspdin, b. 1779, d. 1855.

Portland Vase, Roman glass funerary urn now in British Museum, probably made in the 1st century B.C. ; bought 1770 by Sir William Hamilton, lent by the Duke of Portland to the British Museum (smashed 1845).

Porto Rico, discovered by Christopher Columbus 1493 ; ceded by Spain to the U.S.A. 1898.

Portola, Gaspar de, Spanish explorer and Governor of the Californias, d. after 1784.

Portora Royal School, Enniskillen, Northern Ireland public school, founded 1618.

Portsmouth, England, granted a Charter by King Richard I 1194.

Portsmouth Grammar School, English public school, founded by Dr William Smith 1732.

Portsmouth, Treaty of, ending the Russo-Japanese war (1904–1905), signed 5 Sept. 1905.

Portugal, declared an independent Monarchy 1143 ; ruled by Spain 1581–1640 ; Bragança monarchy 1640–1910 ; proclaimed a Republic 1910 ; ruled by Salazar since 1932 ; present constitution adopted 1933.

Portuguese East Africa (Mozambique), discovered by Vasco da Gama's fleet 1498 ; first colonised 1505 ; created an overseas territory 1951.

Portuguese Guinea, discovered 1446 by the Portuguese Nuno Tristão ; created a separate colony 1879 ; status to overseas territory 1951.

Portuguese India, discovered 1498 by the Portuguese navigator Vasco da Gama ; first colonised 1505 ; status changed to overseas territory 1951.

Portuguese Timor, first colonised 1586 ; created an independent province 1896 ; overseas territory 1951.

Portuguese West Africa (Angola), discovered by the Portuguese navigator Diogo Cão 1482–1485.

Positivism, philosophical system, developed 1822 by the French philosopher Auguste Comte, b. 1798, d. 1857.

Positrons, positive particles, discovered 1932 by the American scientist Carl David Anderson, b. 1905.

Post, Mrs Emily, American arbiter of social etiquette, b. 1873, d. 1960.

Post, Wiley, American pioneer aviator, b. 1899, died in an aircrash 1935.

Post Office Savings Bank, system introduced in Britain 1861.

Postage Stamps, Adhesive, first used in Britain 6 May 1840.

Postage Stamps, Hand-struck, first used in Britain 1661.

Postal Orders, first used in Britain 1 Jan. 1881.

Postcards, Stamped, introduced in Britain 1870.

Postcards, with adhesive stamps, use permitted in Britain from 1894.

Postgate, John, English pioneer in preventing the adulteration of food, b. 1820, d. 1881.

Potassium, discovered 1807 by the English chemist Sir Humphry Davy, b. 1778, d. 1829.

Potato Famine, in Ireland, 1845 to 1849.

Potatoes, introduced into England 1587 by Sir Walter Raleigh, b. 1552, d. 1618.

Potemkin, Gregory Alexandrovich, Russian statesman, b. 1739, d. 1791.

Potgieter, Everhardes Johannes, Dutch poet (*Florence*, 1868), b. 1808, d. 1875.

Pot Lids, decorated lids of jars and pots, produced in England mainly 1847 to 1880.

Potsdam Agreement, World War II, 17 July to 2 Aug. 1945.

Pott, Percivall, English pioneer in modern surgery, b. 1714, d. 1788.

Potter, Beatrix, English writer and illustrator of children's books (*Jemima Puddleduck*), b. 1866, d. 1943.

Potter, Sir Thomas, joint-founder of the *Manchester Guardian*, b. 1773, d. 1845.

Poulenc, Francis, French composer (*Mouvement perpetuel*), b. 1899.

Pound, Ezra, American-born poet (*Cantos*, 1925 onwards), b. 1885.

Pound, Imperial standard weight established in Britain 1844.

Pourtalès, Louis François de, Swiss-born naturalist, b. 1824, d. 1880.

Poussin, Nicolas, French painter (*Venus and Adonis*), b. 1594, d. 1665.

Powell, Humphrey, English printer who established 1551 Ireland's first printing-press at Dublin, lived until after 1556.

Powell, Vavasour, Welsh itinerant preacher, b. 1617, d. 1670.

Power, Tyrone, sen., English-born actor, b. 1869, d. 1931.

Power Loom, Cartwright's, invented 1785 by Edmund Cartwright, b. 1743, d. 1823.

Powys, John Cowper, English writer (*A Glastonbury Romance*, 1933), b. 1872.

Powys, Llewellyn, English author (*Apples be Ripe*, 1930), b. 1884, d. 1939.

Powys, Theodore Francis, English novelist (*Mr Tasker's Gods*, 1925), b. 1875, d. 1953.

Poynings' Law, regulating Irish government, passed 1495 by Sir Edward Poynings, Lord-Deputy of Ireland, b. 1459, d. 1521.

Prado, Spain, national museum of paintings and sculpture, founded 1819.

Praed, Winthrop Mackworth, English poet (*Molly Mog*), b. 1802, d. 1839.

Pragmatism, idea introduced 1878 by the American scientist Charles Sanders Peirce, b. 1839, d. 1914.

Prague, Czech capital, in existence by 600.

Prague, Treaty of, ending the war between Austria and Prussia, signed 23 Aug. 1866.

Prague University, founded by the Emperor Charles IV 1348.

Praseodymium, rare earth element, discovered 1885, by the Austrian chemist Baron von Welsbach, b. 1858, d. 1929.

Pratt, Charles, Earl Camden, Lord Chancellor, b. 1714, d. 1794.

Pratt, Silas Gamaliel, American composer (*Zenobia*, 1882), b. 1846, d. 1916.

Pratt Institute, New York, founded 1887.

Pratt Institute, Pittsburg, founded by Silas Gamaliel Pratt 1906.

Praxiteles, Greek sculptor, b. about 390, d. about 332 B.C.

Prayer Book, English, First published 1549, second 1552 ; Elizabethan 1559, revised 1661 ; attempted revision 1928.

Pre-Cambrian Period, Earth history, more than 520 million years ago.

Prefabricated House, First, a tollhouse created on the West Bromwich–Birmingham highway about 1830 ; dismantled 1926.

Premium Bonds, first issued in Britain 1956.

Premonstratensian Canons, founded 1120 by St Norbert, b. about 1080, d. 1134.

Pre-Raphaelites, English art movement, flourished in the mid-19th century.

Presbyterianism, modern founder John Calvin, b. 1509, d. 1564 ; introduced to Scotland 1559–1560 by John Knox, b. about 1505, d. 1572 ; established again 1638–1641, established finally 1690.

Prescott, William Hickling, American historian (*The Conquest of Mexico*, 1843), b. 1796, d. 1859.

Press Association, London, founded 1868.

Press Council, Great Britain, first met 21 July 1953.

Pressburg, Treaty of, between France and Austria, signed 26 Dec. 1805.

Prester John, mythical mediæval monarch of Asia.

Preston By-pass, British motorway, opened 5 Dec. 1958.

Prestonpans, Battle of, between the Jacobites and Government forces 21 Sept. 1745.

Pretoria, Capital of the Union of South Africa, founded 1855.

Pretorius, Andries Wilhelmus Jacobus, founder of the Transvaal, b. 1799, d. 1853.

Prevost, Sir George, Governor-General of Canada (1811–1816), b. 1767, d. 1816.

Prévost, Marcel, French novelist (*Les Demi-vièrges*, 1894), b. 1862, d. 1941.

Prévost, The Abbé (Antoine François Prévost d'Exiles), French novelist (*Manon Lescaut*, 1731), b. 1697, d. 1763.

Price, Hugh, founder 1571 of Jesus College, Oxford, b. about 1495, d. 1574.

Pride's Purge, of the Long Parliament, carried out 1648 by the Parliamentary general Thomas Pride, d. 1658.

Prideaux, Humphrey, English theologian and scholar, b. 1648, d. 1724.

Priestley, John Boynton, English writer (*The Good Companions*, 1929), b. 1894.

Priestley, Joseph, English scientist, b. 1733, d. 1804.

Primaticcio, Francesco, Italian painter (*Diane de Poitiers*), b. 1504, d. 1570.

Prime Minister, office introduced in Britain 1721–1742, but not legally recognised until 1905.

Primitive Methodists, movement founded 1811 by the English Methodist Hugh Bourne, b. 1772, d. 1852.

Primrose, William, Scottish viola player, b. 1903.

Primrose League, British Conservative organisation, founded in 1883 by Lord Randolph Churchill, b. 1849, d. 1894.

Prince, Thomas, English Governor of Massachusetts, b. 1600, d. 1673.

Prince Andrew, b. 19 Feb. 1960.

Prince Charles, b. 14 Nov. 1948.

Prince Edward Island, Canada, discovered 1534 by the French navigator Jacques Cartier, b. 1491, d. 1557.

Princess Anne, b. 15 Aug. 1950.

Princess Margaret, b. 21 Aug. 1930 ; married 6 May 1960.

Princeton, New Jersey, first settled 1696.

Princeton, Battle of, American War of Independence, 3 Jan. 1777.

Principe, Portuguese overseas territory, discovered by the Portuguese 1471.

Printer's Device, first known example printed in Fust and Schoeffer's Mainz Psalter, 1484.

Printing, known in China and Japan by 8th century, movable type invented 1041 ; invented (in Europe) at Mainz about 1440 ; movable type used by Gutenberg in 1454 ; steam press (1810) and cylinder press (1811) invented by the German inventor Friedrich Koenig (1774–1833).

Printing Offices, Provincial, suppressed by order of the Star Chamber 23 June 1585.

Prior, Matthew, English poet (*To a Child of Quality*), b. 1664, d. 1721.

Priscian, Roman grammarian, lived in the late 5th and early 6th centuries.

Priscillian, Spanish theologian, burnt at the stake 385.

Prisons, first used in England for punishment, during 16th century.

Privy Councillor, first woman, Miss Margaret Bondfield (1873–1953), appointed 1929.

Prize Fight, last held in England, between Sayers and Heenan 17 April 1860.

Probabilities, Theory of, modern approach founded by the French philosopher Blaise Pascal, b. 1623, d. 1662.

Probus, Roman Emperor (276–282), killed 282.

Proclus, Greek philosopher, b. about 410, d. 485.

Procopius, Byzantine historian, d. about 562.

Proctor, Richard Anthony, English astronomer, b. 1837, d. 1888.

Proctor, Robert George Collier, English bibliographer, b. 1868, d. 1903.

Prohibition, came into effect nationally in the U.S.A. 17 Jan. 1920 ; repealed 1933.

Prokofiev, Sergei Sergeievich, Russian composer (*Peter and the Wolf*, 1936), b. 1891, d. 1953.

Promenade Concerts, London, founded 1895 by the English composer and conductor Sir Henry Wood, b. 1869, d. 1944.

Prontosil (sulphonamide drug), curative powers discovered 1935 by the German bacteriologist Gerhard Domagk, b. 1895.

Propertius, Latin poet (*Cynthia*, 25 B.C.), b. about 48, d. about 14 B.C.

Protactinium, metallic element, isolated 1930 by the Russian-born chemist Aristid V. Grosse, b. 1905.

Protagoras, Greek philosopher, lived in the 5th century B.C.

Proterozoic Era, earth history, more than 520 million years ago.

Protestant Episcopal Church, U.S.A., founded 1789.

Prothero, Sir George Walter, English historian, b. 1848, d. 1922.

Protogenes, Greek painter, lived in the late 4th century B.C.

Proton, unit of positive charge, the hydrogen nucleus of the atom, identified 1912 by the New Zealand-born scientist Lord Rutherford, b. 1871, d. 1937.

Protoplasm, discovered in the 18th century ; first so named 1846 by the German botanist Hugo von Mohl, b. 1805, d. 1872.

Protozoa, unicellular animals, discovered 1674 by the Dutch scientist Antony van Leeuwenhoek, b. 1632, d. 1723.

Proudhon, Pierre Joseph, French social reformer, b. 1809, d. 1865.

Proust, Marcel, French novelist (*A la recherche du temps perdu*, 1913–1927), b. 1871, d. 1922.

Prout, Ebenezer, English music theorist (*Harmony*, 1889), b. 1835, d. 1909.

Proxima Centauri, star nearest to the Earth, discovered 1916 by the Scottish astronomer Robert T. A. Innes, b. 1861, d. 1933.

Prudentius, Aurelius Clemens, Spanish poet (*Contra Symmachum*), b. 348, d. 410.

Prud'hon, Pierre Paul, French painter (*L'Assomption*, 1816), b. 1758, d. 1823.

Prussia, kingdom 1701–1918.

Prussian Blue, discovered by the German scientist Johann Konrad Dippel, b. 1673, d. 1734.

Prussic Acid, discovered 1782 by the Swedish chemist Karl Scheele, b. 1742, d. 1786.

Prynne, William, Puritan champion and pamphleteer, b. 1600, d. 1669.

Pryor, Roger Atkinson, New York Supreme Court judge and Confederate general, b. 1828, d. 1919.

' **Psalmanazar,** George ', French-born imposter, b. about 1679, d. 1763.

Psychoanalysis, study founded by the Austrian psychoanalyst Sigmund Freud, b. 1856, d. 1939.

Ptolemy I Soter, King of Egypt (323–285 B.C.), d. 283 B.C.

Ptolemy II Philadelphus, King of Egypt (285–about 246 B.C.), d. about 246 B.C.

Ptolemy III Euergetes, King of Egypt (about 246–about 222 B.C.), d. about 222 B.C.

Ptolemy IV Philopator, King of Egypt (221–204 B.C.), d. 204 B.C.

Ptolemy V Epiphanes, King of Egypt (204–181 B.C.), d. 181 B.C.

Ptolemy VI Philometor, King of Egypt (181–145 B.C.), killed in battle 145 B.C.

Ptolemy VII Physcon, King of Egypt (145–117 B.C.), d. 117 B.C.

Ptolemy VIII Lathyros, King of Egypt (117–107, 89–81 B.C.), d. 81 B.C.

Ptolemy IX Alexander, King of Egypt 107–89 B.C.) killed about 89 B.C.

Ptolemy X, Alexander II, King of Egypt (80 B.C.), killed 80 B.C.

Ptolemy XI Auletes, King of Egypt (80–58, 55–51 B.C.) d. 51 B.C.

Ptolemy XII, King of Egypt (51–about 47 B.C.), drowned about 47 B.C.

Ptolemy XIII, King of Egypt (47–44 B.C.) killed 44 B.C.

Ptolemy XIV Cæsarion, King of Egypt (47–30 B.C.), b. 47, murdered 30 B.C.

Ptolemy, Claudius, Alexandrian geographer, lived in the 2nd century.

Pu Yi, Henry, last Emperor of China (1908–1912), first Emperor of Manchukuo (1934–1945), b. 1905.

Public Libraries Act, First, permitting the establishment of English public libraries, passed 1850.

Public Observation Platforms, introduced 1932 by the American financier John Davison Rockefeller, jun., b. 1874.

Public Safety, Committee of, French Revolution, established 1793.

Public Trustee Office, London, opened 1908.

Publishers' Cloth, introduced into Britain 1820 by the British publisher William Pickering, b. 1796, d. 1854.

Puccini, Giacomo, Italian composer (*Tosca*, 1900), b. 1858, d. 1924.

Puddling Furnace, invented 1784 by the British ironmaster Henry Cort, b. 1740, d. 1800.

Puerto Rico, discovered by Christopher Columbus 1493 ; ceded by Spain to the U.S.A. 1898.

' **Puffing Billy** ', pioneer locomotive, invented 1813 by the inventor William Hedley, b. 1779, d. 1843.

Puget, Pierre, French artist (*Milo of Crotona*, 1683), b. 1622, d. 1694.

Pughe, William Owen, Welsh antiquary and lexicographer, b. 1759, d. 1835.

Pugin, Augustus Charles, French-born architect, b. 1762, d. 1832.

Pulaski, Count Casimir, Polish soldier in Washington's army, b. 1748, d. of wounds 1779.

Pulcheria, Byzantine Empress (450–453), b. 399, d. 453.

Pulitzer Prizes, for American writing, founded 1917 through the philanthropy of the Hungarian-born newspaper owner Joseph Pulitzer, b. 1847, d. 1912.

Pullman Sleeping Car, invented 1864 by the American financier George Mortimer Pullman, b. 1831, d. 1897.

Pultava, Battle of, between the Russians and the Swedes 8 July 1709.

Pumping Engine, Atmospheric, invented about 1708 by the English engineer Thomas Newcomen, b. 1663, d. 1729.

Punch, British periodical, founded 17 July 1841 by the English engraver Ebenezer Landells (1808–1860) and the English writer Mark Lemon (1809–1870).

Punch and Judy, puppet play, origins (probably Italian) uncertain ; introduced into England via France in the 17th century.

Punic War, First, between Rome and Carthage, 264 to 241 B.C.

Punic War, Second, between Rome and Carthage, 218 to 201 B.C.

Punic War, Third, between Rome and Carthage, 149 to 146 B.C.

Punjab, India, annexed by Britain 1849 ; constituted an autonomous province 1937 ; partitioned between India and Pakistan 1947.

Purcell, Henry, English composer (*Dido and Æneas*, 1689), b. about 1658, d. 1695.

Purchas, Samuel, English compiler (*Purchas, His Pilgrimage*, 1613), b. about 1575, d. 1626.

Purchase Tax, introduced in Britain 1940.

Purdue University, Lafayette, Indiana, founded 1874.

Purim, Jewish festival, celebrated 14th and 15th days of Adar.

Pusey, Edward Bouverie, English theologian, b. 1800, d. 1882.

Pushkin, Alexander Sergeievich, Russian writer (*Ruslan and Ludmilla*, 1820), b. 1799, killed in a duel 1837.

Putnam, Frederick Ward, American anthropologist, b. 1839, d. 1915.

Putnam, George Palmer, American publisher, b. 1814, d. 1872.

Puttenham, Richard, English writer (believed to have written *The Arte of English Poesie*, 1589), b. about 1520, d. about 1601.

Puvis de Chavannes, Pierre, French painter (*St Geneviève*), b. 1824, d. 1898.

Pygmies, African, first discovered 1870 by the German ethnologist Georg August Schweinfurth, b. 1836, d. 1925.

Pym, John, English, Puritan leader, b. 1584, d. 1643.

Pynson, Richard, French-born pioneer printer in England, d. 1530.

Pyramids, Battle of the, between Napoleon and the Mamelukes, 21 July 1798.

Pyrenees, Peace of the, ending war between France and Spain, Nov. 1659.

Pyridine, organic base, discovered 1851, by the Scottish chemist Thomas Anderson, b. 1819, d. 1874.

Pyroscope, invented by the Scottish mathematician Sir John Leslie, b. 1766, d. 1832.

Pyrrho of Elis, Greek philosopher, b. about 360, d. 270 B.C.

Pyrrhus, Greek king, b. about 318, d. 272 B.C.

Pyruvic Acid, organic acid, first obtained 1835 by the Swedish chemist Baron Berzelius, b. 1779, d. 1848.

Pytchley Hunt, Northamptonshire and Leicestershire, first Master Earl Spencer from 1750 to about 1790.

Pythagoras, Greek philosopher and mathematician, b. about 582, d. 500 B.C.

Q

' Q ' (Sir Arthur Quiller-Couch), English writer (*Troy Town*, 1888), b. 1863, d. 1944.

Quare, Daniel, English clockmaker and inventor 1687 of repeating watches, b. 1648, d. 1724.

Qatar, Persian Gulf State, in special treaty relations with Britain, regulated by a treaty signed 3 Nov. 1916.

Quadragesima, the forty days of Lent ; sometimes restricted to the first Sunday in Lent.

Quadrant, Reflecting, invented 1731 by the English mathematician John Hadley, b. 1682, d. 1744.

Quadrille, first introduced into Britain 1815.

Quadruple Alliance, of the Allies against Napoleon, 1814–1815.

Quadruple Treaty, guaranteeing the constitutional monarchies of Spain and Portugal, signed by France and Britain 1834.

Quakers (Society of Friends), founded 1647 by the English shoemaker George Fox, b. 1624, d. 1690 ; first Quaker M.P. elected 1833.

Quantitive Analysis, theory developed 1754 by the British scientist Joseph Black, b. 1728, d. 1799.

Quantum Theory, formulated 1900 by the German physicist Max Planck, b. 1858, d. 1947.

Quaritch, Bernard, German-born bookseller, b. 1819, d. 1899.

Quarles, Francis, English poet (*Emblems,* 1635), b. 1592, d. 1644.

Quarter Days, in England and Ireland, 25 Mar., 24 June, 29 Sept., 25 Dec. ; in Scotland, 2 Feb., 15 May, 1 Aug., 11 Nov.

Quarter Sessions, British court of record, held 4 times a year by Statute since 1363.

Quarterly Review, began publication 1809 ; first Editor : William Gifford, b. 1756, d. 1826 ; publisher : John Murray, b. 1778, d. 1843.

Quaternary Period, the last million years of Earth history.

Quaternions, vector analysis, invented 1852 by the Scottish mathematician, Sir William Rowan Hamilton, b. 1805, d. 1865.

Quatre Bras, Battle of, between the British and the French, 16 June 1815.

Quebec, Canada, founded 3 July 1608 by the French navigator Samuel de Champlain (1567–1635).

Quebec Act, concerning the government and territory of the Province of Quebec, 1774.

Quebec Conference, World War II, held 11–24 Aug. 1943.

Queen Alexandra's Day, first held 26 June 1912. The emblem was then an artificial rose.

Queen Anne's Bounty, ecclesiastical fund, founded in England 1703.

Queen Elizabeth, Atlantic passenger liner, launched 27 Sept. 1938.

Queen Elizabeth's Grammar School, Blackburn, founded by Thomas Earl of Derby, 1509 ; re-established and Chartered by Queen Elizabeth I 1567.

Queen Mary, Atlantic passenger liner, launched 26 Sept. 1934.

Queen Mary Land, Antarctica, discovered 1912 by the English Captain John King Davis, b. 1884.

Queen Maud Land, Antarctica, placed under Norwegian sovereignty 1939.

Queens' College, Cambridge University, founded 1448, by Queen Margaret of Anjou ; refounded by Elizabeth Widville, consort of King Edward IV 1465.

Queen's College, The, Oxford University, founded by Robert de Eglesfield 1340–1341.

Queen's University, Belfast, came into being 1909. Previously Queen's College, Belfast.

Queensberry Rules, for glove-fighting, initiated 1867 by Lord Queensberry, b. 1844, d. 1900.

Queensland, Australia, formed into separate colony 1859.

Quérard, Joseph Marie, French bibliographer, b. 1797, d. 1865.

Quetta, India, founded 1876.

Quetta Earthquake, 31 May 1935.

Quevedo, Francisco Gomez de, Spanish writer (*Sueños,* 1627), b. 1580, d. 1645.

Quiberon Bay, Battle of, between English and French fleets 20 Nov. 1759.

Quietism, contemplative mystical movement, founded 1675 by the Spanish theologian Miguel de Molinos, b. 1640, d. 1697.

Quiller-Couch, Sir Arthur, (' Q ') English writer (*Troy Town,* 1888), b. 1863, d. 1944.

Quilter, Roger, English composer (*Where the Rainbow Ends,* 1911), b. 1877, d. 1953.

Quin, James English actor, b. 1693, d. 1766.

Quincey, Thomas de, English writer (*Confessions of an Opium-eater*, 1821), b. 1785, d. 1859.

Quinet, Edgar, French historian, b. 1803, d. 1875.

Quinine, discovered 1820 by the French scientists Pierre Joseph Pelletier (1788–1842) and Joseph Bienaimé Caventou (1795–1877).

Quinquagesima, the fifty days immediately preceding Easter ; or, the Sunday before Ash Wednesday.

Quintana, Manuel Jose, Spanish writer (*Pelayo*, 1805), b. 1772, d. 1857.

Quintero, Serafin (1871–1938) and Joaquin (1873–1944) Alvarez, Spanish playwrights (*El Genio Alegre*, 1906).

Quintilian, Roman orator (*Institutio Oratoria*), b. about 35, d. 95.

Quirinal Palace, Rome, designed 1574 by the Italian architect Domenico Fontana, b. 1543, d. 1607.

Quisling, Vidkun, Norwegian puppet Premier (1942–1945) and traitor, b. 1887, executed 1945.

Quito, capital of Ecuador, annexed by the Spaniards 1533, created a city 1541.

Quiz Programme, First, broadcast in Canada 15 May 1935.

Quiz Programme, First British, the Inter-Regional Spelling Competition (now Regional Round) broadcast 25 Nov. 1937 onwards.

Quorn Hunt, predominantly Leicestershire, county first hunted 1698–1753 by Thomas Boothby ; first Master Hugo Meynell from 1753 to 1800.

R

R 101, British dirigible, first trials 14 Oct. 1929 ; flew the Atlantic 30 July 1930 ; crashed at Beauvais 5 Oct. 1930.

R.A.F., (Royal Air Force), established 1918.

Raabe, Peter, German music historian (*Franz Liszt*, 1931), b. 1872, d. 1945.

Rabbi ben Ezra (Abraham ben Meir ibn Ezra), Spanish Jewish scholar, b. about 1092, d. 1167.

Rabbinical Bible, first published 1516–1517 by the Christian printer Daniel Bomberg, d. 1549.

Rabelais, François, French writer (*Gargantua*, about 1532), b. 1483, d. 1553.

Rabies, effective treatment developed 1885 by the French scientist Louis Pasteur, b. 1822, d. 1895.

Rachel, Elisa (Elisa Rachel Félix), Swiss-born actress, b. 1821, d. 1858.

Rachmaninoff, Sergei, Russian-born composer (*Rhapsody on a theme by Paganini*), b. 1873, d. 1943.

Racine, Jean, French playwright (*Phèdre*, 1677), b. 1639, d. 1699.

Rackham, Arthur, English artist and illustrator, b. 1867, d. 1939.

Radar, first practical demonstration made 1935 by a team led by the British scientist Sir Robert Watson-Watt, b. 1892.

Radcliffe, Anne, English novelist (*The Mysteries of Udolpho*, 1794), b. 1764, d. 1823.

Radcliffe Observatory, Oxford University, founded 1771, through the benefaction of the executors of the English physician John Radcliffe, b. 1650, d. 1714.

Radek, Karl (Sobelsohn), Russian Bolshevik leader, b. 1885.

Radetzky, Josef, Count of Radetz, Austrian Field-Marshal, b. 1766, d. 1858.

Radiation, theory developed 1900 by the German physicist Max Planck (1858–1947) ; and also 1896 by the German physicist Wilhelm Wien (1864–1938).

Radio Photographs, first transmitted from Britain to the U.S.A. 1924.

Radio Signals, first detected 1888 ; first sent across the Atlantic (Cornwall to Newfoundland) 1901 by the Italian inventor Guglielmo Marconi, b. 1874, d. 1937.

Radio Telegraph Service, First, opened between Britain and Canada 1907.

Radio Telephone Service, First, initiated 1927.

Radio Telephone System for Motorists, introduced in Britain 25 Sept. 1959.

Radio Times, British periodical, first published 28 Sept. 1923.

Radio Tuning, Selective, basic principles of the method defined 1898 by the British physicist Sir Oliver Lodge, b. 1851, d. 1940.

Radio Waves, discovered 1888 by the German physicist Heinrich Rudolf Hertz (1857–1894); theory developed 1868 by the Scottish physicist James Clerk Maxwell (1831–1879).

Radioactivity, discovered 1896 by the French scientist Antoine Henri Becquerel, b. 1852, d. 1908.

Radiometer, invented 1873–1876 by the English scientist Sir William Crookes, b. 1832, d. 1919.

Radisson, Pierre Esprit, French explorer, b. about 1632, d. about 1710.

Radium, discovered 1898 by the French scientist Pierre Curie (1859–1906); isolated 1902 by Mme Curie.

Radley College, Berkshire, English public school, founded by the Rev. William Sewell; opened 1847; incorporated by Royal Charter 1890.

Radon, radioactive element, discovered 1900 by the German scientist F. E. Dorn.

Raeburn, Sir Henry, Scottish painter (*The Macnab*), b. 1756, d. 1823.

Raemaekers, Louis, Dutch cartoonist, b. 1869, d. 1956.

Raff, Joseph Joachim, Swiss-born composer (*Im Walde*), b. 1822, d. 1882.

Raffles, Sir Stamford, British founder (1819) of Singapore, b. 1781, d. 1826.

Raglan, Fitzroy James Henry Somerset, Baron, commanded the British troops at the Crimea, b. 1788, d. 1855.

Rahere, founder 1123 of St Bartholomew's Hospital, London, d. 1144.

Raikes, Robert, English founder (1780) of Sunday schools, b. 1735, d. 1811.

Railway, mining railways in use in Europe in 16th century; first public railway (Wandsworth to Croydon) opened 1803; first recorded journey (Mumbles) 1807; first public steam (Stockton to Darlington) opened 1825; first public electric (City and South London) opened 1890.

Railway Letter Stamps, first issued in Britain 1891.

Railway Nationalisation, during wars 1914–1919 and 1939–1946; finally 1948.

Railway Ticket Dating Machine, First, invented 1837 by the British inventor Thomas Edmondson, b. 1792, d. 1851.

Raimondi, Marcantonio, Italian engraver, b. about 1480, d. about 1534.

Raines Law, 1896, relating to liquor sales in New York State, framed by the American politician John Raines, b. 1840, d. 1909.

Rainier, Prince, of Monaco, b. 1923; married Miss Grace Kelly 19 Apr. 1956.

Rais, Gilles de, Marshal of France, b. 1404, hanged 1440.

Rákóczy, Francis II, Prince of Transylvania, b. 1676, d. 1735.

Raleigh, Sir Walter, English mariner and explorer, b. 1552, beheaded 1618.

Ramadan, Islamic month of fasting during the day (Feb.–Mar.).

Raman Effect, physics, discovered 1928 by Sir Chandrasekhara Venkata Raman, b. 1888.

Rambouillet, Catherine de Vivonne, Marquise de, French patron of men of letters, b. 1588, d. 1665.

Rameau, Jean Philippe, French composer (*Dardanus*, 1739), b. 1683, d. 1764.

Rameses I, King of Egypt (about 1315–1314 B.C.), d. about 1314 B.C.

Rameses II, King of Egypt (about 1292–1225 B.C.), d. about 1225 B.C.

Rameses III, King of Egypt (about 1198–1167 B.C.), d. about 1167 B.C.

Ramillies, Battle of, between the British and the French, 23 May 1706.

Ramsay, Allan, Scottish poet (*The Gentle Shepherd*, 1725), b. 1686, d. 1758.

Ramsay, Sir William, Scottish scientist, b. 1852, d. 1916.

Ramsden, Jesse, English instrument-maker, b. 1735, d. 1800.

Ramus, Petrus (Pierre de la Ramée), French philosopher, b. 1515, killed 1572.

Ramuz, Charles Ferdinand, Swiss novelist, b. 1878, d. 1947.

Ranavalona III, last Queen of Madagascar (1883–1916), b. 1861, d. 1916.

Randall, John English, shipbuilder, b. 1755, d. 1802.

Randolph, Sir Thomas, Earl of Moray, Regent of Scotland, d. 1332.

Randolph, Thomas, English writer (*Amyntas*, 1638), b. 1605, d. 1635.

Randolph, William, English founder (1693) of William and Mary College, Virginia, b. 1650, d. 1711.

Ranelagh, London pleasure gardens, opened to the public 1742 ; closed 1803.

Ranjit Singh, Sikh ruler (1799–1838).

Ranjitsinhji, Prince, Indian cricketer, b. 1872, d. 1933.

Ranke, Leopold von, German historian, b. 1795, d. 1886.

Rankin, Thomas, Scottish Methodist reformer, b. 1738, d. 1810.

Rankine, William John Macquorn, Scottish civil engineer and molecular physicist, b. 1820, d. 1872.

Rapallo, Treaties of, settling the frontiers between Yugoslavia and Italy, signed 1920 ; between Germany and Russia, signed 1922.

Rapee, Erno, Hungarian conductor, b. 1891, d. 1945.

Raphael, Italian painter (*St Catherine*), b. 1483, d. 1520.

Rapin du Thoyras, Paul de, French historian, b. 1661, d. 1725.

Rappard, Professor William, Swiss political scientist, b. 1883, d. 1958.

Rashi (Rabbi Solomon ben Ishak), French Jewish scholar, b. 1040, d. 1105.

Rasmussen, Knud Johan Victor, Danish Polar explorer, b. 1879, d. 1933.

Raspe, Rudolf Eric, German-born writer (*Baron Munchhausen*, 1785), b. 1737, d. 1794.

Rasputin (Grigori Yefimovich Novych), Russian court intriguer, b. 1871, assassinated 15 Dec. 1916.

Ratcliffe, Samuel Kerkham, English journalist, b. 1868, d. 1958.

Ratcliffe College, Leicestershire, English public school, founded with funds provided by Lady Mary Arundell of Wardour 1844, opened 1847.

Ratdolt, Erhard, German pioneer printer b. about 1443, d. about 1528.

Rathbone, William, English founder (1859) of the District Nurse movement, b. 1819, d. 1902.

Rathenau, Walter, German statesman, b. 1867, assassinated 1922.

Rationing, Food, in Britain, World War I, 1916–1918 ; World War II, began 8 Jan. 1940, ended 1953. In Germany, World War II, began 27 Aug. 1939.

Rationing, 'Points', World War II, began in Britain 1 Dec. 1941.

Ravel, Maurice, French composer (*Tombeau de Couperin*, 1919), b. 1875, d. 1937.

Ravenna, chief residence of the Roman emperors, 404–476, and of Byzantine exarchs, 540–751 ; ceded to Papacy 756, recovered from Venetians 1509.

Rawalpindi, Treaty of, concluding the 3rd Afghan War, signed 8 Aug. 1919.

Rawlins, Thomas, English medallist and playwright, b. about 1620, d. 1670.

Rawlinson, Sir Henry Crewicke, English Assyriologist, b. 1810, d. 1895

Rawsthorne, Alan, English composer (*Cortège*, 1945), b. 1905.

Ray, John, English naturalist, b. 1627, d. 1705.

Ray Society, London, for the publication of works on natural history, founded in honour of John Ray 1844.

Rayleigh, John William Strutt, Baron, English scientist, b. 1842, d. 1919.

Raymond I, Count of Toulouse 852–864.

Raymond II, Count of Toulouse 918–924.

Raymond III, Count of Toulouse 924–950.

Raymond IV, Count of Toulouse (1093–1105) and crusader, d. 1105.

Raymond V, Count of Toulouse 1148–1194.

Raymond VI, Count of Toulouse (1194–1222), d. 1222.

Raymond VII, Count of Toulouse (1222–1249), d. 1249.

Raymond, Ernest, English writer (*Tell England*, 1922), b. 1888.

Raymond le Gros (Raymond Fitzgerald), English ruler of Ireland, d. about 1182.

Rayon Fibre, first successfully manufactured 1889 by the French chemist Hilaire, Comte de Chardonnet, b. 1839, d. 1924.

Razor, Safety, invented 1901 by the American manufacturer King Camp Gillette, b. 1855, d. 1932.

Read, Charles, English novelist (*The Cloister and the Hearth*, 1861), b. 1814, d. 1884.

Read, Sir Herbert, English poet and critic, b. 1893.

Reade's Kettledrum, condenser for the microscope, invented 1861 by the chemist Joseph Bancroft Reade, b. 1801, d. 1870.

Reading, Rufus Isaacs, Marquess of, British lawyer and Viceroy of India (1921–1926), b. 1860, d. 1935.

Reading University, founded 1892 as the University Extension College ; university status 1926.

Reagan, John Henninger, American statesman, b. 1818, d. 1905.

Real Academia Español, founded at Madrid July 1713.

Reaper, invented 1826 by the Scottish inventor Patrick Bell (1799–1869). First practical machine invented 1831 by the American Cyrus Hall McCormick (1809–1884).

Réaumur Scale, temperature, invented by the French scientist Rene Antoine Ferchault de Réaumur, b. 1683, d. 1757.

Rebecca Riots, Wales, 1839 and 1843.

Recamier, Mme, French leader of society, b. 1777, d. 1849.

Rechabites, Independent Order of, temperance society, founded at Salford 1835.

Recife, Brazil, founded 1536.

Reclus, Jean-Jacques, French geographer and anarchist, b. 1830, d. 1905.

Record Office, First British local, established at Bedford 1923.

Records, Public, first brought under the superintendence of the Master of the

Rolls in Britain by Act of Parliament 1838.

Red Cross, International, founded at Geneva 1864.

'Red Sunday', Russian revolt, took place at St Petersburg 22 Jan. 1905.

Redmond, John Edward, Irish patriot, b. 1856, d. 1918.

Redouté, Pierre Joseph, French botanical artist, b. 1759, d. 1840.

Reed, Talbot Baines, English writer of books for boys, b. 1852, d. 1903.

Reed, Walter, American bacteriologist, b. 1851, d. 1902.

Reeves, John Sims, English operatic singer, b. 1818, d. 1900.

Reflex and Voluntary Action, distinguished 1833–1837 by the English physiologist Marshall Hall, b. 1790, d. 1857.

Reformation, started 1517 by the German reformer Martin Luther, b. 1483, d. 1546.

Reformatory, First British, opened at Redhill 1850.

Refraction, Double, theory made public 1810 by the French physicist Etienne Louis Malus, b. 1775, d. 1812.

Refraction of Light, law postulated 1621 by the Dutch scientist Willebrord Snell, b. 1591, d. 1626.

Refrigerated Railway Waggons, first used in the U.S.A. 1877.

Refrigerators, invented 1867 by the French inventor Charles Tellier, b. 1828, d. 1913.

Regency Period, approximately 1810 to 1830.

Reger, Max, German composer (*Sinfonietta*), b. 1873, d. 1916.

Regiomontanus (Johannes Müller), German astronomer, b. 1436, d. 1476.

Regional Broadcasting, in Britain, began with the opening of the transmitting station at Brookmans Park 21 Oct. 1929.

Registered Trade Mark, First, the Red Badge of Messrs Bass & Co.'s Pale Ale, created 1855.

Registrar-General, First British, Thomas Henry Lister (1800–1842) appointed 1836.

Registration, of births, marriages and deaths, instituted in Britain by Thomas Cromwell, b. about 1485, beheaded 1540 ; made compulsory 1837.

Regnault, Henri, French painter (*Salome*, 1870), b. 1843, killed in battle 1871.

Regnier, Mathurin, French satirical writer (*Macette*), b. 1573, d. 1613.

Regulus, Marcus Atilius, Roman hero, lived in the 3rd century B.C.

Rehan, Ada, Irish-born actress, b. 1860, d. 1916.

Reichenbach, Hans, German-born exponent of the philosophy of science, b. 1891, d. 1953.

Reichstadt, Napoléon Francis Joseph Charles, Duc de (Napoleon II), b. 1811, d. 1832.

Reichstag, German Parliament, reconstituted 1867–1871 ; building burnt 27 Feb. 1933 ; trial began at Leipzig 21 Sept. 1933.

Reid, Mayne, Irish-born writer (*The White Chief*, 1859), b. 1818, d. 1883.

Reid, Sir William, Governor (1839–1846) of the Bermudas, b. 1791, d. 1858.

Reign of Terror, French Revolution, 1793–1794.

Reinach, Salomon, French archæologist (*Apollo*, 1902–1903), b. 1858, d. 1932.

Reinhardt, Max, Austrian pioneer of the Modern Theatre, b. 1873, d. 1943.

Réjane, Gabrielle, French actress, b. 1857, d. 1920.

Relativity, Special Theory of, propounded 1905 ; General Theory of, propounded 1916—both by the German-born scientist Albert Einstein, b. 1879, d. 1955 ; Kinematical Theory of, propounded 1933 by E. A. Milne.

Relief Map, Earliest (of Peru), prepared for the 9th Inca, d. 1191.

Remarque, Erich Maria, German-born novelist (*All Quiet on the Western Front*, 1929), b. 1897.

Rembrandt Harmens van Rijn, Dutch painter (*Woman Taken in Adultery*, 1644), b. 1606, d. 1669.

Remington, Frederick, American artist, b. 1861, d. 1909.

Remonstrance, Grand, parliamentary indictment of Charles I, Nov. 1641.

Remonstrants, Dutch religious movement, founded 1609.

Remusat, Charles François Marie, Comte de, French writer and politician, b. 1797, d. 1875.

Renaissance, of Italian art, between 14th and 16th centuries.

Renan, Ernest, French theologian (*La Vie de Jesus*, 1863), b. 1823, d. 1892.

Reni, Guido, Italian painter (*Deeds of Hercules*, 1617–1621), b. 1575, d. 1642.

Rennie, John, Scottish civil engineer, b. 1761, d. 1821.

Renoir, Pierre Auguste, French painter (*Les Grands Boulevards*), b. 1841, d. 1919.

Renwick, James, Scottish Covenanter, b. 1662, executed 1688.

Reparations, German, after World War I, paid 1921–1931.

Repeating Watches, invented 1687 by the English clockmaker Daniel Quare, b. 1648, d. 1724.

Repington, Cardinal Philip, Bishop of Lincoln, d. 1424.

Repplier, Agnes, American essayist (*To Think of Tea*, 1932), b. 1858, d. 1950.

Repton School, Derbyshire, English public school, founded under the will of Sir John Port 1557.

Republic, French, First 1793–1804, Second 1848–1852, Third 1875–1940, Fourth 1946–1958, Fifth since 1958 ; English 1649–1660 ; Spanish 1873–1874, 1931–1939 ; Portuguese since 1910 ; Italian since 1946 ; German 1918–1933, 1949 to date.

Republican Party, U.S.A., present-day party formed 1854.

Respighi, Ottorino, Italian composer (*La Boutique Fantasque*, 1919), b. 1879, d. 1936.

Restif de la Bretonne, Nicolas Edmé, French writer (*Monsieur Nicolas*, 1794–1797), b. 1734, d. 1806.

Restoration, English, of King Charles II, 29 May 1660.

Restoration, French, of King Louis XVIII, 1814.

Reszke, Jean de, Polish operatic singer, b. 1850, d. 1925.

Retarded Potentials, relativity theory, made public 1867 by the German scientist Ludwig Lorenz, b. 1829, d. 1891.

Retreat from Mons, World War I, Aug. 1914.

Retz, Jean François Paul de, Cardinal de, Abbot of St Denis and politician, b. 1614, d. 1679.

Reuchlin, Johann, German scholar and pioneer in Hebrew grammar, b. 1455, d. 1522.

Réunion, Indian Ocean, discovered 1507 by the Portuguese navigator Diego Fernandes Pereira ; formally annexed by France 1643 ; an overseas department of France since 1946.

Reuter, Paul Julius (Josephat), Baron de, German-born pioneer in the speedy transmission of news, b. 1821, d. 1899.

Reuters, press agency, founded by the German-born Paul Julius Reuter 1849.

Revere, Paul, American revolutionary, b. 1735, d. 1818.

Revised Version of the Bible, completed 1884.

Rexists, Belgian Fascist party, founded 1935 by Léon Degrelle.

Reykjavik, Iceland capital, founded about 875.

Reymont, Władisław Stanisław, Polish novelist (*The Promised Land*, 1898), b. 1868, d. 1925.

Reynolds, George Nugent, Irish poet (*Kathleen O'More*, 1800), b. about 1770, d. 1802.

Reynolds, Sir Joshua, English painter (*Nelly O'Brien*), b. 1723, d. 1792.

Reza Shah Pahlavi, ruler of Persia from 1921 and Shah (1925–1941), b. 1877, d. 1944.

Rhankaves, Alexandres, Greek statesman, b. 1810, d. 1892.

Rhee, Syngman (Li Sung-man), ruler of South Korea 1948–1960.

Rheims Cathedral, construction began 1210, mostly completed by 1298 ; West front erected in the 14th century.

Rheinberger, Josef, Liechtenstein composer of organ sonatas, b. 1839, d. 1901.

Rhenium, metallic element, discovered 1925.

Rhine, Confederation of the, of German states, formed by Napoleon 1806 ; collapsed 1813.

Rhineland, occupied by French 1792–1813 ; by Allies 1918–1930 ; taken over by Hitler 7 Mar. 1936.

Rhode Island, U.S.A., first settled 1636 ; entered the Union 1790.

Rhodes, Cecil John, Central African pioneer, b. 1853, d. 1902.

Rhodes, Island of, seized by the Knights Hospitallers 1309 ; ceded to the Turks 1522 ; seized by the Italians 1912 ; ceded to Greece 1947.

Rhodes, Colossus of, statue built about 285 B.C. ; destroyed by an earthquake 224 B.C.

Rhodes Scholarships, for the education at Oxford of overseas students, set up 1902 by the will of Cecil John Rhodes (1853–1902).

Rhodesia, chartered as the territory of the British South Africa Company (1884–1899), deriving its name from Cecil John Rhodes (1853–1902) ; Central African Federation Bill received Royal Assent 14 July 1953.

Rhodesia, Northern, administered by the British South Africa Company until 1923, then became a British Protectorate ; federated with Southern Rhodesia and Nyasaland 1953.

Rhodesia, Southern, administered by the British South Africa Comapny until 1923, then became a self-governing British Colony ; federated with Northern Rhodesia and Nyasaland 1953.

Rhodesia and Nyasaland, Federation of, came into being 1 Aug. 1953.

Rhodesia University, multi-racial, foundation stone laid 1953.

Rhodium, metallic element, discovered 1803 by the English scientist William Hyde Wollaston, b. 1766, d. 1828.

Rhondda, Margaret Haig Thomas, Viscountess, founder and editor (1920–1958) of *Time and Tide*, b. 1883, d. 1958.

Ribault, Jean, French navigator and pioneer colonist in North America, b. about 1520, killed 1565.

Ribbentrop, Joachim von, German Nazi leader, b. 1893, hanged 1946.

Ribbing Machine, for stocking manufacture, invented 1759 by the English manufacter Jedediah Strutt, b. 1726, d. 1797.

Ribera, Jusepe de, Spanish-born painter (*St Sebastian*), b. 1591, d. 1652.

Ricardo, David (Israel), English economist (*Principles of Political Economy*, 1817), b. 1772, d. 1823.

Ricci, Matteo, Italian missionary in China, b. 1552, d. 1610.

Rice, Elmer, American playwright (*Counsellor-at-law*, 1931), b. 1892.

Rich, Richard, English traveller and writer (*Newes from Virginia*, 1610), lived in the late 16th and early 17th centuries.

Richard I, Coeur de Lion, Crusader and King of England (1189–1199), b. 1157, killed in battle 1199.

Richard II, King of England (1377–1399), b. 1367, murdered 1400.

Richard III, King of England (1483–1485), b. 1452, killed in battle 1485.

Richard de Bury, English divine and book collector (*Philobiblon*), b. 1281, d. 1345.

Richard of Cirencester, English historian (*Speculum Historiale*), d. about 1401.

Richard of Devizes, English historian of the late 12th century.

Richards, Alfred Bate, English writer and first Editor (1855) of the *Daily Telegraph*, b. 1820, d. 1876.

Richards, Frank, English writer (the ' Billy Bunter ' series for boys), b. 1875.

Richardson, Dorothy, English novelist (*Pilgrimage*), b. 1873, d. 1957.

Richardson, Jonathan, English painter (*Matthew Prior*), b. 1665, d. 1745.

Richardson, Samuel, English novelist (*Pamela*, 1740), b. 1689, d. 1761.

Richelieu, Cardinal Armand Jean du Plessis, Duc de, French statesman, b. 1585, d. 1642.

Richemont, Henri Louis Victor Hébert, Comte de, pretender to the Throne of France, d. 1853.

Richepin, Jean, French writer (*Monsieur Scapin*, 1886), b. 1849, d. 1926.

Richmond, George, English painter (*William Wilberforce*), b. 1809, d. 1896.

Richter, Ernst Friedrich, German composer and writer on harmony, b. 1808, d. 1879.

Richter, Hans, Hungarian-born conductor (particularly of Wagner's works), b. 1843, d. 1916.

Richthofen, Manfred, Freiherr von, German aviator in World War I, b. 1892, d. 1918.

Ricordi, Giovanni, Italian music publisher, b. 1785, d. 1853.

Riddell, George Allardice, Baron, newspaper proprietor, b. 1865, d. 1934.

Ridley, Nicholas, Bishop of London, b. about 1500, burnt at the stake 1555.

Ridolfi, Roberto di, Italian intriguer in England, b. 1531, d. 1612.

Ridpath, George, Scottish writer and journalist, d. 1726.

Riemann, Hugo, German music historian, b. 1849, d. 1919.

Riemenschneider, Tilman, German sculptor (*Adam and Eve*), b. about 1468, d. 1531.

Rienzi, Cola di, Italian reformer, b. about 1313, murdered 1354.

Rifle, Enfield, invented by the Frenchman Claude Minié, b. 1814, d. 1879 ; Lee-Enfield introduced in Britain 1895 ; the Belgian FN. 30 adopted by Britain 19 Jan. 1954.

Riga, Latvian capital, founded 1200.

Rigaud, Hyacinthe, French painter (*Louis XIV*), b. 1659, d. 1743.

Rigaud, Stephen Peter, English mathematician and astronomer, b. 1774, d. 1839.

Righton, Edmond, English actor, d. 1899.

Rights, Declaration (Feb.) and Bill (Oct.) of, 1689.

Rights of Man, Declaration of, issued by the French Constituent Assembly 1789.

Riley, James Whitcomb, American poet (*Love Lyrics*, 1899), b. 1853, d. 1916.

Riley, John, English painter to the Court, b. 1646, d. 1691.

Rilke, Rainer Maria, German poet (*Duinese Elegies*, 1923), b. 1875, d. 1926.

Rimbaud, Arthur, French poet (*Les Illuminations*, 1886), b. 1854, d. 1891.

Rimini, Francesca da, Italian heroine, wife of Giovanni Malatesta and mistress of Paolo il Bello, murdered about 1285.

Rimmer, William, English-born artist (*A Dying Centaur*), b. 1816, d. 1879.

Rimsky-Korsakov, Nikolai Andreievich, Russian composer (*Le Coq d'Or*, 1910), b. 1844, d. 1908.

Rinehart, William Henry, American sculptor, b. 1825, d. 1874.

Ring, Wedding, changed from right to left hand in English Prayer Book of 1549, and in *Rituale Romanum* of 1614.

Rio de Janeiro, capital of Brazil, site believed to have been discovered by the Portuguese navigator Andre Gonçalves 1502.

Rio de Oro (Spanish Sahara), formally annexed by Spain 1885.

Ripley, Thomas, English architect, b. about 1683, d. 1758.

Ripon, George Frederick Samuel Robinson, Marquess of, statesman, b. 1827, d. 1909.

Risorgimento, movement for Italian unity in 19th century.

Ritchie, Charles Thomas, Baron Ritchie, British statesman, b. 1838, d. 1906.

Ritschl, Albrecht, German theologian, b. 1822, d. 1889.

Ritson, Joseph, English antiquary (*Bibliographia Poetica*, 1802), b. 1752, d. 1803.

Rittenhouse, David, American astronomer, b. 1732, d. 1796.

Ritter, Hermann, German inventor (1876) of the viola alta, b. 1849, d. 1926.

Rivera, Diego, Mexican painter of murals, b. 1886, d. 1957.

River Plate, Battle of the, between British cruisers and the German *Graf Spee*, Dec. 1939.

Rivers, Richard Woodville, Earl, High Constable of England, executed 1469.

Rizzio, David, Italian secretary to Mary Queen of Scots, b. about 1533, murdered 1566.

Ro, artificial language produced 1919 by the American Foster.

Robbia, Luca della, Italian sculptor, b. about 1400, d. 1482.

Robert I, King of France 922–923), killed in battle 923.

Robert II, King of France (96–1031), d. 1031.

Robert I, King of Scotland (1306–1329), b. 1274, d. 1329.

Robert II, King of Scotland (1371–1390), b. 1316, d. 1390.

Robert III, King of Scotland (1390–1406), b. about 1340, d. 1406.

Robert of Gloucester, English historian, probably lived in the 13th and 14th centuries.

Robert the Bruce, King of Scotland (1306–1329), b. 1274, d. 1329.

Robert Gordon's College, Aberdeen, founded 1729.

Roberts, Frederick Sleigh, Earl, C.-in-C. India (1885–1893), b. 1832, d. 1914.

Roberts, Richard, Welsh inventor, b. 1789, d. 1864.

Robertson, James, Scottish Governor of New York, b. about 1720, d. 1788.

Robertson, Sir John, Australian statesman, b. 1816, d. 1891.

Robertson, Thomas William, English playwright (*Caste*, 1867), b. 1829, d. 1871.

Robeson, Paul, American negro singer, b. 1898.

Robespierre, Maximilien Marie Isidore, French Revolutionary leader, b. 1758, guillotined 1794.

' Robin Hood ', legendary English hero, may have lived about 1200, or possibly a century later.

Robinson, Henry Crabb, English diarist, b. 1775, d. 1867.

Robinson, Mary (' Perdita '), English actress and mistress of Prince of Wales, b. 1758, d. 1800.

'Rob Roy ' (Robert Macgregor), Scottish outlaw, b. 1671, d. 1734.

Robsart, Amy, wife of Robert Dudley, Earl of Leicester, b. about 1532, d. 1560.

Robson, Dame Flora, English actress, b. 1902.

Rochambeau, Jean Baptiste Donatien de Vimeur, Comte de, French soldier in Washington's army, b. 1725, d. 1807.

Rochdale Canal, constructed (opened 1804) by the Scottish civil engineer John Rennie, b. 1761, d. 1821.

Rochester, John Wilmot, Earl of, poet (*Poems on Several Occasions*, 1680), b. 1647, d. 1680.

Rock Drill, invented 1871 by the American inventor Simon Ingersoll, b. 1818, d. 1894.

Rockall Island, Outer Hebrides ; first British landing 1810 ; formally annexed by the Royal Navy 1955.

Rockefeller Foundation, established 1913 through the philanthropy of the American financier John Davison Rockefeller, b. 1839, d. 1937.

Rocker, Rudolf, German-born anarchist leader, b. 1873, d. 1958.

'Rocket, The', first successful high-speed locomotive, built 1829 by George Stephenson (1781–1848) and Robert Stephenson (1803–1859).

Rockingham, Charles Watson Wentworth, Marquess of, Prime Minister (1765–1766, 1782), b. 1730, d. 1782.

Rocroi, Battle of, between the French and the Spaniards, 19 May 1643.

Roderick, King of Connaught and last High King of Ireland, d. 1198.

Rodgers, Richard, American composer (with Oscar Hammerstein, *Oklahoma*, 1943), b. 1902.

Rodin, Auguste, French sculptor (*Le Baiser*, 1898), b. 1840, d. 1917.

Rodney, Admiral George Brydges, b. 1719, d. 1792.

Rodrigues, Indian Ocean, discovered by the Portuguese 1645 ; formally ceded to Britain 1814.

Roebling, John Augustus, German-born civil engineer, b. 1806, d. 1869.

Roedean, English girls' public school, founded by the Misses Lawrence at Brighton 1885 ; moved to present site 1898.

Roerich, Nicholas, Russian painter (particularly of the Himalayas), b. 1874, d. 1947.

Rogation Days, the three days before Ascension Day.

Roger I, of Sicily, b. 1031, d. 1101.

Roger II, King of Sicily (1112–1154), b. 1093, d. 1154.

Roger the Great, Bishop (1102–1139) of Salisbury, d. 1139.

Roger de Wendover, English historian (*Flores Historiarum*), d. 1236.

Rogers, Henry Darwin, American geologist, b. 1808, d. 1866.

Rogers, Samuel, English poet (*Italy*, 1822–1828), b. 1763, d. 1855.

Rogers, Will, American humorist, b. 1879, d. in an air crash 1935.

Rogers, William, English educationalist, b. 1819, d. 1896.

Roget's Thesaurus, compiled 1852 by the English scholar Peter Mark Roget, b. 1779, d. 1869.

Rojas, Fernando de, Spanish novelist (*La Celestina*), b. about 1465, d. about 1526.

Roland, Chanson de, French version of the Roland epic dating from the 11th century ; Roland traditionally died fighting on 15 Aug. 778.

Rolfe, Frederick ('Baron Corvo'), English novelist (*Hadrian the Seventh*, 1904), b. 1860, d. 1913.

Rolfe, John, English colonist in Virginia, b. 1585, d. 1622.

Rolland, Romain, French writer (*Jean Christophe*, 1904), b. 1866, d. 1944.

Rolle, Richard, English writer (*The Pricke of Conscience*), b. about 1290, d. 1349.

Rollo, Sir William, Royalist soldier, executed 1645.

Rolvaag, Ole Edvart, Norwegian-born novelist, b. 1876, d. 1931.

'Romains,' Jules' (Louis Farigoule), French writer (*Les Hommes du bon volonté*, 1932–1946), b. 1885.

Roman Era, began 21 Apr. 753 B.C.

Roman Type, first used in England by the French-born printer Richard Pynson, d. 1530.

Romanes Lectures, Oxford University, founded 1891 by the Canadian-born scientist George John Romanes, b. 1848, d. 1894.

Romanus, Pope 897.

Romanus I, Byzantine Emperor (919–944), d. 948.

Romanus II, Byzantine Emperor (959–963), d. 963.

Romanus III, Byzantine Emperor (1028–1034), d. 1034.

Romanus IV, Byzantine Emperor (1068–1071), d. 1071.

Romberg, Sigmund, Hungarian composer (*The Student Prince*, 1924), b. 1887, d. 1951.

Rome, traditional date of foundation 21 Apr. 753 B.C.

Rome, University of, founded 1244.

Romer, Carl Ferdinand von, German geologist, b. 1818, d. 1891.

Römer, Olaus, Danish astronomer (calculated velocity of light in 1675), b. 1644, d. 1710.

Romilly, Sir Samuel, English legal reformer, b. 1757, committed suicide 1818.

Romney, George, English painter (*Lady Hamilton*), b. 1734, d. 1802.

Romulus Augustulus, Roman Emperor (last in West) 475–476.

Ronald, Sir Landon, English conductor, b. 1873, d. 1938.

Ronsard, Pierre de, French poet (*Hymne de la France*, 1549), b. 1524, d. 1585.

Röntgen Rays, discovered about 1895 by the German scientist Wilhelm von Röntgen, b. 1845, d. 1923.

Roof-top Landing, first successfully made in Paris 1913 by the French aviator Jules Vedrines, b. 1881, d. 1919.

Roosevelt, Mrs Eleanor, b. 1884.

Roosevelt, Franklin Delano, U.S. President (1933–1945), b. 1882, d. 1945.

Roosevelt, Theodore, U.S. President (1901–1909), b. 1858, d. 1919.

Roosevelt Dam, U.S.A., constructed 1906–1911.

Root, Elihu, American statesman, b. 1845, d. 1937.

Roper, Margaret, scholar and daughter of Sir Thomas More, b. 1505, d. 1544.

Rops, Félicien, Belgian artist (*Buveuse d'absinthe*, 1865), b. 1833, d. 1898.

Rorschach Test, devised by the Swiss psychiatrist Hermann Rorschach in 1942.

Rosa, Carl, German-born founder of the Carl Rosa Opera Company, b. 1843, d. 1889.

Rosa, Salvator, Italian painter (*Death of Socrates*), b. 1615, d. 1673.

Rosamund, Fair (Rosamund Clifford), mistress of King Henry II, d. about 1176.

Rosaniline, red dye, discovered 1858 by the German scientist August Wilhelm von Hofmann, b. 1818, d. 1892.

Roscius Gallus, Quintus, Roman actor, b. about 126, d. 62 B.C.

Roscoe, William, English writer (*Lorenzo de' Medici*, 1796), b. 1753, d. 1831.

Rose of Lima, St, first canonised saint in the New World, b. 1586, d. 1617.

Rosebery, Archibald Philip Primrose, Earl of, Prime Minister (1894–1896) and Liberal leader, b. 1847, d. 1929.

Rosegger, Peter, Austrian writer (*Mann und Weib*, 1879), b. 1843, d. 1918.

Rosenberg, Isaac, English poet, b. 1890, killed 1918.

Roses, Wars of the, between the houses of Lancaster and York, 1455–1485.

Rosetta Stone, deciphered 1821–1828 by the French Orientalist Jean François Champollion, b. 1790, d. 1832.

Rosh ha-Shanah, (Feast of the Trumpets), the Jewish New Year, 1st day of Tishri.

Rosicrucians, occult society in 17th century, revived in 18th century and several times since.

Ross, Sir James Clark, Scottish explorer, b. 1800, d. 1862.

Ross, Sir John, Scottish explorer, b. 1777, d. 1856.

Ross, Sir Ronald, India-born pioneer in the cure of malaria, b. 1857, d. 1932.

Ross, Thomas, Scottish libeller of Scottish courtiers, b. about 1575, beheaded 1618.

Rossall School, Lancashire, English public school, founded 1844; incorporated by Royal Charter 1890.

Rosse, William Parsons, Earl of, astronomer, b. 1800, d. 1867.

Rossellino, Antonio, Italian sculptor, b. 1427, d. about 1479.

Rossetti, Christina Georgina, English poet (*Goblin Market*, 1862), b. 1830, d. 1894.

Rossetti, Dante Gabriel, English painter (*Dante's Dream*) and poet, b. 1828, d. 1882.

Rossi, Charles, English sculptor (*James Wyatt*), b. 1762, d. 1839.

Rossini, Gioacchino, Italian composer (*The Barber of Seville*, 1816), b. 1792, d. 1868.

Rostand, Edmond, French playwright (*Cyrano de Bergerac*, 1897), b. 1868, d. 1918.

Rosyth, Scotland, naval base, construction begun 1909.

Rotary International, founded U.S.A. 1905 ; Britain 1914.

Rotary Printing Press, invented 1846 by the American inventor Richard March Hoe, b. 1812, d. 1886.

Rothamsted Experimental Station, world's first agricultural experimental station, founded 1843 by the English agriculturist Sir John Bennet Lawes, b. 1814, d. 1900.

Rothenstein, Sir John, Director of the Tate Gallery since 1938, b. 1901.

Rothenstein, Sir William, English painter (*T. E. Lawrence*), b. 1872, d. 1945.

Rotherhithe-Stepney Tunnel, London, opened 12 June 1908.

Rothermere, Harold Sidney Harmsworth, Viscount, British newspaper publisher, b. 1868, d. 1940.

Rothschild, Meyer Amshel, German financier, b. 1743, d. 1812.

Rotor Ships, invented 1924 by the German engineer Anton Flettner, b. 1885.

Rouault, Georges, French painter (*Henri Lebasçue*), b. 1871, d. 1958.

Roubillac, Louis François, French-born sculptor (*Handel*, 1738), b. 1695, d. 1762.

Rouen, Siege of, by King Henry V of England, 1418–1419.

Rouen Cathedral, construction began 1206.

Rouget de l'Isle, Claude Joseph, French composer of the *Marseillaise* (1792), b. 1760, d. 1836.

Roundheads, nickname of Parliamentary supporters during the English Civil War period of the mid-17th century.

Rousseau, Henri, French painter (*La Chasse au tigre*), b. 1844, d. 1910.

Rousseau, Jean Jacques, Swiss-born writer (*Du Contrat social*, 1762), b. 1712, d. 1778.

Routledge, George, English publisher, b. 1812, d. 1888.

Rouvray, Battle of (Battle of the Herrings), between the English and the French, 1429.

Roux, Pierre Paul Emile, French bacteriologist, b. 1853, d. 1933.

Rover Scouts, movement formed in Britain 1919.

Rowan, Archibald Hamilton, United Irishman, b. 1751, d. 1834.

Rowe, Nicholas, English writer (*Tamerlane*, 1702), b. 1674, d. 1718.

Rowlandson, Thomas, English artist (*Dance of Death*, 1814–1816), b. 1756, d. 1827.

Rowley, William, English playwright (*A Woman Never Vext*, 1632), b. about 1585, d. about 1642.

Rowley Poems, ' 15th-century poems ' written 1765 onwards by the English poet Thomas Chatterton, b. 1752, committed suicide 1770.

Rowntree, Joseph, English Quaker educationist, b. 1801, d. 1859.

Rowton Houses, poor men's hotels in London, founded 1892 onwards by the philanthropist Baron Rowton, b. 1838, d. 1903.

Roxana, wife of Alexander the Great, killed 311 B.C.

' Roy, Rob ' (Robert Macgregor), Scottish rebel, b. 1671, d. 1734.

Royal Academy of Arts, London, founded 1768.

Royal Aeronautical Society, founded 1866 as the Aeronautical Society of Great Britain ; present name since 1919.

Royal Air Force, formed 1918.

Royal Albert Hall, London, opened by Queen Victoria, 29 Mar. 1871.

Royal and Ancient Golf Club of St Andrews, founded 1754.

Royal Astronomical Society, London, founded 1820, chartered 1831.

Royal Automobile Club, London, founded 1897.

Royal Canadian Mounted Police, founded as the North-West Mounted Police 1873 ; assumed present title 1920.

Royal College of Physicians, London, founded 1518.

Royal College of Surgeons, London, founded 1800.

Royal Dutch Petroleum Company, established at The Hague 16 June 1890.

Royal Exchange, London, founded 1566–1571 by the English financier Sir Thomas Gresham, b. 1519, d. 1579.

Royal Flying Corps, approved by King George V as title for the aeronautical branch of the Armed Forces 1912 ; superseded by R.A.F. in 1918.

Royal George, The, sank at Portsmouth 1782.

Royal Grammar School, High Wycombe, English public school, founded in the reign of King Edward VI by the Mayor and burgesses of High Wycombe ; moved to present site 1914.

Royal Grammar School, Newcastle-upon-Tyne, English public school, founded by Thomas Horsley at the beginning of the 16th century ; Royal Charter granted by Queen Elizabeth 1600.

Royal Grammar School, Worcester, English public school, origins uncertain, earliest recorded mention 1290.

Royal Hospital, Chelsea, built 1682–1692 by the English architect Sir Christopher Wren (1632–1723) ; opened 1694.

Royal Hunt Cup, Ascot, first run 1843.

Royal Institute of International Affairs, London, founded 1920.

Royal Institution of Great Britain, London, founded 1799.

Royal London Homeopathic Hospital, founded 1849 by Dr Frederick Hervey Foster Quin, b. 1799, d. 1878.

Royal Marine Corps, constituted 1664 as the Duke of York and Albany's Maritime Regiment of Foot.

Royal Marriage Act, passed 1772.

Royal Masonic School, Bushey, English public school, founded 1798.

Royal Military Academy, Sandhurst (combining Sandhurst and Woolwich), came into being 2 Apr. 1946.

Royal Naval Reserve, formed in Britain under the Royal Naval Reserve (Volunteers) Act of 1859.

Royal Oak, torpedoed by the Germans in World War II, 14 Oct. 1939.

Royal Observatory, Greenwich, founded 1675.

Royal Opera House, Covent Garden, London, opened 15 May 1858. Preceded by two other opera houses, both destroyed by fire.

Royal Society for the Prevention of Cruelty to Animals, London, founded 1824.

Royal Society of Arts, London, founded 1754.

Royal Society of British Artists, London, founded 1823.

Royal Society of London, organised 1660 ; constituted by Royal Charter 1662.

Royal Society of Painters in Watercolours, London, founded 1804.

Royce, Josiah, American philosopher, b. 1855, d. 1916.

Royden, Maude, English leader of the women's movement and preacher, b. 1876, d. 1956.

Ruadri, King of Connaught and last High King of Ireland, d. 1198.

Ruanda-Urundi, Africa, ceded 1919 to Belgium as a mandatory of the League of Nations ; trusteeship territory by United Nations' agreement 1949.

Rubber, synthetic, first produced 1891 by the English chemist, Sir William Tilden, b. 1842, d. 1926.

Rubber, Vulcanisation of, patented by the English merchant Thomas Hancock, b. 1786, d. 1865 ; pioneered 1839 by the American manufacturer Charles Goodyear, b. 1800, d. 1860.

Rubber Factory, First, built 1819 in London by the English merchant Thomas Hancock, b. 1786, d. 1865.

Rubber Trees, first cultivated at the Royal Botanic Gardens, Kew ; introduced by Sir Henry Wickham (1846–1928) into the Far East about 1885.

Rubbra, Edmund Duncan, English composer and conductor, b. 1901.

Rubens, Peter Paul, Flemish painter (*The Descent from the Cross*, 1614), b. 1577, d. 1640.

Rubidium, chemical element, discovered by the German scientists Bunsen (1791–1860) and Gustav Robert Kirchhoff (1824–1887).

Rubinstein, Anton, Russian pianist and composer (*Dmitri Donskoi*, 1851), b. 1829, d. 1894.

Rubinstein, Nikolai, Russian pianist, b. 1835, d. 1881.

Rude, François, French sculptor (*Jeanne d'Arc*, 1852), b. 1784, d. 1855.

Rudolf I, German king (1273–1291), b. 1218, d. 1291.

Rudolf II, Holy Roman Emperor (1576–1612), b. 1552, d. 1612.

Rueda, Lope de, Spanish playwright (*Medora*), b. about 1510, d. about 1565.

Rufinus, Tyrannius, Italian theologian, b. about 342, d. 410.

Rugby Football, started by William Webb Ellis of Rugby School 1823 ; legalised 1846.

Rugby League, seceded from Rugby Union 1895 as Northern Union ; adopted present name 1922.

Rugby School, English public school, founded by Lawrence Sheriff 1567.

Rugby Union, British, founded 1871.

Ruhmkorff, Heinrich Daniel, German physicist, b. 1803, d. 1877.

Rule Britannia, first published 1740 ; words by the Scottish poet James Thomson (1700–1748) ; music by the English composer Thomas Arne (1710–1778).

Rumania, Wallachia and Moldavia united 1856 ; principality 1866–1881 ; monarchy 1881–1947 ; communist régime since 1948.

Rumelia, Eastern, ruled by Bulgaria since 1878.

Rumford, Benjamin Thompson, Count von, American-born scientist, b. 1753, d. 1814.

Rump Parliament, England, 6 Dec. 1648 to 20 Apr. 1653, and 1659.

Runciman, Walter, Baron Runciman, British shipowner, b. 1847, d. 1937.

Rupert of the Rhine, Prince, b. 1619, d. 1682.

Rupert, German king (1400–1410), b. 1352, d. 1410.

Rush, Benjamin, American physician and abolitionist, b. 1745, d. 1813.

Rush-Bagot Convention, providing for an unarmed frontier between the U.S.A. and Canada, signed 1817.

Rushworth, John, English surgeon and promotor of dispensaries, b. 1669, d. 1736.

Ruskin, John, English art critic and writer (*The Stones of Venice*, 1851–1853), b. 1819, d. 1900.

Russell, Bertrand, English philosopher (*History of Western Philosophy*, 1946), b. 1872.

Russell, George (' AE '), Irish writer, b. 1867, d. 1935.

Russell, Lord John, Earl Russell, British statesman (Prime Minister 1846–1852, 1865–1866), b. 1792, d. 1878.

Russell, John Scott, Scottish naval architect (the *Great Eastern*), b. 1808, d. 1882.

Russell, William Howard, British war-correspondent, b. 1820, d. 1907.

Russia, Mongol domination 1242–1368, Muscovite ascendancy 1328–1613 ; Romanov Empire 1613–1917 ; revolutionary period 1917–1922 ; U.S.S.R. formed 1922.

Russian Navy, founded by Count Feodor Apraksin, b. 1671, d. 1728.

Russian Revolutions, abortive revolution, Jan.–Oct. 1905 ; February Revolution, 8–14 Mar. 1917 ; October Revolution, 7 Nov. 1917 ; Civil War, 1917–1922 ; U.S.S.R. formed Dec. 1922.

Russo-Japanese War, began 1904 ; ended 1905.

Russo-Turkish Wars, 1696 ; 1768–1774 ; 1787–1791 ; 1806–1812 ; 1828–1829 ; 1853–1855 ; 1877–1878.

Rutebeuf, French troubadour, lived in the 13th century.

Rutgers University, New Jersey, U.S.A., founded as Queen's College 1766 ; became Rutger's College 1825.

Ruth, ' Babe ' (George Herman Ruth), American champion baseball player, b. 1895, d. 1948.

Ruthenium, metallic element, discovered 1845 by the German chemist Karl Ernst Claus, b. 1796, d. 1864.

Rutherford, Daniel, Scottish physician and discoverer 1772 of Nitrogen, b. 1749, d. 1819.

Rutherford, Ernest, Baron, New Zealand born scientist, b. 1871, d. 1937.

' **Rutherford, Mark** ' (William Hale White), English writer (*The Revolution in Tanner's Lane*, 1887), b. 1831, d. 1913.

Rutherford, Samuel, Scottish covenanter, b. about 1600, d. 1661.

' **Ruthven,** Raid of ', 1582, named after one of the conspirators William Ruthven, Baron Ruthven, b. about 1541, beheaded 1584.

Ruwenzori, Mt., Tanganyika, first climbed by the Duke of the Abruzzi 1906.

Ruysbroek, Jan van, Dutch mystical writer (*De Vera Contemplatione*), b. 1293, d. 1381.

Ruysdael, Jakob, Dutch painter (*Dutch Dunes*), b. 1628, d. 1682.

Ruyter, Michael Adriaanszoon de, Dutch Admiral, b. 1607, d. 1676.

Rydal School, Colwyn Bay, British public school founded by Thomas G. Osborn, 1885.

Rye House Plot, conspiracy of Whigs to assassinate King Charles II, Apr. 1683.

Rylands Library, John, Manchester, founded 1899 by his widow in memory of John Rylands, b. 1801, d. 1888.

Rymer, Thomas, English archæologist and compiler (*Foedera*, 1704–1735), b. 1641, d. 1713.

Rysbrack, John Michael, Flemish sculptor (*John Howard*), b. about 1693, d. 1770.

Ryswick, Treaty of, ending the war between France and the Allies, signed Sept. 1697.

S

SOS, international distress call signal, adopted by the International Radiotelegraph Conference 1912.

S.S.A.F.A. (Soldiers', Sailors' and Airmen's Families Association), London, founded 1885 ; incorporated by Royal Charter 1926.

Saar, placed under the control of the League of Nations 1919 ; reverted to Germany 1935 ; administered by France 1945–1956 ; returned to Germany 1957–1959.

Saar Offensive, World War II, 9–30 Sept. 1939.

Saarinen, Eliel, Finnish-born architect and town planner, b. 1873.

Sabata, Victor de, Italian conductor and composer (*Gethsemani*, 1925), b. 1892.

Sabatier, Louis Auguste, French theologian, b. 1837, d. 1901.

Sabatini, Rafael, Italian writer (*Scaramouche*, 1921), b. 1875, d. 1950.

Sabbath, Jewish day of rest, seventh day of week ; Christian day of rest, first day of week (Lord's Day) since 4th century.

Sabin, Joseph, English-born bibliographer of Americana, b. 1821, d. 1881.

Sabinian, Pope 604–607.

Saccharin, discovered 1879 by the American scientist Ira Remsen (1846–1927) and C. Fahlberg.

Sacheverell, Henry, English clergyman and pamphleteer, b. about 1674, d. 1724.

Sachs, Hans, German writer of *Meisterlieder*, b. 1494, d. 1576.

Sackville, Charles, Earl of Dorset, English poet, b. 1638, d. 1706.

Sackville, Thomas, Earl of Dorset, English playwright (with Norton, *Gorboduc*, 1561), b. 1536, d. 1608.

Sackville-West, Victoria, English writer (*All Passion Spent*, 1931), b. 1892.

Sade, Donatien Alphonse François, Marquis de, French writer (*Justine*, 1791), b. 1740, d. 1814.

Sadi, Persian poet (*Gulistan*, 1258), b. about 1184, d. 1292.

Sadleir, Michael, English publisher and writer (*Fanny by Gaslight*, 1940), b. 1888, d. 1957.

Sadler, Windham William, Irish aeronaut, b. 1796, d. 1824.

Sadler's Wells, London theatre, opened in 1765 ; reconstructed 1879 ; closed 1916 ; reopened 1931.

Sadowa, Battle of (Königgrätz), between Austrians and Persians, 3 July 1866.

Safety Bicycle, invented 1874 by the English inventor H. J. Lawson at Brighton.

Safety Lamp, Miner's, invented 1815 by the English scientist Sir Humphry Davy, b. 1778, d. 1829.

Safety Razor, invented 1901 by the American manufacturer King Camp Gillette, b. 1855, d. 1932.

' **Sagan,** Françoise ' (Françoise Quoirez), French writer (*Bonjour tristesse*, 1956), b. 1936.

Sage, Russell, American financier, b. 1816, d. 1906.

Sahagun, Bernardino de, Spanish missionary and historian of Mexico, b. about 1499, d. 1590.

Sahara, French and Spanish territories defined by treaty of 1900.

Sailors' Rests, founded by the English philanthropist Agnes Elizabeth Weston, b. 1840, d. 1918.

St Albans Abbey, England, original church built 303 ; construction of Abbey begun 1077 ; Abbey consecrated 1115.

St Albans School, English public school, said to have been founded by Abbot Ulsinus 948.

St Andrews University, Scotland, founded by Bishop Wardlaw 1411.

St Andrews Cathedral, Scotland, built 1159–1318.

St Andrew's Day, 30 Nov.

St Anne's College, Oxford University, founded 1879.

St Anthony's College, Oxford University, founded 1950.

St Bartholomew, Massacre of the Huguenots in Paris, 24 Aug.–17 Sept. 1572.

St Bees School, Cumberland, English public school, founded by Edmund Grindal, Archbishop of Canterbury, 1583.

St Benedict's School, Ealing, English public school, founded by Abbot Hugh Edmund Ford 1902.

St Benet's Hall, Oxford University, founded 1947.

St Catharine's College, Cambridge University, founded by Robert Woodlark, Provost of King's College, 1473.

St Catherine's Society, Oxford University, founded 1868.

St Columba's College, Dublin, Irish public school, founded 1843 ; incorporated by Royal Charter 1913.

St Cyr, French military training school, founded 1686.

St David's Cathedral, Wales, constructed 1176–1198.

St David's Day, 1 Mar.

St Dunstan's College, London, English public school, origins uncertain but certainly earlier than 1446 ; refounded 1888.

St Dunstan's, Regent's Park. London, home for blinded soldiers and sailors founded 1915 by the English newspaper owner and philanthropist Sir Arthur Pearson, b. 1866, d. 1921.

St Edmund Hall, Oxford University, reputed to have been founded 1226.

St Edmund's School, Canterbury, founded 1749 ; transferred to Canterbury 1855.

St Edward's School, Oxford, English public school, founded by the Rev Thomas Chamberlain 1863.

St Evremond, Charles, French soldier and poet, b. about 1613, d. 1703.

St Exupéry, Antoine de, French writer (*Vol de nuit*, 1931) and aviator, b. 1900, killed in battle 1944.

St George's Day, 23 Apr.

St Gaudens, Augustus, American sculptor (*Abraham Lincoln*, 1887), b. 1848, d. 1907.

St Germain, Treaty of, settling the fate of Austria, signed 1919.

St Gotthard Pass, carriage road constructed 182c–1830.

St Gotthard Tunnel, construction began 1872 ; completed 1880 ; railway opened 1882.

St Helena, South Atlantic, discovered by the Portuguese navigator João de Nova 1502 ; formally annexed by the British East India Company 1661 ; Crown Colony since 1834.

St Hilda's College, Oxford University, founded 1893.

St James's Gazette, the British newspaper, founded 1880, absorbed into the *Evening Standard* 1905.

St James's Palace, London, built by King Henry VIII, 1532–1533.

St John, Henry, Viscount Bolingbroke, statesman, b. 1678, d. 1751.

St John, Oliver, Chief Justice of England, b. about 1598, d. 1673.

St John's College, Cambridge University, founded by Lady Margaret, Countess of Richmond and Derby, 1511.

St John's College, Oxford University, founded 1555 by Alderman Sir Thomas White, b. 1492, d. 1567.

St John's School, Leatherhead, English public school, founded 1851 ; Royal Charter 1922.

St Just, Louis de, French Revolutionary leader, b. 1767, guillotined 1794.

St Katharine's Dock, Port of London, built by the Scottish engineer Thomas Telford (1757–1834) between 1826 and 1829.

St Kitts Nevis, British West Indies, discovered by Christopher Columbus 1493 ; ceded to the British 1713.

St Laurent, Louis Stephen, Canadian statesman, b. 1882.

St Lawrence College, Ramsgate, English public school, founded 1879 ; incorporated 1892.

St Lawrence River, North America, explored 1535–1536 by the French navigator Jacques Cartier, b. 1491, d. 1557.

St Lawrence Seaway Project, officially launched 1954 ; opened to deep-draught merchant shipping 25 Apr. 1959 ; officially opened 26 June 1959.

St Leger, Doncaster, first run 1776.

St Lucia, British West Indies, believed to have been discovered 1502 by Christopher Columbus ; finally ceded to Britain by France 1814.

St Mark's, Venice, reconstructed 1437–1452 by the Italian Michelozzo, b. 1396, d. 1472.

St Martin-in-the-Fields, London, built 1722–1726 by the Scottish architect James Gibbs, b. 1682, d. 1754.

St Mary Redcliffe, Bristol, built 1325–1475.

St Olave's and St Savior's Grammar School, London, founded by the bequest of the merchant Henry Leeke 1561.

St Patrick's Cathedral, New York, constructed 1858–1879.

St Patrick's Day, Mar. 17.

St Paul's Cathedral, London, constructed 1675–1710 by Sir Christopher Wren, b. 1632, d. 1723.

St Paul's School, London, English public school, founded by John Colet (1467–1519), Dean of St Paul's, 1509.

St Peter's, Rome, constructed 1445–1626.

St Peter's College, Radley (Radley College), Berkshire, English public school, founded by the Rev. William Sewell, opened 1847 ; incorporated by Royal Charter 1890.

St Peter's Hall, Oxford University, founded 1929.

St Peter's School, York, English public school, founded at least as early as the 6th century.

St Pierre, Charles, French writer and reformer, b. 1658, d. 1743.

St Pierre, Jacques Henri Bernardin de, French writer (*Paul et Virginie,* 1787), b. 1737, d. 1814.

St Saëns, Camille, French composer (*Samson and Delilah,* 1877), b. 1835, d. 1921.

St Simon, Claude Henri, Comte de, French political reformer, b. 1760, d. 1825.

Saint-Simon, Louis de Rouvroy, Duc de, French writer (*Memoirs,* 1752), b. 1675, d. 1755.

St Swithin's Day, 15 July.

S. Tomé, Portuguese overseas territory, discovered by the Portuguese 1470.

St Valentine's Day (Old Candlemas), 14 Feb.

St Vincent, John Jervis, Earl of, Admiral of the Fleet, b. 1735, d. 1823.

St Vincent, British West Indies, believed to have been discovered by Christopher Columbus 1498 ; finally ceded to Britain by France 1783.

Ste-Beuve, Charles Augustin, French writer and critic (*Causeries du Lundi*, 1863–1870), b. 1804, d. 1869.

Ste-Chapelle, Paris, constructed 1245–1248.

Saintsbury, George, English literary historian and critic, b. 1845, d. 1933.

Saladin, Sultan of Egypt and soldier, b. 1137, d. 1193.

Salazar, Antonio de Oliveira, Portuguese Prime Minister since 1932, b. 1889.

Sale, George, English translater (1734) of the Koran, b. about 1697, d. 1736.

Salicylic Acid, discovered 1838 by the Italian chemist Rafaelle Piria, b. 1815, d. 1865.

Salinas, Pedro, Spanish poet and literary critic (*Jorge Manrique*, 1947), b. 1892.

Salisbury, John de Montacute, Earl of, diplomat and soldier, b. about 1350, beheaded 1400.

Salisbury, Robert Arthur Talbot Gascoyne-Cecil, Marquess of, Prime Minister (1885–1892, 1895–1902), b. 1830, d. 1903.

Salisbury Cathedral, England, construction began 1220 ; consecrated 1258.

Saliva, Digestive action of, discovered by the Italian scientist Lazaro Spallanzani, b. 1729, d. 1799.

Salk Vaccine, against poliomyelitis, developed 1954 by the American scientist Jonas Edward Salk, b. 1914.

Sallust, Roman historian, b. 86, d. 34 B.C.

Salmasius, Claudius (Claude de Saumaise), French scholar, b. 1588, d. 1653.

Salomon, Dr Erich, German pioneer in the use of the miniature camera and in candid-camera technique, b. 1886, probably killed at Auschwitz 1944.

Salt, Sir Titus, English wool manufacturer, b. 1803, d. 1876.

Salt Lake City, Utah, U.S.A., founded 1847.

Salten, Felix, Austrian writer (*Bambi*, 1923), b. 1869, d. 1945.

Salter, Arthur, Baron Salter, English economist, b. 1881.

Salters Company, London livery company, origins uncertain ; chartered by King Edward III, 1377.

Saltonstall, Richard, English colonist of Massachusetts, b. 1586, d. 1658.

' Saltykov, Mikhail ' (Evgrafovich Shchedrin), Russian writer (*Fables*, 1885), b. 1826, d. 1889.

Salvador, El, became an independent republic 1839 ; new constitution granted 1950.

Salvarsan, a drug curing syphilis, discovered 1908 by the German bacteriologist Paul Ehrlich, b. 1854, d. 1915.

Salvation Army, religious movement, founded in London 1865 by General William Booth, b. 1829, d. 1912.

Salvator Rosa, Italian painter (*Death of Socrates*), b. 1615, d. 1673.

Salzburg Festival, in honour of Mozart, founded 1877.

Samarium, metallic element discovered 1879 by the French scientist Paul Emile Lecoq de Boisbaudran, b. 1838, d. 1912.

Samoa, American, discovered 1722 ; created neutral territory 1889 ; ceded to the U.S.A. 1899–1904 and 1925.

Samuel, Herbert, Viscount Samuel British statesman, b. 1870.

San Francisco Conference, World War II, held 25 Apr.–26 June 1945.

San Francisco Earthquake, took place 18–19 Apr. 1906.

San Marino, world's smallest republic founded 9th to 10th centuries ; independence recognised by the Papacy 1631 ; under Italian protection since 1860.

San Martin, Jose de, South American liberator, b. 1778, d. 1850.

San Nicandro, Italy, place of Judaic sect, led by Donato Manduzio, b. 1885, converted 1930, d. 1948.

San Quentin, California, state prison opened 1852.

Sancho I, King of Portugal (1185–1211), d. 1211.

Sancho II, King of Portugal (1223–1248), b. about 1210, d. 1248.

Sanctuary, Right of, abolished in England 1623–1624.

' Sand, George ' (Armandine Dupin), French writer (*Lélia,* 1833), b. 1804, d. 1876.

Sand River Convention, recognising the establishment of the independent South African Republic (The Transvaal), signed by Britain 17 Jan. 1852.

Sandburg, Carl, American poet (*Cornhuskers,* 1918), b. 1878.

Sandby, Paul, English artist, b. 1725, d. 1809.

Sandhurst Royal Military College, founded 1799 by the Duke of York ; occupied present site 1812.

Sandow, Eugene, strong man and wrestler, b. 1867, d. 1925.

Sandringham House, Norfolk, British royal residence, purchased by King Edward VII, 1861 ; rebuilt 1871.

Sandwich, Edward Montagu, Earl of, Admiral, b. 1625, killed in battle 1672.

Sandwich Islands, now the Hawaiian Islands, discovered by Captain James Cook 1778 ; formally annexed to the U.S.A. 1898.

Sandys, Sir Edwin, organiser of the colony of Virginia, b. 1561, d. 1629.

Sandys, George, English poet (*Hymn to my Redeemer*) and translator, b. 1578, d. 1644.

Sangallo, Antonio di, Italian architect, b. about 1485, d. 1546.

Sanger, ' Lord ' George, English circus manager, b. 1825, murdered 1911.

Sanger, John, English circus manager, b. 1816, d. 1889.

Sankey, Ira David, American hymn-writer, b. 1840, d. 1908.

Sansovino, Jacopo, Italian sculptor and architect, b. 1486, d. 1570.

Santa Anna, Antonio Lopez de, Mexican statesman and soldier, b. 1795, d. 1876.

Santa Claus (St Nicholas), Bishop of Myra in Lycia, lived in the 11th century.

Santa Cruz Archipelago, discovered 1595 by the Spanish navigator Alvaro Mendana (d. 1595).

Santa Fe Trail, U.S.A.–Mexican trading route, mainly used 1822 to 1861.

Santa Sophia, Istanbul, built 532–537 on the site of two previous churches ; converted into a mosque 1453.

Santayana, George, Spanish-born philosopher and writer, b. 1863, d. 1952.

Santillana, Iñigo Lopez de Mendoza, Marquis of, Spanish poet (*Comedieta de Ponza*), b. 1398, d. 1458.

Santos-Dumont, Alberto, Brazil-born pioneer aviator, b. 1873, d. 1932.

São Paulo, Brazil, founded by the Portuguese 1554.

Sappho, Greek poetess, lived in the 6th century B.C.

Sarajevo, Yugoslavia (Capital of Bosnia), scene of the murder of the Archduke Franz Ferdinand 28 June 1914.

Sarasate, Pablo de, Spanish violinist, b 1844, d. 1908.

Saratoga, Battle of, between the Americans and the British, 17 Oct. 1777.

Sarawak, Borneo, government obtained 1841 by Sir James Brooke ; placed under British protection 1888 ; ceded to the Crown 1946 by Sir Charles Brooke, the third Rajah.

Sardinia, ruled by Spain 1292–1713 ; ruled by Savoy from 1720.

Sardou, Victorien, French playwright (*Madame Sans Gêne,* 1893), b. 1831, d. 1908.

Sargent, John Italian-born painter of American descent (*Suggia*), b. 1856, d. 1925.

Sargent, Sir Malcolm, English conductor, b. 1895.

Sargon I, King of Babylonia, lived in the 39th century B.C.

Sargon II, King of Assyria (722–705 B.C.) murdered 705 B.C.

Sarmiento, Domingo Faustino, President (1868–1874) of Argentina, b. 1811, d. 1888.

Saroyan, William, American writer (*The Daring Young Man on the Flying Trapeze,* 1934), b. 1908.

Sarsfield, Patrick, Earl of Lucan, soldier and administrator, died of wounds 1693.

Sarto, Andrea del, Italian painter (*Birth of the Virgin*, 1514), b. 1486, d. 1531.

Sartre, Jean Paul, French writer (*Les Mains Sales*, 1948), b. 1905.

Saskatchewan, Canada, created a separate Province 1905.

Sassanids, ruled Persia 226–651.

Sassoon, Siegfried, English writer (*Memoirs of a Fox-hunting Man*, 1928), b. 1886.

Satellite, First American earth (Explorer I), successfully launched, Cape Canaveral, Florida, 31 Jan. 1958.

Satellite, First Russian earth, successfully launched 4 Oct. 1957 ; second 3 Nov. 1957.

Satie, Erik, French composer (*Gymnopédies*, 1888), b. 1866, d. 1925.

Saturday, seventh day of the week.

Saturday mid-day closing, in Britain, started in Liverpool about 1843 ; Manchester 1844.

Saturn, rings described 1655 by the Dutch astronomer Christiaan Huygens, b. 1629, d. 1695.

Saturninus, Lucius Appuleius, Roman tribune, killed 100 B.C.

Saud, Ibn, King of Saudi Arabia (1926–1953), b. about 1880, d. 1953.

Saudi Arabia, formally proclaimed a Kingdom 1932.

Saumarez, James Saumarez, Baron de, British admiral, b. 1757, d. 1836.

Saunders, Sir Edwin, British pioneer in training in dentistry, b. 1814, d. 1901.

Saussure, Horace Benedict de, Swiss physicist and Alpinist, b. 1740, d. 1799.

Savage, Edward, American artist (*The Washington Family*), b. 1761, d. 1817.

Savage, Richard, English poet (*The Wanderer*, 1729), b. about 1697, d. 1743.

Savannah, first steam-propelled ship, crossed the Atlantic 1819.

Savary, Anne Jean Marie René, Duke of Rovigo, French general and diplomat, b. 1774, d. 1833.

Savery, Thomas, English military engineer and inventor, b. about 1650, d. 1715.

Savigny, Friedrich Karl von, German jurist (*Das Recht des Besitzes*, 1803), b. 1779, d. 1861.

Savile, Sir Henry, English classical scholar and philanthropist, b. 1549, d. 1622.

Savings Bank, first examples established by Priscilla Wakefield at Rotherham (1804) and by Henry Duncan at Ruthwell, Scotland (1810).

Savoy, elected by plebiscite to be annexed to France 1860 ; Dukes of Savoy ruled Sardinia from 1720 and Italy from 1860–1946.

Savonarola, Girolamo, Italian reformer, b. 1452, excommunicated 1497, executed 1498.

Saxaphone, invented 1846 by the Belgian musical instrument-maker Adolphe Sax, b. 1814, d. 1894.

Saxe, Maurice, Comte, Marshal of France, b. 1696, d. 1750.

Saxhorn, invented 1843–1845 by the Belgian musical instrument-maker Adolphe Sax, b. 1814, d. 1894.

Saxo-Grammaticus, Danish historian, b. about 1150, d. about 1205.

Saxton, Christopher, English map designer, lived in the late 16th century.

Say, Leon, French statesman, b. 1826, d. 1896.

Saye and Sele, William Fiennes, Viscount (‘ Old Subtlety ’), promotor of the colonisation of Providence Island, b. 1582, d. 1662.

Sayers, Tom, English pugilist, b. 1826, d. 1865.

Scævola, Quintus Mucius, Roman consul, murdered 82 B.C.

Scaliger, Joseph Justus, French scholar and critic, b. 1540, d. 1609.

Scaliger, Julius Cæsar, Italian-born philosopher and scientist, b. 1484, d. 1558.

Scapa Flow, Scotland, scene of the scuttling of the German battleships, 23 June 1919.

Scarlatti, Alessandro, Italian composer, b. 1659, d. 1725.

Scarlatti, Domenico, Italian composer, b. 1685, d. 1757.

Scarron, Paul, French writer (and husband of Mme de Maintenon), b. 1610, d. 1660.

Schacht, Hjalmar, German statesman and banker, b. 1877.

Schadow, Johann Gottfried, German sculptor (*Frederick the Great*), b. 1764, d. 1850.

Scharnhorst, Gerhard Johann David von, German general, b. 1755, d. 1813.

Scharnhorst, German battleship, sunk by the British Navy off North Cape 26 Dec. 1943.

Scharwenka, Xaver, German composer (*Meisterschule des Klavierspiels*), b. 1850, d. 1924.

Scheele, Carl Wilhelm, Swedish chemist, b. 1742, d. 1786.

Scheer, Admiral Reinhard, German Naval Chief, b. 1863, d. 1928.

Scheffer, Ary, Dutch-born painter (*Mignon*, 1836), b. 1795, d. 1858.

Schelling, Friedrich Wilhelm Joseph von, German philosopher, b. 1775, d. 1854.

Scherer, Wilhelm, German historian of language and literature, b. 1841, d. 1886.

Schiaparelli, Giovanni, Italian astronomer, b. 1835, d. 1910.

Schick Test, for immunity from diphtheria, discovered 1913 by the Hungarian-born scientist Bela Schick, b. 1877.

Schiller, Friedrich von, German writer (*Die Räuber*, 1782), b. 1759, d. 1805.

Schirmer, Gustav, German-born music publisher, b. 1829, d. 1893.

Schism, Great, between Western and Eastern Churches, complete 1054.

Schism of Photius, from which arose about 880 the Eastern Orthodox Church, occasioned by the actions of the Patriarch Photius, b. about 820, d. about 891.

Schism, Papal, 1378–1417.

Schlegel, August, German critic and writer, b. 1767, d. 1829.

Schlegel, Friedrich, German poet, b. 1772, d. 1829.

Schleswig-Holstein, under Danish rule 1460–1864, under Prussian rule from 1864.

Schlieffen, Alfred, Graf von, German soldier and strategist, b. 1833, d. 1913.

Schliemann, Heinrich, German excavator of Troy, b. 1822, d. 1890.

Schnabel, Artur, Austrian-born pianist, b. 1882, d. 1957.

Schnitger, Arp, German organ-builder, b. 1648, d. 1720.

Schnitzer, Eduard (Emir Pasha), German-born doctor and administrator in Turkey, Egypt and Central Africa, b. 1840, d. 1892.

Schnitzler, Arthur, Austrian writer (*Professor Bernhardi*, 1912), b. 1862, d. 1931.

Scholes, Percy, English musicologist, b. 1877, d. 1958.

Schomberg, Frederick Herman Schomberg, Duke of, German-born C.-in-C. of British forces in Ireland (1689–1690), b. 1615, killed in battle 1690.

Schomburgk, Richard, German-born botanist in Australia, b. 1811, d. 1890.

Schönberg, Arnold, Austrian-born composer (*Pierrot Lunaire*, 1912), b. 1874, d. 1951.

School of Musketry (Small Arms School), Hythe, England, opened 1853 ; to be closed 1963.

Schopenhauer, Arthur, German philosopher (*The World as Will and Idea*, 1819), b. 1788, d. 1860.

Schott, Bernhard, German music publisher, d. 1817.

Schreiner, Olive, South African writer (*Story of an African Farm*, 1883), b. 1859, d. 1922.

Schrödinger, Ermin, Austrian-born scientist, b. 1887, awarded the Nobel Prize (Physics) 1933.

Schubert, Franz, German composer (*Erlkönig*, 1815), b. 1797, d. 1828.

Schulz-Beuthen, Heinrich, German composer (*Aschenbrödel*, 1879), b. 1838, d. 1915.

Schumann, Clara (*née* Wieck), German pianist, b. 1819, d. 1896.

Schumann, Elizabeth, German-born operatic singer, b. 1891, d. 1952.

Schumann, Robert, German composer (*Carnaval*, 1834–1835), b. 1810, d. 1856.

Schuyler, General Philip John, American Revolutionary leader, b. 1733, d. 1804.

Schwann, Theodor, German physiologist, b. 1810, d. 1882.

Schwarzenburg, Felix, Austrian statesman, b. 1800, d. 1852.

Schweitzer, Dr Albert, Alsatian musician, theologian and medical missionary, b. 1875.

Scientist, term first introduced 1840 by the Master of Trinity College, Cambridge, William Whewell.

Scientific and Industrial Research, Department of, London, established 1916.

' Scinde Dawk ', first Indian postage stamp, issued 1 July 1852.

Scipio Africanus, Roman General, b. about 236, d. 183 B.C.

Scipio Africanus, the younger, Roman general, b. 185, d. 129 B.C.

Scipio, Quintus Cæcilius Metellus Pius, Roman consul and colonial administrator, committed suicide 46 B.C.

Scopas, Greek sculptor, lived in the 4th century B.C.

Scopes Trial, Dayton, Tennessee, held 1925.

Scoresby, William, English navigator in Arctic regions, b. 1760, d. 1829.

Scot, Michael, Scottish astronomer and alchemist, b. about 1175, d. about 1234.

Scotland, Crown united with that of England 1603 ; Kingdoms united 1707.

Scotland Yard, New, designed 1891 by the Scottish architect Richard Norman Shaw, b. 1831, d. 1912.

Scott, Charles Prestwich, English editor (of *Manchester Guardian*, 1872–1929) and politician, b. 1846, d. 1932.

Scott, Cyril, English composer (*Oboe Concerto*, 1948), b. 1879.

Scott, Robert Falcon, Antarctic explorer, b. 1868, d. 1912.

Scott, Sir Walter, Scottish poet and novelist (*Waverley*, 1814), b. 1771, d. 1832.

Scottish Labour Party, founded 1888 by the Scottish socialist Keir Hardie, b. 1856, d. 1915.

Scotus, Duns, Scottish philosopher, b. about 1266, d. 1308.

Screw-propeller, invented 1836 by the English inventor Sir Francis Pettit Smith, b. 1808, d. 1874.

Screw Threads, standardised 1841 by the English mechanical engineer Sir Joseph Whitworth, b. 1803, d. 1887.

Scriabin, Alexander Nikolaievich, Russian composer (*Poème Satanique*), b. 1872, d. 1915.

Scribe, Eugène, French playwright (*Valérie*, 1822), b. 1791, d. 1861.

Scribner, Charles, American publisher, b. 1821, d. 1871.

Scripps, Edward Wyllis, American newspaper publisher, b. 1854, d. 1926.

Scroggs, Sir William, Lord Chief Justice of England, b. about 1623, d. 1683.

Scrope, Richard le, Archbishop of York (1398–1405), b. about 1350, executed 1405.

Scudéry, Madeleine de, French writer (*Clélie*, 1654–1661), b. 1607, d. 1701.

Scurvy, fruit-juice first used against, in 1601 by Sir James Lancaster, d. 1620.

Scuttling, of German Grand Fleet 21 June 1919 ; of *Graf Spee*, 17 Dec. 1939.

' Sea Devil ' (Graf Felix von Luckner), German naval officer, b. 1886.

Sea Scouts, movement started in Britain 1908 ; adopted present name 1912.

Sea Serpent, sighted in the South Atlantic by the crew of H.M. corvette *Daedalus* 1843.

Seaplane, first invented 1911 by the American aviation pioneer and inventor Glenn Hammond Curtiss, b. 1878, d. 1930.

Searchlights, pioneer model invented 1763 by the Liverpool dockmaster William Hutchison, b. 1715, d. 1801.

Seaton, Edward Cator, English promoter of vaccination, b. 1815, d. 1880.

Seaweed Propagation, method discovered 1886 by the French botanists Edouard Bornet (1828–1911) and Gustave Adolphe Thuret (1817–1875).

Sebastian, King of Portugal (1557–1578), b. 1554, killed in battle 1578.

Sebastiano del Piombo, Italian painter (*Raising of Lazarus*), b. about 1485, d. 1547.

Sebright School, Worcestershire, English public school, founded by William Sebright, Town Clerk of London 1620.

Secondary Education, free in Great Britain since 1944.

Secularism, founded 1846 by the English co-operator George Jacob Holyoake, b. 1817, d. 1906.

Sedan, Battle of, between the Germans and the French, 1 Sep. 1870 ; German break-through at, May 1940.

Sedburgh School, English public school, founded 1525 by the Provost of Eton, Dr Roger Lupton, d. 1540.

Seddon, Frederick Henry, English murderer, b. 1870, hanged 1912.

Sedgemoor, Battle of, between King James II and the Duke of Monmouth 6 July 1685.

Sedgwick, Rev. Adam, English geologist, b. 1785, d. 1873.

Sedgwick, Robert, Major-General of Massachusetts forces, d. 1656.

Sedley, Sir Charles, English writer (*Bellamira*, 1687), b. about 1639, d. 1701.

Seed Drill, invented 1731 by the English agricultural writer Jethro Tull, b. 1674, d. 1741.

Seed Testing, scientific method originated 1869 by the German plant physiologist Friedrich Nobbe, b. 1830, d. 1922.

Seeley, Sir John Robert, English writer (*Ecce Homo*, 1865), b. 1834, d. 1895.

Segovia, Andrès, Spanish guitarist, b. 1893.

Seiber, Mátyás, composer (*Ulysses*, 1949), b. 1905, d. 1960

Seguier, William, English artist and first Keeper of the National Gallery, b. 1771, d. 1843.

Seignobos, Charles, French historian, b. 1854, d. 1942.

Seismograph, earth tremor reader, invented by the Chinese Chang Heng 132.

Seismic Exploration Method, of discovering petroleum, introduced by the Royal Dutch Shell Group in Mexico 1922.

Seismic Reflection Method, of discovering petroleum, introduced by the Royal Dutch Shell Group in Texas 1932.

Sejanus, Lucius Aelius, Roman prefect, murdered 31.

Selborne, Roundell Palmer, Earl of, Lord Chancellor, b. 1812, d. 1895.

Selby, William, English-born organist and composer, b. 1738, d. 1798.

Selden, John, English jurist (*Table Talk*, 1689), b. 1584, d. 1654.

Selenium, discovered 1817 by the Swedish chemist Baron Berzelius, b. 1779, d. 1848.

Selenous Acid, first obtained 1827 by the German chemist Eilhard Mitscherlich, b. 1794, d. 1863.

Seleucid Dynasty, ruled Syria 312–64 B.C.

Seleucid Era, began 1 Sept. 311 B.C.

Seleucus I, Middle Eastern ruler, b. about 356, assassinated 281 B.C.

Seleucus II, Middle Eastern ruler (246–227 B.C.), d. 227 B.C.

Seleucus III, Middle Eastern ruler (227–223 B.C.), assassinated 223 B.C.

Seleucus IV, Middle Eastern ruler (187–176 B.C.), assassinated 176 B.C.

Seleucus V, Middle Eastern ruler (126 B.C.), assassinated 126 B.C.

Seleucus VI, Middle Eastern ruler (96–95 B.C.), assassinated 95 B.C.

Self-starter, for automobiles, invented 1911 by the inventor Charles Franklin Kettering, b. 1876, d. 1958.

Selfridge's, Oxford Street department store, London, opened 15 Mar. 1909. Founded by the American merchant Gordon Selfridge, b. 1858, d. 1947.

Selim I, Sultan of Turkey (1512–1521), b. 1465, d. 1521.

Selim II, Sultan of Turkey (1566–1574), b. 1524, d. 1574.

Selim III, Sultan of Turkey (1789–1808), b. 1762, strangled 1808.

Seljuk (or Jalalian) **Era,** began 15 Mar. 1079.

Selkirk, Alexander, the real ' Robinson Crusoe ', b. 1676, d. 1721.

Selous, Frederick Courteney, English explorer, b. 1851, killed 1917.

Selwyn, George Augustus, first Bishop of New Zealand (1842–1867), b. 1809, d. 1878.

Selwyn College, Cambridge University, founded in memory of Bishop George Augustus Selwyn 1882.

Semaphore Signalling, system pioneered 1666 by Lord Worcester ; developed 1792 by Claude Chappé and 1796 by Lord George Murray ; perfected 1803 by Admiral Home Riggs Popham.

Semmelweiss, Ignatz Philipp, Hungarian discoverer of antisepsis, b. 1816, d. 1865.

Semmering Pass, the Alps, railway constructed 1848–1854.

Sempill, Robert, Scottish poet (*Life and Death of Habbie Simpson*, 1640), b. about 1595, d. about 1665.

Senancour, Etienne Pivert de, French writer (*Obermann*, 1804), b. 1770, d. 1846.

Seneca, Roman orator, b. about 54 B.C., d. A.D. 39.

Seneca, Roman philosopher, b. about 4 B.C., committed suicide A.D. 65.

Senefelder, Alois, German inventor 1798 of lithography, b. 1771, d. 1834.

Senior, Nassau William, English economist, b. 1790, d. 1864.

Senlac, Battle of (Battle of Hastings), between the Normans and the English Oct. 1066.

Sennacherib, King of Assyria (705–681 B.C.), murdered 681 B.C.

Sensory and Motor Nerves, distinguished 1807 by Sir Charles Bell, b. 1774, d. 1842.

September, ninth month of the year.

Septuagint, Greek version of the Old Testament believed to have been made 270 B.C.

Sequoyah, American Indian leader of the Cherokee nation, b. about 1770, d. 1843.

Serapeum, Ruins of, discovered 1850 by the French Egyptologist Auguste Ferdinand François Mariette, b. 1821, d. 1881.

Serbia, ruled by Turks 1459–1829 ; occupied by Austrians 1915–1918 ; part of Yugoslavia since 1918.

Serfs, emancipated in Prussia 1807 ; liberated from Imperial Russian domination 1861.

Sergius I, St, Pope 687–701.

Sergius II, Pope 844–847.

Sergius III, Pope 904–911.

Sergius IV, Pope 1009–1012.

Serra, Junípero, Spanish missionary in California, b. 1713, d. 1784.

Sertorius, Quintus, Roman general and administrator in Spain, assassinated 72 B.C.

Servetus, Michael (Miguel Serveto), Spanish theologian, b. 1511, burnt at the stake 1553.

Service, Robert William, English-born writer (*Songs of a Sourdough*, 1907), b. 1876, d. 1958.

Servile Wars, Sicily 103–101 B.C. ; Italy 73–71 B.C.

Sesostris I, King of Egypt (1980–1933 B.C.), d. 1933 B.C.

Sesostris II, King of Egypt (1906–1887 B.C.), d. 1887 B.C.

Sesostris III, King of Egypt (1887–1849 B.C.), d. 1849 B.C.

Sesshu, Japanese painter, b. 1421, d. 1507.

Sessions, Roger, American composer (*Montezuma*, 1947), b. 1896.

Seth, Andrew, Scottish philosopher, b. 1856, d. 1931.

Seti I, King of Egypt (1313–1292 B.C.) d. 1292 B.C.

Seti II, King of Egypt (1209–1205 B.C.), d. 1205 B.C.

Seton, Ernest Thompson, English-born writer and artist, b. 1860, d. 1946.

Settle, Elkanah, English poet and playwright (*The Empress of Morocco*, 1671), b. 1648, d. 1724.

Seurat, Georges, French pointilliste painter (*Une Baignade*, 1884), b. 1859, d. 1891.

Seven Days' Battles, near Richmond, Virginia, American Civil War 26 June to 2 July 1862.

Seven Sleepers of Ephesus, allegedly slept from 247 to 447.

Seven Weeks' War, between Prussia and Austria (and her allies), 1866.

Seven Years' War, between Prussia (and England) and the Allies, 1756–1763.

Sevenoaks School, English public school, founded 1432 by the Lord Mayor of London Sir William Sevenoke, b. about 1378, d. about 1433.

Seventeen Year Locust, a cicada whose development from egg to adult needs seventeen years.

Sévérac, Déodat de, French composer (*Le Parc aux cerfs*), b. 1873, d. 1921.

Severinus, Pope 640.

Severn, Joseph, English painter (*Spectre Ship*), b. 1793, d. 1879.

Severn Tunnel, England, construction begun 1873 ; completed 1886.

Severus, Roman Emperor (193–211), b. 146, d. in Britain 211.

Severus, Roman Emperor (306–307), d. 307.

Sévigné, Marquise de, French writer (*Lettres*), b. 1626, d. 1696.

Seward, Anna, *The Swan of Litchfield*, English poet and letter-writer, b. 1747, d. 1809.

Sewell, Anne, English writer (*Black Beauty*, 1877), b. 1820, d. 1878.

Sewing Machine, models patented by Charles Weisenthal (1755) and Thomas Saint (1790) ; Thimonnier produced a machine (1830) ; models patented by Newton and Archbold (1841) ; Singer used Howe's needle for his model (1850).

Sextant, invented 1731 by the Englishman John Hadley, b. 1682, d. 1744.

Seychelles, Indian Ocean, probably discovered by the Portuguese about 1500 ; annexed by France 1744 ; ceded to Britain 1814.

Seymour, Edward, the Protector, Earl of Hertford and Duke of Somerset, b. about 1506, beheaded 1552.

Seymour of Sudeley, Thomas Seymour, Baron, Lord High Admiral, b. about 1508, executed 1549.

Sforza, Francesco, Duke of Milan, b. 1401, d. 1466.

Shackleton, Sir Ernest, Antarctic explorer, b. 1874, d. 1922.

Shadwell, Thomas, English writer (*Bury Fair*, 1689), b. about 1642, d. 1692.

Shaftesbury, Anthony Ashley Cooper, 1st Earl of, English politician, b. 1621, d. 1683.

Shaftesbury, Anthony Ashley Cooper, 3rd Earl of, English philosopher, b. 1671, d. 1713.

Shaftesbury, Antony Ashley Cooper, 7th Earl of, English philanthropist, b. 1801, d. 1885.

Shah Jehan, Mogul Emperor of Delhi (1627–1658), and builder of the Taj Mahal, d. 1666.

Shakers, Society of, religious movement, seceded from Quakers 1747 under James and Jane Wardley ; first settlement in America founded 1776 by Ann Lee, b. 1736, d. 1784.

Shakespeare, William, English dramatist, b. 1564, d. 1616.

Shakespeare Memorial Theatre, new building opened at Stratford-on-Avon 23 Apr. 1932.

Shang Yin Dynasty, China, 1766 to 1122 B.C.

Shannon, Charles, English artist (*The Toilet of Venus*), b. 1865, d. 1937.

Sharp, Cecil James, English collector of English folk songs and dances, b. 1859, d. 1924.

Sharp, Granvillle, English anti-slavery pioneer, b. 1735, d. 1813.

Sharp, William (' Fiona Macleod ') Scottish novelist (*The Immortal Hour*, 1900), b. 1855, d. 1905.

Sharpe, Daniel, English geologist, b. 1806, d. 1856.

Shaw, George Bernard, Irish-born playwright (*Man and Superman*, 1903), b. 1856, d. 1950.

Shaw, Martin, English composer (*Mr Pepys*, 1926), b. 1876, d. 1958.

Shaw, Richard Norman, Scottish architect, b. 1831, d. 1912.

Shchedrin, Nikolai Evgrafovich (' M. E. Saltykov '), Russian writer (*The Golovlyov Family*, 1876), b. 1826, d. 1889.

Shearer, Moira, Scottish ballerina, b. 1926.

Shee, Sir Martin Archer, Irish painter (*Prospero and Miranda*), b. 1770, d. 1850.

Shee, Sir William, first British Roman Catholic judge since the Revolution, b. 1804, d. 1868.

Sheffield University, founded 1879 as Firth College by the English manufacturer Mark Firth (1819–1880;) constituted a University College 1897; achieved University status 1905.

Sheldonian Theatre, Oxford, built 1669 by the Archbishop of Canterbury, Gilbert Sheldon, b. 1598, d. 1677.

Shelley, Mary Wollstonecraft, English writer (*Frankenstein*, 1818), b. 1797, d. 1851.

Shelley, Percy Bysshe, English poet (*Queen Mab*, 1813), b. 1792, drowned at sea 1822.

Shenstone, William, English poet (*The Schoolmistress*, 1742), b. 1714, d. 1763.

Sheppard, Jack, English highwayman, b. 1702, hanged 1724.

Sheraton, Thomas, English cabinet-maker, b. 1751, d. 1806.

Sherborne School, English public school, origins (probably 8th century) uncertain, refounded by King Edward VI 1550.

Sheridan, Richard Brinsley, Irish play-wright (*School for Scandal*, 1776), b. 1751, d. 1816.

Sherman, General William Tecumseh, American general (march to the sea, Nov.–Dec. 1864), b. 1820, d. 1891.

Sherriff, Robert Cedric, English-born dramatist (*Journey's End*, 1928), b. 1896.

Sherrington, Sir Charles, British physiologist, b. 1859, d. 1952.

Sherwood, Robert Emmet, American playwright (*The Petrified Forest*), b. 1896, d. 1955.

Shields, Alexander, Scottish Coven-anter, b. about 1660, d. 1700.

Shi'a, Islamic religious movement, founded about 658.

Shiloh, Battle of, American Civil War, 6–7 April 1862.

Ship, First gas-turbine propelled (H.M.S. *Grey Goose*), fitted with two Rolls-Royce RM 60 engines 1955.

Ship, First guided-missile (H.M.S. *Girdle Ness*), commissioned 1956.

Ship, First ocean-going iron (*The Great Britain*), built 1843 by the British engineer Isambard Brunel, b. 1806, d. 1859.

Ship, First steam-propelled (*Savannah*), crossed the Atlantic 1819.

Ship, First turbine-propelled (*Turbinia*), invented 1897 by the British engineer Sir Charles Parsons, b. 1854, d. 1931.

Ship Money, first levied in England 1007. Also levied, without Parliament's consent, by King Charles I, 1634–1636.

Shipton, Mother, English witch and prophet, reputed to have been born about 1487 as Ursula Southill, and to have died 1561.

Shirley, Sir Anthony, English adven-turer, b. 1565, d. about 1635.

Shirley, James, English playwright (*The Traitor*, 1631), b. 1596, d. 1666.

' **Sholem Aleichem** ' (see ' Aleichem, Sholem ').

Shore, Jane, mistress of King Edward IV, d. about 1527.

Shore, John, King's Trumpeter in Ordinary, b. 1662, d. 1752.

Short, James, optician and astronomer, b. 1710, d. 1768.

Shorthand, First, with signs, invented 1588 by the Englishman Dr Timothy Bright, b. 1551, d. 1615.

Shorthouse, Joseph Henry, English novelist (*John Inglesant*, 1881), b. 1834, d. 1903.

Shostakovich, Dmitri, Russian com-poser (*Lady Macbeth of Mzensk*, 1934), b. 1906.

Shrewsbury, Treaty of, recognising Llewelyn II's overlordship of Wales, signed 1265.

Shrewsbury School, English public school, founded by King Edward VI 1552 ; refounded by Queen Elizabeth 1571.

Shrove Tuesday, first day of Lent, and the day before Ash Wednesday.

' **Shute,** Nevil ' (Nevil Shute Norway), novelist (*A Town Like Alice*, 1949), b. 1899, d. 1960.

Siam, absolute monarchy until 1932 ; constitutional monarchy 1932–1951 ; reversion to 1932 constitution effected 1951.

Sibelius, Jean, Finnish composer (*Finlandia*, 1899), b. 1865, d. 1957.

Siberch, John, of Siegburg, set up the first printing press in Cambridge 1521.

Sicilian Vespers, massacre of French residents in Sicily, 31 Mar. 1282.

Sicily, conquered by Arabs in 8th century, by Normans in 11th century ; ruled by Aragonese 1301–1713, by Bourbons 1735–1860.

Sickert, Walter Richard, German-born painter (*Victor Lecour*, 1922), b. 1860, d. 1942.

Siddons, Mrs Sarah, English actress, b. 1755, d. 1831.

Sidgwick, Henry, English philosopher and champion of the admission of women to universities, b. 1838, d. 1900.

Sidmouth, Henry Addington, Viscount, statesman, b. 1757, d. 1844.

Sidney, Algernon, English democrat, b. 1622, executed 1683.

Sidney, Sir Philip, English writer (*Defence of Poesie*, 1591) and soldier, b. 1554, killed 1586.

Sidney Sussex College, Cambridge University, founded under the will of the Lady Frances Sidney, Countess Dowager of Sussex, 1596.

Siebold, Philipp Franz von, German ethnographer and naturalist (particularly with regard to Japan), b. 1796, d. 1866.

Siegen, Ludwig von, Dutch-born engraver and inventor (1642) of the mezzotint process, b. about 1609, d. 1680.

Siemens, Ernst Werner von, German electrical engineer, b. 1816, d. 1892.

Siemens, Sir William, German-born electrical engineer, b. 1823, d. 1883.

Siena, University of, founded 1247.

Sienkiewicz, Henryk, Polish novelist (*Quo Vadis ?*, 1896), b. 1846, d. 1916.

Sierra Leone, earliest English settlement 1787 ; crown colony 1808–1960.

Sièyes, Emmanuel Joseph, French statesman, b. 1748, d. 1836.

Sigebert, King of the Franks, assassinated 575.

Sigismund, Holy Roman Emperor (1433–1437), b. 1368, d. 1437.

Sigismund I, King of Poland (1506–1548), b. 1467, d. 1548.

Sigismund II, King of Poland (1548–1572), b. 1520, d. 1572.

Sigismund III, King of Poland (1587–1632), b. 1566, d. 1632.

Sign Language, for deaf and dumb people, developed 1765 by the French priest Charles Michel, Abbe de l'Epée, b. 1712, d. 1789.

Signac, Paul, French painter (*Le Pont des Arts*, 1914), b. 1863, d. 1935.

Signorelli, Luca, Italian painter (*Eternal Destiny of Man*), b. about 1442, d. 1523.

Sigurdsson, Jon, Icelandic statesman, b. 1811, d. 1879.

Sikh Religion, founded by the Indian religious leader Nanak, b. 1469, d. 1538.

Sikh War, First, India, between the British and the Sikhs, 1845–1846.

Sikh War, Second, India, between the British and the Sikhs, 1848–1849.

Sikkim, Protectorate of the Government of India, officially brought under British protection 1890.

Sikorsky, Igor Ivan, Russian-born inventor of the helicopter, b. 1889.

Silesia, a Bohemian fief 1335–1740 ; Prussian 1740–1871 ; German 1871–1945 ; Polish since 1945.

Silesian Wars, between Prussia and Austria, 1740–1742, 1744–1745 and 1756–1762.

Silicones, study developed 1899–1941 by the English chemist Frederick S. Kipping (1863–1949) ; practical applications discovered 1941 by J. F. Hyde.

Silk, traditionally invented 2640 B.C. ; silkworms brought to Constantinople about A.D. 550 ; first silk mill in U.S.A. established 1839.

Silk, Artificial, made 1883 by the English electro-chemist Sir Joseph Wilson Swan (1828–1914). Industry founded about 1885 by the French scientist Hilaire, Comte de Chardonnet (1839–1924).

Silurian Period, Earth history, 350 million years ago.

' Silurist, The ' (Henry Vaughan), poet, b. 1622, d. 1695.

Silverius, St, Pope 536–537.

Silvester I, St, Pope 314–336.

Silvester II (Gerbert), Pope 999–1003.

Silvester III, Pope 1045.

Silvester IV, Anti-Pope 1105.

Silvestrians, monastic order founded by St Silvester, d. 1267.

Simeon I, Tsar of Bulgaria, reigned 893–927.

Simeon II, Tsar of Bulgaria (1943–1946), b. 1937.

Simeon Stylites, St, b. 387, d. 459.

Simhath Torah (Rejoicing of the Law), Jewish holiday, 23rd day of Tishri.

Simnel, Lambert, pretender, b. about 1475, d. after 1525.

Simon, Sir John, British public health pioneer, b. 1816, d. 1904.

Simon, John, Viscount, British lawyer and statesman, b. 1873, d. 1954.

Simon de Montfort, English baronial leader, b. about 1208, killed in battle 1265.

Simplicius, Pope 468–483.

Simplon Pass, over the Alps, built 1800–1807 ; Tunnel built 1898–1906.

Simpson, Maxwell, British chemist, b. 1815, d. 1902.

Simson, William, Scottish painter (*Solway Moss-Sunset*, 1831), b. 1800, d. 1847.

Sinclair, Upton, American novelist (*Boston*, 1928), b. 1878.

Sind War, between British and Baluchi forces, Mar. 1843.

Sinding, Christian, Norwegian composer (*Rustle of Spring*), b. 1856, d. 1941.

Singapore, founded 1819 by the British administrator Sir Stamford Raffles (1781–1826) ; held by Japanese 1942–1945 ; independent State within the Commonwealth since 1959.

Sinigaglia, Leone, Italian composer (*Danze Piemontese*), b. 1868, d. 1944.

Sinn Fein, political party, founded 1905 by the Irish patriot Arthur Griffith, b. 1872, d. 1922.

Siphon, principle discovered 1577 by the Scottish mathematician William Welwood, d. after 1622.

Sirisius, St, Pope 384–399.

Sisinnius, Pope 708.

Sisley, Alfred, French painter (*Le Canal du Loing*), b. 1839, d. 1899.

Sleeping-cars, Railway, invented about 1864 by the American financier George Mortimer Pullman, b. 1831, d. 1897.

Sismondi, Jean Charles Leonard de, Swiss-born economist and historian, b. 1773, d. 1842.

Sitting Bull, American Indian chief, b. about 1837, killed 1890.

Sitwell, Dame Edith, English writer (*Bath*, 1932), b. 1887.

Sitwell, Sir Osbert, English writer (*Miracle on Sinai*, 1933), b. 1892.

Sitwell, Sacheverell, English writer (*Southern Baroque Art*, 1924), b. 1897.

Siward the Strong, Earl of Northumberland, d. 1055.

Six-shooter Automatic, invented 1836 by the American inventor Samuel Colt, b. 1814, d. 1862.

Sixtus I, St, Pope 115–125.

Sixtus II, St, Pope 257–258, martyred 258.

Sixtus III, St, Pope 432–440.

Sixtus IV, (Francesco della Rovere), Pope 1471–1484, b. 1414, d. 1484.

Sixtus V (Felice Peretti), Pope 1585–1590, b. 1521, d. 1590.

Skanderbeg (Iskander Bey or George Castriota), Albanian leader, b. about 1403, d. 1468.

Skeat, Walter William, English philologist, b. 1835, d. 1912.

Skelton, John, English poet (*Phyllyp Sparowe*, 1542–1546), b. about 1460, d. 1529.

Skinners Company, London livery company, founded in the 12th century ; first Charter granted by King Edward III 1327.

Skyscraper, First, erected in Chicago 1884–1885 ; designed by the American architect William Le Baron Jenney, b. 1832, d. 1907.

Skywriting, in England, first done 1922 over Epsom Downs by the British aviator J. C. Savage.

Slater, Oscar (Leschziner), German-born victim of wrongful imprisonment (1909–1928) for murder, b. about 1872, d. 1948.

Slave Trade, British, abolished 1805–1807.

Slavery, declared illegal in Britain 1772 ; abolished in British possessions 1834 ; in French possessions 1848 ; in the U.S.A. 1863.

Slaves, First negro, introduced into an English colony, landed at Virginia 1620.

Slimming, by the elimination of starch in diet, made popular by the English undertaker William Banting, b. 1797, d. 1878.

Sloane, Sir Hans, Irish-born physician, b. 1660, d. 1753.

Slocum, Henry Warner, American soldier and politician, b. 1827, d. 1894.

Sluter, Claus, Dutch sculptor (*Well of Moses*), d. 1406.

Small Arms School (School of Musketry), Hythe, England, opened 1853, to be closed 1963.

Smart, Christopher, English poet (*Song to David*, 1763), b. 1722, d. 1771.

Smeaton, John, English civil engineer and designer 1759 of the Eddystone Lighthouse, b. 1724, d. 1792.

Smedley, Francis Edward, English novelist (*Frank Fairlegh*, 1850), b. 1818, d. 1864.

Smetana, Bedrich, Bohemian composer (*The Bartered Bride*, 1866), b. 1824, d. 1884.

Smiles, Samuel, Scottish writer (*Self-help*, 1859), b. 1812, d. 1904.

Smirke, Sir Robert, English architect (The British Museum), b. 1781, d. 1867.

Smith, Adam, Scottish economist (*The Wealth of Nations*, 1776), b. 1723, d. 1790.

Smith, Bernard, German-born, organ builder, b. about 1630, d. 1708.

Smith, Sir Francis Pettit, English inventor, b. 1808, d. 1874.

Smith, George Joseph, English murderer (The Brides in the Bath), b. 1872, hanged 1915.

Smith, Joseph, American founder 1827 of the Mormon Church, b. 1805, murdered 1844.

Smith, Stephenson Percy, English-born authority on the Maoris, b. 1840, d. 1922.

Smith, Sydney, British divine, journalist and wit, b. 1771, d. 1845.

Smith, William, ' father of British geology ', b. 1769, d. 1839.

Smithsonian Institution, Washington, D.C., established 1846, through the endowment of the French-born scientist James Smithson, b. 1765, d. 1829.

Smoke Abatement, first attempted in London 1306.

Smolensk, Battle of, between the French and the Russians 16–17 Aug. 1812.

Smollett, Tobias, Scottish novelist (*Roderick Random*, 1748), b. 1721, d. 1771.

Smuts, Jan Christiaan, South African statesman (Prime Minister 1919–1924, 1939–1948), b. 1870, d. 1950.

Smybert, John, Scottish-born artist (*Bishop Berkeley and his Family*, 1731), b. 1688, d. 1751.

Smyth, Dame Ethel, English composer (*The Wreckers*, 1909), b. 1858, d. 1944.

Smyth, James Carmichael, Royal physician and fever expert, b. 1741, d. 1821.

Smyth, Sir James Carmichael, British colonial administrator and abolitionist, b. 1779, d. 1838.

Snorri Sturlason, Icelandic historian (*Heimskringla*), b. 1179, killed 1241.

Snow, Sir Charles Percy, English scientist and writer (*The Masters*, 1951), b. 1905.

Snow, John, British anæsthetist, b. 1813, d. 1858.

Snowden, Philip, Viscount Snowden, British statesman, b. 1864, d. 1937.

Snowdonia, first British national park, founded by gift of 300 acres near Snowdon to the National Trust 21 Jan. 1935.

Snyders, Frans, Flemish painter (*Stag-Hunt*), b. 1579, d. 1657.

Soane, Sir John, English architect, b. 1753, d. 1837.

Soap Opera, originated in Chicago about 1928.

Soap Tax, imposed in England 1712 ; abolished 1853.

Sobieski, John (John III), King of Poland (1674–1696), b. 1624, d. 1696.

Social Insurance, first begun in Germany 1883 ; begun in Britain 1911 ; Beveridge Report on Social Security 1942 ; system reorganised 1946.

Social Democratic Foundation, founded as Democratic Foundation 1881.

Socialist League, founded by seceders from S.D.F. in 1884.

Socialist Parties (Founded) : Germany 1869 ; France (several) 1870's and 1880's ; Portugal 1875 ; Denmark 1878 ; Spain 1879 ; Belgium 1885 ; Holland and Switzerland 1888 ; Sweden 1889 ; Norway 1890 ; Italy 1892 ; Russia 1898 ; Finland 1899. In England, Labour Representation Committee formed 1900, became Labour Party 1906 ; Socialist Labour Party formed 1903, became Socialist Party of Great Britain 1904.

Society for the Prevention of Cruelty to Animals, Royal, founded London 1824.

Society for the Prevention of Cruelty to Children, U.S.A. founded 1874 by the American lawyer Elbridge Thomas Gerry, b. 1837, d. 1927.

Society for the Prevention of Cruelty to Children, National, founded London 1884.

Society for Promoting Christian Knowledge, founded 1698 by the English philanthropist Dr Thomas Bray, b. 1656, d. 1730.

Society for Propagating the Gospel in Foreign Parts, London, founded 1701.

Society for Psychical Research, London, founded 1882.

Society of Antiquaries, London, founded 1707, reconstituted 1717, granted Royal Charter 1751.

Society of Friends (Quakers), founded 1647 by the George Fox, b. 1624, d. 1690.

Society of Indexers, London, founded by G. Norman Knight 1957.

Society Islands, Polynesia, discovered 1607 by the Portuguese explorer Pedro Fernandez de Queiros (1560–1614).

Socotra, island in the Aden Protectorate, ceded to Britain 1878 ; formally annexed 1886.

Socrates, Greek philosopher, b. about 470, condemned to death 399 B.C.

Soddy, Frederick, English scientist, b. 1877, d. 1956.

Sodium, discovered 1807 by the English scientist Sir Humphry Davy, b. 1778, d. 1829.

Sodoma, Giovanni, Italian painter (*Christ Scourged*), b. 1477, d. 1549.

Sol-fa, Tonic, invented about 1845 by the English musician Sarah Ann Glover, b. 1785, d. 1867.

Solar Compass, invented 1836 by the American William Austin Burt, b. 1792, d. 1858.

Solar Parallax, deduced 1639 by the English astronomer Jeremiah Horrocks, b. about 1617, d. 1641.

Solar Year, length determined by the Greek astronomer Hipparchus, *fl.* 160–125 B.C.

Solari, Cristoforo, Italian sculptor (tomb of Beatrice d'Este), d. about 1525.

Solferino, Battle of, between the French and the Sardinians and Austrians, 24 June 1859.

Solid Fuel Injection Principle, invented 1890 by the English engineer Herbert Ackroyd-Stuart.

Solihull School, English public school, origins uncertain, first recorded mention 1560.

'**Sologub,** Feodor ' (Feodor Kuzmich Teternikov), Russian writer, b. 1863, d. 1927.

Solomon Islands, discovered 1568 by the Spanish navigator Alvaro de Mendaña ; British protectorate established 1893–1899.

Solstice, Summer, longest day, 21 or 22 June, according to the year.

Solstice, Winter, shortest day, 21 or 22 Dec., according to the year.

Solvay Process, ammonia-soda process for making sodium carbonate, invented 1863 by the Belgian industrial chemist Ernest Solvay, b. 1838, d. 1922.

Somalia, Italian protectorate 1899–1941 ; British military administration 1941–1949 ; UN trusteeship 1950–1960 ; granted independence 1960.

Somaliland, British, British protectorate established 1887 ; achieved independence 1960.

Somaliland, French, overseas territory of the French Republic, acquired by the French government between 1856 and 1883.

Somaliland, Italian, see **Somalia** above.

Somers, Sir George, English discoverer 1609 of the Bermudas, b. 1554, d. 1610.

Somerset, Edward Seymour, Duke of (The Protector), b. about 1506, beheaded 1552.

Somerset, Robert Carr, Earl of, Scottish politician, b. 1590, d. 1645.

Somerville, Mary, British scientist, b. 1780, d. 1872.

Somerville, William, English poet (*The Chase*, 1735), b. 1675, d. 1742.

Somerville College, Oxford University, founded 1879.

Somme, Battle of the, World War I, 24–25 Sept. 1914 and July–Oct. 1916.

Sontag, Henriette, German operatic singer, b. 1806, d. 1854.

Sontius, River, scene of the battle between Theodoric, King of the Ostrogoths and Odoacer 15 Mar. 496.

Sophia, Electress of Hanover, b. 1630, d. 1714.

Sophia Alekseievna, Regent of Russia (1682–1689), b. 1657, d. 1704.

Sophia Charlotte, Queen of Prussia, b. 1668, d. 1705.

Sophia Dorothea, Electress of Hanover, b. 1666, d. 1726.

Sophocles, Greek playwright (*Œdipus Coloneus*), b. about 496, d. about 405 B.C.

Sophonisba, Queen of Numidia, d.

Sopwith, Sir Thomas Octave, British pioneer aviator, b. 1888.

Soqotra, island in the Aden Protectorate, ceded to Britain 1878 ; formally annexed 1886.

Sorabji, Cornelia, Indian barrister, b. 1866, d. 1954.

Sorbonne, Paris, founded 1253 by the French priest Robert de Sorbon, b. 1201, d. 1274.

Sordello, Italian troubadour, lived in the 13th century, b. about 1422.

Sorel, Agnes, mistress of King Charles VII of France, d. 1450.

Sorel, Georges, French political theorist (*Réflexions sur la Violence*, 1908), b. 1847, d. 1922.

Sorolla y Bastida, Joaquin, Spanish painter (*King Alfonso*), b. 1863, d. 1923.

Sotatsu, Japanese painter (*Matsushima*), b. 1576, d. 1643.

Soter, Pope 166–175.

Sotheby's, London auction rooms, founded by Samuel Baker 1744.

Soufflot, Jacques Germaine, French architect, b. 1709, d. 1780.

Soule, Pierre, French-born American diplomat and statesman, b. 1802, d. 1870.

Soult, Nicolas Jean de Dieu, statesman and Marshal of France, b. 1769, d. 1851.

Sousa, John Philip, American composer (*El Capitan*, 1896), b. 1854, d. 1932.

Sound Recording, first done by machine 1876 (Edison's phonograph) ; first gramophone disk made 1887 by Berliner.

South, Sir James, English astronomer, b. 1785, d. 1867.

South, Robert, English Court preacher, b. 1634, d. 1716.

South Africa, Union of, came into being 31 May 1910 ; achieved independence 1961.

South Australia, formed into a British province 1836.

South Carolina, discovered 1497 by John Cabot ; settled permanently 1670 ; re-admitted to the Union 1868.

South Dakota, first reached 1742 by

South-East Asia Collective Defence Treaty, signed at Manila 8 Sept. 1954.

South Pole, first reached 14 Dec. 1911 by the Norwegian explorer Roald Amundsen, b. 1872, d. 1928.

South Sea Bubble : South Sea Company incorporated 1711 ; financial collapse 1720 ; fraud exposed 1721.

South-West Africa, annexed by Germany 1884 ; League of Nations mandated territory administered by the Union of South Africa 1920 onwards.

Southampton, Henry Wriothesley, Earl of, patron of William Shakespeare, b. 1573, d. 1624.

Southampton, Thomas Wriothesley, Earl of, statesman, b. 1505, d. 1550.

Southampton University, founded 1902 ; achieved university status 1952.

Southcott, Joanna, English self-styled prophet, b. 1750, d. 1814.

Southern Rhodesia, administered by the British South Africa Company until 1923 ; formally annexed to H.M. Dominions 1923 ; federated with North Rhodesia and Nyasaland 1953.

Southerne, Thomas, Irish-born playwright (*Oroonoko*, 1696), b. 1660, d. 1746.

Southey, Robert, English poet (*Joan of Arc*, 1796), b. 1774, d. 1843.

Southwell, Robert, English poet and Jesuit martyr, b. about 1561, hanged 1595.

Southwood, Julius Salter Elias, Viscount, British newspaper publisher, b. 1873, d. 1946.

Souvestre, Emile, French novelist (*Derniers Bretons*, 1835–1837), b. 1806, d. 1854.

Soviet Republic, proclaimed 21 Mar. 1919.

Soyer, Alexis, Reform Club chef, b. 1809, d. 1858.

Space-time Concept, first mooted by the Dutch scientist Hendrik Antoon Lorentz, b. 1853, d. 1928.

Spain, Muslim invasion 711 ; last Muslims expelled 1492 ; ruled by Hapsburgs 1516–1700, by Bourbons 1700–1808, 1814–1870, 1874–1931 ;

republics 1873–1874, 1931–1939 ; dictatorship of Primo de Rivera 1923–1930, of Franco since 1939.

Spangenberg, Bishop August Gottlieb, founder of the Moravian Church in America, b. 1704, d. 1792.

Spanish Armada, assembled 1587 ; defeated by the English 29 July 1588.

Spanish Civil War, began 16 July 1936 ; ended 31 Mar. 1939.

Spanish Guinea, settled by the Spanish at the end of the 18th century.

Spartacus, leader of the Roman slaves, killed in battle 71 B.C.

Speaker of the House of Commons, post instituted 1377.

Specific Gravity, principle discovered by the Greek scientist Archimedes, b. 287, d. 212 B.C.

Spectacles, known in Europe in 14th century ; use common in 15th.

Spectator, The, British periodical, 1711–1712, edited by the English writer Joseph Addison (1672–1719) and Sir Richard Steele (1672–1729) ; British periodical, founded 1828 by Robert Rintoul, b. 1787, d. 1858.

Spectrograph, invented 1919 by the English experimental physicist Francis William Aston, b. 1877, d. 1945.

Spectroheliograph, for photographing the sun, invented 1910 by the American astronomer George Ellery Hale, b. 1868, d. 1938.

Spectrum, of sunlight, discovered 1666 by Sir Isaac Newton, b. 1642, d. 1727.

Spectrum Analysis, originated 1859 by the German scientist Robert Wilhelm Bunsen (1811–1899) and Gustav Robert Kirchhoff (1824–1887).

Spee, Maximilian, Graf von, German naval commander, b. 1861, died in a naval battle 1914.

Speed, John, English map-maker, b. about 1552, d. 1629.

Speke, John Hanning, English discoverer 1862 of the source of the Nile, b. 1827, d. 1864.

Spellman, Cardinal Francis J., Archbishop of New York (since 1939), b. 1889.

Spencer, Herbert, English philosopher (*Man versus the State*, 1884), b. 1820, d. 1903.

Spencer, Sir Stanley, English painter (*Resurrection, Cookham*, 1922–1927), b. 1891, d. 1959.

Spender, Stephen, English poet, b. 1909.

Spengler, Oswald, German philosopher (*The Decline of the West*, 1918–1922), b. 1891, d. 1936.

Spenser, Edmund, English poet (*The Faerie Queene*, 1589–1596), b. about 1552, d. 1599.

Sperry, Elmer Ambrose, American inventor, b. 1860, d. 1930.

Spin, aeronautic, first voluntary, performed 1915 by English pilot J. C. Brooke ; first scientifically investigated 1917 by English physicist F. A. Lindemann.

Spinello Aretino, Italian painter (*Madonna and Saints*, 1391), d. about 1410.

Spinning Frame, Arkwright's, invented 1768 by the English inventor Sir Richard Arkwright, b. 1732, d. 1792.

Spinoza, Benedict (Baruch Despinoza), Dutch philosopher (*Ethics*), b. 1632, d. 1677.

Spiral Nebulæ, discovery publicly announced 1850 by the astronomer the Earl of Rosse, b. 1800, d. 1867.

Spiritualism, modern, began at Hydeville, U.S.A., in 1847–1848.

Spitfires, last fly-past over London commemorating the Battle of Britain, Sunday, 20 Sept. 1959.

Spithead, British Fleet mutiny at, 16 Apr. 1797.

Spode, Josiah, English potter, b. 1754, d. 1827.

Spohr, Ludwig, German composer and violinist, b. 1784, d. 1859.

Spoonerisms, originated by the English don the Rev. William Archibald Spooner, b. 1844, d. 1930.

Spottiswoode, John, Archbishop of St Andrews, b. 1565, d. 1639.

Spotsylvania Courthouse, Battle of, American Civil War, 8–21 May 1864.

Spring, about 21 Mar. to 21 June in the Northern Hemisphere.

Spurgeon, Charles Haddon, English Baptist leader, b. 1834, d. 1892.

Spurs, Battle of the, between the English and the French, 16 Aug. 1513.

Sputnik, Russian earth satellite, first launched 4 Oct. 1957.

Spyri, Johanna, Swiss writer (*Heidi*), b. 1827, d. 1901.

Squarcione, Francesco, Italian painter (*Madonna with Child*), b. 1394, d. 1474.

Squire, Sir John, English writer, b. 1884, d. 1958.

Staël, Mme de, French writer (*Delphine*, 1802), b. 1766, d. 1817.

Stafford, Edward, Duke of Buckingham, Lord High Constable, b. 1478, beheaded 1521.

Stafford, Henry, Duke of Buckingham, politician, b. about 1454, beheaded 1483.

Stahl, Georg Ernst, German propounder (1731) of the phlogiston theory, b. 1660, d. 1734.

Stainer, Sir John, English composer (*The Crucifixion*, 1887), b. 1840, d. 1901.

Stainless Steel, invented 1916 by the Englishman Harry Brearley at Sheffield.

Stair, John Dalrymple, Earl of, soldier and diplomat, b. 1673, d. 1747.

' Stalin, Joseph ' (Joseph Vissarionovich Dzhugashvili), Russian dictator b. 1879, d. 1953.

Stambuliski, Alexander, Bulgarian statesman, b. 1879, d. 1923.

Stambulov, Stefan, Bulgarian statesman, b. 1854, assassinated 1895.

Stamford School, English public school, founded by William Radcliffe of Stamford 1532.

Stamp Act, passed 1764 ; repealed 1766.

Stamp Booklets, first used in Britain 1904.

Stamp Duty, introduced in England 1694.

Stamped Envelopes, First British, designed by the Irish artist William Mulready (1786–1863) ; issued 1840.

Standard Oil Company, founded 1870 by the American financier John Davison Rockefeller, b. 1839, d. 1937.

Standard, Battle of the, between the English and the Scottish 22 Aug. 1138.

Standish, Myles, English coloniser of New Plymouth, b. 1584, d. 1656.

Stanford, Sir Charles Villiers, Irish composer (*The Canterbury Pilgrims*, 1884), b. 1852, d. 1924.

Stanford University, California, founded 1891 through an endowment from the American railway builder Leland Stanford, b. 1824, d. 1893.

Stanhope, Lady Hester, English traveller, b. 1776, d. 1839.

Stanhope, Philip Dormer, Earl of Chesterfield, statesman, b. 1694, d. 1773.

Stanislaus I, King of Poland (1705–1709, 1733), b. 1677, d. 1766.

Stanislaus II, King of Poland (1764–1795), b. 1732, d. in prison 1798.

Stanislavski, Constantin Sergeivich, Russian actor and producer, b. 1863, d. 1938.

Stanley, Sir Henry Morton, Welsh explorer, b. 1841, d. 1904. Meeting with David Livingstone (1813–1873) 10 Nov. 1871.

Stanley, John, English organist and composer (*Zimri*, 1760), b. 1713, d. 1786.

Stannary Parliament, Cornwall, last held at Truro 1752.

Stanton, Mrs Elizabeth Cady, American champion of women's rights, b. 1815, d. 1902.

Star, The, British newspaper, founded 1888 ; absorbed by the *Evening News* 1960.

Star Chamber, English prerogative court inaugurated in the 14th century, abolished by the Long Parliament 1641.

Stark, James, English painter (*The Valley of the Yare*), b. 1794, d. 1859.

Stark Effect, polarisation of light, discovered 1913 by the German physicist Johannes Stark, b. 1874, d. 1957.

Stationers' Company, London, livery company incorporated 1557 ; Charter confirmed by Queen Elizabeth I 1559 ; monopoly ended 1842.

Statius, Latin poet (*Silvæ*), d. 96.

Statue of Liberty, New York harbour, designed 1876 by the French sculptor

Frédéric Auguste Bartholdi (1834–1904) ; unveiled 28 Oct. 1886.

Staunton, Howard, English chess player b. 1810, d. 1874.

Stavisky, Alexandre, French swindler b. 1886, d. 1934.

Stead, William Thomas, English editor and reformer, b. 1849, drowned at sea 1912.

Steam Engine, invented 1698 by the English military engineer Captain Thomas Savery, b. about 1650, d. 1715.

Steam Hammer, invented 1839 by the Scottish engineer James Nasmyth, b. 1808, d. 1890.

Steam Pumping Engine, invented 1705 by the English mechanic Thomas Newcowen, b. 1663, d. 1729 ; developed and perfected 1767 by the Scottish engineer James Watt, b. 1736, d. 1819.

Steam Plough, invented 1850–1860 by the English engineer John Fowler, b. 1826, d. 1864.

Steam Turbine, driving high-speed electric generator, invented 1884 by Sir Charles Parsons, b. 1854, d. 1931.

Steamboat, First, the *Charlotte Dundas* built 1801 by the British engineer William Syminton, b. 1763, d. 1831.

Steamboat, First practical, invented 1787 by the American inventor John Fitch, b. 1743, d. 1798.

Stearin, fat formed from glycerine and stearic acid, discovered by the French scientist Michel Eugène Chevreul, b. 1786, d. 1889.

Steel, cast by the crucible process, invented about 1750 by the English clockmaker Benjamin Huntsman, b. 1704, d. 1776.

Steel Rails, first made about 1858 by the British engineer Sir John Brown, b. 1816, d. 1896.

Steele, Sir Richard, Irish-born writer (*The Spectator*, 1711–1712), b. 1672, d. 1729.

Steen, Jan, Dutch painter (*Music master*), b. 1626, d. 1679.

Steer, Wilson, English painter (*Chepstow Castle*), b. 1860, d. 1942.

Stein, Sir Aurel, Hungarian-born archæologist in Asia, b. 1862, d. 1943.

Stein, Gertrude, American writer (*The Autobiography of Alice B. Toklas,* 1933), b. 1872, d. 1946.

Steinach, Eugen, Austrian pioneer in rejuvenation, b. 1861, d. 1944.

Steiner, Rudolf, Hungarian-born philosopher and educationist, b. 1861, d. 1925.

Steinitz, William, German-born chess champion, b. 1836, d. 1900.

Steinmetz, Charles Proteus, German-born electrical engineer, b. 1865, d. 1923.

Steinway G., Sons, piano manufacturers, firm founded Brunswick about 1825 ; New York 1853 ; London 1875 ; Hamburg 1880.

Stellar Parallax, study developed and advanced by the German astronomer Wilhelm Struve, b. 1793, d. 1864.

'Stendhal ' (Marie Henri Beyle), French novelist (*Le Rouge et le Noir,* 1831), b. 1783, d. 1842.

Steno, Nicolaus, Danish scientist, b. 1631, d. 1686.

Stephen, St, King of Hungary (1001–1038), b. about 977, d. 1038.

Stephen I, St, Pope 254–257.

Stephen II, Pope 752.

Stephen III, Pope 752–757.

Stephen IV, Pope 768–772.

Stephen V, Pope 816–817.

Stephen VI, Pope 885–891.

Stephen VII, Pope 896–897, murdered 897.

Stephen VIII, Pope 928–931.

Stephen IX, Pope 939–942.

Stephen X, (Frederick), Pope 1057–1058.

Stephen, King of England (1135–1154), b. about 1097, d. 1154.

Stephen I, King of Hungary (998–1038), b. 977, d. 1038.

Stephen II, King of Hungary (1114–1131), b. 1100, d. 1131.

Stephen III, King of Hungary (1161–1173).

Stephen IV, King of Hungary (1162), d. 1166.

Stephen V, King of Hungary (1270–1272), b. 1239, d. 1272.

Stephen, the Great, Prince of Moldavia, b. 1431, d. 1504.

Stephen, Sir James Fitzjames, English jurist and writer, b. 1829, d. 1894.

Stephen, Sir Leslie, English writer (editor of the *Dictionary of National Biography*), b. 1832, d. 1904.

Stephen Harding, St, founder of the Cistercian Order, d. 1134.

Stephens, Alexander Hamilton, American statesman, b. 1812, d. 1883.

Stephens, Catherine, Countess of Essex, British singer and actress, b. 1794, d. 1882.

Stephens, George, English runic archæologist, b. 1813, d. 1895.

Stephens, James, Irish writer (*The Crock of Gold,* 1912), b. 1882, d. 1950.

Stephenson, George, English civil engineer and inventor, b. 1781, d. 1848.

Stephenson, Robert, English civil engineer, b. 1803, d. 1859.

' Stepniak, Sergei ' (Sergei Mikhailovich Kravchinski), Russian revolutionary émigré and writer, b. 1852, d. 1895.

Stereochemistry, study initiated 1874 by the Dutch scientist Jacobus Hendricus van't Hoff, b. 1852, d. 1911.

Stereoscope, invented about 1838 by the English scientist Sir Charles Wheatstone, b. 1802, d. 1875.

Stereotype Process, invented 1725 by the Scottish inventor William Ged, b. 1690, d. 1749.

Sterling, John, Scottish writer (*The Election,* 1841), b. 1806, d. 1844.

Sterling, taken off the British gold standard 20 Sept. 1931.

Stern, Julius, German conductor, b. 1820, d. 1883.

Sternberg, Constantin, Russian-born pianist and minor composer, b. 1852, d. 1924.

Sterne, Laurence, Irish-born writer (*Tristram Shandy,* 1760–1767), b. 1713, d. 1768.

Stethoscope, invented by the French physician René Théophile Hyacinthe Laënnec, b. 1781, d. 1826.

Stetson Hats, manufactured by the American industrialist John Batterson Stetson, b. 1830, d. 1906.

Steuben, Frederick William, Baron von, German-born soldier in American service, b. 1730, d. 1794.

Stevens, Alfred, English painter and sculptor (The Wellington monument, 1856–1892), b. 1818, d. 1875.

Stevens, Henry, American bibliographer, London, b. 1819, d. 1886.

Stevens, John, American inventor 1813 of the ironclad, b. 1749, d. 1838.

Stevenson, Adlai, American politician, b. 1900.

Stevenson, David, Scottish civil engineer, b. 1815, d. 1886.

Stevenson, Robert, Scottish engineer, b. 1772, d. 1850.

Stevenson, Robert Louis, Scottish writer (*Treasure Island*, 1883), b. 1850, d. 1894.

Stevenson, Thomas, Scottish engineer and meteorologist, b. 1818, d. 1887.

Stewart, Balfour, Scottish meteorologist, b. 1828, d. 1887.

Stewart, Dugald, Scottish philosopher, b. 1753, d. 1828.

Stewart, Robert, Duke of Albany, Regent of Scotland, b. about 1340, d. 1420.

Stiegel, Henry William, American pioneer glass manufacturer, b. 1729, d. 1785.

Stieler, Adolf, German cartographer, b. 1775, d. 1836.

Stifter, Adalbert, Bohemian-born writer (*Studien*, 1844–1851), b. 1805, d. 1868.

Stigand, Archbishop of Canterbury, d. 1072.

Stilicho, Flavius, Roman general, assassinated 408.

Still, Andrew Taylor, American founder 1874 of osteopathy, b. 1828, d. 1917.

Stillingfleet, Edward, Bishop of Worcester (1689–1699), b. 1635, d. 1699.

Stirling, James, Scottish mathematician, b. 1692, d. 1770.

Stirling, James Hutchison, Scottish philosopher, b. 1820, d. 1909.

Stirner, Max (Kaspar Schmidt), German anarchist (*The Ego and His Own*), b. 1806, d. 1856.

Stockmar, Christian Friedrich, Baron von, adviser to Queen Victoria, b. 1787, d. 1863.

Stockport Grammar School, English public school, founded by the Lord Mayor of London, Sir Edmond Shaa, 1487.

Stockton, Frank R., American novelist and short story writer (*The Lady or the Tiger?* 1884), b. 1834, d. 1902.

Stoicism, philosophical system founded in the 4th century B.C. by Zeno of Citium, b. 340, d. 270 B.C.

Stoker, Bram, Irish writer (*Dracula*, 1897), b. 1847, d. 1912.

Stokes, Sir George Gabriel, Irish-born physicist, b. 1819, d. 1903.

Stokes, Margaret M'Nair, Irish archæologist, b. 1832, d. 1900.

Stokowski, Leopold, English-born conductor, b. 1882.

Stolberg-Stolberg, Friedrich Leopold, Graf zu, German poet (*Timoleon*, 1784), b. 1750, d. 1819.

Stolypin, Piotr Arkadevich, Russian statesman, b. 1863, assassinated 1911.

Stone, Lucy, American champion of women's rights and abolitionist, b. 1818, d. 1893.

Stone, Nicholas, English architect, b. 1586, d. 1647.

Stone Age, Old, between ten thousand and one million years ago.

Stone Age, Middle, between 4,500 and 10,000 years ago.

Stone Age, New, between 4,000 and 4,500 years ago.

Stonyhurst College, English public school, founded originally at St Omer's 1592 ; re-opened in England 1794.

Stopes, Dr Marie, English pioneer in family planning, b. 1880, d. 1958.

Storm, Theodor, German writer (*Gedichte*, 1852), b. 1817, d. 1888.

Storting, Norwegian Parliament, founded 1814.

Stoss, Veit, German sculptor (*Annunciation*), b. 1438, d. 1533.

Stothard, Thomas, English painter (*The Canterbury Pilgrims*), b. 1755, d. 1834.

Stow, John, English antiquary (*Survey of London*, 1598), b. 1525, d. 1605.

Stowe, Mrs Harriet Beecher, American writer (*Uncle Tom's Cabin,* 1851–1852), b. 1811, d. 1896.

Stowe Collection of Manuscripts, now in the British Museum, collected by the English antiquary Thomas Astle, b. 1735, d. 1803.

Stowe School, modern English public school, founded 1923.

Strabo, Greek geographer, b. about 64 B.C., d. about A.D. 22.

Strachan, John, Scottish Bishop of Toronto (1839–1867), b. 1778, d. 1867.

Strachey, John St Loe, English editor of *The Spectator* (1896–1925), b. 1860, d. 1927.

Strachey, Lytton, English writer (*Eminent Victorians,* 1918), b. 1880, d. 1932.

Stradella, Alessandro, Italian composer (*Esther*), b. about 1645, murdered 1682.

Stradivari, Antonio, Italian violin-maker, b. 1644, d. 1737.

Strafford, Thomas Wentworth, Earl of, British statesman, b. 1593, executed 1641.

Strang, William, British artist (*Rudyard Kipling*), b. 1859, d. 1921.

Strange, Sir Robert, Scottish engraver, b. 1721, d. 1792.

Straparola, Giovanni Francesco, Italian writer (*Piacevoli notti,* 1550–1554), b. about 1495, d. about 1557.

Strasbourg, ceded to France under the Treaty of Ryswyck 1697.

Stratford, John de, Archbishop of Canterbury (1333–1348), d. 1348.

Strathallan School, Scottish public school, founded at Bridge of Allan by the first Headmaster H. Riley 1912 ; moved to present site 1920.

Strathcona and Mount Royal, Donald Alexander Smith, Baron, Scottish-born statesman in Canada, b. 1820, d. 1914.

Straus, Oskar, Austrian composer (*The Chocolate Soldier,* 1908), b. 1870, d. 1954.

Strauss, Johann, Austrian composer (*Die Fledermaus,* 1874), b. 1825, d. 1899.

Strauss, Richard, German composer (*Der Rosenkavalier,* 1911), b. 1864, d. 1949.

Stravinsky, Igor, Russian-born composer (*The Fire Bird,* 1910), b. 1882.

Street, George Edmund, English architect, b. 1824, d. 1881.

Street Lighting, in England, first oil 1681 ; first gas, about 1812 ; first electricity, about 1880.

Streptomycin, first isolated 1943 by the Russian-born scientist Selman Abraham Waksman, b. 1888, awarded Nobel Prize 1952.

Stresemann, Gustav, German statesman, b. 1878, d. 1929.

Stretcher-bearers, introduced about 1792 by the Baron Pierre François Percy, b. 1754, d. 1825.

Stribling, Thomas Sigismund, American novelist (*The Store,* 1932), b. 1881.

Strickland, Agnes, English historian (*Lives of the Queens of England,* 1840–1848), b. 1796, d. 1874.

Strijdom, Johannes Gerhardus, Prime Minister (1954–1958) of the Union of South Africa, b. 1893, d. 1958.

Strike, General, in Britain, 3 to 13 May 1926.

Strike, Right to, legalised in Britain 1824.

Strindberg, Johan August, Swedish playwright (*Miss Julie,* 1888), b. 1849, d. 1912.

Strip Cartoons, originated by the German artist Wilhelm Busch, b. 1832, d. 1908.

Stroheim, Erich von, film actor, b. 1886, d. 1957.

Strongbow, Richard (Richard de Clare), Earl of Pembroke and Strigul, d. 1176.

Strontium, metallic element, discovered 1808 by the English chemist Sir Humphry Davy, b. 1778, d. 1829.

Strozzi, Bernardo, Italian painter, b. 1581, d. 1644.

Struensee, Johann Friedrich, German-born statesman in Denmark, b. 1731, executed 1772.

Strutt, Joseph, English antiquary, b. 1749, d. 1802.

Struve, Friedrich Georg Wilhelm, German astronomer, b. 1793, d. 1864.

Struve, Peter Berngardovich, Russian writer and politician, b. 1870, d. 1944.

Strychnine, discovered 1818 by the French chemists Pierre Joseph Pelletier (1788–1842) and Joseph Bienaimé Caventou (1795–1877).

Strype, John, English historian (*Cranmer*, 1694), b. 1643, d. 1737.

' Stuart, La belle' (Frances Teresa Stuart, Duchess of Richmond and Lennox), mistress of Charles II, b. 1647, d. 1702.

Stuart, John, Earl of Bute, statesman, b. 1713, d. 1792.

Stuart, John McDouall, Scottish explorer, first (1860) to reach the centre of Australia, b. 1815, d. 1866.

Stubbs, George, English painter (*Mares and Foals*), b. 1724, d. 1806.

Stubbs, Henry, English writer (*The Commonwealth of Oceana*, 1660), b. 1632, d. 1676.

Stukeley, William, English antiquary, b. 1687, d. 1765.

Sturdee, Sir, Frederick Charles Doveton, Admiral of the Fleet, b. 1859, d. 1925.

Sture, Sten, Regent of Sweden and founder of the University of Uppsala, b. about 1440, d. 1503.

Sturge, Joseph, English reformer and philanthropist, b. 1793, d. 1859.

Sturlason, Snorri, Icelandic historian (*Heimskringla*), b. 1179, killed 1241.

Sturt, Charles, English explorer of Australia, b. 1795, d. 1869.

Stuyvesant, Peter, Dutch Governor of New Amsterdam (now New York), b. about 1602, d. 1682.

Stylites, Simeon, St, d. about 459.

Suarez, Francisco, Spanish theologian, b. 1548, d. 1617.

Sub-machine Gun, invented 1921 by the American inventors John Taliaferro Thompson (1860–1940) and John N. Blish.

Submarine, First atomic-powered, the U.S. submarine *Nautilus*, launched 21 Jan. 1954.

Submarine, First navigable, invented 1620 by the Dutch scientist Cornelis Jacobszoon Drebbel, b. 1572, d. 1633.

Submarine, first British model launched at Barrow 2 Oct. 1901.

Submarine Telephone Cable, longest, laid between Scotland and Norway 1954.

Submarine Telephone System, First long-distance, laid across the Atlantic 1956.

Submarine Warfare, World War I, declared by Germany 4 Feb. 1915.

Suckling, Sir John, English poet (*Why so pale and wan, fond lover ?* 1637), b. 1609, believed to have committed suicide 1642.

Sucre, Antonio José de, South American liberator and President of Bolivia (1826–1828), b. 1795, assassinated 1830.

Sudan, achieved self-government 1953 ; independence as a democratic republic proclaimed 1956.

Sudermann, Hermann, German playwright (*Die Ehre*, 1888), b. 1857, d. 1928.

Sue, Eugène, French novelist (*Le Juif errant*, 1844–1845), b. 1804, d. 1857.

Suetonius, Roman historian, b. 75, d. 160.

Suez Canal, Egypt, concession granted 1855 to French engineer Ferdinand de Lesseps (1805–1894) ; Company formed 1858 ; construction begun Apr. 1859 ; completed Aug. 1869 ; opened 17 Nov. 1869 ; Isma'il's shares in Company bought by British Government 1875 ; British occupation of Zone 1882 ; Convention signed 1888 ; British evacuated Zone 1955 ; Canal nationalised by Egyptian Government July 1956 ; British and French invasion of Zone Nov. 1956 ; forces withdrawn Dec. 1956.

Suffren St Tropez, Pierre André de, French admiral, b. 1729, d. 1788.

Sugar, Grape, discovered 1799 by the French scientist Joseph Louis Proust, b. 1754, d. 1826.

Sugar in Beet, discovered 1747 by the German physicist Andreas Sigismund Marggraf, b. 1709, d. 1782.

Suger, French statesman, b. about 1081, d. 1151.

Suggia, Mme Guilhermina, Spanish cellist, b. 1888, d. 1950.

Sui Dynasty, China, 581–618.

Suicides, buried at crossroads transfixed by a stake until 1834.

Suidas, Greek lexicographer, who probably lived in the 10th century.

Sukkoth (Feast of Tabernacles), Jewish holiday 15th day of Tishri.

Suleiman, Sultan of Adrianople 1402–1410.

Suleiman I, Sultan of Turkey (1520–1566), b. 1494, d. 1566.

Suleiman II, Sultan of Turkey (1687–1691), b. 1641, d. 1691.

Sulfanilamide, first synthetised 1908 by the German scientist P. Gelmo.

Sulla, Lucius Cornelius, Roman statesman and soldier, b. 138, d. 78 B.C.

Sullivan, Sir Arthur, English composer (*The Mikado*, 1885), b. 1842, d. 1900.

Sullivan, Barry, Irish actor, b. 1821, d. 1891.

Sullivan, Sir Edward, Lord Chancellor of Ireland (1883–1885), b. 1822, d. 1885.

Sully, Maximilien de Béthune, Duc de, French statesman, b. 1560, d. 1641.

Sully-Prudhomme, Réne François Armand, French poet (*L'Idéal*, 1865), b. 1839, d. 1907.

Sulphonamide Drugs, first produced 1935 (Prontosil) and 1938 (M & B).

Sumatra, Indonesia, settled about 1510 by the Portuguese ; taken over by the Dutch about 1596 onwards ; included in the independent Republic of Indonesia, established 1949.

Summer, 21 June to 21 Sep., in the Northern Hemisphere.

Summer Solstice, longest day, 21 June or 22, according to the year.

Summer Time, in Britain, introduced 21 May 1916 ; made permanent institution by House of Commons vote 17 July 1925.

Sumner, John Bird, Archbishop of Canterbury (1848–1862), b. 1780, d. 1862.

Sumter, Fort, Battle of, American Civil War, 12–14 Apr. 1861.

Sun, distance from earth, first reliably calculated 1673 by Cassius and Riches ; rotation first observed 1610 by Galileo.

Sun Spots, discovered by Joannes Fabricius, b. 1587, d. 1615.

Sun Yat-Sen, Chinese revolutionary leader, b. 1867, d. 1925.

Sunday, first day of the week.

Sunday Schools, founded in Gloucester 1780 by the English publisher and reformer Robert Raikes, b. 1735, d. 1811.

Sunday Times, The, British newspaper, founded 1822.

Sung Dynasty, China 960–1279.

Superconductivity, of metals, discovered 1911 by the Dutch scientist Heike Kamerlingh Onnes.

Suppé, Franz von, Austrian-born composer (*Poet and Peasant*), b. 1819, d. 1895.

Supply, British Ministry of, in existence 1939–1959.

Supremacy, Acts of, separating the Anglican from the Catholic Church, signed by Henry VIII in 1534 and by Queen Elizabeth in 1559.

Surgeon, First British woman (Miss Eleanor Davies-Colley), admitted to the Royal College of Surgeons 1911.

Surgeons' Company, London, founded 1746.

Surgical Instruments, steam sterilisation introduced 1886 by the German scientist Ernst von Bergmann, b. 1836, d. 1907.

Surinam (Netherlands Guiana), first settled by the English 1630 ; ceded to the Netherlands 1667.

Surrealism, art movement, manifesto issued 1924 by the French poet André Breton, b. 1896.

Surrey, Henry Howard, Earl of, English poet and soldier, b. about 1517, beheaded 1547.

Surtees, Robert Smith, English novelist (*Handley Cross*, 1843), b. 1803, d. 1864.

Suso, Heinrich, German mystic (*Das Büchlein der Wahrheit*, about 1329), b. 1300, d. 1366.

Sussex, Thomas Radclyffe, Earl of, Lord Lieutenant of Ireland (1560–1564), b. about 1526, d. 1583.

Suttee (*Sati*), compulsory or voluntary widow-sacrifice, made illegal in India 1829.

Sutter, John Augustus, American pioneer, b. 1803, d. 1880.

Sutton, Thomas, English founder (1611) of Charterhouse School, b. 1532, d. 1611.

Sutton Hoo, Suffolk, ship-burial treasure discovered 1939.

Sutton Valence School, English public school, founded 1576, by the English merchant and philanthropist William Lambe, b. 1495, d. 1580.

Suvorov, Aleksandr Vasilievich, Russian Field-Marshal, b. 1729, d. 1800.

Svendsen, Johan, Norwegian composer (*Norwegian Rhapsody*) and violinist, b. 1840, d. 1911.

Svalbard Archipelago, Norwegian sovereignty recognised 1920 ; officially incorporated in Norway 1925.

Sverdrup, Otto, Norwegian explorer in the Arctic, b. 1855, d. 1930.

Sverre, King of Norway (1177–1202), d. 1202.

' Svevo, Italo ' (Ettore Schmitz), Italian writer, b. 1864, d. 1928.

Swabian League, The Great, formed by Frederick III 1488 ; disintegrated 1534.

Swammerdam, Jan, Dutch scientist, b. 1637, d. 1680.

Swan, Sir Joseph Wilson, English pioneer in electric lighting and photography, b. 1828, d. 1914.

' Swan of Lichfield, The ' (Anna Seward), English poet and letter-writer, b. 1747, d. 1809.

Swarthmore College, Pennsylvania, founded by the Society of Friends 1864.

Swarthout, Gladys, American operatic singer, b. 1904.

Swaziland, protected by the South African Republic 1894–1899 ; administered by the Governor of the Transvaal 1903–1907 ; administered by a British High Commissioner since 1907.

Sweden, Christian since about 1000 ; ruled by Vasas 1521–1810, by Bernadottes since 1810.

Swedenborg, Emanuel, Swedish theologian (*Heavenly Arcana*, 1749–1756), b. 1688, d. 1772.

Swedenborgian Church, organised 1788 by Robert Hindmarsh, b. 1759, d. 1835.

' Swedish Nightingale ' (Jenny Lind), operatic singer, b. 1820, d. 1887.

Sweelinck, Jan, Dutch organist and composer (*Cantationes Sacræ*), b. 1562, d. 1621.

Sweet, Henry, English philologist, b. 1845, d. 1912.

Swete, Henry Barclay, British theologian, b. 1835, d. 1917.

Sweynheym, Conrad, pioneer German printer in Italy, lived in the 15th century.

Swift, Jonathan, Irish divine and writer (*Gulliver's Travels*, 1726), b. 1667, d. 1745.

Swinburne, Algernon Charles, English poet (*Atalanta in Calydon*, 1865), b. 1837, d. 1909.

Swithin, St, Bishop of Winchester, d. 862.

Swithin's Day, St, 15 July.

Switzerland, state formed 1291–1798 ; unified Helvetic Republic established 1798 ; present area and neutrality achieved 1815.

Sydenham, Thomas, English physician and medical pioneer, b. 1624, d. 1689.

Sydney, New South Wales, founded 1788.

Sydney Harbour Bridge, officially opened 19 Mar. 1932.

' Sylva, Carmen ' (Elizabeth, Queen of Rumania), b. 1843, d. 1916.

Sylvester I, St, Pope 313–335, d. 335.

Sylvester II, Pope 999–1003, d. 1003.

Sylvester, Joshua, English writer and translator (mainly from the French), b. 1563, d. 1618.

Symbolism, artistic and literary movement, originated in Paris 1886–1889.

Symington, William, British marine engineer, b. 1763, d. 1831.

Symmachus, St, Pope 498–514.

Symonds, John Addington, English writer and translator, b. 1840, d. 1893.

Symons, George James, English meteorologist, b. 1838, d. 1900.

Syndicalism, revolutionary doctrine formulated by Fernand Pelloutier, b. 1867, d. 1901.

Synge, John Millington, Irish playwright (*The Playboy of the Western World*, 1907), b. 1871, d. 1909.

Synod of the Clergy, first held in England at Hertford 673.

Synthetic Geometry, theory developed by the Swiss mathematician Jakob Steiner, b. 1796, d. 1863.

Synthetic Oil Production, initiated 1850 by the Scottish scientist James Young, b. 1811, d. 1883.

Syphilis, bacillus discovered 1905 by the German scientists Erich Hoffman (1868–1959) and Fritz Schaudinn ; curative drug ' Salvarsan ' discovered 1908 by the German bacteriologist Paul Ehrlich, b. 1854, d. 1915.

Syracuse University, New York State, founded 1849 ; moved to present site 1870.

Syria, ruled by Turks 1517–1918 ; French Mandate 1923–1946 ; joined Egypt in the United Arab Republic 1958.

Széchenyi, Count Stephen, Hungarian statesman, b. 1791, committed suicide 1860.

Szigeti, Joseph, Hungarian-born violinist, b. 1892.

Szymanowski, Karol, Polish composer (*Symphonie Concertante*, 1933), b. 1883, d. 1937.

T

Tabari, Abu Ja'far, Arab historian, b. 839, d. about 923.

Tabernacles, Feast of (Sukkoth), Jewish holiday, 15th day of Tishri.

Table Turning, in Spiritualist seances, began in the U.S.A. 1848, reached Europe 1852.

Tabora, capital of Western Province, Tanganyika, founded by Arab slave and ivory traders about 1820.

Tabriz, capital of Azerbaijan Province, Persia, reputed to have been founded

by Zobeidah, wife of Harun-el-Rashid, 791.

Tacca, Pietro, Florentine sculptor, b. 1577, d. 1640.

Tacitus, Roman emperor (275–276), d. 276.

Tacitus, Cornelius, Roman historian, b. about 55, d. about 116.

Tacoma Narrows, American suspension bridge, collapsed after construction 1940.

Taddeo di Bartolo, Sienese painter, b. about 1362, d. about 1422.

Tadema, Sir, Lawrence Alma-, Dutch-born painter, b. 1836, d. 1912.

Tadzhikstan, Soviet Socialist Republic, admitted to the U.S.S.R. 1929.

Taffeta, in its earliest form, introduced into England in the 14th century.

Taft, William Howard, U.S. President (1909–1913), b. 1857, d. 1930.

Taganrog, Sea of Azov port, founded 1769 on the site of a fortress erected by Peter the Great, 1698.

Taglioni, Maria, Italian ballerina, b. 1804, d. 1884.

Tagore, Rabindranath, Indian poet and philosopher (*Gitanjali*, 1912), b. 1861, d. 1941.

Tahirites, ruling family in Khorassan, Persia 813–872.

Tahiti, largest of the French Society Islands, discovered 1767 by the English naval captain Samuel Wallis, b. 1728, d. 1804.

Taillefer, 11th century bard, struck the first blow at the Battle of Hastings, 1066.

Taine, Hippolyte, French historian, b. 1828, d. 1893.

Tait, Archibald Campbell, Archbishop of Canterbury (1869–1882), b. 1811, d. 1882.

Taiwan (Formosa), ceded to Japan by China 1895 ; seized by Chiang Kai-shek 1945 and held after evacuation of Chinese mainland in 1949.

Taj Mahal, Agra, India, mausoleum built (1632) by the Emperor Shah Jehan (d. 1666) for his favourite wife Mumtaz Mahal.

Takahashi, Korekiyo, Japanese statesman, b. 1854, d. 1936.

Talana Hill, nr. Dundee, north Natal, scene of the first Battle of the Boer War 20 Oct. 1899.

Talavera, Battle of, between the English and the French 27–28 July 1809.

Talbot, William Henry Fox, English pioneer in photography, b. 1800, d. 1877. Invented instantaneous photography 1851.

Taliesin, Welsh bard, reputed to have lived in the 6th century.

'Talkies', first shown in commercial cinemas 1928.

Talking Books, for the blind, first sponsored 1934 by the American lawyer Robert Forsythe Irwin, b. 1892.

Tallage, special tax on English towns, first levied in the reign of King Henry I, ceased with the 1332 levy, formally abolished 1340.

Tallahassee, capital of Florida, reputed to have been founded by the Spaniards 1638.

Talleyrand-Périgord, Charles Maurice de, French diplomat and statesman, b. 1754, d. 1838.

Tallien, Jean Lambert, French Revolutionary leader, b. 1769, d. 1820.

Tallinn, Estonia, founded by Waldemar II of Denmark 1219.

Tallis, Thomas, English composer (*Song of Forty Parts*), b. about 1505, d. 1585.

Talmud, Rabbinical thesaurus, recension completed during the 5th century; first complete edition published 1520–1523 by the Christian printer Daniel Bomberg, d. 1549.

Tamar Bridge, linking Devon and Cornwall, to be completed 1961.

Tamerlane, Tartar conqueror, b. about 1336, d. 1405.

Tammany Hall, New York political organisation, founded about 1789. Tammany Hall Scandal took place 1870.

Tancred, crusader, b. about 1078, d. 1112.

Tandy, James Napper, United Irishman, b. 1740, d. 1803.

T'Ang Dynasty, China 618–906.

Tanganyika, German territory 1884–1914; conquered by British forces 1914–1918; mandated territory of the League of Nations 1920–1946; United Nations trusteeship since 1946; achieved responsible government 1960.

Tanganyika, Lake, discovered 1858 by the English explorers Burton (1821–1890) and John Hanning Speke (1827–1864).

Tangier, ruled by Portugal 1471–1662, England 1662–1684, Morocco 1684–1904; international zone created 1923, terminated 1956.

Tank Corps, British Army, formation authorised 28 July 1917.

Tanks, tested and so-named 29 Jan. 1916, first used by the British Army on the Somme 15 Sept. 1916.

Tannenberg, Battle of, between Teutonic Order and Poles 1410; and between the Germans and the Russians 26–31 Aug. 1914.

Tanner, Thomas, English antiquary (*Notitia Monastica*, 1695), b. 1674, d. 1735.

Tannhaüser, German minnesinger, lived in the 13th century.

Tantalum, metallic element, discovered 1802 by A. G. Ekeberg.

Tâoism, religious movement, thought to have been founded by the Chinese sage Lâo-tsze, who lived in the late 7th and early 6th centuries B.C.

Tardieu, André Pierre Gabriel Amédée, French statesman, b. 1876, d. 1945.

Tarkington, Booth, American writer (*Penrod*, 1914), b. 1869, d. 1946.

Tarleton, Sir Banastre, English general in the American War of Independence, b. 1754, d. 1833.

Tarlton, Richard, English actor, d. 1588.

Tarquin (Lucius Tarquinius Superbus), Roman king, b. 534, d. 510 B.C.

Tartini, Giuseppe, Italian violinist and composer (*Trillo del Diavolo*), b. 1692, d. 1770.

Tasman, Abel Janszoon, Dutch navigator, b. about 1603, d. about 1659.

Tasmania, discovered 1642 by the Dutch navigator Abel Janszoon Tasman, b. about 1603, d. about 1659.

Tassili Rock Paintings, Sahara, discovered by the Camel Corps officer Lieutenant Brenans 1933.

Tasso, Torquato, Italian poet (*La Gerusa-lemme Liberata*, 1576), b. 1544, d. 1595.

Tata, Jamsetji Nasarwanji, Indian pioneer industrialist and philanthropist, b. 1839, d. 1904.

Tate, Sir Henry, English manufacturer and philanthropist, b. 1819, d. 1899.

Tate, Nahum, Irish-born poet-laureate (*Panacea*, 1700), b. 1652, d. 1715.

Tate Gallery, London, officially opened 21 July 1897 ; founded by the English manufacturer Sir Henry Tate (1819–1899) ; reassumed its original name 1932.

Tatham, Charles Heathcote, British architect, b. 1772, d. 1842.

Tatler, The, 1709–1711, edited by the Irish-born writer Sir Richard Steele, b. 1672, d. 1729.

Tattersall's, London horse auction and sporting centre, founded 1776 by the English horse-auctioneer Richard Tattersall, b. 1724, d. 1795.

Tauber, Richard, Austrian-born operatic singer, b. 1892, d. 1948.

Täuber-Arp, Sophie, Swiss painter (*Moved Circles*, 1934), b. 1889.

Tauchnitz, Karl Christoph Traugott, German publisher and printer, b. 1761, d. 1836.

Taunton School, English public school, founded 1847.

Taussig, Frank William, American economist, b. 1859, d. 1940.

Taverner, John, English composer of masses and motets, b. about 1495, d. 1545.

Taverner, Jean Baptiste, French traveller and merchant in the East, b. 1605, d. 1689.

Taxi-cabs, first official recognition of their existence shown in the draft of proposed cab regulations for London, issued by the Home Secretary 21 Jan. 1907.

Tay Bridge, Scotland, opened 1887.

Taylor, Alfred Swaine, English medical jurist (*The Principles and Practice of Medical Jurisprudence*, 1865), b. 1806, d. 1880.

Taylor, Jeremy, English theologian (*Holy Living*, 1650, and *Holy Dying*, 1651), b. 1613, d. 1667.

Taylor, John ('The Water-Poet'), English writer (*The Pennyles Pilgrimage*, 1618), b. 1580, d. 1653.

Taylor, Zachary, U.S. President (1849–1850), b. 1784, d. 1850.

Tchaikovsky, Piotr Ilyich, Russian composer (*Eugen Onegin*, 1879), b. 1840, d. 1893.

Te Deum, the 'Ambrosian Chant', probably composed in the 5th century.

Tea, traditionally invented 2737 B.C. by the Chinese emperor Shen Nung ; reached Holland 1610 ; first recorded reference in Britain 1658 ; Indian tea reached Britain 1839.

Teach, Edward (Blackbeard), English pirate, killed 1718.

Teasdale, Sarah, American poet (*Rivers to the Sea*, 1915), b. 1884, d. 1935.

Technetium (Masurium), discovered 1925 by I. and W. Noddack. Confirmed by C. Perrier and E. Segré of the University of California, 1937.

Tecumseh, American Indian Chief, b. 1768, killed in battle 1813.

Tedder, Arthur William, Baron, Marshal of the Royal Air Force, b. 1890.

Teheran Conference, World War II, between the Allied statesmen Roosevelt, Stalin and Churchill 28 Nov. to 1 Dec. 1943.

Teixeira, Pedro, Portuguese explorer in South America, d. 1640.

Tel-Aviv, Israel ; coastal city, founded 1909, capital since 1948.

Telegraph, invented 1832 by the American inventor Samuel Morse, b. 1791, d. 1872.

Telegraph, Ocular, invented 1792 by the French engineer Claude Chappe, b. 1763, d. 1805.

Telegraph Cable, first laid across English Channel 1851 ; first Atlantic, laid 1857.

Telegraph Line, First practical, patented 1837 by the English inventors Sir William Fothergill Cooke (1806–1879) and Sir Charles Wheatstone (1802–1875) ; monopoly granted to Post Office 1869.

Telegraph Line, First, set up between Washington and Baltimore 1844 by the American inventor Samuel Morse, b. 1791, d. 1872.

Telemann, George Philipp, German composer (*Der Tag des Gerichts*), b. 1681, d. 1767.

Telepathy, first so named 1882 by the English writer Frederick William Henry Myers, b. 1843, d. 1901.

Telephone, invented 1860 by Reis ; patented 1876 by the Scottish-born inventor Alexander Graham Bell, b. 1847, d. 1922.

Telephone Cable, First multi-channel, laid across the Atlantic 1956.

Telephone Exchange, First all-electronic, to be installed in north London 1961.

Telephone Service, First automatic, inaugurated in London 1927.

Telephone System, British, taken over by the General Post Office 1912.

Telephone Weather Forecasting Service, began in Britain 1956.

Telescope, traditionally invented by Roger Bacon in the 13th century ; model presented 2 Oct. 1608 to Dutch General Estates by the optician Hans Lippershym, d. 1619.

Telesphorus, St, Pope 125–136.

Television, first demonstrated 1926 by the Scottish inventor John Logie Baird, b. 1888, d. 1946.

Television, Colour, first publicly demonstrated in Glasgow 1927 ; the two-colour system demonstrated 1944 by the Scottish inventor John Logie Baird, b. 1888, d. 1946.

Television, Commercial, began in Britain 1955.

Television Broadcast, First B.B.C. experimental, 1929, first B.B.C. experimental programme broadcast 1932.

Television Theatre, First, opened at Brighton, 1953.

Telford, Thomas, Scottish engineer, b. 1757, d. 1834.

Tell, William, mythical Swiss patriot of 13th century.

Tellier, Charles, French inventor 1867 of the refrigerator, b. 1828, d. 1913.

Tellurium, white metal-element, discovered by Reichenstein 1782.

Tempest, Marie, English actress, b. 1864, d. 1942.

Templars, Order of the Knights, founded about 1118, ended 1314.

Temple, Jerusalem, first destroyed by Nebuchadnezzar 586 B.C. ; second built 516 B.C., destroyed by Titus A.D. 70.

Temple, Sir William, statesman and writer, b. 1628, d. 1699.

Temple Bar, Fleet Street, London, built 1672 by Sir Christopher Wren (1632–1723) ; re-erected at Theobalds Park, Essex, 1878.

Teniers, David, the elder, Flemish painter (*Temptation of St Anthony*), b. 1582, d. 1649.

Teniers, David, the younger, Flemish painter (*The Prodigal Son*), b. 1610, d. 1690.

Tenison, Thomas, Archbishop of Canterbury (1694–1715), b. 1636, d. 1715.

Tennant, Smithson, English chemist and discoverer (1804) of iridium, b. 1761, d. 1815.

Tennessee, U.S.A., first settled 1757 ; admitted to the Union 1796.

Tennessee University, U.S.A., founded at Knoxville 1794.

Tennessee Valley Authority, U.S.A., established 1933.

Tenniel, Sir John, English illustrator of Lewis Carroll's *Alice's Adventures in Wonderland* (1865), b. 1820, d. 1914.

Tennis, Lawn, origins in outdoor real tennis, played in France in 18th century. Invented as ' sphairistike ' by Major Wingfield in 1874, and Lawn Tennis Association formed 1888.

Tennis, Royal, played in France in 11th century ; played in England by Henry VII as early as 1497.

Tennis Court Oath, French Revolution, 20 June 1789.

Tennyson, Lord Alfred, English poet (*In Memoriam*, 1850), b. 1809, d. 1892.

Ter Borch, Gerard, Dutch painter (*Guitar Lesson*), b. 1617, d. 1681.

Terbium, metallic element, discovered by the Swedish chemist Karl Gustav Mosander, b. 1797, d. 1858.

Terence, Roman playwright (*Phormio*), b. about 185, d. about 159 B.C.

Teresa, St (Teresa de Cepeda y Ahu-mada), b. 1515, d. 1582.

Terpander, ' Father of Greek music ', lived in the 7th century B.C.

Territorial Army, inaugurated at Buckingham Palace 1907. Yeomanry and Volunteer Force units transferred to the newly-constructed Territorial Force 1958.

Terry, Dame Ellen, English actress, b. 1848, d. 1928.

Terry, Sir Richard, English composer of church music, b. 1865, d. 1938.

Tertiary Period, Earth history between 1 and 70 million years ago.

Tertis, Lionel, English viola-player, b. 1876.

Tertullian, Roman theologian (*Apologeticus*, 197), b. about 155, d. about 220.

Teschen, The Peace of, averting war between Austria and Prussia, signed 13 May 1779.

Tesla, Nikola, Croatian-born electrician and inventor, b. 1857, d. 1943.

Test Act, British measure against Catholic office-holding, 1673 ; extended to Peers 1678 ; repealed 1828-1829.

Tetrazzini, Luisa, Italian operatic singer, b. 1871, d. 1940.

Tetzel, Johann, German ecclesiastic, b. 1455, d. 1519.

Teutoburg Forest, Battle of the, between the Cherusei and the Romans A.D. 9.

Teutonic Knights, military order of Crusaders, founded 1189-1191.

Tewfik Pasha, Khedive of Egypt, b. 1852, d. 1892.

Texas, U.S.A., proclaimed a Republic 1836 ; admitted to the Union 1845.

Texas Rangers, mounted military police, formed 1836.

Texas University, Austin founded 1883.

Textile Institute, Manchester, founded 1910.

Teyte, Dame Maggie, English operatic singer, b. 1889.

Thackeray, William Makepeace, India-born novelist (*Vanity Fair*, 1847-1848), b. 1811, d. 1863.

Thailand, absolute monarchy until 1932 ; constitutional monarchy 1932-1951 ; reversion to 1932 constitution effected 1951.

Thales, Greek statesman and philosopher, b. about 624, d. about 548 B.C.

Thallium, metallic element, discovered 1861 by the English scientist Sir William Crookes, b. 1832, d. 1919.

Thames, River Steamboat Service inaugurated 1905.

Thames Conservancy, founded as The Conservators of the River Thames 1857.

Thames Rowing Club, founded as the City of London Rowing Club 1860 ; assumed present name 1862.

Thames Tunnel, constructed 1825-1843 by the French-born engineer Sir Marc Isambard Brunel, b. 1769, d. 1849.

Thanksgiving Day, U.S.A., commemorating the 1623 harvest, celebrated the 4th Thursday in November. First national Thanksgiving Day 26 Nov. 1789.

Thayer's Law of Camouflage, defined 1910 by the American painter Abbott Henderson Thayer, b. 1849, d. 1921.

Theatre, First permanent English, opened in London 1576.

Theatre, First television, opened at Brighton 1953.

Theatre Footlights, first used in Britain 1672.

Theatre-in-the-Round, first used in cinematography by Grimion Samson at the Paris Exhibition 1900.

Theatre Lighting, first gas 1803 (Lyceum, London) ; first electric 1846 (Opéra, Paris).

Theatres, English, closed by the Puritans 1642 ; reopened 1660.

Thelwall, John, English reformer, b. 1764, d. 1834.

Themistocles, Greek general, b. about 525, d. 459 B.C.

Theobald, Archbishop of Canterbury, d. 1161.

Theocritus, Greek poet, b. before 300, d. after 270 B.C.

Theodora, Byzantine empress, d. 548.

Theodore, Anti-Pope 687.

Theodore I, Pope 642–649.

Theodore II, Pope 897–898.

Theodore I, Tsar of Russia (1584–1598), b. 1557, d. 1598.

Theodore II, Tsar of Russia (1605), b. 1589, murdered 1605.

Theodore III, Tsar of Russia (1676–1682), b. 1661, d. 1682.

Theodore of Mopsuestia, Syrian theologian, b. about 350, d. about 428.

Theodore of Tarsus, Archbishop of Canterbury (668–690), b. 602, d. 690.

Theodoret, Syrian theologian, b. 393, d. 458.

Theodoric, Anti-Pope 1100.

Theodoric, King of the Ostrogoths (493–526), b. about 454, d. 526.

Theodosius I, Byzantine emperor (379–395), b. about 346, d. 395.

Theodosius II, Byzantine emperor (408–450), b. 401, d. 450.

Theodosius III, Byzantine emperor (716–717).

Theognis, Greek poet, lived in the 6th and 5th centuries B.C.

Theophrastus, Greek philosopher, b. about 371 d. about 287, B.C.

Theosophical Society, founded in the U.S.A. 1875 by the Russian-born Mme Helena Blavatsky (1831–1891) ; in Britain by the English leader Annie Besant (1847–1933).

Theresa of Avila, St, b. 1515, d. 1582.

Thérèse of Lisieux, St (Little Flower of Jesus), b. 1873, d. 1897.

Thermidor, French Revolutionary calendar month of July–Aug.

Thermionic Emission, observed 1883 by the American scientist Thomas Alva Edison, b. 1847, d. 1931.

Thermionic Valve, diode developed 1900 by Fleming; triode developed 1907 by Lee de Forest ; tetrode developed 1916 by von Schottky.

Thermionics, study developed by the English physicist Sir Owen Willans Richardson, b. 1879, d. 1959.

Thermochemistry, study developed by the German scientist Germain Henri Hess, b. 1802, d. 1850.

Thermodynamics, study founded by the German scientist Rudolf Julius Emanuel Clausius, b. 1822, d. 1888.

Thermoelectricity, discovered 1821 by the German physicist Thomas Seebeck, b. 1770, d. 1831.

Thermonuclear Fusion, basic research successfully carried out in Britain by Z.E.T.A. at Harwell 1957.

Thermopylæ, Battle of, between Greeks and Persians 480 B.C.

Thibaut IV, King of Navarre and troubadour, b. 1201, d. 1253.

Thicknesse, Philip, English soldier and writer, b. 1719, d. 1792.

Thierry, Augustin, French historian, b. 1795, d. 1856.

Thiers, Adolphe, French statesman, b. 1797, d. 1877.

Thimonnier, Barthélemy, French tailor and inventor (1830) of a sewing machine, b. 1793, d. 1859.

Third-Class Travel, British Railways, abolished 3 June 1956.

Third Programme, B.B.C., inaugurated 29 Sept. 1946.

Third Republic, France 1871–1940.

Thirkell, Mrs Angela, English writer (Love Among the Ruins, 1948), b. 1890.

Thirty-nine Articles, of the Church of England, agreed by Convocation 1563 ; enforced by Parliament 1571 ; revised 1604.

Thirty Years War, religious wars in Germany 1618–1648.

Thistle, Order of the, founded by James III of Scotland about 1480 ; revived in 1687 and 1703.

Thistlewood, Arthur, English conspirator and murderer, b. 1770, hanged 1820.

Thomas, Ambroise, French composer (Mignon, 1866), b. 1811, d. 1896.

Thomas, Dylan, Welsh writer (Under Milk Wood, 1954), b. 1914, d. 1953.

Thomas, Honoratus Leigh, English surgeon, b. 1769, d. 1846.

Thomas Aquinas, St, Italian philosopher and theologian (Summa Theologiæ), b. 1227, d. 1274.

Thomas á Becket, St, Archbishop of Canterbury (1162–1170), b. about 1118, martyred 1170.

Thomas á Kempis, German theologian (*The Imitation of Christ*), b. about 1397, d. 1471.

Thomas Cook's, Travel agents, founded 1841 by the English pioneer Thomas Cook, b. 1808, d. 1892.

Thomas of Erceldoune ('Thomas the Rhymer'), Scottish prophet and writer, lived in the 13th century.

Thomason, George, English bookseller and collector of contemporary pamphlets, d. 1666.

Thompson, David, English-born explorer in Canada, b. 1770, d. 1857.

Thompson, Edith, English murderess, b. 1893, hanged 1922.

Thompson, Francis, English poet (*The Hound of Heaven*, 1893), b. 1859, d. 1907.

Thompson, John Taliaferro, American inventor 1921 of the sub-machine ('Tommy') gun, b. 1860, d. 1940.

Thomson, Elihu, English-born engineer, b. 1853, d. 1937.

Thomson, James, Scottish poet (*The Seasons*, 1726–1730), b. 1700, d. 1748.

Thomson, John Turnbull, Scottish pioneer surveyor in New Zealand, b. 1821, d. 1884.

Thomson, Sir Joseph John, English scientist (postulated existence of electrons, 1893), b. 1856, d. 1940.

Thomson, Robert William, Scottish engineer and inventor 1845 of pneumatic tyres, b. 1822, d. 1873.

Thomson, Virgil, American composer (*Four Saints in Three Acts*, 1934), b. 1896.

Thoreau, Henry David, American writer (*Walden*, 1854), b. 1817, d. 1862.

Thoresby, John, statesman and Archbishop of York (1351–1373), d. 1373.

Thoresby, Ralph, English antiquary, b. 1658, d. 1725.

Thorium, radioactive element, discovered 1828 by the Swedish chemist Baron Jöns Jakob Berzelius, b. 1779, d. 1848.

Thorndike, Dame Sybil, English actress, b. 1882.

Thornton, William, British-born architect (1793–1827) of the U.S. Capitol, d. 1827.

Thornton, Robert, English antiquary, b. 1623, d. 1678.

Thorvaldsen, Bertel, Danish sculptor, b. 1770, d. 1844.

Thothmes I, King of Egypt 1557–1501 B.C.

Thothmes II, King of Egypt 1501 B.C.

Thothmes III, King of Egypt 1501–1447 B.C.

Thothmes IV, King of Egypt 1420–1411 B.C.

Thou, Jacques Auguste de, French historian, b. 1553, d. 1617.

Thrale, Mrs Hester Lynch (Mrs Piozzi), friend of Dr Samuel Johnson, b. 1741, d. 1821.

Thrasybulus, Greek statesman, killed about 390 B.C.

Three Choirs Festival, annual West Country festival, founded 1724.

Three-speed Gear, Sturmey-Archer, first patented 1901 by the Raleigh Bicycle Company.

Threshing-Machine, First, invented 1784 by the Scottish millwright Andrew Meikle, b. 1719, d. 1811.

Throckmorton, Sir Nicholas, English diplomat, b. 1515, d. 1571.

Thucydides, Greek historian of the Pelopponesian War, b. about 460, d. about 398 B.C.

Thulium, a metal of the rare earths, discovered 1879 by Per Teodor Cleve.

Thurber, James American humorous artist and writer (*The Middle-aged Man on the Flying Trapeze*), b. 1894.

Thuret, Gustave Adolphe, French botanist and discoverer 1886 (with the French botanist Edouard Bornet) of a method of seaweed propagation, b. 1817, d. 1875.

Thurloe, John, English statesman, b. 1616, d. 1668.

Thurlow, Edward Thurlow, Baron, Lord Chancellor, b. 1731, d. 1806.

Thursday, the fifth day of the week.

Thurstan, Archbishop of York, d. 1140.

Tibbet, Lawrence, American operatic singer, b. 1896.

Tiberius, Roman Emperor (A.D. 14–37), b. 42 B.C., d. A.D. 37.

Tibullus, Albius, Roman poet, b. about 54, d. 18 B.C.

Tichborne, Chidiock, English conspirator, b. about 1558, executed 1586.

Tichborne Claimant, The, the Australian butcher, Arthur Orton, b. 1834 ; claimed Tichborne inheritance 1871–1872 ; tried for perjury 1873–1874 ; imprisoned 1874–1884 ; d. 1898.

Tickell, Thomas, English poet (*Colin and Lucy*), b. 1686, d. 1740.

Ticker-tape Machine, invented by the American inventors, Thomas Alva Edison (1847–1931) and Franklin Leonard Pope (1840–1895).

Tieck, Ludwig, German novelist (*Magelone*, 1796), b. 1773, d. 1853.

Tiepolo, Giovanni Battista, Italian painter (*St Catherine of Siena*), b. about 1694, d. 1769.

Tiffany, Charles Lewis, American jeweller, b. 1812, d. 1902.

Tigranes, King of Armenia (96–55 B.C.), b. 140, d. 55 B.C.

Tillett, Benjamin, English labour leader, b. 1860, d. 1943.

Tillotson, John Archbishop of Canterbury (1691–1694), b. 1630, d. 1694.

Tilly, Johann Tserklaes, Count of, Imperial general, b. 1559, killed 1632.

Tilsit, Treaty of, between Napoleon and Russia, 1807.

Timæus, Greek philosopher, lived in the 5th and 4th centuries.

Time and Tide, British periodical, founded 1920 by Lady Rhondda, b. 1883, d. 1958.

Times, The, founded London 1785 by the English merchant John Walter, b. 1739, d. 1812 ; present name since 1788.

Timoleon, Greek statesman, b. about 410, d. about 337 B.C.

Timon of Athens, lived in the 5th century, B.C.

Tindal, Mathew, English theologian, b. 1653, d. 1733.

Tintoretto (Jacopo Robusti), Italian painter (*The Miracle of St Mark*), b. 1518, d. 1594.

Tippecanoe, Battle of, between the Americans and the Indians, 7 Nov. 1811.

'Tipperary, It's a long way to', favourite song in World War I, composed 1912 by the English song-writer Jack Judge, b. 1878, d. 1938.

Tippett, Michael, English composer (*The Midsummer Marriage*, 1955), b. 1905.

Tippoo Sahib, Sultan of Mysore, b. 1749, killed in battle 1799.

Tiptoft, John, Earl of Worcester, ' the Butcher of England ', b. about 1427, executed 1470.

Tirpitz, German warship, destroyed by the British Navy in World War II, 12 Nov. 1944.

' Tirso de Molina ' (Gabriel Téllez), Spanish playwright (*El Burlador de Sevilla*, 1630), b. 1571, d. 1648.

Tisserand, François Félix, French astronomer, b. 1845, d. 1896.

Tissue Culture, devised 1907 by the American biologist Ross Harrison, b. 1870.

Titanic, Atlantic passenger liner, sank on her maiden voyage 15 Apr. 1912.

Titanium, under the name Menachinite, discovered 1791 by the English scientist the Rev. William Gregor, b. 1761, d. 1817. Called Titanium 1795.

Tit-Bits, British periodical, founded 1881 by George Newnes, b. 1851, d. 1910.

Titian (Tiziano Vercelli), Italian painter (*Sacred and Profane Love*), b. about 1486, d. 1576.

Tito, Marshal Josip Broz (ruler of Yugoslavia since 1945, President since 1953), b. 1892.

Titus, Roman Emperor (79–81), b. 40, d. 81.

Tobacco, brought from America to Europe in 16th century ; introduced 1560 into France by the French ambassador to Portugal, Jean Nicot, b. 1530, d. 1600.

Tobacco Pipe, Indian, brought by Ralph Lane, first Governor of Virginia to Sir Walter Raleigh 1586.

Tobruk, World War II, taken by the British 22 Jan. 1941 ; recaptured after an eight - months siege by Rommel 21 June 1942.

Tocqueville, Alexis de, French politician and writer (*Ancien Régime et la Revolution*, 1856), b. 1805, d. 1859.

Togo, Heihachito, Japanese naval pioneer, b. 1847, d. 1934.

Togoland, British, surrendered by Germany to the British and French 1914 ; union with Ghana approved by the United Nations 1956.

Toleration, religious, granted to German rulers by the Peace of Augsburg 1555 ; in Transylvania by John Sigismund 1568 ; in France by Edict of Nantes 1598 ; in England by the Act of Toleration 1639.

Toller, Ernst, German playwright, b. 1893, committed suicide 1939.

Tolstoy, Count Leo, Russian writer (*War and Peace*, 1864–1868), b. 1828, d. 1910.

' Tom Thumb ', General (Charles Sherwood Stratton), American dwarf, b. 1838, d. 1883.

' Tom Thumb, The ' first railway engine built 1830 in the U.S.A., constructed by the American inventor Peter Cooper, b. 1791, d. 1883.

Tomato, brought from South America to Europe in 16th century.

Tomkins, Thomas, British calligrapher (*The Beauties of Writing*, 1777), b. 1743, d. 1816.

Tommasini, Vincenzo, Italian composer (*Medea*, 1906), b. 1878, d. 1950.

Tommy Gun, invented 1921 by the American inventors John Taliaferro Thompson (1860–1940) and John N. Blish.

Tompion, Thomas, English clockmaker, b. 1639, d. 1713.

Tonbridge School, English public school, founded by Sir Andrew Judd 1553 ; Chartered by King Edward VI 1553.

Tone, Wolfe, United Irishman, b. 1763, committed suicide 1798.

Tonga, South Pacific, discovered by the Dutch 1616, and by Abel Janszoon Tasman 1643 ; proclaimed a British Protectorate 1900.

Tonic Sol-fa System, invented about 1845 by the English musician Sarah Ann Glover, b. 1785, d. 1867.

Tonson, Jacob, English publisher, b. about 1656, d. 1736.

Tonti, Henri de, Italian-born explorer in North America, b. about 1650, d. 1704.

Tontine, annuity system, introduced about 1653 by the Italian banker Lorenzo Tonti, b. about 1633, d. about 1689.

Tooke, John Horne, English politician and writer (*The Diversions of Purley*, 1786–1798), b. 1736, d. 1812.

Topelius, Zakarias, Finnish writer, b. 1818, d. 1898.

Töpffer, Rodolphe, Swiss writer (*Rose et Gertrude*, 1845), b. 1799, d. 1846.

Topham, Thomas, British strong man, b. about 1710, committed suicide 1749.

Toplady, Augustus Montague, English divine and hymn-writer (*Rock of Ages*, 1775), b. 1740, d. 1778.

Tories, British political group, first so named 1679.

Toronto University, Canada, founded 1827.

Torpedo, Motor, invented by the American engineer Herschel Clifford Parker, b. 1867.

Torpedo, Submarine, invented 1866 by the English engineer Robert Whitehead, b. 1823, d. 1905.

Torquemada, Tomás de, leader 1483 of the Spanish Inquisition, b. 1420, d. 1498.

Torrens, Sir Robert Richard, Irish-born statesman in Australia, b. 1814, d. 1884.

Torricelli, Evangelista, Italian inventor of the barometer, b. 1608, d. 1647.

Torrigiano, Pietro, Italian sculptor (*Henry VII's Tomb*), b. 1472, d. 1522.

Toscanini, Arturo, Italian conductor, b. 1867, d. 1957.

Tosti, Sir Francesco Paolo, singing-master to the British Royal family and composer, b. 1846, d. 1916.

Tostig, Earl of the Northumbrians, killed 1066.

Tottel, Richard, English publisher (*Miscellany*, 1557), d. 1594.

Toulon, scene of the sabotaging of the French Fleet in World War II 27 Nov. 1942.

Toulouse-Lautrec, Henri de, French painter, b. 1864, d. 1901.

Tourneur, Cyril, English playwright (*The Atheist's Tragedy*, about 1611), b. about 1575, d. 1626.

Tourniquet, invented in the Thirty Years War by the German surgeon Fabriz von Hilden, b. 1560, d. 1634.

Tourniquet, Screw, invented by the French surgeon Jean Louis Petit, b. 1674, d. 1750.

Tours, Battle of, between Charles Martel and the Saracens, 732.

Toussaint l'Ouverture, François Dominique, Governor-General of (Haiti) Santo Domingo, b. a slave about 1743, d. 1803.

Tovey, Sir Donald, English music-ologist, b. 1875, d. 1940.

Townshend, Charles Townshend, Viscount, British statesman and agricultural pioneer, b. 1674, d. 1738.

Toynbee Hall, London, founded 1885 as a memorial to the British social reformer Arnold Toynbee, b. 1852, d. 1883.

Toynbee, Arnold, British historian (*A Study of History*, 1934–1954), b. 1889.

Trachoma, main cause of blindness, virus first isolated by the Chinese scientist F. F. T'ang 1957.

Tracts for the Times, Oxford Group tracts issued in defence of the Church of England as a divine institution 1833 to 1841.

Trades Union Congress, Great Britain, formed 1868.

Trafalgar, Battle of, between Lord Nelson and the French and Spanish fleets, 21 Oct. 1805.

Traherne, Thomas, English poet, b. about 1637, d. 1674.

Trajan, Roman Emperor (98–117), b. about 54, d. 117.

Tramway, First, opened in New York 26 Nov. 1832 ; first introduced into England by G. F. Train 1860 ; first English electrified tramway Leeds 1891 ; last tram in London ran 6 July 1952.

Transandine Railway Tunnel, between Chile and Argentine, opened 1910.

Transatlantic Cable, first laid 1858.

Transatlantic Flight, first non-stop solo flight (Long Island to Paris) made 20–21 May 1927 by the American aviator Charles Augustus Lindbergh (b. 1902). First woman Transatlantic flier, Amelia Earhart (b. 1898) flew Newfoundland to Wales 18 June 1928.

Transatlantic Cable Signal, First, received 14 Dec. 1901 at St John's, Newfoundland, by the Italian radio pioneer Guglielmo Marconi, b. 1874, d. 1937.

Transatlantic Telephone Cables, between the United Kingdom, Canada and the U.S.A. inaugurated 1956.

Transcendental Club, formed in U.S.A. 1836.

Transfer Machine, First automatic, designed by M. Taylor and F. G. Woollard at Morris Motors 1923.

Transfinite Numbers, theory postulated 1915 by the German mathematician Georg Cantor, b. 1845, d. 1918.

Transformer, World's largest electric, built in England 1958.

Transistors, first demonstrated by scientists of the Bell Telephone Laboratories 1948.

Trans-Siberian Railway, construction begun 1891, completed 1906.

Transvaal, independence recognised by Britain 1852 ; annexed by Britain 1877 ; independence restored 1881 ; reconquered 1902.

Transvaal Gold-bearing Lode, discovered 1883.

Transverse-propelled Ship, First (the *Oriana*), launched 1959.

Transylvania, ruled by Austria 1698–1848, 1849–1867 ; by Hungary 1867–1920 ; by Rumania 1920–1940, and since 1945.

Trappist Order, founded 1664 by Armand de Rancé, b. 1626, d. 1700.

Trasimeno, Battle of Lake, between Hannibal and the Romans, 217 B.C.

Trebizond, Asia Minor, founded 756 B.C. (as Trapezoz) ; site of Empire of Comneni 1204-1461 ; captured by Turks 1461 and renamed Trabzon.

Tree, Sir Herbert Beerbohm, English actor-manager, b. 1853, d. 1917.

Treitschke, Heinrich von, German historian, b. 1834, d. 1896.

Trelawny, Edward John, English writer, b. 1792, d. 1881.

Trelawny, Sir Jonathan, Bishop of Winchester (1707–1721), b. 1650, d. 1721.

Trent, Council of, Catholic ecumenical council, held 1545 to 1563.

Trent College, English public school, founded 1866.

Trevisa, John of, English writer and translator, b. 1326, d. 1412.

Trevithick, Richard, English engineer, b. 1771, d. 1833.

Trianon, Treaty of, between Hungary and the Allies, signed 4 June 1920.

Triassic Period, Earth history, 195 million years ago.

Trieste, ruled by Austria 1382–1918, by Italy 1918–1945 ; free territory 1942–1954 ; partitioned by Italy and Yugoslavia 1954.

Trinity College, Cambridge University, founded by King Henry VIII 1546.

Trinity College, Glenalmond, Scottish public school, founded 1841 ; opened 1847.

Trinity College, Oxford University, founded 1555 by Sir Thomas Pope, d. 1559.

Trinity Hall, Cambridge University, founded by William Bateman, Bishop of Norwich, 1350.

Trinity House, London, origins in the mediæval Guild of Mariners, developing into the Corporation of Trinity House of Deptford Strond which was granted its first Charter by King Henry VIII, 1514.

Trinity School of John Whitgift, English public school founded by the Archbishop of Canterbury, John Whitgift, b. 1530, d. 1604.

Triode Valve (Audion), invented 1906 by the American inventor Lee de Forest, b. 1873.

Triple Alliances, in Europe, 1668, 1717, 1820, 1827, 1881, 1882.

Tristan da Cunha, Atlantic island, discovered Mar. 1506 by the Portuguese navigator Tristão da Cunha, b. about 1460, d. about 1540 ; settled 1810, annexed by Britain 1816.

Troeltsch, Ernst, German theologian, b. 1865, d. 1923.

Trolley-bus, first used in England 1909.

Trollope, Anthony, English novelist (*Barchester Towers*, 1857), b. 1815, d. 1882.

Trollope, Mrs Frances, English writer (*Domestic Manners of the Americans*, 1832), b. 1780, d. 1863.

‘ **Trotsky,** Leon ’ (Lev Davidovich Bronstein), Russian Revolutionary leader, b. 1877, exiled 1929, assassinated 1940.

Troy, destroyed about 1200 B.C. ; site at Hissarbik discovered 1801 by the English archæologist Sir William Gell (1777–1836) ; excavations carried out by the German archæologist Henrich Schliemann (1822–1890).

Troy Ounce, for precious metals and stones, legalised in Britain 1853.

Truck Act, prohibiting payment in kind, passed by Parliament 1831.

Truman, Harry S., U.S. President (1945–1953), b. 1884.

Trumbull, John, American painter, b. 1756, d. 1843.

Trunk Call Dialling, first introduced in Britain at Bristol, 5 Sept. 1959.

Truro School, English public school, founded 1879.

Truth, founded 1877 and edited by the English scholar Henry Labouchere, b. 1831, d. 1912 ; ceased publication 1957.

Tsushima, Naval battle of, between the Japanese and Russian fleets, 27 May 1905.

Tuberculosis, bacillus discovered 1882 by the German bacteriologist Robert Koch, b. 1843, d. 1910.

Tubman, William Vacanarat Shadrach, President (since 1943) of Liberia, b. 1895.

Tucker, Benjamin, American anarchist, b. 1854, d. 1939.

Tucuman, Congress of, declared the independence of Argentina 9 July 1816.

Tuesday, the third day of the week.

Tuke, Sir Brian, ' Master of the Postes ', d. 1545.

Tulane University, New Orleans, founded 1834.

Tull, Jethro, English agricultural pioneer and inventor of the seed drill, 1731, b. 1674, d. 1741.

Tungsten, metallic element, discovered 1781 by the Swedish chemist Carl Wilhelm Scheele, b. 1742, d. 1786.

Tungsten, Ductile, discovered 1906 by the American scientist William David Collidge, b. 1873.

Tungsten, Metallic, isolated 1783 by the Spanish chemist Fauste d'Elhuyar, b. 1755, d. 1833.

Tuning Fork, said to have been invented 1711 by the English trumpeter and lutenist John Shore, d. 1752.

Tunney, Gene, American ex-world heavyweight champion, b. 1898.

Tunstall, Cuthbert, Master of the Rolls and Bishop of Durham (1530–1559), b. 1474, d. 1559.

Turbine, First reaction, built 1839.

Turbine, Steam, invented 1884 by the British engineer Sir Charles Parsons, b. 1854, d. 1931.

Turbo-Alternator, World's largest (550,000 kW.), ordered for Thorpe Marsh Power Station, England, by the Central Electricity Generating Board 1958.

Turbo-Alternator Set, First, manufactured by the British engineer Sir Charles Parsons, b. 1854, d. 1931.

Turbo-Jet, First (the De Havilland Comet I), entered airline service 1958.

Turbo-Prop Airliner, First (the Bristol Britannia), entered scheduled service 1 Feb. 1957.

Turbo-Prop Engine, First (the Rolls-Royce Dart), 1947.

Turenne, Henri de la Tour d'Auvergne, Vicomte de, French soldier, b. 1611, killed in battle 1675.

Turgenev, Ivan Sergeievich, Russian novelist (*A Sportsman's Sketches*, 1846), b. 1818, d. 1883.

Turgot, Anne Robert Jacques, French statesman, b. 1727, d. 1781.

Turgot, Bishop of St Andrews, d. 1115.

Turina, Joaquín, Spanish composer (*Sinfonia Sevillana*), b. 1882, d. 1949.

Turks, rebelled against Avars 552, defeated Byzantine army 1071, defeated by Mongols 1243 ; Ottomans crossed Dardanelles 1345, defeated Serbs at Kossovo 1389, defeated by Timur 1402, captured Constantinople 1453. Ottoman Empire collapsed 1922 and republic of Turkey proclaimed 1923.

Turner, Joseph Mallord William, English painter (*The Grand Canal, Venice*), b. 1775, d. 1851.

Turner, Thomas, English potter who introduced 1780 The Willow Pattern, b. 1749, d. 1809.

Turpin, Dick, English highwayman, b. 1705, hanged 1739.

Tussaud's, Mme, London waxworks, opened 1835 by the Swiss-born showwoman Mme Marie Tussaud (1760–1850). New building opened 1928.

Tutankhamun, tomb of, discovered 1922.

' Twain, Mark ' (Samuel Langhorne Clemens), American writer (*Tom Sawyer*, 1876), b. 1835, d. 1910.

Twelfth Night (Old Christmas Day or, The Feast of the Three Kings), celebrated on night of 5 Jan.

Twentieth Century, The, founded 1877 as *The Nineteenth Century* by the English architect Sir James Knowles, b. 1831, d. 1908.

Two Thousand Guineas, Newmarket, first run 1809.

Tycho Brahe, Danish astronomer, b. 1546, d. 1601.

Tyler, John Tyler, U.S. President (1841–1845), b. 1790, d. 1862.

Tyler, Wat, English rebel leader, killed 1381.

Tyndale, William, English translator of the Bible, b. about 1494, strangled and burnt at the stake 1536.

Tyndall, John, Irish-born scientist, b. 1820, d. 1893.

Typewriter, model constructed 1873 by Sholes and Glidden ; modern version (Underwood) constructed 1898 by F. X. Wagner.

Typhoid Fever, bacillus described by Eberth 1880.

Typhus, bacillus described by Ricketts 1910.

Tyres, pneumatic (see **Pneumatic Tyres**).

Tyrrell, Anthony, English spy, b. 1552, d. about 1610.

Tzetzes, John, Byzantine scholar, b. about 1110, d. 1180.

U

U.F.O. (Unidentified Flying Objects), first noticed by the American Kenneth Arnold June 1947.

U.N.E.S.C.O. (United Nations Educational, Scientific and Cultural Organisation), established 4 Nov. 1946.

U.N.I.C.E.F. (United Nations Children's Fund), established 1946.

U.N.O. (see **United Nations**).

Ubaldini, Petruccio, Italian-born writer and illuminator, b. about 1524, d. about 1600.

Überweg, Friedrich, German philosopher, b. 1826, d. 1871.

Uccello, Paolo, Italian artist (*Deluge,* about 1445), b. about 1396, d. 1475.

Udall, Nicholas, English playwright (*Ralph Roister Doister,* about 1553), b. 1505, d. 1556.

Uganda, British Protectorate since 1894.

Ugolino da Siena, Italian painter, lived in the 14th century.

Uhde, Fritz von, German painter, b. 1848, d. 1911.

Ulfilas, translator of the Bible into Gothic, b. about 311, d. 383.

Ulloa, Francisco de, Spanish navigator of the Californian coast, d. about 1540.

Ulpian, Roman jurist, killed about 228.

Umberto I, King of Italy (1878–1900), b. 1844, assassinated 1900.

Umberto II, King of Italy (1946), b. 1904.

Unamuno, Miguel de, Spanish writer, b. 1864, d. 1937.

Underground Railroad, system by which negro slaves were enabled to escape through the northern states of America, 1825 onwards.

Underground Railway, first opened in London 1863 (Metropolitan Railway); first electric line opened 1890 (City & South London Railway).

Undset, Sigrid, Norwegian novelist (*Kristin Lavransdatter*), b. 1882, d. 1949.

'Unidentified Flying Objects' (U.F.O.), first noticed by the American Kenneth Arnold, June 1947.

Uniformity, Acts of, 1549, 1552, 1559, 1662.

Union, Act of, between England and Scotland 1707; between Britain and Ireland 1800.

Union, Decree of (*Lætentur cæli*), uniting the Latin and Greek churches, issued 6 July 1439.

Union of Soviet Socialist Republics, Russia, formed 1922.

Union Pacific Railway, U.S.A., built mainly 1862–1869.

United Boys' Brigade of America, founded 1887.

United Church of Christ, formed in the U.S.A. through the union of the General Council of the Congregational Christian Churches with the Evangelical and Reformed Church 1957.

United Kingdom (Great Britain), formed 1801.

United Nations, formed 1942; organisation set up 1945.

United States of America, declared independence 1776; Constitution established 1787.

Universal Postal Union, founded at Berne 9 Oct. 1875.

University College, London University, opened 1828.

University College, Oxford University, once believed to have been founded 872; in existence by 1170.

University College School, London, English public school, founded 1830; moved to present site 1907.

Unwin, Mrs Mary, friend of the poet William Cowper, b. 1724, d. 1796.

Uppingham School, English public school, founded by Archdeacon Johnson 1584.

Uranus, planet discovered 13 Mar. 1781 by the German-born astronomer William Herschel, b. 1738, d. 1822.

Ure, Mary, Scottish actress, b. 1935.

d'Urfey, Thomas, English playwright (*The Comical History of Don Quixote,* 1694–1696), b. about 1653, d. 1723.

Urien, British prince, lived in the 6th century.

Urquhart, Sir Thomas, Scottish writer and translator, b. about 1611, d. 1660.

Urquiza, Justo José de, President (1854–1860) of Argentina, b. 1800, assassinated 1870.

Ursinus, Zacharias, German theologian who, with Caspar Olevianus (1536–1587) published 1563 the Heidelburg Catechism, b. 1536, d. 1583.

Ursuline Order, of nuns, founded 1535.

Uruguay, independence established 1828.

Ussher, James, Archbishop of Armagh and writer, b. 1581, d. 1656.

Utah, U.S.A., settled 1847 ; organised as a Territory 1850 ; admitted to the Union 1896.

Utah University, Salt Lake City, founded 1850 ; reopened under present name 1867.

Utamaro, Kitagawa, Japanese artist, b. 1753, d. 1806.

Utrillo, Maurice, French painter, b. 1883, d. 1955.

Uttman, Barbara, German woman who introduced 1561 pillow lace-making into Germany, b. 1514, d. 1575.

V

Vaccination, against smallpox, pioneered by Lady Mary Wortley Montagu (1689–1762) ; revived 1796 by Edward Jenner (1749–1823).

Vaccine, Salk, developed 1954 by the American scientist Jonas Edward Salk, b. 1914.

Vacuum Flask, invented by the Scottish scientist Sir James Dewar, b. 1842, d. 1923.

Vaihinger, Hans, German philosopher, b. 1852, d. 1933.

Valdivia, Pedro de, Spanish conquistador in Chile, killed 1554.

Valency, Double, Isomerism, study developed 1893 by the Swiss chemist Alfred Werner, b. 1866, d. 1919.

Valens, Byzantine Emperor (364–378), killed in battle 378.

Valentine, St, martyred about 270.

Valentine, Pope 827.

St Valentine's Day, Feb. 14.

Valentinian I, Roman Emperor (364–375), b. 321, d. 375.

Valentinian II, Roman Emperor (375–392), b. 371, d. 392.

Valentinian III, Roman Emperor (425–455), d. 419, assassinated 455.

Valentino, Rudolph, film actor, b. 1895, d. 1926.

Valera, Eamon, de, Irish statesman (Prime Minister 1927–1948, 1951–1954, 1957–1959), b. 1882.

Valerian, Roman Emperor, 253–260.

Valéry, Paul, French writer, b. 1871, d. 1945.

Valle-Inclan, Ramón del, Spanish novelist, b. 1870, d. 1936.

Vallet, Edouard, Swiss painter (*Sunday in the Valais,* 1919), b. 1876, d. 1929.

Valois Dynasty, ruled France 1328–1589.

Valotton, Félix, Swiss painter (*The Rape of Europa,* 1908), b. 1865, d. 1925.

Valparaiso, Chile, founded 1536.

Valve, Thermionic, diode developed 1900 by Fleming ; triode developed 1907 by Lee de Forest ; tetrode developed 1916 by W. von Schottky.

Van Buren, Martin, U.S.A. President (1837–1841), b. 1782, d. 1862.

Van Der Meer, Jan, Dutch painter, b. 1628, d. 1691.

Van Doren, Carl, American writer, b. 1885, d. 1950.

Van Gogh, Vincent, Dutch painter (*Sunflowers*), b. 1853, committed suicide 1890.

Van Dyck, Sir Anthony, Flemish-born painter (*Charles I*), b. 1599, d. 1641.

Van Loon, Hendrick, American writer (*Story of Mankind,* 1921), b. 1882, d. 1944.

Van Rensselaer, Killian, Dutch merchant, b. 1595, d. 1644.

Van Vechten, Carl, American novelist (*Nigger Heaven*), b. 1880.

Vanadium, metallic element, discovered by Sefström 1830.

Vanbrugh, Sir John, English playwright and architect, b. 1664, d. 1726.

Vancouver, George, British navigator b. 1758, d. 1798.

Vandals, crossed Rhine 406 ; entered Spain 409 ; crossed to Africa 429 ; sacked Rome 455 ; defeated by Belisarius 533.

Vanderbilt, Cornelius, American financier, b. 1794, d. 1877.

Vanderbilt University, Tennessee, founded 1872.

Vane, Sir Henry, statesman, b. 1613, executed 1662.

Vanhomrigh, Esther, Dean Swift's ' Vanessa ', b. 1690, d. 1723.

Varro, Marcus Terentius, Roman writer, b. 116, d. 27 B.C.

Vasco da Gama, Portuguese explorer and navigator, b. about 1460, d. about 1525.

Vascular Surgery, initiated by the French surgeon Alexis Carrel, b. 1873, d. 1945.

Vatican, papal residence since 1377.

Vatican Council, Catholic general council, held 1869–1870.

Vaughan, Henry (*The Silurist*), Welsh poet, b. 1622, d. 1695.

Vaughan, William, coloniser of Newfoundland, b. 1577, d. 1641.

Vaughan Williams, Ralph, English composer (*Hugh the Drover,* 1911–1914), b. 1872, d. 1958.

Vauxhall Gardens, open from about 1661 to 1859.

Veblen, Thorstein, American sociologist, b. 1857, d. 1929.

Veidt, Conrad, film actor, b. 1894, d. 1943.

Velazquez, Diego Rodriquez de Silva, Spanish painter (*The Rokeby Venus*), b. 1599, d. 1660.

Venezuela, independence proclaimed 1811, secured 1830.

Venice, independent republic under Doge 697–1797 ; ruled by Austria 1797–1805, 1815–1848, 1849–1866.

Venizelos, Eleutherios, Greek statesman, b. 1864, d. 1936.

Verdi, Giuseppe, Italian composer (*Rigoletto,* 1851), b. 1813, d. 1901.

Verdun, Battle of, between Germans and French, Feb.–Apr. 1916

Vere, Edward de, Earl of Oxford, poet, b. 1550, d. 1604.

Vereeniging, Treaty of, between English and Boers, signed 1902.

Verhaeren, Emile, Belgian poet, b. 1855, d. 1916.

Verlaine, Paul, French poet, b. 1844, d. 1896.

Vermeer, Jan, Dutch painter, b. 1632, d. 1675.

Vermont, U.S.A., first settled 1724 ; admitted to the Union 1791.

Veronese (Paolo Caliari), Italian painter, b. 1528, d. 1588.

Versailles, Treaty of, signed 28 June 1919.

Vertue, George, English engraver, b. 1684, d. 1756.

Vespasian, Roman Emperor (69–79), b. 11, d. 79.

Vespucci, Amerigo, Italian explorer, b. 1451, d. 1512.

Vestris Mme (Lucia Elizabeth Mathews), actress, b. 1797, d. 1856.

Veto, abolished in Polish Diet 1791 ; last used by British sovereigns 1707 ; established in U.N. Security Council 1945.

Vianney, Jean Marie (The Curé d'Ars), French priest, b. 1787 d. 1859.

Viceroy, title of ruler of India 1858–1947.

Vichy, place of French government 1940–1947.

Victoria, Queen, b. 1819, d. 1901.

Victoria and Albert Museum, London, opened 18 May 1852.

Victoria College, Jersey, public school, founded in commemoration of a visit of Queen Victoria to the island and opened 1852.

Victoria Cross, premier British decoration for valour, founded by Queen Victoria 1856.

Victorian Order, Royal, founded by Queen Victoria 1896.

Vidocq, François, Eugène French criminal and detective, b. 1775, d. 1857.

Vienna, besieged by Turks 1529 and 1683 ; Congress of, 1814–1815.

Viet Nam, Democratic Republic of, Communist régime since 1945.

Viet Nam, Republic of, independence within the French Union proclaimed 1949 ; sovereignty achieved 1954.

Vieuxtemps, Henri, Belgian violinist and composer, b. 1820, d. 1881.

Vigfusson, Gudbrandr, Icelandic scholar, b. 1828, d. 1889.

Vigny, Alfred de, French writer, b. 1797, d. 1863.

Villa-Lobos, Heitor, Brazilian comcomposer (*Vidapura*, 1918), b. 1887, d. 1959.

Villiers, Barbara, Countess of Castlemaine, Duchess of Cleveland, b. 1641, d. 1709.

Villiers, George, Duke of Buckingham, English courtier, b. 1592, assassinated 1628.

Villiers, George, Duke of Buckingham, courtier and statesman, b. 1628, d. 1687.

Villon, François, French criminal and poet, b. 1431, disappeared 1463.

Vinegar Bible, so-called for its ' Parable of the Vinegar ' (*i.e.* Vineyard), published 1717.

Vintners Company, London livery company, origins uncertain ; first recorded reference 1321 ; Letters Patent granted 1363 ; first Charter 1437.

Violin Playing, first made the subject of formal tuition 1730 by the Italian violinist Francesco Geminiani, b. 1687, d. 1762.

Virchow Rudolf, German founder of the science of modern pathology, b. 1821, d. 1902.

Virgil (Publius Vergilius Maro), Roman, poet (*Æneid*), b. 70, d. 19 B.C.

Virginia, U.S.A., first settled 1607, entered the Union 1788.

Vitalis, Ordericus, English historian, b. 1075, d. about 1143.

Vitruvius (Marcus Vitruvius Pollio), Roman architect in 1st century B.C.

Vivaldi, Antonio, Italian composer (*La Stravaganza*), b. about 1676, d. 1741.

Vivisection, Law regulating, passed 1876.

Vodka, manufacture of, prohibited in Russia 1914–1925.

Vogelweide, Walther von der, German Minnesinger and poet (*The Palestine Song*), d. about 1230.

Volta, Alessandro, Italian physicist, b. 1745, d. 1827.

Voltaire, François Marie Arouet de, French writer (*Candide*, 1759), b. 1694, d. 1778.

Volunteers of America, founded by Generals Ballington Booth and Maud Ballington Booth 1896.

Von Stroheim, Erich, film actor, b. 1886, d. 1957.

Vortigern, British leader, lived in the 5th century.

Vulcanisation of Rubber, patented 1843 by the English merchant Thomas Hancock, b. 1786, d. 1865.

Vulgate, Latin translation of Bible, made 382–405 by St Jerome.

Vulpius, Melchior, German composer (*The Matthew Passion*), b. about 1560, d. 1615.

W

Waals, Johannes Diderik van der, Dutch scientist and Nobel Prize winner, b. 1837, d. 1923.

Wadham College, Oxford University, founded 1612 by bequest of Nicholas Wadham, d. 1609.

Wafd, Egyptian political party, formed 1919.

Wagner, Cosima, wife of Richard Wagner, b. 1837, d. 1930.

Wagner, Richard, German composer (*Lohengrin*, 1848), b. 1813, d. 1883.

Wagram, Battle of, between Napoleon and the Austrians 5–6 July 1809.

Wain, John, English novelist (*Hurry on Down*, 1953), b. 1925.

Wainewright, Thomas Griffiths, the English poisoner and artist, b. 1794, d. 1852.

Waitangi, Treaty of, signed with the Maoris in New Zealand, 6 Feb. 1840.

Wake Island, Pacific, World War II ; American defence against the Japanese 7–23 Dec. 1941.

Wakefield Grammar School, English public school, founded by Royal Charter 1591.

Waksman, Dr Selman Abraham, Russian-born discoverer 1943 of streptomycin, b. 1888, awarded Nobel Prize 1952.

Walburga, St, b. about 710, d. about 777.

Waldenses, Christian heretic sect, founded during 12th century by Peter Walds of Lyons.

Waldteufel, Emil, French composer of dance music (*Estudiantina*), b. 1837, d. 1915.

Wales, finally subdued by England 1284 (rebelled 1400–1410) ; united with England 1536–1547 ; first Archbishop of (The Bishop of St Asaph), enthroned 1 June 1920.

Walker, George, Governor of Londonderry, b. 1618, killed in battle 1690.

Walkinshaw, Clementina, mistress of the Young Pretender, b. about 1726, d. 1802.

Wall Game, held at Eton College on St Andrew's Day, 30. Nov.

Wallace, Alfred Russel, English naturalist, b. 1823, d. 1913.

Wallace, Lew, American writer (*Ben Hur*, 1880), b. 1827, d. 1905.

Wallace, Sir William, Scottish leader, b. about 1274, executed 1305.

Wallace Collection, The, London, bequeathed by the widow of Sir Richard Wallace (1818–1890), opened 1900.

Wallasey Grammar School, English public school, origins uncertain ; first recorded mention 1595.

Wallenstein, Albrecht von, Bohemian soldier, b. 1583, assassinated 1634.

Waller, Edmund, English poet and politician, b. 1606, d. 1687.

Waller, Sir William, soldier and politician, b. about 1597, d. 1668.

Wallis, John, English mathematician, b. 1616, d. 1703.

Wallis, Samuel, English naval captain and discoverer 1767 of Tahiti, b. 1728, d. 1804.

Walpole, Horace, Earl of Orford, English writer (*The Castle of Otranto*, 1764), b. 1717, d. 1797.

Walpole, Hugh, New Zealand-born novelist (*Rogue Herries*, 1930), b. 1884, d. 1941.

Walpole, Robert, Earl of Orford, British statesman (virtual Prime Minister 1721–1742), b. 1676, d. 1745.

Walpurga, St, English Abbess of Heidenheim, d. about 779.

Walsh, John, English publisher of music, d. 1736.

Walsingham, Sir Francis, British statesman, b. about 1530, d. 1590.

Walsingham, Thomas, English historian (*Chronica Majora*), d. about 1422.

' Walter, Bruno ' (Bruno Walter Schlesinger), German-born conductor, b. 1876.

Walter, John, English merchant and founder 1785 of *The Times*, b. 1739, d. 1812.

Walther von der Vogelweide, German Minnesinger and poet (*The Palestine Song*), d. about 1230.

Walton, Izaak, English writer (*The Compleat Angler*, 1653), b. 1593, d. 1683.

Walton, Sir William, English composer (*Façade*, 1922), b. 1902.

Wan Li Period, China, 1573–1619.

Warbeck, Perkin, French-born pretender, b. 1474, executed 1499.

Warburg Institute, University of London, founded by Professor Aby Warburg, b. 1866, d. 1929.

Warburton, William, Bishop of Gloucester (1759–1779), b. 1698, d. 1779.

Ward, Mrs Humphry (Mary Augusta Ward), Tasmanian-born novelist (*Robert Elsmere*, 1888), b. 1851, d. 1920.

Warham, William, Archbishop of Canterbury (1504–1532), b. about 1450, d. 1532.

' Warlock, Peter ' (Philip Heseltine), English composer (*The Curlew*), b. 1894, d. 1930.

Warner, Sylvia Townsend, English writer (*Lolly Willowes*, 1926), b. 1893.

' Warwick the Kingmaker ', Richard Neville, Earl of Warwick, b. 1428, killed 1471.

Warwick School, English public school, probably founded about 914 ; re-founded by King Henry VIII 1545.

Washington, Booker Taliaferro, American negro educationist, b. about 1859, d. 1915.

Washington, George, U.S. President (1789–1797), b. 1732, d. 1799.

Washington, D.C., capital of U.S.A., founded 1791.

Washington, U.S.A., created a Territory 1853 ; admitted to the Union 1889.

Washington, Treaty of, between the U.S.A. and Great Britain, signed 1871.

Wassermann, August von, German scientist and inventor 1906 o⁺ the Wassermann Test, b. 1866, d. 1925.

Wassermann, Jakob, novelist (*Christian Wahnschaffe*, 1919), b. 1873, d. 1934.

Water, first analysed 1783 by the French chemist Antoine Laurent Lavoisier, b. 1743, d. 1794.

Water-closets, invented 1596 by the English poet Sir John Harington, b. 1561, d. 1612.

' Water-Poet, The ' (John Taylor), English writer (*The Pennyles Pilgrimage*, 1618), b. 1580, d. 1653.

Waterhouse, Alfred, British architect, b. 1830, d. 1905.

Waterloo, Battle of, 18 June 1815.

Waterloo Bridge, London ; old bridge built by the Scottish engineer John Rennie (1761–1821). New bridge opened to vehicles 1942 ; formally opened 1945.

Waterlow, Sir Sydney Hedley, English printer and philanthropist, b. 1822, d. 1906.

Watermarks, in paper, first known example made about 1282.

Waterproof Clothing, invented 1823 by the Scottish chemist Charles Macintosh, b. 1766, d. 1843.

Watson, George Lennox, British yacht designer, b. 1851, d. 1904.

Watson, Richard, Bishop of Llandaff and scientist, b. 1737, d. 1816.

Watt, James, Scottish engineer and inventor, b. 1736, d. 1819.

Watt, Robert, Scottish physician and bibliographer, b. 1774, d. 1819.

Watteau, Antione, French painter (*The Embarkation for Cythera*, 1717), b. 1684, d. 1721.

Watts, Sir George Frederick, English painter (*Paolo and Francesca*, 1848), b. 1817, d. 1904.

Watts, Isaac, English Hymn-writer (*Jesus Shall Reign*), b. 1674, d. 1748.

Waugh, Evelyn, English writer (*Brideshead Revisited*, 1945), b. 1903.

Wave Mechanics, defined 1923 by the French scientist Prince Louis de Broglie, b. 1892.

Wavell, Archibald Percival Wavell, Earl, Viceroy of India (1943–1947), b. 1883, killed 1953.

Waynflete, William of, Bishop of Winchester and founder 1458 of Magdalen College, Oxford, b. about 1395, d. 1486.

Weather Map, First, drawn 1820 by the German astronomer and physicist Heinrich Wilhelm Brandes, b. 1777, d. 1834.

Weather Prediction, study founded by the French scientist Jean Baptiste Pierre Antoine de Monet, Chevalier de Lamarck, b. 1744, d. 1829.

Weaver, John, English dancing-master, b. 1673, d. 1760.

Webb, Beatrice (1858–1943) and Sidney (1859–1947), British sociologists, married 1892.

Weber, Carl Maria, German composer (*Der Freischütz*, 1821), b. 1786, d. 1826.

Webern, Anton von, Austrian composer (*Passacaglia*, 1908), b. 1883, d. 1945.

Webster, John, English playwright (*The White Devil*, 1612), b. about 1580, d about 1625.

Webster, Noah, American dictionary-maker (first published 1806, but present dictionary dates from 1828), b. 1758, d. 1843.

Wedekind, Frank, German writer, b. 1864, d. 1918.

Wedgwood, Josiah, English potter, b. 1730, d. 1795.

Wedgwood, Thomas, English inventor and the first (1802) photographer, b. 1771, d. 1805.

Wednesday, the fourth day of the week.

Week, the seven days from midnight on Saturday to midnight the following Saturday ; adopted in Roman Empire from Jewish custom about 500.

Wei Dynasty, China, 368 to 557.

Weight Reduction, by the elimination of starch in diet, popularised by the English undertaker, William Banting, b. 1797, d. 1878.

Weill, Kurt, composer (*Die Dreigroschenopfer*, 1928), b. 1900.

Weingartner, Felix, conductor, b. 1863, d. 1942.

Weishaupt, Adam, German philosopher and founder 1776 of the Illuminati, b. 1748, d. 1830.

Weizmann, Dr Chaim, Polish-born scientist, Zionist leader and first President of Israel, b. 1874, d. 1952.

Wellesley, Richard Colley Wellesley, Marquis, Governor-General of India (1797–1805), b. 1760, d. 1842.

Wellesz, Egon, Austrian composer (*Alkestis*, 1924), b. 1885.

Wellingborough School, English public school, founded 1478 ; moved to present site 1881.

Wellington, Arthur Wellesley, Duke of, British soldier and statesman, b. 1769, d. 1852.

Wellington College, English public school, founded by public subscription in honour of the memory of the Duke of Wellington 1853.

Wellington School, Somerset, English public school, founded 1841.

Wells, Herbert George, English writer (*Kipps*, 1905), b. 1866, d. 1946.

Wells, Fargo & Co., American express company, founded 1852.

Welsbach Mantle, invented by the Austrian chemist Baron von Welsbach, b. 1858, d. 1929.

Welsh, Thomas, English singer, b. about 1780, d. 1848.

Welsh Literature, recorded before 600.

Welwyn Garden City, built 1920.

' Wembley Exhibition ' : British Empire Exhbition, Wembley, opened 23 Apr., closed 1 Nov. 1924.

Wentworth, William Charles, Australian pioneer, b. 1793, d. 1872.

Werfel, Franz, Austrian writer, b. 1890, d. 1945.

Werner, Alfred, Swiss chemist who developed 1893 the study of double valency, b. 1866, d. 1919.

Wesker, Arnold, English playwright (*Roots*, 1959), b. 1932.

Wesley, Charles, English hymn-writer (*Jesu, Lover of My Soul*), b. 1707, d. 1788.

Wesley, John, founder 1738 of Methodism, b. 1703, d. 1791.

West, Benjamin, American painter (*The Death of General Wolfe*, 1771), b. 1738, d. 1820.

' West, Rebecca ' (Cicely Fairfield), English writer (*The Meaning of Treason*, 1949), b. 1892.

West Aden Protectorate Federation (Federation of Arab Amirates of the South), inaugurated 11 Feb. 1959.

West Virginia, U.S.A., separated from Virginia 1861, admitted to the Union 1863.

Western Australia, founded 1829 ; reached overland 1875 on third attempt (1875–1876) by the Australian explorer Ernest Giles, b. 1835, d. 1897.

Western European Union, first Assembly opened at Strasbourg 1955.

Western Pacific High Commission, British Commonwealth, created 1877.

Westminster Abbey, rebuilding begun 1245.

Westminster Assembly, religious body, sat 1643–1649.

Westminster Cathedral, England, opened 1903 ; consecrated 1910.

Westminster Gazette, The, British newspaper, founded 1892 ; absorbed into *The Daily News* 1928.

Westminster School, English public school, origins uncertain ; first recorded mention 1339 ; finally established by Queen Elizabeth I, 1560.

Westminster, Statute of, regulating British Commonwealth relations, passed 1931.

Weston, Agnes Elizabeth, English founder of the Royal Sailors' Rests, b. 1840, d. 1918.

Westphalia, Kingdom of, existed 1807–1814.

Westphalia, Peace of, ending the Thirty Years War, signed 1648.

Wetterhorn, 12,162 ft. peak nr. Grindelwald, first climbed by the Swiss guides Bannholzer and Jaun 1844.

Weyden, Roger van der, Flemish painter (*The Last Judgment*), b. about 1400, d. 1464.

Weyprecht, Karl, German discoverer 1873 of Franz Josef Land in the Arctic, b. 1838, d. 1881.

Whaling Commission, International, set up 1946.

Wharton, Henry, English scholar, b. 1664, d. 1695.

Wheatstone Bridge, invented by the English scientist Sir Charles Wheatstone, b. 1802, d. 1875.

Whigs, British political group, first so named 1679 ; split 1791.

Whipsnade Zoo, opened to the public 1931.

Whistler, James McNeill, American-born painter (*Portrait of My Mother*), b. 1834, d. 1903.

Whiston, Joseph, London bookseller, d. 1780.

Whitaker's Almanack, founded 1868 by the English publisher Joseph Whitaker, b. 1820, d. 1895.

Whitby, Synod of, held 664.

White, Gilbert, English naturalist (*The Natural History and Antiquities of Selbourne*, 1789), b. 1720, d. 1793.

White, William Hale ('Mark Rutherford'), English writer (*Catherine Furze*, 1893), b. 1831, d. 1913.

White Lotus Day, commemorating the death of the founder of the Theosophical Society, Mme Blavatsky (1831–1891).

White Russia, Soviet Republic declared 1919.

White Ship, The, sank with Prince William 1120.

' **White Woman of the Genesee,** The ' (Mrs Mary Jemison), b. 1743, d. 1833.

Whitehead, Alfred Worth, British philosopher, b. 1861, d. 1947.

Whitefield, George, English Calvinist Methodist, b. 1714, d. 1740.

Whitehead, Robert, English inventor and torpedo manufacturer, b. 1823, d. 1905.

Whiteman, Paul, American jazz conductor, b. 1890.

Whitfield, Henry, founder of Guildford, Connecticut, d. about 1660.

Whitgift School, Croydon, founded 1596 by the Archbishop of Canterbury, John Whitgift, b. 1530, d. 1604.

Whitley Councils, concerning British labour conditions largely founded 1917 by John Henry Whitley, Speaker of the House of Commons, b. 1866, d. 1935.

Whitman, Walt, American poet (*Leaves of Grass*, 1855), b. 1819, d. 1892.

Whitsunday (Pentecost), seventh Sunday after Easter.

Whittingham, Charles, English printer, b. 1767, d. 1840.

Whittington, Dick, Lord Mayor (1397) of London, b. about 1358, d. 1423.

Whittle, Sir Frank, English pioneer in jet propulsion, b. 1907.

Whitworth, Sir Joseph, English mechanical engineer who standardised 1841 screw threads, b. 1803, d. 1887.

Whymper, Edward, English climber 1865 of the Matterhorn, b. 1840, d. 1911.

Whyte-Melville, George John, Scottish writer, b. 1821, d. 1878.

Wickham, Sir Henry, pioneer rubber planter, b. 1846, d. 1928.

Widor, Charles Marie, French composer (*Symphonie Romaine*), b. 1844, d. 1937.

Wiemkin, Walter Kurt, Swiss painter (*Life*, 1935), b. 1907.

Wien, Wilhelm, German physicist and exponent of the theory of radiation, b. 1864, d. 1938.

Wieniawski, Henri, Polish violinist and composer (*Légende*), b. 1835, d. 1880.

Wilberforce, Samuel, English divine, b. 1805, d. 1873.

Wilberforce, William, English suppressor of slavery, b. 1759, d. 1833.

Wild, Jonathan, English receiver and informer, b. about 1682, hanged 1725.

Wilde, Oscar, Irish-born wit and writer (*The Importance of being Earnest*, 1895), b. 1856, d. 1900.

Wilfrid, St, English divine, b. 634, d. 710.

Wilhelm, Karl Friedrich, German composer (*Die Wacht am Rhein*, 1854), b. 1815, d. 1873.

Wilhelmina, Queen (1890-1948) of the Netherlands, b. 1880.

Wilhelmshaven, first German military port, opened officially 17 June 1869.

Wilkes, John, English politician, b. 1727, d. 1797.

Wilkins, Sir Hubert, Australian explorer, b. 1888, d. 1958.

William I, King of Prussia and Emperor of Germany, b. 1797, succeeded his brother 1861, proclaimed Emperor 1871, d. 1888.

William II, Emperor of Germany, b. 1859, succeeded 1888, abdicated 1918, d. 1942.

William the Conqueror (William I), b. about 1027, conquered England 1066, d. 1087.

William Rufus (William II), King of England (1087–1100), b. about 1056, shot 1100.

William of Orange (William III), King of England, Scotland and Ireland (1689–1702), b. 1650, d. 1702.

William IV, King of Great Britain and Ireland (1830–1837), b. 1765, d. 1837.

William of Malmesbury, English historian, b. about 1095, d. 1143.

William of Ockham, English philosopher, d. about 1349.

William of Wykeham, Bishop of Winchester and founder 1379 of New College, Oxford, and 1382 of Winchester College, b. 1324, d. 1404.

William the Lyon, King of Scotland (1165–1214), b. 1143, d. 1214.

William the Silent, Prince of Orange, b. 1533, killed 1584.

William II Land, Antarctica, discovered 1903 by the German explorer Erich von Drygalski, b. 1865, d. 1949.

William and Mary, College of, Williamsburg, Virginia, founded 1693 by the English colonist William Randolf, b. 1650, d. 1711.

William Hulme's Grammar School, English public school, founded by the Hulme Trust 1887.

Williams, Sir George, founder 1844 of the Y.M.C.A., London, b. 1821, d. 1905.

Williams, Ralph Vaughan, English composer (*Hugh the Drover*, 1911–1914), b. 1872, d. 1958.

Williams, Tennessee (Thomas Lanier Williams), American writer (*A Streetcar Named Desire*, 1947), b. 1912.

Williams, Walter, last surviving veteran (Confederate) of the American Civil War, b. 1843, d. 1960.

Williams's Library, Dr, London, founded by the nonconformist leader Daniel Williams, b. about 1643, d. 1716.

Williamson, Alexander William, English chemist, b. 1824, d. 1904.

Willibrord, St, English missionary, b. about 658, d. 739.

Willis, Henry, English organ-builder, b. 1821, d. 1901.

Willow Pattern, introduced 1780 by the English potter Thomas Turner, b. 1749, d. 1809.

Wilson, Angus, English writer (*Hemlock and After*, 1952), b. 1913.

Wilson, John, English lutenist and composer, b. 1595, d. 1673.

Wilson, John ('Christopher North'), Scottish writer (*Recreations*, 1842), b. 1785, d. 1854.

Wilson, Woodrow, U.S. President (1913–1921), b. 1856, d. 1924.

'Wilson, Beau' (Edward Wilson), London man about town, killed 1694.

Wilson Cloud Chamber, invented 1911 by the Scottish scientist Charles Thomson Rees Wilson (Nobel Prize, 1927), b. 1869, d. 1959.

Wilson's Fourteen Points, announced by President Wilson 8 Jan., accepted by Germany 27 Oct. 1918.

Wilton Carpet, introduced into Britain from the U.S.A. about 1878.

Winchester Cathedral, England, constructed about 1079 to 1093.

Winchester College, English public school, founded 1382 by the Bishop of Winchester, William of Wykeham, b. 1324, d. 1404.

Window Tax, enacted in England 1695, finally repealed 1851.

Windmill, first mentioned in Persia in 7th century ; first mentioned in England in 1191.

Windsor, adopted by the British Royal Family as the family title 17 July 1917.

Wine and Food Society, London, held first meeting at the Café Royal 14 Nov. 1933.

Wingate, Orde Charles, British soldier, b. 1903, killed 1944.

Winslow, Edward, English Governor of Plymouth Colony, b. 1595, d. 1655.

Winstanley, Gerrard, English communist, active 1648–1652.

Winter, Thomas (' Tom Spring '), boxer, b. 1795, d. 1851.

Winterhalter, Franz Xaver, German-born painter (*The Prince Consort*), b. 1806, d. 1873.

Winthrop, John, English Governor of Massachusetts, b. 1588, d. 1649.

Winthrop, John, English Governor of Connecticut, b. 1606, d. 1676.

Wireless Telegraphy, brought into being 1895 by the Italian inventor Guglielmo Marconi, b. 1874, d. 1937.

Wisconsin, U.S.A., first settled 1670 ; created a Territory 1836 ; admitted to the Union 1848.

Wiseman, Cardinal Nicholas, first Archbishop of Westminster, b. 1802, d. 1865.

Wiseman, Richard, Royal surgeon, b. about 1622, d. 1676.

Witch, The last Lancashire, Mary Nutter, b. 1856, d. 1928.

Witches : last trial (Jane Wenham, d. 1730) in England 1712 ; last in Scotland 1722 ; statutes against witchcraft repealed 1736.

Wittelsbach Dynasty, ruled Bavaria 1180–1918.

Wittgenstein, Ludwig, Austrian-born philosopher, b. 1889, d. 1951.

Woffington, Peg, Irish-born actress, b. about 1714, d. 1760.

Wolcot, John (' Peter Pindar '), English writer (*The Lousiad*, 1785), b. 1738, d. 1819.

Wolf, Hugo, Austrian composer (*Der Corregidor*, 1896), b. 1860, d. 1903.

Wolf Cubs, junior Boy Scout movement, first organised in Britain 1916.

' Wolf of Badenoch, The ', Alexander Stewart, Earl of Buchan and Lord of Badenoch, b. about 1343, d. about 1405.

Wolfe, James, English general, b. 1727, killed 1759.

Wolf-Ferrari, Ermanno, Italian-born composer (*I Gioielli della Madonna*, 1911), b. 1876, d. 1948.

Wollstonecraft, Mary, English social reformer (*Vindication of the Rights of Women*, 1792), b. 1759, d. 1797.

Wolseley, Garnet Joseph Wolseley, Viscount, Irish-born Field - Marshal and Army reformer, b. 1833, d. 1913.

Wolsey, Cardinal Thomas, English divine and statesman, b. about 1475, d. 1530.

Wolverhampton Grammar School, English public school, founded by Sir Stephen Jenyns 1512 ; moved to present site 1875.

Woman Minister, first was Nina Bang, Minister of Education in Denmark (1924–1926) ; in England, Margaret Bondfield, Minister of Labour (1929–1931).

Woman Prime Minister, first was Mrs Sirimaro Bandaranaike in Ceylon 1960.

Women's Legion, voluntary British wartime organisation of drivers founded by the Marchioness of Londonderry (1879–1959).

Women's Suffrage, New Zealand 1893, Australia 1902, Finland 1907, Norway 1913, Britain 1918–1928, U.S.A. 1920, France 1944, Italy 1945.

Women's Voluntary Service, founded by Lady Reading 1938.

à Wood, Anthony, English antiquary, b. 1632, d. 1695.

Wood, Mrs Henry (Ellen Wood), English novelist (*East Lynne*, 1861), b. 1814, d. 1887.

Wood, Sir Henry, English conductor and composer, b. 1869, d. 1944.

Wood's Halfpence, referring to the 1722 patent granting sole privilege of coining halfpence and farthings for circulation in Ireland to the ironmaster William Wood (1671–1730). Patent surrendered 1725.

Woodhouse Grove School, English public school, founded 1812.

Woodville, Anthony, Earl Rivers, Defender and Director of Papal Causes in England, b. about 1442, executed 1483.

Woolf, Virginia, English writer (*Mrs Dalloway*, 1925), b. 1882, d. 1941.

Woolner, Thomas, English sculptor (*Tennyson*, 1857), b. 1825, d. 1892.

Worcester, Battle of, between Parliamentary and Royalist forces, 3 Sept. 1651.

Worcester Cathedral, built 1084–1089 ; burnt 1202 ; restored 1218.

Worcester Porcelain, manufactured since 1781.

Worcester Royal Grammar School, origins uncertain ; earliest recorded mention 1290 ; granted a Charter by Queen Elizabeth I, 1561.

Worde, Wynkyn de, Alsace-born pioneer printer in England, d. about 1534.

Wordsworth, Dorothy, English writer, b. 1771, d. 1855.

Wordsworth, William, English poet (*The Prelude*, 1805), b. 1770, d. 1850.

Work, Henry Clay, American composer (*Marching Through Georgia*), b. 1832, d. 1884.

Worker-Priest Movement, French, instituted 1943, banned by the Vatican 1959.

Worksop College, English public school, founded by the Duke of Newcastle 1895.

World Association of Girl Guides and Girl Scouts, formed in London 1928.

World Council of Churches, constituted 23 Aug. 1948.

World Health Organisation, constitution drawn up 1946 ; confirmed a specialised agency of the United Nations 1948.

World War I, 28 July 1914 to 11 Nov. 1918.

World War II : 1 Sept. 1939 to 15 Aug. 1945. German invasion of Poland 1 Sept. 1939, of Norway 7 Apr. 1940, of Low Countries 10 May 1940 ; surrender of France 17 June 1940 ; German attack on Russia 22 June 1941 ; Japanese attack on U.S.A. 7 Dec. 1941 ; Italian surrender 9 Sept. 1943 ; D-Day 6 June 1944 ; German surrender 8 May 1945 ; Japanese surrender 14 Aug. 1945 ; Victory Day celebrations 8 June 1946 ; Peace Conference, Paris 20 July–15 Oct. 1946.

Worms, Diet of, called to condemn Luther 1521.

Worth, Charles Frederick, English-born dressmaker, b. 1825, d. 1895.

Wotton, Sir Henry, diplomat and writer, b. 1568, d. 1639.

Wren, Sir Christopher, English architect (St Paul's Cathedral, 1675–1711), b. 1632, d. 1723.

Wright, Frank Lloyd, American architect, b. 1869, d. 1959.

Wright, Orville, American pioneer aviator, b. 1871, d. 1948.

Wright, Wilbur, American pioneer aviator, b. 1867, d. 1912. Orville and Wilbur Wright flew their first plane 17 Dec. 1903.

Wulfstan, St, Bishop of Worcester, b. about 1012, d. 1095.

Wulfstan, Archbishop of York, d. 1023.

Wyatt, Sir Francis, Governor of Virginia, b. about 1575, d. 1644.

Wyatt, Sir Thomas, English lyric poet, b. 1503, d. 1542.

Wyatt, Sir Thomas, English rebel, b. about 1521, executed 1554.

Wycherley, William, English playwright (*The Country Wife*, 1675), b. about 1640, d. 1715.

Wyclif, John, English religious reformer, b. about 1320, d. 1384. His version of the Bible (the early version) completed about 1382–1384 ; the later version completed about 1388.

Wykeham, William of, Bishop of Winchester, and founder 1379 of New College, Oxford, and 1382 of Winchester College, b. 1324, d. 1404.

Wynkyn de Worde, Alsace-born pioneer printer in England, d. about 1534.

Wyoming, U.S.A., first settled 1834 ; Territory 1868 ; admitted to the Union 1890.

X

Xenon, element, discovered 1898 by Ramsay and Travers.

Xenophon, Greek writer (*Anabasis*), b. about 430, d. 355 B.C.

X-Rays, discovered 1895 by the German scientist Wilhelm von Röntgen, b. 1845, d. 1923.

XYZ Mission, to arrange Franco-American treaty, 1798.

Y

Yale, Elihu, American administrator, b. 1648, d. 1721.

Yale Locks, invented by the American inventor Linus Yale, b. 1821, d. 1868.

Yale University, Connecticut, founded as a school 1701 ; first called Yale College 1716 ; chartered 1745 ; Yale University since 1887.

Yalta, Conference of, Feb. 1945.

Yamamoto, Gombei, Japanese Prime Minister, b. 1852, d. 1933.

Yard, Imperial standard, length established in Britain 1844.

Yarrow, Sir Albert Fernandez, English engineer and inventor, b. 1842, d. 1932.

Year of Confusion, first of the Julian Calendar and including 80 extra days, 46 B.C.

Yeardley, Sir George, Governor of Virginia, b. about 1580, d. 1627.

Yeats, William Butler, Irish writer, b. 1865, d. 1939.

Yellow Book, The, English quarterly literary journal in which appeared many outstanding contributions by late 19th century writers, and artists, published 1894 to 1897.

Yellow Fever, cause discovered 1900 by the American bacteriologist Walter Reed, b. 1851, d. 1902.

Yellowstone National Park, first American national park to be designated, 1872.

Yiddish Language, earliest known document, dated 1396.

Yokohama, Japanese port, first opened to foreign trade through the intervention of Commodore Perry, 1859.

Yonge, Charlotte Mary, English writer (*The Heir of Redclyffe*, 1853), b. 1823, d. 1901.

York Minster, present structure erected mainly 1291–1345, with important addition in the middle of the 15th century.

Yorktown, Virginia, Siege of, in which Cornwallis surrendered to Washington 1781.

Yosemite National Park, California, designated 1890.

Youmans, Vincent, American composer (*No, no Nanette*, 1924), b. 1898, d. 1946.

Young, Sir Allen William, explorer in the Arctic, b. 1827, d. 1915.

Young, Andrew, Scottish hymn-writer (*There is a Happy Land*, 1838), b. 1807, d. 1889.

Young, Arthur, English agricultural administrator and writer, b. 1741, d. 1820.

Young, Brigham, American Mormon leader, b. 1801, d. 1877.

Young, Edward, English poet (*Night Thoughts*, 1742), b. 1683, d. 1765.

Young, James, Scottish chemist and founder 1856 of the paraffin industry, b. 1811, d. 1883.

Young, Loretta, American actress, b. 1913.

Young, Thomas, English scientist, b. 1773, d. 1829.

Young England, romantic conservative group, active 1842–1848.

Young Ireland, nationalist group, active 1842–1848.

Young Italy, nationalist group, founded 1831 by Giuseppe Mazzini, b. 1805, d. 1872.

Young Men's Christian Association, founded in London 1844 by Sir George Williams, b. 1821, d. 1905.

Young Women's Christian Association, founded in London by Lady Kinnaird, b. 1816, d. 1888.

Youth Hostels Association, founded 1930.

Ypres, First Battle of, World War I, 19 Oct.–22 Nov. 1914.

Ypres, Second Battle of, World War I, 22 Apr.–25 May 1915.

Ypres, Third Battle of, World War I, July–Aug. 1917.

Yriarte, Tomás de, Spanish poet and composer, b. 1750, d. 1791.

Ysaÿe, Eugène, Belgian violinist and conductor, b. 1858, d. 1931.

Ytterbium, chemical element, discovered 1878 by the French scientist Jean Charles Gallisard de Marignac, b. 1817, d. 1894.

Yttrium, chemical element discovered by the scientist Johan Gadolin 1794.

Yüan Dynasty, China, 1280–1368.

Yugoslavia, kingdom proclaimed 1 Dec. 1918 ; constitution established 1921 ; monarchist dictatorship 1929–1941 ; Communist régime since 1945.

Yule, Sir Henry, Scottish administrator in India, b. 1820, d. 1889.

Yuletide, the Christmas festival.

Yung Chêng Period, China 1723–1735.

Yung Lo Period, China 1403–1424.

Z

Z.E.T.A. (Zero Energy Thermonuclear Assembly), commenced operations at Harwell Aug. 1957.

Zachary, St, Pope 741–752.

Zack, Leon, Russian-born abstract artist, b. 1892.

Zaehnsdorff, Joseph, Hungarian-born London bookbinder, b. 1816, d. 1886.

Zagreb University, Yugloslavia, founded 1669.

Zaharoff, Sir Basil, Turkish-born cosmopolitan financier and armaments manufacturer, of Greek descent and British nationality, b. 1849, d. 1936.

Zakharoff, Andreyan Dmitrievich, Russian architect, b. 1761, d. 1811.

Zamenhof, Lazarus Ludovic, Polish inventor 1887 of Esperanto, b. 1859, d. 1917.

Zandonai, Riccardo, Italian composer (*Francesca da Rimini*, 1914), b. 1883, d. 1944.

Zangwill, Israel, English Jewish novelist (*Children of the Ghetto*, 1892), b. 1864, d. 1926.

Zanzibar, first visited by the English 1591 ; united with Pemba under one sovereign, Seyyid Said bin Sultan 1822 ; placed under British protection by the Sultan and formally declared a British protectorate 1890 ; constitutional government established 1891 ; slavery abolished by the Sultan 1897 ; new constitution granted 1956.

Zapata, Emiliano, Mexican revolutionary leader, b. about 1879, murdered 1919.

Zapf, Hermann, German type designer, b. 1910

Zarubin, Georgi, Soviet Deputy Foreign Minister, b. 1900, d. 1958.

Zeebrugge Raid, World War I, 22 Apr. 1918.

Zeeman, Pieter, Dutch scientist and Nobel Prize winner 1902, b. 1865, d. 1943. Discovered the Zeeman effect 1896.

Zeiss, Carl, German optical instrument manufacturer and founder of the firm of that name, b. 1816, d. 1888.

Zeller, Eduard, German theologian, b. 1814, d. 1908.

Zemstvos, Russian provincial assemblies formed 13 Jan. 1864.

Zen Buddhism, founded about 520 when Bodhi-Dharma (480–528) went to China.

Zeno, Roman Emperor (474–491) at Constantinople, d. 491.

Zeno of Citium, Greek philosopher, b. 340, committed suicide 270 B.C.

Zeno of Elea, Greek philosopher, b. about 490, d. about 430 B.C.

Zenobia, Queen of Palmyra, d. about 285.

Zephyrinus, St, Pope 199–217.

Zeppelins, invented 1900 by the German Count Ferdinand von Zeppelin, b. 1838, d. 1917. Zeppelin L21 destroyed at Cuffley 3 Sept. 1916 ; L33 in Essex 24 Sept. 1916.

Zero, Absolute, approximately achieved 1921 at the University's physical laboratory at Leyden.

Zetkin, Klara, German communist leader, b. 1857, d. 1933.

Zeuss, Johann Kaspar, German pioneer (1853) in the study of Celtic philology, b. 1806, d. 1856.

Zevi, Sabbatai, Jewish false Messiah, b. about 1621, d. 1676.

Zhdanov, Andrei Aleksandrovich, Soviet general, b. 1896, d. 1948.

Zhukov, Georgi Konstantinovich, Soviet Field-Marshal, b. 1896.

Zhukovskii, Vassily Andreievich, Russian poet, b. 1783, d. 1852.

Ziegfeld, Florenz, American producer of the Ziegfeld Follies from 1917, b. 1869, d. 1932.

Zimbabwe, Southern Rhodesian ruins of disputed origin, built between 12th and 16th centuries, discovered 1868.

Zimbalist, Efrem, Russian - born violinist, b. 1889.

Zimisces, John, Byzantine emperor 969–976, b. about 925, d. 976.

Zincography, illustration process, invented in Paris 1850.

Zingarelli, Nicola Antonio, Italian composer (*Giulietta e Romeo*, 1769), b. 1752, d. 1837.

Zinkeisen, Anna, Scottish artist, b. 1901.

Zinoviev Letter, forged instructions for Communist uprising in Great Britain, published Oct. 1924. Claimed to have been written by Grigori Evseievich Zinoviev, Russian revolutionary leader, b. 1883, shot 1936.

Zinzendorf, Nikolaus Ludwig, German leader of the Moravian Community, b. 1700, d. 1760.

Zionist Congress, first world, held at Basle 1897.

Zionist Movement, Modern, founded 1897 by Theodor Herzl, b. 1860, d. 1904.

Zirconia, mineral discovered 1789 by the German chemist Martin Heinrich Klaproth, b. 1743, d. 1817.

Zirconium, chemical element, isolated 1824 by the Swedish chemist Baron Berzelius, b. 1779, d. 1848.

Zita, St, b. about 1215, d. 1272. Canonised 1696.

Zita, Empress of Austria, b. 1892.

Zizka, John, Hussite leader, b. about 1370, d. 1424.

Zoe, Byzantine empress (1028–1050), d. 1050.

Zoega, Georg, Danish-born archæologist, b. 1755, d. 1809.

Zoffany, John, English-born painter, b. 1725, d. 1810.

Zog (Ahmed Beg Zogu), King of Albania (1928–1939), b. 1895.

Zola, Emile, French novelist (*Thérèse Raquin*, 1866), b. 1840, d. 1902.

Zollverein, German Customs Union, formed 1834.

Zöllner, Johann Karl Friedrich, German scientist, b. 1834, d. 1882.

Zomba, Nyasaland capital, founded about 1880.

Zoological Society, London, founded 1826 by Sir Stamford Raffles, b. 1781, d. 1826.

Zorn, Anders, Swedish artist, b. 1860, d. 1920.

Zoroaster (Zarathustra), Persian religious leader and founder of Zoroastrianism, b. about 659, d. about 582 B.C.

Zorrilla, José, Spanish poet (*Don Juan Tenorio,* 1844), b. 1817, d. 1893.

Zoshchenko, Mikhail Mikhailovich, Russian wrtier, b. 1895, d. 1958.

Zosimus, Greek historian active at mid-5th century.

Zozimus, St, Pope 417–418.

Zsigmondy, Richard, Austrian pioneer in the development of colloid chemistry, b. 1865, d. 1929.

Zschokke, Alexander, Swiss sculptor (*René Auberjonois,* 1947), b. 1894.

Zuccarelli, Francesco, Italian painter. b. 1702, d. 1788.

Zuccaro, Federigo, Italian painter, b. 1543, d. 1609.

Zuccaro, Taddeo, Italian painter (and brother of Federigo), b. 1529, d. 1566.

Zucchi, Antonio Pietro, Italian painter, b. 1726, d. 1795.

Zuckerman, Sir Solly, South African-born anatomist, b. 1904.

Zuckmayer, Carl, German playwright (*Der Hauptmann von Köpenick*, 1931), b. 1896.

Zuider Zee, the Netherlands, reclamation of inundated land planned 1891 by the Dutch engineer and statesman Dr C. Lely (1854–1929) ; inaugurated 1 May 1919 ; last gap closed 28 May 1932 ; repaired 1945.

Zukor, Adolph, Hungarian-born film industry pioneer, b. 1873.

Zuloaga, Ignacio, Spanish painter, b. 1870, d. 1945.

Zululand, first war 1879 ; second 1906. Zululand annexed to Natal 30 Dec. 1897.

Zumalacarregui, Tomás, Spanish general, b. 1788, d. 1835.

Zurbaran, Francisco de, Spanish painter (*Apotheosis of St Thomas Aquinas*), b. 1598, d. 1662.

Zutphen, Siege of, Sept. 1586.

Zweig, Arnold, German novelist (*Sergeant Grischa*, 1927), b. 1887.

Zweig, Stefan, Austrian writer, b. 1881, committed suicide 1942.

Zwingli, Huldreich, Swiss religious reformer, b. 1484, killed 1531.

Zymose, yeast-cell fermenting agent, discovered 1903 by the German scientist Eduard Buchner, b. 1860, d. 1917.

ANNIVERSARIES
PEOPLE AND EVENTS

1st JANUARY

New Year's Day. Bank Holiday in Scotland. Julian Calendar began in 45 B.C. The Festival of the Circumcision.

Needle and Thread Ceremony

On this day the Bursar of Queen's College, Oxford, presents to each guest at the 'gaudy' a needle and thread—'aiguille' and 'fil', a pun on the name of Robert de Eglesfield, founder of the College (1340)—with the words 'Take this and be thrifty'

People
1449   Lorenzo de' Medici (Il Magnifico) born.
1515   Louis XII, King of France, died.
1559   Christian III, King of Denmark and Norway, died.
1651   Charles II crowned at Scone.
1697   Joseph de Plex, Governor-General of India under the French, born.
1704   Thomas Newton, Bishop of Bristol, born.
1766   The 'Old Pretender' died.
1767   Maria Edgeworth, the novelist, born.
1800   Francis Egerton, Earl of Shrewsbury, statesman and poet, born.
1854   Francis Place, radical reformer, died.
1857   John Britton died.
1863   Baron Pierre de Coubertin, reviver of the Olympic Games, born.
1894   Heinrich Rudolf Hertz, physicist, died.
1899   Edmund Righton, actor, died.
1925   Francis Carruthers Gould, cartoonist, died.

Events
1804   Haiti declared its independence.
1887   Queen Victoria proclaimed Empress of India at Delhi.
1910   Labour Exchanges Act came into operation.
1957   The Saar territory returned to Germany.
1960   The French Cameroons achieved independence.

2nd JANUARY

Berchtold's Day (Switzerland).

People
1322   Philip V, King of France, died.
1647   Nathaniel Bacon, American pioneer, born.
1727   General James Wolfe, born.
1861   Frederick William IV of Prussia died.
1891   A. W. Kinglake, writer and traveller, died.
1892   Sir George Airy, astronomer, died.
1898   Sir Edward Bond, antiquarian, died.

Events
1492   Spanish army took Granada from the Moors.
1905   Port Arthur, Manchuria, captured by the Japanese.
1946   King Zog of Albania deposed *in absentia*.

3rd JANUARY

Feast of St Geneviève, patron saint of Paris.

People
106BC Cicero born.
1497   Beatrice d'Este, patron of the arts and diplomat, died.

1641   Jeremiah Horrocks, astronomer, died.
1670   George Monck, Duke of Albemarle, died.
1795   Josiah Wedgwood, English potter, died.
1803   Douglas Jerrold, humorous writer, born.
1840   Father Damien, missionary, born.
1858   Rachel, actress, died.
1875   David Wark Griffith, pioneer film director, born.
1883   Lord Attlee, statesman, born.
1894   Elizabeth Palmer Peabody, kindergarten pioneer, died.
1915   James Elroy Flecker, poet, died.
1931   Marshal Joffre died.

Events
1521   Martin Luther excommunicated.
1777   Battle of Princeton.
1933   Royal Charter granted to the National Playing Fields Association.

4th JANUARY

People
1581   Archbishop Usher born.
1642   Sir Isaac Newton, scientist, born.
1785   Jakob Grimm, philologist and folklorist, born.
1809   Louis Braille, benefactor of the blind, born.
1813   Sir Isaac Pitman, shorthand pioneer, born.
1825   Ferdinand IV, King of Naples, died.
1878   Augustus John, artist, born.
1891   Charles Keene, artist, died.
1913   Louis Paul Cailletet, chemist, died.
1958   Dr Ralph Vaughan Williams, composer, died.
1960   Albert Camus, novelist, died.

Events
1642   King Charles I attempts the arrest of five members of Parliament
1896   Utah achieves Statehood.
1948   Burma becomes an independent Republic.

5th JANUARY
Wassail Eve (Britain).

People
1066   King Edward the Confessor died.
1589   Catherine de' Medici died.
1762   The Empress Elizabeth of Russia died.
1779   Stephen Decatur, American naval commander, born.
1782   Robert Morrison, missionary in China, born.
1816   Sir George Prevost, soldier and statesman, died.
1824   Jeremiah Daniel Murphy, boy linguist, died.
1840   Charles Whittingham, founder of the Chiswick Press, died.
1855   King Camp Gillette, manufacturer, born.
1858   Marshal Radetzky died.
1885   Humbert Wolfe, poet, born.
1922   Sir Ernest Shackleton, explorer, died.
1940   Humbert Wolfe, poet, died.
1941   Amy Johnson, aviator, died.
1943   George Washington Carver, American negro leader, died.

Events
1477   The battle of Nancy.
1919   National Socialist Party founded in Germany.

6th JANUARY

Epiphany.   Twelfth Night.   Old Christmas Day.   Christmas Day (Spain).   Feast of
the Three Kings.

People
1367   King Richard II born.
c1412   Joan of Arc born.
1714   Percival Pott, surgeon, born.
1800   William Brownrigg, chemist, died.
1831   Rodolphe Kreutzer, violinist, died.
1838   Max Bruch, composer, born.
1840   Fanny Burney (Madame d'Arblay), novelist, died.
1878   Carl Sandburg, poet, born.
1919   Theodore Roosevelt, statesman, died.

Events
871   Battle of Ashdown Forest.
1540   King Henry VIII and Anne of Cleves married.
1558   Calais surrendered to the French.
1579   Union of Arras.
1912   New Mexico achieves Statehood.
1944   Jet propulsion invented.

7th JANUARY
Christmas Day (Russia).

People
1502   Pope Gregory XIII born.
1655   Pope Innocent X died.
1715   François Fénelon, writer, died.
1718   Israel Putnam, American pioneer, born.
1758   Allan Ramsay, poet, died.
1768   Joseph Bonaparte, King of Naples, born.
1794   Eilhard Mitscherlich, chemist, born.
1800   Millard Fillmore, statesman, born.
1830   Sir Thomas Lawrence, painter, died.
1873   Adolph Zukor, film industry pioneer, born.
1889   Arthur Clifford Hartley, engineer, born.
1912   Sophia Louisa Jex-Blake, champion of women's rights, died.
1932   André Maginot, statesman, died.
1958   Dr Hubert Ripka, Czech patriot, died.

Events
1558   Calais regained by the English.
1789   First American national election.

8th JANUARY
People
1198   Pope Celestine III died.
1337   Giotto di Bondoni, artist, died.

1536   Catherine of Aragon died.
1642   Galileo Galilei, astronomer, died.
1825   Eli Whitney, inventor, died.
1871   Viscount Craigavon born.
1896   Jaromir Weinberger, composer, born.
1941   Lord Baden-Powell died.
1958   Rt. Hon. Walter Elliot, statesman, died.

Events
1815   Battle of New Orleans.
1916   Allied operations in Gallipoli ended.
1918   President Wilson's ' Fourteen Points ' announced.
1926   Ibn Saud proclaimed King of the Hedjaz.

9th JANUARY
People
1554   Pope Gregory XV born.
1590   Simon Vouet, artist, born.
1735   Earl St Vincent, admiral, born.
1757   Bernard de Fontenelle, writer, died.
1843   William Hedley, inventor, died.
1859   Mrs Carrie Chapman Catt, suffragette, born.
1870   Joseph Baermann Strauss, bridge builder, born.
1873   The Emperor Napoleon III died.
1881   Lascelles Abercrombie, poet, born.
1890   Karel Čapek, playwright, born.
1913   Richard Nixon, statesman, born.

Events
1916   The complete evacuation of the Gallipoli Peninsula announced.
1924   The formation in Britain of the Rural Party.

10th JANUARY
People
1276   Pope Gregory X died.
1480   Margaret of Austria, Duchess of Savoy, born.
1645   Archbishop Laud executed.
1738   Ethan Allen, American patriot, born.
1761   Admiral Boscawen died.
1778   Carl Linnæus, naturalist, died.
1855   Mary Russell Mitford, writer, died.
1880   Grock, the clown, born.
1949   Erich von Drygalski, geophysicist and geographer, died.

Events
1308   The Templars created in England.
1840   Penny post came into operation in Britain.
1890   Cleopatra's tomb discovered.
1920   Treaty of Versailles ratified in Paris.
1946   First United Nations General Assembly held in London.

11th JANUARY
Hilary Law Sittings begin.

People

1494	Domenico Ghirlandaio, artist, died.
1753	Sir Hans Sloane, physician, died.
1757	Alexander Hamilton, statesman, born.
1762	L. F. Roubillac, sculptor, died.
1807	Ezra Cornell, philanthropist, born.
1815	Sir John Alexander Macdonald, statesman, born.
1825	Bayard Taylor, traveller and writer, born.
1829	Friedrich Schlegel, poet, died.
1842	William James, philosopher, born.
1843	Francis Scott Key, lawyer and poet, died.
1857	Fred Archer, jockey, born.
1858	Gordon Selfridge, merchant, born.
1882	Theodor Schwann, physiologist, died.

Events

1790	United Belgium formed.
1861	Juarez occupied Mexico City.
1946	Albania declared a Republic.

12th JANUARY

People

690	Benedict Biscop, churchman, died.
1519	The Emperor Maximilian I died.
1588	John Winthrop, statesman, born.
1628	Charles Perrault, writer, born.
1729	Edmund Burke, statesman, born.
1746	J. H. Pestalozzi, educationalist, born.
1751	Ferdinand IV, King of Naples, born.
1852	Marshal Joffre born.
1860	Sir Charles Oman, historian, born.
1878	Ferencz Molnar, playwright, born.
1960	Neville Shute, novelist, died.

Events

1604	Hampton Court Conference began.
1866	The Aeronautical Society of Great Britain (now the Royal Aeronautical Society) founded.
1916	Britain's annexation of the Gilbert and Ellice Islands became effective.

13th JANUARY
Canute's Day (Sweden).

People

86BC	Gaius Marius, Roman general, died.
1239	John of Fornsete, composer, died.
1691	George Fox, Quaker, died.
1864	Stephen Collins Foster, song writer, died.
1879	Sir William Reid Dick, sculptor, born.
1941	James Joyce, writer, died.

Events
1771 The *Tatler* first issued.
1864 The Zemstvos, or provincial assemblies, formed in Russ a.

14th JANUARY
Mallard Day (All Souls : Oxford).

People
1575 Barbara Uttman, lace-maker, died.
1640 Lord Coventry, statesman, died.
1742 Edmund Halley, astronomer, died.
1806 Matthew Fontaine Maury, hydrographer, born.
1847 The Rev. Wilson Carlile, founder of the Church Army, born.
1850 Pierre Loti, writer, born.
1867 J. D. A. Ingres, artist, died.
1875 Dr Albert Schweitzer born.
1890 Lord Napier of Magdala died.
1892 Cardinal Manning died.
1907 Sir James Fergusson, statesman, died.
1929 Dr Cornelis Lely, statesman and engineer, died.

Events
1814 Norway ceded to the King of Sweden by the King of Denmark.
1858 Orsini's (unsuccessful) attempt on Napoleon III's life.
1935 Oil pipeline (Kirkuk to Haifa) inaugurated.
1943 Casablanca Conference began.

15th JANUARY

People
  69 The Emperor Galba assassinated.
1342 Philip the Bold, Duke of Burgundy, born.
1622 Molière, playwright, born.
1815 Emma, Lady Hamilton, mistress of Lord Nelson, died.
1893 Fanny Kemble, actress, died.
1896 Matthew B. Brady, photographer, died.
1909 Ernest Reyer, musician, died.
1912 Henry Labouchere, editor, died.
1915 Sir George Nares, explorer, died.

Events
1535 The Act of Supremacy.
1759 The British Museum opened.
1778 Hawaii discovered by Captain Cook.
1790 Lettres de cachet abolished in France.
1916 Von Papen expelled from the U.S.A.
1922 The Irish Free State came into being.

16th JANUARY

People
1599 Edmund Spenser, poet, died.
1794 Edward Gibbon, historian, died.
1809 General Sir John Moore died.
1891 Léo Delibes, composer, died.

Events
1547   The first Russian Tsar (Ivan the Terrible) crowned.
1556   The Emperor Charles V abdicated from his Spanish throne.
1809   Battle of Coruña.
1839   Aden annexed to British India.
1906   The conference of Algeciras began.
1909   The Shackleton Expedition reached the Magnetic South Pole.
1920   Prohibition came into force in the United States.
1929   *The Listener* commences publication.
1956   President Nasser issued a Constitution proclaiming Egypt an independent Republic.

17th JANUARY
St Anthony's Day.

People
395   The Emperor Theodosius I died.
1504   Pope Pius V born.
1600   Pedro Calderon de la Barca, playwright, born.
1706   Benjamin Franklin, statesman, scientist and writer, born.
1781   Robert Hare, chemist, born.
1860 (o.s.)   Anton Chekhov, playwright, born.
1863   David Lloyd George, statesman, born.
1871   David, Earl Beatty, First Sea Lord, born.
1903   Quintin Hogg, Polytechnic founder, died.

Events
1377   The Papal See was transferred from Avignon back to Rome.
1852   The Sand River Convention signed.
1920   Volstead Act reinforced prohibition in the United States.

18th JANUARY

People
1779   Peter Mark Roget, thesaurus-writer, born.
1782   Daniel Webster, statesman, born.
1840   Austin Dobson, poet, born.
1841   A. E. Chabrier, composer, born.
1856   Joseph Haydn, compiler of the *Dictionary of Dates*, died.
1863   Konstantin Stanislavski, actor-manager, born.
1890   Alexander Shaw, surgeon, died.
1936   Rudyard Kipling, poet and novelist, died.

Events
1562   The Council of Trent reconvened after a suspension of 10 years.
1604   Hampton Court Conference ended.
1871   The German Empire proclaimed.
1912   Captain Scott reaches the South Pole.
1943   The siege of Leningrad raised.

19th JANUARY

People
1544   Francis II, King of France, born.
1547   The Earl of Surrey, poet and soldier, beheaded.

1736 James Watt, inventor, born.
1737 Bernardin de St-Pierre, writer, born.
1807 Robert E. Lee, Confederate general, born.
1809 Edgar Allan Poe, writer, born.
1813 Sir Henry Bessemer, engineer, born.
1839 Paul Cézanne, artist, born.
1881 Auguste Mariette, Egyptologist, died.

Events
1563 The Heidelberg Catechism published.
1840 Captain Wilkes discovered Antarctic coast.
1899 Condominium of the United Kingdom and Egypt over the Sudan established.
1954 Britain approves the adoption of the Belgian FN 30 rifle.

20th JANUARY
St Agnes' Eve.   Inauguration Day (U.S.A.).

People
1612 The Emperor Rudolph II died.
1779 David Garrick, actor, died.
1790 John Howard, prison reformer, died.
1870 Guillaume Lekeu, composer, born.
1891 Mischa Elman, violinist, born.
1900 John Ruskin, art critic, died.
1915 Lord Ardilaun, philanthropist, died.
1926 Charles M. Doughty, traveller and poet, died.
1936 King George V died.

Events
1265 First assembly of the House of Commons.
1793 King Louis XVI condemned to death.
1918 Naval battle of Imbros.
1936 Edward VIII proclaimed King.
1943 The Casablanca Conference ended.

21st JANUARY
Feast of St Agnes.

People
1118 Pope Paschal II died.
1609 Joseph Justus Scaliger, scholar and critic, died.
1743 John Fitch, inventor, born.
1766 James Quin, actor, died.
1793 King Louis XVI guillotined.
1813 John Charles Frémont, explorer, born.
1814 Bernardin de St Pierre, writer, died.
1824 ' Stonewall ' Jackson, Confederate general, born.
1829 Oscar II, King of Sweden and Norway, born.
1840 Sophia Louisa Jex-Blake, champion of women's rights, born.
1855 Ernest Chausson, composer, born.
1855 John Moses Browning, inventor, born.
1857 Samuel Wilson Parr, chemist, born.
1892 Robert Forsythe Irwin, sponsor of Talking Books for the Blind, born.
1901 Elisha Gray, inventor, died.
1924 Lenin died.

Events

1769 The letters of Junius began publication.
1772 The letters of Junius last appeared.
1907 Britain first officially recognises the existence of taxi-cabs.
1935 Snowdonia, Britain's first national park, established.
1954 The U.S. submarine *Nautilus*, first atomic-powered ship, launched.

22nd JANUARY
St Vincent's Day.

People

1561 Lord Bacon, statesman and writer, born.
1690 Nicolas Lancret, painter, born.
1729 Gottfried Ephraim Lessing, writer, born.
1775 André Ampère, physicist, born.
1788 Lord Byron, poet, born.
1796 Karl Ernst Claus, chemist, born.
1799 Horace Bénédict de Saussure, physicist and Alpinist, died.
1849 August Strindberg, playwright, born.
1858 Beatrice Webb, social reformer, born.
1887 Sir Joseph Whitworth, mechanical engineer, died.
1901 Queen Victoria died.
1906 George Jacob Holyoake, co-operator and secularist, died.
1931 Anna Pavlova died.
1942 Richard Sickert, artist, died.

Events

1905 ' Red Sunday ' in St Petersburg.
1924 First Labour Premier takes office in Britain.
1944 Anzio landings in Italy begin.

23rd JANUARY

People

1002 The Emperor Otto III died.
1766 William Caslon, printer, died.
1806 William Pitt, statesman, died.
1832 Edouard Manet, artist, born.
1833 Admiral Lord Exmouth, died.
1837 John Field, composer of nocturnes, died.
1841 Benoît-Constant Coquelin, actor, born.
1875 Charles Kingsley, poet and novelist, died.
1878 Rutland Boughton, composer, born.
1896 Charlotte, Grand Duchess of Luxembourg, born.
1956 Sir Alexander Korda, film producer, died.

Events

1571 Royal Exchange, London, opened.
1579 Treaty of Utrecht.
1719 The Principality of Liechtenstein constituted.
1943 Tripoli captured by the British.

24th JANUARY

People

1712 Frederick the Great of Prussia born.
1732 Pierre de Beaumarchais, playwright, born.

1746   Gustavus III, King of Sweden, born.
1749   Charles James Fox, statesman, born.
1818   John Mason Neale, hymn-writer, born.
1862   Edith Wharton, novelist, born.
1883   Friedrich Flotow, composer, died.

Events
1616   Cape Horn first rounded by Willem Schouten.
1848   Gold first discovered in California.
1908   First Boy Scout troop formed in England.
1915   Naval Battle of the Dogger Bank.

25th JANUARY
Feast of the Conversion of St Paul.

People
844   Pope Gregory IV died.
1138   Pope Anacletus II died.
1540   Edmund Campion, Jesuit martyr, born.
1627   Robert Boyle, physicist, born.
1640   Robert Burton, writer, died.
1640   The first Duke of Devonshire, born.
1736   Joseph Louis Lagrange, scientist, born.
1746   Mme de Genlis, writer, born.
1759   Robert Burns, poet, born.
1841   Lord Fisher, naval strategist, born.
1857   Lord Lonsdale, sportsman, born.
1866   Emile Vandervelde, statesman, born.
1886   Wilhelm Furtwängler, conductor, born.
1914   Sir John Tenniel, artist, died.
1960   Rutland Boughton, composer, died.

Events
1787   Abortive attempt to seize the U.S. Arsenal at Springfield, Mass.
1934   John Dillinger, bank robber, captured in Tucson, Arizona.
1952   Vincent Massey appointed first Governor-General of Canada.

26th JANUARY
Australia Day (Wattle Day).

People
1763   King Charles XIV of Sweden, born.
1778   Ugo Foscolo, poet, born.
1823   Edward Jenner, pioneer in vaccination, died.
1880   General Douglas MacArthur, born.
1885   General Gordon assassinated at Khartoum.
1939   W. B. Yeats, poet, died.

Events
1564   The decrees or definitions of the Council of Trent confirmed by Pope Pius IV
1837   Michigan achieves Statehood.
1871   The Rugby Union founded.
1885   Khartoum falls to the Mahdi's troops.

1939   Barcelona falls to the Spanish Nationalists.
1949   The first test photograph made at Mt. Palomar Observatory.
1950   India proclaimed a Republic within the Commonwealth.

27th JANUARY
Feast of St John Chrysostom.

People
1720   Samuel Foote, actor and playwright, born.
1756   Wolfgang Amadeus Mozart, composer, born.
1775   Friedrich Wilhelm Joseph von Schelling, philosopher, born.
1814   Eugène Viollet-le-Duc, architect, born.
1823   Edouard Lalo, composer, born.
1832   Lewis Carroll, writer and mathematician, born.
1851   John James Audubon, ornithologist, died.
1859   Kaiser Wilhelm II of Germany born.
1873   The Rev. Adam Sedgwick, geologist, died.
1878   Sir Edward Creasy, military historian, died.
1885   Jerome Kern, composer, born.
1901   Giuseppe Verdi, composer, died.

Events
1926   John Logie Baird gave first demonstration of television.

28th JANUARY

People
1457   King Henry VII born.
1547   King Henry VIII died.
1596   Sir Francis Drake, navigator, died.
1613   Sir Thomas Bodley, book-collector, died.
1621   Pope Paul V died.
1706   John Baskerville, printer, born.
1725   Peter the Great, Tsar of Russia, died.
1791   L. J. Hérold, composer, born.
1833   General Gordon born.
1861   Henri Murger, writer, died.
1947   Reynaldo Hahn, composer, died.
1960   Arthur Clifford Hartley, inventor, died.

Events
1521   The Diet of Worms began.
1846   Battle of Aliwal, first Sikh War.
1871   Paris surrendered to the German army.
1918   Latvia declared her independence.
1936   Burial of King George V.

29th JANUARY

People
1119   Pope Gelasius II died.
1688   Emanuel Swedenborg, theologian, born.
1696   Ivan V, Tsar of Russia, died.
1737   Thomas Paine, reformer, born.
1782   Daniel Auber, composer, born.

1820   King George III died.
1843   William McKinley, statesman, born.
1860   (N.S.) Anton Chekhov, playwright, born.
1866   Romain Rolland, novelist, born.
1872   Sir William Rothenstein, painter, born.
1917   The Earl of Cromer died.
1928   Earl Haig died.
1942   Bion Joseph Arnold, electrical engineer and inventor, died.

Events
1635   Académie Française formally established.
1728   *The Beggar's Opera* first performed.
1820   George IV proclaimed King.
1856   The Victoria Cross instituted.
1861   Kansas achieved Statehood.
1935   The London County Council approves the Green Belt scheme.

30th JANUARY
Anniversary of King Charles the Martyr.   Feast of St Basil.

People
1730   Peter II, Tsar of Russia, died.
1775   Walter Savage Landor, writer, born.
1801   Horatia, daughter of Nelson and Lady Hamilton, born.
1882   Franklin Delano Roosevelt, statesman, born.
1888   Edward Lear, artist and writer, died.
1889   Crown Prince Rudolf of Austria and Mary Vetsera committed suicide (the
         Mayerling tragedy).
1891   Charles Bradlaugh, reformer, died.
1948   Orville Wright, aviator, died.
1948   Mahatma Gandhi assassinated.

Events
1649   King Charles I executed.
1840   The Emperor of China forbade all trade with Britain.
1853   The wedding of Napoleon III and Eugénie.
1858   The Hallé Orchestra gave its first regular public concert.
1933   Adolf Hitler appointed Chancellor.
1959   First British drive-in bank opened at Liverpool.

31st JANUARY

People
1606   Guy Fawkes, conspirator, hanged.
1797   Franz Schubert, composer, born.
1885   Anna Pavlova, ballerina, born.
1892   C. H. Spurgeon, Baptist pastor, died.
1933   John Galsworthy, novelist and playwright, died.
1938   Princess Beatrix of the Netherlands born.

Events
1858   The *Great Eastern* launched.
1939   Leon Trotsky exiled from Russia.

1st FEBRUARY
Feast of St Bridget.

People
1552 Sir Edward Coke, legal expert, born.
1859 Victor Herbert, composer, born.
1891 Alexander Kipnis, operatic singer, born.
1903 Sir George Stokes, mathematician and physicist, died.
1908 King Carlos I of Portugal assassinated.

Events
1790 U.S. Supreme Court holds first meeting.
1811 Bell Rock Lighthouse started operating.
1910 First British State Labour Exchanges opened.
1917 Germany began unrestricted submarine warfare.
1939 The White Paper on Civil Defence in Britain published.
1941 The British Air Training Corps founded.
1957 First turbo-prop airliner entered into scheduled service in Britain.
1958 Egypt merged with Syria in the United Arab Republic.
1958 The European Nuclear Energy Agency founded within the O.E.E.C.

2nd FEBRUARY
Candlemas.   Festival of the Purification of the Virgin.   Scottish Quarter Day.

People
1594 Giovanni da Palestrina, composer, died.
1875 Fritz Kreisler, violinist and composer, born.
1882 James Joyce, writer, born.
1901 Jascha Heifetz, violinist, born.
1905 Robert Eitner, musicologist, died.
1958 Imre Horváth, Hungarian Foreign Minister, died.

Events
1534 The Great Swabian League dissolved.
1558 The University of Jena inaugurated.
1808 Rome occupied by General Miollis.
1943 The Germans capitulate at Stalingrad.

3rd FEBRUARY
St Blaze's Day.

People
1399 John of Gaunt died.
1809 Felix Mendelssohn-Bartholdy, composer, born.
1811 Horace Greeley, editor of the *New York Tribune*, born.
1821 Dr Elizabeth Blackwell, first English woman doctor, born.
1826 Walter Bagehot, ' The spare Chancellor ', born.
1842 Sidney Lanier, poet, born.
1853 Hudson Maxim, inventor, born.
1873 Lord Trenchard, police commissioner, born.
1891 Air Marshal Gossage born.
1935 John Henry Whitley, Speaker of the House of Commons, died.
1948 Oscar Slater, victim of wrongful imprisonment, died.

Events
1830   Greece declared a kingdom by the Protocol of London.
1945   The Yalta Conference began.

4th FEBRUARY

People
211   The Roman Emperor Severus died at York.
1002   The Emperor Otto III died.
1617   Louis Elzevier, printer, died.
1693   George Lillo, playwright, born.
1805   Harrison Ainsworth, novelist, born.
1825   Birket Foster, artist, born.
1836   Sir William Gell, archæologist, died.
1881   Thomas Carlyle, historian, died.
1902   Charles Augustus Lindbergh, aviator, born.
1915   Mrs M. E. Braddon, novelist, died.
1950   Lord Norman, banker, died.

Events
1861   The Montgomery Convention met.
1874   Battle of Kumasi, Ashanti Campaign.
1915   Submarine warfare declared by Germany.
1938   Hitler took command of the German Army.
1948   Ceylon assumed Dominion status within the Commonwealth.
1952   The United Nations Disarmament Commission first met.

5th FEBRUARY

People
1788   Sir Robert Peel born.
1799   John Lindley, botanist, born.
1810   Ole Bull, violinist, born.
1837   Dwight Lyman Moody, missionary, born.
1840   Sir Hiram Stevens Maxim, inventor, born.
1840   John Boyd Dunlop, inventor, born.
1900   Adlai Stevenson, politician, born.

Events
1818   Charles XIV proclaimed King of Sweden.
1862   ' Greenbacks ' first issued by Abraham Lincoln.
1920   The Royal Air Force College, Cranwell, founded.

6th FEBRUARY

People
1140   Thurstan, Archbishop of York, died.
1515   Aldus Manutius, printer, died.
1626   Mme de Sévigné, writer, born.
1665   Queen Anne born.
1670   Frederick III, King of Denmark, died.
1685   Charles II died.
1748   Adam Weishaupt, philosopher, born.
1804   Joseph Priestley, scientist, died.

1838   Sir Henry Irving, actor, born.
1890   Anthony Fokker, aeroplane designer, born.
1952   King George VI died.

Events
1840   The Treaty of Waitangi.
1840   New Zealand becomes a British Colony.
1922   The Limitation of Armaments Conference, Washington, ended.
1934   The Stanislavsky riots in Paris.
1952   Queen Elizabeth II succeeded to the throne.
1959   National Day of New Zealand first changed to 6th February.

7th FEBRUARY
People
1447   Pope Eugene IV died.
1478   Sir Thomas More, martyr, born.
1801   John Rylands, manufacturer, born.
1812   Charles Dickens, novelist, born.
1820   Samuel Holyoke, hymn-writer, died.
1823   Mrs Radcliffe, novelist, died.
1837   Gustavus IV, King of Sweden, died.
1878   Pope Pius IX died.
1885   Sinclair Lewis, novelist, born.
1894   ' Babe ' Ruth, baseball player, born.
1923   The Earl of Harewood born.
1937   Elihu Root, statesman, died.

Events
1831   The Belgian Constitution published.
1941   Benghazi captured by the British.

8th FEBRUARY
People
1580   William Herbert, Earl of Pembroke, born.
1587   Mary, Queen of Scots, executed.
1741   André Grétry, composer, born.
1819   John Ruskin, art critic, born.
1820   William Tecumseh Sherman, general, born.
1866   John Henry Whitley, Speaker of the House of Commons, born.
1884   Lord Brabazon of Tara, pioneer motorist and aviator, born.
1888   Dame Edith Evans, actress, born.

Events
1861   The Confederate States of America formed.
1904   The outbreak of the Russo-Japanese War.
1910   The Boy Scouts of America formally incorporated.

9th FEBRUARY
St Apollonia's Day.
People
1773   William Henry Harrison, statesman, born.
1860   John St Loe Strachey, editor, born.

1860 Sir John David McClure (McClure of Mill Hill), born.
1865 Erich von Drygalski, geophysicist and geographer, born.
1894 Adolphe Sax, musical-instrument maker, died.
1960 Alexandre Benois, theatre designer, died.

Events
1830 Charles Sturt, the explorer, discovered the termination of the Murray River.
1849 The Republic of Rome proclaimed.
1867 Nebraska achieved Statehood.
1870 The United States Weather Service established.
1934 The Balkan Entente signed at Athens.
1943 The Japanese evacuated Guadalcanal Island.

10th FEBRUARY

People
1306 John Comyn, claimant to the Scottish throne, killed.
1775 Charles Lamb, essayist, born.
1795 Ary Scheffer, painter, born.
1824 Samuel Plimsoll, mercantile marine benefactor, born.
1829 Pope Leo XII died.
1834 Lionel Lukin, inventor of lifeboats, died.
1846 Ira Remsen, chemist, born.
1868 William Allen White, editor, born.
1876 A. J. Sodermann, composer, died.
1890 Boris Pasternak, writer, born.
1912 Lord Lister, surgeon, died.
1939 Pope Pius XI died.

Events
1635 The Académie Française founded.
1696 The Assassination Plot against William of Orange exposed.
1763 The Peace of Paris ceded Canada to Britain.
1840 Queen Victoria and Prince Albert married.
1840 Upper and Lower Canada united.
1931 New Delhi officially opened.
1947 The U.S.S.R. signed a peace treaty with Finland.

11th FEBRUARY

People
 731 Pope Gregory II died.
1435 Joanna II, Queen of Naples, died.
1535 Pope Gregory XIV, born.
1650 René Descartes, philosopher, died.
1657 Bernard de Fontenelle, writer, born.
1763 William Shenstone, poet, died.
1801 William Hutchinson, mariner, died.
1819 William Rathbone, philanthropist, born.
1821 Auguste Mariette, Egyptologist, born.
1847 Thomas Alva Edison, inventor, born.
1920 Farouk, King of Egypt, born.
1960 Ernst von Dohnanyi, composer, died.

Events

1847   The Abel Ministry protested in a memorandum against the King of Bavaria's demand for the naturalisation of his Spanish mistress Lola Montez.
1858   First miracles of Lourdes.
1929   The Vatican City created an independent sovereign state.
1959   The Federation of Arab Amirates of the South (the West Aden Protectorate Federation) inaugurated.

12th FEBRUARY

People

1554   Lady Jane Grey and Lord Guildford Dudley executed.
1624   George Heriot, jeweller and royal banker, died.
1637   Jan Swammerdam, naturalist, born.
1663   Cotton Mather, writer on witchcraft, born.
1690   Charles Le Brun, painter, died.
1746   Tadeusz Kosciusko, Polish patriot, born.
1760   Jan Dussek, composer, born.
1768   Francis II, last Holy Roman Emperor, born.
1804   Immanuel Kant, philosopher, died.
1809   Charles Robert Darwin, scientist, born.
1809   Abraham Lincoln, statesman, born.
1828   George Meredith, poet and novelist, born.
1860   Sir William Napier, general, died.
1870   Marie Lloyd, music hall comedian, born.
1912   Armauer Hansen, physician, died.

Events

1709   Alexander Selkirk (prototype of Robinson Crusoe) taken off Juan Fernandez Island.
1945   The Yalta Conference ended.
1950   The European Broadcasting Union formed.

13th FEBRUARY

People

990   Ethelgar, Archbishop of Canterbury, died.
1130   Pope Honorius II died.
1615   Pope Innocent XII born.
1728   John Hunter, physiologist, born.
1754   Prince Talleyrand born.
1834   Heinrich Caro, chemist, born.
1849   Lord Randolph Churchill born.
1873   Feodor Chaliapin, operatic singer, born.
1883   Richard Wagner, composer, died.
1892   Grant Wood, painter, born.
1908   James Knowles, editor and architect, died.
1950   Rafael Sabatini, novelist, died.
1958   Dame Christabel Pankhurst, suffragette, died.

Events

1689   William III and Mary proclaimed King and Queen.
1692   The massacre of Glencoe.
1772   Kerguelen Island discovered by the navigator Yves Joseph de Kerguelen-Trémarec.

1798 General Berthier entered Rome unopposed.
1859 The Corps of Commissionaires founded.
1866 The James-Younger gang robbed the bank at Liberty, Missouri (their first bank robbery).
1943 The Nuffield Foundation founded.

14th FEBRUARY
St Valentine's Day. Old Candlemas.

People
1400 Richard II probably murdered.
1779 Captain Cook, navigator, murdered.
1840 John Oldham, engineer, died.
1845 Quintin Hogg, founder of the Polytechnic, born.
1859 George Washington Gale Ferris, engineer, born.
1869 Professor C. T. R. Wilson, scientist, born.
1945 Sir William Rothenstein, painter, died.

Events
1488 The Great Swabian League formed.
1797 Battle of Cape St Vincent.
1859 Oregon achieved Statehood.
1912 Arizona achieved Statehood.
1939 The *Bismarck* launched.
1958 The Arab Federation of Iraq and Jordan proclaimed.

15th FEBRUARY
People
1368 The Emperor Sigismund born.
1680 Jan Swammerdam, naturalist, died.
1809 Cyrus Hall McCormick, inventor, born.
1845 Elihu Root, statesman, born.
1857 M. I. Glinka, composer, died.
1874 Sir Ernest Henry Shackleton, explorer, born.
1886 Air Marshal Sir Cyril Newall born.
1923 Charles Simon Clermont-Ganneau, orientalist, died.

Events
1898 The *Maine* blown up in Havana Harbour.
1937 The Balkan Entente Conference held at Athens.
1942 The Japanese captured Singapore.

16th FEBRUARY
People
1497 Philip Melanchthon, reformer, born.
1519 Gaspard de Coligny, general, born.
1620 Frederick William, The Great Elector, born.
1740 Giambattista Bodoni, printer, born.
1754 Richard Mead, Royal physician, died.
1834 Ernst Haeckel, naturalist, born.
1838 Henry Adams, historian, born.
1848 Hugo de Vries, botanist, born.

1876 G. M. Trevelyan, historian, born.
1878 Selim Palmgren, composer, born.
1898 Katharine Cornell, actress, born.

Events
1824 The Athenæum Club, London, founded.
1871 The capitulation of the fortress of Belfort to the German army.
1940 The Battle of the *Altmark*.
1945 Bataan, Philippines, taken by the Americans.

17th FEBRUARY

People
1673 Molière, playwright, died.
1688 James Renwick, Scottish Covenanter, executed.
1740 Horace Bénédict de Saussure, physicist and Alpinist, born.
1766 Thomas Robert Malthus, economist, born.
1781 René Thédore Hyacinthe Laënnec, physician, born.
1856 Heinrich Heine, poet, died.
1862 Sir Edward German, composer, born.
1884 Charles Stuart Calverley, poet and parodist, died.
1902 Marian Anderson, singer, born.
1934 Albert, King of the Belgians, died.
1948 The Imam Yahya, King of the Yemen, murdered.

Events
1871 The Pact of Bordeaux signed.
1944 The White Paper concerning the National Health Service published.

18th FEBRUARY

People
999 Pope Gregory V died.
1478 The Duke of Clarence put to death in the Tower.
1516 Mary I, Queen of England, born.
1546 Martin Luther, reformer, died.
1564 Galileo Galilei, astronomer, born.
1564 Michelangelo Buonarroti, artist, died.
1745 Count Alessandro Volta, physicist, born.
1790 Marshall Hall, physiologist, born.
1795 George Peabody, philanthropist, born.
1855 Jean Jules Jusserand, diplomat and historian, born.
1860 Anders Zorn, painter, born.
1922 Sir John David McClure (McClure of Mill Hill) died.

Events
1678 The *Pilgrim's Progress* published.
1725 The Order of the Bath ' revived '.
1861 The Italian Parliament opened.
1915 The German submarine blockade of Britain began.
1951 The King of Nepal proclaimed a constitutional monarchy.

19th FEBRUARY

People
1473 Nicolaus Copernicus, astronomer, born.
1622 Sir Henry Savile, classical scholar and philanthropist, died.

1718   Lord Rodney, admiral, born.
1789   Sir William Fairbairn, engineer and inventor, born.
1825   Maurus Jókai, novelist, born.
1843   Adelina Patti, singer, born.
1846   Charles Simon Clermont-Ganneau, orientalist, born.
1859   Svante August Arrhenius, physicist, born.
1865   Sven Hedin, traveller, born.
1885   Louis Elsberg, laryngologist, died.
1893   Sir Cedric Hardwicke, actor, born.
1941   Sir Hamilton Harty, conductor, died.
1951   André Gide, writer, died.

Events
1674   The Peace of Westminster.
1797   The Peace of Tolentino.
1803   Ohio achieved Statehood.
1861 (o.s.)   Liberation of the serfs in Russia.

20th FEBRUARY
People
1431   Pope Martin V died.
1437   James I, King of Scotland, assassinated.
1482   Luca della Robbia, sculptor, died.
1717   David Garrick, actor, born.
1790   The Emperor Joseph II died.
1808   Honoré Daumier, artist, born.
1810   Andreas Hofer, Tirolese patriot, executed.
1820   Henri Vieuxtemps, violinist, born.
1834   George Du Maurier, artist and novelist, born.
1861   Eugène Scribe, playwright, died.
1960   Sir Leonard Woolley, archæologist, died.

Events
1909   First Manifesto of Futurism (art movement) issued.
1915   The Panama-Pacific International Exposition opened at San Francisco.
1917   The U.S.A. bought the Dutch West Indies.
1938   The Foreign Secretaryship resigned by Anthony Eden.

21st FEBRUARY
International Youth Day of Struggle against Colonialism
(U.S.S.R. and Countries of Eastern Europe).
People
1513   Pope Julius II died.
1595   Robert Southwell, poet and Jesuit martyr, hanged.
1677   Baruch Spinoza, philosopher, died.
1728   Peter III, Tsar of Russia, born.
1741   Jethro Tull, agricultural writer, died.
1779   Friedrich Karl von Savigny, jurist, born.
1801   Cardinal Newman born.
1821   Georg Friedrich von Martenz, jurist and diplomatist, died.
1824   Eugène de Beauharnais, Prince of Venice, died.
1836   Léo Delibes, composer, born.
1907   W. H. Auden, poet, born.
1941   Sir Frederick Grant Banting, scientist, killed in an air-crash.

Events
1916　Battle of Verdun began.
1946　Indian naval mutiny at Bombay.
1952　Identity cards abolished in Britain.

22nd FEBRUARY

People
1440　Ladislaus V, King of Hungary, born.
1756　Georg Friedrich von Martenz, jurist and diplomatist, born.
1788　Arthur Schopenhauer, philosopher, born.
1797　Baron Münchhausen died.
1810　Frédéric Chopin, composer, born.
1819　James Russell Lowell, poet, born.
1826　Charles Willson Peale, painter, died.
1845　Sydney Smith, reformer, died.
1857　Lord Baden-Powell born.
1857　Heinrich Rudolf Hertz, physicist, born.
1875　Sir Charles Lyell, geologist, died.
1890　Benno Moiseiwitsch, pianist, born.
1892　Edna St Vincent Millay, poet, born.
1958　Maulana Azad, statesman, died.

Events
1649　The Westminster Assembly ended.
1797　The last invasion of Britain : the French at Fishguard.
1819　Spain ceded Florida to the U.S.A.

23rd FEBRUARY

People
1447　Pope Eugene IV died.
1468　Johannes Gutenberg, printer, died.
1516　Ferdinand V, King of Castile and Leon, died.
1633　Samuel Pepys, diarist and statesman, born.
1685　George Frideric Handel, composer, born.
1792　Sir Joshua Reynolds, painter, died.
1821　John Keats, poet, died.
1929　Sir Edward Marshall Hall, lawyer, died.
1931　Dame Nellie Melba, singer, died.
1934　Sir Edward Elgar, composer, died.
1955　Paul Claudel, writer and diplomat, died.

Events
1820　The Cato Street Conspiracy.
1836　The Siege of El Alamo, San Antonio, Texas, began.
1901　The United States Steel Corporation founded.
1942　' Lease-Lend ' made reciprocal between the U.S.A. and Britain.

24th FEBRUARY
St Matthias' Day.

People
1545　Don John of Austria born.
1693　James Quin, actor, born.

1815 Robert Fulton, inventor, died.
1822 Thomas Coutts, banker, died.
1825 Thomas Bowdler, editor, died.
1852 George Moore, writer, born.
1856 Nicholas Lobatchevsky, mathematician, died.
1860 Daniel Berkeley Updike, typographer, born.
1873 Thomas Guthrie, promoter of Ragged Schools, died.
1880 Sir Samuel Hoare, statesman, born.
1938 Wilhelm Wien, physicist, died.

Events
1525 The battle of Pavia.
1829 Cadiz made a free port.
1848 King Louis Philippe abdicated.

25th FEBRUARY
People
1601 Robert, Earl of Essex, favourite of Queen Elizabeth, executed.
1713 Frederick I, King of Prussia, died.
1723 Christopher Wren, architect, died.
1778 José de San Martín, South American patriot, born.
1841 Pierre Auguste Renoir, artist, born.
1852 Thomas Moore, poet, died.
1860 Robert Coombes, champion sculler, died.
1866 Benedetto Croce, philosopher, born.
1873 Enrico Caruso, operatic singer, born.
1879 Charles Peace, murderer, hanged.
1890 Dame Myra Hess, pianist, born.
1922 Landru, murderer, executed.

Events
1570 Pope Pius V excommunicated Queen Elizabeth I and declared her a usurper.
1913 First Federal income tax became law in the U.S.A.
1947 The State of Prussia liquidated.

26th FEBRUARY
People
1154 Roger II, King of Sicily, died.
1266 Manfred, King of Sicily, killed in battle.
1564 Christopher Marlowe, playwright, baptised.
1802 Victor Hugo, writer, born.
1808 Honoré Daumier, artist, born.
1846 ' Buffalo Bill ' born.
1879 Frank Bridge, composer, born.

Events
 493 The capitulation of Ravenna to Theodoric.
1266 The Battle of Benevento.
1848 The Second French Republic proclaimed.
1938 Lord Halifax became Foreign Secretary.

27th FEBRUARY

People

1706 John Evelyn, diarist, died.
1795 Francis Marion, American patriot and soldier, died.
1807 Henry Wadsworth Longfellow, poet, born.
1823 Ernest Renan, philosopher and theologian, born.
1848 Dame Ellen Terry, actress, born.
1848 Sir Hubert Parry, composer, born.
1850 Henry Edward Huntington, railway promoter, born.
1854 Félicité Robert de Lamennais, church reformer, died.
1899 Charles Herbert Best, scientist, born.

Events

1558 Russia's first trade mission to England reaches London.
1933 The burning of the Reichstag.

28th FEBRUARY

People

1468 Pope Paul III, born.
1513 Robert Fabyan, historian, died.
1533 Michel Eyquem de Montaigne, essayist, born.
1648 Christian IV, King of Denmark, died.
1683 René-Antoine, Ferchault de Réaumur, scientist, born.
1820 Sir John Tenniel, artist and illustrator, born.
1821 Rachel, actress, born.
1865 Sir Wilfred Grenfell, medical missionary, born.
1869 Alphonse de Lamartine, poet, died.
1873 Viscount Simon, statesman, born.
1890 Vaslav Nijinsky, dancer, born.
1909 Stephen Spender, poet, born.
1916 Henry James, writer, died.
1941 Alfonso, ex-King of Spain, died.

Events

1900 Ladysmith relieved (Boer War).
1922 The British Protectorate over Egypt ended.

29th FEBRUARY
Leap Year.

People

 468 St Hilary, Pope, died.
 992 St Oswald, Archbishop of York, died.
1528 Patrick Hamilton, Scottish martyr, burnt at the stake.
1604 Archbishop Whitgift died.
1712 Louis Joseph, Marquis de Montcalm, soldier, born.
1736 Ann Lee, founder of the Society of Shakers, born.
1792 Gioacchino Antonio Rossini, composer, born.
1940 Edward Frederic Benson, writer, died.

Events

1880 The Junction of the galleries under the St. Gothard Pass effected.
1884 The Battle of Trinkitat.
1892 The Behring Sea Arbitration Treaty signed.
1908 Stanley Baldwin first returned for Parliament.
1912 Military revolt in Peking.

1st MARCH
St David's Day.

People

1510   Francisco d'Almeida, first Portuguese Viceroy of India, died.
1643   Girolamo Frescobaldi, organist and composer, died.
1757   Sir Samuel Romilly, lawyer, born.
1792   The Emperor Leopold II died.
1837   William Dean Howells, novelist, born.
1848   Augustus St Gaudens, sculptor, born.
1883   Prince Gorchakov died.
1938   Gabriele d'Annunzio, writer, died.

Events

1498   Moçambique discovered by Vasco da Gama's fleet.
1562   The massacre of the Huguenots at Vassy.
1711   The first number of *The Spectator* published.
1781   The articles of Confederation and Perpetual Union ratified by all States in North America.
1935   The Saar returned to Germany.
1935   King George's Jubilee Trust Fund launched.
1950   Chiang Kai-shek resumed the Presidency of the National Republic of China.

2nd MARCH

People

483   Pope Simplicius died.
986   Lothair, King of the West Franks, died.
1545   Sir Thomas Bodley, book-collector, born.
1578   George Sandys, poet and translator, born.
1676   Franz Rakoczy, Hungarian patriot, born.
1791   John Wesley, Methodist, died.
1793   Sam Houston, statesman, born.
1797   Horace Walpole, Earl of Orford, writer, died.
1810   Pope Leo XIII born.
1824   Friedrich Smetana, composer, born.
1835   Francis II, last Holy Roman Emperor, died.
1840   Zerah Colburn, calculating prodigy, died.
1855   Nicholas I, Emperor of Russia, died.
1876   Pope Pius XII born.
1916   Carmen Silva, Queen Elizabeth of Rumania, died.

Events

1836   A group of 59 citizens of Mexico founded the Republic of Texas.
1924   The Turkish National Assembly abolished the Caliphate.
1943   Battle of the Bismarck Sea began.
1956   Independence restored to Morocco.

3rd MARCH
Feast of Dolls (Japan).

People

1583   Lord Herbert of Cherbury, poet, born.
1606   Sir William D'Avenant, poet and dramatist, baptised.
1633   George Herbert, poet, buried.
1652   Thomas Otway, playwright, born.

1703 Robert Hooke, scientist, died.
1756 William Godwin, political writer, born.
1792 Robert Adam, architect, died.
1793 William Macready, actor, born.
1818 Simon Ingersoll, inventor, born.
1831 George Mortimer Pullman, inventor, born.
1842 Frederick Gustavus Burnaby, traveller and soldier, born
1847 Alexander Graham Bell, inventor, born.
1853 Vincent Van Gogh, artist, born.
1869 Sir Henry Wood, conductor and composer, born.
1932 Ernest Howard Griffiths, physicist, died.
1945 Edwin Evans, musicologist, died.

Events
1845 Florida achieved Statehood.
1848 Louis-Philippe arrived in England after his abdication.
1861 Serfdom abolished in Russia.
1918 The Treaty of Brest-Litovsk signed.

4th MARCH
People
561 Pope Pelagius I died.
1193 Saladin, Sultan of Egypt, died.
1394 Prince Henry the Navigator born.
1748 Count Casimir Pulaski, soldier, born.
1756 Sir Henry Raeburn, artist, born.
1788 James Robertson, Governor of New York, died.
1952 Sir Charles Sherrington, physiologist, died.
1953 Sergei Prokofiev, composer, died.

Events
1681 King Charles II granted William Penn a Patent for territory in North America.
1789 The Constitution of the United States of America came into force.
1791 Vermont achieved Statehood.
1824 The Royal National Lifeboat Institution founded.
1880 The Forth Bridge opened.
1890 The Forth Bridge officially opened.
1919 The Comintern formed.
1943 The Battle of the Bismarck Sea ended.

5th MARCH
People
1512 Gerard Mercator, mapmaker, born.
1534 Antonio Allegri da Correggio, artist, died.
1561 The nephews of Pope Paul IV executed.
1778 Thomas Arne, composer, died.
1790 Flora Macdonald, Scottish patriot, died.
1815 Franz Anton Mesmer, physician and theologian, died.
1817 Sir Austen Henry Layard, archæologist, born.
1852 Lady Gregory, dramatist, born.
1853 Howard Pyle, artist, born.
1879 Lord Beveridge, economist, born.
1887 Heitor Villa-Lobos, composer, born.

1927 Ira Remsen, chemist, died.
1930 Lorin Maazel, musical prodigy, born.
1953 Joseph Stalin died.

Events
1770 The Boston Massacre.
1946 (Sir) Winston Churchill's ' Iron Curtain ' speech at Fulton.
1956 The Telephone Weather Forecasting Service began in Britain.

6th MARCH
People
1475 Michelangelo Buonarroti, artist, born.
1616 Francis Beaumont, playwright, died.
1806 Elizabeth Barrett Browning, poet, born.
1867 Artemus Ward, humorist, died.
1872 Johan Bojer, novelist, born.
1885 Ring Lardner, humorous writer, born.
1902 William Rathbone, philanthropist, died.
1915 Lord Cadogan, statesman, died.
1932 John Philip Sousa, composer, died.
1935 Oliver Wendell Holmes, U.S. Supreme Court judge, died.

Events
1836 The Siege of El Alamo, San Antonio, Texas, ended.
1957 The State of Ghana established.

7th MARCH
Feast of St Thomas Aquinas.
People
1724 Pope Innocent XIII died.
1756 André Michaux, botanist, born.
1769 Richmal Mangnall, educationalist, born.
1792 Sir John Herschel, astronomer, born.
1802 Sir Edwin Landseer born.
1810 Admiral Lord Collingwood died.
1839 Ludwig Mond, chemist, born.
1849 Luther Burbank, botanist, born.
1850 Thomas Masaryk, statesman, born.
1875 Maurice Ravel, composer, born.
1883 John Richard Green, historian, died.
1903 Dr Hely Hutchinson Almond, educationalist, died.

Events
1871 Simon Ingersoll's invention of the rock drill made public.
1876 Alexander Graham Bell patented his first telephone.
1936 The Rhineland reoccupied by Hitler.

8th MARCH
People
1702 King William III died.
1714 C. P. E. Bach, composer, born.
1803 The Duke of Bridgewater, canal pioneer, died

1841   Oliver Wendell Holmes, U.S. Supreme Court judge, born.
1844   King Charles XIV of Sweden died.
1858   Ruggiero Leoncavallo, composer, born.
1865   Frederick William Goudy, typographer, born.
1869   Hector Berlioz, composer, died.
1879   Otto Hahn, nuclear physicist, born.
1887   Paul Féval, novelist, died.
1889   John Ericsson, inventor, died.

Events
1801   The British Army landed at Aboukir.
1865   Construction began of the Amsterdam—North Sea Canal.
1912   Foundation stone of the London County Hall laid.
1917   Russian Revolution began at Petrograd.
1949   Independence of Viet Nam within the French Union proclaimed.

9th MARCH

People
1451   Amerigo Vespucci, navigator, born.
1606   Edmund Waller, poet, born.
1661   Cardinal Mazarin, statesman, died.
1749   The Comte de Mirabeau, politician and writer, born.
1763   William Cobbett, writer, born.
1824   Leland Stanford, railway pioneer, born.
1847   Mary Anning, fossil-collector, died.

Events
1862   The Battle of *Monitor* and *Merrimac*.
1958   The Kingdom of the Yemen combined with the United Arab Republic to form the United Arab States.

10th MARCH

People
1772   Friedrich Schlegel, poet, born.
1776   Louise, Queen of Prussia, born.
1787   William Etty, artist, born.
1810   Henry Cavendish, scientist, died.
1810   Sir Samuel Ferguson, poet, born.
1844   Pablo Sarasate, violinist, born.
1858   Henry Watson Fowler, expert on English usage, born.
1864   Maximilian II, King of Bavaria, died.
1885   Tamara Karsavina, ballet-dancer, born.
1892   Arthur Honegger, composer, born.
1895   Charles Worth, dress designer, died.
1934   F. Anstey, writer, died.
1943   Laurence Binyon, poet, died.
1948   Jan Masaryk, statesman, died.

Events
1848   The U.S. Senate ratified the Treaty of Guadelupe Hidalgo.
1880   The Salvation Army sent a pioneer party to the United States.
1906   The Bakerloo Tube, London, opened.
1915   The Battle of Neuve-Chapelle began.

11th MARCH

People

1514 Donato Bramante, architect, died.
1544 Torquato Tasso, poet, born.
1770 William Huskisson, statesman, born.
1801 Paul I, Tsar of Russia, murdered.
1819 Sir Henry Tate, manufacturer and philanthropist, born.
1820 Benjamin West, painter, died.
1820 Sir Alexander Mackenzie, explorer, died.
1847 Johnny Appleseed, American pioneer, died.
1858 William Hodson, of Hodson's Horse, killed at Lucknow.
1885 Sir Malcolm Campbell, motor racing champion, born.
1899 Frederick IX, King of Denmark, born.
1936 Admiral Earl Beatty died.
1941 Sir Walford Davies, composer, died.
1955 Sir Alexander Fleming, bacteriologist, died.

Events

1702 The *Daily Courant*, London's first daily newspaper, first issued.
1888 The Great Blizzard started in the U.S.A.
1917 The fall of Baghdad.
1938 German troops entered Austria.
1941 ' Lease-Lend ' for Britain (from the U.S.A.) became law.

12th MARCH
Feast of St Gregory the Great.

People

417 Pope Innocent I died.
604 Pope Gregory the Great died.
1613 André le Nôtre, landscape architect, born.
1628 John Bull, composer, died.
1685 Bishop Berkeley, philosopher, born.
1710 Thomas Arne, composer, born.
1711 Abraham Darby, jun., ironmaster, born.
1790 John Frederic Daniell, chemist, born.
1838 Sir William Henry Perkin, scientist, born.
1863 Gabriele d'Annunzio, writer, born.
1880 Kemal Atatürk, statesman, born.
1915 Heinrich Schulz-Beuthen, composer, died.
1925 Sun Yat-sen, Chinese leader, died.

Events

1789 The United States Post Office established.
1854 The Allies sign a treaty of alliance.
1912 The Girl Scouts movement started in the U.S.A.
1917 Revolution broke out in Russia.
1938 Austria annexed by Germany.

13th MARCH

People

1619 Richard Burbage, actor, died.
1733 Joseph Priestley, scientist, born.
1741 The Emperor Joseph II born.

1770   Daniel Lambert, fat man, born.
1855   Percival Lowell, astronomer, born.
1858   The assassin Orsini executed.
1860   Hugo Wolf, composer, born.
1877   Charles Cowden Clarke, lecturer and man of letters, died.
1884   Sir Hugh Walpole, novelist, born.

Events
1758   Halley's comet came to its perihelion—as Halley had predicted in 1682.
1781   The planet Uranus discovered by Sir William Herschel.
1884   Standard time established in the U.S.A.

14th MARCH
People
1682   Jakob van Ruisdael, painter, died.
1748   Field-Marshal Wade, builder of military roads in Britain, died.
1757   Admiral Byng executed at Portsmouth.
1803   Friedrich Gottlieb Klopstock, poet, died.
1804   Johann Strauss, the elder, composer, born.
1820   King Victor Emmanuel born.
1835   Giovanni Virginio Schiaparelli, astronomer, born.
1854   Paul Ehrlich, scientist, born.
1860   Louis Antoine Jullien, conductor, died.
1868   Maxim Gorky, novelist, born.
1879   Albert Einstein, scientist, born.
1915   Walter Crane, artist, died.

Events
1864   Lake Albert discovered by Sir Samuel White Baker.
1915   The German battleship *Dresden* sunk.
1917   The German retreat to the Hindenburg Line began.
1925   The first trans-Atlantic broadcast made.
1939   Slovakia declared an independent State.

15th MARCH
People
44BC   Julius Caesar assassinated.
  493   Odoacer slain by Theodoric, King of the Ostrogoths.
1767   Andrew Jackson, statesman, born.
1842   Luigi Cherubini, composer, died.
1881   Lord Salter, economist, born.
1891   Sir Joseph William Bazalgette, engineer, died.

Events
1079   The Jalalian (or Seljuk) Era began.
1820   Maine achieved Statehood.
1848   Hungarian revolution began in Budapest.
1909   Selfridge's, London department store, opened.
1917   The Tsar of Russia abdicated.
1919   The American Legion founded.
1939   German troops invaded Bohemia and Moravia.
1939   The Hungarians occupied part of Ruthenia.
1959   Northern Nigeria became a self-governing territory.

16th MARCH

People
1457 Laszló Hunyadi, Hungarian patriot, decapitated.
1533 Lord Berners, translator, died.
1751 James Madison, statesman, born.
1787 Georg Simon Ohm, physicist, born.
1792 Gustavus III, King of Sweden, shot.
1822 Rosa Bonheur, painter, born.
1839 Stephen Peter Rigaud, mathematician and astronomer, died.
1856 Eugène, Prince Imperial of France, born.
1878 Emil Cammaerts, writer, born.
1878 William Banting, undertaker and pioneer in slimming, died.
1892 E. A. Freeman, historian, died.
1940 Selma Lagerlöf, writer, died.

Events
1517 The Fifth Lateran Council ended.
1660 The Long Parliament finally dissolved.
1802 The United States Military Academy established at West Point.
1815 William of Orange proclaimed William I, King of the Netherlands.
1909 The first meeting of the Port of London Authority held.

17th MARCH
St Patrick's Day.

People
  45 Titus Labienus, Roman tribune, killed.
1040 Harold Harefoot, King of the English, died.
1394 Sir John Hawkwood, White Company commander, died.
1473 James IV, King of Scotland, born.
1715 Bishop Burnet, historian, died.
1781 The Corn Law Rhymer, Ebenezer Elliott, born.
1787 Edmund Kean, actor, born.
1817 Pasquale Stanislao Mancini, statesman, born.
1846 Kate Greenaway, artist, born.
1892 Edward Augustus Freeman, historian, died.
1958 Sir Hubert Wilkins, explorer, died.

Events
1766 The Stamp Act repealed by Parliament.
1776 British troops withdrew from Boston.
1948 The Brussels Treaty, on Western Union, signed.

18th MARCH

People
1227 Pope Honorius III died.
1455 Fra Angelico, painter, died.
1584 Ivan the Terrible died.
1609 Frederick III, King of Denmark, born.
1740 Jean Antoine Houdon, sculptor, born.
1745 Sir Robert Walpole, statesman, died.
1768 Laurence Sterne, writer, died.
1782 John Caldwell Calhoun, statesman, born.
1812 John Horne Tooke, politician, died.

1830 Fustel de Coulanges, historian, born.
1832 Sir James Fergusson, statesman, born.
1837 Grover Cleveland, statesman, born.
1842 Stéphane Mallarmé, poet, born.
1844 Nikolai Rimsky-Korsakov, composer, born.
1858 Rudolf Diesel, inventor, born.
1869 Neville Chamberlain, statesman, born.
1876 Ferdinand Freiligrath, poet, died.
1913 King George of Greece assassinated.
1936 Eleutherios Venizelos, statesman, died.

Events
1123 The First Lateran Council began.
1208 Great Yarmouth granted first charter by King John.
1848 The Italian Revolution broke out in Milan.
1890 Prince Bismarck resigned from the German Chancellorship.
1891 The London–Paris telephone system operated.
1915 H.M.S. *Irresistible* sunk in the Dardanelles.

19th MARCH
Feast of St Joseph.

People
1687 Robert Cavelier, Sieur de la Salle, assassinated in Texas.
1711 Bishop Ken died.
1813 David Livingstone, explorer, born.
1821 Sir Richard Burton, traveller and writer, born.
1872 Sergei Diaghilev, ballet master, born.
1873 Max Reger, composer, born.
1930 The Earl of Balfour, statesman, died.

Events
1859 *Faust* first performed in Paris.
1932 Sydney Harbour Bridge officially opened.

20th MARCH
People
43BC Ovid, poet, born.
1413 King Henry IV of England died.
1549 Thomas Seymour, Lord High Admiral of England, executed.
1656 Archbishop Usher died.
1717 Abraham Darby, ironmaster, died.
1727 Sir Isaac Newton, scientist, died.
1828 Henrik Ibsen, playwright, born.
1834 Charles William Eliot, writer, born.
1866 Rikard Nordraak, composer, died.
1890 Beniamino Gigli, singer, born.
1894 Louis Kossuth, Hungarian statesman, died.
1925 Lord Curzon, statesman, died.
1929 Marshal Foch died.

Events
1602 The Dutch East India Company founded.
1806 The foundation stone of Dartmoor Prison laid.

1815   Napoleon arrives at Fontainebleau (the beginning of ' The Hundred Days ').
1819   The Burlington Arcade, London, opened.
1848   Ludwig I, King of Bavaria, abdicated.
1935   The British Council established.
1956   France recognised the independence of Tunisia.

21st MARCH
Feast of St Benedict.

People
1556   Archbishop Cranmer burnt at the stake.
1685   Johann Sebastian Bach, composer, born.
1724   Daniel Quare, clockmaker, died.
1729   John Law, financier, died.
1763   Jean Paul Richter, humorist, born.
1771   Thomas Dibdin, actor, born.
1804   The Duc d'Enghien shot.
1806   Benito Juárez, statesman, born.
1839   Modest Moussorgsky, composer, born.
1842   Carl Rosa, impresario, born.
1843   Robert Southey, poet, died.
1857   William Scoresby, Arctic explorer, died.
1936   Aleksandr Konstantinovich Glazunov, composer, died.

Events
1801   The Battle of Alexandria.
1859   The Scottish National Gallery, Edinburgh, opened.
1871   The first Reichstag officially opened.
1918   The Battle of the Somme began.
1919   The Soviet Republic proclaimed.
1953   The Sudan achieved self-government.

22nd MARCH
People
1459   The Emperor Maximilian I born.
1599   Sir Anthony Van Dyck born.
1687   Jean Baptiste Lully, composer, died.
1785   The Rev. Adam Sedgwick, geologist, born.
1797   Wilhelm I, Emperor of Germany, born.
1832   Wolfgang von Goethe, poet, died.
1846   Randolph Caldecott, artist, born.
1858   Hans Meyer, geographer, born.
1868   Hamish MacCunn, composer, born.
1868   Robert Andrews Millikan, scientist, born.
1903   Dean Frederick William Farrar, theologian, died.

Events
1312   The Pope abolished the Order of the Templars.
1765   The Stamp Act came into force.
1939   Memel annexed by Germany.
1945   The Arab League founded at Cairo.
1946   Transjordan recognised by Britain as a sovereign independent state.

23rd MARCH

People

1369 Pedro the Cruel, King of Castile and Leon, killed in single combat with his
       brother.
1430 Margaret of Anjou, Queen of England, born.
1555 Pope Julius III died.
1699 John Bartram, botanist, born.
1769 William Smith, geologist, born.
1817 James Percy, metallurgist, born.
1819 August Friedrich Ferdinand von Kotzebue, playwright, killed.
1854 Alfred, Lord Milner, statesman, born.
1881 Egon Petri, composer, born.
1921 E. W. Hornung, novelist, died.
1946 Gilbert Newton Lewis, chemist, died.
1953 Raoul Dufy, painter, died.

Events

1848 First officially organised band of settlers landed at Dunedin, New Zealand.
1956 Pakistan proclaimed Islamic Republic within the Commonwealth.

24th MARCH

People

1455 Pope Nicholas V died.
1490 Georg Agricola, mineralogist, born.
1603 Queen Elizabeth I died.
1711 William Brownrigg, chemist, born.
1773 Lord Chesterfield died.
1834 William Morris, writer, artist and reformer, born.
1844 Bertel Thorwaldsen, sculptor, died.
1855 Andrew William Mellon, financier, born.
1864 Karl Ernst Claus, chemist, died.
1866 Marie Amélie Thérèse, Queen of France, died.
1884 François Mignet, historian, died.
1916 Enrique Granados, composer, died.
1921 Déodat de Sévérac, composer, died.

Events

1267 St Louis of France called his Knights to Paris in preparation for his second
       crusade.
1603 Accession of King James I.
1603 Union of England and Scotland.
1933 Concentration camps created in Germany.
1942 The national loaf introduced in Britain.

25th MARCH

Feast of the Annunciation of the Virgin.   Lady Day.   Greek Independence Day.
                          Maryland Day.

People

1133 Henry II, King of England, born.
1347 St Catherine of Siena born.
1767 Joachim Murat, King of Naples, born.
1801 ' Novalis ', poet, died.

1813   Field-Marshal Kutuzov died.
1820   Anne Brontë, novelist, born.
1867   Arturo Toscanini, conductor, born.
1881   Bela Bartok, composer, born.
1918   Claude Debussy, composer, died.

Events
1409   The Council of Pisa assembled.
1802   The Treaty of Amiens signed.
1821   Greece proclaimed her independence.
1924   Greece proclaimed a Republic.
1936   Britain signed a Naval Treaty with France and the U.S.A.
1957   Euratom established by Treaty signed at Rome.
1957   The European Economic Community established by Treaty signed at Rome.

26th MARCH
People
1516   Konrad von Gesner, naturalist, born.
1546   Sir Thomas Elyot, diplomat, died.
1726   Sir John Vanbrugh, architect and playwright, died.
1769   Honoratus Leigh Thomas, surgeon, born.
1826   John VI, King of Portugal, died.
1827   Ludwig van Beethoven, composer, died.
1859   A. E. Housman, poet, born.
1865   Thomas Hancock, founder of the rubber trade, died.
1868   King Fuad I of Egypt born.
1874   Robert Frost, poet, born.
1902   Cecil Rhodes, statesman, died.
1923   Sarah Bernhardt, actress, died.
1945   Lloyd George, statesman, died.

Events
1639   First patent signed for the Drury Lane Theatre.
1674   Second Drury Lane Theatre opened.
1838   Sir George Grey discovered aboriginal cave-drawings in Western Australia.
1917   Battle of Gaza.

27th MARCH
People
1378   Pope Gregory XI died.
1615   Marguerite de Valois died.
1625   King James I died.
1785   Louis XVII, King of France, born.
1797   Alfred de Vigny, poet, born.
1813   Nathaniel Currier, lithographer, born.
1845   Wilhelm Konrad von Röntgen, physicist, born.
1851   Vincent d'Indy, composer, born.
1889   John Bright, statesman, died.
1899   Birket Foster, artist, died.
1923   Sir James Dewar, physicist, died.

Events
1794   The United States Navy created.

28th MARCH

People

193   The Emperor Pertinax assassinated.
1592 Johann Amos Comenius, reformer, born.
1660 King George I born.
1749 The Marquis de Laplace, mathematician, born.
1760 Peg Woffington, actress, died.
1819 Sir Joseph William Bazalgette, engineer, born.
1840 Emin Pasha, traveller, born.
1862 Aristide Briand, statesman, born.
1871 Willem Mengelberg, conductor, born.
1902 Flora Robson, actress, born.
1937 Karol Szymanowski, composer, died.
1941 Virginia Woolf, writer, died.
1943 Sergei Rachmaninoff, composer, died.

Events

1854 The Allies declared war on Russia.
1939 The Spanish Civil War ended.
1941 The Battle of Matapan.

29th MARCH

People

1058 Pope Stephen X died.
1751 Thomas Coram, philanthropist, died.
1769 Marshal Soult born.
1772 Emanuel Swedenborg, scientist and theologian, died.
1790 John Tyler, statesman, born.
1792 Gustavus III, King of Sweden, died.
1815 Sir Bartle Frere, statesman, born.
1837 Mrs Fitzherbert, wife of King George IV, died.
1840 Sir John Keltie, geographer, born.
1847 Prince Jules de Polignac, diplomat and statesman, died.
1853 Elihu Thomson, scientist, born.
1866 John Keble, divine and poet, died.
1869 Sir Edward Lutyens, architect, born.
1902 Sir William Walton, composer, born.
1931 Margaret McMillan, nursery school pioneer, died.

Events

1461 The Battle of Towton.
1871 The Royal Albert Hall, London, officially opened.

30th MARCH

People

1707 Sebastien de Vauban, military engineer, died.
1746 Francisco José de Goya, artist, born.
1783 William Hunter, anatomist, died.
1840 Beau Brummel died.
1842 John Fiske, historian, born.
1842 Madame Vigée-Lebrun, painter, died.
1853 Vincent van Gogh, painter, born.
1883 Jo Davidson, sculptor, born.
1960 Edward Evans, composer of the British manual alphabet, for the deaf-blind, died.

Events
1867   Alaska purchased from Russia by the U.S.A.
1912   The Treaty of Fez concluded.

31st MARCH

People
1499   Pope Pius IV born.
1547   Francis I, King of France, died.
1596   René Descartes, philosopher, born.
1621   Philip III, King of Spain, died.
1732   Franz Josef Haydn, composer, born.
1763   Abraham Darby, jun., ironmaster, died.
1809   Nikolai Gogol, writer, born.
1809   Edward FitzGerald, poet, born.
1811   Robert Wilhelm Bunsen, scientist, born.
1837   John Constable, painter, died.
1850   John Caldwell Calhoun, statesman, died.
1855   Charlotte Brontë, novelist, died.
1900   The Duke of Gloucester born.
1915   Lord Rothschild died.
1945   Hans Fischer, scientist, died.

Events
1282   The Sicilian Vespers (massacre of the French in Sicily).
1814   The Surrender of Paris.
1921   The independence of Mongolia proclaimed.

1st APRIL
April Fools' Day

People
1548   Sigismund I, King of Poland, died.
1578   William Harvey, Royal physician, born.
1815   Prince Bismarck, statesman, born.
1852   Edwin Austin Abbey, artist, born.
1868   Edmond Rostand, playwright, born.
1873   Sergei Rachmaninoff, composer, born.
1940   John Atkinson Hobson, economist, died.

Events
1918   The Royal Air Force formed.
1935   The Green Belt Scheme for the environs of London came into force.
1945   The Battle of Okinawa began.
1954   The U.S. Air Force Academy created.
1958   The Yeomanry and Volunteer Force units transferred to the newly constituted British Territorial Force.

2nd APRIL.

People
742   Charlemagne born.
1305   Jeanne, Queen of Navarre, died.
1416   Ferdinand I, King of Aragon, died.
1791   The Comte de Mirabeau, politician and writer, died.

1805   Hans Christian Andersen, writer, born.
1817   Tadeusz Kosciuszko, statesman, died.
1827   Holman Hunt, painter, born.
1836   Louis Elsberg, laryngologist, born.
1840   Emile Zola, novelist, born.
1862   Nicholas Murray Butler, philosopher, born.
1914   Sir Alec Guinness, actor, born.

Events
1559   The Peace of Cateau Cambrésis.
1792   The United States Mint established.
1801   The Naval Battle of Copenhagen.
1927   The Oxford and Cambridge Boat Race first broadcast.
1930   Hailé Selassié proclaimed Emperor of Ethiopia.
1939   The official end of the Spanish Civil War.
1946   The Royal Military Academy, combining Sandhurst and Woolwich, established at Sandhurst.
1951   NATO Allied Command, Europe, came into being.

3rd APRIL
People
1245   Philip III, King of France, born.
1287   Pope Honorius IV died.
1367   Henry IV, King of England, born.
1593   George Herbert, poet, born.
1764   John Abernethy, surgeon, born.
1783   Washington Irving, writer and diplomat, born.
1822   Edward Everett Hale, writer, born.
1826   Bishop Reginald Heber, hymn-writer, died.
1897   Johannes Brahms, composer, died.
1901   Richard D'Oyly Carte, impresario, died.
1925   Jean de Reszke, singer, died.
1942   Paul Gilson, composer, died.
1958   Lord Percy of Newcastle, diplomat, died.

Events
1860   First Pony Express set out across the United States.
1941   Benghazi captured by Rommel.
1949   Arab armistice with Israel.

4th APRIL
People
1490   Matthias Corvinus, King of Hungary, died.
1588   Frederick II, King of Denmark, died.
1617   John Napier, inventor and mathematician, died.
1648   Grinling Gibbons, artist, born.
1752   Nicola Antonio Zingarelli, composer, born.
1758   John Hoppner, painter, born.
1774   Oliver Goldsmith, writer, died.
1807   Joseph Lalande, astronomer, died.
1817   Marshal Masséna died.
1823   Sir William Siemens, inventor, born.

1843   Hans Richter, conductor, born
1932   Wilhelm Ostwald, scientist, died.
1939   Ghazi, King of Iraq, died.

Events
1460   The University of Basle opened.
1931   Faisal II acceded to the throne of Iraq.
1947   I.C.A.O. came into being.
1949   The North Atlantic Treaty signed at Washington.
1959   Senegal and Sudan combined in the Federation of Mali.

5th APRIL

People
1588   Thomas Hobbes, philosopher, born.
1649   Elihu Yale, merchant, born.
1732   Jean Honoré Fragonard, painter, born.
1765   Edward Young, poet, died.
1784   Ludwig Spohr, composer, born.
1794   Georges-Jacques Danton, statesman, guillotined
1795   Sir Henry Havelock, general, born.
1811   Robert Raikes, Sunday School founder, died.
1827   Lord Lister, surgeon, born.
1837   Algernon Charles Swinburne, poet, born.
1856   Booker T. Washington, negro leader, born.
1869   Albert Roussel, composer, born.
1896   Henri François Marion, philosopher, died.

Events
1614   The Addled Parliament began sitting.
1955   Sir Winston Churchill resigned the Premiership.

6th APRIL

People
1483   Raphael Sanzio, artist, born.
1528   Albrecht Dürer, artist, died.
1605   John Stow, historian, died.
1773   James Mill, philosopher and historian, born.
1869   Louis Raemaekers, artist, born.
1870   Oscar Straus, composer, born.
1874   Harry Houdini, professional magician, born.
1893   Vicat Cole, painter, died.

Events
1712   Slave revolt in New York.
1851   Cardinal Manning converted to Catholicism
1862   The Battle of Shiloh began.
1909   Commander Peary reached the North Pole.
1917   The U.S.A. declared war on Germany.
1939   Britain and the U.S.A. agreed on 50-year joint control of the Phœnix Islands.
1944   P.A.Y.E. introduced in Britain.
1955   Sir Anthony Eden became Prime Minister.

7th APRIL

People
1199 Richard Cœur de Lion killed in battle.
1506 St Francis Xavier born.
1614 El Greco, painter, died.
1668 Sir William D'Avenant, poet, and playwright, died.
1770 William Wordsworth, poet, born.
1780 William Ellery Channing, Unitarian, born.
1836 William Godwin, writer, died.
1850 William Lisle Bowles, poet, died.
1891 David Low, cartoonist, born.
1947 Henry Ford, pioneer motor manufacturer, died.

Events
1862 The Battle of Shiloh ended.
1906 The Conference of Algeciras ended.
1936 President Zamora of Spain deposed.
1948 The World Health Organisation confirmed a specialised agency of the United Nations.
1956 Spain relinquished her protectorate in Morocco.

8th APRIL

People
1143 John II, Byzantine emperor, killed accidentally.
1492 Lorenzo de' Medici, statesman, died.
1605 Philip IV, King of Spain, born.
1818 August Wilhelm von Hofmann, chemist, born.
1850 William Henry Welch, scientist, born.
1858 Anton Diabelli, music publisher and composer, died.
1860 Count Stephen Szechenyi, statesman, died.
1869 Harvey Williams Cushing, man of medicine, born.
1875 Albert I, King of the Belgians, born.
1937 Sir Henry Hadow, musicologist, died.
1941 Marcel Prévost, novelist, died.
1950 Vaslav Nijinsky, ballet-dancer, died.

Events
1213 The Assembly of Soissons.
1812 Louisiana achieved Statehood.
1858 The hour bell of Big Ben cast.
1898 Battle of Atbara.
1904 The Entente Cordiale: signature of the Anglo-French agreement.

9th APRIL

People
1483 King Edward IV died.
1553 François Rabelais, writer, died.
1626 Francis Bacon, statesman and writer, died.
1761 William Law, theologian, died.
1772 François Marie Charles Fourier, social reformer, born.
1802 Elias Lönnrot, Finnish folklorist, born.
1804 Jacques Necker, statesman, died.

319

1807   John Opie, painter, died.
1821   Charles Baudelaire, poet, born.
1835   Leopold II, King of the Belgians, born.
1865   Charles Proteus Steinmetz, electrician, born.
1870   Lenin born.
1889   Efrem Zimbalist, violinist, born.
1898   Paul Robeson, singer, born.
1906   The Rt. Hon. Hugh Gaitskell born.
1933   Siegfried Karg-Elert, composer, died.
1940   Mrs Patrick Campbell, actress, died.

Events
1865   General Robert E. Lee surrendered to General Ulysses S. Grant at Appomattox.
1917   The Canadians stormed Vimy Ridge.
1942   Dr Temple elected Archbishop of Canterbury.

10th APRIL

People
1512   James V, King of Scotland, born.
1583   Hugo Grotius, jurist, born.
1585   Pope Gregory XIII died.
1599   Gabrielle d'Estrées, King Henri IV's mistress, died
1778   William Hazlitt, essayist and critic, born.
1794   Commodore Perry of the U.S. Navy born.
1813   Joseph Louis Lagrange, scientist, died.
1829   William Booth, Salvation Army founder, born.
1847   Joseph Pulitzer, journalist, born.
1904   Isabella II, Queen of Spain, died.
1954   Auguste Lumière, pioneer in cinematography, died

Events
1790   The United States patent system established.
1814   Battle of Toulouse.
1841   The *New York (Herald) Tribune* first published
1848   The Chartists presented their Petition to Parliament.
1864   Maximilian made Emperor of Mexico.

11th APRIL

People
1492   Marguerite d'Angoulême, Queen of Navarre, born.
1767   Jean Baptiste Isabey, painter, born.
1770   George Canning, statesman, born.
1794   Edward Everett, statesman, born.
1839   John Galt, novelist, died.
1934   Sir Gerald Du Maurier, actor-manager, died.

Events
1310   The public trial of the Templars in Paris began.
1713   The Treaty of Utrecht signed.
1814   The Treaty of Fontainebleau signed.
1814   Napoleon abdicated.
1814   Louis XVIII acceded to the throne of France.
1935   The Stresa Conference began.

12th APRIL

People

1443 Archbishop Chichele died.
1684 Niccolo Amati, violin-maker, died.
1704 Jacques Bénigne Bossuet, orator and historian, died.
1726 Dr Charles Burney, historian of music, born.
1748 William Kent, architect, died.
1777 Henry Clay, statesman, born.
1792 The Earl of Durham, statesman, born.
1814 Dr Charles Burney, historian of music, died.
1938 Feodor Chaliapin, singer, died.
1945 Franklin Delano Roosevelt, statesman, died.

Events

1782 Admiral Rodney defeated the French fleet in the West Indies.
1861 The American Civil War began.
1861 The Battle of Fort Sumter began.
1944 King Victor Emmanuel III of Italy abdicated.

13th APRIL

People

1593 The Earl of Strafford, statesman, born.
1695 Jean de La Fontaine, writer, died.
1743 Thomas Jefferson, statesman, born.
1748 Joseph Bramah, inventor, born.
1817 George Jacob Holyoake, co-operator and secularist, born.
1852 Frank Winfield Woolworth, merchant, born.
1868 Sir John Blackwood McEwen, composer, born.
1944 Lord Lonsdale, sportsman, died.

Events

1367 The Battle of Navarrete.
1598 The Edict of Nantes issued.
1829 The Catholic Emancipation Act became law.
1868 Magdala, Abyssinia, finally taken by the British.

14th APRIL
Pan American Day (throughout the Americas).

People

911 Pope Sergius III died.
1471 Warwick the Kingmaker killed in battle.
1578 Philip III, King of Spain, born.
1629 Christiaan Huygens, physicist, born.
1759 George Frideric Handel, composer, died.
1769 General Barthélemy Joubert born.
1865 Abraham Lincoln, statesman, assassinated (died 15th).
1883 William Farr, statistician, died.
1900 Osman Pasha, Field-Marshal, died.
1904 Sir John Gielgud, actor, born.
1951 Ernest Bevin, statesman, died.

Events

1828 Webster's *Dictionary* first published.
1849 Hungary declared its independence.
1861 Battle of Fort Sumter ended.
1868 William Griggs publicly announced the invention of photochromolithography.
1890 The Pan American Union established at the first International Conference of American States.
1912 S.S. *Titanic* sank (night of 14/15) on maiden voyage.
1931 Alfonso XIII, King of Spain, abdicated.
1935 The Stresa Conference ended.

15th APRIL

People

69 The Emperor Otho committed suicide.
1053 Godwin, Earl of the West Saxons, died.
1446 Filippo Brunelleschi, architect, died.
1741 Charles William Peale, artist, born.
1764 Madame de Pompadour died.
1812 Théodore Rousseau, artist, born.
1814 John Lothrop Motley, historian, born.
1817 Benjamin Jowett, classical scholar and theologian, born.
1840 Thomas Drummond, engineer and inventor, died.
1843 Henry James, writer, born.
1868 Signe Lund, composer, born.
1874 Johannes Stark, physicist, born.
1894 Charles Marignac, chemist, died.

Events

1598 The Edict of Nantes signed by King Henri IV.
1920 Sacco and Vanzetti accused of murder.
1942 Malta awarded the George Cross by King George VI.

16th APRIL

People

1533 William the Silent, Prince of Orange, born.
1660 Sir Hans Sloane, physician and collector, born.
1682 John Hadley, mathematician, born.
1766 Sir John Leslie, mathematician, born.
1786 Sir John Franklin, explorer, born.
1838 Ernest Solvay, industrial chemist, born.
1741 Charles Willson Peale, painter, born.
1844 Anatole France, novelist, born.
1850 Madame Tussaud, waxworks founder, died.
1871 John Millington Synge, poet and playwright, born.
1881 Lord Halifax, statesman, born.
1889 Charles Chaplin, actor, born.
1904 Samuel Smiles, writer, died.
1940 Princess Margrethe of Denmark born.

Events

1521 Martin Luther arrived at the Diet of Worms.
1746 Battle of Culloden.
1797 The mutiny of the Fleet of Spithead.

1855 The Declaration of Paris signed.
1912 The *Daily Herald* began publication.
1912 The Channel first flown by a woman.
1948 The Organisation for European Economic Co-operation set up.

17th APRIL
People
1711 The Emperor Joseph I died.
1833 Vicat Cole, painter, born.
1837 John Pierpont Morgan, the elder, born.
1876 Ian Hay, writer, born.
1954 Theodore Komisarjevsky, theatre director, died.

Events
1521 Martin Luther examined by the Diet of Worms.
1559 The Act of Supremacy partly re-enacted.
1839 The Republic of Guatemala established.
1897 Turkey declared war on Greece.
1951 The University College of North Staffordshire formally opened.

18th APRIL
People
1552 John Leland, antiquary, died.
1587 John Foxe, martyrologist, died.
1689 Judge Jeffreys died in the Tower of London.
1802 Erasmus Darwin, physician and writer, died.
1817 George Henry Lewes, writer, born.
1819 Franz von Suppé, composer, born.
1878 Humphrey Verdon Roe, aviation pioneer, born.
1882 Leopold Stokowski, conductor, born.
1940 H. A. L. Fisher, historian, died.
1955 Albert Einstein, scientist, died.

Events
1775 Paul Revere's ride from Charleston to Lexington.
1906 The San Francisco earthquake and fire began.
1949 The Republic of Ireland Act, 1948, came into operation.
1951 The European Steel and Coal Community set up.
1955 The First Bandoeng Conference began.

19th APRIL
Primrose Day.
People
1054 Pope Leo IX died.
1560 Philip Melanchthon, reformer, died.
1588 Paolo Veronese, artist, died.
1645 Antony van Diemen, explorer, died.
1689 Queen Christina of Sweden died.
1757 Admiral Lord Exmouth born.
1772 David Ricardo, economist, born.
1813 Benjamin Rush, physician and abolitionist, died.
1824 Lord Byron, poet, died.

1832   José Echegaray, writer and scientist, born.
1874   Owen Jones, architect, died.
1881   Lord Beaconsfield, statesman, died.
1893   John Addington Symonds, critic and poet, died.

Events
1775   Battle of Lexington.
1839   The Treaty of London signed.
1906   The San Francisco earthquake ended.
1923   The Proclamation of the Constitution of the Kingdom of Egypt as an hereditary
       constitutional monarchy.
1956   Prince Rainier of Monaco married Miss Grace Kelly.

20th APRIL

People
1809   James David Forbes, scientist, born.
1820   Arthur Young, agricultural pioneer, died.
1889   Adolf Hitler born.
1893   Joan Miró, painter, born.
1947   Christian X, King of Denmark, died.

Events
1653   The Long Parliament dissolved (temporarily) by Cromwell.
1896   The Bimetallist Conference met at Brussels.
1904   The appointment of a Royal Commission on Ecclesiastical Disorders announced.

21st APRIL

People
1073   Pope Alexander II died.
1109   Archbishop Anselm died.
1142   Peter Abelard died.
1509   King Henry VII died.
1671   John Law, financier, born.
1699   Jean Racine, playwright, died.
1736   Prince Eugene of Savoy died.
1782   Friedrich Froebel, education pioneer, born.
1816   Charlotte Brontë, novelist, born.
1818   Josh Billings, humorist, born.
1896   Léon Say, statesman, died.
1926   Queen Elizabeth II born.
1946   Lord Keynes, economist, died.
1958   Sarah Margery Fry, social reformer, died.

Events
753BC Traditional date of the foundation of Rome.
1836   Battle of San Jacinto.
1869   The Metaphysical Society founded by James Knowles.
1906   The San Francisco fire ended.

22nd APRIL

People
1451   Isabella, Queen of Castile and Leon, born.
1707   Henry Fielding, novelist, born.
1724   Immanuel Kant, philosopher, born.

1766   Madame de Staël, writer, born.
1794   Lamoignon-Malesherbes, statesman, guillotined.
1892   Edouard Lalo, composer, died.
1912   Kathleen Ferrier, singer, born.
1916   Yehudi Menuhin, violinist, born.

Events
1500   Brazil discovered by Pedro Alvarez Cabral.
1823   The Baltic Exchange formally established (17th-century coffee-house origins) as the Baltic Club, London.
1834   The Quadruple Treaty signed.
1834   St Helena became a Crown Colony.
1915   Poison gas first used by the Germans.
1918   Battle of Zeebrugge began.

23rd APRIL
St George's Day.

People
1564   William Shakespeare born (traditional date).
1616   William Shakespeare died.
1616   Miguel de Cervantes, novelist, died.
1697   Admiral Lord Anson born.
1728   Captain Samuel Wallis, navigator, born.
1775   J. M. W. Turner, painter, born.
1791   James Buchanan, statesman, born.
1812   Louis Antoine Jullien, conductor, born.
1818   J. A. Froude, historian, born.
1850   William Wordsworth, poet, died.
1858   Max Planck, physicist, born.
1858   Dame Ethel Smyth, composer, born.
1861   Lord Allenby born.
1891   Sergei Prokofiev, composer, born.
1899   Vladimir Nabokov, writer, born.
1952   Elizabeth Schumann, singer, died.

Events
1826   The Turks captured Missolonghi.
1860   The explorer John McDouall Stuart reached the centre of the Continent of Australia.
1896   The first public film show (at New York).
1918   The Battle by Zeebrugge ended.
1924   The British Empire Exhibition, Wembley, opened.
1932   The new Shakespeare Memorial Theatre opened at Stratford-on-Avon.
1952   The oil pipe-line, Kirkuk to Banias, completed.
1959   Britain's first Heliport opened on the Thames.

24th APRIL
People
1743   Edmund Cartwright, inventor, born.
1815   Anthony Trollope, novelist, born.

1817   Charles Marignac, chemist, born.
1856   Marshal Pétain born.
1889   Sir Stafford Cripps born.

Events
1800   The Library of Congress, Washington, established.

25th APRIL
Feast of St Mark the Evangelist.   Anzac Day.

People
1214   St Louis, King of France, born.
1284   King Edward II born.
1482   Margaret of Anjou, Queen of England, died.
1533   William the Silent born.
1599   Oliver Cromwell born.
1710   James Ferguson, astronomer, born.
1734   Johann Konrad Dippel, doctor and alchemist, died.
1769   Sir Marc Isambard Brunel, engineer, born.
1792   John Keble, divine and poet, born.
1800   William Cowper, poet, died.
1874   Guglielmo Marconi, radio pioneer, born.
1882   J. K. F. Zöllner, scientist, died.
1897   The Princess Royal born.

Events
1792   The Marseillaise composed by Rouget de Lisle.
1792   The guillotine first erected in Paris at the Place de Grève.
1859   Work commenced on the construction of the Suez Canal.
1915   Allied operations in Gallipoli began.
1916   Anzac Day first celebrated in London.

26th APRIL

People
121   Marcus Aurelius, Roman Emperor, born.
1573   Marie de' Medici, Queen of France, born.
1711 (o.s.)   David Hume, historian, born.
1731   Daniel Defoe, writer, died.
1765   Emma, Lady Hamilton, mistress of Lord Nelson, born.
1782   Marie Amélie Thérèse, Queen of France, born.
1785   John James Audubon, ornithologist, born.
1798   Ferdinand Delacroix, painter, born.
1812   Friedrich Flotow, composer, born.
1834   Artemus Ward, humorist, born.
1877   Sir Alliott Verdon-Roe, aviation pioneer, born.
1880   Michel Fokine, choreographer, born.
1881   Alexander Savine, composer, born.
1910   Björnstjerne Björnson, writer, died.

Events
1478   The Pazzi Conspiracy.
1521   The Diet of Worms ended.
1915   The (Secret) Pact of London.
1923   The marriage of King George VI and Queen Elizabeth.

1925   The election of President Hindenburg.
1928   Madame Tussaud's new building opened in London.
1937   Guernica, Spain, destroyed by German aircraft.

27th APRIL

People
1404   Philip the Bold, Duke of Burgundy, died.
1521   Ferdinand Magellan, navigator, died.
1682   Theodore III, Tsar of Russia, died.
1737   Edward Gibbon, historian, born.
1791   Samuel Finlay Breese Morse, inventor, born.
1820   Herbert Spencer, philosopher, born.
1822   General Ulysses S. Grant born.
1873   William Macready, actor, died.
1891   Loftus Perkins, engineer and inventor, died.
1893   Norman Bel Geddes, designer, born.

Events
1296   Battle of Dunbar.
1746   Battle of Culloden.
1910   (27–28 April) Louis Paulhan won the *Daily Mail* London–Manchester flight.
1955   First Bandoeng Conference ended.
1960   Togoland achieved its independence.

28th APRIL

People
  32   The Emperor Otto born.
1442   King Edward IV born.
1710   Thomas Betterton, actor, died.
1758   James Monroe, statesman, born.
1772   Count von Struensee, statesman, executed.
1801   Lord Shaftesbury, social reformer, born.
1831   John Abernethy, surgeon, died.
1889   Dr Antonio de Oliveira Salazar, statesman, born.
1935   Sir Alexander Mackenzie, composer, died.
1936   King Fuad I of Egypt died.
1940   Luisa Tetrazzini, operatic soprano, died.
1945   Benito Mussolini executed.

Events
1770   Botany Bay discovered by Captain Cook.
1789   The mutiny on the *Bounty*.
1919   The League of Nations founded.
1936   King Farouk ascended throne of Egypt.
1939   The Anglo-French Naval Agreement denounced by Hitler.
1952   Japan regained her sovereignty.

29th APRIL

People
1380   St Catherine of Siena died.
1658   John Cleveland, poet, died.
1676   Admiral de Ruyter died.

1769 The Duke of Wellington born.
1818 Alexander II, Emperor of Russia, born.
1864 Abraham Gesner, geologist, died.
1879 Sir Thomas Beecham, conductor, born.
1895 Sir Malcolm Sargent, conductor, born.
1901 The Emperor Hirohito of Japan born.
1958 Professor William Rappard, political scientist, died.

Events
1945 The German Army in Italy surrendered unconditionally to the Allies.
1986 Halley's Comet will return to perihelion.

30th APRIL
Feast of St Catherine of Siena.

People
1524 The Chevalier de Bayard killed.
1632 Jan, Count of Tilly, general, died.
1777 J. K. F. Gauss, mathematician, born.
1870 Franz Lehár, composer, born
1889 Carl Rosa, impresario, died.
1909 Queen Juliana of the Netherlands born.
1912 Wilbur Wright, aviator, died.
1945 Adolf Hitler committed suicide.

Events
1789 General Washington inaugurated first President of the U.S.A.
1803 The U.S.A. purchased Louisiana from France.
1926 General strike began in Britain.

1st MAY
May Day. Labour Day.

People
1218 King Rudolph I born.
1572 Pope Pius V died.
1602 William Lilly, astrologer, born.
1672 Joseph Addison, writer, born.
1700 John Dryden, poet and playwright, died.
1764 Benjamin Henry Latrobe, architect, born.
1820 Richmal Mangnall, educationalist, died.
1850 The Duke of Connaught born.
1873 David Livingstone, explorer, died.
1878 The Duke of Montrose born.
1885 Viscount Alexander of Hillsborough, statesman, born.
1904 Antonin Dvořák, composer, died.

Events
1517 ' Evil May Day ' in London.
1851 The Great Exhibition opened at Crystal Palace.
1876 Queen Victoria proclaimed Empress of India.
1898 Battle of Manila Bay.
1919 The reclamation of the Zuider Zee inaugurated.
1953 The European Productivity Agency created.

2nd MAY

People

1519   Leonardo da Vinci, artist, died.
1551   William Camden, historian, born.
1601   Athanasius Kircher, scientist and inventor, born.
1729   Catherine the Great, Empress of Russia, born.
1772   ' Novalis ', poet, born.
1779   John Galt, novelist, born.
1821   Mrs Thrale (Mrs Hester Piozzi) died.
1844   William Beckford, writer, died.
1859   Jerome Klapka Jerome, writer, born.
1860   Theodor Herzl, founder of Zionism, born.
1864   Giacomo Meyerbeer, composer, died.
1892   The Baron von Richthofen, aviator, born.
1905   Alan Rawsthorne, composer, born.
1935   King Faisal II of Iraq born.
1957   Senator Joe McCarthy, politician, died.

Events

1668   Treaty of Aix-le-Chapelle.
1670   The Hudson Bay Company chartered.
1813   Battle of Lutzen.
1945   Berlin surrendered to the Allies.
1953   King Faisal II ascended the throne of Iraq.
1953   King Hussein ascended the throne of Jordan.
1955   Public service of VHF sound broadcasting introduced in Britain.

3rd MAY

People

1469   Niccolo Machiavelli, diplomat and writer, born.
1761   August Friedrich Ferdinand von Kotzebue, playwright, born.
1763   George Psalmanazar, adventurer, died.
1844   Richard D'Oyly Carte, impresario, born.
1845   Thomas Hood, poet, died.
1849   Prince von Bülow, statesman, born.
1860   John Scott Haldane, physiologist, born.
1912   Emil Leopold Boas, Hamburg-Amerika general manager, died.

Events

1500   Admiral Pedro Alvares Cabral discovered Brazil.
1512   The Fifth Lateran Council began.
1791   The Polish Constitution reformed.
1951   The Festival of Britain opened.

4th MAY

People

1655   Bartolommeo Cristofori, harpsichord maker, born.
1734   Sir James Thornhill, painter, died.
1769   Sir Thomas Lawrence, painter, born.
1776   J. F. Herbart, philosopher, born.
1796   William Hickling Prescott, historian, born.
1825   Thomas Henry Huxley, scientist, born.
1889   Cardinal Francis J. Spellman born.

Events

1471	Battle of Tewkesbury.
1780	The Derby first run.
1789	The States-General met in Paris.
1833	The Convention of Kutayah.
1839	The Cunard Company founded.
1865	Argentine, Brazil and Uruguay make an alliance against Paraguay.
1886	The Colonial and Indian Exhibition officially opened at South Kensington.

5th MAY

Feast of Flags (Japan).

People

1352	Rupert, German King, born.
1705	The Emperor Leopold I died.
1747	The Emperor Leopold II born.
1813	Søren Kierkegaard, philosopher, born.
1818	Karl Marx, revolutionary writer, born.
1819	Stanislaw Moniuszko, composer, born.
*1821	Napoleon died at St Helena.
1826	The Empress Eugénie of France born.
1837	Nicola Antonio Zingarelli, composer, died.
1882	Sir Douglas Mawson, explorer, born.
1883	Lord Wavell born.
1887	Sir Charles R. Fairey, aeroplane designer, born.
1892	August Wilhelm von Hofmann, chemist, died.
1902	Bret Harte, writer, died.
1904	Maurus Jókai, novelist, died.

Events

*1659	St Helena occupied by Captain John Dutton of the East India Company.
1789	The States General assembled at Versailles.
1811	The Battle of Fuentes de Onoro.
1865	First train robbery in the U.S.A. carried out near North Bend, Ohio.
1936	Italian troops captured Addis Ababa.
1942	The Battle of the Coral Sea began.
1949	Statute establishing the Council of Europe signed in London.
1955	The Federal Republic of Germany became a sovereign independent country.

6th MAY

People

1574	Pope Innocent X born.
1638	Cornelis Jansen, theologian, died.
1758	Marshal Masséna born.
1758	Citizen Robespierre born.
1856	Sigmund Freud, psychoanalyst, born.
1856	Robert Edwin Peary, explorer, born.
1859	Alexander von Humboldt, naturalist and explorer, died.
1861	Rabindranath Tagore, writer, born.
1880	Field-Marshal Lord Ironside born.
1882	Peter Konjović, composer, born.
1910	King Edward VII died.
1949	Maurice Maeterlinck, writer, died.
1952	Dr. Maria Montessori, educationalist, died.

Events

1092 Lincoln Cathedral consecrated.
1536 The Bible ordered by King Henry VIII to be placed in every church.
1626 Manhattan bought from the Indians for a few trinkets, by Peter Minuit.
1840 The first postage stamp issued.
1882 Epping Forest dedicated for the perpetual use of the people by Queen Victoria.
1882 The Phoenix Park, Dublin, murders.

7th MAY

People

721 St John of Beverley died.
973 The Emperor Otto the Great died.
1763 Prince Joseph Poniatowski, general, born.
1812 Robert Browning, poet, born.
1833 Johannes Brahms, composer, born.
1840 Peter Ilyich Tchaikovsky, composer, born.
1847 Lord Rosebery, statesman, born.
1868 Lord Brougham, statesman, died.
1892 Archibald MacLeish, poet, born.
1940 George Lansbury, Labour Party leader, died.
1941 Sir James Frazer, social anthropologist, died.
1942 Felix Weingartner, conductor, died.

Events

1663 The first Drury Lane Theatre opened.
1832 Greece proclaimed an independent kingdom.
1915 The *Lusitania* torpedoed by the Germans.
1945 German unconditional surrender ending World War II.
1955 Inaugural meeting of the Western European Union Council.

8th MAY
St Michael's Day.   Furry Day (Helston, Cornwall).

People

1786 Thomas Hancock, founder of the rubber trade, born.
1794 Antoine Lavoisier, chemist, guillotined.
1828 Jean Henri Dunant, Red Cross founder, born.
1834 Loftus Perkins, engineer and inventor, born.
1873 John Stuart Mill, philosopher, died.
1884 Midhat Pasha, statesman, died.
1944 Dame Ethel Smyth, composer, died.
1947 Harry Gordon Selfridge, department store pioneer, died.

Events

1559 The Act of Uniformity signed by the Queen.
1864 The Battle of Spotsylvania Courthouse began.
1895 The Treaty of Shimonoseki signed.
1942 The Battle of the Coral Sea ended.
1945 VE Day in Britain.
1945 The unconditional surrender of the German armed forces.

9th MAY

People
1439　Pope Pius III born.
1688　Frederick William, the Great Elector, died.
1800　John Brown, abolitionist, born.
1805　Johann Christoph Friedrich von Schiller, poet and playwright, died.
1850　Joseph Louis Gay-Lussac, scientist, died.
1860　Sir James Barrie, writer, born.
1880　Gustave Flaubert, novelist, died.
1874　Lilian Baylis, theatre manager, born.
1904　Sir Henry Morton Stanley, explorer, died.
1946　King Vittorio Emanuele III abdicated.
1949　Prince Louis II of Monaco died.

Events
1671　Colonel Blood attempted to steal the Crown Jewels.
1926　The North Pole first flown over by Richard E. Byrd.
1932　Piccadilly Circus first lit by electricity.
1936　The King of Italy proclaimed Emperor of Abyssinia.

10th MAY

People
1696　Jean de la Bruyère, essayist, died.
1727　A. R. J. Turgot, statesman, born.
1774　Louis XV, King of France, died.
1838　James, Viscount Bryce, statesman, born.
1845　Benito Pérez Galdos, writer, born.
1850　Sir Thomas Lipton, merchant and sportsman, born.
1863　' Stonewall ' Jackson, Confederate general, died.
1890　General Sir Thomas Eastwood born.
1914　Sir William Alexander Smith, founder of the Boys' Brigade, died.

Events
1775　Fort Ticonderoga captured by Ethan Allen.
1869　The Central Pacific and Union Pacific Railways linked up west of Ogden, thus
　　　completing the first transcontinental U.S. railway.
1871　Peace of Frankfurt-am-Main.
1893　Imperial Institute, London, officially opened.
1929　Rhodes House, Oxford, officially opened.
1940　Neville Chamberlain resigned the Premiership.
1940　(Sir) Winston Churchill appointed Prime Minister.

11th MAY

People
1778　The Earl of Chatham, statesman, died.
1812　Spencer Perceval, Prime Minister, assassinated.
1828　Alfred Stevens, painter, born.
1849　Madame Récamier, social leader, died.
1854　Ottmar Mergenthaler, inventor, born.
1871　Sir John Herschel, astronomer, died.
1888　Irving Berlin, composer, born.
1896　Josip Slavenski, composer, born.
1916　Max Reger, composer, died.

Events
1745   Battle of Fontenoy.
1858   Minnesota achieved Statehood.
1920   Oxford University passed statute admitting women to degrees.

12th MAY

People
1003   Pope Silvester II died.
1496   Gustavus Vasa, King of Sweden, born.
1641   The Earl of Strafford executed.
1784   James Sheridan Knowles, playwright, born.
1803   Baron von Liebig, chemist, born.
1812   Edward Lear, artist and writer, born.
1820   Florence Nightingale, nursing pioneer, born.
1828   Dante Gabriel Rossetti, painter, born.
1842   Jules Massenet, composer, born.
1845   August Schlegel, poet and critic, died.
1845   Gabriel Fauré, composer, born.
1871   Sir John Herschel, astronomer, died.
1880   Lincoln Ellsworth, aviator, born.
1884   Friedrich Smetana, composer, died.
1935   Marshal Pilsudski, statesman, died.

Events
1588   The ' Day of the Barricades ' in France.
1906   Horatio Bottomley began the publication of *John Bull*.
1926   General strike ended in Britain.
1937   The coronation of King George VI.
1949   The Berlin Blockade lifted.

13th MAY
Festival of All Saints.

People
1619   Johan van Oldenbarneveldt, statesman, executed.
1655   Pope Innocent XIII born.
1717   The Empress Maria Theresa born.
1769   John VI, King of Portugal, born.
1785   F. C. Dahlmann, historian, born.
1792   Pope Pius IX born.
1840   Alphonse Daudet, novelist, born.
1842   Sir Arthur Sullivan, composer, born.
1857   Sir Ronald Ross, scientist, born.
1867   Sir Frank Brangwyn, artist, born.
1883   James Young, chemist, died.
1884   Cyrus Hall McCormick, inventor, died.
1925   Lord Milner, statesman, died.
1930   Fridtjof Nansen, explorer, died.

Events
1607   First permanent English settlement made at Jamestown, Virginia.
1777   Button Gwinnett, American patriot, mortally wounded in a duel.
1779   The Peace of Teschen signed.
1830   The Presidency of Quito became the Republic of Ecuador.

14th MAY
Feast of St John Nepomuk.

People

1316   The Emperor Charles IV born.
1553   Marguerite de Valois born.
1610   Henri IV of France assassinated.
1643   King Louis XIII died.
1771   Thomas Wedgwood, the first photographer, born.
1771   Robert Owen, reformer, born.
1870   Bruce Rogers, typographer, born.
1885   Otto Klemperer, conductor, born.
1936   Field-Marshal Lord Allenby died.

Events

1264   The Battle of Lewes.
1796   Edward Jenner made his first successful experiment in vaccination.
1811   The independence of Paraguay proclaimed.
1842   The *Illustrated London News* first published.
1940   The Home Guard formed in Britain.
1948   Israel proclaimed an independent State.

15th MAY

People

1833   Edmund Kean, actor, died.
1847   Daniel O'Connell, Irish patriot, died.
1858   Robert Hare, chemist, died.
1859   Pierre Curie, scientist, born.
1932   Premier Tsuyoshi Inukai assassinated in Tokyo.

Events

1525   The Battle of Frankenhausen.
1602   The first white man (Captain Bartholomew Goswold) set foot in New England.
1858   The (third) Royal Opera House opened at Covent Garden.
1862   The creation of the U.S. Department of Agriculture.
1918   U.S.A. inaugurated world's first regular air mail service
1935   The first broadcast quiz programme made in Canada.
1943   The Third International dissolved.

16th MAY

People

1611   Pope Innocent XI born.
1703   Charles Perrault, story-teller, died.
1777   Button Gwinnett, American patriot, died.
1804   Elizabeth Palmer Peabody, kindergarten pioneer, born.
1830   J. B. J. Fourier, mathematician, died.
1835   Felicia Hemans, hymn-writer, died.
1899   Sir Frederick McCoy, palæontologist, died.
1902   Jan Kiepura, singer, born.
1929   Lilli Lehmann, singer, died.
1931   Samuel Wilson Parr, chemist, died.

Events
1633 Charles I crowned King of Scotland at Edinburgh.
1811 Battle of Albuera.
1875 The Kentucky Derby first run.

17th MAY

People
1510 Sandro Botticelli, artist, died.
1575 Archbishop Parker, church historian, died.
1749 Edward Jenner, surgeon, born.
1810 Thomas Rankin, Methodist reformer, died.
1834 Heinrich Wilhelm Brandes, astronomer and physicist, died.
1838 Prince Talleyrand, statesman, died.
1935 Paul Dukas, composer, died.

Events
1630 The belts of the planet Jupiter first recognised.
1692 The French Fleet destroyed off Cap La Hague.
1814 The independence of Norway proclaimed.
1900 Mafeking relieved by the British.
1916 The Summer Time Act came into force in Britain.

18th MAY

People
1410 Rupert, German King, died.
1742 Lionel Lukin, inventor of lifeboats, born.
1812 John Bellingham, assassin (of the Prime Minister, Spencer Perceval), hanged.
1830 Carl Goldmark, composer, born.
1836 Wilhelm Steinitz, chess champion, born.
1868 Nicholas II, Emperor of Russia, born.
1883 Walter Gropius, architect, born.
1909 George Meredith, writer, died.
1909 Isaac Albeniz, composer, died.
1917 John Nevil Maskelyne, professional magician, died.

Events
1756 Britain declared war on France.
1843 The Free Church of Scotland founded.
1845 Don Carlos relinquished his rights to the Spanish crown in favour of his son
1900 Mafeking Night in Britain.
1900 Tonga proclaimed a British protectorate.
1922 The BBC (as the British Broadcasting Company) founded.
1943 U.N.R.R.A. founded.
1943 The Hot Springs Conference began.
1944 The independence of Iceland proclaimed.

19th MAY

People
1218 The Emperor Otto IV died.
1536 Anne Boleyn beheaded.
1762 J. G. Fichte, philosopher, born.
1767 Sir George Prevost, soldier and statesman, born.

1795   James Boswell, biographer of Dr Johnson, died.
1861   Dame Nellie Melba, singer, born.
1935   T. E. Lawrence killed in a road accident.

Events
1579   Treaty of the Malcontents with the Prince of Parma signed.
1643   Battle of Rocroi.
1802   The order of the Légion d'Honneur created.
1906   The Simplon Tunnel opened officially.

20th MAY

People
1506   Christopher Columbus born.
1799   Honoré de Balzac, novelist, born.
1805   G. G. Gervinus, literary and political historian, born.
1806   John Stuart Mill, philosopher, born.
1834   The Marquis de Lafayette, statesman, died.
1864   John Clare, poet, died.
1882   Sigrid Undset, novelist, born.
1896   Clara Schumann, pianist, died.
1956   Sir Max Beerbohm, writer, died.

Events
1259   The Treaty of Abbeville signed.
1775   The Mecklenburg declaration of independence adopted at Charlotte, North Carolina.
1867   The foundation stone of the Royal Albert Hall, South Kensington, officially laid.
1927   The Treaty of Jedda signed.
1927   Colonel Lindbergh starts first non-stop solo trans-Atlantic flight.
1956   The first American hydrogen bomb to be dropped over Bikini atoll.

21st MAY
The Feasts of St Helen and St Constantine.

People
1471   Henry VI, King of England, murdered.
1471   Albrecht Dürer, artist, born.
1527   Philip II, King of Spain, born.
1542   Hernando de Soto, soldier and explorer, died.
1688   Alexander Pope, poet, born.
1736   The Duke of Bridgwater, canal pioneer, born.
1771   Christopher Smart, poet, died.
1780   Elizabeth Fry, prison reformer, born.
1818   Lord Playfair, chemist, born.
1850   Gustav Lindenthal, civil engineer, born.
1855   Emile Verhaeren, poet, born.
1878   Glenn Hammond Curtiss, aviator and inventor, born.
1884   Lord Auchinleck born.
1887   Air-Marshal Sir Philip Joubert born.
1895   Franz von Suppé, composer, died.

Events
1502   João de Nova discovered the island of St Helena.
1553   Lady Jane Grey forced to marry Lord Guildford Dudley.

1602 Capt. Bartholomew Gosnold landed at Martha's Vineyard (now No Man's Land), Massachusetts.
1864 The Battle of Spotsylvania Courthouse ended.
1871 The Treaty of Frankfurt ratified.
1894 The Manchester Ship Canal officially opened.
1927 Colonel Lindbergh reached Paris at the end of his first solo non-stop trans-Atlantic flight.

22nd MAY

People
1382 Joanna I, Queen of Naples, executed.
1813 Richard Wagner, composer, born.
1859 Sir Arthur Conan Doyle, writer, born.
1868 Julius Plücker, scientist, died.
1907 Sir Laurence Olivier, actor, born.
1925 Field-Marshal French (the Earl of Ypres) died.
1932 Lady Gregory, playwright, died.

Events
1216 Louis VIII of France invaded England, landing at Stonor.
1200 The Treaty of Le Goulet signed.
1931 Whipsnade Zoo opened to the public.
1939 The Italo-German alliance signed in Berlin.

23rd MAY

People
1498 Girolamo Savonarola, reformer, strangled and burnt at the stake.
1701 Captain Kidd, pirate, hanged.
1707 Carl Linnaeus, botanist, born.
1734 Franz Anton Mesmer, physician and theologian, born.
1799 Thomas Hood, poet, born.
1906 Henrik Ibsen, playwright, died.

Events
1660 King Charles II sailed from Scheveningen for England on his return from exile.
1706 Battle of Ramillies.
1797 The Mutiny at the Nore.

24th MAY
Commonwealth Day.

People
1089 Lanfranc, Archbishop of Canterbury, died.
1543 Nicolaus Copernicus, astronomer, died.
1686 Daniel Gabriel Fahrenheit, physicist, born.
1743 Jean Paul Marat, revolutionary leader, born.
1814 The Empress Josephine died.
1819 Queen Victoria born.
1855 Sir Arthur Pinero, playwright, born.
1870 Jan Christian Smuts, statesman, born.
1879 William Lloyd Garrison, abolitionist, died.

1887 Alexander Archipenko, sculptor, born.
1912 Joan Hammond, singer, born.
1959 John Foster Dulles, statesman, died.

Events
1809 Dartmoor Prison opened.
1815 The Lachlan River (Australia) discovered by the explorer George William Evans.
1822 The Battle of Pinchincha.
1844 Samuel Morse sent the first public message over his electric telegraph between Washington and Baltimore.
1902 Empire Day first celebrated.
1909 Bristol University granted a Royal Charter.
1935 Prince Frederick (Frederick IX) of Denmark married Princess Ingrid of Sweden.
1959 Empire Day renamed Commonwealth Day.

25th MAY
Independence Day (Argentine).

People
1085 Pope Gregory VII died.
1681 Pedro Calderón, playwright, died.
1803 Ralph Waldo Emerson, writer, died.
1805 William Paley, theologian, died.
1826 Tom Sayers, pugilist, born.
1828 John Oxley, explorer of Australia, died.
1865 P. Zeeman, physicist, born.
1879 Lord Beaverbrook born.
1899 Rosa Bonheur, artist, died.
1934 Gustav Holst, composer, died.

Events
1735 The Battle of Bitonto.
1911 President Porfirio of Mexico resigned.
1921 The first British woman barrister qualified.
1923 Transjordan (now Jordan) achieved independence.
1953 The world's first atomic shell fired in Nevada.
1955 A British expedition climbed Kanchenjunga.

26th MAY
Feast of St Augustine of Canterbury.

People
1391 Charles, Duc d'Orléans, poet, born.
1613 Sir Harry Vane, statesman, born.
1623 Sir William Petty, economist, born.
1703 Samuel Pepys, statesman and diarist, died.
1799 Alexander Pushkin, writer, born.
1822 Edmond de Goncourt, writer, born.
1844 Jacques Laffitte, banker and politician, died.
1867 Queen Mary, wife of King George V, born.
1893 Eugene Goossens, composer, born.

1922 Ernest Solvay, industrial chemist, died.
1939 Charles Horace Mayo, surgeon, died.

Events
1637 Pequod Fort, Connecticut, destroyed.
1660 King Charles II landed at Dover.
1805 Napoleon crowned King of Italy.
1828 Kaspar Hauser, the wild boy, found in the Nuremberg market-place.
1871 Ismailia annexed to Egypt.
1906 Vauxhall Bridge, London, officially opened.
1913 The first British woman magistrate appointed.

27th MAY
People
1564 John Calvin, reformer, died.
1661 The Earl of Argyll beheaded.
1756 Maximilian I, King of Bavaria, born.
1799 Jacques François Fromental Elie Halévy, composer, born.
1878 Isadora Duncan, dancer, born.

Events
1679 The Habeas Corpus Act became law.
1905 The Naval Battle of Tsushima.
1937 The Golden Gate Bridge, San Francisco, opened.
1952 The European Defence Community set up.
1958 General de Gaulle acclaimed saviour of France.

28th MAY
People
1738 Dr Joseph Guillotine, adviser on capital punishment, born.
1759 William Pitt, the younger, statesman, born.
1779 Thomas Moore, poet, born.
1807 Jean Louis Rodolphe Agassiz, naturalist, born.
1849 Anne Brontë, novelist, died.
1883 Sir George Dyson, composer, born.
1884 Edvard Beneš, statesman, born.

Events
1812 The Treaty of Bucharest signed.
1932 The closing of the 20-mile dyke connecting North Holland with Friesland, reduced the Zuider Zee to an inland lake.
1937 Neville Chamberlain appointed Prime Minister.
1940 The Belgian Army surrendered to the Germans.

29th MAY
Oak Apple Day.
People
1500 Bartolomeu Diaz, explorer, lost at sea.
1630 King Charles II born.
1736 Patrick Henry, orator and statesman, born.
1829 Sir Humphry Davy, scientist, died.
1846 Sir Henry Wickham, pioneer rubber planter, born.

1860   Isaac Albeniz, composer, born.
1874   G. K. Chesterton, writer, born.
1884   Sir Bartle Frere, statesman, died.
1898   Lord Playfair, chemist, died.
1917   John F. Kennedy, statesman, born.
1935   Joseph Suk, composer, died.

Events

1453   Constantinople fell to the Turks.
1660   King Charles II entered London (traditionally, Restoration Day).
1848   Wisconsin achieved Statehood.
1940   The evacuation of Dunkirk began.
1953   Sir Edmund Hillary and the Sherpa Tensing climbed Mount Everest.

30th MAY
Feast of St Joan of Arc. Memorial Day (U.S.A.).

People

1431   St Joan of Arc burnt at the stake.
1640   Peter Paul Rubens, artist, died.
1672   Peter the Great, Tsar of Russia, born.
1744   Alexander Pope, poet, died.
1778   François Marie Arouet de Voltaire, writer, died.

Events

1656   The Grenadier Guards formed.
1814   The first Treaty of Paris signed.
1869   Memorial Day (Decoration Day) first observed in the U.S.A.
1913   The Treaty of London signed.

31st MAY
Union Day (Union of South Africa).

People

1809   Josef Haydn, composer, died.
1819   Walt Whitman, poet, born.
1837   Joseph Grimaldi, clown, died.
1857   Pope Pius XI born.
1860   Walter Sickert, artist, born.
1863   Sir Francis Younghusband, explorer, born.
1923   Prince Rainier III of Monaco born.

Events

1669   Samuel Pepys ended his Diary.
1902   The Peace of Vereeniging.
1910   The Colony of Natal merged in the Union of South Africa.
1916   The Naval Battle of Jutland.
1952   The Volga-Don Canal opened.

1st JUNE

People

1593   Christopher Marlowe, playwright, buried.
1637   Jacques Marquette, missionary and explorer, born.
1793   Henry Francis Lyte, hymn-writer, born.

1801   Brigham Young, Mormon, born.
1804   Mikhail Ivanovich Glinka, composer, born.
1815   James Gillray, caricaturist, died.
1815   Otto I, King of Greece, born.
1846   Pope Gregory XVI died.
1878   John Masefield, poet, born.
1879   Eugène, Prince Imperial of France, killed in the Zulu campaign.
1941   Hugh Walpole, novelist, died.

Events
1792   Kentucky achieved Statehood.
1794   The Battle of the 1st of June.
1796   Tennessee achieved Statehood.
1835   Otto I assumes the government of Greece.
1920   The first Archbishop of Wales enthroned.
1939   The submarine *Thetis* lost.
1941   The Hot Springs Conference ended.
1946   A combined television and sound broadcasting receiving licence introduced in Britain.

2nd JUNE
People
959   Odo, Archbishop of Canterbury, died.
1453   Alvaro de Luna, Constable of Castile, executed.
1624   John Sobieski, King of Poland, born.
1701   Madeleine de Scudéry, novelist, died.
1776   Robert Foulis, printer, died.
1817   George Henry Cortiss, engineer, born.
1835   Pope Pius X born.
1840   Thomas Hardy, writer, born.
1857   Sir Edward Elgar, composer, born.
1863   Felix Weingartner, conductor, born.

Events
1780   Lord George Gordon's ' No Popery ' riots began.
1864   Greek troops occupied Corfu.
1895   Japan took formal possession of Formosa from China.
1953   The coronation of Queen Elizabeth II.

3rd JUNE
People
1657   William Harvey, Royal physician, died.
1771   Sydney Smith, reformer, born.
1808   Jefferson Davis, statesman, born.
1832   Charles Lecocq, composer, born.
1865   King George V born.
1875   Georges Bizet, composer, died.
1899   Johann Strauss, the younger, composer, died.

Events
1621   The Dutch West Indies Company founded.
1665   The Naval Battle of Lowestoft.
1745   The Battle of Hohenfriedberg (3–4 June).

1887   The foundation stone of the opening lock of Kiel Canal laid.
1937   The Duke of Windsor married Mrs Wallis Warfield.
1940   The evacuation of Dunkirk ended.
1956   British 3rd Class railway travel abolished.

4th JUNE
Eton College Celebrations on the birthday of George III.

People

1738   King George III born.
1792   General Burgoyne, soldier and playwright, died.
1867   Field-Marshal Mannerheim born.
1891   Erno Rapee, conductor, born.
1931   Ibn Hussein, King of the Hejaz, died.
1945   Georg Kaiser, composer, died.
1951   Sergei Koussevitsky, conductor, died.

Events

1831   Leopold, Duke of Kendal, elected first King of the Belgians.
1859   The Battle of Magenta.
1878   The Anglo-Turkish Convention signed.
1944   The Allies enter Rome.

5th JUNE
Feast of St Boniface.

People

1316   Louis X, King of France, died.
1625   Orlando Gibbons, composer, died.
1660   Sarah, Duchess of Marlborough, born.
1723   Adam Smith, economist, born.
1826   Carl von Weber, composer, died.
1826   Ivar Hallström, composer and pianist, born.
1883   Lord Keynes, economist, born.
1897   Madame Chiang Kai-shek born.
1916   Lord Kitchener perished at sea.

Events

1783   The Balloon invented by the brothers Montgolfier.
1863   Protocol between Britain, France and Russia provided for the incorporation of
         the Ionian Islands with Greece.
1942   The Battle of Midway Island began.
1947   The Marshall Plan announced.

6th JUNE
People

1502   John III, King of Portugal, born.
1557   John III, King of Portugal, died.
1599   Diego de Velasquez, painter, born.
1606   Pierre Corneille, dramatist, born.
1755   Nathan Hale, American patriot, born.
1756   John Trumbull, artist, born.
1762   Admiral Lord Anson died.

1826   Léon Say, statesman, born.
1832   Jeremy Bentham, philosopher, died.
1840   Sir John Stainer, composer, born.
1860   Dean Inge, theologian, born.
1868   Robert Falcon Scott, explorer, born.
1875   Thomas Mann, novelist, born.
1881   Henri Vieuxtemps, violinist and composer, died.
1903   Aram Khachaturiyan, composer, born.
1934   Albert, Prince of Liège, born.
1935   Field-Marshal Lord Byng died.
1935   George Grossmith, actor and writer, died.
1941   Louis Chevrolet, pioneer automobile designer, died.

Events
1520   Field of the Cloth of Gold.
1863   The King of Denmark accepted the Greek Crown on behalf of Prince William (George I).
1918   The Battle of Belleau Wood began.
1942   The Battle of Midway Island ended.
1944   D-Day.
1954   The birth of Eurovision through the direct relay on the European network of the *Fête des Narcisses* at Montreux.

7th JUNE

People
555   Pope Vigilius died.
632   Mahomet died.
1329   Robert Bruce, King of Scotland, died.
1761   John Rennie, engineer, born.
1778   Beau Brummel born.
1859   David Cox, artist, died.
1866   E. W. Hornung, novelist, born.
1873   Sir Landon Ronald, conductor, born.
1879   Knud Rasmussen, explorer, born.

Events
1494   The Treaty of Tordesilas signed.
1614   The Addled Parliament dissolved.
1905   Norway proclaimed the dissolution of the union of Norway and Sweden.
1906   The *Lusitania* launched.
1917   The Battle of Messines.
1935   Baldwin appointed Prime Minister.
2004   The next transit of Venus over the sun.

8th JUNE

People
1714   Sophia, Electress of Hanover, died.
1724   John Smeaton, civil engineer, born.
1772   Robert Stevenson, engineer, born.
1795   The death of Louis XVII, King of France, announced.
1809   Tom Paine, political writer and philanthropist, died.
1814   Charles Reade, novelist, born.

1831   Mrs Sarah Siddons, actress, died.
1857   Douglas Jerrold, humorist, died.
1865   Sir Joseph Paxton, architect and ornamental gardener, died.
1869   Frank Lloyd Wright, architect, born.
1876   George Sand, writer, died.
1942   Morley Roberts, novelist, died.

Events
1815   The Congress of Vienna ended.
1930   King Carol returned to the throne of Rumania.
1946   Victory Day celebration in Britain.

9th JUNE
People
1640   The Emperor Leopold I born.
1681   William Lilly, astrologer, died.
1781   George Stephenson, engineer, born.
1810   Otto Nicolai, composer, born.
1870   Charles Dickens, novelist, died.

Events
1904   First concert of the London Symphony Orchestra.
1904   First meeting of the Ladies' Automobile Club, London.

10th JUNE
People
1190   Barbarossa, Holy Roman Emperor, died.
1580   Luis Vaz de Camoens, poet, died.
1688   James Stuart, the Old Pretender, born.
1727   King George I died.
1859   Sir James Guthrie, artist, born.
1899   Ernest Chausson, composer, died.
1921   Prince Philip born.
1934   Frederick Delius, composer, died.
1942   Stanley Lupino, comedian, died.
1956   Marie Laurencin, painter, died.

Events
1727   George II proclaimed King.
1809   Napoleon excommunicated.
1826   The final revolt of the Janissaries in Turkey began.
1829   First Oxford and Cambridge University Boat Race.
1854   Crystal Palace officially opened.
1918   Battle of Belleau Wood ended.
1940   Italy declared war on Great Britain.
1946   Italy became a republic.

11th JUNE
People
1488   James III, King of Scotland, assassinated.
1588   George Wither, poet, born.
1665   Sir Kenelm Digby, writer, died.

1776   John Constable, painter, born.
1847   Sir John Franklin, explorer, died.
1859   Prince Metternich died.
1864   Richard Strauss, composer, born.
1942   Geoffrey Toye, conductor and composer, died.

Events
1509   King Henry VIII married Catherine of Aragon.
1903   King Alexander of Serbia and Queen Draga assassinated in Belgrade.
1935   DERV fuel first marketed as a separate product in Britain.

12th JUNE
People
1759   William Collins, poet, died.
1802   Harriet Martineau, writer, born.
1806   John Augustus Roebling, engineer, born.
1819   Charles Kingsley, poet and novelist, born.
1842   Dr Thomas Arnold, headmaster of Rugby, died.
1842   Rikard Nordraak, composer and folksong collector, born.
1859   Jacob Bell, founder of the Pharmaceutical Society, died.
1897   Sir Anthony Eden, statesman, born.

Events
1458   Magdalen College, Oxford, founded.
1908   The Rotherhithe-Stepney Tunnel, London, opened.

13th JUNE
People
  39   Gnaeus Julius Agricola, statesman, born.
1231   St Anthony of Padua died.
1396   Philip the Good, Duke of Burgundy, born.
1752   Fanny Burney (Mme D'Arblay), novelist, born.
1795   Dr Thomas Arnold, headmaster of Rugby, born.
1831   James Clerk-Maxwell, physicist, born.
1865   William Butler Yeats, poet, born.
1869   Eduard Poldini, composer, born.
1886   Ludwig II, King of Bavaria, drowned.
1888   Elizabeth Schumann, singer, born.
1958   Pierre Flandin, statesman, died.

Events
1700   Peter the Great concluded peace with the Porte.
1900   The Boxer Rising in China.
1946   King Umberto II of Italy left the country.
1956   Last British troops left the Suez base.
1958   Algiers rising that brought President de Gaulle to power.

14th JUNE
Flag Day (U.S.A.).

People
1594   Orlando di Lasso, composer, died.
1662   Sir Harry Vane, statesman, beheaded.

1809   Admiral Keppel born.
1811   Harriet Beecher Stowe, writer, born.
1883   Edward FitzGerald, poet, died.
1884   Count John McCormack, singer, born.
1927   J. K. Jerome, writer, died.
1936   G. K. Chesterton, writer, died.

Events
1381   King Richard II persuaded the Essex rebels to return home.
1645   The Battle of Naseby.
1777   The Stars and Stripes adopted by the Continental Congress.
1800   The Battle of Marengo.
1900   The Hawaiian Islands constituted as United States territory.
1940   The Germans entered Paris.
1958   The withdrawal of French forces from Morocco announced.

15th JUNE
Feast of St Vitus.

People
923   Robert I, King of France, killed in battle.
1330   Edward, the Black Prince, born.
1381   Wat Tyler killed at Smithfield.
1467   Philip the Good, Duke of Burgundy, died.
1563   George Heriot, jeweller and royal banker, born.
1605   Thomas Randolph, poet, baptised.
1815   ' Phiz ' (Hablot K. Browne), artist, born.
1843   Edvard Grieg, composer, born.
1844   Thomas Campbell, poet, died.
1851   Ernest Howard Griffiths, physicist, died.
1858   Ary Scheffer, painter, died.
1860   General Sir Charles Monro born.
1865   Paul Gilson, composer, born.
1876   Hussein Auni, statesman, assassinated.
1888   Frederick III, Emperor of Germany, died.
1889   Michail Eminescu, poet, died.
1893   Franz Erkel, composer, died.
1909   St John Hankin, playwright, died.

Events
1215   Magna Carta signed.
1752   Benjamin Franklin demonstrated electricity by means of a kite.
1836   Arkansas achieved Statehood.
1858   The Massacre of the Christians at Jedda.
1919   Alcock and Brown complete first non-stop trans-Atlantic flight.
1944   First flying-bomb attacks on London.

16th JUNE
People
1514   Sir John Cheke, classical scholar, born.
1722   The Duke of Marlborough died.
1801   Julius Plücker, scientist, born.
1842   Otto Flügel, philosopher, born.

1858   King Gustav V of Sweden born.
1930   Elmer Ambrose Sperry, inventor, died.
1937   Simeon II, ex-Tsar of Bulgaria, born.

Events
1487   The Battle of Stoke.
1755   Boston troops captured the French fort in Nova Scotia.
1815   The Battle of Quatre Bras.
1826   The insurrection of the Janissaries at Constantinople ended.
1880   The Berlin Conference.
1930   Mixed bathing in the Serpentine, Hyde Park, first permitted.
1940   The Soviet Union sends an ultimatum to Estonia.

17th JUNE

People
1239   King Edward I born.
1682   King Charles XII of Sweden born.
1696   John III, King of Poland, died.
1703   John Wesley born.
1719   Joseph Addison, writer, died.
1762   P. J. de Crébillon, poet, died.
1800   The Earl of Rosse, astronomer, born.
1808   E. J. Potgieter, writer, born.
1808   Henrik Wergeland, writer, born.
1810   Ferdinand Freiligrath, poet, born.
1818   Charles François Gounod, composer, born.
1845   Richard Barham, poet, died.
1882   Igor Stravinsky, composer, born.
1958   Imre Nagy, statesman, executed.

Events
1745   The French surrendered Louisburg, Cape Breton Island, to the British.
1775   The Battle of Bunker Hill.
1789   The Third Estate constituted themselves the French National Assembly.
1860   *Great Eastern* left the Needles on her first trans-Atlantic voyage.
1869   Wilhelmshaven, Germany's first military port, officially inaugurated.
1873   The Roumelian Railway opened.
1905   The River Steamboat Service on the Thames began.
1940   Latvia occupied by the Russians.
1940   The evacuation of the British Expeditionary Force from France completed.
1944   Iceland proclaimed an independent Republic.

18th JUNE

People
1749   Ambrose Philips, poet, died.
1835   William Cobbett, writer and politician, died.
1857   Henry Clay Folger born.
1868   Nicolas Horthy, statesman, born.
1871   George Grote, historian, died.
1880   John Augustus Sutter, pioneer in the U.S.A., died.
1936   Maxim Gorki, writer, died.

Events
1429   The Battle of Patay.
1812   War between Britain and the U.S.A. began.
1815   The Battle of Waterloo.
1928   The Atlantic first flown by a woman aviator (Amelia Earhart).
1953   Egypt proclaimed a Republic.

19th JUNE

People
1566   King James I born.
1623   Blaise Pascal, philosopher, born.
1782   Félicité Robert de Lamennais, church reformer, born.
1809   Richard Monckton Milnes, Lord Houghton, poet and reformer, born.
1820   Sir Joseph Banks, naturalist, died.
1834   Charles Haddon Spurgeon, Baptist, born.
1838   Heinrich Schulz-Beuthen, composer, born.
1861   Earl Haig of Bemersyde born.
1867   The Emperor Maximilian of Mexico shot.
1889   John Percy, metallurgist, died.
1937   Sir James Barrie, writer, died.

Events
1828   The capitulation of Brahilov.
1850   The Earl of Rosse publicly announced his discovery of the Spiral Nebulæ.
1895   The Kiel Canal opened.
1910   The first Zeppelin airliner (*Deutschland*) launched.

20th JUNE

People
1819   Jacques Offenbach, composer, born.
1837   King William IV died.
1870   Jules de Goncourt, writer, died.

Events
1314   The Battle of Bannockburn.
1789   The oath of the Tennis Court.
1791   Louis XVI's attempted flight to Varennes
1792   The mob invaded the Tuileries.
1837   Queen Victoria ascended the throne.
1863   West Virginia achieved Statehood.
1927   Greyhound racing began at White City, London.
1931   The Hoover Moratorium declared in the United States.

21st JUNE
The Summer Solstice (except in Leap Years).

People
1002   Pope Leo IX born.
1377   King Edward III died.
1529   John Skelton, poet, died.
1631   John Smith, coloniser of Virginia, died.
1639   Increase Mather, President of Harvard, born.
1652   Inigo Jones, architect, died.

1852   Friedrich Froebel, educationalist, died.
1882   Rockwell Kent, artist, born.
1884   The Prince of Orange died.
1884   Field-Marshal Sir Claude Auchinleck born.
1908   Nikolai Rimsky-Korsakov, composer, died.
1940   John Taliaferro Thompson, soldier and inventor, died.

Events
1619   Dulwich College, London, founded.
1788   The American Constitution came into force.
1843   The Royal College of Surgeons, London, founded.
1919   The German Fleet scuttled at Scapa Flow.
1942   Tobruk fell to the Germans.

22nd JUNE
The Summer Solstice in Leap Years.
People
1101   Roger I of Sicily died.
1276   Pope Innocent V died.
1527   Niccolo Machiavelli, diplomat and writer, died.
1535   Bishop John Fisher executed.
1748   Thomas Day, writer, born.
1763   E. N. Méhul, composer, born.
1809   Mary Victoria Cowden-Clarke, Shakespeare's concordancer, born.
1830   Theodore Leschetizky, pianist, born.
1846   Benjamin Robert Haydon, painter, committed suicide.
1851   Thomas Edmondson, inventor, died.
1874   Howard Staunton, chess-player, died.
1887   Sir Julian Huxley, biologist, born.
1907   Anne Morrow Lindbergh born.

Events
1476   The Battle of Morat.
1559   Queen Elizabeth's Prayer Book issued.
1679   The Battle of Bothwell Bridge.
1774   The Quebec Act received the Royal Assent.
1817   Windham William Sadler crossed the St George's Channel by balloon.
1900   The Wallace Collection, London, opened.
1907   The Northern Underground Line, London, opened.
1933   The Social Democrat Party suppressed in Germany.
1945   The Battle of Okinawa ended.

23rd JUNE
Midsummer Night.
People
1596   Johan Baner, Swedish commander, born.
1703   Marie Leszczynska, Queen of France, born.
1763   The Empress Josephine, wife of Napoleon, born.
1836   James Mill, philosopher and historian, died.
1839   Lady Hester Stanhope, traveller, died.
1894   The Duke of Windsor born.
1924   Cecil Sharp, folk-music collector, died.

Events
1585   The Star Chamber suppressed all provincial printing offices.
1611   The navigator Henry Hudson cast adrift to perish.
1683   William Penn signed a treaty of peace and friendship with the Indians.
1757   The Battle of Plassey.
1793   The beginning of the Reign of Terror in France.
1828   The surrender of Anapa.
1848   The rising of the Red Republicans in France.
1945   Mindanas reconquered by the Americans.

24th JUNE
The Feast of St John the Baptist. Midsummer Day.

People
1065   Ferdinand I, King of Castile and Leon, died.
1340   John of Gaunt, Duke of Lancaster, born.
1519   Lucrezia Borgia, Duchess of Ferrara, died.
1542   St John of the Cross born.
1643   John Hampden, statesman, died.
1650   The Duke of Marlborough born.
1768   Marie Leszczynska, Queen of France, died.
1768   Lazare Hoche, soldier, born.
1771   Eleuthère Irénée du Pont, American powder manufacturer, born.
1813   Henry Ward Beecher, divine, born.
1850   Lord Kitchener born.
1870   Adam Lindsay Gordon, poet of Australia, committed suicide.
1909   Sir William Penney, scientist, born.

Events
1314   The Battle of Bannockburn.
1497   John Cabot reached the North American shore.
1717   The Mother Grand Lodge of Freemasonry inaugurated in London.
1839   The Battle of Nessib.
1859   The Battle of Solferino.
1860   The training of nurses in Britain started at St Thomas's Hospital, London.
1948   The Russian blockade of Berlin began.
1956   Col. Nasser elected President of the Republic of Egypt.

25th JUNE

People
1483   Earl Rivers executed.
1483   Lord Richard Grey executed.
1634   John Marston, dramatist, died.
1736   John Horne Tooke, politician and philologist, born.
1876   George Armstrong Custer, American pioneer, died.
1879   Sir William Fothergill Cooke, electrician, died.
1897   Hans Barth, pianist and composer, born.
1908   Grover Cleveland, statesman, died.
1912   Sir Lawrence Alma-Tadema, artist, died.
1913   Esteban Eitler, composer, born.

Events
841   The Battle of Fontenoy.
1530   The Confession of Augsburg read to the Diet.

1876   The Battle of Little Big Horn (Custer's Last Stand).
1950   The Korean War began.

26th JUNE

People
363   Julian the Apostate, emperor, died of wounds.
1541   Francisco Pizarro, conquistador, assassinated.
1666   Sir Richard Fanshawe, diplomat and translator, died.
1763   George Morland, painter, born.
1793   Gilbert White, writer on natural history, died.
1824   Lord Kelvin, scientist, born.
1827   Samuel Crompton, inventor, died.
1830   King George IV died.
1836   C. J. Rouget de Lisle, writer of the Marseillaise, died
1846   Honoratus Leigh Thomas, surgeon, died.
1892   Pearl S. Buck, writer, born.
1938   E. V. Lucas, essayist, died.
1945   Erno Rapee, conductor, died.

Events
1830   William IV ascended the throne.
1846   The Corn Laws repealed.
1853   The Russians issue a manifesto against Turkey.
1857   Queen Victoria distributed Victoria Crosses at Hyde Park.
1862   The Seven Days' Battles began.
1909   The present buildings of the Victoria and Albert Museum opened officially.
1912   The first Queen Alexandra Day held.
1917   The American Expeditionary Force reached France.
1945   The United Nations Charter signed at San Francisco.

27th JUNE

People
1829   James Smithson, scientist, died.
1846   Charles Stewart Parnell, Irish Nationalist leader, born.
1872   Paul Lawrence Dunbar, poet, born.
1880   Helen Keller, blind and deaf scholar, born.
1888   Guilhermina Suggia, 'cellist, born.

Events
1743   The Battle of Dettingen.
1900   The Central London Electric Railway opened.
1944   Cherbourg taken by the Allies.

28th JUNE

People
767   Pope Paul I died.
1476   Pope Paul IV born.
1491   King Henry VIII born.
1712   Jean Jacques Rousseau, writer and philosopher, born
1805   Giuseppe Mazzini, Italian leader, born.
1815   Robert Franz, composer, born.
1831   Joseph Joachim, violinist, born.
1855   Field-Marshal Lord Raglan died.
1867   Luigi Pirandello, playwright, born.

1871   Luisa Tetrazzini, singer, born.
1873   Alexis Carrel, scientist, born.
1914   The Archduke Ferdinand and his morganatic wife assassinated at Sarajevo.
1915   Victor Trumper, cricketer, died.

Events
1776   The British repulsed at Charleston.
1778   The Battle of Monmouth, New Jersey.
1815   Louis XVIII returned in state to Paris (the end of " The Hundred Days ").
1910   The first Zeppelin airliner (*Deutschland*) crashed.
1910   Westminster Cathedral consecrated.
1919   The Treaty of Versailles signed.
1948   The Anglo-U.S. airlift to Berlin began.

29th JUNE
The Feasts of St Peter and St Paul.

People
1577   Peter Paul Rubens, painter, born.
1810   Robert Schumann, composer, born.
1841   Sir Henry Morton Stanley, explorer, born (traditional date).
1858   George Washington Goethals, Panama Canal builder, born.
1861   William James Mayo, surgeon, born.
1868   George Ellery Hale, astronomer, born.
1890   Alexander Parkes, chemist, died.
1892   Alexandres Rhankaves, poet, scholar and statesman, died.
1911   Prince Bernhard of the Netherlands born.
1941   Ignaz Jan Paderewski, pianist and statesman, died.

Events
1734   The Battle of Parma.
1954   The Potomac Charter issued.

30th JUNE

People
1792   Thomas Edmondson, inventor, born.
1843   Sir Herbert Stewart, soldier, born.
1861   Elizabeth Barrett Browning, poet, died.

Events
1688   William of Orange invited to England.
1825   Ibrahim Pasha took Tripolitza.
1860   The British Association's first annual meeting held at Oxford.
1855   The Newspaper Stamp Tax abolished in Britain.
1924   The first International Power Conference held at Wembley.
1934   The ' Night of the Long Knives ' (or, ' The Bloodbath ') in Germany.
1960   The Belgian Congo's independence proclaimed.

1st JULY
Canada Day.

People
1534   Frederick II, King of Denmark, born.
1574   Bishop Joseph Hall, satirist, born.

1589   Christopher Plantin, printer, died.
1646   Gottfried Wilhelm, Baron Leibniz, philosopher, born.
1725   Field-Marshal the Comte de Rochambeau born.
1742   Georg Christoph Lichtenberg, physicist, born.
1804   George Sand, writer, born.
1839   Mahmud II, Sultan of Turkey, died.
1860   Charles Goodyear, inventor, died.
1872   Louis Blériot, pioneer aviator, born.
1904   George Frederick Watts, painter, died.
1909   Sir William Curzon Wyllie, administrator, assassinated.
1925   Eric Satie, composer, died.

Events
1643   The Westminster Assembly began.
1690   The Battle of the Boyne.
1852   First Indian postage stamps issued.
1858   The Darwinian theory of evolution by natural selection first communicated to
         the Linnean Society.
1862   The Battle of Malvern Hill.
1863   Slavery ceased in the Dutch West Indies.
1863   The Battle of Gettysburg began.
1867   The German federal constitution came into force.
1867   The Provinces of Canada united under the British North American Act.
1873   Prince Edward Island admitted to the Union of Canada.
1885   The sovereignty of King Leopold over the Congo proclaimed.
1920   The British civil administration of Palestine began.
1933   London Passenger Transport Board took control of London's passenger
         transport.
1944   The Bretton Woods Conference began.
1946   The first atom bomb test took place over Bikini atoll.

2nd JULY
People
 936   King Henry the Fowler died.
1489   Thomas Cranmer, Archbishop of Canterbury, born.
1566   Nostradamus, astrologer, died.
1714   Christoph Willibald Gluck, composer, born.
1724   Friedrich Gottlieb Klopstock, poet, born.
1778   Jean Jacques Rousseau, philosopher, died.
1809   John Jordan, poet, died.
1850   Sir Robert Peel, statesman, died.
1862   Sir William Henry Bragg, scientist, born.
1881   James Abram Garfield, statesman, shot (and died 19th Sept.).
1903   Olav V, King of Norway, born.
1914   Joseph Chamberlain, statesman, died.
1917   Sir Herbert Beerbohm Tree, actor-manager, died.
1932   Manuel II, ex-King of Portugal, died.

Events
1644   The Battle of Marston Moor.
1860   Queen Victoria fired first shot at inaugural meeting of the National Rifle
         Association.
1862   The Seven Days' Battles ended.
1940   The Vichy Government set up in France.

3rd JULY

People

1423	Louis XI, King of France, born.
1642	Marie de' Medici, Queen of France, died.
1728	Robert Adam, architect, born.
1738	John Singleton Copley, painter, born.
1746	Henry Grattan, statesman, born.
1816	Mrs Dorothy Jordan, actress and royal mistress, died (generally accepted date).
1908	Joel Chandler Harris, humorous writer, died.

Events

323	The Battle of Adrianople.
1194	The Battle of Fréteval.
1608	The settlement of Quebec began.
1620	The Treaty of Ulm signed.
1778	The Massacre at Wyoming, Pennsylvania.
1815	King Louis XVIII entered Paris.
1863	The Battle of Gettysburg ended.
1890	Idaho achieved Statehood.
1898	The Naval Battle of Santiago.
1953	Nanga Parbat climbed by a German-Austrian expedition.

4th JULY

Independence Day in the United States of America.

People

1623	William Byrd, composer, died.
1681	Agatha, Tsarina of Russia, died.
1761	Samuel Richardson, novelist, died.
1804	Nathaniel Hawthorne, novelist, born.
1807	Giuseppe Garibaldi, Italian patriot and leader, born.
1826	Stephen Collins Foster, song-writer, born.
1826	John Adams, statesman, died.
1826	Thomas Jefferson, statesman, died.
1831	James Monroe, statesman, died.
1848	François René, Vicomte de Chateaubriand, writer, died
1857	Joseph Pennell, etcher, born.
1872	Calvin Coolidge, statesman, born.
1910	Giovanni Virginio Schiaparelli, astronomer, died.
1934	Madame Curie, scientist, died.
1942	Prince Michael born.

Events

1187	The Battle of Hittin.
1399	Henry of Lancaster (Henry IV) landed at Ravenspur, Yorkshire.
1636	Providence, Rhode Island, founded.
1653	Barebones Parliament began sitting.
1776	The American declaration of independence.
1817	Work on the Erie Canal began.
1828	Don Miguel assumed the title of King of Portugal.
1829	The first London bus ran from Marylebone Road to the Bank.
1863	The surrender of Vicksburg.
1883	The Statue of Liberty presented to the United States.
1904	The construction of the Panama Canal began.
1946	The Republic of the Philippines established.

5th JULY

People
1709 Etienne de Silhouette, statesman, born.
1755 Mrs Sarah Siddons, actress, born.
1764 Ivan VI, Emperor of Russia, murdered.
1781 Sir Stamford Raffles, administrator, born.
1801 Admiral David Glasgow Farragut born.
1804 George Sand, writer, born.
1803 George Borrow, writer, born.
1810 Phineas Taylor Barnum, circus pioneer, born.
1826 Sir Stamford Raffles, administrator, died.
1843 Bishop Mandell Creighton, historian, born.
1853 Cecil Rhodes, statesman, born.
1877 Wanda Landowska, musician, born.
1878 Josef Holbrooke, composer, born.
1880 Jan Kubelik, violinist, born.
1894 Sir Austen Henry Layard, archæologist, died.
1929 Hans Meyer, geographer, died.

Events
1187 Guy de Lusignan, King of Jerusalem, defeated by Saladin.
1841 Thomas Cook's, travel agents, founded.
1933 The German Catholic Party dissolved.
1948 The British National Health Service came into operation.
1955 The first Assembly of the Western European Union opened at Strasbourg.

6th JULY
Feast of St Thomas More.

People
1189 King Henry II died.
1415 John Huss, reformer, burnt at the stake.
1553 King Edward VI died.
1572 Sigismund II, King of Poland, died.
1747 John Paul Jones, naval adventurer, born.
1755 John Flaxman, sculptor, born.
1759 Sir William Pepperell, soldier, died.
1796 Nicholas I, Emperor of Russia, born.
1832 The Emperor Maximilian of Mexico, born.
1847 Lord Runciman, shipowner, born.
1883 Viscount Malvern, statesman, born.
1893 Guy de Maupassant, writer, died.
1933 Robert Kajanus, musician, died.

Events
1439 The Decree of Union issued (uniting the Latin and Greek churches).
1560 The Treaty of Edinburgh signed.
1685 The Battle of Sedgemoor.
1809 The Battle of Wagram.
1829 The Treaty of London signed.
1859 Queensland, Australia, formed into a separate colony.
1907 Brooklands Motor Racecourse opened.
1923 The U.S.S.R. formally constituted.

1950 The Oder-Neisse Line declared the permanent frontier between Germany and Poland (by the German Democratic Republic and Poland only).
1952 The last London tram ran.

7th JULY
Feasts of St Cyril and St Methodius.

People
1307 King Edward I died.
1535 Sir Thomas More executed.
1752 Joseph Marie Jacquard, inventor, born.
1816 Richard Brinsley Sheridan, playwright, died.
1860 Gustav Mahler, composer, born.
1884 Lion Feuchtwanger, novelist, born.
1930 Sir Arthur Conan Doyle, writer, died.

Events
1807 The Treaty of Tilsit signed.
1871 The Netherlands ceded Dutch possessions in Guinea to Britain.
1898 Hawaii annexed by the United States.
1924 The British Government abandoned the Channel Tunnel scheme.

8th JULY

People
1621 Jean de La Fontaine, writer, born.
1623 Pope Gregory XV died.
1695 Christian Huygens, physicist, died.
1726 John Ker, spy, died in prison.
1797 Edmund Burke, political writer, died.
1819 Admiral Sir Francis Leopold M'Clintock, explorer, born.
1822 Percy Bysshe Shelley, poet, died.
1823 Sir Henry Raeburn, painter, died.
1836 Joseph Chamberlain, statesman, born.
1838 Count Zeppelin, inventor, born.
1882 Sir John Anderson, statesman, born.
1882 Percy Grainger, composer, born.
1939 Havelock Ellis, physician and scholar, died.
1943 Sir Harry Oakes, gold prospector and multi-millionaire, murdered.

Events
1709 The Battle of Poltava.
1832 Oporto taken by Don Pedro.
1833 The Treaty of Unkiar Skelessi signed.
1864 The Battle of Monocacy.
1924 Hitler resumed leadership of the National Socialist Party in Germany.

9th JULY

People
1228 Archbishop Stephen Langton died.
1440 Jan van Eyck, painter, died.
1746 Philip V, King of Spain, died.
1764 Ann Radcliffe, novelist, born.
1777 Henry Hallam, historian, born.

1819 Elias Howe, inventor, born.
1839 John Davison Rockefeller, sen., born.
1856 Nikola Tesla, inventor, born.
1863 Baron von Stockmar, statesman, died.
1909 The Marquess of Ripon, statesman, died.
1932 King Camp Gillette, manufacturer, died.

Events
1386 The Battle of Sempach.
1553 Lady Jane Grey proclaimed Queen of England.
1755 General Braddock's troops attacked by the French and Indians near Fort Duquesne.
1810 Holland united to France.
1816 The Congress of Tucumán.
1816 Argentina declares its independence from Spain.
1857 Madeleine Smith acquitted at Edinburgh of the murder of her lover.
1860 Massacre of the Christians in Damascus began.
1937 The Treaty of Saadabad signed.
1944 Caen captured by the Allies.

10th JULY
People
1290 Ladislaus IV, King of Hungary, murdered.
1451 James III, King of Scotland, born.
1509 John Calvin, reformer, born.
1559 King Henry II of France killed.
1605 Theodore II, Tsar of Russia, murdered.
1723 Sir William Blackstone, jurist, born.
1759 Pierre Joseph Redouté, painter, born.
1792 Captain Marryat, writer, born.
1805 Thomas Wedgwood, the first photographer, died.
1834 James Abbott McNeill Whistler, painter, born.
1835 Henri Wieniawski, composer, born.
1886 Field-Marshal Lord Gort, born.
1888 Toyohiko Kagawa, reformer and writer, born.
1893 Henry Nettleship, scholar, died.
1920 Lord Fisher, Admiral of the Fleet, died.
1923 Albert Chevalier, singer and composer, died.

Events
1890 Wyoming achieved Statehood.
1931 The King George V Dock, Glasgow, opened.
1938 Rheims Cathedral reopened.

11th JULY
People
1274 Robert Bruce, King of Scotland, born.
1319 Jean, Sire de Joinville, crusader and historian, died.
1657 Frederick I, King of Prussia, born.
1732 Joseph Lalande, astronomer, born.
1754 Thomas Bowdler, literary editor, born.
1767 John Quincy Adams, statesman, born.

1797 Charles Macklin, actor, died.
1811 Sir William Robert Grove, lawyer and scientist, born.
1817 The Rev. William Gregor, chemist and mineralogist, died.
1838 John Wanamaker, merchant, born.
1859 William Richard Hamilton, antiquarian, died.
1903 William Ernest Henley, poet, died.
1926 Gertrude Bell, traveller, died.
1937 George Gershwin, composer, died.
1941 Sir Arthur Evans, archæologist, died.
1946 Paul Nash, artist, died.
1957 The Aga Khan died.

Events
1302 The Battle of the Spurs (Battle of Courtrai).
1637 The number of typefounders in England restricted to four by Star Chamber
        decree.
1708 The Battle of Oudenarde.
1804 Alexander Hamilton fatally wounded in a duel with Aaron Burr.
1859 The Treaty of Villafranca signed.
1860 Massacre of the Christians at Damascus ended.

12th JULY
Orangeman's Day (Northern Ireland).
People
100BC Julius Cæsar born.
1536 Desiderius Erasmus, reformer, died.
1584 William, Prince of Orange, assassinated.
1730 Josiah Wedgwood, potter, born.
1803 Thomas Guthrie, promoter of Ragged Schools, born.
1804 Alexander Hamilton, statesman, died.
1817 Henry David Thoreau, writer, born.
1847 Karl Barth, conductor and pianist, born.
1849 Sir William Osler, physician, born.
1849 Horace Smith, writer, died.
1850 Robert Stevenson, engineer, died.
1854 George Eastman, photographic pioneer, born.
1895 Kirsten Flagstad, singer, born.
1910 The Hon. C. S. Rolls, pioneer aviator, killed.
1935 Alfred Dreyfus died.

Events
1691 The Battle of Aughrim.
1806 The formation of the Confederation of the Rhine.
1831 Belgium separated from Holland.
1843 Marlborough College founded.
1878 The British took possession of Cyprus.
1906 Alfred Dreyfus vindicated and rehabilitated.

13th JULY
People
1380 Bertrand du Guesclin, Constable of France, died.
1755 General Edward Braddock died.
1779 William Hedley, inventor, born.

1793   John Clare, poet, born.
1793   Jean Paul Marat, statesman, assassinated.
1811   James Young, chemist, born.
1816   Gustav Freytag, novelist, born.
1859   Sidney Webb, Lord Passfield, economist, born.
1886   Clifford Bax, playwright, born.
1890   John Charles Frémont, explorer, died.
1951   Arnold Schönberg, composer, died.

Events

1762   *Coup d'état* in Russia dethroning Peter III.
1787   The North-west Ordinance, for the government of U.S. western territories,
        passed.
1798   Wordsworth wrote his ' Lines ' composed a few miles above Tintern Abbey.
1868   The Scottish Reform Act passed.
1878   The Treaty of Berlin signed.
1878   Rumania proclaimed independent.
1919   The airship *R* 34 landed in England after its flight from the U.S.A.
1953   The foundation stone of the multi-racial University of Rhodesia laid.

14th JULY
Bastille Day (France).

People

1223   Philip Augustus, King of France, died.
1602   Cardinal Mazarin, statesman, born.
1816   Francisco de Miranda, Venezuelan leader, died.
1816   The Comte de Gobineau, traveller and writer, born.
1817   Madame de Staël, writer, died.
1858   Mrs Emmeline Pankhurst, champion of women's rights, born.
1904   Stephanus Johannes Paulus Kruger, Boer leader, died.
1910   Marius Petipa, ballet-master and choreographer, died.
1911   Terry-Thomas, actor, born.
1958   King Faisal of Iraq assassinated.

Events

1789   The storming of the Bastille began.
1790   Louis XVI swore to maintain the Constitution of France.
1831   The Battle of Minsk.
1833   The Oxford Movement launched.
1953   The Central African Federation Bill received the Royal Assent.

15th JULY
St Swithin's Day

People

1291   King Rudolph I died.
1573   Inigo Jones, architect, born.
1606   Rembrandt van Rijn, painter, born.
1685   The Duke of Monmouth beheaded.
1704   Bishop August Gottlieb Spangenberg, founder of the Moravian Church of
        America, born.
1839   Winthrop Mackworth Praed, poet, died.
1865   Lord Northcliffe, newspaper proprietor, born.
1948   General John Joseph Pershing died.
1958   General Nuri-es-Said assassinated in Baghdad.

Events
1099 Jerusalem captured by the Crusaders.
1662 The Royal Society received a Royal charter.
1741 The Russian navigator Tchivikov landed in California.
1840 The Treaty of London signed.
1841 Mehemet made hereditary Viceroy of Egypt.
1870 The Franco-Prussian War began.
1912 Social insurance came into effect in Britain.

16th JULY

People
1216 Pope Innocent III died.
1723 Sir Joshua Reynolds, painter, born.
1821 Mrs Mary Baker Eddy, religious leader, born.
1827 Josiah Spode, potter, died.
1828 Jean Antoine Houdon, sculptor, died.
1857 Pierre Jean de Béranger, writer, died.
1859 General Charles Murray Cathcart, died.
1872 Roald Amundsen, explorer, born.
1877 Béla Schick, pediatrician, born.
1892 John MacGregor, traveller and writer, died.
1896 Edmond de Goncourt, writer, died.
1918 Nicolas II, Tsar of Russia, shot.
1932 Lord Plumer, administrator and soldier, died.
1953 Hilaire Belloc, writer, died.

Events
1790 The District of Columbia established.
1945 The first atomic bomb explosion carried out in New Mexico.
1951 Leopold III, King of the Belgians, abdicated.

17th JULY

People
1674 Isaac Watts, hymn-writer, born.
1763 John Jacob Astor, capitalist, born.
1790 Adam Smith, economist, died.
1793 Charlotte Corday, assassin, executed.
1810 Martin Tupper, writer, born.
1832 A. J. Sodermann, composer, born.
1845 Earl Grey, statesman, died.
1875 Sir Donald Tovey, composer, born.
1903 James Abbott McNeill Whistler, painter, died.

Events
1791 The Champs de Mars massacre.
1821 Florida formally ceded to the U.S.A. by Spain.
1841 *Punch* first issued.
1870 The French declaration of war against Prussia signed.
1917 The Royal Family adopted the name Windsor as a family title.
1936 The Spanish Civil War began.
1940 The Baghdad Railway completed.
1945 The Potsdam Conference began.

18th JULY

People

1100   Godfrey of Bouillon, crusader, died.
1552   The Emperor Rudolf II born.
1721   Antoine Watteau, painter, died.
1762   Peter III, Tsar of Russia, murdered.
1792   John Paul Jones, naval adventurer, died.
1811   William Makepeace Thackeray, writer, born.
1817   Jane Austen, writer, died.
1848   W. G. Grace, cricketer, born.
1853   H. A. Lorentz, physicist, born.
1864   Lord Snowden, statesman, born.
1865   Laurence Housman, writer, born.
1872   Benito Juárez, statesman, died.
1873   Ferdinand David, composer, died.
1892   Thomas Cook, travel agent, died.
1894   Leconte de Lisle, poet, died.
1938   Marie, Queen of Rumania, died.

Events

1870   The infallibility of the Pope and the universality of his episcopate proclaimed
        by the Vatican Council.
1918   The Second Battle of the Marne.
1925   The first part of Hitler's *Mein Kampf* published.
1934   The Mersey Tunnel formally opened.

19th JULY
Feast of St Vincent de Paul.

People

1810   Louise, Queen of Russia, died.
1814   Matthew Flinders, explorer, died.
1814   Samuel Colt, inventor, born.
1834   Edgar Degas, artist, born.
1839   Maurice de Guérin, poet, died.
1865   Charles Horace Mayo, surgeon, born.
1896   A. J. Cronin, novelist, born.
1873   William Wilberforce, Bishop of Winchester, died.

Events

1333   The Battle of Halidon Hill.
1821   The Coronation of King George IV.
1870   Neutrality proclaimed by the British Government in the Franco-Prussian War.
1904   The building of Liverpool Cathedral began.
1919   Peace celebrations at the end of World War I.
1924   Liverpool Cathedral consecrated.
1930   The King's Prize at Bisley first won by a woman.

20th JULY

People

1031   Robert II, King of France, died.
1304   Francesco Petrarch, poet, born.
1835   Ernest Giles, explorer, born.
1838   Augustin Daly, theatre manager, born.

1860 Margaret McMillan, nursery school pioneer, born.
1873 J. M. D. de Sévérac, composer, born.
1873 Alberto Santos-Dumont, aviator, born.
1897 Jean Ingelow, poet, died.
1903 Pope Leo XIII, died.
1937 Guglielmo Marconi, inventor, died.

Events
1845 The first white man (Charles Sturt) entered Simpson's Desert in Central Australia.
1877 The first Battle of Plevna.
1927 Oscar Slater declared to have been wrongfully imprisoned for 19 years.
1932 Von Papen's *coup d'état* in Prussia.
1934 The German S.S. became an independent party.
1944 The attempt on Hitler's life.
1946 The Paris Peace Conference began.

21st JULY
Belgian Independence Day.
People
1664 Matthew Prior, poet, born.
1764 Sir Sidney Smith, naval commander, born.
1796 Robert Burns, poet, died.
1809 Daniel Lambert, fat man, died.
1880 Count Keyserling, philosopher and traveller, born.
1924 Lenin died.
1928 Ellen Terry, actress, died.

Events
1588 The beginning of the assembly of the Spanish Armada.
1595 Alvaro Mendaña discovered the Marquesas Islands.
1773 The Pope dissolved the Society of Jesus.
1798 The Battle of the Pyramids.
1831 Leopold proclaimed King of the Belgians.
1861 The first Battle of Bull Run.
1873 The James-Younger gang carried out the train robbery near Adair, Iowa (the first train robbery in the West).
1897 The Tate Gallery, London, officially opened.
1944 The Americans occupied Guam.
1953 The first meeting of the Press Council in London.

22nd JULY
People
1478 Philip the Handsome, King of Spain, born.
1812 The Comte d'Antraigues and his wife murdered by their servant.
1822 Gregor Johann Mendel, botanist, born.
1832 The Emperor Napoleon II died.
1844 The Rev. William Archibald Spooner, originator of Spoonerisms, born.
1852 William Poel, dramatic producer, born.
1860 ' Baron Corvo ', writer, born.
1892 Dr Seyss Inquart, statesman, born.
1906 Russell Sayer, financier, died.

1909   Detlev von Liliencron, poet, died.
1922   Michael Collins, Irish leader, killed.
1950   Mackenzie King, statesman, died.

Events
1298   The Battle of Falkirk.
1812   The Battle of Salamanca.
1847   The Mormons entered Salt Lake City.
1932   The Imperial Economic Conference began at Ottawa.
1944   The Bretton Woods Conference ends.
1946   The constitution of the World Health Conference drawn up.
1953   Construction of Calder Hall atomic station began.

23rd JULY

People
1403   Hotspur killed in battle.
1562   Goetz von Berlichingen, soldier, died.
1883   Lord Allenbrooke born.
1886   Don Salvador de Madariaga, writer and diplomat, born.
1892   Hailé Selassié, Emperor of Ethiopia, born.
1930   Glenn Hammond Curtiss, aviator, died.
1951   Marshal Pétain, statesman, died.
1955   Cordell Hull, statesman, died.

Events
1403   The Battle of Shrewsbury.
1858   The Jewish Disabilities Removal Act passed.
1870   The Emperor Napoleon III appointed the Empress Eugénie Regent of France.

24th JULY

People
1345   Jacob van Artevelde, statesman, murdered.
1783   Simón Bolívar born.
1802   Alexandre Dumas, père, writer, born.
1842   John Sell Cotman, painter, died.
1864   Franz Wedekind, dramatist, born.
1880   Ernest Bloch, composer, born.
1883   Captain Matthew Webb, swimmer, died.
1894   Simon Ingersoll, inventor, died.
1898   Amelia Earheart, aviator, born.

Events
1704   Admiral Sir George Rooke took Gibraltar from the Spaniards.
1837   The Indian post office established.
1847   Brigham Young approved the site of Salt Lake City.
1882   A Holy War in Egypt declared by Arabi Pasha.
1923   The Treaty of Lausanne signed.
1927   The Menin Gate unveiled.
1956   The first guided-missile ship commissioned.

25th JULY

The Feasts of St James the Great and St Christopher.

People
1492   Pope Innocent VIII died.
1814   Charles Dibdin, playwright and song-writer, died.

1834 Samuel Taylor Coleridge, poet, died.
1843 Charles Macintosh, inventor, died.
1848 The Earl of Balfour, statesman, born.
1876 Elizabeth, Queen of the Belgians, born.
1934 Dr Dollfuss, statesman, murdered.

Events
1139 The Moors defeated Alfonso I of Portugal.
1581 The Netherlands proclaim their independence from Spain.
1799 Napoleon defeated the Turks near Aboukir.
1859 The last performance at Vauxhall Gardens, London.
1909 Louis Blériot flew the Channel.
1943 Mussolini fell and was arrested.
1948 The Brussels Treaty concerning Western Union came into force.
1952 The European Steel and Coal Community came into being.

26th JULY
Feast of St Anne.

People
1471 Pope Paul II died.
1659 Moll Cutpurse died.
1678 The Emperor Joseph I born.
1782 John Field, composer, born.
1802 William Mackworth Praed, poet, born.
1856 George Bernard Shaw, writer, born.
1867 Otto I, King of Greece, died.
1874 Sergei Koussevitsky, conductor, born.
1881 George Borrow, writer, died.
1894 Aldous Huxley, writer, born.
1909 Peter Thorneycroft, statesman, born.

Events
1847 The independence of Liberia proclaimed.
1869 The Royal Assent given to the Irish Church Bill.
1956 The Suez Canal Company nationalised compulsorily.

27th JULY

People
1689 John Graham of Claverhouse, Viscount Dundee, killed.
1777 Heinrich Wilhelm Brandes, astronomer and physicist, born.
1847 John Walter II, editor, died.
1870 Bertram Borden Boltwood, chemist, born.
1877 Ernst von Dohnányi, composer, born.
1881 Hans Fischer, scientist, born.
1904 Selwyn Lloyd, statesman, born.
1942 Sir Flinders Petrie, Egyptologist, died.

Events
1689 The Battle of Killiecrankie.
1809 The Battle of Talavera began.
1830 Revolution broke out in Paris.
1866 The Atlantic telegraph cable completed.
1953 The Korean armistice signed.
1955 Austria regained her sovereignty.

28th JULY

People
388   Theodosius I overthrew Maximus near Aquileia.
1750 Johann Sebastian Bach, composer, died.
1760 Sir John Cope died.
1794 Louis de St Just, French Revolutionary Leader, guillotined.
1811 Giulia Grisi, operatic singer, born.
1860 J. R. Tanner, historian, born.
1939 William James Mayo, surgeon, died.

Events
1656 The Battle of Warsaw begins.
1790 Forth and Clyde Canal opened.
1809 The Walcheren Expedition set out.
1809 The Battle of Talavera ended.
1821 Peru declared her independence from Spain.
1914 Austria declared war on Serbia.
1917 The formation of the British Tank Corps authorised.
1938 No-surcharge airmail to Australia and New Zealand inaugurated.
1943 Italian Fascist Party dissolved.

29th JULY
Feasts of St Olaf and St Theodor.

People
1108 Philip I, King of France, died.
1833 William Wilberforce, philanthropist, died.
1841 Armauer Hansen, physician, born.
1846 John Owens, merchant and philanthropist, died.
1856 Robert Schumann, composer, died.
1867 Enrique Granados, composer, born.
1869 Booth Tarkington, writer, born.
1877 William Beebe, naturalist, born.
1883 Benito Mussolini, statesman, born.
1887 Sigmund Romberg, composer, born.
1890 Vincent van Gogh, painter, died.
1897 General Sir Neil Ritchie born.
1913 Joseph Grimond, politician, born.
1946 Gertrude Stein, writer, died.

Events
1588 The Spanish Armada routed.
1899 The Permanent Court of Arbitration established at The Hague.
1945 The BBC Light Programme began.
1945 The Treaty of Moscow signed.

30th JULY

People
1511 Giorgio Vasari, art critic and historian, born.
1718 William Penn, Quaker, writer and founder of Pennsylvania, died.
1771 Thomas Gray, poet, died.
1784 Denis Diderot, encyclopædist, died.
1857 Thorstein Veblen, economist, born.
1859 Sir Henry Lunn born.

1863 Henry Ford, motor-car manufacturer, born.
1884 Mark Pattison, writer, died.
1894 Walter Pater, writer, died.
1898 Prince Bismarck died.
1898 Henry Moore, sculptor, born.

Events
1656 The Battle of Warsaw ended.
1877 The Second Battle of Plevna.
1930 The airship *R* 101 flew the Atlantic.
1934 Dr Schuschnigg appointed Chancellor of Austria.
1948 The world's first Port Radar Station opened at Liverpool.

31st JULY
Feast of St Ignatius Loyola.

People
1527 The Emperor Maximilian II born.
1556 St Ignatius Loyola died.
1750 John V, King of Portugal, died.
1803 John Ericsson, inventor, born.
1849 Alexander Petöfi, poet, died.
1886 Franz Liszt, composer, died.
1935 Gustav Lindenthal, civil engineer, died.
1950 Madame Suggia, 'cellist, died.

Events
1917 The Third Battle of Ypres began.
1934 The murderers of Dollfuss executed.
1954 The mountain K 2 (Godwin-Austen) climbed by an Italian expedition.

1st AUGUST
Lammas Day. Swiss Independence Day.

People
 527 The Emperor Justin I died.
1137 Louis VI, King of France, died.
1589 King Henri III of France murdered.
1714 Queen Anne died.
1743 Richard Savage, poet, died.
1744 The Chevalier de Lamarck, naturalist, born.
1770 William Clark, explorer, born.
1779 Francis Scott Key, lawyer and poet, born.
1790 John Knox, philanthropist, died.
1815 Richard Henry Dana, writer, born.
1819 Herman Melville, writer, born.
1821 Mrs Inchbald, novelist, died.
1936 Louis Blériot, pioneer aviator, died.

Events
1714 George I proclaimed king.
1715 Doggett's Coat and Badge Race first rowed on the Thames.
1793 The French adopted the metrical system.
1798 The Battle of the Nile.
1831 New London Bridge opened.

1834   Slavery abolished in all British possessions.
1876   Colorado achieved Statehood.
1883   Inland parcel post began in Britain.
1914   The Central Powers declared war on Russia.
1934   Hitler became Reichsführer.

2nd AUGUST

People

1100   William Rufus killed.
1640   Gérard Audran, engraver, born.
1754   Major L'Enfant, planner of Washington, born.
1788   Thomas Gainsborough, painter, died.
1820   John Tyndall, physicist, born.
1823   Edward Augustus Freeman, historian, born.
1835   Elisha Gray, inventor, born.
1849   Mehemet Ali, Pasha of Egypt, died.
1858   Sir William Watson, poet, born.
1916   Hamish McCunn, composer, died.
1921   Enrico Caruso, singer, died.
1934   President Hindenburg died.

Events

1718   The Quadruple Alliance concluded in London.
1858   The government of India transferred from the East India Company to the British Government.
1858   British Columbia constituted a Crown Colony.
1914   Germany declared war on France.
1945   The Potsdam Conference ended.

3rd AUGUST

People

1460   James II, King of Scotland, killed.
1721   Grinling Gibbons, artist, died.
1792   Sir Richard Arkwright, inventor, died.
1819   Sir George Stokes, mathematician and physicist, born.
1857   Eugène Sue, novelist, died.
1867   Lord Baldwin, statesman, born.
1872   King Haakon of Norway born.
1887   Rupert Brooke, poet, born.
1896   Sir William Robert Grove, lawyer and scientist, died.
1907   Augustus St Gaudens, sculptor, died.
1916   Sir Roger Casement hanged.
1924   Joseph Conrad, novelist, died.

Events

1610   Henry Hudson discovered Hudson Bay
1759   Eugene Aram, murderer, tried at York.
1830   The July Revolution in France ended.
1858   The source of the Nile discovered by John Speke.
1882   Suez occupied by British marines.
1940   Latvia admitted to the Soviet Union.
1949   The Council of Europe came into being.

4th AUGUST
Feast of St Dominic.

People

1060 Henri I, King of France, died.
1265 Simon de Montfort, Earl of Leicester, killed in battle.
1578 King Sebastian of Portugal killed in battle.
1598 Lord Burghley, statesman, died.
1640 Robert Spencer, Earl of Sunderland, born.
1792 Percy Bysshe Shelley, poet, born.
1792 Edward Irving, founder of the Irvingites, born.
1804 Admiral Lord Duncan died.
1810 Maurice de Guérin, poet, born.
1816 Russell Sage, financier, born.
1839 Walter Pater, writer, born.
1859 Knut Hamsun, writer, born.
1900 Queen Elizabeth, the Queen Mother, born.

Events

1265 The Battle of Evesham.
1511 Albuquerque captured Malacca.
1578 The Battle of Al Kasr al Kebir.
1853 Newspaper advertisements duty abolished in Britain.
1892 Sir Wilfred Grenfell, medical missionary, arrived in Labrador.
1914 Germany invaded Belgium.
1914 Britain declared war on Germany.

5th AUGUST

People

 882 Louis III, King of France, died.
1799 Admiral Lord Howe died.
1809 A. W. Kinglake, traveller and writer, born.
1811 Ambroise Thomas, composer, born.
1827 Manoel da Fonseca, statesman, born.
1850 Guy de Maupassant, writer, born.
1858 Alexis Soyer, chef, died.
1896 Friedrich Engels, Marxist, died.

Events

1864 The Battle of Mobile Bay.
1890 A French protectorate declared over Madagascar.
1939 British trans-Atlantic airmail service inaugurated.
1955 The European Monetary Agreement signed.
1955 The French Southern and Antarctic Territories created.

6th AUGUST
Feast of the Transfiguration.

People

 258 Pope Sixtus II martyred.
1272 Stephen V, King of Hungary, died.
1458 Pope Callistus III died.
1504 Archbishop Parker, theologian, born.
1623 Anne Hathaway, wife of William Shakespeare, died.
1637 Ben Jonson, dramatist, died.

1644 Louise de la Vallière, mistress of Louis XIV, born.
1651 François de Salignac de la Mothe Fénélon, dramatist, born.
1660 Diego Velasquez, painter, died.
1759 Eugene Aram, murderer, hanged.
1775 Daniel O'Connell, Irish patriot, born.
1809 Alfred, Lord Tennyson, poet, born.
1820 Lord Strathcona, statesman, born.
1866 John Mason Neale, hymn-writer, died.
1900 Wilhelm Liebknecht, socialist, died.

Events
1806 Francis II renounced the crown of the Holy Roman Empire.
1825 Bolivia declared her independence from Peru.
1896 Madagascar and its dependencies declared a French colony.
1915 The Allied landings at Suvla in the Dardanelles began.
1945 The first atomic bomb dropped on Hiroshima.

7th AUGUST
People
1657 Admiral Blake died.
1831 Dean Frederick William Farrar, theologian, born.
1834 Joseph Marie Jacquard, inventor, died.
1868 Sir Granville Bantock, composer, born.
1881 Dr E. G. Jansen, statesman, born.
1885 Dornford Yates, novelist, born.
1913 Colonel S. F. Cody, aviator, killed in a flying accident.
1941 Rabindranath Tagore, writer, died.

Events
1409 The Council of Pisa dissolved.
1479 The Battle of Guinegatte.
1485 Henry Tudor (Henry VII) landed at Milford Haven.
1790 Alexander McGillivray, chief of the Muskogian Indians, signed a treaty of peace and friendship with President Washington.
1830 Louis Philippe accepted the crown of France.
1858 Ottawa selected as capital of Canada.
1925 Summer Time Act made permanent in Britain.

8th AUGUST
People
 869 Lothair, King of Lotharingia, died.
1673 John Ker, spy, born.
1827 George Canning, statesman, died.
1856 Madame Vestris, actress, died.
1857 Cécile Chaminade, composer, born.
1899 Lord Evershed, administrator, born.
1901 Ernest Orlando Lawrence, inventor, born.

Events
 870 The Treaty of Mersen signed.
1288 Pope Nicholas IV proclaimed a crusade against Ladislaus IV of Hungary.
1588 The Spanish Armada destroyed.
1588 Queen Elizabeth reviewed her troops at Tilbury.

1902   The British Academy, London, granted a Royal Charter.
1918   The Battle of Amiens began.
1919   The Treaty of Rawalpindi signed.
1940   The Battle of Britain began.

9th AUGUST

People

1593   Izaak Walton, writer, born.
1631   John Dryden, poet and playwright, born.
1757   Thomas Telford, engineer, born.
1788   Adoniram Judson, missionary, born.
1848   Captain Marryat, writer, died.
1875   Reynaldo Hahn, composer, born.
1886   Sir Samuel Ferguson, poet, died.
1896   Léonide Massine, choreographer, born.
1919   Ruggiero Leoncavallo, composer, died.
1919   Ernst Haeckel, naturalist, died.

Events

378   The Battle of Adrianople.
1690   The Siege of Limerick began.
1842   The Canada-U.S.A. Frontier defined.
1858   The first Atlantic cable completed.
1890   Heligoland formally transferred to Germany.
1945   An atomic bomb dropped on Nagasaki.
1946   The Arts Council of Great Britain incorporated.

10th AUGUST
St Lawrence's Day.

People

1673   Johann Konrad Dippel, doctor and alchemist, born.
1740   Samuel Arnold, hymn-writer, born.
1759   Ferdinand VI, King of Spain, died.
1782   Sir Charles Napier, naval reformer, born.
1810   The Count di Cavour, statesman, born.
1821   Jay Cooke, banker, born.
1823   Charles Keene, artist, born.
1845   Karl Wilhelm Naundorff, pretender to the Throne of France, died.
1853   The Comte de Richemont, pretender to the Throne of France, died.
1865   Aleksandr Konstantinovich Glazunov, composer, born.
1874   Herbert Hoover, statesman, born.

Events

1388   The Battle of Otterburn.
1557   The Battle of St Quentin.
1675   Greenwich Observatory founded.
1792   The ' suspension ' of the French Royalty by the Legislative Assembly.
1809   Ecuador finally revolted against Spanish domination.
1846   The Smithsonian Institution established in Washington.
1910   Airmail service first organised in Britain.
1920   The Treaty of Sèvres.
1952   The High Authority (Luxemburg) of the European Steel and Coal Community inaugurated.
1954   The St Lawrence Seaway Project officially launched.

11th AUGUST

People

1433 John I, King of Portugal, died.
1456 János Hunyadi, Hungarian patriot, died.
1656 Prince Octavio Piccolomini, military commander, died.
1737 Joseph Nollekens, sculptor, born.
1821 Octave Feuillet, novelist, born.
1823 Charlotte M. Yonge, novelist, born.
1857 Marshall Hall, physiologist, died.
1885 Richard Monckton Milnes, Lord Houghton, poet and reformer, died.
1890 Cardinal Newman, died.
1919 Andrew Carnegie, philanthropist, died.

Events

1711 The first Ascot race meeting held.
1936 Ribbentrop appointed ambassador to London.
1939 The Axis Conference at Salzburg began.
1942 The new Waterloo Bridge, London, opened to traffic.
1943 The Quebec Conference opened.
1952 King Talal deposed by the Parliament of Jordan.

12th AUGUST
Grouse Shooting begins.

People

1350 Philip VI, King of France, died.
1484 Pope Sixtus IV, died.
1676 King Philip, American Indian Chief, killed.
1689 Pope Innocent XI, died.
1715 Nahum Tate, playwright, died.
1753 Thomas Bewick, engraver, born.
1762 King George IV, born.
1774 Robert Southey, poet, born.
1774 Stephen Peter Rigaud, mathematician and astronomer, born.
1832 Dr Hely Hutchinson Almond, educationalist, born.
1848 George Stephenson, engineer, died.
1862 Julius Rosenwald, philanthropist, born.
1866 Jacinto Benavente, playwright, born.
1870 General Sir Hubert Gough born.
1884 Frank Swinnerton, writer, born.
1955 Thomas Mann, writer, died.

Events

1676 The Indian War in New England ended.
1678 Titus Oates' Popish Plot made known to King Charles II.
1898 The U.S.A. formally annexed Hawaii.
1944 The ' Pluto ' Pipeline came into action.

13th AUGUST
Old Lammas Day.

People

1667 Jeremy Taylor, theologian, died.
1765 Francis I, Emperor, died.
1843 Sir A. L. Liberty, merchant, born.

371

1879   John Ireland, composer, born.
1896   Sir John Millais, painter, died.
1910   Florence Nightingale, nursing pioneer, died.
1912   Jules Massenet, composer, died.
1937   Lord Runciman, shipowner, died.
1946   H. G. Wells, writer, died.

Events
1704   The Battle of Blenheim.
1792   The Dauphin incarcerated in the Temple.

14th AUGUST
People
1040   Duncan I, King of Scotland, murdered (traditional date).
1464   Pope Pius II died.
1552   Paolo Sarpi, statesman, born.
1740   Pope Pius VII born.
1778   Augustus Montague Toplady, hymn-writer, died.
1840   Richard von Krafft-Ebing, physician, born.
1859   The Curé d'Ars died.
1860   Ernest Thompson Seton (' Ernest Seton Thompson '), writer and naturalist, born.
1861   Bion Joseph Arnold, electrical engineer and inventor, born.
1867   John Galsworthy, writer, born.
1870   Admiral David Glasgow Farragut died.
1887   Richard Jefferies, writer, died.
1938   Sir Landon Ronald, conductor, died.
1951   William Randolph Hearst, newspaper proprietor, died.
1956   Bertold Brecht, playwright, died.

Events
1385   The Battle of Aljubarrota.
1814   The independence of Norway, in a personal union with Sweden, proclaimed.
1920   The Little Entente formed.
1941   The Atlantic Charter made public.
1945   The Emperor Hirohito accepted the Allies' surrender terms.
1947   India established as a Dominion.
1947   Pakistan established as a Dominion.

15th AUGUST
Feast of the Assumption of the Blessed Virgin Mary.
People
1057   Macbeth, King of Scotland, slain in battle.
1769   Napoleon born.
1771   Sir Walter Scott, writer, born.
1785   Thomas De Quincey, writer, born.
1799   General Barthélemy Joubert killed in battle.
1802   Nikolaus Lenau, poet, born.
1842   Sir William Tilden, chemist, born.
1845   Walter Crane, artist, born.
1875   Samuel Coleridge-Taylor, composer, born.
1879   Ethel Barrymore, actress, born.

1883   Ivan Meštrović, sculptor, born.
1888   T. E. Lawrence, traveller, writer and soldier, born.
1890   Jacques Ibert, composer, born.
1907   Joseph Joachim, violinist, died.
1927   Bertram Borden Boltwood, chemist, died.
1935   Wiley Post, aviator, died.
1935   Will Rogers, humourist, died.
1950   Princess Anne born.

Events
1057   The Battle of Lumphanan.
1237   Berlin founded.
1799   The Battle of Novi.
1914   The Panama Canal officially opened.
1915   The Allied landings at Suvla in the Dardanelles completed.
1945   VJ-Day.
1948   The Republic of Korea (South Korea) proclaimed.

16th AUGUST
People
1678   Andrew Marvell, poet, died.
1854   Duncan Phyfe, cabinet-maker, died.
1860   Lord Hawke, cricketer, born.
1879   Herbert Joseph Spinden, anthropologist, born.
1906   Prince Francis Joseph II of Liechtenstein born.
1941   John Coates, singer, died.

Events
1513   The Battle of the Spurs.
1777   The Battle of Bennington, Vermont.
1779   The Battle of Camden, South Carolina.
1812   The Battle of Smolensk began.
1819   The Peterloo Massacre.
1825   The Republic of Bolivia proclaimed.
1870   The Battle of Vionville.

17th AUGUST
People
1753   Joseph Dobrovsky, philologist, born.
1761   William Carey, missionary, born.
1786   Frederick the Great died.
1786   David Crockett, American pioneer, born.
1834   Pierre Léonard Léopold Benoît, composer, born.
1840   Wilfrid Scawen Blunt, poet, born.
1850   Honoré de Balzac, novelist, died.
1880   Ole Bull, violinist, died.
1928   Sir George Otto Trevelyan, writer, died.
1955   Fernand Léger, artist, died.

Events
1812   The Battle of Smolensk ended.
1945   Indonesia proclaimed an independent Republic.

18th AUGUST

People

1559 Pope Paul IV died.
1587 Virginia Dare, first white child of English parentage to be born in America, born on Roanoke Island, North Carolina.
1765 Francis I, Holy Roman Emperor, died.
1774 Meriweather Lewis, explorer, born.
1792 Earl Russell, statesman, born.
1803 James Beattie, poet, died.
1809 Matthew Boulton, engineer, died.
1834 Marshall Field, merchant, born.
1869 Count Reventlow, publicist, born.
1874 Sir William Fairbairn, engineer and inventor, died.
1884 Basil Cameron, conductor, born.
1922 William Henry Hudson, naturalist and writer, died.

Events

1870 The Battle of Gravelotte.
1917 The Verdun offensive began.

19th AUGUST

People

1560 The Admirable Crichton born.
1601 Michael the Brave died.
1646 John Flamstead, first astronomer royal, born.
1662 Blaise Pascal, philosopher, died.
1790 Edward John Dent, chronometer maker, born.
1819 James Watt, engineer, died.
1823 Robert Bloomfield, poet, died.
1843 Charles M. Doughty, traveller and poet, born.
1871 Orville Wright, pioneer aviator, born.
1881 Georges Enesco, composer, born.
1928 Viscount Haldane, statesman and reformer, died.
1934 Sir Nigel Playfair died.
1944 Sir Henry Wood, conductor and composer, died.

Events

1561 Mary, Queen of Scots, returned from France.
1792 The French Revolutionary Tribunal set up.
1861 The passport system introduced in the U.S.A.
1958 *Triton*, U.S. nuclear submarine (largest submarine ever built) launched.

20th AUGUST

Feast of St Bernard of Clairvaux.

People

1153 St Bernard of Clairvaux died.
1648 Lord Herbert of Cherbury, poet, died.
1672 Jan de Witt, statesman, died.
1701 Sir Charles Sedley, playwright, died.
1778 Bernardo O'Higgins, Chilean patriot, born.
1779 The Baron Berzelius, chemist, born.
1818 Emily Brontë, writer, born.
1823 Marco Bozzaris, Greek patriot, died.
1823 Pope Pius VII died.

1833   Benjamin Harrison, statesman, born.
1854   Friedrich Wilhelm Joseph von Schelling, philosopher, died.
1860   Raymond Poincaré, statesman, born.
1860   Richard Flexmore, clown, died.
1902   Christian Bérard, painter, born.
1912   William Booth, Salvation Army leader, died.
1915   Paul Ehrlich, scientist, died.
1932   Gino Watkins, explorer, died.
1956   Cardinal Griffin died.

Events
1914   The Germans entered Brussels.
1932   The Imperial Economic Conference at Ottawa ended.

21st AUGUST
People
1165   Philip II, King of France, born.
1567   St Francis de Sales born.
1754   William Murdock, engineer and inventor, born.
1762   Lady Mary Wortley Montagu, traveller, died.
1765   King William IV born.
1798   Jules Michelet, historian, born.
1890   Charles West Cope, painter, died.
1930   Princess Margaret born.
1940   Trotsky assassinated in Mexico.
1951   Constant Lambert, composer, died.

Events
1808   The Battle of Vimiero.
1810   Marshal Bernadotte chosen Crown Prince of Sweden.
1918   The Battle of Bapaume-Peronne began.
1944   The Dumbarton Oaks Conference began.

22nd AUGUST
People
1241   Pope Gregory IX died.
1607   Captain Bartholomew Gosnold, navigator, died.
1741   Jean la Pérouse, sailor and explorer, born.
1760   Pope Leo XII born.
1818   Warren Hastings, administrator, died.
1847   Sir Alexander Mackenzie, composer, born.
1850   Nikolaus Lenau, poet, died.
1862   Claude Debussy, composer, born.
1889   John Sanger, circus manager, died.
1940   Sir Oliver Lodge, scientist and writer, died.

Events
1138   The Battle of the Standard.
1485   The Battle of Bosworth Field.
1642   Civil War in England began.
1864   The International Red Cross founded.
1910   Korea formally annexed by Japan.
1932   The first experimental television programme broadcast from the BBC, London.

23rd AUGUST

People

408   Flavius Stilichus, general, assassinated.
1540   Guillaume Budé, classical scholar, died.
1628   The Duke of Buckingham assassinated.
1754   King Louis XVI born.
1768   Sir Astley Cooper, surgeon, born.
1769   The Baron de Cuvier, anatomist, born.
1785   Oliver Hazard Perry, naval officer, born.
1802   John Randall, shipbuilder, died.
1849   William Ernest Henley, poet, born.
1864   Eleutherios Venizelos, statesman, born.
1889   Sir Geoffrey Faber, publisher, born.
1905   Constant Lambert, composer, born.
1927   Sacco and Vanzetti executed at Charleston, Massachusetts.
1937   Albert Roussel, composer, died.
1942   Michel Fokine, choreographer, died.

Events

1328   The Battle of Cassel.
1905   The Treaty of Portsmouth, N.H., signed.
1914   Japan declared war on Germany.
1914   Namur captured by the Germans.
1914   The Battle of Mons.
1939   The Soviet–German agreement signed.
1948   The World Council of Churches formed.

24th AUGUST
Feast of St Bartholomew.

People

1540   Francesco Parmigianino, artist, died.
1572   General Gaspard de Cologny, Huguenot, killed.
1680   Colonel Thomas Blood, adventurer, died.
1759   William Wilberforce, statesman, born.
1770   Thomas Chatterton, poet, committed suicide.
1831   Field-Marshal August, Graf Gneisenau, died.
1841   Theodore Hook, writer, died.
1846   Adam Krusenstern, circumnavigator of the world, died.
1883   Lord Woolton born.
1906   Alfred Stevens, painter, died.
1958   Dr J. G. Strijdom, statesman, died.

Events

1572   The Massacre of St Bartholomew.
1814   British troops captured Washington, D.C.
1943   The Quebec Conference ended.

25th AUGUST
Feast of St Louis.

People

79   Pliny the Elder, naturalist, died.
1270   St Louis of France died.
1530   Ivan IV, ' the Terrible ', Tsar of Muscovy, born.

1744 J. G. von Herder, poet, born.
1767 Louis de St Just, French Revolutionary leader, born.
1776 David Hume, philosopher, died.
1786 Ludwig I, King of Bavaria, born.
1822 Sir William Herschel, astronomer, died.
1839 Bret Harte, writer, born.
1845 Ludwig II, King of Bavaria, born.
1867 Michael Faraday, scientist, died.
1908 Henri Antoine Becquerel, physicist, died.

Events
1825 The independence of Uruguay proclaimed.
1830 Revolution against Netherlands broke out in Brussels.
1860 Victoria Bridge, Montreal, officially opened.
1914 The Germans sacked Louvain.
1919 Daily service by air between London and Paris began.
1921 The Treaty of Berlin signed.
1939 President Roosevelt made peace appeal to Hitler.
1944 The Allies liberated Paris.

26th AUGUST

People
1278 King Ottocar II killed in battle.
1584 Franz Hals, painter, born.
1676 Sir Robert Walpole, statesman, born.
1743 Antoine Laurent Lavoisier, chemist, born.
1819 Albert, Prince Consort, born.
1833 Henry Fawcett, statesman and economist, born.
1833 Stephen Joseph Perry, astronomer, born.
1850 Louis Philippe died.
1873 Lee de Forest, inventor, born.
1900 Friedrich Wilhelm Nietzsche, philosopher, died.
1910 William James, psychologist, died.
1944 Prince Richard born.

Events
55BC Julius Caesar's first invasion of Britain.
1346 The Battle of Crecy.
1914 Louvain destroyed by the Germans.
1914 The Battle of Tannenberg began.
1920 Women's suffrage came into force in the U.S.A.
1936 The Anglo-Egyptian Alliance signed.

27th AUGUST

People
551BC Confucius, philosopher, born.
1576 Titian, painter, died.
1590 Pope Sixtus V died.
1635 Lope de Vega, poet, died.
1770 Georg Wilhelm Friedrich Hegel, philosopher, born.
1879 Sir Rowland Hill, pioneer in postal services, died.
1886 Eric Coates, composer, born.
1908 Sir Donald Bradman, cricketer, born.
1919 General Louis Botha, statesman, died.

Events

1776   The Battle of Long Island.
1859   The first oil well drilled in West Pennsylvania.
1928   The Kellogg Pact signed.

28th AUGUST
The Feast of St Augustine, Bishop of Hippo.

People

1749   Wolfgang von Goethe, writer, born.
1790   Sir George Sinclair, writer, born.
1828   Count Leo Tolstoy, writer, born.
1833   Sir Edward Burne-Jones, painter, born.
1840   Ira David Sankey, revivalist, born.
1859   Leigh Hunt, writer, died.
1863   Eilhard Mitscherlich, chemist, died.
1943   Tsar Boris III of Bulgaria died.
1958   Dr Ernest Lawrence, inventor, died.

Events

 489   The Battle of Sontius.
1914   The Battle of Heligoland Bight.

29th AUGUST

People

1619   Jean Baptiste Colbert, statesman, born.
1632   John Locke, philosopher, born.
1645   Hugo Grotius, statesman, died.
1799   Pope Pius VI died.
1809   Oliver Wendell Holmes, writer, born.
1817   John Leech, artist, born.
1853   Sir Charles Napier, statesman, died.
1862   Maurice Maeterlinck, writer, born.
1876   Félicien David, composer, died.
1877   Brigham Young, Mormon leader, died.
1890   Richard Gardiner Casey, statesman, born.
1919   Louis Botha, statesman, died.
1930   The Rev. William Archibald Spooner, originator of Spoonerisms, died.

Events

1526   The Battle of Mohatz.
1782   The loss of *The Royal George*.
1835   Melbourne, Australia, founded.
1842   The Treaty of Nanking, ending the Opium War, signed.
1882   ' The Ashes ' instituted.
1929   The airship *Graf Zeppelin* completed the circumnavigation of the world.

30th AUGUST

People

1334   Pedro the Cruel, King of Castile and Leon, born.
1483   Louis XI, King of France, died.
1871   Lord Rutherford, scientist, born.

1890   Marianne North, painter, died.
1890   Thomas Nuttall, soldier, died.
1940   Professor Sir J. J. Thomson, scientist, died.

Events
1721   The conclusion of the Peace of Nystad.
1860   First British tramway inaugurated at Birkenhead.

31st AUGUST

People
1422   King Henry V died.
1688   John Bunyan died.
1811   Théophile Gautier, writer, born.
1821   Hermann von Helmholtz, physicist, born.
1864   Ferdinand Lassalle, socialist, died.
1880   Queen Wilhelmina of the Netherlands born.
1887   Friedrick Adolf Paneth, scientist, born.
1931   Sir Hall Caine, writer, died.

Events
1914   The Battle of Tannenberg ended.
1957   Malaya achieved independence.

1st SEPTEMBER

People
1159   Pope Adrian IV (the Englishman Nicholas Breakspear) died.
1566   Edward Alleyn, philanthropist, born.
1715   King Louis XIV died.
1729   Richard Steele, writer, died.
1804   Zerah Colburn, calculating prodigy, born.
1854   Engelbert Humperdinck, composer, born.
1874   Edwin Evans, musicologist, born.
1877   Francis William Aston, experimental physicist, born.
1912   Samuel Coleridge-Taylor, composer, died.
1943   W. W. Jacobs, humorous writer, died.

Events
1853   The first triangular Cape of Good Hope stamps issued.
1860   Foundation stone of the Parliament Buildings, Ottawa, laid.
1870   The Battle of Sedan ended.
1894   The use of postcards with adhesive stamps first permitted in Britain.
1939   The German Army invaded Poland.
1939   The BBC Home Service began.
1944   General Montgomery appointed Field Marshal.
1951   The Pacific Security Pact signed.

2nd SEPTEMBER

People
1685   Lady Alice Lisle, supporter of religious dissent, beheaded.
1726   John Howard, prison reformer, born.
1839   ' Single-Tax ' Henry George born.
1851   William Nicol, physicist, died.

379

1853   Wilhelm Ostwald, scientist, born.
1865   Sir William Rowan Hamilton, mathematician, died.
1877   Frederick Soddy, scientist, born.
1937   Baron Pierre de Coubertin, reviver of the Olympic Games, died.

Events
31BC   The Battle of Actium.
1666   The Great Fire of London began.
1898   Omdurman captured by Lord Kitchener.
1930   The first non-stop trans-Atlantic flight Paris–New York.
1945   The surrender of the Japanese armed forces to the Allies signed on the U.S.
        battleship *Missouri*.
1958   China opened its first television station at Peking.

3rd SEPTEMBER
People
1592   Robert Greene, dramatist, died.
1658   Oliver Cromwell died.
1728   Matthias Boulton, engineer, born.
1739   George Lillo, dramatist, died.
1847   James Hannington, first Bishop of Eastern Equatorial Africa, born.
1948   President Beneš of Czechoslovakia died.

Events
 590   Gregory the Great consecrated Pope.
1650   The Battle of Dunbar.
1651   The Battle of Worcester.
1783   The Treaty of Paris signed.
1916   The first Zeppelin destroyed in England.
1939   Britain and France declare war on Germany.
1939   Excess Profits Tax came into force in Britain.

4th SEPTEMBER
People
1768   François René de Chateaubriand, writer, born.
1824   Anton Bruckner, composer, born.
1892   Darius Milhaud, composer, born.
1907   Edvard Grieg, composer, died.

Events
1260   The Battle of Monte Aperto.
1870   The Third Republic proclaimed in France.
1909   The first Boy Scout Rally held at Crystal Palace.

5th SEPTEMBER
People
1187   Louis VIII, King of France, born.
1548   Catherine Parr, Queen-Dowager of England, died.
1585   Cardinal Richelieu, statesman, born.
1638   King Louis XIV born.
1733   Christoph Martin Wieland, poet, born.
1781   Anton Diabelli, music publisher and composer, born.

1791   Giacomo Meyerbeer, composer, born.
1808   John Home, poet, died.
1831   Victorien Sardou, playwright, born.

Events
1774   The first Continental Congress assembled at Philadelphia.
1905   The Treaty of Portsmouth signed.

6th SEPTEMBER

People
1757   The Marquis de Lafayette, statesman, born.
1766   John Dalton, scientist, born.
1858   Hiroshige, artist, died.
1860   Jane Addams, social reformer, born.
1869   Sir Walford Davies, composer, born.
1923   King Peter of Yugoslavia born.
1939   Arthur Rackham, artist, died.

Events
1620   The *Mayflower* set sail from Plymouth.
1651   The future King Charles II hid in an oak tree after the Battle of Worcester.
1666   The Great Fire of London ended.
1901   President McKinley shot.
1914   The Battle of the Marne began.
1940   The second phase of the Battle of Britain ended.
1954   The Manila Conference began.

7th SEPTEMBER

People
1312   Ferdinand IV, King of Castile and Leon, died.
1496   Ferdinand II, King of Naples, died.
1533   Queen Elizabeth I born.
1707   The Comte de Buffon, naturalist, born.
1735   Thomas Coutts, banker, born.
1736   Captain John Porteous hanged by the Edinburgh mob.
1782   Susan Ferrier, novelist, born.
1833   Hannah More, religious writer, died.
1867   John Pierpont Morgan the younger born.
1910   Holman Hunt, painter, died.
1930   Baudouin, King of the Belgians, born.
1956   Charles Burgess Fry, cricketer, died.

Events
1822   Brazil proclaimed her independence from Spanish domination.
1940   The London Blitz began.

8th SEPTEMBER

People
1157   Richard Cœur de Lion born.
1474   Ludovico Ariosto, poet, born.
1560   Amy Robsart, wife of the Earl of Leicester, died.
1644   Francis Quarles, poet, died.
1656   Bishop Hall, satirist, died.

1767   August Wilhelm von Schlegel, poet and translator, born.
1778   Klemens Brentano, poet and novelist, born.
1804   Eduard Mörike, poet, born.
1841   Antonin Dvořak, composer, born.
1894   Hermann von Helmholtz, physicist, died.
1933   King Faisal of Iraq died.
1949   Richard Strauss, composer, died.

Events
1664   The Dutch surrendered New Amsterdam (now New York) to the English.
1760   Montreal capitulated to the British.
1909   Colonel Cody, aviator, remained in the air for the British record time of one hour.
1944   The first V2 landed in England.
1951   San Francisco Treaty of Peace with Japan signed.
1954   The Manila Conference ended.

9th SEPTEMBER

People
1087   William the Conqueror died.
1513   James IV, King of Scotland, killed in battle.
1583   Sir Humphrey Gilbert, explorer, drowned at sea.
1585   Cardinal Richelieu, statesman, born.
1737   Luigi Galvani, scientist, born.
1846   Henri François Marion, philosopher, born.
1855   Houston Stewart Chamberlain, writer, born.
1882   The Earl of Harewood born.
1954   André Derain, artist, died.

Events
1513   The Battle of Flodden Field.
1850   California achieved Statehood.
1914   The Battle of the Marne ended.
1939   The Saar offensive began.
1943   The Allies landed at Salerno.

10th SEPTEMBER

People
 954   Louis IV, King of France, died.
1487   Pope Julius III born.
1578   Pierre Lescot, architect, died.
1624   Thomas Sydenham, physician, born.
1753   John Soane, architect, born.
1771   Mungo Park, explorer, born.
1797   Mary Wollstonecraft, champion of rights for women, died.
1834   Sir J. R. Seeley, historian and essayist, born.
1890   Franz Werfel, writer, born.

Events
1547   The Battle of Pinkie.
1813   The Battle of Lake Erie.
1919   The Treaty of St Germain signed.

11th SEPTEMBER

People
1524 Pierre de Ronsard, poet, born.
1611 Marshal Turenne born.
1618 Thomas Ross, libeller, beheaded.
1700 James Thomson, poet, born.
1823 David Ricardo, economist, died.
1860 Ben Tillett, Labour leader, born.
1862 O. Henry, writer, born.
1877 Sir James Jeans, scientist, born.
1950 Field-Marshal Smuts, statesman, died.

Events
1709 The Battle of Malplaquet.
1877 The third Battle of Plevna.
1909 Halley's Comet first observed at Heidelberg.
1922 The British mandate proclaimed in Palestine.

12th SEPTEMBER

People
1362 Pope Innocent VI died.
1494 Francis I, King of France, born.
1733 François Couperin, composer, died.
1764 Jean-Philippe Rameau, composer, died.
1786 William Cotton, merchant and philanthropist, born.
1818 Richard Jordan Gatling, inventor, born.
1819 Field-Marshal Blücher died.
1852 The Earl of Oxford and Asquith, statesman, born.
1874 François Pierre Guillaume Guizot, historian and statesman, died.
1889 Fustel de Coulanges, historian, died.
1948 Rupert D'Oyly Carte, impresario, died.

Events
1609 The Hudson River discovered by Henry Hudson.
1683 Vienna besieged by the Turks.
1814 The defence of Baltimore.
1932 The dissolution of the Reichstag in Germany.
1940 Five boys from Montignac discovered the painted caves at Lascaux.
1943 Mussolini rescued from prison by the Germans.
1948 The Korean People's Republic (North Korea) proclaimed.

13th SEPTEMBER

People
1506 Andrea Mantegna, artist, died.
1520 Lord Burghley, statesman, born.
1557 Sir John Cheke, classical scholar, died.
1592 Michel de Montaigne, writer, died.
1598 Philip II, King of Spain, died.
1759 General Wolfe died.
1759 The Marquis de Montcalm mortally wounded (died 14th).
1803 John Barry, naval officer, died.
1806 Charles James Fox, statesman, died.
1819 Clara Schumann, pianist, born.

1851   Walter Reed, bacteriologist, born.
1860   General Pershing, born.
1874   Arnold Schönberg, composer, born.
1894   Emmanuel Chabrier, composer, died.
1944   W. Heath Robinson, artist, died.

Events
1515   The Battle of Marignan began.
1759   The Battle of Quebec.
1791   Louis XVI took his oath as Constitutional Monarch of France.
1814   Francis Scott Key wrote the words of ' The Star-Spangled Banner '.
1918   The Battle of St Mihiel.
1943   General Chiang Kai Shek elected President of the Chinese Republic.

14th SEPTEMBER
People
258   St Cyprian martyred.
407   St John Chrysostom died.
1321   Dante Alighieri, poet, died.
1646   The Earl of Essex, Parliamentary general, died.
1735   Robert Raikes, Sunday School pioneer, born.
1743   Nicolas Lancret, painter, died.
1759   The Marquis de Montcalm died.
1760   Luigi Cherubini, composer, born.
1774   Lord William Bentinck, statesman, born.
1817   Theodor Storm, poet and novelist, born.
1852   The Duke of Wellington died.
1852   Augustus Pugin, architect, died.
1901   William McKinley, statesman, died of wounds.
1909   Peter Scott, artist, born.
1916   José Echegaray, writer and scientist, died.
1937   Thomas Masaryk, statesman, died.

Events
1515   The Battle of Marignan ended.
1752   The Gregorian calendar adopted in Britain.
1829   The Treaty of Adrianople signed.
1860   Niagara Falls illuminated for the first time.
1917   Russia proclaimed a Republic.

15th SEPTEMBER
People
1583   Albrecht Wenzel Eusebius von Wallenstein, statesman, born.
1613   François de La Rochefoucauld, writer, born.
1666   Sophia Dorothea, Electress of Hanover, born.
1712   The Earl of Godolphin, statesman, died.
1789   James Fenimore Cooper, novelist, born.
1830   William Huskisson, statesman, killed.
1834   Heinrich von Treitschke, historian, born.
1857   William Howard Taft, statesman, born.
1859   Isambard Kingdom Brunel, engineer, died.
1876   Bruno Walter, conductor, born.
1887   General Sir Bernard Paget, born.

Events

1784   Lunardi made his first balloon ascent in England.
1821   The Central American republics proclaimed their independence from Spanish domination.
1830   The Manchester–Liverpool Railway opened.
1916   Tanks first used in World War I.
1938   Hitler and Chamberlain met at Berchtesgaden.
1946   The Bulgarian People's Republic proclaimed.
1952   The British handed over the sovereignty of Eritrea to Ethiopia.

16th SEPTEMBER

People

655   Pope Martin I died.
1498   Tomás de Torquemada, Inquisitor-General, died.
1519   John Colet, theologian, died.
1638   King Louis XIV born.
1736   Gabriel Daniel Fahrenheit, physicist, died.
1745   Field-Marshal Kutuzov born.
1797   Sir Anthony Panizzi, librarian, born.
1823   Francis Parkman, historian, born.
1824   Louis XVIII, King of France, died.
1858   Andrew Bonar Law, statesman, born.
1858   Sir Edward Marshall-Hall, lawyer, born.
1893   Sir Alexander Korda, film producer, born.
1911   Edward Whymper, mountaineer, died.
1932   Sir Ronald Ross, professor of tropical medicine, died.
1945   Count John McCormack, singer, died.
1946   Sir James Jeans, scientist, died.

Events

1620   The Pilgrim Fathers sailed from Plymouth.
1639   Van Tromp defeated the Spanish fleet.
1810   The Mexican revolt against Spain began.
1859   Lake Nyasa discovered by David Livingstone.
1861   Post Office Savings Banks introduced in Britain.
1862   The Battle of Antietam began.
1941   Reza Khan Pahlavi, Shah of Iran, abdicated.

17th SEPTEMBER
Constitution Day in the United States.

People

1552   Pope Paul V born.
1665   Philip IV, King of Spain, died.
1701   King James II died.
1730   The Baron von Steuben, army reformer, born.
1743   The Marquis de Condorcet, philosopher, born.
1771   Tobias Smollett, novelist, died.
1863   Alfred de Vigny, poet, died.
1907   Ignaz Brüll, pianist and composer, died.
1929   Stirling Moss, racing motorist, born.
1958   Friedrich Adolf Paneth, scientist, died.

Events
1745 Edinburgh occupied by the Young Pretender.
1862 The Battle of Antietam ended.
1871 The Mont-Cenis Tunnel opened.
1949 The first meeting of the North Atlantic Treaty Council held.

18th SEPTEMBER

People
1180 Louis VII, King of France, died.
1709 Dr Samuel Johnson, writer, born.
1721 Matthew Prior, poet, died.
1765 Pope Gregory XVI born.
1775 Andrew Foulis, Scottish printer, died.
1792 Bishop August Gottlieb Spangenberg, founder of the Moravian Church in America, died.
1797 General Lazare Hoche died.
1819 Jean Bernard Léon Foucault, scientist, born.
1830 William Hazlitt, writer and critic, died.
1860 Joseph Locke, civil engineer, died.
1905 Greta Garbo, actress, born.

Events
1810 The independence of Chile proclaimed.
1851 The *New York Times* began publication.
1914 The Home Rule Bill received the Royal Assent.
1918 The Battle of Megiddo began.

19th SEPTEMBER

People
1551 Henri III, King of France, born.
1802 Lajos Kossuth, statesman, born.
1867 Arthur Rackham, artist, born.
1881 James Abram Garfield, statesman, died.

Events
1356 The Battle of Poitiers.
1734 The Battle of Luzzara.
1870 The Siege of Paris (by the Germans) began.
1950 The European Payments Union set up.

20th SEPTEMBER

People
1803 Sir Titus Salt, manufacturer and philanthropist, born.
1803 Robert Emmet, Irish patriot, executed.
1863 Jakob Grimm, writer and philologist, died.
1876 Sir Titus Salt, manufacturer and philanthropist, died.
1898 Theodor Fontane, poet and novelist, died.
1908 Pablo de Sarasate, violinist, died.
1933 Mrs Annie Besant, theosophist, died.

Events
1258   Salisbury Cathedral consecrated.
1562   The Treaty of Hampton Court signed.
1697   The Treaty of Ryswick signed.
1792   The Battle of Valmy.
1854   The Battle of Alma.
1857   Delhi recaptured by the British.
1861   The Battle of Lexington.
1906   The *Mauretania* launched.
1909   The South Africa Act received the Royal Assent.
1909   The Labour Exchanges Act, setting up the first British labour exchanges, received the Royal Assent.
1931   Sterling taken off the Gold Standard.
1932   The Methodist Church of Great Britain and Ireland came into being.
1959   Last fly-past of Hurricanes over London commemorating the Battle of Britain.

21st SEPTEMBER
The Feast of St Matthew.

People
1327   King Edward II murdered.
1452   Girolamo Savonarola, reformer, born.
1549   Marguerite d'Angoulême, Queen of Navarre, died.
1645   Louis Jolliet, explorer, born.
1722   John Home, poet, born.
1756   John Loudon McAdam, highway engineer, born.
1832   Louis Paul Cailletet, chemist, born.
1860   Arthur Schopenhauer, philosopher, died.
1866   H. G. Wells, writer, born.
1869   Field-Marshal Lord Chetwode born.
1874   Gustav Holst, composer, born.
1883   Karol Szymanowski, composer, born.
1953   Roger Quilter, composer, died.
1957   Haakon VII, King of Norway, died.

Events
1745   The Battle of Prestonpans.
1792   Beginning (midnight) of the era of the French Republic and the French Revolutionary Calendar.
1933   The Reichstag Fire Trial opened at Leipzig.
1949   The Federal Republic of Germany formally came into existence.
1949   The People's Republic of China proclaimed.

22nd SEPTEMBER
People
1241   Snorri Sturlason, historian, killed.
1606   Richard Busby, schoolmaster, born.
1694   Lord Chesterfield, literary patron and writer, born.
1776   Nathan Hale, American patriot, hanged.
1788   Theodore Hook, humorous writer, born.
1791   Michael Faraday, scientist, born.
1826   Johann Peter Hebel, poet, died.
1851   Mrs Sherwood, writer, died.

1880 Dame Christabel Parkhurst, suffragette, born.
1914 Alain-Fournier, writer, killed in action.
1952 Ian Hay, novelist, died.

Events
1586 The Battle of Zutphen.
1792 France declared a Republic.
1955 Commercial television inaugurated in Britain.
1955 General Perón, President of Argentina, deposed.

23rd SEPTEMBER
Autumnal Equinox.

People
63BC Augustus Caesar, Roman emperor, born.
1625 Johan de Witt, statesman, born.
1650 Jeremy Collier, historian of the theatre, born.
1713 Ferdinand VI, King of Spain, born.
1764 Robert Dodsley, bookseller, died.
1783 Peter Cornelius, painter, born.
1854 Dr Cornelis Lely, statesman and engineer, born.
1874 Sir Ernest Barker, political scientist, born.
1880 Lord Boyd Orr born.
1889 Wilkie Collins, novelist, died.
1939 Sigmund Freud, psychoanalyst, died.

Events
1642 The Battle of Worcester.
1779 The naval battle between the *Bonhomme Richard* and the *Serapis* off Flamborough Head.
1803 The Battle of Assaye.
1940 The George Cross and the George Medal instituted.
1955 Pakistan joined the Baghdad Pact.

24th SEPTEMBER
People
768   Pepin III, King of the Franks, died.
1143 Pope Innocent II died.
1717 Horace Walpole, writer, born.
1762 William Lisle Bowles, poet, born.
1795 Antoine Barye, sculptor, born.
1813 André Grétry, composer, died.
1860 Samuel Crockett, novelist, born.
1890 Sir Alan Herbert, writer, born.
1892 Patrick Gilmore, bandmaster and composer, died.

Events
1841 Sir James Brooke obtained the government of Sarawak for the Sultan of Brunei.
1916 The second Zeppelin destroyed in England.
1916 Krupps Works at Essen bombed by the French.

25th SEPTEMBER
People
1066 Harald Haardraade, King of Norway, killed in battle.
1506 Philip the Handsome, King of Spain, died.

1680   Samuel Butler, satirist, died.
1683   Jean-Philippe Rameau, composer, born.
1793   Felicia Hemans, hymn-writer, born.
1849   Johann Strauss, the elder, composer, died.
1896   Robert Gerhard, composer, born.

Events
1066   The battle of Stamford Bridge.
1513   Balboa discovered the Pacific.
1857   The relief of Lucknow began.
1882   The reconstituted Polytechnic, Regent St., London, opened.
1915   The Battle of Loos began.
1956   Trans-Atlantic telephone cables inaugurated between Britain and North America.

26th SEPTEMBER
Dominion Day in New Zealand.

People
1626   Bishop Lancelot Andrewes, theologian, died.
1750   Admiral Lord Collingwood born.
1898   George Gershwin, composer, born.
1942   The Rev. Wilson Carlile, founder of the Church Army, died.
1945   Bela Bartok, composer, died.

Events
1815   Holy Alliance made between the Emperors of Russia and Austria and the King of Prussia.
1907   New Zealand declared a Dominion.
1918   The Battle of the Meuse-Argonne began.
1934   The *Queen Mary* launched.
1938   The Sudeten German crisis began.

27th SEPTEMBER

People
1404   William of Wykeham died.
1627   Jacques Bénigne Bossuet, orator and historian, born.
1660   St Vincent de Paul died.
1696   St Alfonso Maria dei Liguori born.
1700   Pope Innocent XII died.
1722   Samuel Adams, American patriot, born.
1792   George Cruikshank, artist, born.
1817   Paul Féval, novelist, born.
1840   Alfred Thayer Mahan, naval historian, born.
1862   Louis Botha, statesman, born.
1879   Cyril Scott, composer, born.
1917   Edgar Degas, artist, died.
1919   Adelina Patti, singer, died.
1921   Engelbert Humperdinck, composer, died.
1928   Sir Henry Wickham, pioneer rubber planter, died.
1944   Aimee Semple McPherson, evangelist, died.

Events
1829   Ararat first climbed by Dr J. J. Parrot.
1938   The *Queen Elizabeth* launched.

28th SEPTEMBER
Feast of St Wenceslaus.

People
1789   Thomas Day, writer, died.
1803   Prosper Mérimée, novelist, born.
1824   Francis Turner Palgrave, anthologist, born
1841   Georges Clemenceau, statesman, born.
1851   Henry Arthur Jones, dramatist, born.
1856   Kate Douglas Wiggin, writer, born.
1870   Florent Schmitt, composer, born.
1873   Emile Gaboriau, writer, died.
1895   Louis Pasteur, scientist, died.

Events
1864   The First International founded.
1918   The Battle of Passchendaele.
1920   The Khaki Election opens.
1923   The *Radio Times* first published.
1958   Guinea opted out of the French Union.
1958   Referendum concerning the Constitution of the Fifth Republic of France held
       throughout the French Union.

29th SEPTEMBER
Feast of St Michael and All Angels.   Michaelmas.

People
1518   Tintoretto, painter, born.
1560   King Gustavus Vasa of Sweden died.
1725   Lord Clive of Plassey born.
1758   Lord Nelson born.
1760   William Beckford, writer, born.
1810   Mrs Gaskell, novelist, born.
1833   Ferdinand VII, King of Spain, died.
1867   Walter Rathenau, statesman, born.
1902   Emile Zola, novelist, died.
1931   Sir William Orpen, painter, died.

Events
490BC The Battle of Marathon.
1613   The New River water supply for London opened.
1818   The Congress of Aix-la-Chapelle began.
1850   The Catholic Hierarchy in Britain inaugurated.
1918   The Hindenburg Line broken by the Allies.
1930   The Pilgrim Trust established.
1938   The Munich Conference.
1946   The BBC Third Programme began.

30th SEPTEMBER

People
 420   St Jerome died.
1628   Sir Fulke Greville, poet, murdered.
1732   Jacques Necker, financier, born.
1770   George Whitfield, religious leader, died.
1772   James Brindley, engineer, died.

1811	Bishop Percy, man of letters, died.
1832	Lord Roberts of Kandahar and Waterford born.
1852	Sir Charles Stanford, composer, born.
1913	Rudolf Diesel, engineer, died.
1930	Lord Birkenhead, statesman, died.

Events

1320	Pope Martin V entered Rome, thus beginning his task of regaining Italy.
1399	The coronation of Henry IV.
1810	The University of Berlin opened.
1929	The first BBC experimental television broadcast took place.
1938	The Munich Agreement signed.
1939	The Saar Offensive ended.
1939	Identity cards were first issued in Britain.
1951	The Festival of Britain ended.

1st OCTOBER

National Holiday in China commemorating the formation of the Central People's Government 1949.

People

1207	King Henry III born.
1578	Don John of Austria died.
1684	Pierre Corneille, playwright, died.
1754	Paul I, Tsar of Russia, born.
1781	James Lawrence, naval officer, born.
1865	Paul Dukas, composer, born.
1873	Sir Edwin Landseer, painter, died.
1878	Othmar Spann, sociologist, born.
1893	Benjamin Jowett, classical scholar and theologian, died.
1904	Vladimir Horowitz, pianist, born.

Events

1529	The Colloquy of Marburg began.
1795	Belgium incorporated in the French Republic.
1802	The Peace of Amiens : preliminary articles signed.
1843	The *News of the World* began publication.
1870	Halfpenny postage introduced in Britain.
1870	Stamped postcards first issued in Britain.
1918	T. E. Lawrence and the Arabs formally entered Damascus.
1938	German troops entered Czechoslovakia.
1953	Andhra constituted a separate State in India.

2nd OCTOBER

People

1452	King Richard III born.
1780	Major John André hanged at Tappan, N.Y.
1786	Admiral Keppel died.
1817	Gunnar Wennerberg, poet, born.
1847	Paul von Hindenberg, statesman and soldier, born.
1851	Field-Marshal Foch born.
1869	Mahatma Gandhi, statesman, born.
1871	Cordell Hull, statesman, born.

1873   Sir Pelham Warner, cricketer, born.
1920   Max Bruch, composer, died.
1931   Sir Thomas Lipton, sportsman, died.

Events
1187   Saladin entered Jerusalem.
1799   The Duke of York captured Alkmaar in the Netherlands.
1901   The first British submarine launched at Barrow.
1909   The first Rugby football match played at Twickenham.
1940   A Royal Charter of incorporation granted to the British Council.
1958   Guinea proclaimed an independent Republic.

3rd OCTOBER
Feast of St Thérèse of Lisieux.

People
1226   St Francis of Assisi died.
1369   Margaret Maultasch, Countess of Tyrol, died.
1658   Miles Standish, leader of the Pilgrim Fathers, died.
1859   Eleanora Duse, actress, born.
1867   Elias Howe, inventor, died.
1875   Gilbert Newton Lewis, chemist, born.
1886   Alain-Fournier, writer, born.
1896   William Morris, artist and writer, died.
1929   Gustav Stresemann, statesman, died.
1953   Sir Arnold Bax, composer, died.

Events
1574   The relief of Leyden.
1691   The surrender of Limerick.
1918   Tsar Ferdinand of Bulgaria abdicated.
1929   Yugoslavia first so named.

4th OCTOBER
Feast of St Francis of Assisi.

People
1289   Louis X, King of France, born.
1669   Rembrandt van Rijn, artist, died.
1720   Giovanni Battista Piranesi, architect, born.
1741   Edmund Malone, Shakespeare scholar, born.
1743   Henry Carey, poet and musician, died.
1787   François Pierre Guillaume Guizot, historian and statesman, born.
1802   Marshal Niel, statesman, born.
1814   Jean François Millet, artist, born.
1821   John Rennie, engineer, died.
1832   William Griggs, inventor, born.
1861   Frederick Remington, artist, born.
1872   Admiral Lord Keyes born.
1881   Field-Marshal von Brauchitsch born.

Events
1535   The first English-language Bible : printing completed.
1830   The independence of Belgium proclaimed.

1883　The Boys' Brigade founded at Glasgow.
1957　The first Soviet earth-satellite launched.

5th OCTOBER

People
1285　Philip III, King of France, died.
1713　Denis Diderot, encyclopædist, born.
1789　William Scoresby, Arctic explorer, born.
1805　Charles, Marquess Cornwallis, statesman, died.
1830　Chester Alan Arthur, statesman, born.
1880　Jacques Offenbach, composer, died.

Events
1930　The airship R101 crashed at Beauvais.
1938　President Beneš of Czechoslovakia resigned.
1947　The Cominform formed at Belgrade.
1958　The constitution of the Fifth Republic of France came into force.

6th OCTOBER

People
1536　William Tyndale, theologian, strangled and burnt.
1769　General Sir Isaac Brock born.
1820　Jenny Lind, singer, born.
1846　George Westinghouse, inventor, born.
1891　Charles Stewart Parnell, Irish patriot, died.
1892　Alfred, Lord Tennyson, poet, died.
1893　Ford Madox Brown, painter, died.

Events
1238　Peterborough Cathedral consecrated.
1571　The Battle of Lepanto.
1895　The Promenade Concerts, London, founded by Sir Henry Wood.
1903　Manchester University formally opened.
1949　The Berlin airlift ended.

7th OCTOBER

People
1468　Sigismondo Malatesta, tyrant and soldier, died.
1543　Hans Holbein the Younger, painter, died.
1573　Archbishop Laud born.
1577　George Gascoigne, poet and playwright, died.
1734　Sir Ralph Abercromby, soldier, born.
1780　Patrick Ferguson, soldier and inventor, killed in action.
1849　James Whitcomb Riley, poet, born.
1893　Sir William Smith, lexicographer, died.
1894　Oliver Wendell Holmes, writer, died.
1918　Sir Hubert Parry, composer, died.
1922　Marie Lloyd, music hall comedian, died.

Events
1391　St Bridget of Sweden canonised.
1571　The Naval Battle of Lepanto.

1906　The Persian Assembly opened by the Shah.
1944　The Dumbarton Oaks Conference ended.
1949　The constitution of the German Democratic Republic enacted.

8th OCTOBER
People
1354　Cola di Rienzi, reformer, murdered.
1469　Fra Filippo Lippi, artist, died.
1754　Henry Fielding, novelist, died.
1837　François Marie Charles Fourier, social reformer, died.
1838　Lord Dowton, philanthropist, born.
1838　John Hay, statesman, born.
1863　Archbishop Whateley, writer, died.
1953　Kathleen Ferrier, singer, died.

Events
1871　The outbreak of the Great Fire of Chicago (ended 11th Oct.).
1912　War broke out in the Balkans against Turkey.
1918　Beirut taken by the British.

9th OCTOBER
Feast of St Denis.　Leif Ericson Day (Norway).
People
1253　Robert Grosseteste, theologian, died.
1757　Charles X of France born.
1835　Charles Camille Saint-Saëns, composer, born.
1859　Alfred Dreyfus born.
1890　Aimee Semple McPherson, evangelist, born.
1907　Viscount Hailsham, statesman, born.
1934　Alexander, King of Yugoslavia, assassinated.
1935　The Duke of Kent born.
1940　Sir Wilfred Grenfell, medical missionary, died.
1958　Pope Pius XII died.

Events
1514　Louis XII, King of France, married Mary Tudor.
1561　The Colloquy of Poissy broke up.
1871　The great Chicago fire began.
1875　The Universal Postal Union founded at Berne.

10th OCTOBER
People
1685　Antoine Watteau, painter, born.
1731　Henry Cavendish, scientist, born.
1738　Benjamin West, painter, born.
1766　Dionys Weber, composer, born.
1797　Thomas Drummond, inventor, born.
1802　Hugh Miller, geologist, born.
1813　Giuseppe Verdi, composer, born.
1825　Paul Kruger, statesman, born.
1827　Ugo Foscolo, poet, died.
1830　Isabella II, Queen of Spain, born.

1861 Fridtjof Nansen, explorer, born.
1877 Lord Nuffield, manufacturer and philanthropist, born.
1894 Dr William Moon, friend of the blind, died.
1900 Helen Hayes, actress, born.
1904 Clemens Alexander Winkler, scientist, died.
1940 Katherine Mayo, reformer and writer, died.

Events
43BC Lyons, France, founded by Lucius Plancus.
1774 The Battle of Point Pleasant.
1845 The United States Naval Academy at Annapolis opened.
1911 The outbreak of the Chinese Revolution.

11th OCTOBER

People
1531 Huldreich Zwingli, reformer, killed.
1542 Sir Thomas Wyatt, poet, died.
1779 Count Casimir Pulaski, soldier, died of wounds.
1821 Sir George Williams, founder of the Y.M.C.A., born.
1837 Samuel Wesley, composer, died.
1884 Mrs Eleanor Roosevelt born.
1889 James Prescott Joule, physicist, died.
1896 Anton Bruckner, composer, died.

Events
1797 The Battle of Camperdown.
1871 The great Chicago fire ended.
1958 The Russian moon rocket first launched.

12th OCTOBER
Columbus Day in the United States.

People
1537 King Edward VI born.
1576 The Emperor Maximilian II died.
1654 Carel Fabritius, painter, killed.
1844 Helen Modjeska, actress, born.
1845 Elizabeth Fry, prison reformer, died.
1859 Robert Stephenson, engineer, died.
1860 Elmer Ambrose Sperry, inventor, born.
1870 General Robert E. Lee died.
1872 Ralph Vaughan Williams, composer, born.
1892 Ernest Renan, philosopher, died.
1915 Nurse Edith Cavell executed by the Germans.
1924 Anatole France, writer, died.

Events
1654 The great explosion at Delft.
1950 The College of Europe, Bruges, opened.

13th OCTOBER

People
1812 General Sir Isaac Brock killed.
1815 Joachim Murat, King of the Two Sicilies, executed

1821   Rudolf Virchow, pathologist, born.
1825   Maximilian I, King of Bavaria, died.
1831   James Knowles, editor and architect, born.
1905   Sir Henry Irving, actor, died.

Events
1307   The arrest of the Templars in Paris.
1890   The funeral service of Mrs ' General ' Booth.
1923   The Fell and Rock Climbing Club handed over to the National Trust 3,000 acres
        in the Lake District.

14th OCTOBER

People
1066   Harold, King of the English, slain in battle.
1630   Sophia, Electress of Hanover, born.
1633   King James II born.
1644   William Penn, Quaker, founder of Pennsylvania, born.
1784   Ferdinand VII, King of Spain, born.
1882   Eamon de Valera, statesman, born.
1890   General Eisenhower born.
1942   Dame Marie Tempest, actress, died.

Events
1066   The Battle of Hastings.
1806   The Battle of Jena.
1809   The Peace of Vienna.
1929   The first trials of the airship *R* 101.
1939   The *Royal Oak* torpedoed in Scapa Flow.
1955   The Province of West Pakistan came into being.

15th OCTOBER

People
70   Virgil, poet, born.
1553   Lucas Cranach, painter, died.
1633   James II, King of Great Britain, born.
1686   Allan Ramsay, poet, born.
1762   Samuel Holyoke, hymn-writer, born.
1836   James Tissot, painter, born.
1844   Friedrich Wilhelm Nietzsche, philosopher, born.
1884   Miloye Miloyevich, composer, born.
1905   Sir Charles Snow (C. P. Snow), scientist and novelist, born.
1934   Raymond Poincaré, statesman, died.

Events
1582   The Gregorian Calendar introduced into Catholic countries.
1846   Ether first publicly demonstrated in its use as an anæsthetic.
1851   The Great Exhibition at Crystal Palace closed.
1928   The airship *Graf Zeppelin* completed its first trans-Atlantic flight.
1946   The Paris Peace Conference ended.
1957   The naval base of Trincomalee handed over to Ceylon by Britain.

16th OCTOBER

People

1430 James II, King of Scotland, born.
1555 Bishop Latimer executed.
1555 Bishop Ridley burnt at the stake.
1591 Pope Gregory XIV died.
1621 Jan Sweelinck, organist, died.
1758 Noah Webster, dictionary-maker, born.
1793 Marie Antoinette guillotined.
1793 John Hunter, surgeon, died.
1797 The Earl of Cardigan, soldier, born.
1803 Robert Stephenson, engineer, born.
1827 Arnold Böcklin, painter, born.
1854 Oscar Wilde, writer, born.
1886 David Ben-Gurion, statesman, born.
1888 Eugene O'Neill, playwright, born.
1946 Sir Granville Bantock, composer, died.

Events

1759 Official opening of Smeaton's Eddystone Lighthouse.
1859 John Brown raided Harper's Ferry.
1869 Girton College, Cambridge University, opened.
1925 The BBC began weekly broadcasts to the Continent.

17th OCTOBER

People

1552 Andreas Osiander, religious reformer, died.
1586 Sir Philip Sidney, statesman, died.
1727 John Wilkes, politician, born.
1757 R. A. F. de Réaumur, scientist, died.
1813 Georg Büchner, playwright, born.
1849 Frédéric Chopin, composer, died.
1921 Ludwig III, King of Bavaria, died.

Events

1346 The Battle of Neville's Cross.
1662 Charles II sold Dunkirk to the French.
1777 General Burgoyne surrendered at Saratoga.
1850 James Young patented Synthetic Oil Production.
1951 The North Atlantic Treaty amended in London by Protocol.
1956 The Calder Hall Atomic Power Station opened.

18th OCTOBER
Feast of St Luke.

People

1405 Pope Pius II born.
1417 Pope Gregory XII died.
1503 Pope Pius III died.
1541 Margaret, Queen of Scotland, died.
1595 Alvaro Mendaña, navigator, died.
1663 Prince Eugene of Savoy born.
1674 Beau Nash born.
1715 Peter II, Tsar of Russia, born.

1735 John Adams, statesman, born.
1753 J. J. R. de Cambacérès, statesman, born.
1777 Heinrich von Kleist, poet and dramatist, born.
1831 Frederick III, Emperor of Germany, born
1859 Henri Bergson, philosopher, born.
1865 Lord Palmerston, statesman, died.
1878 James Truslow Adams, historian, born.
1893 Charles-François Gounod, composer, died.
1893 Sidney George Holland, statesman, born.
1931 Thomas Alva Edison, inventor, died.

Events
1685 King Louis XIV revoked the Edict of Nantes.
1775 Falmouth (now Portland, Maine) bombarded by the British.
1826 The last State Lottery drawn in Britain.
1905 Aldwych, London, opened.
1905 Kingsway, London, opened.
1937 Rheims Cathedral reconsecrated.

19th OCTOBER

People
1216 John Lackland (King John) died.
1605 Sir Thomas Browne, writer, born.
1745 Jonathan Swift, satirist, died.
1758 Johan Roman, composer, died.
1784 Leigh Hunt, writer, born.
1817 Tom Taylor, playwright, born.
1875 Sir Charles Wheatstone, physicist, died.
1909 Cesare Lombroso, criminologist, died.
1937 Lord Rutherford, scientist, died.

Events
1781 Lord Cornwallis surrendered at Yorktown.
1807 Sir Humphry Davy publicly announced his discovery of sodium.
1912 The Treaty of Ouchy signed.
1954 Anglo-Egyptian agreement concerning the Suez Canal base signed.

20th OCTOBER

People
1524 Thomas Linacre, Royal physician, died.
1632 Sir Christopher Wren, architect, born.
1784 Lord Palmerston, statesman, born.
1822 Thomas Hughes, writer, born.
1842 Grace Darling died.
1858 John Burns, statesman, born.
1859 John Dewey, philosopher, born.
1867 Sarah Ann Glover, inventor of the Tonic Sol-fa system, died.
1890 Sir Richard Burton, traveller and writer, died.
1894 J. A. Froude, historian, died.

Events
480BC The Battle of Salamis.
1805 The Battle of Ulm.

1827 The Battle of Navarino.
1944 The Allies captured Aachen.

21st OCTOBER

People
1558 Julius Cæsar Scaliger, philosopher and scientist, died.
1687 Edmund Waller, poet, died.
1760 Hokusai, painter, born.
1772 Samuel Taylor Coleridge, poet, born.
1777 Samuel Foote, actor and playwright, died.
1790 Alphonse de Lamartine, poet, born.
1805 Lord Nelson died.
1833 Alfred Nobel, manufacturer and philanthropist, born.
1943 Admiral Sir Dudley Pound died.

Events
1803 The Louisiana Purchase ratified.
1805 The Battle of Trafalgar.
1909 Halley's comet sighted from Cambridge Observatory.
1929 The BBC began regional broadcasting services.
1940 Purchase tax introduced in Britain.

22nd OCTOBER

People
1383 Ferdinand I, King of Portugal, died.
1565 Jean Grolier, statesman, died.
1659 Abel Tasman, explorer, died.
1689 John V, King of Portugal, born.
1806 Thomas Sheraton, cabinet-maker, died.
1811 Franz Liszt, composer, born.
1843 Stephen Moulton Babcock, scientist, born.
1845 Sarah Bernhardt, actress, born.
1859 Ludwig Spohr, composer, died.
1882 Janos Arany, poet, died.
1890 Sir Archibald Sinclair, statesman, born.
1933 Sir John Fortescue, historian, died.
1935 Lord Carson, statesman, died.

Events
1721 The official birthday of the Russian Empire.
1883 The Metropolitan Opera House in New York opened.
1910 Crippen convicted.

23rd OCTOBER

People
42BC Brutus committed suicide.
1658 Thomas Pride, Parliamentary General, died.
1805 Adalbert Stifter, writer, born.
1845 George Saintsbury, literary historian and critic, born.
1845 Sarah Bernhardt, actress, born.
1906 Paul Cézanne, painter, died.
1915 W. G. Grace, cricketer, died.

23rd October

Events

42BC The Second Battle of Philippi.
1642 The Battle of Edgehill.
1917 The Battle of Caporetto began.
1942 The Battle of El Alamein began.
1944 The Naval Battle of the Philippines began.
1956 The Hungarian Revolt began.

24th OCTOBER
Feast of St Raphael the Archangel.

People

1601 Tycho Brahe, astronomer, died.
1632 Anthony van Leeuwenhoek, naturalist, born.
1645 Sir William Rollo, Royalist, executed.
1767 Jacques Laffitte, banker and politician, born.
1811 Ferdinand Hiller, composer, born.
1897 Francis Turner Palgrave, anthologist, died.
1918 Charles Lecocq, composer, died.
1951 Prince Carl of Sweden died.

Events

1648 The Treaty of Westphalia signed.
1685 The Edict of Nantes revoked by King Louis XIV.
1861 The transcontinental telegraph line across the U.S.A. completed.

25th OCTOBER
Feast of St Crispin.

People

1400 Geoffrey Chaucer, poet, died.
1510 Giorgione, painter, died.
1735 James Beattie, poet, born.
1760 King George II died.
1800 Lord Macaulay, historian, born.
1825 Johann Strauss, the younger, composer, born.
1838 Georges Bizet, composer, born.
1861 Friedrich Karl von Savigny, jurist, died.
1864 Aleksandr Gretchaninov, composer, born.
1888 Richard Evelyn Byrd, aviator and explorer, born.
1890 Floyd Bennett, aviator, born.
1920 Terence James MacSwiney, Irish patriot, died of starvation.

Events

1415 The Battle of Agincourt.
1760 George III proclaimed King.
1854 The Charge of the Light Brigade at Balaklava.
1924 The Zinoviev Letter published in Britain.
1944 The Naval Battle of the Philippines ended.
1956 A military pact, signed by Egypt, Syria and Jordan, placed their armed forces under Egyptian command.

26th OCTOBER

People

1440	Gilles de Rais, Marshal of France, hanged.
1694	Johan Roman, composer, born.
1757	Karl, Freiherr von Stein, statesman, born.
1759	Georges Danton, statesman, born.
1764	William Hogarth, artist, died.
1800	Helmuth, Graf von Moltke, soldier, born.
1866	Viscount Sankey, lawyer, born.
1919	Mohammad Reza Pahlavi, Shah of Iran, born.
1913	' Baron Corvo ', writer, died.

Events

1825	The Erie Canal opened to traffic.
1905	Sweden agreed to the repeal of the union of Sweden and Norway.
1907	The Territorial Army inaugurated in Britain.
1918	The independence of Czechoslovakia proclaimed.
1956	The United Nations approved the establishment of the International Atomic Energy Agency.

27th OCTOBER

People

1553	Michael Servetus, theologian, burnt at the stake.
1670	Vavasour Powell, itinerant preacher, died in prison.
1760	Graf Gneisenau, soldier, born.
1782	Nicolò Paganini, violinist, born.
1854	Sir William Alexander Smith, founder of the Boys' Brigade, born.
1856	Albrecht Rodenbach, poet, born.
1858	Theodore Roosevelt, statesman, born.
1899	Edward Lyon Berthou, inventor, died.

Events

1775	The Continental Congress established the United States Navy.
1806	Berlin captured by the French.
1870	The capitulation of Metz to the German army.
1930	The Courtauld Institute of Art established in London.
1930	The London Naval Treaty ratified.

28th OCTOBER

People

901	Alfred the Great died.
1412	Margaret, Queen of Denmark, Norway and Sweden, died.
1466	Desiderius Erasmus, reformer, born.
1485	Rodolphus Agricola, scholar and theologian, born.
1585	Cornelis Jansen, theologian, born.
1696	Marshal Saxe born.
1704	John Locke, philosopher, died.
1728	Captain Cook, navigator and explorer, born.
1792	John Smeaton, civil engineer, died.
1899	Ottmar Mergenthaler, inventor, died.
1914	Jonas Edward Salk, scientist, born.

Events
1636   Harvard College founded.
1886   The Statue of Liberty dedicated.
1918   The Czechoslovak State came into existence.

29th OCTOBER

People
1618   Sir Walter Raleigh executed.
1656   Edmund Halley, astronomer, born.
1740   James Boswell, Dr Johnson's biographer, born.
1759   John Keats, poet, born.
1783   Jean d'Alembert, mathematician and philosopher, died.
1804   George Morland, artist, died.
1864   John Leech, artist, died.
1879   Franz von Papen, politician, born.
1885   James Hannington, first Bishop of Eastern Equatorial Africa, murdered.
1897   Paul Joseph Goebbels, Nazi leader, born.
1911   Joseph Pulitzer, newspaper publisher, died.
1950   Gustaf V, King of Sweden, died.

Events
1888   The Convention of Constantinople declared the Suez Canal open to the vessels
       of all nations and free from blockade.
1918   The German mutiny began.
1945   The Atomic Energy Research Establishment set up at Harwell.
1956   The Suez Canal attack began.
1956   The international status of the Tangier Zone abolished.

30th OCTOBER

People
1741   Angelica Kauffmann, artist, born.
1751   Richard Brinsley Sheridan, playwright, born.
1823   Edmund Cartwright, inventor, died.
1860   Lord Dundonald, naval commander, died.
1883   Ralph Hale Mottram, novelist, born.
1894   Peter Warlock, composer, born.
1895   Gerhard Domagk, pathologist, born.
1910   Henri Dunant, founder of the International Red Cross, died.
1923   Andrew Bonar Law, statesman, died.
1932   Lord Methuen died.

Events
1841   Fire at the Tower of London.
1928   The experimental transmission of still pictures by television began in Britain.

31st OCTOBER
Hallowe'en.

People
1620   John Evelyn, diarist, born.
1632   Jan Vermeer, painter, born.
1638   Meyndert Hobbema, painter, born.

1867 The Earl of Rosse, astronomer, died.
1886 Chiang Kai-shek, statesman, born.
1905 William Francis Grimes, archæologist, born.

Events
1517 Luther nailed his theses on indulgences to the church door at Wittenberg.
1815 Sir Humphry Davy's invention of the miner's safety lamp.
1864 Nevada achieved Statehood.
1902 The Pacific cable completed at Suva.
1909 The National University of Ireland, Dublin, came into being.
1909 Queen's University, Belfast, came into being.
1917 Beersheba captured by the Allies.
1925 The Persian Majles deposed the Shah, Sultan Ahmad.
1940 The Battle of Britain ended.

1st NOVEMBER
People
846   Louis II, King of France, born.
1500 Benvenuto Cellini, artist, born.
1636 Nicolas Boileau, poet, born.
1714 John Radcliffe, physician, died.
1770 Alexander Cruden, concordancer, died.
1778 Gustavus IV, King of Sweden, born.
1793 Lord George Gordon died.
1865 John Lindley, botanist, died.
1894 Alexander III, Emperor of Russia, died.
1896 Edmund Blunden, poet, died.
1903 Theodor Mommsen, historian and archæologist, died.

Events
1755 The great earthquake at Lisbon.
1814 The Congress of Vienna opened.
1914 The Battle of Coronel.
1922 Broadcasting licences (10s.) introduced in Britain.
1924 The British Empire Exhibition, Wembley, closed.
1956 Andhra, India, reconstituted and enlarged and renamed Andhra Pradesh.
1956 The States Reorganisation Act came into force in India.

2nd NOVEMBER
All Souls' Day.
People
1148 St Malachy died.
1470 King Edward V born.
1483 The Duke of Buckingham executed.
1600 Richard Hooker, theologian, died.
1734 Daniel Boone, American pioneer, born.
1755 Marie Antoinette born.
1795 James Knox Polk, statesman, born.
1818 Sir Samuel Romilly, lawyer, committed suicide.
1827 Paul de Lagarde, Biblical scholar and orientalist, born.
1865 William Gamaliel Harding, statesman, born.
1887 Jenny Lind, singer, died.
1950 George Bernard Shaw, dramatist, died.

Events
1308   Castellat, last of the Templar's stronghold, fell.
1889   North and South Dakota achieved Statehood.
1917   The Balfour Declaration.
1953   The first television theatre opened at Brighton.
1959   M1 motorway officially opened.

3rd NOVEMBER
People
1779   Field-Marshal Lord Gough born.
1793   Stephen Fuller Austin, statesman, born.
1794   William Cullen Bryant, poet, born.
1801   Karl Baedeker, guidebook publisher, born.
1832   Sir John Leslie, mathematician, died.
1879   Vilhjálmur Stefánsson, explorer, born.
1901   Leopold III, King of the Belgians, born.
1954   Henri Matisse, artist, died.

Events
1640   The Long Parliament assembled.
1706   Abruzzi destroyed by an earthquake.
1840   Acre taken by the Allies.
1903   The independence of Panama proclaimed.
1916   Qatar and Britain signed a treaty of friendship.
1918   The mutiny at Kiel.

4th NOVEMBER
People
1702   Admiral Benbow died.
1740   Augustus Montague Toplady, hymn-writer, born.
1787   Edmund Kean, actor, born.
1840   Auguste Rodin, sculptor, born.
1847   Felix Mendelssohn, composer, died.
1856   Paul Delaroche, painter, died.
1858   Sir Frank Benson, actor-manager, born.
1859   Joseph Rowntree, Quaker educationalist, died.
1862   Eden Phillpotts, writer, born.
1879   Will Rogers, humorist, born.
1891   Sir Frederick Grant Banting, physician, born.
1924   Gabriel Fauré, composer, died.

Events
1918   The German Revolution began.
1942   The Battle of El Alamein ended.
1948   The Indian Constitution formally introduced in the Constituent Assembly.
1957   The second Soviet earth-satellite launched.

5th NOVEMBER
Guy Fawkes' Day.
People
1459   Sir John Fastolf, soldier, died.
1494   Hans Sachs, poet and dramatist, born.

1807 Angelica Kauffman, painter, died.
1854 Susan Ferrier, novelist, died.
1895 Walter Gieseking, pianist, born.
1955 Maurice Utrillo, painter, died.

Events
1605 Guy Fawkes' attempt on the Houses of Parliament.
1688 William of Orange landed at Torbay.
1854 The Battle of Inkerman.
1956 First experimental ' live-picture ' colour television transmission in Britain.

6th NOVEMBER
People
1406 Pope Innocent VII died.
1612 Henry Frederick, Prince of Wales, died.
1632 Gustavus Adolphus, King of Sweden, killed in battle.
1650 William II of Orange died.
1656 John IV (The Fortunate), King of Portugal, died.
1671 Colley Cibber, writer, born.
1771 Alois Senefelder, inventor of lithography, born.
1793 John Murray, publisher, died.
1814 Adolphe Sax, musical instrument-maker, born.
1833 Jonas Lie, novelist, born.
1842 William Hone, writer, died.
1854 John Philip Sousa, composer, born.
1860 Admiral Sir Charles Napier died.
1870 Viscount Samuel, statesman, born.
1884 Henry Fawcett, statesman and economist, died.
1892 Sir John Alcock, pioneer aviator, born.
1893 Peter Tchaikovsky, composer, died.
1913 Sir W. H. Preece, radio pioneer, died.
1939 Adolf Max, Burgomaster of Brussels, died.

Events
1860 Abraham Lincoln elected President of the United States.
1956 The Suez Canal cease-fire.
1956 The Kariba Hydro-Electric Project High Dam construction begun.

7th NOVEMBER
People
1723 Sir Godfrey Kneller, painter, died.
1810 Franz Erkel, composer, born.
1846 Ignaz Brüll, pianist and composer, born.
1853 Edwin Herbert Hall, scientist, born.
1860 Joseph Hocking, novelist and Methodist preacher, born.
1867 Madame Curie, scientist, born.
1888 Sir Chandrasekhara Venkata Raman, physicist, born.
1912 Richard Norman Shaw, architect, died.

Events
1619 Elizabeth, daughter of James I, crowned Queen of Bohemia.
1631 Transit of Mercury (first observation of the transit of a planet) observed by Pierre Gassendi.

1811   The Battle of Tippecanoe.
1903   The Civic inauguration of Liverpool University.
1917   The October Revolution in Russia.

8th NOVEMBER
People
1226   Louis VIII, King of France, died.
1308   Duns Scotus, philosopher, died.
1674   John Milton, poet, died.
1793   Madame Roland, revolutionary, guillotined.
1828   Thomas Bewick, engraver, died.
1834   J. K. F. Zöllner, scientist, born.
1865   Tom Sayers, pugilist, died.
1867   Ilmari Krohn, musician, born.
1868   Viscount Lee of Fareham, statesman, born.
1883   Sir Arnold Bax, composer, born.
1886   Fred Archer, jockey, committed suicide.
1890   César Franck, composer, died.
1908   Victorien Sardou, playwright, died.
1933   Mohammed Nadir Shah of Afghanistan assassinated.

Events
1861   The U.S. warship *San Jacinto* overhauled the British mailship *Trent* in the
         Bahama channel.
1889   Montana achieved Statehood.
1923   The Munich Putsch of Hitler.
1942   The Allies land in North Africa.

9th NOVEMBER
People
1623   William Camden, historian, died.
1677   Archbishop Sheldon died.
1721   Mark Akenside, poet, born.
1818   Ivan Turgenev, writer, born.
1841   King Edward VII born.
1880   Sir Giles Scott, architect, born.
1908   Lord Duveen, art dealer, died.
1937   Ramsay MacDonald, statesman, died.
1940   Neville Chamberlain, statesman, died.
1951   Sigmund Romberg, composer, died.
1953   King Ibn Saud died.
1953   Dylan Thomas, poet, died.

Events
1858   The first concert of the New York Symphony Orchestra.
1907   The Cullinan Diamond presented to the King on behalf of the people of the
         Transvaal.
1908   Britain's first woman Mayor elected at Aldeburgh.
1914   The *Emden* destroyed.
1917   Clemenceau elected Premier of France.
1918   The Kaiser abdicated.
1918   The German Republic proclaimed.
1918   The independence of Poland proclaimed.

1923   Hitler's Putsch at Munich defeated.
1943   The U.N.R.R.A. Agreement signed.
1944   The beginning of the Moscow Conference.

10th NOVEMBER
People
461   Pope Leo the Great died.
1444   Wladislaus III, King of Hungary, died.
1483   Martin Luther, reformer, born.
1549   Pope Paul III died.
1556   Richard Chancellor, navigator, lost at sea.
1668   François Couperin, composer, born.
1683   King George II born.
1697   William Hogarth, artist, born.
1728   Oliver Goldsmith, writer, born.
1759   Friedrich Schiller, writer, born.
1796   Catherine II, Empress of Russia, died.
1846   Martin Wegelius, musician, born.
1852   Gideon Algernon Mantell, geologist and palæontologist, died.
1861   Robert T. A. Innes, astronomer, born.
1873   H. B. Rabaud, composer, born.
1880   Jacob Epstein, sculptor, born.
1887   Arnold Zweig, writer, born.
1893   John Phillips Marquand, novelist, born.
1924   Sir Archibald Geikie, geologist, died.
1938   Kemal Ataturk, statesman, died.

Events
1559   Queen Elizabeth confirmed the Charter of the Stationers' Company.
1775   The United States Marine Corps formed.
1798   Alois Senefelder discovered the lithographic process.
1915   The Gilbert and Ellice Islands annexed by Britain.

11th NOVEMBER
Martinmas.
People
1599   Prince Octavio Piccolomini, military commander, born.
1642   A. C. Boulle, cabinet-maker, born.
1729   L. A. de Bougainville, navigator, born.
1821   Fedor Dostoievski, novelist, born.
1855   Søren Kierkegaard, philosopher, died.
1858   Hugh Lee Pattinson, metallurgical chemist, died.
1882   Gustaf VI, King of Sweden, born.
1926   Sir William Tilden, chemist, died.
1936   Sir Edward German, composer, died.
1945   Jerome Kern, composer, died.

Events
1889   Washington achieved Statehood.
1918   The Battle of the Meuse-Argonne ended.
1918   Armistice Day : World War I.
1920   The Unknown Soldier buried in Westminster Abbey
1920   The Cenotaph in Whitehall, London, unveiled

12th NOVEMBER
People
1035 King Canute the Great died.
1202 King Canute VI of Denmark died.
1555 Bishop Gardiner, theologian, died.
1595 Sir John Hawkins, navigator, died.
1615 Richard Baxter, divine, born.
1671 Thomas Fairfax, Parliamentary general, died.
1684 Admiral Vernon born.
1755 Gerhard Johann David von Scharnhorst, Prussian general, born.
1769 Mrs Opie, novelist, born.
1841 Lord Rayleigh, physicist, born.
1854 Charles Kemble, actor, died.
1865 Mrs Gaskell, novelist, died.

Events
1630 The Day of Dupes (in France).
1847 Chloroform first used as an anæsthetic in an operation in Britain.
1893 The Durand Agreement, defining the frontier between Afghanistan and India, signed.
1921 The Limitation of Armaments Conference began at Washington.
1927 The first automatic telephone service inaugurated in London.
1933 The first plebiscite under Hitler's régime held in Germany.
1944 The *Tirpitz* sunk.

13th NOVEMBER
People
 867 Pope Nicholas the Great died.
1093 Malcolm III, King of the Scots, killed.
1312 King Edward III born.
1460 Prince Henry the Navigator died.
1736 George Sale, orientalist, died.
1782 Esaias Tegner, writer, born.
1792 E. J. Trelawny, traveller and writer, born.
1825 Charles Frederick Worth, dress designer, born.
1831 James Clerk-Maxwell, physicist, born.
1833 Edwin Booth, actor, born.
1849 William Etty, artist, died.
1850 Robert Louis Stevenson, writer, born.
1853 John Drew, writer, born.
1854 George Whitefield Chadwick, composer, born.
1861 Arthur Hugh Clough, poet, died.
1862 Ludwig Uhland, poet, died.
1882 Gottfried Kinkel, poet, died.
1897 Ernest Giles, explorer, died.
1907 Francis Thompson, poet, died.
1916 Percival Lowell, astronomer, died.

Events
1564 The Tridentine Creed promulgated.
1804 Captain Samuel Wallis, navigator, died.
1875 Ernest Giles reached Perth, Australia, overland.
1929 The Bank for International Settlements founded.
1930 The planet Pluto discovered.

14th NOVEMBER

People

565	The Emperor Justinian I died.
1635	' Old Parr ' (born about 1483), died.
1716	Gottfried Wilhelm Leibniz, philosopher, died.
1734	Louise de Keroualle, mistress of King Charles II, died.
1765	Robert Fulton, inventor, born.
1797	Sir Charles Lyell, geologist, born.
1816	John Curwen, musician, born.
1825	Jean Paul Richter, humorist, died.
1831	G. W. F. Hegel, philosopher, died.
1840	Claude Monet, painter, born.
1843	Sir W. R. Anson, jurist, born.
1863	Leo Hendrik Baekeland, inventor, born.
1889	Jawaharlal Nehru, statesman, born.
1891	Sir Frederick Grant Banting, scientist, born.
1909	Senator Joe McCarthy born.
1914	Lord Roberts of Kandahar and Waterford died.
1915	Theodore Leschetizky, pianist, died.
1916	Henryk Sienkiewicz, novelist, died.
1935	King Hussein of Jordan born.
1946	Manuel de Falla, composer, died.
1948	The Prince of Wales born.
1955	Robert E. Sherwood, writer, died.

Events

1770	Bruce discovered the source of the Blue Nile.
1918	The Czechoslovak State formally declared to be a Republic.
1922	British daily broadcasting began from 2LO.
1936	The Waterways clauses of the Versailles Treaty denounced by Germany.
1959	The world's largest atomic reactor opened at Dounreay.

15th NOVEMBER

People

1397	Pope Nicholas V born.
1607	Madeleine de Scudéry, writer, born.
1630	Johannes Kepler, astronomer, died.
1638	Catharine of Braganza born.
1671	Johann Komensky (Comenius), educational reformer, died.
1708	The Earl of Chatham, statesman, born.
1738	Sir William Herschel, astronomer, born.
1741	J. K. Lavater, poet and physiognomist, born.
1776	Per Henrik Ling, pioneer in gymnastic training, born.
1787	Christoph Willibald Gluck, composer, died.
1802	George Romney, painter, died.
1848	Count de Rossi, statesman, assassinated.
1854	Emil Leopold Boas, Hamburg-Amerika Line general manager, born.
1862	Gerhardt Hauptmann, dramatist, died.
1863	Frederik VII, King of Denmark, died.
1882	Felix Frankfurter, American Supreme Court judge, born.
1889	Manuel II, King of Portugal, born.
1959	Professor Charles Thomas Rees Wilson, physicist, died.

Events
1315   The Battle of Morgarten.
1831   The Treaty of London.
1889   Brazil became a Republic.

16th NOVEMBER

People
42BC   Tiberius, Roman emperor, born.
1272   Henry III, King of England, died.
1632   Gustavus Adolphus of Sweden killed.
1724   Jack Sheppard, highwayman, hanged.
1766   Rodolphe Kreutzer, violinist, born.
1776   James Ferguson, astronomer, died.
1811   John Bright, statesman, born.
1839   William de Morgan, artist and novelist, born.
1841   Ferencz Kossuth, statesman, born.
1889   George S. Kaufman, playwright, born.
1895   Paul Hindemith, composer, born.

Events
1532   The Battle of Cajamarca.
1632   The Battle of Lützen.
1824   The Murray River discovered by the Australian explorer Hamilton Hume.
1846   Austria annexed Cracow.
1869   The formal opening of the Suez Canal at Port Said.
1907   Oklahoma achieved Statehood.
1917   The Allies entered Jaffa.
1918   Hungary proclaimed an independent Republic.

17th NOVEMBER

People
1093   St Margaret, Queen of Scotland, died.
1558   Reginald, Cardinal Pole, died.
1558   Queen Mary I died.
1587   J. van den Vondel, poet, born.
1665   John Earle, writer, died.
1747   A. R. Le Sage, novelist and dramatist, died.
1755   Louis XVIII, King of France, born.
1858   Robert Owen, social reformer, died.
1880   Group-Captain Sir Louis Greig, born.
1907   Admiral Sir Francis Leopold McClintock, explorer, died.
1917   Auguste Rodin, sculptor, died.
1959   Heitor Villa-Lobos, composer, died.

Events
1869   Procession of ships make the first passage through the Suez Canal.

18th NOVEMBER

People
1785   Sir David Wilkie, painter, born.
1789   Louis Daguerre, pioneer in photography, born.
1827   Wilhelm Hauff, poet and novelist, died.

1830   Adam Weishaupt, philosopher, died.
1831   Karl von Clausewitz, general and military writer, died.
1836   Sir W. S. Gilbert, playwright, born.
1851   Ernest Augustus, King of Hanover, died.
1860   Ignaz Jan Paderewski, pianist, composer and statesman, born.
1863   Richard Dehmel, poet, born.
1889   Amelita Galli-Curci, singer, born.
1899   Eugene Ormandy, conductor, born.
1922   Marcel Proust, writer, died.

Events
1822   Hetton Line (Co. Durham), first real railway on a prepared surface, and oldest British mineralogical railway, opened.
1883   Standard time introduced in the U.S.A.
1903   The U.S.A. and Panama signed a treaty concerning the construction, government and use of the Panama Canal and the Canal Zone.
1903   The independence of Panama proclaimed.
1905   Prince Carl of Denmark formally elected as King Haakon VII of Norway.

19th NOVEMBER
People
1600   King Charles I born.
1665   Nicolas Poussin, artist, died.
1692   Thomas Shadwell, poet and dramatist, died.
1770   Bertel Thorwaldsen, sculptor, born.
1770   Adam Krusenstern, circumnavigator of the world, born.
1805   Ferdinand de Lesseps, engineer, born.
1828   Franz Schubert, composer, died.
1831   James Abram Garfield, statesman, born.
1883   Sir William Siemens, inventor, died.

Events
1946   The first General Conference of U.N.E.S.C.O. held in Paris.
1951   The world's first atomic central heating plant started operating at Harwell.

20th NOVEMBER
People
1591   Sir Christopher Hatton, statesman, died.
1751   George Graham, mechanician, died.
1752   Thomas Chatterton, poet, born.
1752   John Shore, King's Trumpeter in Ordinary, died.
1761   Pope Pius VIII born.
1841   Sir Wilfrid Laurier, statesman, born.
1847   Henry Francis Lyte, hymn-writer, died.
1855   Josiah Royce, philosopher, born.
1858   Selma Lagerlöf, writer, born.
1864   Sir Percy Cox, administrator, born.
1894   Anton Rubinstein, composer, died.
1910   Count Leo Tolstoy, writer, died.
1925   Queen Alexandra died.
1935   Admiral Lord Jellicoe died.
1938   Queen Maud of Norway died.
1945   Francis William Aston, experimental physicist, died.

Events
1759 The Naval Battle of Quiberon Bay.
1917 The Battle of Cambrai.
1945 The Nuremberg War Crimes Tribunal began to sit.
1947 The wedding of Queen Elizabeth II.

21st NOVEMBER
People
1579 Sir Thomas Gresham, founder of the Royal Exchange, died.
1682 Claude Lorrain, painter, died.
1694 François Marie Arouet de Voltaire, writer, born.
1695 Henry Purcell, composer, died.
1811 Heinrich von Kleist, poet and dramatist, committed suicide.
1835 James Hogg, the Ettrick Shepherd, died.
1863 Field-Marshal Sir Claude Jacob, Constable of the Tower of London, born.
1871 Lord Kindersley, statesman, born.
1877 Siegfried Karg-Elert, composer, born.
1895 William Gerhardi, writer, born.
1916 The Emperor Franz Josef died.
1942 General Hertzog died.

Events
1818 The Congress of Aix-la-Chapelle ended.
1843 The vulcanisation of rubber patented.
1890 The Lincoln Judgment (concerning the jurisdiction of the Archbishop of Canterbury) delivered.
1918 The surrender of the German battle fleet to the Allies.
1944 The Moscow Conference ended.
1955 The inaugural meeting of the Permanent Council of the Baghdad Pact (now C.E.N.T.O.) at Baghdad.
1958 The construction of the Forth Road Bridge begun.

22nd NOVEMBER
People
1594 Sir Martin Frobisher, explorer, died.
1643 The Sieur de la Salle, explorer, born.
1767 Andreas Hofer, Tirolese patriot, born.
1774 Lord Clive died.
1808 Thomas Cook, travel agent, born.
1819 George Eliot, novelist, born.
1849 Friedrich von Bernhardi, Pan-German advocate, born.
1857 Sir Henry Havelock, general, died.
1859 Cecil Sharp, folk-music collector, born.
1869 Andrè Gide born.
1873 L. S. Amery, statesman, born.
1896 George Washington Gale Ferris, engineer, died.
1890 Charles de Gaulle, soldier and statesman, born.
1900 Sir Arthur Sullivan, composer, died.
1913 Benjamin Britten, composer, born.
1944 Sir Arthur Eddington, scientist, died.

Events
1497   Vasco da Gama doubled the Cape of Good Hope.
1921   The Anglo-Afghan Treaty concluded in Kabul.
1956   The Olympic Games opened at Melbourne.

23rd NOVEMBER

People
912   The Emperor Otto the Great born.
1457   Ladislaus V, King of Hungary, died.
1585   Thomas Tallis, composer, died.
1616   Richard Hakluyt, geographer, died.
1726   Sophia Dorothea, Electress of Hanover, died in captivity.
1804   Franklin Pierce, statesman, born.
1837   J. van der Waals, physicist, born.
1860   Marie Bashkirtseff, diarist, born.
1876   Manuel de Falla, composer, born.
1910   Crippen executed at Pentonville.
1934   Sir Arthur Pinero, playwright, died.

Events
1858   The General Medical Council held its first meeting in London.

24th NOVEMBER

People
1468   The Bastard of Orleans died.
1504   Isabella, Queen of Castile and Leon, died.
1572   John Knox, reformer, died.
1632   Baruch Spinoza, philosopher, born.
1693   Archbishop Sancroft, leader of the Seven Bishops, died.
1694   François Marie Arouet de Voltaire, writer, born.
1713   Laurence Sterne, writer, born.
1713   Father Junipero Serra, missionary, born.
1784   Zachary Taylor, statesman, born.
1801   Ludwig Bechstein, writer, born.
1815   Grace Darling born.
1848   Lord Melbourne, statesman, died.
1848   Lilli Lehmann, operatic singer, born.
1857   Sir Henry Havelock, soldier, died.
1869   Antonio Carmona, statesman, born.
1929   Georges Clemenceau, statesman, died.
1937   Lilian Bayliss, theatre manager, died.
1940   Lord Craigavon, statesman, died.

Events
1639   The transit of Venus first observed by Jeremiah Horrocks.
1642   Tasman discovered Van Diemen's Land.
1793   The Republican calendar adopted in France.

25th NOVEMBER

People
1562   Lope de Vega, poet and playwright, born.
1626   Edward Alleyn, actor, died.

1686   Nicolaus Steno, scientist, died.
1748   Isaac Watts, hymn-writer, died.
1775   Charles Kemble, actor, born.
1835   Andrew Carnegie, philanthropist, born.
1841   Sir Francis Legatt Chantrey, sculptor, died.
1877   Harley Granville Barker, actor and critic, born.
1378   Georg Kaiser, playwright, born.
1881   Pope John XXIII born.

Events
1542   The Battle of Solway Moss.
1783   British troops evacuated New York.
1859   The London Irish Volunteer Rifles formed.
1892   Baron Pierre de Coubertin proposed the revival of the Olympic Games.
1918   French troops entered Strasbourg.
1937   The first British quiz programme broadcast.

26th NOVEMBER
People
399   Pope Siricius died.
1607   John Harvard, philanthropist, born.
1731   William Cowper, poet, born.
1761   John Rich, father of British pantomime, died.
1810   Lord Armstrong, inventor and engineer, born.
1836   John Loudon McAdam, highway engineer, died.
1851   Marshal Soult died.
1857   Joseph von Eichendorff, writer, died.
1869   Queen Maud of Norway born.
1896   Coventry Patmore, poet, died.
1917   Sir Leander Starr Jameson, statesman, died.
1930   Otto Sverdrup, explorer, died.

Events
1789   First national Thanksgiving Day (celebrating the harvest of 1623) in the United States.
1941   The independence of Lebanon proclaimed.
1949   The new Constitution of India passed by the Constituent Assembly.

27th NOVEMBER
People
1635   Madame de Maintenon born.
1680   Athanasius Kircher, scientist and inventor, died.
1758   Perdita (Mary Robinson), actress, born.
1809   Fanny Kemble, actress, born.
1811   Andrew Meikle, millwright and inventor, died.
1874   Charles Austin Beard, historian, born.
1953   Eugene O'Neill, playwright, died.
1955   Arthur Honegger, composer, died.

Events
1518   Daniel Bomberg completed the Rabbinical Bible.
1912   Spain established a protectorate in Morocco.
1919   The Treaty of Neuilly signed.
1942   The French Fleet sabotaged at Toulon.

28th NOVEMBER

People
1757   William Blake, poet and painter, born.
1780   The Empress Maria Theresa died.
1811   Maximilian II, King of Bavaria, born.
1812   Ludwig Lindeman, composer, born.
1829   Anton Rubinstein, composer, born.
1855   Adam Mickiewicz, poet, died.
1859   Washington Irving, writer and diplomat, died.
1892   Thomas Wood, musician, born.
1895   José Iturbi, pianist and conductor, born.
1911   ' Lord ' George Sanger, circus pioneer, murdered.
1954   Enrico Fermi, atomic scientist, died.

Events
1660   The Royal Society formally founded.
1885   The British entered Mandalay.
1905   The Sinn Fein Party organised.
1912   The independence of Albania proclaimed.

29th NOVEMBER

People
1314   Philip IV, King of France, died.
1378   The Emperor Charles IV died.
1489   Margaret, Queen of Scotland, born.
1516   Giovanni Bellini, painter, born.
1530   Cardinal Wolsey died.
1569   Antonio Ferreira, poet, died.
1632   Jean Baptiste Lully, composer, born.
1682   Prince Rupert died.
1695   Anthony à Wood, antiquary, died.
1802   Wilhelm Hauff, poet and novelist, born.
1832   Louisa May Alcott, writer, born.
1856   Theobald von Bethmann Hollweg, statesman, born.
1869   Giulia Grisi, operatic singer, died.
1872   Horace Greeley, editor of the *New York Tribune*, died.
1898   Clive Staples Lewis, writer, born.
1924   Giacomo Puccini, composer, died.
1954   Sir George Robey, actor, died.

Events
1945   Yugoslavia proclaimed a Republic.

30th NOVEMBER
Eton College Wall Game.   St Andrew's Day.

People
1554   Sir Philip Sidney, poet and statesman, born.
1628   John Bunyan baptised.
1654   John Selden, jurist and antiquary, died.
1667   Jonathan Swift, writer, born.
1750   Marshal Saxe died.
1807   William Farr, statistician, born.
1809   Mark Lemon, editor of *Punch*, born.

1817 Theodor Mommsen, historian, born.
1835 Mark Twain, writer, born.
1856 Viscount Haldane, statesman and reformer, born.
1858 Sir Jagadis Chandra Bose, scientist, born.
1862 James Sheridan Knowles, playwright, died.
1874 Sir Winston Churchill born.
1900 Oscar Wilde, writer, died.
1901 Edward John Eyre, explorer and statesman, died.
1910 Jem Mace, pugilist, died.
1954 Wilhelm Furtwängler, conductor, died.

Events
1924 Radio photographs first transmitted from Britain to the U.S.A.
1936 The Crystal Palace destroyed by fire.

1st DECEMBER
People
1135 Henry I, King of England, died.
1455 Lorenzo Ghiberti, sculptor, died.
1521 Pope Leo X died.
1525 Blanche of Castille died.
1755 Maurice Greene, Master of the King's Band, died.
1823 Ernest Reyer, musician, born.
1825 Alexander I, Emperor of Russia, died.
1830 Pope Pius VIII died.
1844 Queen Alexandra born.
1847 Patrick Murphy, weather prophet, died.
1849 Ebenezer Elliott, Corn Law poet, died.
1866 William Cotton, merchant and philanthropist, died.
1867 President Moscicki of Poland born.

Events
1918 The British Second Army entered Germany.
1919 The first British woman Member of Parliament (Lady Astor) took her seat in the House of Commons.
1925 A pact of mutual agreement between Belgium and Britain signed in London.
1932 The Tate Gallery reassumed its original name.
1933 Hitler, as Reich Chancellor, signed a decree identifying the Nazi Party with the State.
1941 ' Points ' rationing began in Britain.
1942 The Beveridge Report on Social Security in Britain issued

2nd DECEMBER
People
1547 Hernando Cortes, conquistador, died.
1825 Pedro II, Emperor of Brazil, born.
1853 Mrs Opie, novelist, died.
1856 Robert Kajanus, musician, born.
1859 John Brown, American abolitionist, hanged.
1859 Georges Seurat, painter, born.
1899 Sir John Barbirolli, conductor, born.
1919 Field-Marshal Sir Evelyn Wood died.
1931 Vincent d'Indy, composer, died.

Events

1254	The Battle of Foggia.
1804	Napoleon crowned by the Pope.
1805	The Battle of Austerlitz.
1823	Birkbeck College (University of London) founded.
1823	The Monroe Doctrine declared.
1852	The proclamation of the Second French Empire.
1861	The Danube Navigation Statute signed.
1942	The first atomic pile began operating in Chicago.
1950	United Nations resolution provided for the handing over (1952) of Eritrea to Ethiopia.

3rd DECEMBER
Feast of St Francis Xavier.

People

1596	Niccolo Amati, violin-maker, born.
1684	Ludwig Holberg, dramatist, born.
1753	Samuel Crompton, inventor, born.
1755	Gilbert Stuart, painter, born.
1766	Robert Bloomfield, poet, born.
1795	Sir Rowland Hill, postal pioneer, born.
1803	Robert Stephen Hawker, poet, born.
1812	Hendrik Conscience, novelist, born.
1826	John Flaxman, sculptor, died.
1857	Christian Daniel Rauch, sculptor, died.
1857	Joseph Conrad, novelist, born.
1877	Alexandre François Debain, inventor, died.
1888	Nonna Otescu, composer, born.
1910	Mrs Mary Baker Eddy, religious leader, died.
1919	Pierre Auguste Renoir, painter, died.

Events

1800	The Battle of Hohenlinden.
1808	Madrid surrendered to Napoleon.
1810	The British captured Mauritius from the French.
1818	Illinois achieved Statehood.
1917	The Battle of Cambrai ended.

4th DECEMBER
People

1334	Pope John XXII died.
1584	John Cotton, divine, born.
1637	Nicholas Ferrar, religious leader, died.
1642	Cardinal Richelieu, statesman, died.
1649	William Drummond of Hawthornden, writer, died
1679	Thomas Hobbes, philosopher, died.
1732	John Gay, poet and playwright, died.
1777	Madame Récamier, social leader, born.
1795	Thomas Carlyle, historian and writer, born.
1798	Luigi Galvani, scientist, died.
1865	Edith Cavell, nurse and patriot, born.
1879	Sir Hamilton Harty, conductor, born.

Events
1563   The Council of Trent dissolved.
1886   The third centenary of the introduction of potatoes into England celebrated.
1896   Brighton Chain Pier completely destroyed during gales.

5th DECEMBER
People
1560   Francis II, King of France, died.
1594   Gerhard Mercator, geographer, died.
1782   Martin Van Buren, statesman, born.
1791   Wolfgang Amadeus Mozart, composer, died.
1830   Christina Rossetti, poet, born.
1859   Admiral Earl Jellicoe born.
1859   Sir Sidney Lee, writer, born.
1867   Marshal Pilsudski, statesman, born.
1870   Alexandre Dumas, père, writer, died.
1870   Vitezšlav Novák, composer, born.
1891   Pedro II, Emperor of Brazil, died.
1899   Sir Henry Tate, manufacturer and philanthropist, died.
1901   Walt Disney, film cartoonist, born.
1925   Wladyslaw Reymont, novelist, died.
1926   Claude Monet, painter, died.
1940   Jan Kubelik, violinist, died.
1959   Prince Duleepsinjhi, cricketer, died.

Events
1492   Columbus discovered the island of Santo Domingo.
1757   The Battle of Leuthen.
1925   Medina capitulated to Ibn Saud.
1933   National prohibition in the U.S.A. repealed.
1956   The union of British Togoland with Ghana approved.
1958   The Preston by-pass officially opened.

6th DECEMBER
Feast of St Nicholas.
People
1421   Henry VI, King of England, born.
1608   General Sir George Monk born.
1721   Lamoignon-Malesherbes, statesman, born.
1732   Warren Hastings, statesman, born.
1778   Joseph Louis Gay-Lussac, scientist, born.
1788   Richard Harris Barham (' Thomas Ingoldsby '), writer, born.
1857   Joseph Conrad, writer, born.
1882   Anthony Trollope, novelist, died.
1892   Ernst Werner von Siemens, inventor, died.
1892   Sir Osbert Sitwell, writer, born.

Events
1492   Columbus discovers Haïti.
1648   Pride's Purge of Parliament.
1857   The Battle of Cawnpore (Kanpur).
1897   The Treaty of Constantinople signed.

1917 The independence of Finland proclaimed.
1921 Ireland accepted Dominion Status.
1925 The Libyan Frontier Agreement between Italy and Egypt signed.

7th DECEMBER
Feast of St Ambrose.

People
983   The Emperor Otto II died.
1254 Pope Innocent IV died.
1542 Mary, Queen of Scots, born.
1549 Robert Kett, rebel leader, hanged.
1598 Giovanni Lorenzo Bernini, architect, born.
1709 Meindert Hobbema, painter, died.
1793 Madame du Barry guillotined.
1810 Theodor Schwann, physiologist, born.
1815 Marshal Ney executed.
1826 John Flaxman, sculptor, died.
1834 Edward Irving, founder of the Irvingites, died.
1863 Pietro Mascagni, composer, born.
1876 Willa Cather, novelist, born.
1879 Rudolf Friml, composer, born.
1911 William Griggs, inventor, died.

Events
1941 The Japanese attack on Pearl Harbour.

8th DECEMBER
People
65BC Horace, writer, born.
1626 Queen Christina of Sweden born.
1708 Francis I, Holy Roman Emperor, born.
1832 Björnstjerne Björnson, dramatist, born.
1859 Thomas De Quincey, writer, died.
1865 Jean Sibelius, composer, born.
1903 Herbert Spencer, philosopher, died.
1956 Princess Marie Louise died.

Events
1660 The first (unnamed) English actress acted on the English stage.
1914 The Naval Battle of the Falkland Islands.

9th DECEMBER
People
1165 Malcolm IV, King of the Scots, died.
1437 The Emperor Sigismund died.
1565 Pope Pius IV died.
1594 Gustavus Adolphus, King of Sweden, born.
1608 John Milton, poet, born.
1641 Sir Anthony Van Dyck, painter, died.
1754 The Marquis of Hastings, statesman, born.
1814 Joseph Bramah, inventor, died.

1848 Joel Chandler Harris ('Uncle Remus'), writer, born.
1902 Richard Austen Butler, statesman, born.
1921 Sir Arthur Pearson, publisher and philanthropist, died.

Events
1813 The Macquarie River (Australia) discovered and named by the explorer George
        William Evans.
1824 The Battle of Ayacucho.
1905 Law promulgating the separation of the Churches from the State in France.
1917 Jerusalem surrendered to the Allies.

10th DECEMBER
People
1495 Hans Memling, artist, died.
1626 Edmund Gunter, mathematician, died.
1805 William Lloyd Garrison, abolitionist, born.
1822 César Franck, composer, born.
1830 Emily Dickinson, poet, born.
1851 Melvil Dewey, pioneer in modern book classification, born.
1865 Leopold I, King of the Belgians, died.
1891 Field-Marshal Lord Alexander born.
1896 Alfred Nobel, manufacturer and philanthropist, died.

Events
1508 The Treaty of Cambrai signed.
1599 The Assembly of the Convention of States at Edinburgh.
1710 The Battle of Villaviciosa.
1768 The Royal Academy, London, founded.
1817 Mississippi achieved Statehood.
1845 Robert William Thomson patented the first pneumatic tyres.
1846 George Jacob Holyoake first publicly announced his philosophy of Secularism.
1898 Cuba became an independent State.
1902 The Aswan Dam completed.
1908 The National Farmers' Union, London, founded.
1928 The new Underground Station in Piccadilly Circus opened.
1936 King Edward VIII abdicated.
1941 The Naval Battle of Malaya.
1945 Waterloo Bridge opened.
1948 The Declaration of Human Rights issued.

11th DECEMBER
People
1475 Pope Leo X born.
1718 King Charles XII of Sweden killed.
1757 Charles Wesley, musician and composer, born.
1803 Hector Berlioz, composer, born.
1843 Casimir Delavigne, writer, died.
1843 Robert Koch, scientist, born.
1909 Ludwig Mond, chemist, died.
1913 Menelek II, Emperor of Ethiopia, died.

Events
1816 Indiana achieved Statehood.
1848 Louis Napoleon elected President of the Republic of France.

1899   The Battle of Magersfontein.
1931   The Statute of Westminster became law.
1936   The Duke of Windsor made his abdication broadcast.
1936   King George VI acceded to the throne.

12th DECEMBER
People
1574   Selim II, Sultan of Turkey, died.
1582   The Duke of Alva, statesman and soldier, died.
1724   Admiral Viscount Hood born.
1731   Erasmus Darwin, physician and writer, born.
1745   John Jay, statesman, born.
1751   Lord Bolingbroke, statesman, died.
1821   Gustave Flaubert, writer, born.
1837   John Richard Green, historian, born.
1849   Sir Mark Isambard Brunel, engineer, died.
1889   Vaclav Stepan, pianist, born.
1889   Robert Browning, poet, died.
1929   John Osborne, playwright and actor, born.
1939   Douglas Fairbanks, film actor, died.

Events
1688   Judge Jeffreys took refuge in the Tower of London from the mob
1901   Marconi received the first trans-Atlantic radio signal.

13th DECEMBER
People
1466   Donatello, sculptor, died.
1521   Pope Sixtus V born.
1521   Manoel I, King of Portugal, died.
1553   King Henri IV of France born.
1565   Konrad von Gesner, botanist, died.
1585   William Drummond of Hawthornden, writer, born.
1675   Jan Vermeer, painter, died.
1784   Dr Samuel Johnson, writer and dictionary-maker, died.
1797   Heinrich Heine, poet, born.
1814   Field-Marshal the Prince de Ligne died.
1816   Ernst Werner von Siemens, inventor, born.
1903   John Piper, painter, born.
1906   The Duchess of Kent born.
1934   William Poel, dramatic producer, died.

Events
1545   The Council of Trent started.
1577   Sir Francis Drake began his voyage round the world from Plymouth
1653   The Barebones Parliament ended.
1862   The Battle of Fredericksburg.
1916   The Germans sent a Peace Note to the Allies.
1939   Naval Battle with the *Graf Spee* began.

14th DECEMBER
People
1417   Sir John Oldcastle (prototype of Shakespeare's Falstaff) hanged.
1503   Nostradamus, astrologer, born.

1542 King James V of Scotland died.
1546 Tycho Brahe, astronomer, born.
1553 Henri IV, King of France, born.
1791 Charles Wolfe, poet, born.
1799 George Washington, statesman, died.
1824 Puvis de Chavannes, artist, born.
1861 Albert, Prince Consort, died.
1873 Jean Louis Rodolphe Agassiz, naturalist, died.
1873 Joseph Jongen, composer, born.
1895 King George VI born.
1901 Paul I, King of the Hellenes, born.
1947 Earl Baldwin of Bewdley, statesman, died.

Events
1819 Alabama achieved Statehood.
1911 Amundsen reached the South Pole.
1911 The first woman surgeon was admitted to the Royal College of Surgeons.
1918 Women first voted in a British General Election.
1939 The Naval Battle of the River Plate.

15th DECEMBER
People
1263 Haakon IV, King of Norway, died.
1683 Isaak Walton, writer (particularly on angling), died
1832 Gustav Eiffel, engineer, born.
1852 Henri Antoine Becquerel, physicist, born.
1859 Dr Ludwig Lazarus Zamenhof, oculist and inventor of Esperanto, born.
1861 Pehr Evind Svinhufvud, statesman, born.
1890 Sitting Bull, American Indian chief, killed.
1916 Gregory Rasputin, monk and Tsarist Court favourite, murdered.

Events
1745 The Battle of Kesselsdorf.
1791 The United States Bill of Rights ratified by the States.
1899 The Battle of Colenso.
1906 The Piccadilly Tube opened.
1916 The Battle of Verdun ended.

16th DECEMBER
Dingaan's Day, Union of South Africa.
People
 714 Pepin II died.
1714 George Whitefield, evangelist, born.
1742 Field Marshal Blücher born.
1770 Ludwig van Beethoven, composer, born.
1775 Jane Austen, novelist, born.
1775 François-Adrien Boieldieu, composer, born.
1790 Leopold I, King of the Belgians, born.
1859 Wilhelm Grimm, philologist and writer, died.
1882 Zoltán Kodály, composer, born.
1899 Noël Coward, playwright, born.
1921 Camille Saint-Saëns, composer, died.

Events
1620   The *Mayflower* arrived at Plymouth Rock, New England.
1653   Oliver Cromwell became Lord Protector.
1773   The Boston Tea Party.
1838   Dingaan's Day, when the Boers crushed the Zulu King Dingaan.
1879   The Transvaal Republic founded.
1925   The construction of the Mersey Tunnel began.
1944   The Battle of the Ardennes began.
1955   The new terminal buildings at London Airport opened.

17th DECEMBER

People
1187   Pope Gregory VIII died.
1493   Paracelsus, scientist, born.
1619   Prince Rupert of the Rhine born.
1724   Thomas Guy, philanthropist, died.
1778   Sir Humphry Davy, scientist, born.
1797   Joseph Henry, scientist, born.
1807   John Greenleaf Whittier, poet, born.
1830   Simón Bolivar, revolutionary leader and statesman in South America, died.
1830   Jules de Goncourt, writer, born.
1833   Kaspar Hauser, the wild boy, died.
1842   Marius Lie, mathematician, born.
1907   Lord Kelvin, scientist, died.
1909   Leopold II, King of the Belgians, died.

Events
1807   The Milan Decree issued.
1858   The Geologists' Association, London, founded.
1903   The Wright brothers flew their first plane at Kitty Hawk, North Carolina.
1938   The Franco-Italian Agreement of 1935 denounced by Italy.
1939   The *Graf Spee* scuttled.
1940   President Roosevelt proposed ' Lease-Lend ' for Britain.

18th DECEMBER

People
1682   The Earl of Nottingham died.
1737   Antonio Stradivarius, violin-maker, died.
1779   Joseph Grimaldi, clown, born.
1786   Carl Maria Weber, composer, born.
1790   Leopold I, King of the Belgians, born.
1818   Philipp Friedrick von Rieger, Czech patriot, born.
1818   Dr William Moon, friend of the blind, born.
1829   The Chevalier de Lamarck, naturalist, died.
1856   Sir J. J. Thomson, scientist, born.
1859   Francis Thompson, poet, born.
1861   Edward Alexander MacDowell, composer, born.
1870   Arseni Nikolaievich Koreshtchenko, composer, born.
1907   Christopher Fry, playwright, born.
1941   Prince William born.

Events

1745   The Battle of Clifton Moor.
1865   Slavery abolished in the United States.
1917   The United States Congress submitted prohibition legislation to the States.
1923   The international zone of Tangier set up.

19th DECEMBER

People

1498   Andreas Osiander, religious reformer, born.
1683   Philip V, King of Spain, born.
1741   Vitus Bering, explorer, died.
1742   Carl Wilhelm von Scheele, chemist, born.
1790   Sir William Edward Parry, explorer, born.
1848   Emily Brontë, novelist, died.
1851   Joseph Mallord William Turner, painter, died.
1852   Albert Abraham Michelson, scientist, born.
1884   Sir Stanley Unwin, publisher, born.
1953   Robert Andrews Millikan, Nobel Prize-winning physicist, died.
1959   Walter Williams, last surviving Veteran of the American Civil War, died, aged 117.

Events

1562   The Battle of Dreux.
1957   The first Heads-of-Government meeting of N.A.T.O., Paris, ended (started 16th Dec.).

20th DECEMBER

People

1590   Ambroise Paré, surgeon, died.
1856   Sir Reginald Blomfield, architect, born.
1868   Harvey Samuel Firestone, manufacturer, born.
1889   Božidar Širola, composer, born.
1894   Robert Menzies, statesman, born.
1954   James Hilton, novelist, died.

Events

1699   Peter the Great's reform of the Russian calendar.
1888   The Battle of Suakin.
1959   The first atomic ice-breaker (the *Lenin*) started operations.

21st DECEMBER

Winter Solstice on an average of two years in every four.   Feast of St Thomas. Forefathers Day (U.S.A.).

People

1375   Giovanni Boccaccio, writer, died.
1639   Jean Baptiste Racine, playwright, born.
1795   Robert Moffat, missionary, born.
1803   Sir Joseph Whitworth, mechanical engineer, born.
1823   Jean Henri Fabre, naturalist and writer, born.
1850   Zdenko Fibich, composer, born.
1879   Stalin born.

21st December

Events

1620   The landing of the Pilgrim Fathers on Plymouth Rock.
1832   The Battle of Konieh.
1845   The Battle of Ferozeshah began.
1846   Anæsthetics first used in surgery in Europe.
1908   The Port of London Authority constituted.
1958   General Charles de Gaulle elected President of the 5th Republic of France.

22nd DECEMBER

Winter Solstice on an average of two years in every four.

People

1552   St Francis Xavier died.
1788   Percival Pott, surgeon, died.
1807   Johan Welhaven, poet, born.
1831   Charles Stuart Calverley, poet and parodist, born.
1839   John Nevil Maskelyne, professional magician, born.
1858   Giacomo Puccini, composer, born (now accepted as the correct date by most authorities).
1867   Théodore Rousseau, painter, died.
1869   Edwin Arlington Robinson, poet, born.
1880   George Eliot, novelist, died.

Events

1845   The Battle of Ferozeshah ended.
1935   (Sir) Anthony Eden appointed Foreign Secretary.
1944   The Battle of the Ardennes ended.
1956   The withdrawal of the forces from the Suez Canal area completed.

23rd DECEMBER

People

1588   Henri de Lorraine, Duc de Guise, assassinated.
1613   Karl Gustav von Wrangel, statesman and soldier, born.
1621   The Earl of Nottingham born.
1631   Michael Drayton, poet, died.
1732   Sir Richard Arkwright, inventor, born.
1761   Alestair Macdonnell, ' Pickle the spy ', died.
1804   Charles Augustin Sainte-Beuve, writer, born.
1812   Samuel Smiles, writer, born.
1888   Lord Rank born.
1843   Marie Stella, Lady Newborough, pretender, died.
1908   Yousef Karsh, photographer, born.
1959   The Earl of Halifax, Viceroy and Governor-General of India, died.

Events

1834   Hansom cabs patented by Joseph Hansom.
1861   Britain presented a Note on the Trent Affair to the U.S. Government.
1913   The Federal Reserve Bank in the United States founded.
1933   The sentences announced at the Reichstag Fire Trial.

24th DECEMBER

Christmas Eve. The Festival of Nine Lessons and Nine Carols (King's College, Cambridge).

People

1167   John Lackland (King John) born.
1491   St Ignatius Loyola born.

1524   Vasco da Gama, navigator, died.
1754   George Crabbe, poet, born.
1791   Eugène Scribe, playwright, born.
1798   Adam Mickiewicz, poet, born.
1809   Kit Carson, American pioneer, born.
1818   James Prescott Joule, physicist, born.
1822   Matthew Arnold, poet, born.
1845   George I, King of the Hellenes, born.
1863   William Makepeace Thackeray, novelist, died.
1881   Juan Ramón Jiménez, Spanish poet, born.
1894   Frances Mary Buss, pioneer in the development of girls' high schools, died.
1935   Alban Berg, composer, died.
1953   Lord Wavell killed.

Events
1814   The Treaty of Ghent signed.
1933   The Codex Sinaiticus arrived in London.
1951   Libya achieved independence.
1951   King Idriss I acceded to the throne of Libya.

25th DECEMBER
Christmas Day.

People
1642   Sir Isaac Newton, scientist, born.
1721   William Collins, poet, born.
1759   Richard Porson, classical scholar, born.
1761   The Rev. William Gregor, chemist and mineralogist, born.
1796   Hugh Lee Pattinson, metallurgical chemist, born.
1808   Richard Porson, classical scholar, died.
1810   Alexandres Rhankaves, scholar, poet and statesman, born.
1842   Dionys Weber, composer, died.
1864   Wilhelm Wien, physicist, born.
1885   Paul Manship, sculptor, born.
1901   The Duchess of Gloucester born.
1938   Karel Čapek, writer, died.

Events
800   Charlemagne crowned first Holy Roman Emperor by Pope Leo III.
1926   The Emperor Hirohito acceded to the throne of Japan.

26th DECEMBER
Feast of St Stephen.   Boxing Day.

People
1716   Thomas Gray, poet, born.
1734   George Romney, painter, born.
1769   Ernst Moritz Arndt, poet, born.
1829   Patrick Gilmore, bandmaster and composer, born.
1837   Admiral George Dewey born.
1838   Clemens Alexander Winkler, scientist, born.
1888   Pasquale Stanislao Mancini, statesman, died.
1931   Melvil Dewey, pioneer in modern book classification, died.
1950   James Stephens, writer, died.

Events
1776   The Battle of Trenton.
1805   The Treaty of Pressburg signed.
1806   The Battle of Pultusk.
1808   Karageorge proclaimed hereditary Chief of the Serbians.
1898   Radium discovered by Pierre and Marie Curie.
1915   The Treaty between Ibn Saud and Britain signed.
1943   The *Scharnhorst* sunk off North Cape.

27th DECEMBER
Feast of St John the Evangelist.
People
1571   Johannes Kepler, astronomer, born.
1585   Pierre de Ronsard, poet, buried.
1717   Pope Pius VI born.
1800   Sir John Goss, composer, born.
1822   Louis Pasteur, scientist, born.
1834   Charles Lamb, essayist, died.
1859   Sir Henry Hadow, musicologist, born.
1889   Stephen Joseph Perry, astronomer, died.
1938   Emile Vandervelde, statesman, died.
1942   Sir Reginald Blomfield, architect, died.

Events
1703   The Methuen Treaty signed.

28th DECEMBER
Childermas (Holy Innocents' Day).
People
1622   St Francis de Sales died.
1775   João Domingos Bomtempo, pianist and composer, born.
1835   Sir Archibald Geikie, geologist, born.
1856   Woodrow Wilson, statesman, born.
1859   Sir John Fortescue, historian, born.
1859   Lord Macaulay, historian, died.
1937   Maurice Ravel, composer, died.
1947   Vittorio Emanuele III, ex-King of Italy, died.

Events
1846   Iowa achieved Statehood.
1908   The Messina earthquake.

29th DECEMBER
People
1170   St Thomas à Becket murdered.
1766   Charles Macintosh, inventor, born.
1800   Charles Goodyear, inventor, born.
1808   Andrew Johnson, statesman, born.
1809   William Ewart Gladstone, statesman, born.
1813   Alexander Parkes, chemist, born.
1843   Carmen Silva, Queen Elizabeth of Rumania, born.
1890   Octave Feuillet, novelist, died.
1894   Christina Rossetti, poet, died.
1926   Rainer Maria Rilke, poet, died.

Events

1775   Sarah Siddons made her début on the London stage.
1843   The Battle of Maharajpur.
1845   Texas achieved Statehood.
1895   The Jameson Raid.
1931   The scientist H. C. Urey publicly announced the discovery of heavy water.
1954   Viet Nam achieved independence.
1959   Durgapur Steel Works, West Bengal, officially opened.
1959   Britain signed the Outer Seven European Free Trade Association Convention

30th DECEMBER

People

1591   Pope Innocent IX died.
1853   André Charles Messager, composer, born.
1865   Rudyard Kipling, writer, born.
1867   Simon Guggenheim, philanthropist, born.
1869   Stephen Leacock, humorous writer, born.
1894   Amelia Jenks Bloomer, champion of women's rights, died.
1899   Sir James Paget, surgeon, died.
1904   Dmitri Kabalevsky, composer, born.
1956   Ruth Draper, actress, died.

Events

1460   The Battle of Wakefield.
1897   Zululand annexed to Natal.
1922   The Treaty of Union adopted by the first Soviet Congress of the U.S.S.R.
1947   King Michael of Rumania abdicated.

31st DECEMBER
New Year's Eve.   St Sylvester's Eve.   Hogmanay.

People

1295   Margaret of Provence, Queen of France, died.
1384   John Wycliffe, reformer, died.
1491   Jacques Cartier, explorer, born.
1514   Andrew Vesalius, surgeon, born.
1668   Itermann Boerhaave, physician, born.
1705   Catherine of Braganza died.
1719   John Flamsteed, first Astronomer Royal, died.
1720   Charles Edward Stewart, the Young Pretender, born.
1738   The Marquess Cornwallis, statesman and soldier, born.
1815   Sir Edward Bond, antiquarian, born.
1830   Mme de Genlis, writer, died.
1851   Frederick Courteney Selous, explorer, born.
1860   John Taliaferro Thompson, soldier and inventor, born.
1868   James David Forbes, scientist, died.
1869   Adolphe Max, Burgomaster of Brussels, born.
1939   Sir Frank Robert Benson, actor-manager, died.
1955   Dr C. F. Garbett died.

Events

1805   Napoleon abandoned the use of the Revolutionary Calendar.
1923   The chimes of Big Ben first broadcast.
1927   The use of the lance in the British Army abandoned, except for ceremonial use.
1940   Firewatching became compulsory in Britain.